Communications
in Computer and Information Science   1651

T0207461

More information about this series at https://link.springer.com/bookseries/7899

Enrico Borgogno-Mondino ·
Paola Zamperlin (Eds.)

Geomatics for Green and Digital Transition

25th Italian Conference, ASITA 2022
Genova, Italy, June 20–24, 2022
Proceedings

Editors
Enrico Borgogno-Mondino ⓘ
University of Torino
Grugliasco, Italy

Paola Zamperlin ⓘ
University of Pisa
Pisa, Italy

ISSN 1865-0929   ISSN 1865-0937 (electronic)
Communications in Computer and Information Science
ISBN 978-3-031-17438-4   ISBN 978-3-031-17439-1 (eBook)
https://doi.org/10.1007/978-3-031-17439-1

This Springer imprint is published by the registered company Springer Nature Switzerland AG
The registered company address is: Gewerbestrasse 11, 6330 Cham, Switzerland

Preface

This volume collects 33 selected articles presented at the Italian Conference on Geomatics and Geospatial Technologies – ASITA 2022 – held in person in Genoa, Italy during June 20–24, 2022, with attendees coming from more than 30 universities, research centers, public institutions, and private companies. The variety of contributing profiles demonstrates the great impact that Geomatics appears to have at all levels of society, even in this unfavorable time of the COVID-19 pandemic.

All scientific disciplines related to Geomatics (cartography, remote sensing, photogrammetry, traditional and GNSS surveying, GIS, and geoinformation) are well represented within this volume, proving that no single field can exist autonomously and that integrated approaches are desirable. The papers were selected from 60 submissions (an acceptance of 55%) following a single-blind review process, with each paper being reviewed by at least 2 Program Committee members with the help of additional reviewers.

During the conference, all accepted papers were organized in thematic sessions, characterized by lively discussions that, starting from the specific technical issues, soon moved to a higher and general level that mostly involved the ongoing EU Next Generation (in Italy, PNRR, the National Plan for Reprise and Resilience) policy. With a special focus on the Italian situation, the complete absence of the word "Geomatics" in the most of governmental documents where the expected strategic goals of PNRR investments were defined was immediately evident. This appeared highly surprising given the numerous actions involving territorial items that PNRR is going to finance. The question that arose was, therefore, is anyone from the Government or Parliament aware of what Geomatics is and does? If not, could this lack of awareness be related to a limited impact in communication that the Geomatics community (i.e, the ASITA Federation) can impress on the system? Or, has Geomatics been trivialized by automation of surveying and data processing, which informatics introduced, making everyone a potential geomatician and therefore merging these skills into more general definitions?

Actually, according to the standard definition, Geomatics "is the discipline concerned with the collection, distribution, storage, analysis, processing, and presentation of geographic data or geographic information" (ISO/TC 211 Geographic information/Geomatics). What seems to be lacking in this definition is a key element, which is the 'consciousness' of all the actions listed. Consciousness means that geomaticians have to be able to continually critically evaluate the results that automatized systems can easily generate. Is this the actual situation? Or, rather, are professionals proposing a "smart" Geomatics that, in spite of any acquired skills, is only made viable by automation?

Geomaticians, once named surveyors, feel that something is going wrong from this side. If the Government, in defining a great number of strategic actions based on territory knowledge, has not recognized the need, and value, of consulting with the Geomatics domain, then somewhere a fault is certainly present.

It is our conviction that the recent – and sudden – technological advancement has made available low-cost tools providing the illusion of an operational autonomy in those fields where users' skills are low or absent, and therefore it is not possible to guarantee information reliability and control. This is not a negligible aspect of the problem, especially when quantitative measures are required. We recognize that the scientific community has moved slowly and is disjointed. This is, perhaps, mainly due to the new and reverted relationship linking the applied sciences with the technological market. Today more than ever, the market needs to anticipate applied sciences requirements, proposing solutions for problems that are yet to come. Scientists and scholars are therefore called to go back along the new product supply chain to get technical specifications (generally not provided to users), which are needed to consciously use devices and test them under the right conditions. In many cases they also have to find suitable and valuable applications for the new and proposed low-cost technology.

Is this healthy for science? Is this safe for sustainable development? Here we only intend to ask the question, leaving the readers to supply their own answer.

It seems to us that it is worth underlining that this reversal of roles, where the market satisfies the needs that it itself has created, has also entered politics. The Next Generation EU program (NGEU) is paradigmatic from this point of view and during the ASITA 2022 conference this issue (somehow) arose implicitly. One of main cross-cutting topics of the conference was to identify the best uses of the PNRR budget, to inform the allocation of funds.

Let's try to explain. If NGEU's economic resources are really needed to respond to the social dramas resulting from the pandemic, why do investment objectives still have to be defined? Otherwise, if the needs are a priori unknown and the political leaders are asking for proposals, something is going wrong. This appears even more critical if we consider the urgency of investment periods, given that NGEU imposes very risky deadlines for the completion of interventions considered "structural".

In this particular social and political context, ASITA 2022 was finally held in person after two years, creating an arena in which all the actors involved (including public and private institutions) could finally share their feelings, doubts, and hopes regarding the near future of research, applications, and investments. This made the event more than a typical conference and the papers presented herein are more than simply a collection of proceedings.

Going back to the initial question of this preface (why Geomatics is missing in PNRR?), ASITA 2022 answered with different voices. Someone supported the idea that the weakness is mainly in the way Geomatics itself communicates, missing the right language. Someone else, on the contrary, stated that actual needs do not require communication, since they are largely evident: if Geomatics is absent from PNRR, it means that PNRR is more interested in activating smart and communicatively effective works than providing solutions to actual needs. And yet, territory-related needs, in Italy, are certainly the most urgent and potentially impactful ones, possibly requiring the highest level of consciousness of skills.

The right answer is probably "blowing in the wind" and, as usual, may be a trade-off between these two positions. Meanwhile, ASITA 2002 has tried to identify some possible solutions.

The first one deals with both communication of Geomatics and consciousness of skills: an Italian National Earth Observation Doctorate was in fact been presented at the conference, supported by the Copernicus Academy network, which is waiting for accreditation from the Italian Ministry of University and Research. Its main goal is the education and preparation of a new generation of high-level technicians for management positions in the institutions that guide the future of territorial knowledge and management.

The second solution is a sort of "declaration of intent" of the whole community to unite the main players within ASITA (the four founding scientific associations relating to cartography, geodesy, GIS, and remote sensing …) as a whole in the dialogue with institutional and private subjects, thus becoming a single accredited interlocutor when a geomatic need arises. This would permit an immediate and unambiguous recognition of the reference speaker in dealing with the knowledge of the territory, allowing a structural and continued updating of territory-related needs and solutions. Additionally, this would trigger an effective process for defining standards for data acquisition and processing in order to recover a leading role for the Geomatics community in the framework of a conscious and sustainable technology transfer process. The discussion is open and hopefully this volume will support the sharing of mutual knowledge people in the field of Geomatics and beyond.

Finally, as editors we are very proud of having gathered these contributions that a valuable reviewers' board had properly selected and helped to improve, making this volume interesting for both civil society and the scientific community.

July 2022

Enrico Borgogno-Mondino
Paola Zamperlin

Organization

Program Committee Chairs

Enrico Borgogno-Mondino   University of Torino, Italy
Paola Zamperlin   University of Pisa, Italy

Program Committee

Maria Antonietta Dessena   ENAS, Italy
Andrea Fiduccia   AMFM GIS Italia, Italy
Antonio Ganga   AMFM GIS Italia, Italy
Alberto Giordano   Texas State University, USA
Francesco Guerra   Università Iuav di Venezia, Italy
Stefano Nicolodi   SIFET, Italy
Filiz Sunar   Istanbul Technical University, Turkey
Paolo Dabove   Politecnico di Torino, Italy
Sandro Bimonte   INRAE, France
Francesco Pirotti   University of Padua, Italy
Domenico Sguerso   University of Genova, Italy
Maria Teresa Melis   University of Cagliari, Italy
Stefania Bertazzon   University of Calgary, Canada
Tiago Gil   University of Brasilia, Brazil
Elena Dai Prà   University of Trento, Italy
Cinzia Podda   University of Sassari, Italy
Monica Sebillo   University of Salerno, Italy
Michele Grimaldi   University of Salerno, Italy

Additional Reviewers

Caterina Balletti
Massimo Blandino
Mariano Bresciani
Samuele Bumbaca
Samuele De Petris
Marco Devecchi
Alessandro Farbo
Vanina Fissore
Gabriele Garnero
Federica Ghilardi

Claudia Giardino
Tommaso Orusa
Luigi Perotti
Marco Prandi
Filippo Sarvia
Marco Scaioni
Fabio Giulio Tonolo
Andrea Virano
Domenico Visintini

Contents

Cultural Heritage and Landscape Analysis

Environmental Monitoring and Analysis

Sustainable Development and Climate Change

Positioning, Navigation and Operational Geodesy

15 Years of the Italian GNSS Geodetic Reference Frame (RDN): Preliminary Analysis and Considerations

Eugenia Giorgini⓪, Enrica Vecchi(✉) ⓪, Luca Poluzzi⓪, Luca Tavasci⓪, Maurizio Barbarella⓪, and Stefano Gandolfi⓪

DICAM, University of Bologna, Bologna, Italy
enrica.vecchi@unibo.it

Abstract. In 2011, the IGMI (Istituto Geografico Militare Italiano) defined the new Italian geodetic reference, materialized by the Rete Dinamica Nazionale (RDN), a cluster of 99 GNSS permanent stations located in Italy and, few of them, in neighbouring areas. RDN also includes some IGS and EPN sites, so that it constitutes a densification of those two networks. The official coordinates of the 99 GNSS stations were initially obtained by computing a limited period of 28 days starting from the end of 2007 and aligned to the datum ETRS89-ETRF2000 at epoch 2008.0. After years of continuously acquired data, other studies published the stations' coordinates together with the associated velocities. This paper presents the updated results of the velocity trends considering the whole dataset now available, consisting of 15 years of data. The analysis considered only the 77 stations that worked consistently for at least five years. The workflow starts with the archive organization and pre-analysis, followed by the geodetic computation using the Precise Point Positioning approach implemented in the GIPSYX software. After the post-processing of the solutions, which included the alignment to the ETRF2000 frame and the analysis of discontinuities, the mean velocities have been computed. The latter were compared to those estimated in a previous work basing on 8 years long dataset. The comparison shows the overall agreement between the linear trends, but also highlights the importance of considering the whole dataset nowadays available to assess the behaviour of those few sites who underwent velocity changes over time.

Keywords: Italian reference network · RDN · Italian velocity field · Precise point positioning · GNSS

1 Introduction

In the last decades, the use of GNSS permanent stations has become a standard in the definition of geodetic reference frames, such as the global ITRF and the European ETRS through the IGS (International GNSS service) (https://igs.org) and EPN (European Permanent Network) (https://epncb.eu) networks respectively. This way allows a continuous monitoring of the positions, with the advantage of being able to update the coordinates

E. Borgogno-Mondino and P. Zamperlin (Eds.): ASITA 2022, CCIS 1651, pp. 3–14, 2022.
https://doi.org/10.1007/978-3-031-17439-1_1

in case of natural movements, also ensuring the possibility of aligning local data using GNSS measurements. CORS (Continuously Operating Reference Station) networks are nowadays used in several technical and scientific contexts, such as the monitoring of crustal movements, landslides, and subsidence, and as a support for surveying activities in real-time.

In Italy, several stations have been installed and maintained by scientific institutes and agencies such as ASI (Italian Space Agency), INGV (National Institute of Geophysics and Vulcanology) and Universities or commercial companies. As established by the Ministerial Decree [1], in 2011 the new Italian geodetic reference frame has been materialized by the Rete Dinamica Nazionale (RDN) and aligned on the new official national datum ETRS89-ETRF2000 (2008.0). The IGMI (Istituto Geografico Militare Italiano) decided to define this GNSS network as a densification of the EPN (European Permanent Network) on a national scale. It was done by selecting already existing permanent stations, without taking charge of their direct management. EUREF (Reference Frame sub-commission for Europe) has recognized the RDN as an EPN class B densification network, including most of the stations located in our territory and meeting the European standards for geodetic reference systems [2–4].

The first release of RDN was composed by 99 GNSS tracking stations, homogeneously distributed on the Italian territory every 3.000 km^2, continuously acquiring and transmitting GNSS data to a Data Processing Centre situated at IGMI [1, 5]. RDN also included some stations belonging to the IGS and EPN networks, some of those located outside the Italian borders [1]. In 2011 the IGMI published an Official Note with the network's official coordinates, obtained by computing the first 28 consecutive days starting from the end of 2007. The dataset of RDN acquisitions is freely and publicly available on the Istituto Geografico Militare repository (ftp://37.207.194.154/), accessible from the official site (http://www.igmi.org/rdn/). This repository also included data from permanent stations which are not formally included in the RDN.

The definition of a dynamic geodetic frame is generally obtained through the precise computation of the stations coordinates at a given epoch and their variations over time, i.e. the average velocity parameters. These data allow to understand the local dynamics and trends which affect each specific site, also being able to update the positions considering a uniform movement over time. Despite the formal definition of the Italian reference, which fixes the coordinates at 2008.0 epoch, the dynamic nature of RDN enables to periodically update the stations coordinates taking into account the natural changes of the crustal surface [6]. The knowledge of the positions and the velocity associated to each station is obtained through refined computation processes which are usually carried out starting on huge amount of data [7, 8]. In 2018, the stations coordinates and the associated velocities obtained using the 2008.0–2016.0 dataset have been published by Barbarella et al. 2018 [3].

This paper aims to present the updated results of the velocity trends considering the whole available dataset, now consisting in fifteen years of data. The analysis follows different steps, starting from the archive organization and pre-analysis, the geodetic computation using the Precise Point Positioning [9, 10] approach, and finally the post-processing of the time-series and the velocity computation. Furthermore, discontinuities in the time-series have been evaluated. Finally, a comparison between the velocities estimated with this last computation and those already published in previous works, based on shorter dataset, is provided.

2 Dataset

The analysed dataset considered for this publication has been selected basing on the list of 99 GNSS stations officially included in the Ministerial Decree 2011. In 2013 about the 20% of the official RDN stations was found to be not correctly working due to several problems [11]. We found the number of stations still working at the time to be 77. Note that one station was found to be not coherent with the one reported in [3], where 78 stations were considered, therefore it was not considered in the following analysis. The spatial distribution of the selected RDN stations is presented in Fig. 1, where different symbols are used to show stations belonging to IGS and EPN networks.

All the available observations with a time span ranging from the end of 2007 to the end of 2021 have been downloaded from the official IGMI repository. Any lack of data detected in the archive have been filled by downloading additional RINEX data from other public repositories (EUREF - igs.bkg.bund.de, INGV - gpsfree.gm.ingv.it). The dataset is made of daily files in RINEX format with 30 s sample rate.

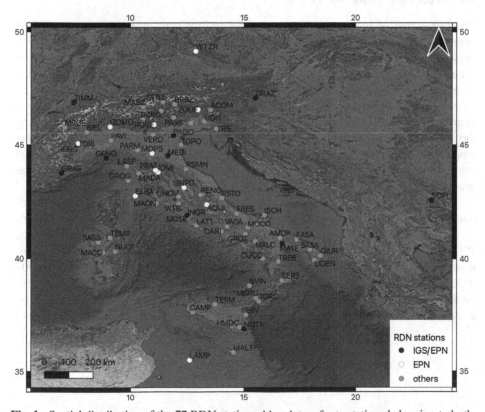

Fig. 1. Spatial distribution of the 77 RDN stations: blue dots refer to stations belonging to both IGS and EPN networks, whereas green dots show EPN sites. Pink dots refer to other stations. (Color figure online)

3 Methods

3.1 Archive Analysis

As already known by previous works [12, 13], the RDN archive does not fulfil the international standards for GNSS data sharing yet, both in terms of files metadata (RINEX headers) and log files. Therefore, the first operational phase consisted of the organization of the dataset to make it homogeneous in order to simplify the following automated elaboration procedures. Moreover, the archive analysis underlined some significant inaccuracy that had to be solved:

- different file formats (compression type, daily/hourly RINEX), RINEX version, and file-name structures;
- RINEX data related to GNSS permanent stations not included in the official RDN network;
- no reporting of instrumental changes or replacements in metadata;
- incomplete maintenance of some stations, with very poor data consistency.

3.2 Processing Using GIPSYX 1.7

The processing of re-organized and complete archive was carried out using the PPP approach implemented in the GIPSYX 1.7 software package [https://gipsy.jpl.nasa.gov], exploiting only GPS data. This method has proved to enable comparable precision and accuracy with those obtained by differential approaches. Moreover, the PPP approach does not require the contemporary acquisition from more than one receiver, making more flexible the data processing of large networks. GIPSYX follows an undifferenced approach, which allows elaborating each station independently from the others, allowing the reprocessing of a single station in case of mistakes [7, 14, 15]. The other great advantage of the PPP is related to the direct alignment of the coordinates onto a global reference frame and the independence from any kind of geodetic infrastructure on the ground [16].

As for the processing parameters, the Vienna Mapping Function was used as tropospheric model and the cut-off angle was set equal to 10°. IGS absolute corrections for antennas calibrations were applied through igs14.atx files. As for the satellite orbits, JPL (Jet Propulsion Laboratory) fiducial products were used, thus allowing direct alignment of the coordinates to the IGb14 (https://lists.igs.org/pipermail/igsmail/2020/007917.html), which is a consistent update of the ITRF2014. ITRS2014 coordinates were then expressed in the ETRS89 by applying the transformation parameters published by Z. Altamimi in Table 3 within the technical note [17], leading to the ETRF2000 frame.

3.3 Post-processing

Having available for each station the time-series of the solutions aligned to the ETRF2000 reference frame, these have been analyzed following different steps:

- transformation of the solutions, expressed in geocentric coordinates, to local topocentric coordinate systems (North, East, Up), together with the propagation of the covariance matrix;
- splitting of the time series basing on discontinuities due to instrumental changes (receiver/antenna) and known from already available metadata;
- visual analysis to check additional discontinuities due to earthquakes or possible local phenomena;
- calculation of the regression lines for each part of the time-series using weighted least squares approach;
- outlier rejection considering a 3σ threshold: outlier solutions have been rejected in all three components even if only one of them had values exceeding the threshold;
- discontinuities resolution after solving the jumps between the consecutive parts of the series, by implementing 1) the Heaviside step function [18], or 2) calculating independent slopes for different time-series spans in the case of steady velocity changes over time;
- computation of the regression lines of the recomposed time series and related slopes. These values are representative of the mean velocity for each station over the whole analysed period (thereafter expressed in mm/years).

4 Result and Discussion

Following the above described steps, the mean velocity in the analyzed period for each of the selected stations has been computed. Figure 2 shows the spatial distribution of the velocities for the planimetric components referred to the ETRF reference frame.

Table 1 reports the velocities of the selected RDN stations considering fifteen years of data. Velocities are expressed in the local topocentric components, North, East and Up, together with the related uncertainties, and all the values are expressed in mm/year. These velocities (Table 1) can be used for different purposes such as geodesy and geodynamics analysis. For example, they can be considered when estimating the crustal deformations affecting the Italian territory and its motion relative to the stable part of the Eurasian plate.

The computed trends are also shown in Fig. 2, which highlight the heterogeneous velocity field in the Italian peninsula, as already observed by Barbarella et al. 2018 [3]. Different clusters of vectors can be observed, mainly related to tectonic boundaries between the Eurasian and African plates. Position rates up to 5 mm/y can be observed in the south and eastern part of Italy, whereas the Alps, Sardinia, and the north-western regions, which are strongly linked to the stable part of Eurasian plate, show almost no residual ETRS89 velocities [19].

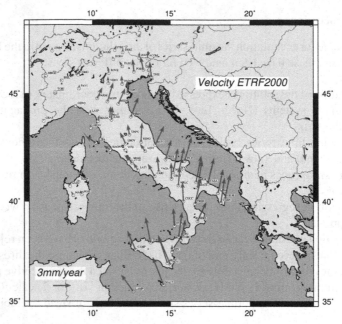

Fig. 2. Velocity vectors map in ETRF estimated in the timespan ranging from 2007–2021 for the 77 RDN stations.

Table 1. Velocities of the RDN stations expressed in the local topocentric components (North, East, Up) and the related uncertainties. Values are expressed in mm/year.

SITE	V_N	V_E	V_U	σV_N	σV_E	σV_U	SITE	V_N	V_E	V_U	σV_N	σV_E	σV_U
ACOM	1,3	0,1	1,0	0,003	0,004	0,012	MRGE	−0,3	−0,2	1,5	0,005	0,004	0,015
AMUR	4,4	0,9	−0,4	0,003	0,003	0,010	MRLC	3,2	0,3	0,7	0,015	0,011	0,018
AQUI	1,2	−0,9	−0,8	0,007	0,008	0,013	MSRU	4,1	0,6	−0,2	0,004	0,004	0,014
BIEL	0,1	−0,2	0,6	0,004	0,003	0,012	NOT1	4,8	−2,1	−1,3	0,005	0,006	0,016
BRBZ	0,7	0,0	1,1	0,005	0,004	0,016	NU01	0,7	−0,3	−0,3	0,020	0,019	0,047
BZRG	0,5	−0,2	1,2	0,006	0,004	0,013	PADO	1,4	−0,1	−0,7	0,008	0,004	0,011
CAMP	3,1	−1,4	0,3	0,013	0,012	0,048	PARM	1,8	0,8	−0,9	0,005	0,003	0,020
CARI	2,1	−1,2	−0,2	0,019	0,013	0,046	PASS	0,8	−0,5	0,4	0,006	0,006	0,016
COMO	0,4	−0,3	−0,3	0,004	0,006	0,010	PAVI	0,6	0,1	−0,8	0,003	0,006	0,009
CUCC	3,2	−0,2	−0,1	0,006	0,013	0,024	PORD	2,1	−0,3	−1,0	0,006	0,004	0,016
EIIV	1,2	0,0	1,0	0,015	0,007	0,016	PRAT	2,0	0,1	−0,2	0,004	0,005	0,014
ELBA	1,1	−1,7	−0,6	0,006	0,007	0,018	RENO	3,2	0,2	0,3	0,019	0,015	0,063
FASA	4,2	1,0	−1,0	0,016	0,020	0,102	ROVE	1,0	−0,1	0,5	0,004	0,004	0,017
FOGG	3,8	0,9	−0,1	0,004	0,004	0,012	RSMN	3,3	1,2	0,6	0,004	0,004	0,013

(continued)

Table 1. (*continued*)

SITE	V_N	V_E	V_U	σV_N	σV_E	σV_U	SITE	V_N	V_E	V_U	σV_N	σV_E	σV_U
FRES	3,2	1,0	−0,7	0,005	0,005	0,015	RSTO	3,1	1,5	−1,0	0,005	0,004	0,010
GENO	0,2	0,2	−0,4	0,004	0,003	0,012	SASA	4,0	0,9	−1,0	0,009	0,014	0,033
GIUR	4,1	0,9	−1,3	0,003	0,003	0,012	SASS	0,5	−0,3	0,4	0,003	0,003	0,012
GRAS	0,2	−0,1	−0,3	0,004	0,003	0,009	SERS	3,1	1,5	0,3	0,004	0,004	0,014
GRAZ	0,6	0,4	−0,4	0,003	0,003	0,011	SOFI	−2,2	0,2	−0,7	0,004	0,004	0,016
GROG	0,6	−0,1	−0,2	0,005	0,005	0,017	STBZ	0,8	0,2	1,1	0,006	0,005	0,018
GROT	2,7	−0,1	0,9	0,003	0,003	0,011	SVIN	2,9	−0,2	0,2	0,007	0,007	0,019
HMDC	4,6	−1,6	−1,2	0,005	0,008	0,018	TEMP	0,4	−0,1	−0,1	0,005	0,007	0,017
IENG	−0,1	0,2	−0,1	0,004	0,003	0,010	TERM	4,2	−0,9	0,9	0,024	0,018	0,069
IGMI	2,2	0,2	−0,6	0,007	0,003	0,013	TGPO	2,1	0,0	−5,2	0,007	0,005	0,015
INGR	1,3	−1,0	−0,4	0,003	0,005	0,010	TGRC	3,4	0,8	0,5	0,013	0,012	0,044
ISCH	4,0	1,2	−0,5	0,003	0,003	0,012	TORI	0,0	0,2	0,4	0,004	0,004	0,012
LAMP	2,8	−2,1	−1,2	0,006	0,007	0,012	TREB	4,4	1,0	0,8	0,013	0,016	0,043
LASP	0,6	0,1	−0,5	0,003	0,003	0,010	TRIE	2,6	−0,3	−0,7	0,003	0,005	0,011
LAT1	1,2	−0,7	1,1	0,004	0,006	0,017	UDI1	2,2	−0,5	−0,5	0,003	0,003	0,011
M0SE	1,0	−1,2	−0,5	0,003	0,003	0,011	UGEN	4,2	0,7	−0,9	0,004	0,003	0,011
MABZ	0,4	0,1	1,9	0,006	0,005	0,019	UNOV	1,9	−1,0	0,5	0,018	0,019	0,065
MACO	0,6	−0,4	0,7	0,011	0,009	0,040	UNPG	1,7	−0,3	−0,7	0,004	0,005	0,012
MADA	0,9	0,2	−0,9	0,004	0,004	0,017	VAGA	2,5	−0,3	0,6	0,019	0,011	0,014
MALT	4,7	−1,8	−0,6	0,005	0,005	0,019	VERO	1,1	−0,1	0,3	0,006	0,005	0,011
MAON	0,7	−1,1	−0,8	0,004	0,003	0,013	VITE	0,2	−0,5	−1,4	0,013	0,020	0,050
MATE	4,6	0,8	0,1	0,003	0,003	0,010	WTZR	0,4	0,0	−0,7	0,004	0,004	0,013
MEDI	2,6	1,2	−2,0	0,005	0,006	0,013	ZIMM	0,5	−0,1	0,6	0,003	0,003	0,010
MOCO	4,0	0,8	−0,2	0,004	0,004	0,013	ZOUF	1,0	0,0	0,7	0,003	0,003	0,010
MOPS	3,2	1,0	−1,8	0,003	0,004	0,013							

Considering the availability of a common dataset computed by Barbarella et al. 2018 [3], relating to a shorter period (2008.0–2016.0), a comparison between the velocities published in that work and those estimated in this study has been performed. Note that positive differences result when our values are higher than Barbarella et al. 2018 ones. Obtained Since similar processing methodologies were used, the main differences between the two datasets lay in the time span increased of 6 years. The vectors in Fig. 3 show the velocity differences for each analyzed site between the two considered datasets. It can be observed that most of the differences are quite negligible having magnitudes in the order of few tenths of mm/y. Only a few stations show higher differences, up to a couple of mm/y. Their spatial distribution does not evidence any systematic effects related to specific areas.

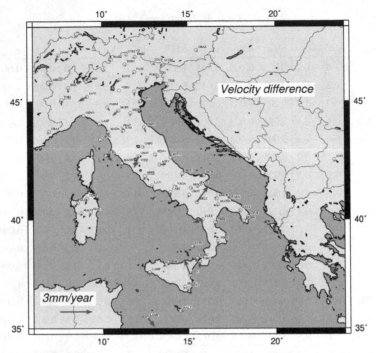

Fig. 3. Vectors of the velocity differences between Barbarella et al. 2018 dataset and the 15-years dataset, for the 77 RDN stations. Positive values mean that Barbarella et al. 2018 velocities are lower than the current dataset ones.

Figure 4 shows the histogram of the residual velocities between the two considered datasets, relating to the three topocentric directions Northing, Easting and Up.

Considering the plan components, only 3 sites have velocity differences higher than 1 mm/y, while most of the differences are less than 0.4 mm/y for the North component and less than 0.2 mm/y for the East one. Residuals along the Northing direction are slightly biased (−0.2 mm/y), suggesting that a reduction of the overall velocity field might have occurred in the last years. This fact should be verified using further data and studied together with geological observations and considerations.

Differences along the Up component are generally higher: 11 sites have residual rates greater than 1 mm/y, while the other sites are characterized by differences lower than 0.5 mm/y.

The highest values of the velocity differences can be due to several factors, primary related to changes in the geomorphology of the site occurred in the period 2016–2022. The geomorphology of the area may affect the velocity depending on the occurrence of local phenomena such as landslides or earthquakes, that may no longer make valid the hypothesis of linearity of the velocity field. This can be evidenced by analysing a significantly longer time span. Figure 5 highlights the differences in the consistency of the two considered datasets in terms of total number of RINEX files analyzed for each station.

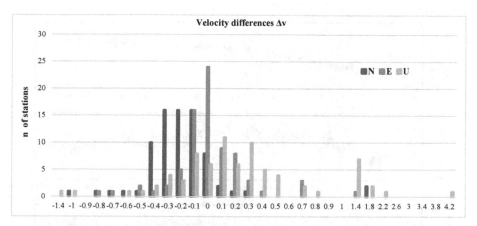

Fig. 4. Histogram of the velocity differences, for the three components of the local topocentric system. X-axis relates to the difference values, y-axis relates to the number of stations for each class of differences. Values are expressed in mm/year. Positive values mean that Barbarella et al. 2018 velocities are lower than the current dataset ones.

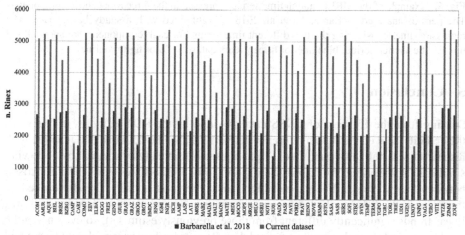

Fig. 5. Consistency histogram of the two considered datasets, in terms of total number of RINEX files analyzed for each selected station. Blue bars refer to Barbarella et al. 2018 [3], red bars refer to the current dataset. (Color figure online)

Figure 6 provides an example of time series who led to different mean velocities, showing data related to MRLC station. Considering the period after 2016 the velocities have changed enough to affect the whole trends. This becomes appreciable only considering the whole time span while it was not evident from the dataset considered in the previous work.

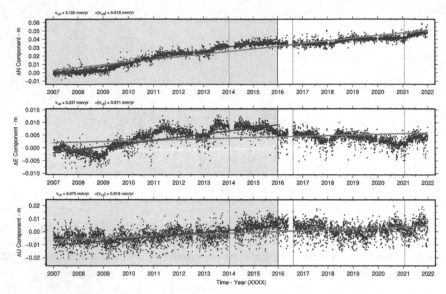

Fig. 6. Example of the MRLC station time series expressed in the three topocentric components. The periods analyzed in Barbarella et al. 2018 is highlighted with a shady background. The regression lines considering the two different time spans, for each component, are showed: red line for the shorter period, blue line for fifteen years dataset. (Color figure online)

5 Conclusion

Starting from the 15 years of GNSS data provided by the RDN stations, in this work the velocity field of the Italian reference network has been calculated and updated with respect to what already published. A previous work already estimated, by following similar data processing, the velocity field relying on a 8 years time-span. The comparison between the two sets of linear trends highlighted the good stability already reached by the frame in 2016 due to the long-term acquisitions. Nevertheless, some stations shown linear trends significantly different from those previously estimated, so evidencing the needs of considering also newly acquired data. These trend variations should be studied to assess whether they depend on local or regional phenomena. Moreover, being the Italian peninsula affected by relevant residual displacements with respect to the Eurasian tectonic plate, after such a long period from the definition of the Italian formal reference, within the geodetic community should rise the need to update the reference coordinates of the RDN network. This ought to be done considering the linear trends evidenced in this paper, also taking care of the fact that jump discontinuities are present in the dataset and, in some cases, the velocity ratios vary over time for the same site. In other words, it might be the time to follow up the international standards for reference frames management as done for the IGS and EPN reference networks. Finally, also the repository used for the RDN data sharing should be integrated with log-files containing stations metadata and all the information for proper use of the GNSS files.

References

1. DPCM 10 November 2011. https://www.gazzettaufficiale.it/eli/id/2012/02/27/12A01799/sg
2. Baroni, L., Cauli, F., Farolfi, G., Maseroli, R.: Final results of the italian Rete Dinamica Nazionale (RDN) of Istituto Geografico Militare Italiano (IGMI) and its alignment to ETRF2000. Bollettino di geodesia e scienze affini **68**(3), 287–320 (2009)
3. Barbarella, M., Gandolfi, S., Tavasci, L.: Monitoring of the Italian GNSS geodetic reference frame. In: Cefalo, R., Zieliński, J., Barbarella, M. (eds.) New Advanced GNSS and 3D Spatial Techniques. LNGC, pp. 59–71. Springer, Cham (2018). https://doi.org/10.1007/978-3-319-56218-6_5
4. Bruyninx, C., et al.: EUREF Permanent Network 2013 (2013)
5. Maseroli, R.: Relazione RDN (2009). http://87.30.244.175/rdn/rdn.php
6. Barbarella, M., Gandolfi, S., Ricucci, L., Zanutta, A.: The new Italian geodetic reference network (RDN): a comparison of solutions using different software packages. In: Proceedings of EUREF Symposium, Florence, Italy (2009)
7. Barbarella, M., Gandolfi, S., Ricucci, L.: Confronto degli spostamenti e velocità di una rete di stazioni permanenti ottenuta con due software di calcolo. In: Atti della 14a Conferenza nazionale ASITA, Brescia (2010)
8. Barbarella, M., Gandolfi, S., Ricucci, L.: Esperienze di calcolo della Rete Dinamica Nazionale. In: Bollettino Sifet (2010)
9. Zumberge, J.F., et al.: Precise point positioning for the efficient and robust analysis of GPS data from large networks. J. Geophys. Res. Solid Earth **102**(B3), 5005–5017 (1997)
10. Kouba, J., Héroux, P.: Precise point positioning using IGS orbit and clock products. GPS Solut. **5**, 12–28 (2001). https://doi.org/10.1007/PL00012883
11. Baroni, L., Maseroli, R.: Rete Dinamica Nazionale: versione 2. In: Atti della 18a Conferenza Nazionale ASITA (Federazione della Associazioni Scientifiche per le Informazioni Territoriali e Ambientali), Firenze, 14–16 ottobre 2014 (2014)
12. Barbarella, M., Gandolfi, S., Poluzzi, L., Tavasci, L.: Il monitoraggio della rete Rete Dinamica Nazionale dal 2009 al 2013. In: Conferenza Nazionale ASITA, pp. 95–102 (2013)
13. Gandolfi, S., Tavasci, L.: Procedure per l'analisi di consistenza e qualità di archivi di reti di stazioni permanenti GNSS: applicazione alla nuova rete dinamica nazionale RDN. Bollettino SIFET **1**(2013), 55–66 (2013)
14. Gandolfi, S., Tavasci, L., Poluzzi, L.: Improved PPP performance in regional networks. GPS Solut. **20**(3), 485–497 (2015). https://doi.org/10.1007/s10291-015-0459-z
15. Gandolfi, S., Poluzzi, L.: Procedure automatiche per il monitoraggio di reti di stazioni permanenti GNSS mediante approccio Precise Point Positioning. Bollettino della società italiana di fotogrammetria e topografia (1), 41–53 (2013)
16. Barbarella, M., Gandolfi, S., Poluzzi, L., Tavasci, L.: Precision of PPP as a function of the observing-session duration. IEEE Trans. Aerosp. Electron. Syst. **54**(6), 2827–2836 (2018). https://doi.org/10.1109/TAES.2018.2831098
17. Altamimi, Z.: EUREF technical note 1: relationship and transformation between the international and the European terrestrial reference systems. Published by EUREF (2018)
18. Davies, J.: Statistics and Data Analysis in Geology. Wiley, New York (1986)
19. Serpelloni, E., Anzidei, M., Baldi, P., Casula, G., Galvani, A.: Crustal velocity and strain-rate fields in Italy and surrounding regions: new results from the analysis of permanent and non-permanent GPS networks. Geophys. J. Int. **161**(3), 861–880 (2005). https://doi.org/10.1111/j.1365-246X.2005.02618.x

A Low-Cost MMS Approach
to the Simultaneous Localization and Mapping
Problem

Enrico Breggion$^{(\boxtimes)}$ ⓘ, Caterina Balletti ⓘ, Paolo Vernier ⓘ, and Francesco Guerra ⓘ

Laboratorio di Fotogrammetria, Università IUAV di Venezia, Santa Croce 191, Venezia, Italy
{ebreggion,balletti,vernier,guerra2}@iuav.it

Abstract. The increasing computational capacity and the reduction of production costs of electronic devices allow the adoption of new approaches to the architectural survey. The purpose of this paper is to analyze and test different low-cost sensors able to acquire odometry, depth data and RGB images processed through SLAM (Simultaneous Localization and Mapping) algorithms to obtain metrically correct point clouds applicable in the normal workflow of the architectural survey. The advantage of these new systems is the time needed to obtain the result. The post-processing time is virtually cleared, and it is not necessary to use targets and control points during acquisition. The capabilities of these sensors are tested both qualitatively and quantitatively by comparing them with the data obtained with traditional surveying systems (laser scanning, photogrammetry, etc.) set as "ground truth". First, the acquisition efficiency of the low-cost sensors under different conditions of use are verified. Subsequently, the different point clouds obtained using different acquisition software are compared. Lastly, pros and cons are evaluated, also from an economic point of view, in relation to traditional surveying systems. The comparisons highlight that the performance of these devices varies considerably depending on the size of the acquired environment. Therefore, they are excellent for the acquisition of small environments as they allow to obtain an accuracy of about ±3 cm in an area of 100 m^2.

Keywords: Simultaneous Localization and Mapping (SLAM) · Mobile Mapping System (MMS) · LiDAR · Stereo camera · Point cloud comparison · Tracking

1 Introduction

Geomatics techniques are well known in the architectural field, such as laser scanning and photogrammetry which are the most used methods.

In the laser scanning survey, the instrument is placed on a static tripod that is moved to cover the entire area of interest. The various performed scans are then georeferenced in a known coordinate system, generally using targets as control points. To georeference the point clouds, targets are topographically surveyed and then adjusted with the classical least squares method. Despite the excellent results gained through this process, the amount of time required by stationing the instruments, acquisition and post-processing

E. Borgogno-Mondino and P. Zamperlin (Eds.): ASITA 2022, CCIS 1651, pp. 15–47, 2022.
https://doi.org/10.1007/978-3-031-17439-1_2

is quite substantial; Moreover, from an economic point of view, this is the most expensive system.

Regarding the photogrammetric process, several digital images are used, in most cases acquired by uncalibrated cameras. The internal and external orientation of the frames is solved automatically through algorithms using an approach known as "Structure from Motion" (SfM). The photographed object (structure) is detected by estimating the position and rotation (motion) of the sensor, which is computed without considering the scaling factor [1]. The analytical solution considers each image statically acquired. Even in this case, the control points (targets) have the same purpose as in the laser scanning and are essential for the absolute orientation and the estimation of the scale factor of the model.

Faster and cheaper surveying methods are increasingly being researched in geomatics [27]. The SLAM (Simultaneous Localization and Mapping) approach through MMS (Mobile Mapping Systems) seems to be the most promising. A great acceleration in the development of these systems has been prompted by two main factors. The first concerns the release on the market of new low-cost high-performance sensors, mainly used for facial recognition, VR/AR applications and self-driving cars; while the second is the continuous implementation of SLAM algorithms. These systems employ the same laser scanning and photogrammetry technologies for surveying but they can solve the localization problem in real-time by using algorithms capable of estimating the position and the rotation of the sensor with respect to a given coordinate system and mapping at the same time [2].

The MMS systems commercially available today are still bulky and expensive. They essentially consist of one or more LiDAR, an inertial system composed of tri-axial accelerometers and gyroscopes, a PC and possibly a camera used for the detection of 2D features and/or for point clouds' coloring; in order to survey large outdoor areas, they also integrate a GNSS system. The aim of this paper is to evaluate the potential and the limitations of several low-cost sensors that are generally used for robotics applications, applying them to architectural surveying. Two different types of devices are used: the first incorporates a LiDAR type sensor, the second integrates a structured light technology sensor. Both devices have been tested using two different software that apply radically different approaches to the problem of spatial localization.

2   Materials and Methods

2.1   Technical Specifications of the Tested Devices

Low-Cost Devices. The analyzed devices are a semi-solid-state LiDAR, a stereo camera and a tracking camera that will be used coupled with the acquisition equipment.

The devices, which have been chosen for the analysis, are produced by Intel®. Thanks to the good availability of support from the online developer community and the increased integration with different acquisition software, these sensors seem to be the most suitable for the purpose. A software that allows to visualize and export the generated point clouds is also provided. To affect the results as little as possible, the default parameters of the various devices are considered for all the analyses. The supplied software does not integrate SLAM algorithms.

Intel® RealSense™ D455 Stereo Camera. The RGB-D camera D455 consists of two infrared sensors, a RGB sensor and a dot pattern projector. It applies the stereoscopic view principle. In this case, the two infrared sensors are placed at a known distance (9.5 cm) and acquire images synchronized with each other. By applying photogrammetric principles and knowing the distance between the two frames, it is possible to determine, through a forward intersection, the space position of a generic point acquired by the system [3]. This process is performed for the entire image surface with a maximum frequency of 30 Hz and at a maximum resolution of 1280×720 points thus generating a dynamic and time-varying point cloud. The system also includes an infrared projector that reproduces, on the detected surface, a known pattern at a wavelength of 850 nm not visible to the naked eye, which allows to improve the surfaces' recognition when it is not possible to identify homologous points in the acquired images (e.g., monochromatic walls). As it has emerged from the tests made and reported later, the device suffers from all the limitations given by the automated photogrammetric process. In fact, as the distance increases, the precision of the points decreases considerably. Moreover, with monochromatic and/or dark surfaces, it is complicated for the software to determine homologous points between the acquired frames, thus increasing the noise of the generated point clouds. The device also includes an inertial system composed of accelerometers and a triaxial gyroscope. Through the RGB sensor it is possible to color the clouds generated by the device. The maximum acquisition distance for depth is 20 m, the recommended operating range is from 0.6 m to 6 m. The cost of this sensor in March 2022 was € 250. A calibration of the device was first performed through the acquisition software [4].

Intel® Realsense™ L515. MEMS (Micro Electro-Mechanical Systems) mirrors LiDAR systems, compared to other types of laser scanners, present many advantages in terms of size, speed and cost, making them ideal for different types of applications. They are also called semi-solid-state LiDAR because the movable parts are limited to the direction of the laser beam, with no need to move any optical components. In this system, a diode emits laser pulses synchronized in real time with the position of a small mirror (diameter of about 1–7 mm [5]). The vibration frequency and the amplitude of its tilt angle define the performance of the LiDAR. The laser pulses are emitted by a diode normal to the scanning direction of the mirror which, moving on two axes, allows the laser beam to be directed over the entire field of view (Fig. 1). By measuring the time elapsed between the emission of the pulse and its return, it is possible to determine the distance of a generic point from the photodetector. The point set acquired from the 2D matrix allows to generate a 3D point cloud. The 2D array of photodetectors defines the resolution of the system. The low number of moving mechanisms and the miniaturization of the components allow to obtain small and cheap devices that suffer less from issues such as mechanical wear, typical of rotating laser scanners. However, the millimetric size of the mirror limits the power of the laser beam: increasing the size of the mirror would compromise the robustness of the system. In addition, larger photodetector arrays prove to be difficult to manufacture, causing a substantial increase in sensor cost [6].

The L515 depth camera consists of a LiDAR (ToF) sensor, a RGB sensor and an inertial module. The LiDAR sensor uses an infrared laser, a MEMS mirror, a photodiode, and an ASIC visual processing module [4]. The MEMS mirror is used to direct the laser beam over the entire field of view. The reflected laser beam is captured by the photodiode and is then processed by the ASIC module, generating a point cloud as output. This process is performed for the entire image surface with a maximum frequency of 30 Hz at a maximum resolution of 1024 × 768 (786,432 dots). In contrast to the D455 device, the processing of the depth data takes place directly within the ASIC module, significantly reducing the computational load on the connected computer. Through the RGB sensor, it is possible to color the generated point clouds. The maximum distance for depth detection is 9 m. As also shown by the preliminary tests performed, the type of material and the lighting have a great influence on the quality of the acquired points. It is advisable to use the sensor indoors, as sunlight disturbs the operation of the device. The cost in March 2022 was about € 350.

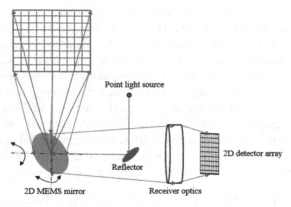

Fig. 1. MEMS mirror LiDAR working principle [6].

Intel® RealSense™ Tracking Camera T265. With the Intel® RealSense™ T265 tracking camera, it is possible to determine the space position without knowing the environment in which the device is located by estimating the 6 unknowns (3 rotations and 3 translations) that allow to define the position time by time (trajectory). Visual-SLAM algorithms, through a combination of cameras and inertial modules, allow to determine the position with a good accuracy [7–24, 25]. Specifically, this module consists of two fisheye sensors, an inertial module and a VPU (Vision Processing Unit) [4]. All V-SLAM algorithms are processed directly within the VPU. The two fisheye sensors, through the detection of feature points between pairs of frames and together with the inertial module, allow to track the position of the sensor through the space. The output data are expressed directly on a Cartesian system at 200 Hz. For each position, the issue of the 6 degrees of freedom is then solved. This device, together with the two previously listed, allows to significantly reduce the computational load given to the processor because all position data are processed directly by the integrated VPU. The cost of this sensor in March 2022 was € 200.

Assembled Low-Cost SLAM Systems. After the calibration phase of the devices, a docking support was designed to allow the use of one of the two depth cameras (D455 or L515) in combination with the T265 tracking camera. The relative position between the two sensors was then calculated (Sect. 2.4) in order to be used by the software to estimate the six unknowns of the acquisition system. The devices were placed on a telescopic rod and then connected to a tablet PC where the two software used for the analysis (RTAB-map and DOT3D Pro) are installed (Fig. 2).

Fig. 2. Low-cost MMS system assembled.

Reference SLAM Systems. The following professional devices have been tested during some presentations held by the manufacturers. Data acquisition and processing have been performed by qualified operators who are familiar with the potentialities and limitations of the devices. The data provided will therefore be considered as the best result obtainable for each of the systems analyzed [8–11] (Table 1).

Table 1. Professional MMS technical specifications

	LiBackpack C50	Kaarta Stencil 2–16	Heron Lite
Weight	6,2 kg	3,9 kg	1.7 kg
LiDAR sensor	Velodyne VLP-16	Velodyne VLP-16	Velodyne puck lite
Range	1–100 m	1–100 m	1–100 m
Acquisition rate	300.000 points/s	300.000 points/s	300.000 points/s
LiDAR accuracy	±3 cm	±3 cm	±3 cm
Output accuracy	±5 cm	±5 cm	±5 cm
FOV	V 30° O 360°	V 30° O 360°	V 30° O 360°
Camera	360°	Feature tracker	/
Price (in march 2022)	55.600 €	49.900 €	54.900 €

2.2 MMS Analytical Measurement Principle

The MMS systems integrate different sensors which, by working together, allow to solve the localization problem [26]. The following formula determinates the generic position of a point in space through an MMS system [12] without considering the contribution of the GNSS sensor that at this moment will not be considered.

$$r_i^{gcs} = r_{ins}^{gcs} + R_{ins}^{gcs} \left(R_{tls}^{ins} R_b^{tls} r_i^b + a_{tls}^{ins} \right) \tag{1}$$

where:

- r_i^{gcs} = generic point i in space, located according to a global coordinate system gcs at instant t;
- r_{ins}^{gcs} = position of the inertial navigation system ins according to the global coordinate system gcs;
- R_{ins}^{gcs} = rotation matrix between the inertial navigation system ins and the global coordinate system gcs;
- R_{tls}^{ins} = rotation matrix between the center of the laser scanner tls and the inertial navigation system ins with fixed angles calculated during the calibration phase;
- R_b^{tls} = rotation matrix between the laser beam b and the laser scanner center tls;
- r_i^b = laser beam b directed to the generic point i;
- a_{tls}^{ins} = position of the center of the laser scanner tls with respect to the inertial navigation system ins calculated during the calibration phase.

The position obtained from the inertial system is continuously updated, starting from a known epoch t until the following epochs $t + n$. The observed quantities have different frequencies: hundreds of Hz for r_{ins}^{gcs} and R_{ins}^{gcs}, tens of KHz for R_b^{tls} and r_i^b. In addition to the synchronization errors between the different systems, there are measurement errors from each of the sensors, so the combined effect propagates to the position of r_i^{gcs}. In each case, the error grows as the distance r_i^b increases, and it is mainly affected by the error resulting from inaccuracies in the rotation matrix R_{tls}^{ins}. Generally, the inertial system would be used for navigation and the laser scanner for mapping, but the advantage of MMS systems is that the data derived from mapping can be used to improve the navigation data to consequentially implement the former with the latter.

From a methodological point of view, the standard workflow consists in dividing the entire point cloud into (n) individual static frames, each with its own previously estimated position. The latter will probably show position inconsistencies, resulting from the errors listed above. For this reason, other procedures are used to reduce the differences between the various clouds, such as Iterative Closest Point (ICP) algorithms [13].

The process of point cloud acquisition and processing can be summarized in five steps:

1. Estimation of the 6 unknowns for each epoch, derived from the inertial system data;
2. Estimation of the best translation and rotation between octree pairs;
3. Cloud registration through ICP algorithms for all scans;
4. Determination of loop closures to distribute the incremental residual derived from sequential scans;

5. Improvement of the entire model using global registration systems called "simultaneous matching" that allow to distribute the error over the entire point cloud.

Commercially available systems can implement different SLAM processes that may be different from the one reported here. The accuracy of the final model depends on the accuracy of the sensors used, especially for the laser scanner. The results are influenced by aspects such as the speed of the operator's walk and the inclination given to the device during the acquisition phase, as well as the geometric and material characteristics of the surveyed object.

2.3 Depth Sensors Performance Evaluation at Different Acquisition Distances

The aim of this test is to verify the performance of the two different devices (Intel® RealSense™ L515 and D455) by comparing the point clouds obtained with a reference dataset generated through the photogrammetric process. In this case, the point clouds generated by the devices have been obtained through the Intel® proprietary visualization software, keeping the default settings for both sensors to affect any post processing filter applied to the clouds as little as possible. No SLAM algorithms were applied, since the purpose was to verify the precision and accuracy of the point clouds generated by a single frame acquired at different distances from the two sensors.

Test Field Features. A wall with different overhangs was used as an experimental field, to which different types of targets were applied. Three different types of targets were used to evaluate which one of them could prove to be the best to use with the two devices. For each type, fifteen items were placed on the wall, distributed randomly over. Leica Geosystem© reflective targets, black coded circular targets generated for automatic recognition by the Agisoft Metashape© software and blue checkerboard targets were used. It has been shown that the latter are the most suitable to use with the two devices, based on two factors: the geometric shape of the checkerboard allows to locate the center of the target more accurately at long distances while the blue color enables to avoid deformation of the point cloud. Using the D455 stereo camera, the black targets generate errors in the identification of common homologous points between the two frames, leading, especially at high distances, to deformation in the point cloud in the area surrounding the targets and causing an incorrect estimation of the distance. With regard to the L515 LiDAR camera, the problem lies in the reflectivity of the material: due to the low power of the laser beam, a lack of points is reported in the cloud, especially on black surfaces. Particular attention was also paid to the printing method used for the targets: especially in the case of laser print, which makes the surface slightly reflective, measurement errors could then occur on both devices (Fig. 3).

Fig. 3. Reference surface area with targets.

Reference Surface Area. Several reasons led to choosing to use a wall inside a room as a reference surface. To avoid deformations in the point clouds, an opaque white surface seems to be the best compromise for both devices. Different stone overhangs are useful to have more control during orientation, as they avoid unwanted slips during cloud registration with ICP. The choice fell on a surface where illumination could be controlled, as sunlight greatly affects the final quality of point clouds generated with the L515 camera. In addition, a horizontal stadia was fixed to the wall to increase redundancy and control of the topography.

Ground Truth and Dataset Alignment. After a series of preliminary tests, a methodology that would not exceed a ±0.2 mm MSE was adopted to obtain an accurate and metrically correct "ground truth" reference data. For this reason, the photogrammetric method was used to obtain the mesh to be compared with the generated point clouds. For the orientation and scaling of the model, the forty-five targets were collimated from three reference stations using a Leica© TCR1103 total station which, once the observations were adjusted, allowed to obtain an accuracy of about ±1 mm. Subsequently, this operation was repeated with the Leica© TCA2003 total station which instead, by using reflective targets, can provide an accuracy of about ±0.1 mm. For non-reflective targets, only the angular directions were measured. Due to the great proximity between the three reference stations, observations were also made using a horizontal stadia. Both sets of observations made with the total stations were subsequently adjusted. They were first treated individually and then together to increase total redundancy. Consequently, the adjusted coordinates were verified through a set of measurements obtained using a regular meter on the distance between some targets, as well as observations taken with the stadia. The obtained coordinates were then rotated in order for the surface of the wall to be parallel to the x-axis of the reference system. Subsequently, ninety-five photos of the wall were taken at about 2 m distance using a Nikon D800 camera with a 20 mm fixed focal length lens and a resolution of 7360×4912 pixels (estimated pixel size 0.37 mm). Additional photos were taken at different distances and angles, in order to avoid reconstruction errors during the orientation phase. Due to the monochromatic texture of the wall, a pattern was projected in order to let the software identify as many homologous feature points as possible. The points obtained through the topographic survey were identified in the photogrammetric model in the absolute orientation phase (average residual 0.17 mm). A mesh was consequently generated and exported.

The clouds generated by the D455 stereo camera and L515 LiDAR camera had to be georeferenced in the same reference system of the "ground truth". In a preliminary phase, a rough alignment was performed manually using four control points and then refined through an ICP algorithm using the CloudCompare software.

Quantitative Evaluation Criteria. Due to the different types of sensor, the default settings given by the acquisition software were maintained for both devices to alter the result as little as possible. The acquisition resolution for both devices was set as high as possible: 1280×720 points for the D455 camera and 1028×768 points for the L515 camera. After some preliminary analyses, the devices were tested in a range going from 0.5 m to 6 m, since beyond this distance it is not possible to accurately identify the targets during alignment. In addition, in indoor environments, where a maximum distance of 6 m should be sufficient, a greater use is expected. The scans were performed 0.5 m from each other.

Cloud to Mesh Comparison. To compare the different clouds, a cloud to mesh (C2M) distance computing algorithm, implemented in the CloudCompare software, was used: this, thanks to the presence of normals on the mesh, allows to calculate both positive and negative deviation values from the reference surface. All the overhanging parts were previously removed from the point clouds to reduce the whole analysis to the plane surface only. In order not to incur in gross errors of comparison, a threshold value of ± 5 cm was set, beyond which the deviation between clouds and mesh was not calculated. The compared data were presented as a colored scalar field (Fig. 4).

Sensitivity. Knowing the density of the different point clouds and the sensitivity of the instruments can be helpful to obtain a more in-depth analysis of these devices' capabilities. The sensitivity of the instrument varies with respect to the distance from the acquired object. It was derived by considering the average distance between the points of the same cloud. Through the software CloudCompare, it is possible to calculate the number of points within the area of a sphere whose diameter can be set as a function of the point cloud density. Using the formula reported below, it was then possible to calculate the average distance between the points [14]:

$$S = \sqrt{\pi \frac{r^2}{N}} \tag{2}$$

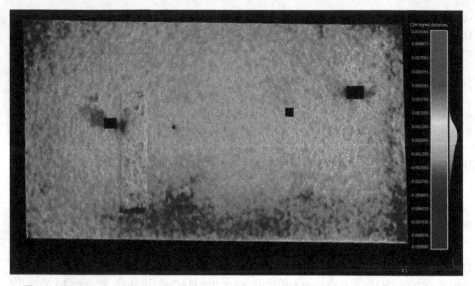

Fig. 4. Signed distances computed to the "ground truth" acquired with the L515 camera.

where:

N = average number of points inside a sphere with radius r.

Through the equation below the density per m^2 of the individual point clouds was determined.

$$D = \frac{N}{\pi r^2} \tag{3}$$

2.4 Pairing T265 Tracking Device with D455 and L515

To let the device understand the 3D world, it is necessary to have a spatial knowledge not only of the surroundings, but also of the position and rotation of the device itself in space. This is made possible by spatially aligning the RealSense™ T265 tracking camera with one of the depth cameras (RealSense™ L515 or D455). The tracking camera estimates its position in space with respect to an initial frame oriented according to gravitational interaction. At the same time, the depth camera generates 3D point clouds of the scene. Together, these inputs can be used to generate an oriented and scaled point cloud of a large scene.

To obtain the correct transformation between the points coming from the depth camera and the positions derived from the tracking camera, it is necessary to know the transformation between the reference system origin of the two devices. The tracking camera is considered as reference and the depth camera is consequently rotated with respect to the position of the former. The parameters needed for the transformation are:

- Translation: 3D translation vector where the offset distance between the origin of the tracking camera and the origin of the depth camera is determined. It is expressed as a 3 × 1 vector in meters and written as tx, ty, tz;

- Rotation: 3D rotation matrix between the origin of the tracking camera and the origin of the depth camera. It is expressed as a 3×3 matrix and written as [[r11, r12, r13], [[r21, r22, r23], [r31, r32, r33]]

The combination of translation and rotation allows to roto-translate a point acquired by the depth camera and to re-place it on the position given by the tracking camera. It is expressed through the transformation matrix [15]:

$$
\begin{matrix}
r_{11} & r_{12} & r_{13} & t_x \\
r_{21} & r_{22} & r_{23} & t_y \\
r_{31} & r_{32} & r_{22} & t_z
\end{matrix}
\tag{4}
$$

The reiteration of this process in time allows to obtain a point cloud composed of (n) frames correctly oriented in space (Fig. 5).

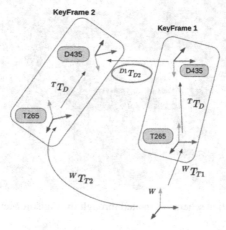

Fig. 5. Relative transformation of the system from the epoch T0 to T1 [23]

Support Design. A rigid bracket, which could be easily 3D printed, was required to assemble together the devices: the first to match the T265 tracking camera with the D455 stereo camera, while the second to match the T265 camera with the L515 LiDAR camera. Both were printed through the stereolithographic process with photopolymerizing resin that allows to obtain particularly accurate models with limited deformation. This printing process was chosen in order to necessarily avoid any deformation resulting in rotation or displacement of the devices over time.

Transformation Matrix. Two different methodologies were used to calculate the transformation matrix. The first method was based on estimating the position and rotation of the acquisition devices through the photogrammetric process. The second approach solved the problem of estimating rotations through the inertial system present on all devices. The methodology used for the actual matching was through the inertial systems, as even in the test phase it produced more accurate data than those obtained with the photogrammetric method.

Transformation Matrix Obtained Through the Photogrammetric Process. Calculating the transformation through the photogrammetric process means to assume that all the devices (D455 + T265) are equipped with CMOS sensors, which can be used to estimate the position and rotation of the origin and, consequently, to obtain the transformation matrix between the two devices. The main problem is to report the rotations and translations obtained in a coordinate system usable by the SLAM software, where the depth camera is considered as reference with coordinates (0, 0, 0) and the tracking camera is rotated accordingly. It is possible to use this method only with the D455 depth camera and not with the L515 LiDAR camera because the latter does not use a sensor that allows to acquire images for depth estimation (Fig. 6).

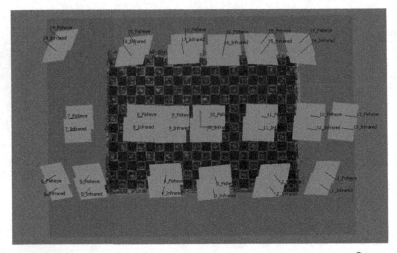

Fig. 6. Tacking position scheme estimated through the Agisoft Metashape © software

The principle behind the automated digital photogrammetric process assumes that an adequate number of images of an object, acquired from different angles, allows to obtain a digital model of the same object, which can be orientated using a known and previously determined topographic coordinate system. Through this process, it is possible to locate the images' origin in the same position they were in the time of acquisition [16]. The camera positions estimated in this step will be used to determine the transformation between the two devices, since the acquisition was performed with both devices mounted on the support.

Therefore, it is necessary to find a metrically measurable object to be detected that will allow to obtain a correct reconstruction of the model. The sensors of the used devices acquire images in grayscale and have a low resolution (<1 megapixel): for this reason, a calibration panel encoded with ChArUco targets was used, since it lets the software to easily identify points on the image and, thanks to the small size (A3 sheet), allows to acquire images at a reasonable distance, covering the entire surface of the sensor. The control points were obtained by placing the surface as a two-dimensional plane. Considering that each of the sides of the panel checkerboard is 4 cm, the coordinates of thirty-two control points were derived accordingly. Images were acquired from nineteen taking points where a pair of frames was taken for each position corresponding to the right sensors of both devices, for a total of thirty-eight frames.

The relative orientation was performed with Agisoft Metashape©. Subsequently, control points were identified on each frame, through which it was possible to orient and scale the model according to the known coordinate system. At this point, it was possible to export the data of the position and rotation of each individual camera, composed of a 3×4 matrix in which the first three columns provide the rotation information, while the last column provides the coordinates of the point according to the previously determined reference system.

For each position, the main problem is therefore to return the position of the frames acquired by the depth camera to the point 0 of the reference system and the rotation of the three axes to a value of 0 and, consequently, to rotate the frames acquired by the tracking camera according to this new reference system. This step is necessary to obtain the same translation and rotation between the two cameras from all the coordinate pairs. The rotation is obtained through the following formula:

$$R = \left(R_t\, R_d^T \right) \tag{5}$$

where:

- $R_t = 3 \times 3$ rotation matrix of the frame acquired with the T265 tracking camera;
- $R_d^T = 3 \times 3$ transposed rotation matrix of the frame acquired with the D455 depth camera.

This equation allows to obtain the difference between the rotation of the depth camera frame and the tracking camera frame. Then, considering that the coordinates of the point Pd/ will have to coincide with the point [0, 0, 0], in order to find the position of the point Pt/, it is necessary to translate it using the coordinates of the point Pd and rotate it using the previously obtained matrix. The formula used for this transformation is:

$$P_{t'} = \left(R_t\, R_d^T \right) (P_t - P_d) \tag{6}$$

where:

- $P_t = $ taking center coordinates [x, y, z] of the frame acquired with the tracking camera T265;
- $P_d = $ taking center coordinates [x, y, z] of the frame acquired with the depth camera D455.

The mean and standard deviation were calculated from the nineteen rotations and translations, which in this case was too high to obtain usable results for device alignment.

Transformation Matrix Obtained Through Visual/Inertial SLAM Process. The problem of determining the relative rotation between the two devices can also be solved using the data obtained through a VI-SLAM process.

In this case, it is only possible to determine the rotation but not the translation, since the global coordinate system of each of the two devices is independent from the other, making it impossible to relate them by an estimation process such as the one presented below.

To achieve this, the ROS (Robot Operating System) application package was used by implementing the RTAB-map software, which allows multiple sensors to be managed simultaneously using VI-SLAM algorithms. The position in space of the two devices can be determined using both the depth sensors and the inertial system. Determining with good accuracy the relative rotation of the two devices is possible thanks to the gyroscope [17], which allows to estimate the variations of orientation with respect to the gravitational axis [9], in combination with the visual SLAM algorithms, which allow to estimate the variation of the odometry over time. By rotating the devices according to different angles and calculating the difference between the direction angles, it is possible to determine the angles ω, φ, κ coincident with the relative rotation between the two devices.

A total of ten pairs of direction angles were acquired and converted from Hamilton quaternions to Euler angles. Then, for each pair, the direction angles derived from the D455 depth camera were subtracted from the direction angles derived from the tracking camera. The mean and standard deviation between the ten observations were then calculated. The translation of the tracking camera relative to the depth camera was derived analytically, knowing the dimensions of the support and the position of the origins derived from the technical specifications [4].

2.5 SLAM Software

In the following paragraph, the two SLAM software used to benchmark the RealSense™ devices will be analyzed. The choice of using different software originates from the assumption that the results may vary considerably depending on the approaches and algorithms used to solve the problem of localization and mapping.

RTAB-Map. RTAB-map (Real-Time Appearance-Based Mapping) is an open source, standalone and cross-platform software capable of handling different sensors implemented through ROS (Robot Operating System) that allows to standardize data coming from different sensors [18]. Odometry management can be addressed using different approaches: odometry from IMU, laser or visual. If proprioceptive odometry (IMU for position estimation) is no longer available or if it is not sufficiently accurate, the odometry derived from the LiDAR or from the visual system will be used. The RTAB-map implements two different types of odometry approaches: Frame-To-Map (F2M) and Frame-To-Frame (F2F). The main difference between these two approaches is that F2F records the newly acquired frame based on the previous frame, while F2M records the new frame with reference to a local feature map created from the previous frames. These two approaches are also implemented for LiDAR sensors and are identified as Scan-To-Map (S2M) and Scan-To-Scan (S2S) and apply the same approach as F2M and F2F, with the difference that point clouds are used instead of 3D visual features.

Regarding the use of stereo cameras as input sources, the process follows the scheme below:

1. Feature identification: when a frame is acquired, the correspondences between the images are computed to derive homologous points between the frames;
2. Feature matching: in the case of F2M, the matching between features is done by searching for the nearest neighbor with respect to the Feature Map, which contains the feature descriptors of the previously acquired frames;
3. Motion prediction: a predictive model of the displacements, based on the previous transformations, is used to predict where the features of the Key Frame (F2F) or Feature Map (F2M) should be in the current frame. Through this procedure, it is possible to limit the search window for feature matching, which allows to improve matching especially when repetitive textured environments are involved. It also reduces the computational load;
4. Motion estimation: used to calculate the current frame transformation, with reference to the Key Frame or Feature Map;
5. Local Bundle Adjustment: the resulting transformation is then refined by improving the feature registration of local groups of frames;
6. Pose update: with the estimated transformation, the odometry is updated. The standard deviation between 3D feature correspondences is also computed;
7. Key Frame and Feature Map update: if the number of inliers computed during the Motion estimation is below a certain threshold, the Key Frame is updated. In the F2F method, the Key Frame is replaced with the current one; in the case of F2M, the Feature Map is updated by adding the unmatched features of the current frame and the position of the matched features that have been refined through the Local Bundle Adjustment.

The odometry estimation process derived from LiDAR follows these steps:

1. Point cloud filtering: the input point cloud is resampled and the normals are computed;
2. ICP registration: the registration of the point cloud is done on the Point Cloud Map (S2M) or on the last frame (S2S) using the Iterative Closest Point (ICP) algorithm. Registration can be done by identifying the Point To Point (P2P) or Point To Plane (P2N) correspondences;
3. Motion prediction: before estimating the transformation, it is necessary to estimate the future position of the device. This is done through a predictive model based on previous transformations;
4. Pose update: after registration, the position of the odometry is updated;
5. Key frame and point cloud map update: if the number of inliers computed during the motion estimation is below a certain threshold, the new frame becomes the Key frame for S2S, while for S2M it is subtracted from the latter, and the remaining points are consequently added to the Point cloud map;
6. If the ICP is unable to estimate the transformation the odometry is lost [19].

Thanks to this software, it is possible to use the devices by combining tracking camera and depth camera.

Dot3D Pro©. Dot3D Pro©, developed by DotProduct©, is a cross-platform software that allows to use various acquisition devices to generate point clouds of small environments. The software comes with a 30-day trial period after which there is a $995/year fee. It comes bundled with an acquisition device manufactured by the company, but it can also be used with Intel© RealSense™ devices. It is not intended to be used in conjunction with tracking + depth devices, as odometry estimation is done only through feature tracking. For the survey of large areas, the use of coded targets is expected [20].

2.6 Quantitative and Qualitative Analysis of SLAM Point Clouds

The aim of this test is to verify the performance of RealSense™ devices using the two SLAM software (RTAB-map and DOT3D Pro) in different use conditions. The survey objects were chosen considering typical scenarios that could be faced during an architectural survey. The survey objects are: the cloister of the Tolentini complex, headquarter of the Università IUAV di Venezia, which allows to test the devices on a large area using the loop closure function; a portion of the building consisting of three rooms, to test the capabilities of the devices in indoor environments and to verify the tracking capability in small and narrow spaces due to the presence of doorways and a portion of a brick wall, to evaluate the details as well as the noise of the various clouds acquired.

The point clouds generated through the devices were then compared with reference point clouds generated with the laser scanner and with the clouds obtained from the commercial SLAM devices: KAARTA stencil, LiBackpack C50 and Heron Lite.

To analytically estimate the accuracy of the point clouds obtained through the low-cost MMS systems by considering only the evaluations made in Sect. 2.3 would not be completely correct, as the errors deriving from the alignment of the single frames, which represent the main problem of localization in space, are not taken into account. Therefore, further comparisons have been performed to analyze the point clouds, both quantitatively and qualitatively.

Experimental Field Characteristics
Tolentini Cloister. The area used for this analysis includes the cloister's portico of the Tolentini complex, headquarter of the Università IUAV di Venezia. Fifty targets were placed in the area of the porch, which have then been collimated to obtain a topographic support on which to align the point clouds. For each device, a path was defined in order to obtain the best result. As regards RealSense™ devices, which have a limited FOV, the path was followed only once, always keeping the devices in the direction of travel (Fig. 7a) to avoid, as demonstrated during the preliminary tests, problems such as the presence of double surfaces in the final point clouds. As for the SLAM reference devices, the followed path was defined by the operator, who determined the optimal acquisition path during the presentation phase. The LiBackPack C50 requires a preliminary and a final calibration phase, where the operator had to walk for a few minutes. To acquire the greatest quantity of points, the route was then carried out alternating inside and outside areas around the porch (Fig. 7b) and repeated several times. With KAARTA Stencil, circular loops were traced both inside and outside the arcade. The path was then

repeated by tilting the device, to also acquire the vaulted part of the porch and the internal facade of the cloister (Fig. 7c). A preliminary calibration step was not necessary. Using Heron lite, two loops were performed: one for the porch part and one for the external part (Fig. 7d). Again, no preliminary calibration step was required.

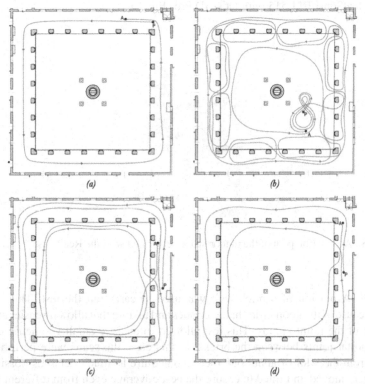

Fig. 7. Acquisition paths of the cloister. (a) RealSense™ devices; (b) LiBackPack C50; (c) KAARTA Stencil®; (d) LiBackPack C50.

The devices used for this test were:

- Intel® RealSense™ D455 + T265 with RTAB-map software;
- Intel® RealSense™ L515 + T265 with RTAB-map software;
- Intel® RealSense™ D455 with Dot3D Pro software;
- KAARTA Stencil®;
- LiBackPack C50;
- Heron® Lite

Indoor Space. To evaluate this application, an internal portion of the Tolentini complex, composed of three connected rooms, was chosen. The path made with the devices was followed to cover the entire surface, tilting them in order to acquire both the ceiling and the floor of the area and providing several acquisitions of the same surface from different distances and angles.

The devices used for this test were:

- Intel® RealSense™ D455 + T265 with RTAB-map
- Intel® RealSense™ L515 + T265 with RTAB-map
- Intel® RealSense™ D455 with DOT3D Pro
- Intel® RealSense™ L515 with DOT3D Pro (Fig. 8)

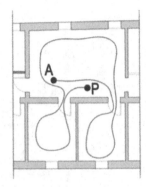

Fig. 8. Acquisition path of the indoor space performed with the RealSense™ devices

Brick Wall. A portion of a brick wall was used to carry out the test. This area was chosen because of the geometric characteristics and texture that allow an easier and better alignment of the point clouds. This test allowed to analyze small geometric elements such as mortar joints between the bricks. In this case, the scans were performed at a distance from the wall of about one meter, to acquire as much detail as possible. The devices were moved and tilted to ensure the best coverage even from different angles.

The devices used for this test were:

- Intel® RealSense™ D455 + T265 with RTAB-map
- Intel® RealSense™ L515 + T265 with RTAB-map
- Intel® RealSense™ D455 with DOT3D Pro
- Intel® RealSense™ L515 with DOT3D Pro

Ground Truth and Dataset Alignment
Tolentini Cloister. The point clouds generated by the devices were compared with the reference "ground truth" which, with sufficient approximation, can be defined as the element corresponding to the real value, which in this case coincides with a point cloud generated by laser scans georeferenced in the same topographic reference system. Fifty targets were collimated with a Leica TCR1103 total station from three reference stations located in the central part of the cloister, then the observations were compensated using Microsurvey Star * Net software. A total of twelve scans were made using the Cam2©

Faro Focus S120 laser scanner, four of which were located in the central part of the cloister and the remaining were evenly distributed within the porch. All the scans were then oriented on the previously acquired topographic points. The resulting point cloud was then subsampled to allow an easier elaboration in the following phases. Subsequently, a mesh was generated starting from the point clouds.

The point clouds generated from the analyzed devices were then aligned to the reference mesh using four control points materialized through the targets. The alignment was then optimized using the ICP algorithm integrated in the CloudCompare software.

Indoor space. In this case, the "ground truth" was obtained through four scans taken with the Cam2© Faro Focus S120 laser scanner, which were subsequently oriented through the proprietary software. It was not necessary to use control points and topography, as the orientation was based on the direct alignment of the scans through the identification of homologous points between them, which allows to have an acceptable error (average error 0.13 mm). A mesh was generated from the point cloud obtained and has then been used in subsequent comparisons. The point clouds generated through the devices were then aligned using four control points for each scan. Subsequently, the alignment was optimized using the ICP algorithm integrated in CloudCompare.

Brick Wall. The reference ground truth was obtained from one of the scans used for the cloister. It was not necessary to use more scans to cover the entire surface because the acquisition was performed orthogonally to the plane, which was sufficiently covered. Starting from the scan, a mash, then used in the comparison phase, was generated. The point clouds generated by the devices have been aligned using four points corresponding to the corners of the window on the wall. The alignment was then optimized using the ICP algorithm present in CloudCompare.

Quantitative Evaluation Criteria. It is hard to define a standard procedure to be used for the comparison between different devices. At the same time, making an exhaustive evaluation only through accuracy data is not sufficient. For this reason, some evaluation criteria were defined to obtain the highest number of comparable data. As far as the acquisition settings of the RealSense™ devices are concerned, they were set-up to obtain the highest number of points in the final cloud. Specifically, the acquisition resolution set for the D455 stereo camera was 1280×720 points and for the L515 LiDAR camera it was 1028×768 points. With regard to the SLAM reference devices used, the parameters varied depending on the system, as they use different proprietary software for acquisition and subsequent processing. Other factors to consider were the speed of acquisition, the inclination of the devices and the movement's smoothness, especially for changes of direction. For this reason, the operator tried to maintain a constant walk throughout the acquisition.

Another consideration, specifically for the commercial MMS, concerns the data processing, because different software which implemented different algorithms were used – none of which open source nor supported by scientific accessible documentation. The processed data provided will be considered as the optimal result of the different systems. For the reasons listed above, the number of points between the clouds of different devices varies greatly. For quantitative comparisons, this value was not considered. The evaluation of the correctness and accuracy of the point clouds was then performed following three different approaches: cloud to mesh, point to point and cloud to features.

Cloud to Mesh Comparison. The algorithm cloud to mesh (C2M) integrated in Cloud-Compare was used to compare the different clouds: unlike a cloud-to-cloud comparison, it allows to calculate both positive and negative deviation values from the reference thanks to the presence of normals on the mesh. All points that cannot directly be compared and easily recognizable as outliers such as double surfaces, misalignments and objects visibly distant from the true surface were first removed through a manual approach. Using automatic filters to clean the clouds would have greatly affected the assessment of the actual performance of the devices. In order not to incur in gross errors of comparison, a threshold value, beyond which the deviation between clouds and mesh was not calculated, was also set. The compared data were presented as a colored scalar field.

Point to Point Comparison. Horizontal profiles with a thickness of about 5 cm were extracted at a height of about one meter from the floor, which were compared to highlight the actual distance between the reference section and those obtained from the devices. At the same time, the noise of the point cloud was estimated through four different measurements of the point cloud thickness (Fig. 9) from which the average was obtained. Via this analysis it is possible to determine the presence of double surfaces and misalignments between frames, as well as to know the actual quality and noise of the point cloud.

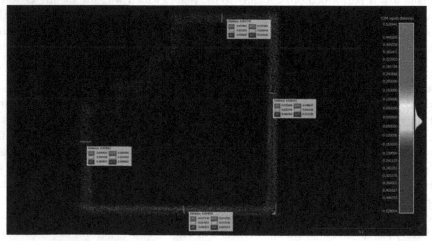

Fig. 9. Horizontal profile of a cloister's pillar with point cloud thickness measured in different positions.

Cloud to Features Comparison. The comparison between the real geometric characteristics and those of the clouds generated through the devices is useful to obtain a deeper analysis of the performance of the devices. However, the comparison must consider the size of the scene as well as the presence of systematic errors arising from the alignment of frames of the same point cloud. For this reason, it is necessary to use an identifiable object to be compared with the reference. The interior room configuration is suitable for this analysis. The use of both longitudinal and vertical sections (Fig. 10) and the comparison of the thickness of the point clouds is useful for a quantitative verification of the characteristics of the devices. The use of a small environment allows to minimize the incidence of the drift of the position estimation on the analysis. This allows to obtain data regarding the recognizability of geometric features rather than tracking errors that are more fully considered with the cloud to mesh comparison of the cloister's clouds.

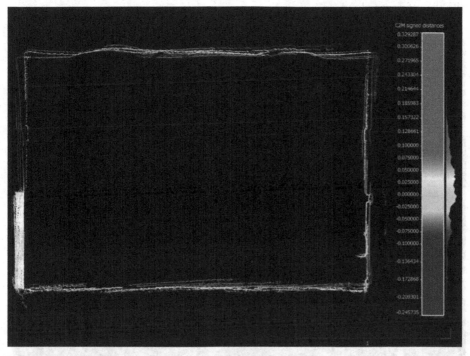

Fig. 10. Dataset compared: RealSense™ L515 RTAB-map point cloud as scalar field and reference data in white.

Qualitative Evaluation Criteria. In addition to the quantitative analysis described above, qualitative evaluations may be useful to provide a more comprehensive assessment of the analyzed systems.

Data Quality and Completeness. If, for the previous analyses, the evaluation of the density of the point clouds is not a parameter that affected the result, an analysis of the number of points in the clouds can be useful to highlight the actual quality and usability of the data. In fact, even if the analyzed area is the same, the number of points between scans varies considerably. Elements such as the movements of the operator, the path taken during acquisition and the scanning speed have a significant impact on the final number of points. The procedure described earlier in paragraph 2.3 was used to estimate the number of points. Another element that affects the readability of the data is given by the coloration: not all devices can color the cloud, but they might present only intensity values obtained through LiDAR.

Detail Recognizability. To obtain a more accurate evaluation, the ability to recognize small details must be considered. A roughness filter was applied through the CloudCompare software, which assigns a roughness value (Fig. 11) – given by the distance between the cloud and the best intersection of a plane based on the nearest points – for each point in the cloud [21]. Through this filter, it is possible to visualize the local geometric variations in the point cloud, which then allow to verify the details quality. The obtained data were represented through a colored scalar field and consequently compared visually with the reference cloud.

Fig. 11. Roughness filter applied to the RealSense™ L515-Dot3D Pro point cloud of the brick wall.

Double Surface Errors and Outliers. Repetition of scans of the same surface can be critical because errors such as double surfaces can negatively affect the result. The evaluation of the approach used by the software for acquisition and processing can be useful to prevent and evaluate this type of errors. Extracting horizontal and vertical profiles of various parts of the clouds is useful to assess the presence of double surfaces. Particular attention was also paid to the thickness of the point cloud, which is in part due to the general noise related to the characteristics of the sensor and in part to the incorrect recording of the acquired individual frames.

3 Results

3.1 Performance Evaluation at Different Distances of RealSense™ Depth Sensors

This evaluation was performed to understand the true capabilities of the RealSense™ devices used. As demonstrated by the various preliminary tests, the performance of the devices varies depending on multiple factors such as lighting, texture and type of material. To obtain comparable data, an attempt to minimize their incidence was made. In the following graphs (Fig. 12), the performance of the L515 camera is slightly higher than that of the D455 camera. With regard to the cloud to mesh comparison, it has been shown that the values change as a function of the distance from the object and that the density of the detected points varies as a function of the angle between the instrument and the detected surface. Therefore, considering that the instrument is placed orthogonally with respect to the surface, the point density decreases concentrically from the projection of the camera center on the wall. This factor assumes that if the analysis was done considering small areas in different positions, the density of the points would vary as a function of the angle of incidence. For this reason, the average value resulting from the analysis is considered with good approximation close to the real value. In addition, the values in the C2M comparison also change: these variations could also be attributed to lens distortion in the case of the D455 camera and to the deformation of the laser dot, due to the angle of incidence, of the L515 camera.

Particular attention was paid to target identification, demonstrating the actual usability of point clouds in a real application. In fact, it was noted that for the D455 camera the identification of the target center above a four-meters distance proves particularly difficult, because even if the device compared to the L515 camera has a higher acquisition resolution, at the same time it has a lower point density due to the wider field of view. As shown on the graphs (Fig. 12 a–b) the values from L515 LiDAR camera are better both for RMS and density of points evaluation.

With regard to the D455 stereo camera, other problems are due to the approach used for the reconstruction of the points' position by the software and to the distance between the two stereoscopic sensors. In fact, during the acquisition phase, it was noticed that the position of a generic point in the cloud varied considerably time by time between frames acquired from the same location, mainly due to errors in the position estimation defined as temporal noise [4]. This problem is also present in the L515 camera but to a lesser extent and localized in small areas of the point cloud. The reliability of the points used to align the clouds is low, because their position varies consistently between acquisitions. For this reason, in the cloud alignment phase, the use of ICP allows to obtain better results than the identification of individual points. Comparing the results obtained with the two depth cameras, it is possible to see that the alignment of the D455 through the targets is particularly difficult, especially at a long distance.

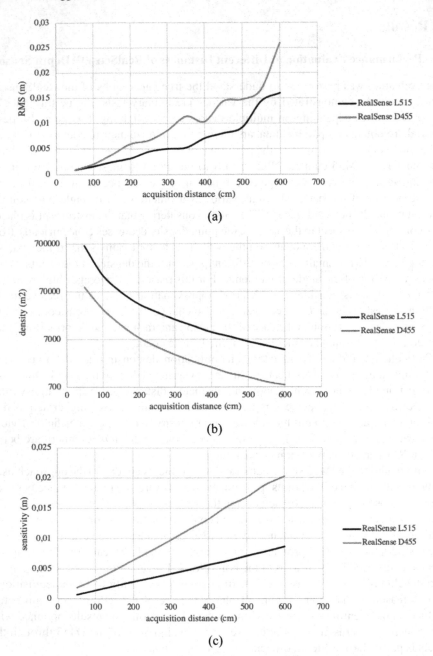

Fig. 12. Graphs: (a) cloud to mesh comparison (b) density variation (c) sensitivity variation.

3.2 Quantitative and Qualitative Analysis of SLAM Point Clouds

Dataset Acquisition

RTAB-Map with Intel® RealSense™ Devices. Thanks to the RTAB-map software, it is possible to acquire point clouds using the T265 tracking camera and the D455 or L515 depth camera. Through the graphical interface, before the acquisition, one may also set different parameters such as scanning range, resolution and acquired frames per second. During acquisition, it was noted that it was possible, with the computer used, to acquire a maximum of about 350 frames before the program stopped responding: this problem is mainly due to the RAM memory of the PC and can be easily solved by using a more powerful processor. Through the software, one might also use only depth cameras without the tracking camera, but in preliminary tests it was noted that the computational load, due to the additional need to estimate the position of the device, made the system slower and unusable. Moreover, this problem caused the loss of tracking after a short time, making the acquired data incomplete and useless.

Particular attention must be paid to the movement path during the acquisition. Abrupt changes of direction and too fast a pace greatly affect the position estimation, causing the misalignment of the point clouds. In most cases, acquiring the same surface multiple times, thus making multiple passes, causes frame alignment errors. Secondly, it is possible to start a post-processing of the acquired data using loop closure detection algorithms in a more accurate way, as well as to improve the alignment of the various frames acquired. Finally, it is possible to globally optimize the point cloud by distributing any registration errors uniformly over it following the same process.

Dot3D Pro® with Intel® RealSense™ Devices. The Dot3D Pro® software allows to acquire point clouds using one of the Realsense™ devices (D455 or L515). In this case, the use of a tracking camera is not expected, as the position estimation is done through the feature tracking of the different acquired clouds. Therefore, the inertial module inside the devices is not used. Through the graphical interface, it is possible to set the acquisition resolution, but it is not possible to modify any other parameter. The acquisition allows to obtain a limited number of points (maximum 160.000.000), beyond which the scanning stops automatically; for the cloister, it was possible to acquire only the lower part of the portico before the scanning stopped. It is necessary to perform much slower movements than with the RTAB-map system because the software loses the tracking very easily: an issue originating from the adopted position estimation approach. This problem occurs more frequently using the L515 camera for two reasons: a more limited field of view compared to the D455 and a maximum acquisition distance of 6 m against the 20 m of the D455. It is however possible, after the loss of tracking, to return to a position already acquired and resume the scanning accordingly, through the selection of a starting frame. As regards to very large environments, it is necessary to use the coded targets provided with the software that allow to improve the alignment of the different clouds and to identify possible loop closures. In the post processing phase, it is possible to optimize the acquired data. The process is done automatically, so it is not possible to know which algorithms and filters are applied to optimize the data. In the specific case of the test performed on the cloister, it was not possible to use the L515 sensor because the entire arcade could not be acquired.

Dataset Evaluation

Tolentini Cloister. The results obtained after the comparisons vary greatly depending on both the devices and the software used. With regards to low-cost devices, the quality of tracking and, consequently, the general geometry of the environments improves considerably when the T265 tracking camera is used in combination with a depth camera. Evaluating the different combinations of tracking and depth camera with RTAB-map software, the L515 LiDAR camera obtained the worst results in the C2M comparison due to the incorrect orientation of the various frames, even if in the performance evaluation tests it proves more accurate and performs better than the D455 stereo camera. The restricted field of view and the maximum acquisition distance limited to 6 m made it necessary to acquire a higher number of frames and that led consequently to poorer results in the orientation phase.

Testing the D455 depth camera with the Dot3D Pro software, the general geometry of the cloister presents some notable distortions distributed on the entire surface of the model caused by an incorrect loop closure (Fig. 13). This problem has always occurred in all the performed preliminary tests despite the use of the coded targets provided with the software. From the local point of view, it shows remarkable results denoted by the low thickness of the cloud. This result shows the aggressive filtering and smoothing mechanisms of the point cloud applied by the software.

Fig. 13. RealSense™ D455 Dot3D Pro cloister plan cloud to mesh comparison

From the qualitative point of view, due to the acquisition scheme parallel to the average trend of the facades, the point clouds are noisy especially for the acquisitions made with the D455 camera. With the L515 camera, the density of the point cloud varies considerably depending on the material acquired. This is due to differences in reflectance between the materials and the low power of the laser emitter integrated in the device.

Regarding the commercial SLAM devices, the results vary considerably, although they all integrate the same LiDAR. In the KAARTA Stencil dataset the presence of outliers is evident and due to an incorrect orientation process of the point clouds acquired by the device. With the LiBackPack C50, the point cloud generated is much more thinned, despite the acquisition path being longer and more complex; in fact, the identification of targets for the orientation was not possible and was then performed through the identification of architectural points. In the Heron Lite dataset, the distribution of points is uniform throughout the cloud. This indicates a subsampling process of the acquired data implemented by the software. The thickness of the point cloud in the section is consistent with the specifications declared by the manufacturer (Table 2).

Table 2. Results obtained through the MMS comparison regarding the cloister test field.

MMS	C2M RMS (m)	Cloud thickness (m)	Density (m2)
L515 + T265 RTAB-map	0,2029	0,0898	16.000
D455 + T265 RTAB-map	0,1071	0,0604	21.000
D455 Dot3D Pro	0,1197	0,0084	126.700
KAARTA Stencil	0,0341	0,0671	36.300
LiBackPack C50	0,0629	0,0689	4.900
Heron Lite	0,0323	0,0537	600

Indoor Space. For this test, unlike for the previously performed analyses, a smaller environment chosen as an experimental field allows a more in-depth evaluation of the ability of RealSense™ devices to maintain a stable tracking functionality through narrower passages, namely doors.

The main problem found is the presence of rotations at the transition point between the various rooms, except for the test performed with the D455 using Dot3D Pro software, where no obvious rotations and deformations are present. The rotations at door level denote a poor ability of the device to determine its own position transiting from a known environment to an unknown one. For the tests performed with the RTAB-map software with both depth cameras, there are outliers in the point clouds that do not allow to define with sufficient precision the real development of the surfaces. With regard to the L515 with Dot3D Pro (Fig. 14), despite the rotations due to the limited field of view and range of the device, a more accurate development of the surfaces has been obtained compared to other devices (Table 3).

Table 3. Results obtained through the MMS comparison regarding the indoor space test field.

MMS	C2M RMS (m)	Cloud thickness (m)
D455 RTAB-map	0,0868	0,0648
L515 RTAB-map	0,1191	0,0253
D455 Dot3D Pro	0,0323	0,0045
L515 Dot3D Pro	0,0624	0,0031

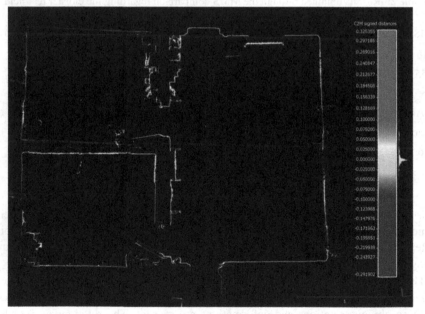

Fig. 14. Dot3D Pro Intel® RealSense™ L515 indoor space's cloud to mesh comparison

Brick Wall. This analysis was performed to evaluate how smaller details are visible and identifiable on the point clouds generated with the RealSense™ devices through the two different acquisition software.

With RTAB-map software, the two depth cameras coupled with the tracking camera have obtained quite similar results: large geometries are easily distinguishable; smaller elements, such as individual bricks, are not noticeable from the noise and are consequently measurable. Specifically for the LiDAR camera, the presence of outliers is more evident, denoting errors in the individual frames' acquired orientation.

In general, more satisfactory results were obtained by using the Dot3D Pro software. With both devices, the development of the surfaces coincides with the ground truth and the identification of smaller elements is easy and precise. In the case of the LiDAR camera, the point cloud obtained presents a slight concave deformation probably due to a systematic drift process typical of the automatic photogrammetric process [22]; despite this deformation, the most precise results were obtained in the comparison of the elements with smaller dimensions (Fig. 15).

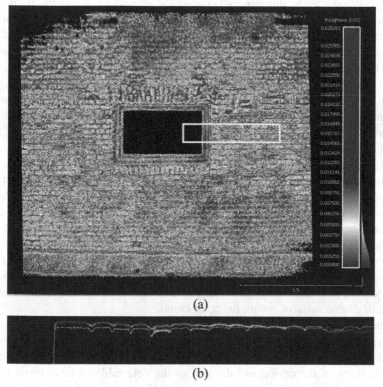

(a)

(b)

Fig. 15. Dot3D Pro Intel® RealSense™ L515 (a) brick wall roughness evaluation (b) section of the cloud to mesh comparison.

4   Conclusions

The purpose of this research was to evaluate the potential of low-cost SLAM acquisition systems applied to architectural surveying. Nowadays MMS systems are one of the most promising technologies in geomatic surveying, as they can acquire larger amounts of data in a shorter time and with no need to transport bulky equipment. The aim is therefore to try to evaluate the performance of these devices by comparing them with classical survey systems and MMS systems already on the market. During the various analyses, we have tried to determine procedures that would allow us to compare the systems as impartially as possible. To achieve this goal, all the variable conditions in which these devices can operate have been considered. For this reason, through an analysis of the characteristics of the two different sensors, LiDAR and stereo camera, it was possible to understand that the performance of these devices varies greatly depending on the material, on the lighting of the environment and especially on the distance between the object of acquisition and the sensor. The tests were performed in different environments to test different configurations. Through the comparison with the reference dataset (Sect. 2.6), it was possible to determine the differences between the ground truth and the point clouds generated through these systems in a rigorous way. It was noted that the values vary considerably depending on the size of the acquired environment and on the distance between the object of acquisition and the sensor. At the same time, a qualitative analysis was carried out considering other factors, such as the recognizability of details, the presence of double surfaces and the density of points acquired by each device. For low-cost systems, considering that the analysis performed using two different software (RTAB-map and Dot3D Pro) showed that the results vary considerably and that the MMS systems on the market all have the same model of LiDAR sensor, the results obtained vary from one device to another, even if the hardware characteristics are similar. Therefore, the biggest obstacle for these new technologies is represented not so much by the characteristics of the sensor but by the ability of the software to correctly process the data derived from them. More specifically, the main difficulty lies in the ability of the system to determine its position in space, estimated through various input devices and algorithms. With low-cost devices, it is evident from the analysis that, by using an additional device (Intel® RealSense™ T265), the estimation of the position is more stable and allows to cover larger areas. At the same time, the estimation of the relative orientation parameters between the two devices proved to be complex and not sufficiently precise, leading to local misalignments between the various frames with the consequent presence of double surfaces within the point cloud.

A complete analysis that compares the various systems (low-cost MMS and commercial reference MMS) is hard to perform, since the field of application varies depending on the characteristics of the device. Two parameters to be considered for this analysis are the accuracy of the device and the size of the detectable surface. From the tests performed, it can be seen that, with reference MMS systems and TLS, the detectable surface can exceed hundreds of meters while maintaining good accuracy; with low-cost MMS systems, the application area is limited to about ten meters, beyond which the accuracy decreases significantly mainly due to the drift in position estimation.

To compare the economic value of the various systems, the most representative parameter was given by the average accuracy obtained through a comparison that considered a common surveyed object (tests performed on the cloister of the Tolentini complex). The RMS obtained from low-cost devices is ±10 cm and that obtained with the reference MMS devices is ±3 cm (Table 4).

For the same accuracy, the price of reference MMS systems is much higher than the value of low-cost devices. For this reason, their use should certainly be taken into consideration in the field of professional surveying. Another useful consideration for the cost-benefit analysis concerns the acquisition time. Both for low cost and reference

Table 4. Summary table with values in minutes calculated on the acquisitions made on the cloister.

	RealSense Dot3D pro	RealSense RTAB-map	KAARTA Stencil	LiBackPack C50	Heron lite	TLS	Photogrammetry
Signalization (minutes)	15	/	/	/	/	60	60
Topography (minutes)	/	/	/	/	/	120	120
Setup (minutes)	5	5	5	10	10	30	5
Acquisition (minutes)	10	15	10	20	10	160	20
Processing (minutes)	60	120	360	360	240	240	900
Instrumentation cost (€)	250–350	450–550	48.900	38.000	55.000	25.000	1.000
Software cost (€)	995/year	/	/	7.600	/	/	3.500
Accuracy (cm)	±10	±15	±3	±6	±3	±0,3	±0,3
Average density (point/m^2)	126.700	19.200	36.300	4.900	600	63.100	105.000

MMS systems, the time spent for acquisition and processing is very similar. For this reason, it is useful to make a comparison with classical survey systems such as laser scanning and photogrammetry: considering that both require a topographic support for georeferencing and orientation and a much longer acquisition and processing time, the advantage given by this technology, despite the lower accuracy, is evident.

By analyzing the obtained results, it is possible to understand that the field of application of low-cost devices is different from other methods of surveying because the point clouds generated by the latter have substantial limitations that make them suitable for use in smaller environments or at least for the acquisition of artifacts at short distances. For these reasons, they are excellent tools for surveying objects of limited size which for their complex geometry would prove difficult to acquire in a sufficiently limited time by using other methods. The substantial advantage that these systems have over the photogrammetric method – which can also be defined as a low-cost technology – is the considerable reduction of processing times and the fact that no additional measurements are required in order to obtain a scaled model.

In conclusion, even if these systems are now still limited both from the software and hardware point of view – thanks to the constant reduction of production costs and the increasingly accelerated technological development – they are one of the most promising surveying methodologies.

Author Contributions. All authors contributed to the study conception and design. Methodology was design by Enrico Breggion and Francesco Guerra. Material preparation, data collection and analysis were performed by Enrico Breggion, Francesco Guerra and Paolo Vernier. Supervision was by Francesco Guerra. The first draft of the manuscript was written by Enrico Breggion and Caterina Balletti and all authors commented on previous versions of the manuscript. All authors read and approved the final manuscript.

References

1. Ozyesil, O., Voroninski, V., Basri, R., Singer, A.: A survey of structure from motion. arXiv: 1701.08493 [cs] (2017)
2. Zhu, Y., Zheng, C., Yuan, C., Huang, X., Hong, X.: CamVox: a low-cost and accurate lidar-assisted visual SLAM system. arXiv:2011.11357 [cs] (2020)
3. OrRiordan, A., Newe, T., Dooly, G., Toal, D.: Stereo vision sensing: review of existing systems. In: 2018 12th International Conference on Sensing Technology (ICST), Limerick, pp. 178–184. IEEE (2018)
4. Intel© RealSense™ technical specifications. https://dev.intelrealsense.com/docs/datasheets. Accessed Sept 2021
5. Wang, D., Watkins, C., Xie, H.: MEMS mirrors for LiDAR: a review. Micromachines **11**, 456 (2020). https://doi.org/10.3390/mi11050456
6. Xu, F., Qiao, D., Song, X., Zheng, W., He, Y., Fan, Q.: A semi-coaxial MEMS-based LiDAR. In: IECON 2019 - 45th Annual Conference of the IEEE Industrial Electronics Society, Lisbon, Portugal, pp. 6726–6731. IEEE (2019)
7. Taketomi, T., Uchiyama, H., Ikeda, S.: Visual SLAM algorithms: a survey from 2010 to 2016. IPSJ Trans. Comput. Vis. Appl. **9**(1), 1–11 (2017). https://doi.org/10.1186/s41074-017-0027-2
8. KAARTA© Stencil technical specifications. https://www.kaarta.com/wp-content/uploads/Stencil_2-16_spec_sheet_04.21-web.pdf. Accessed Sept 2021
9. Zhang, J., Singh, S.: LOAM: lidar odometry and mapping in real-time. In: Robotics: Science and Systems X. Robotics: Science and Systems Foundation (2014)
10. LiBackPack C50 technical specifications. https://greenvalleyintl.com/hardware/libackpack/. Accessed Feb 2022
11. Heron Lite techinical specifications. https://gexcel.it/it/soluzioni/heron-mobile-mapping/heron-lite. Accessed Feb 2022
12. Tucci, G., Visintini, D., Bonora, V., Parisi, E.: Examination of indoor mobile mapping systems in a diversified internal/external test field. Appl. Sci. **8**, 401 (2018). https://doi.org/10.3390/app8030401
13. He, Y., Liang, B., Yang, J., Li, S., He, J.: An iterative closest points algorithm for registration of 3D laser scanner point clouds with geometric features. Sensors **17**, 1862 (2017). https://doi.org/10.3390/s17081862
14. CloudCompare density estimation. https://www.cloudcompare.org/doc/wiki/index.php?title=Density. Accessed Feb 2022
15. Intel© RealSense™ depth and tracking cameras alignment. https://dev.intelrealsense.com/docs/depth-and-tracking-cameras-alignmentnt. Accessed Feb 2022
16. Dore, P.: Fondamenti di fotogrammetria. Fototopografia da terra e da aerei. Zanichelli (1938)
17. Technical specifications Bosh BMI055. https://www.bosch-sensortec.com/media/boschsensortec/downloads/datasheets/bst-bmi055-ds000.pdf. Accessed Sept 2021
18. Huletski, A., Kartashov, D.: A SLAM research framework for ROS. In: Proceedings of the 12th Central and Eastern European Software Engineering Conference in Russia on - CEE-SECR 2016, Moscow, Russian Federation, pp. 1–6. ACM Press (2016)
19. Labbé, M., Michaud, F.: RTAB-Map as an open-source lidar and visual simultaneous localization and mapping library for large-scale and long-term online operation: LABBÉ AND MICHAUD. J. Field Robot. **36**, 416–446 (2019). https://doi.org/10.1002/rob.21831
20. Dot3D Pro software features. https://www.dotproduct3d.com/dot3dpro.html. Accessed Feb 2022
21. CloudCompare roughness filter. http://www.cloudcompare.org/doc/wiki/index.php?title=Roughness. Accessed Feb 2022

22. Brown, D.C.: Unflatness of plates as a source of systematic error in close-range photogrammetry. Photogrammetria **40**, 343–363 (1986). https://doi.org/10.1016/0031-8663(86)900 20-7
23. Tsykunov, E., Ilin, V., Perminov, S., Fedoseev, A., Zainulina, E.: Coupling of localization and depth data for mapping using Intel RealSense T265 and D435i cameras. arXiv:2004.00269 [cs] (2020)
24. Dabove, P., Lingua, A.M., Piras, M.: Photogrammetric visual odometry with unmanned ground vehicle using low cost sensors. In: 2018 IEEE/ION Position, Location and Navigation Symposium (PLANS) Monterey, CA, pp. 426–431. IEEE (2018)
25. De Agostino, M., Lingua, A., Nex, F., Piras, M.: GIMPhI: a novel vision-based navigation approach for low cost MMS. In: IEEE/ION Position, Location and Navigation Symposium, Indian Wells, CA, USA, pp. 1238–1244. IEEE (2010)
26. Di Pietra, V., Grasso, N., Piras, M., Dabove, P.: Characterization of a mobile mapping system for seamless navigation. Int. Arch. Photogramm. Remote Sens. Spat. Inf. Sci. **XLIII-B1–2020**, 227–234 (2020). https://doi.org/10.5194/isprs-archives-XLIII-B1-2020-227-2020
27. Calantropio, A., Patrucco, G., Sammartano, G., Losè, L.T.: Sensori low-cost per il mapping speditivo di beni culturali. Primi test su di una steadycam low-cost. Bollettino SIFET n. 3. Sezione Scienza (2017)

Low-Cost Hardware PPP-RTK AR Time-to-Fix and Positioning Performance Assessment: A Preliminary Static Test

Matteo Cutugno[1]([✉])(iD), Umberto Robustelli[2](iD), and Giovanni Pugliano[1](iD)

[1] Department of Civil, Architectural and Environmental Engineering,
University of Naples Federico II, Naples, Italy
{matteo.cutugno,giovanni.pugliano}@unina.it
[2] Department of Engineering, University of Naples Parthenope, Naples, Italy
umberto.robustelli@uniparthenope.it
http://www.unina.it , http://www.uniparthenope.it

Abstract. Over the last years, researchers are struggling to develop solutions and services for smart and sustainable urban mobility creating dynamic shared spaces for both vehicles and pedestrians. Also, the deployment of autonomous vehicles has boosted the interest in precise, accurate, and robust position, navigation, and timing (PNT). Most of these services will be based primarily on the location of the vehicle relative to other vehicles, objects, and pedestrians in its vicinity. Therefore, the importance of a robust, ubiquitous, and reliable PNT can't be overlooked. In the mass-market scenario, the challenge will be developing low-cost navigation equipment capable of providing navigation solutions that meet the accuracy, integrity, continuity, and availability requirements. This paper reports some preliminary tests aiming to investigate the phase-ambiguity fixing performance of a commercial precise point positioning real-time kinematic (PPP-RTK) correction service, employing a low-cost receiver. To assess the ambiguity resolution performance, we forced the receiver to restart the ambiguity search generating enough samples for statistic analysis. In this test, PPP-RTK has revealed a promising technique for decimetre-level accuracy positioning with low-cost receivers. Integer ambiguity fixed solutions reveal a DRMS of 0.09 m whereas float solutions reveal a DRMS of 0.45 m. When PPP-RTK corrections are not available, SPP/DGNSS solutions reveal a DRMS of 1.36 m. The test showed that the employment of cost-effective equipment along with the exploitation of correction services allows reaching decimetre/sub-metre accuracy in about 20 s and sub-decimetre accuracy in about 2 min once the integer ambiguity is fixed.

Keywords: Carrier-phase ambiguity · Low-cost positioning · Smart mobility · PPP-RTK · Time-to-fix

1   Introduction

During the last years, climate changes and pandemics have pushed decision-makers to undertake actions to change city paradigms, aiming to create healthy, livable, and sustainable cities. The research community is struggling to develop solutions that tackle last-mile pollution and congestion as well as improve autonomous delivery, active mobility, sustainable logistics, and creating dynamic shared spaces for both vehicles and pedestrians. Smart mobility encourages the integration of innovative solutions and services to accelerate change towards sustainable urban mobility. Also, the deployment of autonomous vehicles has boosted the interest in precise, accurate, and robust position, navigation, and timing (PNT). Autonomous vehicles that are available for a large portion of the population will soon become a reality on road networks. Most of these services will be based primarily on the location of the vehicle relative to other vehicles, objects, and pedestrians in its vicinity. Therefore, the importance of a robust, ubiquitous, and reliable PNT can't be overlooked. In the mass-market scenario, the challenge will be developing low-cost navigation equipment for land vehicles capable of providing a navigation solution that meets the accuracy, integrity, continuity, and availability requirements [2]. The adoption of high-accuracy positioning within the mass market is also supported by other factors such as the availability of multi-constellation and multi-frequency receivers, the access to raw measurements in Android 7+, the fall in hardware prices, and the deployment of several commercial correction services [1]. Until some years ago, accuracy was a prerogative of high-grade geodetic receivers. Today high accuracy can be achieved also with low-cost receivers thanks to several factors, among all: the increased availability of GNSS interoperable constellations as well as the accessibility to several augmentation techniques both satellite- and ground-based. Given the potential advantage of bringing high accuracy and precision positioning to consumer-grade devices, a new impetus has been given to the study and implementation of these augmentation techniques. GNSS has been the most widely used system for navigation. However, despite its capability to provide absolute navigation information, this system suffers from problems related to signal propagation, especially in urban environments, where buildings, trees, and other structures hinder the reception of GNSS signals [11]. In addition, low-cost receivers can't assure the required performance if compared to high-grade ones. For these reasons, to employ low-cost receivers for navigation purposes, their performance must be augmented. Then, the increasing demand for high-accuracy and high-integrity navigation solutions can be fulfilled by low-cost GNSS receivers with implemented augmentation techniques. This research aimed to investigate the phase-ambiguity fixing performance of a commercial precise point positioning real-time kinematic (PPP-RTK) correction service, employing a low-cost receiver. Hence, to simulate urban-canyon conditions where GNSS signals can be lost, tests comprehending consecutive shutdowns of the receiver have been carried out. Ambiguity resolution (AR) fixing time and positioning performances have been investigated.

The remainder of this paper is organized as follows: Sect. 2 briefly presents the methodology of PPP-RTK. Section 3 presents the experiment, and Sect. 4 provides results and discussion. Lastly, Sect. 5 draws conclusions and sets future goals.

2 Methodology

The methodology's development contemplates the experimentation of a low-cost receiver augmented by a PPP-RTK correction service. Aiming to provide robust subdecimetre-level accuracy positioning with a stand-alone low-cost receiver, different GNSS techniques are available, among all: real-time kinematic (RTK), precise point positioning (PPP), and the hybridisation of these (PPP-RTK). The most advanced adaptation of RTK is network RTK (NRTK). It has been the most popular GNSS signal augmentation technology for many industries such as surveying and agriculture and it is particularly prevalent in regions with well-developed Continuously Operating Reference Station (CORS) networks like Europe. NRTK provides near-instant, high-accuracy positioning up to 1 cm +1 ppm [1]. In this technique, each CORS transfers its observations to a control center; the latter calculates systematic effects modeling corrections over the entire serviced area. In this manner, rovers inside the network area connect to a server receiving corrections via a direct bi-directional communication channel. This allows the rover to resolve the ambiguities of the differenced carrier phase data and to estimate the coordinates of its position. The unfeasibility of this technique for the mass-market implementation resides in the non-trivial communication requirements since a bi-directional communication channel is required; thus a large-scale implementation would not be compatible with the actual infrastructure's capacity. On the other hand, PPP is a global precise positioning service, requiring the availability of precise reference satellite orbit and clock products. It exploits a network of CORS. Combining the precise satellite positions and clocks with a dual-frequency GNSS receiver, PPP minimizes GNSS errors to achieve better accuracy positioning. The corrections are delivered to the user via satellite L-band or through internet protocol (IP), resulting in decimetre-level accuracy with light ground infrastructure requirements. To resolve any local biases, such as the ionosphere and troposphere effects, multipath, and satellite geometry, PPP solutions typically take a period of 5–30 min, mostly for atmospheric error modeling, thus resulting in long AR times [3].

To overcome limitations related to these positioning techniques, the research community is hybridising PPP and RTK obtaining benefits from both technologies [12,18]. The principles of this hybridization have been described by Teunissen et al. in [13] where the analytical expressions for the variance matrices of the ambiguity-fixed and ambiguity-float PPP-RTK corrections have been illustrated. Subsequently, Khodabandeh et al. in [7] provided an analytical study of the quality of the PPP-RTK corrections as well as their impact on the user AR performance. Khodabandeh in [6] conducted an analytical study showing that the number of satellites and number of frequencies work in tandem to increase the correction latency, yet ensuring successful single-receiver AR. Indeed, PPP-RTK appears to be a promising technique for present and future urban mobility. The concept behind PPP-RTK is to improve PPP estimations by adding the atmospheric delay corrections which are derived from a local reference network; in this manner, the near-instantaneous AR is attainable for rovers inside the network, reducing considerably fixing times [17]. As reported by Wübbena et al. in [16], PPP-RTK exploits a 2D distribution of atmospheric errors created based on the raw measurements of the network of CORS; the quality of this "map" defines the AR capability of the service. Odijk et al. in [8] present and discuss the underlying principles of PPP-RTK demonstrating its GPS-based performance; Wang et al. in [15] tried to achieve rapid centimeter-level positioning for vehicle navigation in urban environments by developing a multi-frequency and multi-GNSS PPP-RTK model. The location-based corrections are most accurate in correspondence to each reference station and degrade as the distance between the rover and the nearest station increases, resulting in longer convergence times [5]. When the rover exceeds the limits of the network, AR is not possible anymore and there is a smooth transition to standard PPP [1]. Therefore, the key factors that make PPP-RTK a highly promising technique for accurate PNT reside in the short convergence times, the smooth degradation to the PPP solution, and the unidirectional data stream broadcast. The performance of a PPP-RTK system is highly dependent on how much data can be provided to the receiver and how fast it can be made available [1]. The quantity and frequency of data that can be delivered to users are limited by the available bandwidth and the data size. These two factors must be well balanced since less quantity of data means a reduction of accuracy and longer convergence times, whilst the reduction of the corrections update rate may introduce latencies that, especially within a high-dynamics application, are not eligible. For this reason, the implementation of 5G infrastructures within European cities is one of the main triggers for the feasibility of the PPP-RTK technique; at this point is well-known that 5G technology ensures transmission speeds previously unreleased as well as the capacity to provide access to a larger number of devices. For such reasons, PPP-RTK can reveal as an appropriate technique for mass-market urban navigation; thus, this paper aims to study how quickly the PPP-RTK technique reaches the positioning performance required by urban mobility applications. The test reported hereinafter has to model appropriately the conditions in an urban environment where satellite signals outage can occur and phase-ambiguity fixing can be lost. Therefore, several shutdowns of the receiver are imposed to investigate time-to-fix and positioning performance both in terms of accuracy and precision.

3   Experimental Setup

The present paper shows a preliminary test of the PPP-RTK technique, employing a low-cost receiver. The hardware employed consisted of a low-cost multi-constellation multi-frequency GNSS receiver, namely the u-blox zed-f9p, connected via SubMiniature (SMA) cable to a geodetic antenna (Topcon PG-A1).

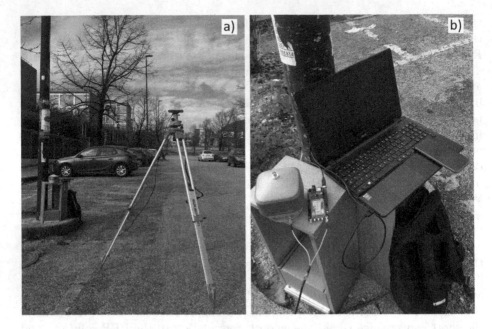

Fig. 1. The location where the experimental data were collected, and the equipment used in the experiment: (a) Topcon PG-A1 antenna, (b) u-blox zed-f9p.

A geodetic receiver sharing the same antenna was employed for comparison purposes. The test refers to a 2 h GNSS acquisition in the L1/E1, L2, and E5b frequencies. The test site is located in Naples, Italy; this scenario is expected to be a quasi-open-sky and low-multipath environment, as shown in Fig. 1. The correction service exploits the IP network and delivers two types of messages in SPARTN 2.0 format [4]: satellite clock corrections every 5 s and satellite orbits, bias, and atmosphere every 30 s. Given that the reference coordinates are expressed in the ETRF2000 (2008.0), a transformation was performed to consider the relationship of the ETRS89 with the International Terrestrial Reference System (ITRS), allowing the comparison with the PPP-RTK correction service solutions. The results were analysed by exploiting MATLAB® software, developed specifically for this work. The latter extracts some information from the binary u-blox proprietary file, e.g. high-precision positions and solution status, among all. The paper consists of a preliminary study, aiming to investigate the time it takes for AR; 15 consecutive hot starts were imposed and almost every 10 min a new ambiguity set was searched. According to the u-blox integration manual [14], in hot start mode, the receiver simulates a short-time shutdown (4 h or less), so that its ephemerides are still valid. Figure 2 depicts the sky-plot of the survey; a cut-off angle of 15° has been defined and the satellite under the cut-off angle are represented in grey whereas the satellites with an elevation angle bigger than 15° are represented with blue lines. The Figure shows that

also satellite E18 from the Galileo constellation has been tracked; according to
[10] and [9], this satellite presents a highly eccentric orbit.

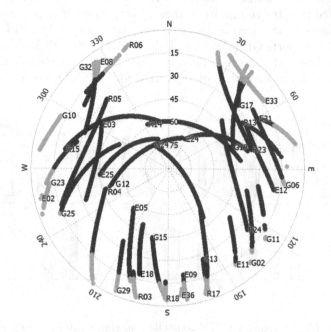

Fig. 2. Skyplot of the survey. The satellites with an elevation angle equal to or less
than 15° are represented with grey lines whereas the satellites with an elevation angle
bigger than 15° are represented with blue lines. (Color figure online)

4   Preliminary Results and Discussion

Figures 3, 4 and 5 depict the mean carrier-to-noise density ratio (C/N_0) comparison between the low-cost and the geodetic receivers for the different GNSS
constellations. Since the receivers share the same geodetic antenna, C/N_0 output indicates the accuracy of the tracked satellite observations and the noise
density as seen by receivers. It also indicates the level of noise present in the
measurements. The lower the signal-to-noise ratio the worse the quality of the
measurements. Figure 3 refers to the GPS constellation; the top row shows that
on L1 frequency PRN 2, 29, and 32 were tracked only by the geodetic receiver
while PRN 10 and 14 were tracked only by the low-cost one; the bottom row,
referred to L2 frequency, demonstrates that PRN 6, 29, and 32 were tracked
only by the geodetic receiver while PRN 10, 14, and 23 only by the low-cost one.
Similarly, Fig. 4 refers to the GLONASS constellation; the top row shows that on
L1 frequency only the geodetic receiver tracks PRN 6, 17, and 18 while only the
low-cost receiver tracks PRN 22; the same situation is depicted by the bottom
row, except for GLONASS satellites that do not provide the second frequency.
Moreover, Fig. 5 refers to the Galileo constellation; the top row shows that, on

E1 frequency, PRN 2, 8, 11, 12, and 18 were tracked only by the geodetic receiver while PRN 31 and 33 only by the low-cost one; bottom row, referred to E5b frequency, depicts the same behaviour, in terms of satellites tracked by receivers. It can be noted that the second frequencies (bottom panels of previous Figures) acquisitions are characterized by lower C/N_0. According to [14], PPP-RTK correction service supports GPS (L1 C/A, L2P, L2C, L5), GLONASS (L1 C/A, L2 C/A), and Galileo (E1, E5A/B). Therefore, the BeiDou constellation, even if it is tracked by u-blox receivers, is not supported for PPP-RTK corrections, so far.

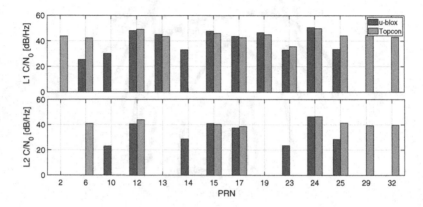

Fig. 3. Mean of C/N_0 values for GPS constellation; comparison between low-cost and geodetic receivers. Blue bars represent the low-cost receiver while red bars represent the geodetic receiver: the top row refers to the GPS L1 band; the bottom row to the GPS L2 band. (Color figure online)

Figure 6 shows the North, the East, and the Vertical error components obtained by the low-cost receiver over time depending on the solution quality status. The top, the middle, and the bottom panels refer to the North, the East, and the Vertical error components, respectively.

In the Figure are shown 15 samples generated for 2 h; each color represents a different solution status (SPP, DGNSS, float, and the fixed RTK): in particular, orange markers represent SPP solutions while yellow markers refer to DGNSS solution; moreover, green color represents float solutions, once fixed solutions were reached the receiver was left running for an extra 5 min interval represented by violet markers. Table 1 reports the time taken by the low-cost receiver either for float and fixed ambiguity estimates after each hot start imposed. Regarding the time to obtain the first ambiguity-float solution, the average is equal to 19 s whereas the shorter is equal to 10 s and the longer to 60 s. Regarding the time to obtain the first ambiguity-fixed solution, the average is equal to 129 s whereas the shorter time is equal to 44 s and the longer one to 457 s. During event 7, the receiver was unable to resolve the integer-ambiguity; therefore, a hot start was imposed after 1413 s. Moreover, during event 8, the fixed status was lost after

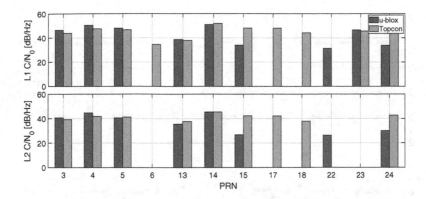

Fig. 4. Mean of C/N_0 values for GLONASS constellation; comparison between the low-cost and the geodetic receivers. Blue bars represent the low-cost receiver while red bars refer to the geodetic receiver: the top row refers to the GLONASS L1 band; the bottom row refers to the GLONASS L2 band. (Color figure online)

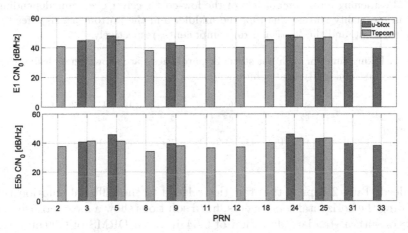

Fig. 5. Mean of C/N_0 values for Galileo constellation; comparison between low-cost and geodetic receivers. Blue bars represent the low-cost receiver, red bars represent the geodetic receiver: the top row refers to the Galileo E1 band; the bottom row refers to the Galileo E5 band. (Color figure online)

38 s without forcing the restart. It is worth noting that these performances were obtained by employing a geodetic antenna, as described in the previous section.

Figure 7 shows the scatter plot of the positioning errors obtained with the low-cost receiver; each color represents a different solution status (SPP/DGNSS, float and fixed RTK). As can be seen from the Figure, the scatter shows exactly what is expected: switching from SPP/DGNSS to RTK float and then RTK fixed, the solutions are gradually less dispersed and more accurate, as confirmed in Table 2.

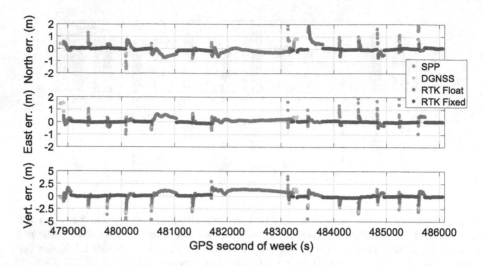

Fig. 6. Positioning error components of the low-cost receiver over time depending on the solution quality status. The top, the middle, and the bottom panels refer to the North, the East, and the Vertical error components, respectively.

Table 1. Fixing time for each hot start. In parenthesis are shown the relative time to obtain the first ambiguity-float solution.

# of hot start	1	2	3	4	5	6	7	8	9	10	11	12	13	14	15
Time to fixed solution (s)	189	51	62	153	457	68	–	72	68	285	44	46	132	46	128
	(60)	(13)	(10)	(14)	(14)	(17)	(12)	(28)	(0)	(16)	(14)	(16)	(16)	(16)	(15)

Indeed, Table 2 depicts the statistics related to the different solution types. Regarding the horizontal components, fixed solutions show a mean position error of 0.08 m with a standard deviation of 0.04 m and a DRMS of 0.09 m; degrading to float solutions the mean position error is equal to 0.39 m with a standard deviation of 0.24 m and a DRMS equal to 0.45 m. Moreover, when PPP-RTK corrections are not applied at all and only SPP/DGNSS solutions are achievable, statistics degrade to a mean position error of 1.11 m with a standard deviation of 0.79 m and a DRMS equal to 1.36 m. Regarding the vertical error statistics, the integer-ambiguity fixed solutions reveal a mean position error of 0.05 m with a standard deviation of 0.13 m and an RMS of 0.14 m. The float solutions vertical error statistics attest to 0.82 m, 0.57 m, and 1.00 m for the mean position error, the standard deviation, and the RMS, respectively. Lastly, when PPP-RTK corrections are not available and SPP/DGNSS solutions are attainable the mean position error is equal to −0.53 m with a standard deviation of 2.04 m and a RMS equal to 2.11 m. As one can notice, integer ambiguity-fixed solutions reveal both high-accuracy and high-precision levels. Considering the statistics reported in Table 2, we can state that the tested system achieves decimetre accuracy

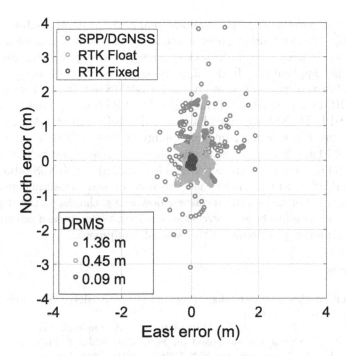

Fig. 7. Scatter plot of the positioning errors. Each color represents a different solution status: orange refers to SPP/DGNSS solutions, green represents RTK float solutions, and violet refers to RTK fixed solutions. (Color figure online)

Table 2. Positioning performance for different type of solution status.

Solution type	# of solutions	Horizontal			Vertical		
		mean (m)	std (m)	DRMS (m)	mean (m)	std (m)	RMS (m)
SPP/DGNSS	336	1.11	0.79	1.36	−0.53	2.04	2.11
RTK float	2913	0.39	0.24	0.45	0.82	0.57	1.00
RTK fixed	3946	0.08	0.04	0.09	0.05	0.13	0.14

in a few seconds; giving some seconds more, the statistics improve, reaching a subdecimetre-level of accuracy once the integer ambiguity is fixed.

5   Conclusions and Future Work

In this paper, PPP-RTK has proved to be a promising technique for decimetre-level positioning performance with low-cost receivers. During the experiment, the time-to-fix has been investigated after consecutive receiver shutdowns. The test showed that the employment of cost-effective equipment along with the exploitation of correction services allows reaching decimetre/sub-metre accuracy in about 20 s and sub-decimetre accuracy in about 2 min once the integer ambiguity is fixed. Results achieved have revealed promising for low-cost urban mobility applications. In detail, as reported in the previous section, integer ambiguity-fixed solutions have revealed a DRMS of 0.09 m whereas the float solution's DRMS was equal to 0.45 m. When PPP-RTK corrections are not available at all, SPP/DGNSS solutions have revealed a DRMS of 1.36 m. Regarding the vertical error component, integer ambiguity-fixed solutions have revealed an RMS of 0.14 m whereas the float solutions RMS was equal to 1.00 m. Lastly, when PPP-RTK corrections are not available at all, SPP/DGNSS solutions have revealed an RMS of 2.11 m. In the past, this level of near-instantaneous accuracy was a prerogative of high-grade receivers; nowadays, thanks to the deployment of ground- and satellite-based correction services, phase measurements can be exploited for precise positioning with low-cost equipment.

References

1. PPP-RTK market and technology report. European Global Navigation Satellite Systems Agency (1) (2019)
2. Ben Afia, A., Escher, A.C., Macabiau, C.: A low-cost GNSS/IMU/Visual monoSLAM/WSS integration based on Federated Kalman Filtering for navigation in urban environments. In: ION GNSS+ 2015, 28th International Technical Meeting of the Satellite Division of The Institute of Navigation, pp. 618–628. ION GNSS 2015, ION, ION, Tampa, FL, United States, September 2015. https://hal-enac.archives-ouvertes.fr/hal-01284973
3. Cai, C., Gao, Y.: Precise point positioning using combined GPS and GLONASS observations. J. Global Position. Syst. **6**, 13–22 (2007). https://doi.org/10.5081/jgps.6.1.13
4. Ferguson, K., Urquhart, L., Leandro, R.: SPARTN: the first open GNSS data standard that enables safe and accurate GNSS localization for automotive applications. In: Proceedings of the 33rd International Technical Meeting of the Satellite Division of The Institute of Navigation (ION GNSS+ 2020), pp. 2092–2106 (2020)
5. Gokdaş, O., Ozlüdemir, M.T.: A variance model in NRTK-based geodetic positioning as a function of baseline length. Geosciences **10**(7), 262 (2020). https://doi.org/10.3390/geosciences10070262, https://www.mdpi.com/2076-3263/10/7/262
6. Khodabandeh, A.: Single-station PPP-RTK: correction latency and ambiguity resolution performance. J. Geodesy **95**(4), 1–24 (2021)
7. Khodabandeh, A., Teunissen, P.: An analytical study of PPP-RTK corrections: precision, correlation and user-impact. J. Geodesy **89**(11), 1109–1132 (2015)
8. Odijk, D., et al.: PPP-RTK by means of s-system theory: Australian network and user demonstration. J. Spatial Sci. **62**(1), 3–27 (2017). https://doi.org/10.1080/14498596.2016.1261373
9. Robustelli, U., Benassai, G., Pugliano, G.: Signal in space error and ephemeris validity time evaluation of Milena and Doresa Galileo satellites. Sensors **19**(8), 1786 (2019). https://doi.org/10.3390/s19081786, http://www.mdpi.com/1424-8220/19/8/1786
10. Robustelli, U., Pugliano, G.: Galileo single point positioning assessment including FOC satellites in eccentric orbits. Remote Sens. **11**(13), 1555 (2019). https://doi.org/10.3390/rs11131555

11. Robustelli, U., Cutugno, M., Pugliano, G.: Positioning domain assessment of multi constellation dual frequency lowcost receivers in an highly degraded scenario. In: Parente, C., Troisi, S., Vettore, A. (eds.) R3GEO 2019. CCIS, vol. 1246, pp. 3–15. Springer, Cham (2020). https://doi.org/10.1007/978-3-030-62800-0_1

12. Teunissen, P., Odijk, D., Zhang, B.: PPP-RTK: results of CORS network-based PPP with integer ambiguity resolution. J. Aeronaut. Astronaut. Aviat. Ser. A **42**, 223–230 (2010)

13. Teunissen, P., Khodabandeh, A.: Review and principles of PPP-RTK methods. J. Geodesy **89**(3), 217–240 (2015)

14. U-blox: U-blox website. https://www.u-blox.com/en. Accessed 8 Mar 2022

15. Wang, B., et al.: Multi-frequency and Multi-GNSS PPP-RTK for vehicle navigation in urban environments. In: EGU General Assembly Conference Abstracts, pp. EGU21-9039 (2021)

16. Wübbena, G., Bagge, A., Schmitz, M.: Network based techniques for RTK applications. In: Proceedings of GPS Symposium, GPS JIN 2001, pp. 14–16, November 2001

17. Wübbena, G., Schmitz, M., Bagge, A.: PPP-RTK: precise point positioning using state-space representation in RTK networks. In: Proceedings of the 18th International Technical Meeting of the Satellite Division of The Institute of Navigation (ION GNSS 2005), pp. 2584–2594, September 2005

18. Zhang, B., Teunissen, P., Odijk, D.: A novel un-differenced PPP-RTK concept. J. Navig. **64**, S180–S191 (2011). https://doi.org/10.1017/S0373463311000361

A Calibration-Free Astrometric Clinometer for Static Monitoring

M. Chersich[1]([⊠]) [iD], D. Bolognini[2] [iD], D. Curone[1] [iD], F. Dacarro[2] [iD], and R. Devoti[3] [iD]

[1] YETITMOVES SRL, Via Ferrata 1, 27020 Pavia, Italy
{mchersich,dcurone}@yetitmoves.it
[2] EUCENTRE, Via Ferrata 1, 27020 Pavia, Italy
{davide.bolognini,filippo.dacarro}@eucentre.it
[3] INGV, Via di Vigna Murata, 605, 00143 Roma, Italy
roberto.devoti@ingv.it

Abstract. Among the various applications of astrometry in astronomical geodesy we must point out the accurate time frame maintenance, the measurement of the Earth rotation, and the study of the local geoid. At the time, the authors have found being no mention of use of astrometry techniques dedicated to measure variations of inclination of a ground infrastructure. We present herein a device composed by a tiny telescope coupled with a CMOS astronomical camera used to acquire star field images overnight. The pointing angle of the telescope is accurately computed by a process called plate-solving and then actualized to account for Earth precession and nutation. A series of tests was conducted for a preliminary assessment of the instrument performances. The results proved that the sensitivity of this cost-effective device is in the range of 10–20 μrad, while long-term repeatability is of the order of tens μrad, comparable to MEMS inclinometers, but without the need of frequent recalibration operations.

Keywords: Astrometry · Clinometer · Monitoring

1 Introduction

After a period of expansion and development, the European infrastructure network has reached an age where owners and managers are facing the problem of maintaining a population of ageing and deteriorating artifacts at an acceptable level of safety, performance, and aesthetics, given the limited financial resources. Moreover, design or construction deficiencies or lack of proper maintenance can result in a faster degradation of construction materials. Assessing the health state of ground infrastructures is crucial in terms of sustainability besides the maintenance optimization results in a less frequent or extensive maintenance-related service interruptions [1].

In this field, Structural Health Monitoring (SHM) provides automated methods for determining adverse changes in the mechanics of a system. Moreover, recent advancements in sensing technology (i.e., micro-electromechanical system (MEMS), acoustic sensors, fiber optics) and latest developments in the Internet of Things (IoT), mobile

E. Borgogno-Mondino and P. Zamperlin (Eds.): ASITA 2022, CCIS 1651, pp. 60–73, 2022.
https://doi.org/10.1007/978-3-031-17439-1_4

networks (5G), and wireless connectivity (Wi-Fi, Bluetooth 5), are finally creating a promising platform for the inspection and evaluation of structural systems. SHM systems (SHMS), based on these new technologies, have the potential to collect precise information about every event, providing a route to proactive maintenance operations.

Space techniques based on Earth observation and Global Navigation Satellite Systems (GNSS) have recently become of paramount importance for continuous monitoring, especially in those countries where hydrogeological hazard is relevant. Both above-mentioned techniques can measure accurately tiny horizontal and vertical displacements of ground or infrastructures. In the next few years, a new generation of cost effective GNSS receivers for the continuous monitoring of buildings featuring very high position accuracy and innovative end-to-end services will outcompete current state-of-the-art systems based on strain monitoring with dedicated gauges and A/D transducers.

However, to decouple translational and rotational movements, the usage of independent ground sensors, i.e., clinometers and/or tiltmeters is still needed. Together with the existing structural response parameters that are primarily adopted in SHM applications (i.e., acceleration, displacement, and strain), the occurrence of tilt during structural deformation provides information that is useful in evaluating the vertical deflection, via the angle of rotation in the case of horizontal members and the drift in the case of vertical members [2]. Current tiltmeters and clinometers are very sensitive to temperature variations and thus they must be calibrated at the factory before operation [3]. Due to ageing, the calibration procedure should be repeated rather frequently to guarantee nominal performances, operation that is often long and expensive and not very easy to carry out, requiring a uninstall-calibration-reinstall operation. This problem is particularly present in MEMS inclinometers, while state-of-art gravity-based tiltmeters can be more resistant, but they cost up to several thousand euros.

1.1 Applications of Astrometry in Geodesy

Precise measurement of the position of stars and other celestial bodies derive from the work of Hipparchus, who in the second century BC discovered the Earth precession. Modern astrometry derives from the works of the astronomer Friederich Bessel, to whom we owe the first measurement of stellar parallax in the 19th century.

During the 20th century, first with the use of photographic techniques and then with the advent of CCD cameras, astrometry has had a substantial boost leading to the measurement of stars position with sub-arcsec accuracy. The Gaia space mission, launched in 2013, has the goal to determine star parallaxes with a median error ranging from 4 μarcsec at 10 mag to 160 μarcsec at 20 mag [4].

Applications of astrometry are the most varied, ranging from the establishment and maintenance of astronomical reference frames to stars proper motion measurement, from monitoring of near-Earth objects for space awareness to discovery of new exo-planets. In a particular application, forming a discipline called geodetic astronomy, astrometry can be used for measuring the Earth rotation axis vector [5], for the geoid determination [6], and for accurate time frame maintenance [7]. Astrometric techniques have been used also in space to determine the attitude of satellites (star-trackers) [8], or, at ground, to determine the gravity-induced deflection from the vertical (digital zenith cameras) [9], and to determine the geodetic coordinates [10].

1.2 Proposed Concept

At the time, the authors have found, in scientific literature, no hint of use of astrometry techniques dedicated to measure variations of inclination of a ground infrastructure. However, the concept herein proposed inherits the principles of operation of a star-tracker and that of a digital zenith camera.

The basic idea is to use a very small telescope coupled with a commercial astronomical camera, fixed to the building or to the infrastructure to be monitored. Overnight many star field images are collected and automatically referenced respect to star catalogues through a process called plate-solving. The boresight is continuously measured, actualized to account for Earth precession and nutation, and normal (averaged) points are formed, one each night of observation. If the building or infrastructure were perfectly stationary the measured azimuth and altitude (in a topocentric reference frame) would be constant over time. If a dissipative force (that is a ground deformation or other external elastic force) acts on the structure or the structure tilts under its own gravitational load, these values would be subject to change over time.

This technique works only at night and when the sky is clear, and thus is suitable only for applications where very slow movements are expected. Being static monitoring based on the very low-frequency domain, the astrometric clinometer finds its natural placement in this application niche. Not least, it can be coupled with third-party MEMS or gravity-referenced electrolytic tiltmeters to maintain calibration over time. In this case, both fast-static and static monitoring is possible.

2 Materials and Methods

The setup used for testing is composed by a tiny telescope with a 32 mm diameter and 130 mm focal length, equipped with a frontal helical focuser, coupled with a cheap astronomical camera based on a AR0130CS CMOS sensor featuring a 1/3−in. CMOS digital image sensor with an active pixel array of 1280H x 960V. The whole optical system features a 5.95 arcsec/pixel image scale and a 3.36 sq. Degrees field of view. During image acquisition a small dew heater band has been placed around the telescope lens to avoid humidity condensation. The camera has been connected to a mini-PC through a USB-C connector.

A specific software has been developed to automatize the image acquisition process. To avoid possible drifts due to the limits in PC clock accuracy (1 s of clock error leads to an error of 15 arcsec in hour angle measurement) a third-party software, synchronizing the PC clock with external time servers (NTP), has been used. Images are saved as Flexible Image Transport System (FITS) files, an open standard commonly used in astronomy and capable of storing metadata in a specific header [11].

Once images have been collected, another software module asynchronously performed the plate-solving, by comparing the acquired star field with a database of star positions. We made use of the UCAC3 star catalogue, a high density, highly accurate, astrometric catalog of 100,766,420 stars covering the entire sky [13]. Stars positions are expressed in the ICRS (International Celestial Reference System) and given at epoch J2000.0.

Plate-solving provided the observed equatorial coordinates, i.e., hour angle (h) and declination (δ) [14] mean equinox and equator of J2000.0. Then the J2000.0 equinox has been converted to actual equinox true of date, using the Standard Of Fundamental Astronomy - SOFA open source library [12], which also accounts for atmospheric refraction, aberration (annual and diurnal), parallaxes, and other biases. Finally, for the target application, we converted the computed equatorial coordinates to local horizontal coordinates, i.e., azimuth (A, measured from the north point, turning positive to the east) and altitude (a, 90° when pointing to the zenith).

It must be noted that the conversion formulae between equatorial and local horizontal coordinates are non-trivial functions of the hour angle h and declination δ [14]. In particular:

1. near the celestial pole ($\delta = 90°$) the hour angle h can be undetermined or erratic. For this reason, we do not show the results of h when pointing to this direction.
2. near the zenith ($a = 90°$) the azimuth can be undermined or erratic. For this reason, we avoided to point to this direction.

On the other hand, pointing near the horizon may lead to inconsistent measurements due to strong atmospheric refraction and light pollution. Altitudes of about 45° has been considered as preferential, considering also that deposits of humidity, snow and dirt can thus be minimized, for example using a small canopy over the protecting glass of the device.

To avoid possible elongations of the star pattern, the exposure time has been limited to 2 s. Considering that the rotation rate of the Earth is 15 arcsec/sec, the maximum elongation (given the 6 arcsec/pixel image scale) resulted to be 5 pixels. Longer exposure time led to less precise measurements in h, especially when pointing at lower declinations.

3 Test Results

3.1 Laboratory Results

Results hereafter presented aim to verify the performances of the system and have been obtained in a controlled environment (laboratory) through the following tests:

1. Fast static, nearly 45 min of observations, pointing to the four cardinal points with $a\sim45°$. Purpose: understand how repeatability is affected when observing different sky zones.
2. Static, over five hours of observation pointing towards the direction with best repeatability in A and a, as obtained from test 1. Purpose: assess possible overnight drifts in A and a due to mismodelling.
3. Kinematic, pointing towards the preferential direction and applying tiny angular displacements in A and a. Purpose: measure the sensitivity of the instrument.
4. Long-term, fixing the astrometric clinometer to a bearing wall of a stable building. Purpose: assess long-term repeatability.

Test 1–3 have been carried out in a roll-off-roof astronomical observatory (45.1436°
N, 9.1699° E), featuring a German equatorial mount (10micron GM2000 HPS), equipped
with two high-precision absolute encoders mounted directly on each axis and featuring
a 0.1 arcsec resolution. This setup allowed sub-arcsec pointing precision. The mount
has been installed on a heavy cylindrical iron pier which is in turn bounded to a massive
reinforced concrete foundation. The mount has been used to change the pointed sky zone
(test 1) and to generate tiny displacements in azimuth and altitude (test 3). In test 2 the
astrometric clinometer has been directly screwed to the observatory pier.

Test 4 has been conducted at a testbed placed on the roof of the EUCENTRE building, exploiting a bearing wall. Here we installed two astrometric clinometers (hereafter
referred as V1 and V2) and a geodetic-grade gravity-referenced electrolytic clinometer
(Jewell Model 701–2) that has been used as benchmark. This instrument uses an absolute
gravity-referenced electrolytic sensor, featuring ultra-high sensitivity (up to <0.1 μrad)
with virtually zero long-term drift.

Fast Static Test
In Table 1 we resume the RMS obtained pointing at the four cardinal points. Each result
has been obtained in a single night and observing for nearly 45 min, acquiring two
images per minute.

Pointing at east and west the RMS resulted to be around 20 μrad for both azimuth
and altitude, while at south (near the meridian/equator crossing) the RMS of azimuth
was nearly 40 μrad, value due to the higher linear velocities involved.

The north direction (at the observatory latitude near the celestial pole) resulted to
be the geometry leading to the lowest variability in azimuth and altitude (<5 μrad) and
thus the most indicated to minimize measurement noise.

Table 1. Fast-static test, RMS of the observed residuals in μrad.

			Equatorial		Horizontal	
			RMS (μrad)			
Boresight	Cardinal point	Number of solved images	hour angle	declination	azimuth	altitude
h ~ 0 deg, δ ~ 0 deg	south	114	27.4	4.3	39.0	4.3
A ~ 270 deg, a ~ 45 deg	west	112	30.9	4.6	22.7	21.9
δ ~ 90 deg	north	119		3.0	4.6	4.8
A ~ 90 deg, a ~ 45 deg	east	110	29.2	4.5	21.1	20.8

Static Test
Static test has been carried out over four nights of observation and fixing the telescope
directly to the observatory pier, pointing toward north, i.e., the direction that optimizes
the repeatability of measurements, as resulted from fast-static test. More than 30 h of
data and a total of 2915 images acquired in four nights have been collected.

Table 2 shows the RMS of the azimuth and altitude residuals of the four data batch
in μrad. The RMS values are slightly higher than the ones computed by fast-static test
(Table 1) due to a non-neglectable drift shown by the time series. The source of this drift
is still under investigation.

Table 2. Static test, RMS of the observed residuals and total drift in μrad.

| | | | Horizontal | | | |
| | | | RMS (μrad) | | drift (μrad) | |
Boresight	Duration (hour)	Number of solved images	azimuth	altitude	azimuth	altitude
A=16.3, a=43.85	6.67	543	5.9	7.8	-6.9	-4.8
A=16.3, a=43.85	7.91	729	5.8	8.0	-2.8	-11.2
A=0.12, a=44.78	5.62	529	7.1	4.3	4.4	-6.0
A=-0.18, a=45.14	12.33	1114	8.1	6.2	-3.8	-3.3

Kinematic Test

The graphics shown in Fig. 1 have been obtained programming the mount to move by tiny changes in azimuth and altitude (24.5 μrad) every twenty images.

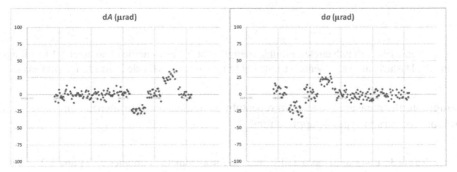

Fig. 1. Effects of a 24.5 μrad displacement in horizontal coordinates are clearly visible.

Empirically, we can infer the sensitivity of the astrometric clinometer to be in the 10–20 μrad range.

Long-Term Test

The time series of the geodetic-grade gravity-referenced electrolytic clinometer used as benchmark, composed by 262 days of consecutive observations (from 13th Jan 2021 to 2nd Oct 2021), shown an RMS less than 1 μrad in both axes and a nearly zero drift. This confirmed that the bearing wall was stable and can be considered a true "zero" for the astrometric solutions.

Figure 2 shows the overnight averages of the residuals obtained with the astrometric device V1 and the average ambient temperature. Data start from 24th Feb 2021 to 11th Sep 2021. A 4th degree polynomial (dashed line) has been superimposed.

As can be inferred from Table 3, the RMS values are of the order of tens of μrad. The astrometric clinometer results are affected by a seasonal oscillatory signal that is clearly anticorrelated with respect to temperature. The occurrence of a possible spurious effect due to temperature variations is still under investigation. Possible candidates are the thermal deformations of the telescope body and the influence of a big conditioning system standing right in front of the testbed. In any case, as we will see in the next

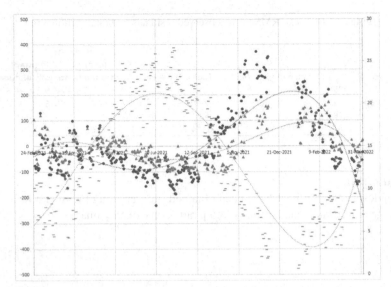

Fig. 2. Residuals (azimuth circles, altitude triangles) of the astrometric clinometer V1 in a long-term test. Dashed curve represents the ambient temperature. Left scale in μrad, right in Celsius.

paragraph, the measured long-term repeatability makes the astrometric clinometer still suitable for certain types of applications.

Table 3. Long-term repeatability in μrad for astrometric clinometers V1 and V2.

		RMS (μrad)	
Clinometer	# observations	azimuth	altitude
V1	172	123	64
V2	88	82	79

3.2 Roncovetro Landslide Monitoring

The "Lavina di Roncovetro" landslide (Fig. 3, on the left) is in the northern-Apennines of the Reggio Emilia Province in Italy, between the hamlets of Roncovetro and Vedriano, and presents rather particular morphometric and kinematic features. It is 2.5 km long with a maximum width of 300 m; the depletion and accumulation zones are separated by a long and narrow landslide body, 30 to 40 m wide [15].

In the northernmost portion of the landslide, in June 2021, the Italian Institute for Geophysics and Volcanology (INGV) installed a single-frequency DISPLAYCE GNSS monitoring system [16] composed by three GNSS (RV02, RV03 and RV04) on the main deformation area, and one GNSS (RV01) outside the crown of the landslide. The calculation of the displacements is carried out through the widely known Double Difference (DD) technique [17].

To check the stability of RV01 and to use it in the future as reference point for the DD measurements, INGV started monitoring possible RV01 movements using, as reference, an external double-frequency geodetic-grade GNSS (Topcon Odyssey RS), located in Castelnuovo Ne' Monti (RE), at about 10 km from the monitoring site. This GNSS permanent station is part of the TopNet network (Topcon Positioning Systems Inc.).

The astrometric clinometer has been installed on the RV01 pole (Fig. 3, on the right), to verify the actual stability of the concrete monumentation used to fix the GNSS antenna, and to separate translations from rotations and understand their correlation, if any.

Fig. 3. Left: Lavina di Roncovetro. Right: RV01 GNSS station and the astrometric clinometer.

The telescope and the CMOS camera have been embedded in an aluminum pipe sealed by a UV/IR-Cut filter screwed on top to protect from external agents (Fig. 3, on the left). The pipe has been cut so to avoid deposits of water or snow and to avoid birds from leaning on the glass. A dew heater band has been placed around the telescope lens to avoid humidity condensations. The protective box contains the electronics, i.e., the GNSS receiver, back-up battery, a mini-PC for astrometric images acquisition and processing and a 4G LTE router for GNSS and astrometric solutions data transmission.

GNSS displacements are expressed in a local topocentric frame whose east and north axis form a plane tangent to the WGS84 ellipsoid and fixed to the GNSS antenna phase center (the topocentric origin), and the up axis points upwards, along the normal to that plane.

To compare GNSS displacements with the astrometric solutions we must transform the azimuth and altitude values to linear displacements expressed in the same ENU local reference system. In Fig. 4 we show a schematic representation of the system.

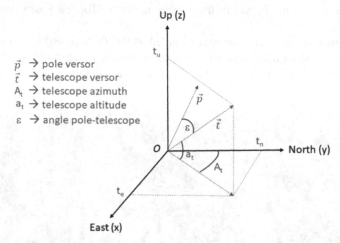

Fig. 4. Pole and telescope versors in the local topocentric reference system ENU.

To transform the astrometric solution (a_t, A_t) into linear displacements we start defining the zenithal distance

$$z_t = \frac{\pi}{2} - a_t \tag{1}$$

Then we have the ENU components of the telescope versor:

$$\begin{cases} t_e = \sin z_t \sin A_t \\ t_n = \sin z_t \cos A_t \\ t_u = \cos z_t \end{cases} \tag{2}$$

and, similarly, the ENU components of the pole versor:

$$\begin{cases} p_e = \sin z_p \sin A_p \\ p_n = \sin z_p \cos A_p \\ p_u = \cos z_p \end{cases} \tag{3}$$

We must set two constraints for the rigid body formed by the pole (holding the GNSS antenna) and the telescope, i.e.:

1. the pole rotates around a fixed pivot, typically located inside the concrete plinth in which the pole is immerged.
2. the pole does not twist, i.e., rotations around the pole axis are not allowed or, equivalently, rotations around the telescope axis are not allowed (from the astronomical point of view, there is no field rotation).

The first assumption translates into the condition that the vertices of the pole and telescope versors moves on a sphere, and thus:

$$\cos \varepsilon = \cos z_t \cos z_p + \sin z_t \sin z_p \cos(A_t - A_p)$$

that, using Eqs. (2), can be rewritten as

$$\cos \varepsilon = t_u \cos z_p + t_n \sin z_p \cos A_p + t_e \sin z_p \sin A_p \tag{4}$$

being ε (the angle formed by the telescope and the pole versors) known and unchanging over time (it depends only on the rigid collar-stirrup system that fixes the telescope to the pole, in our case, approximately 45°).

The second assumption means that the straight line obtained as intersection of the plane formed by telescope and pole versors (*tp* plane), and the NE plane (local horizon) does not rotate. The plane equation is given by:

$$\det \begin{pmatrix} x & y & z \\ t_e & t_n & t_u \\ p_e & p_n & p_u \end{pmatrix} = 0$$

that is to say

$$x \cdot \det \begin{pmatrix} t_n & t_u \\ p_n & p_u \end{pmatrix} - y \cdot \det \begin{pmatrix} t_e & t_u \\ p_e & p_u \end{pmatrix} + z \cdot \det \begin{pmatrix} t_e & t_n \\ p_e & p_n \end{pmatrix} = 0$$

which leads to

$$x \cdot (t_n \cdot p_u - t_u \cdot p_n) - y \cdot (t_e \cdot p_u - t_u \cdot p_e) + z \cdot (t_e \cdot p_n - t_n \cdot p_e) = 0$$

Being the intersection of the *tp* plane with the NE plane the place of the points such as $z = 0$, then we have:

$$y = \frac{t_n \cdot p_u - t_u \cdot p_n}{t_e \cdot p_u - t_u \cdot p_e} \cdot x$$

This is the equation of the straight line obtained by the intersection of the *tp* plane with the horizon. The non-twisting pole constrain means that the angular coefficient of the straight line must be constant in time. This value (γ) may be found, for example, if, during the installation, we level the pole (pole pointing to zenith). In this case, we have $p_{n_0} = 0$, $p_{e_0} = 0$ and $p_{u_0} = 1$, i.e.

$$\gamma = \frac{t_{n_0}}{t_{e_0}}$$

with t_{n_0} and t_{e_0} the values computed from the first astrometric solution through Eqs. (2).

The two fundamental equations then are:

$$\begin{aligned} t_u \cos z_p + t_n \sin z_p \cos A_p + t_e \sin z_p \sin A_p - \cos \varepsilon = 0 \\ t_e \cos z_p - \gamma t_u \sin z_p \sin A_p - t_n \cos z_p + t_u \sin z_p \cos A_p = 0 \end{aligned} \tag{5}$$

We have two non-linear equations for two unknowns (z_p and A_p), that can be found using a proper root finding algorithm, supplying the Jacobian (the matrix of partial derivatives) and thus providing the gradient of each target function. For the results shown hereafter we used the Powell's dogleg method [18], a robust algorithm allowing fast convergence when other methods have failed.

Results

Since its installation at the Lavina di Roncovetro landslide on 16th June 2021, the astrometric clinometer proved to be affordable in terms of acquisition rate. The camera (as on 22nd May 2022) acquired about 239.964 images for a total number of 276 normal points out of 340 available nights, with 81% acquisition rate.

The GNSS data coming from the reference station in Castelnuovo Ne' Monti (RE) span the period from 6th August 2022 to 29th March 2022, so the results hereafter shown are limited to this period. Furthermore, being the vertical movements not so representative of the deformation in the given time frame, we will limit the results to planimetric movements only.

In Fig. 5 we show the GNSS planimetric displacements of RV01. As we can see, despite the point has been installed outside the crown of the landslide, it moved southward by more than 20 mm, with an estimated velocity of about 45 mm/yr. The east displacement is more contained with a roughly oscillating behavior confined to few mm.

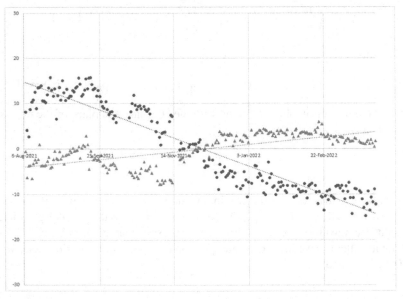

Fig. 5. GNSS (RV01) planimetric displacements (N circles, E triangles) and fitting regressions. Vertical scale is in mm.

In Fig. 6 (N component in grey and E component in yellow), we show the NE movements obtained with the astrometric clinometer and computed through Eqs. (5). As we can see, the dispersion of the residuals is very low with respect to GNSS, indicating a better precision of the astrometric solutions. Short gaps are attributable to cloudy nights, i.e., when the astrometric clinometer did not acquire any image.

In the same figure (N component in blue and E component in orange) we superimposed the graph of the GNSS displacements after having removed the rotation component. This graph represents the pure translation due to the landslide. It is interesting to note that the translational velocity of the GNSS antenna is slower than what initially indicated by the GNSS measurements (Table 4).

Moreover, rotations and translations follow a similar trend, featuring a correlation of 0.88 in the north component and 0.69 in the east component. This is a clear indication that the rotation of the pole is induced mainly by the landslide movement and, to a lesser extent, by an intrinsic instability of the holding plinth.

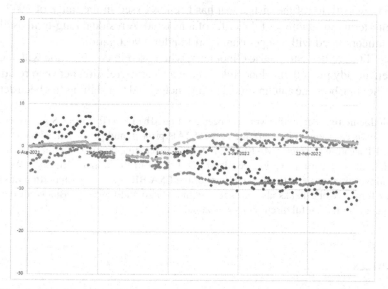

Fig. 6. Translations (N circles, E triangles) and rotations (N long dashes, E short dashes) of the GNSS antenna. Vertical scale is in mm.

In Table 4 we show the planimetric velocities before and after the removal of the rotational component.

Table 4. Velocity of the landslide before and after the removal of the rotational components.

	Velocity (mm/yr)	
	translation+rotation	translation only
N	-45	-28
E	12	7

4 Conclusions

Clinometers have proved to be essential components of a structural health monitoring system. In less expensive devices, compensation for the temperature drift error is not very sophisticated, and such tiltmeters may show nonlinear output in reaction to changes in temperature and erratic drifts or other behaviors that would be difficult to predict without accurate and toilsome calibration procedures. The opportunity, in the future, to use clinometers weakly dependent on temperature and ageing will give the chance to drastically reduce the periodic calibration costs, keeping the long-term accuracy and reliability of the data.

The astrometric clinometer herein presented has shown good performances, comparable with MEMS clinometers but without the drawback of frequent recalibration operations. The sensitivity of the instrument has been assessed in the range of 10–20 μrad while long-term repeatability of the order of tens μrad. A residual long-term oscillatory pattern anticorrelated with temperature is still under investigation.

Capabilities of the astrometric clinometer, when used in combination with a GNSS, have been already proved on a landslide, where a clear correlation between rotations of the pole (holding both the antenna and the clinometer) and translations has been detected.

Acknowledgements. Part of this work has been co-funded by ESA (European Space Agency) and ASI (Italian Space Agency) in the frame of the iSTAR project, and partly funded by Ministry of Ecological Transition (formerly MATT) through the project "Integrated and multi-scale approach for the definition of earthquake-induced landslide hazard in the Italian territory". We wish to thank Andrea Cosentino and Roberto Giuliani of the ESA BIC Lazio for supporting this project in various forms. A big thanks also goes to Cosimo Marzo and Giuseppe Bianco of the Italian Space Agency for the useful discussions and valuable advice.

References

1. Wenzel, H.: Health Monitoring of Bridges. Wiley, New York (2009). https://doi.org/10.1002/9780470740170
2. Panuntun, R.B., Aminullah, A., Suhendro, B., Wardana, P.K.: Bridge displacement estimation using tiltmeter data. J. Civ. Eng. Forum 5(2) (2019). https://doi.org/10.22146/jcef.43670
3. Chersich, M., Bolognini, D., Curone, D., Dacarro, F.: A calibration-free astrometric tiltmeter for static SHM. In: Cunha, A., Caetano E. (eds.) 10th International Conference on Structural Health Monitoring of Intelligent Infrastructure, Porto, Portugal (2021)
4. Perryman, M.A.C.: Overview of the Gaia mission in astrometry in the age of the next generation of large telescopes. In: Seidelmann, P.K., Monet, A.K.B. (eds.) ASP Conference Series, vol. 338 (2005)
5. Bizouard, C., Capitaine, N., Ron, C., Vondrák, J.: Principal term of nutation from the combination of VLBI observations and optical astrometry. Int. Astron. Union Colloq. 165, 481–486 (1997)
6. Machotka, R., Kuruc, M., Volařík, T.: Local quasigeoid model creation from astrogeodetic measurements. Stud. Geophys. Geod. 57, 27–46 (2013)
7. Johnston, K.J., de Vegt, C.: Reference frames in astronomy. Annu. Rev. Astron. Astrophys. 37, 97–125 (1999)

8. Liebe, C.C.: Accuracy performance of star trackers - a tutorial. IEEE Trans. Aerosp. Electron. Syst. **38**, 587–599 (2002)
9. Hirt, C., Bürki, B., Somieski, A., Seeber, G.: Modern: determination of vertical deflections using digital zenith cameras. J. Surv. Eng. **136**, 1–12 (2010)
10. Izadmehr, M., Ghomi, M.K.: Design and construction of a portable high resolution positioner using star patterns. Astrophys. Space Sci. **364**(5), 1 (2019). https://doi.org/10.1007/s10509-019-3565-5
11. Pence, W.D., Chiappetti, L., Page, C.G., Shaw, R.A., Stobie, E.: Definition of the flexible image transport system (FITS), version 3.0. A&A 524 (2010)
12. International Astronomical Union. SOFA - Standard of Fundamental Astronomy. https://www.iausofa.org/
13. Finch, C.T., Zacharias, N., Wycoff, G.L.: UCAC3: astrometric reductions. Astron. J. **139**, 2200–2207 (2010)
14. Roy, A.E., Clarke, D.: Astronomy, Principles and Practice, 4th edn. Institute of Physics Publishing, Bristol and Philadelphia (2003). ISBN 0-7503-0917-2
15. Bertolini, G.: La Lavina di Roncovetro, Quaderni di Geologia Applicata, 8–2 (2001)
16. Zuliani, D., Tunini, L., Di Traglia, F., Chersich, M., Curone, D.: Cost-effective, single-frequency GPS network as a tool for landslide monitoring. Sensors **22**, 3526 (2022). https://doi.org/10.3390/s22093526
17. Hofmann-Wellenhof, B., Lichtenegger, H., Collins, J.: GPS Theory and Practice. Springer, New York (2001). ISBN 978-3-211-83534-0. https://doi.org/10.1007/978-3-7091-6199-9
18. Powell, M.J.D.: A new algorithm for unconstrained optimization. In: Rosen, J.B., Mangasarian, O.L., Ritter, K. (eds.) Nonlinear Programming, pp. 31–66. Academic Press, New York (1970)

Data Exploitation: Services and Tools

Exploiting Copernicus Data via Access Hubs and Processing Tools

Lorenza Apicella$^{(\boxtimes)}$ ⓘ, Monica De Martino$^{(\boxtimes)}$ ⓘ, and Alfonso Quarati ⓘ

Institute for Applied Mathematics and Information Technologies - National Research
Council, Genoa, Italy
{lorenza.apicella,demartino,quarati}@ge.imati.cnr.it

Abstract. To take full advantage of the enormous amount of free and
open Earth Observation data provided by the Copernicus Programme,
users have to be aware of the several data access and processing tools
available and to be able to exploit them to develop satellite-based applications. To this end, we provide an overview of Copernicus data access
hubs and processing tools and compare them based on their features for
their suitability in supporting users in developing satellite applications
based on Copernicus data.

Keywords: Copernicus Programme · Open data · Satellite imagery ·
Data access hub · Processing tool

1 Introduction

Earth Observation (EO) data is pivotal for many scientific, industrial, and government applications worldwide [9]. Changes on Earth's surface are largely due
to human decision-making at multiple scales. Thus, a better understanding of the
state, trend, and effects of land changes, is essential for the sustainable development goals [10,14] as advocated by the 8th Environmental Action Program [12],
setting the line of the environmental and climate policy action of the European
Union (EU) for reducing greenhouse gas emissions by 2030.

The European Copernicus Programme[1] is one of the main sources of satellite
EO and in-situ free and open data, accessible by any citizen, and any organisation around the world, for sustaining relevant social and economic advancements
to the EU. It is managed by the European Commission (EC) in partnership
with the European Space Agency (ESA[2]), the European Organisation for the
Exploitation of Meteorological Satellites (EUMETSAT[3]), the European Centre
for Medium-Range Weather Forecasts (ECMWF[4]), EU Agencies and Mercator Océan[5]. Copernicus addresses the provision of EO data through a group

---

[1] www.copernicus.eu.
[2] www.esa.int/.
[3] www.eumetsat.int/.
[4] https://www.ecmwf.int/.
[5] https://www.mercator-ocean.eu/en/.

E. Borgogno-Mondino and P. Zamperlin (Eds.): ASITA 2022, CCIS 1651, pp. 77–88, 2022.
https://doi.org/10.1007/978-3-031-17439-1_5

of missions called *Sentinels* and the contributing missions, which collect multi-spectral images of Europe and almost the totality of the Earth. Information extracted from this data is also released by Copernicus core services for six thematic areas: land, marine, atmosphere, climate, emergency and security. Copernicus's high-resolution data releasing via free and open data policy established a crucial paradigm shift in EU policies for global environmental management and security [9]. Notwithstanding its undeniable potential, the huge amount of data daily collected by Copernicus satellites risk, like other public Open Data sources [19–21], to be hardly used. A Copernicus User Uptake strategy [1] has been undertaken by the EC in 2016, promoting several initiatives [24] to raise user awareness, and increase their skills, thus ensuring that Copernicus data benefits expectations materialize. In this wake, the EO-UPTAKE project[6] was funded by the Liguria Region, Italy, in 2019, to promote the development and the dissemination of skills and competencies for the exploitation of Copernicus data and services.

From the experience gained on EO-UPTAKE [19], we argue that a possible factor hindering the use of Copernicus data can be related to the perceived complexity of the Copernicus ecosystem, which may lead end-users to wonder what data is available, as well as how data can be discovered, accessed and used. Copernicus products are accessible by several platforms and elaborated through various processing tools. Therefore, while EO experts may have the knowledge and possess the necessary tools to develop satellite-based applications, users with low EO and Remote Sensing (RS) skills are likely to face three issues: "Which tools are available to access and process RS data?", "What are the main features of these tools?" and "What applications can one build with Copernicus data?".

While in our previous works we addressed the last issue, exemplifying the use of Copernicus product in the areas of Natural Disaster Management [5], Urban Monitoring [3], and Agriculture [6], in this paper, we address the other two issues. We first present an overview of some relevant access hubs and processing tools, then briefly analyze their main features and how their exploitation by non-expert users can support Copernicus-based applications development.

2   Background

Copernicus Upstream Sector is the infrastructural part of the programme where the satellites, i.e. the *space segment*, acquire and distribute data to the *ground segment*, for data stream operations and calibration. It currently includes three Sentinel missions, namely Sentinel-1 (S-1A, S-1B), Sentinel-2 (S-2A, S-2B), and Sentinel-3 (S-3A, S-3B), plus two single satellites, Sentinel-5 Precursor (S-5P) and Sentinel-6 Michael Freilich[7] (S-6) presently in orbit. They deliver multi-spectral images, i.e. different images of the same spatial and temporal interval, acquired on different wavelengths of the electromagnetic spectrum. Multi-spectral imaging measures light in a small number of spectral bands (typically 3

---

[6] www.gisig.eu/eouptake.
[7] https://www.nasa.gov/sentinel-6/overview.

to 15) for EO and environmental monitoring. Satellite products present different spatial, temporal, spectral, radiometric resolutions.

The Copernicus Downstream Sector is the part of the programme where data are processed and published, thus playing the essential role of transforming the spatial data produced by satellite platforms into EO products and services directly usable by the end-users [18]: Copernicus provides *Sentinel products*, i.e. satellite multi-spectral images, metadata and other files, plus a set of *core service resources*, where Sentinel products and other types of data are processed in ready-to-use thematic information [6]. All this data is available and accessible from different access points.

Except for S-5P data, distributed in NetCDF[8] format, S[1-2-3-6] products are disseminated using the Standard Archive Format for Europe specification (SAFE[9]), designed to act as a common format for archiving and conveying data within ESA EO archiving facilities, with Sentinel-specific features. The SENTINEL-SAFE format wraps in a zip folder image data, XML product metadata and other information related to the Sentinel mission and the pre-processing levels, as detailed in a 'data format' section of the Sentinel's user guide[10].

2.1 Copernicus Data Access Hubs

Sentinel satellites imagery is made freely available and accessible through several access points. ESA and EUMETSAT manage respectively the Copernicus Open Access Hub (COA[11]), and the EUMETSAT Data Centre[12]. Moreover, Google Earth Engine (GEE[13]) and the Sentinel Hub[14] platform, managed by Sinergise, provides access either to Sentinel and other satellite products (see Table 1).

The COA Hub is the primary point of access to the free and open Sentinel products [22]. Through the Open Hub and S-5P Pre-Ops Hub, one can discovery and download, via Guided User Interface (GUI), respectively S-[1-2], S-3 land monitoring and S5-P products. The Advanced Program Interface (API) hub provides S-[1-2-3-5P] products, by searching and accessing via scripting queries.

EUMETSAT Data Centre is a long-term archive making available to users one of Europe's largest and most comprehensive collections of meteorological data, providing, on request, either Sentinel S-3 marine products and S-6, and other mission products. Accessing meteorological data is done through registering in the ESA Earth Observation Portal (eoPortal[15]) and ordering through the Online Ordering Application-EUMETSAT's data catalog. Users can access Data Centre collections in the EUMETSAT Product Navigator[16], which allows prod-

---

[8] https://www.unidata.ucar.edu/software/netcdf/.
[9] https://Earth.esa.int/SAFE/.
[10] https://sentinels.copernicus.eu/web/sentinel/user-guides.
[11] https://scihub.copernicus.eu/.
[12] https://www.eumetsat.int/eumetsat-data-centre.
[13] https://code.earthengine.google.com/.
[14] https://www.sentinel-hub.com/.
[15] https://eoportal.org/web/eoportal/home.
[16] https://navigator.eumetsat.int/start.

Table 1. Products and resources provided by data access hubs and core services.

	Sentinel	Other missions	Thematic resources
COA	S[1-2-5P], S-3 land products		
EUMETSAT Data Centre	S-3 marine products, S-6	Meteosat, Jason[1-2] Metop[A-B-C], Eumetsat SAFs, AVHRR	
GEE	S[1-2-3-5P]	Landsat, MODIS.	GEE Thematic Resources
Sentinel Hub	S[1-2-3-5P]	Landsat, MODIS, Envisat, Prova-V, GIBS	Copernicus core services, Planet-NICFI
CLMS			Global, European, local land products
CAMS			Atmospheric data
C3S			Climate data
CMEMS			Ocean products data
CEMS			On demand mapping, early warning and monitoring data

ucts lists browsing even without credentials, and redirects users to the Ordering system for the download.

GEE provides access to several satellite collections (S-[1-2-3-5P], Landsat, and a wide variety of products and thematic resources[17] out of the Copernicus Programme), including geo-spatial datasets at planetary-scale. Users can browse such resources by the *Explorer* interface providing a single access hub.

Sentinel Hub provides free access to a range of satellite imagery (such as Sentinel, Landsat, Envisat, and Proba) and core service resources through EO Browser tool. It also grants pay-per-use access to commercial satellite missions products, such as Airbus SPOT, Pleiades, PlanetScope, WorldView/GeoEye, available in the data catalogues of Sentinel Hub.

Besides the Sentinel imagery, the Copernicus Programme disseminates the thematic information of the core services. Such ready-to-use preprocessed resources are derived from Sentinels' and other satellite products to serve specific use-cases, thus they may be especially interesting for users with less experience with EO data. These thematic resources are accessible through the six Copernicus core service hubs[18] namely: the Copernicus Atmosphere Monitoring Service (CAMS), the Copernicus Marine Environment Monitoring Service (CMEMS), the Copernicus Land Monitoring Service (CLMS), the Copernicus Climate Change Service (C3S); the Copernicus Emergency Management Service (CEMS), and the Copernicus Security Service (CSS). Apart from CSS, whose products are not available to all users, the other services are provided for free.

---

[17] https://developers.google.com/earth-engine/datasets/catalog.
[18] https://www.copernicus.eu/en/copernicus-services.

Table 2. Processing tools

	Pre-processing tools	Thematic processors	Classifiers	Management tools
SNAP	Subset, resample, reprojection	Optical, radar	Supervised, unsupervised	Graph, batch processing, statistics, Python console, metadata explorer
GEE	Subset, resample, reprojection	Optical, radar	Supervised, unsupervised	Graph, batch processing, statistics, Python console
Sentinel Hub				Timelapses generator, data fusion and 3D visualization
Q-GIS	Subset, reprojection		Supervised	3D visualization, raster/vector converter, batch processing, attribute tables edits, custom statistics, Python console

2.2 Copernicus Data Processing Tools

ESA and other geospatial data service providers offer specific tools to deploy Copernicus data processing and analysis workflows (see Table 2). ESA has promoted the development of a set of free open-source toolboxes for the scientific exploitation of Sentinel missions S-[1-2-3], atmospheric and altimetry toolboxes, and other tools for further satellite missions (e.g. ESA SMOS[19], PROBA-V[20]).

A common architecture for all toolboxes is the Sentinel Application Platform (SNAP[21]), a desktop application for the scientific exploitation of EO data. SNAP allows image navigation and visualization, the information extraction and the analysis of satellite images both for Sentinels as well as other third-party missions. It also offers a graph framework, for products batch processing and a Python console for a scripting processing management[22].

GEE and EO Browser, other than supply access points to various satellite platforms, also provide geo-spatial processing services for these resources. GEE supplies a processing tool, the *Code Editor*, for the development of complex geospatial workflows with APIs, supported by a *client library* with ready to use and editable scripts. It is freely available for academic and research use, while for commercial it presents a pay-for model (with increased computational speed and higher processing power with the granted support of EO-experts). Sentinel Hub, through EO Browser, grants a 30 days trial period offering customized data browsing visualization, the execution of simple processing steps (i.e. the calculation of vegetation indices and simple *band math*), and the download of the resulting maps. It also offers a *data fusion* functionality to combine Sentinel data with other collections in a single image, and a *time-lapse* tool, for the video-rendering of satellite images time-series. Moreover, Sentinel Hub allows the development of ad-hoc applications through the RESTful API interface, enabling standardized import of RS products into Geographic Information System (GIS).

---

[19] https://earth.esa.int/eogateway/missions/smos.
[20] https://earth.esa.int/eogateway/missions/proba-v.
[21] www.step.esa.int/main/toolboxes/snap.
[22] https://step.esa.int/main/toolboxes/snap/.

Developing EO applications often implies the use of GIS software, allowing data processing, analysis, integration and visualisation of the final result (e.g. with the insertion of the scale and other geographical references etc.). Quantum GIS (QGIS[23]) is an open-source desktop application for importing and processing Sentinel products using dedicated plugins freely exploitable by users.

3   Exploiting Hubs and Tools: Highlights

The development of most of the EO-based applications [4], from agriculture [8], to forestry [23], from renewable energy [2] to urban monitoring [15], shares the same type of workflow, schematized in Fig. 1, consisting of four phases: i) *data selection and download*; ii) *pre-processing*, which prepares the satellite images for the iii) *processing*, which elaborates and/or analyzes them, based on the objectives of the application in order to iv) *present the results*. To carry out these phases, users can exploit the most suitable access hubs and tools according to the core business of their application and their competencies in RS and EO. Based on the experience gained in the EO-UPTAKE project in developing three application scenarios [3,5,6], we present in the following some of the features and functionalities of these hubs and tools by highlighting their appropriateness according to user task and needs.

For *selecting and downloading* Copernicus resources, users must identify the most suitable functionalities offered by the various tools, according to their needs and the project to be deployed requirements. For instance, if an application requires to operate on data from different missions, users should adopt tools offering multiple satellite products to optimize the time spent for the study areas selection and the covered period. While COA Hub provides only Sentinel products, EUMETSAT Data Centre, GEE, and Sentinel Hub offer Sentinel archives along with other collections, such as Landsat 5, 7 and 8, Envisat Meris, MODIS, Proba-V and GIBS products. Some of these collections are offered according to a pay-per-use model requiring subscription fees based on users' necessities, e.g. on EUMETSAT hubs, the so-called *non-essential data* are licensed under specific conditions[24]. Notwithstanding these fees, users may need paid data than a free product, for example, when the resolution of the former is better: Airbus SPOT and Pleiades collections present data with a spatial resolution of up to 30 cm, 30 times higher than S-2 products.

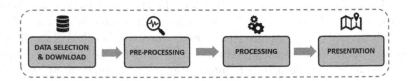

Fig. 1. Satellite based application workflow

---

[23] www.qgis.org/en/site/.
[24] https://www.eumetsat.int/eumetsat-data-licensing.

By the level of their information technology skills, users may exploit data hubs via GUI or API. All the analyzed access points provides API access for consulting, downloading, and processing bulk datasets. API access is recommended for users who make huge employment of Copernicus data, but it requires the basic knowledge of the hub technical features along with adequate competencies of programming. GUI or Web-UI access is recommended for users newly approaching RS and EO datasets.

COA Hub is currently the primary means of accessing Sentinel data [7], through its GUI users can specify the extent of the Area Of Interest (AOI) by drawing a bounding box or a polygon. Users may also exploit a search interface with information regarding the sensing period, the satellite, the platform, the sensor mode, the polarization, the application of a cloud filter to select a proper cloud coverage percentage, the selection of the orbit number, etc. If a relevant product is found, the product can be pre-loaded into a personal cart or directly downloaded. The download procedure has to be performed for each product singularly with the GUI. COA Hub also allows bulk downloading up to 100 products, using a metalink file of the personal cart (however the use of a command-line is required for this task).

A simple entry-level approach to Copernicus products is provided by EO Browser, which allows users (even without credentials) to view and download single images from different collections for the selected AOI and period, and to download a single band at a time, i.e. not for the entire satellite product. The download options are comprehensive of geo-referenced high-resolution images, entire multi bands products for logged-in users.

Data access from EUMETSAT Data Centre works differently, it offers users a products list that can be filtered by a keyword search or a thematic panel in the *ordering application* of the hub. Once pre-selected the chosen product can be downloaded following the online step-by-step ordering application instructions: starting with the product selection, the filtering procedure for a specific date, time and AOI, the choice of a delivery format and method and, finally, the *check-out*, i.e. the end of the procedure.

Copernicus core services can be accessed through the individual thematic portals. Unlike data access portals, these hubs provide multiple thematic maps accessible in the data section of the hubs, e.g. the Atmosphere Data Store for CAMS and the Climate Data Store for C3S. Such hubs provide the thematic time series of the past years, e.g. CLMS Global and European Land Services, provide vegetation, energy, water, cryosphere maps of indices and parameters, as well as land cover and land use maps. The analysis and visualization of the actual situation are also provided, e.g. with CAMS Ensemble modelling of European air quality maps or via CMEMS Ocean data visualisation tools. Short and long term forecasts are available to users, e.g. the climate future projections and the seasonal forecasts of Climate Data Store. The Climate Data Store Toolbox allows users to process the retrieved data by deploying and running their Python applications on its online work-space. Despite their advantage of supplying users with ready-to-use data, Copernicus services do not always meet the spatial or temporal requirements needed for implementing a high-resolution local monitoring [6]. In our previous study of land monitoring [5], we decided not to adopt a ready-to-use classification map, provided by the CLMS dating back to 2018, since we needed a more recent resource for the scenario. In the study of the Surface Urban Heat Island (UHI) effect monitoring [3], we initially considered the use of a resource supplied by the Climate Data Store, i.e. a collection of day and night UHI intensity time-series of 100 European cities[25] represented as annual maps showing the average summer and winter values, in the period between 2008 and 2017. Nonetheless, we did not exploit such resources because our investigation covered 2020.

The *Pre-processing* phase is crucial in EO analysis since it allows to set up the raw downloaded satellite products to be subsequently processed and investigated to extract information and integrate these images with further data and resources [13,17]. Both SNAP and GEE allow perform the main pre-processing steps such as: i) the visual quality check, i.e. for detecting the presence of clouds that could prevent the use of optical and thermal satellite images; ii) the clipping of the AOI, as this allows to carry out the following processing steps by optimizing the computational resources; iii) the re-sample of the products according to a target band resolution; iv) the reprojection on a proper geographical coordinate system. SNAP provides an intuitive graphical interface to perform such steps with ready-to-use preset commands directly on the zipped satellite product. Furthermore, it allows to efficiently perform pre-processing operations on *virtual bands*, i.e. a single raster file or a layer that can be visualized and elaborated without being saved or written on the disk. This procedure is available for all the pre-processing and processing steps, allowing to store only the final result rather than all the intermediate images, favouring more efficient storage management. Even QGIS allows users to work on virtual levels, although it does not have pre-processing presets like the other tools. Users should also consider that, to import data into QGIS, the satellite product bands need to be extracted individually from the product .zip file and converted in .bigTIFF format.

During the *Processing* phase, users can use tools like SNAP and GEE (see Table 2), which supply thematic processors for performing calculations between bands with ready-to-use formulas, based on different data products, i.e. optical or radar, and themes. For example, SNAP provides a *Thematic Land processor* in the optical menu, containing numerous indices, e.g. the Normalized Difference Vegetation Index (NDVI), a dimensionless index to estimate the density of green on an area of land, the Soil Adjusted Vegetation Index (SAVI), often used in arid regions, the Normalized Difference Water Index (NDWI), related to the plant water content and other parameters useful for thematic land analysis. In the context of precision farming, for monitoring the health of vineyards located in the Ligurian province of La Spezia [6], we calculated, by SNAP, the NDVI by carrying out a single preset processing step. Figure 2 depicts the SNAP GUI

---

[25] https://cds.climate.copernicus.eu/cdsapp#!/Software/app-health-urban-heat-islands-current-climate?tab=app.

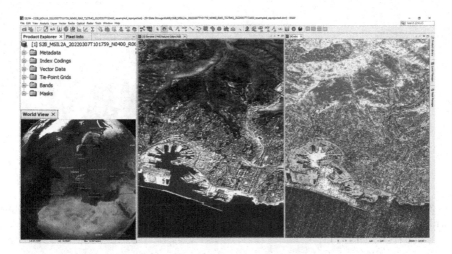

Fig. 2. Computing NDVI with SNAP GUI, for Genoa central area, based on a S2 RGB (Color figure online)

with the NDVI (right panel) calculated on Genoa, based on a S-2 image (March 7th 2022), with the relative RGB image (central panel).

Furthermore, users can also develop their ad-hoc functions and algorithms operating on the different bands of multi-spectral products, using customizable *band math* processors. For instance, QGIS's bandwidth mathematical tool supported us in the study of the surface UHI [3], where we calculated the monthly mean temperature difference between rural and urban areas.

SNAP, GEE, and QGIS provide a set of statistical and graph processors for calculating and comparing satellite images as a function of indices such as mean, median, mean square error. The *band math* functionality makes the analysis options almost unlimited and fully customizable.

Land cover (LC) and land use classifications enormously benefit from the availability of satellite images [17], thus from the presence of RS *classifiers* provided by processing tools. The classification process can be executed in supervised or unsupervised mode, which are both made available by SNAP and GEE, while QGIS provide an external plugin for the supervised classification of satellite images. In the flooding risk assessment in the proximity of a Ligurian artificial lake [5] we performed an LC classification with SNAP supervised k-NN classifier [11]. We firstly created a training vector set for five LC classes and obtained an updated classification starting from a recent image of S-2.

An essential functionality proper of GIS systems, such as QGIS, enables the in-depth inspection and analysis of the attributes tables of raster and vector files, by performing queries and analysis for individual fields to extract specific information from the processed images or the thematic resources.

The ***presentation of the results*** can be accomplished either with images, videos or with the production of graphs and statistics derived from the analysis of products and resources. The satellite processing workflow outcome, i.e. any

Fig. 3. 3D view of Genoa's central area with land cover and buildings All layers are downloadable from the Geoportal of the Liguria Region [16]

transformation of the starting image, should be enriched with some contextual information aimed at making it more interpretable by users. QGIS provides the tools for the geographical contextualization of the AOI, available in *the print layout editor*, such as a scale bar, the geographical grid of reference and the set up of a proper legend with custom features (See Fig. 3). QGIS and EO Browser also allow the visualization of the results in 3D. In particular, QGIS 3D visualization enables the integration of data of different types, for example, by putting together a Digital Terrain Model with an index obtained from a satellite image for a given area, producing a more rich result in terms of information as shown in the Genoa map of Fig. 3. A helpful feature provided by GEE and EO Browser to improve the presentation of the results is the creation of time-lapses, suitable for representing the trend of time series obtained from a set of elaborated satellite images representative of a given parameter of interest: for example, the visualization of the temporal variations of a vegetation index for an AOI subject to the strong presence of anthropogenic activity.

One can entirely or partly automate the satellite workflow's phases by describing the various steps and the data flow. GEE and SNAP enable this function through a *graph generator* that allows users to define the workflow graphically. Once created, the same graph can be run in batch mode enabling the sequential execution on a dataset of multiple products. QGIS users can automatically perform entire workflows with the support of a Python scripts console.

4   Conclusions

The enormous volume of free and open data made available by Copernicus offers economic and scientific opportunities, which can only be fully grasped if all potentially interested users know how to recognize and exploit them for their own needs. In developing satellite-based applications, each workflow phase, from the selection of the data to the representation of the final results, can be carried out with different approaches, depending on the level of computer skills and technical knowledge of the users. For this reason, users, especially those less accustomed to working with satellite data, must know, and be able to distinguish, the available tools to discover, access, and process Copernicus' information assets. To supply a reference framework to those users, we first identified some platforms and tools for accessing and processing data, providing an overview of their main characteristics and features. Furthermore, we briefly discussed and compared the suitability of these tools in supporting the main steps of the workflow related to the development of applications on satellite images.

Acknowledgements. The work has been carried out within the Italian Ligurian Region funded project EO-UPTAKE. We thank the Geographical Information Systems International Group (GISIG) in Genoa (Italy), for his precious collaboration as project partner, in particular, Roderic Molina and Silva Gorni.

References

1. Copernicus User Uptake (2016). https://copernicus.eu/sites/default/files/2018-10/Copernicus_User_Uptake_Engaging_with_Users_0
2. Alfadda, A., Rahman, S., Pipattanasomporn, M.: Solar irradiance forecast using aerosols measurements: a data driven approach. Solar Energy **170**, 924–939 (2018). https://doi.org/10.1016/j.solener.2018.05.089
3. Apicella, L., Quarati, A., Martino, M.D.: Analysing the surface Urban Heat Island effect with Copernicus data. In: Kö, A., Francesconi, E., Kotsis, G., Tjoa, A.M., Khalil, I. (eds.) EGOVIS 2021. LNCS, vol. 12926, pp. 61–72. Springer, Cham (2021). https://doi.org/10.1007/978-3-030-86611-2_5
4. Apicella, L., Quarati, A., Gorni, S., Molina, R., De Martino, M.: Copernicus users uptake: an overview of downstream applications. In: Borgogno-Mondino, E., Zamperlin, P. (eds.) ASITA 2021. CCIS, vol. 1507, pp. 3–14. Springer, Cham (2022). https://doi.org/10.1007/978-3-030-94426-1_1
5. Apicella, L., Quarati, A., Rosim, S., De Martino, M.: User uptake of Copernicus resources: a use case for land monitoring. In: 2021 IEEE International Geoscience and Remote Sensing Symposium, IGARSS, pp. 5688–5691 (2021). https://doi.org/10.1109/IGARSS47720.2021.9554087
6. Apicella, L., De Martino, M., Quarati, A.: Copernicus user uptake: from data to applications. ISPRS Int. J. Geo-Inf. **11**(2) (2022). https://doi.org/10.3390/ijgi11020121
7. Bereta, K., et al.: The Copernicus app lab project: easy access to Copernicus data. In: EDBT (2019)
8. Borgogno-Mondino, E., de Palma, L., Novello, V.: Investigating Sentinel 2 multispectral imagery efficiency in describing spectral response of vineyards covered with plastic sheets. Agronomy **10**(12) (2020). https://doi.org/10.3390/agronomy10121909
9. Doldrina, C.: Open data and earth observations: the case of opening up access to and use of earth observation data through the global earth observation system of systems. J. Intell. Prop. Info. Tech. & Elec. Com. L. **6**, 73 (2015)
10. Dong, J., Metternicht, G., Hostert, P., Fensholt, R., Roy Chowdhury, R.: Remote sensing and geospatial technologies in support of a normative land system science: status and prospects. Curr. Opin. Environ. Sustain. **38**, 44–52 (2019). https://doi.org/10.1016/j.cosust.2019.05.003

11. Duda, R., Hart, P.: Pattern Classification and Scene Analysis, vol. 3. Wiley, New York (1973)
12. EC: General Union Environment Action Programme to 2030 (2020). https://ec. europa.eu/environment/pdf/8EAP/2020/10/8EAP-draft.pdf
13. Filipponi, F.: Sentinel-1 GRD preprocessing workflow. Proceedings **18**(1) (2019). https://doi.org/10.3390/ECRS-3-06201. https://www.mdpi.com/2504-3900/18/1/11
14. Giuliani, G., et al.: Knowledge generation using satellite earth observations to support sustainable development goals (SDG): a use case on land degradation. Int. J. Appl. Earth Observ. Geoinf. (2020). https://doi.org/10.1016/j.jag.2020.102068
15. Hidalgo García, D., Arco Díaz, J.: Modeling of the Urban Heat Island on local climatic zones of a city using Sentinel 3 images: urban determining factors. Urban Clim. **37**, 100840 (2021). https://doi.org/10.1016/j.uclim.2021.100840
16. Liguria Region: Geoportal Liguria Region (2018). Edifici E Manufatti - C.T.R. Sc. 1:5000–2007/2013 - II Edizione 3d/Db Topografico; Uso Del Suolo Sc. 1:10000 - Ed. 2018 (merged classes); DTM - Modello Digitale Del Terreno - Liguria Ed. 2017. https://geoportal.regione.liguria.it
17. Phiri, D., Simwanda, M., Salekin, S., Nyirenda, V.R., Murayama, Y., Ranagalage, M.: Sentinel-2 data for land cover/use mapping: a review. Remote Sens. **12**(14) (2020). https://doi.org/10.3390/rs12142291
18. PWC: Copernicus Ex-Ante benefits assessment. Final report (2017). https://www. copernicus.eu/sites/default/files/2018-10/Copernicus-Ex-Ante-Final-Report_0_0. pdf
19. Quarati, A., De Martino, M.: Geospatial open data usage and metadata quality. ISPRS Int. J. Geo-Inf. **10** (2021). https://doi.org/10.1177/0165551520961048
20. Quarati, A., Raffaghelli, J.E.: Do researchers use open research data? Exploring the relationships between usage trends and metadata quality across scientific disciplines from the Figshare case. J. Inf. Sci. (2020). https://doi.org/10.1177/0165551520961048
21. Quarati, A.: Open Government Data: usage trends and metadata quality. J. Inf. Sci., 1–24 (2021). https://doi.org/10.1177/01655515211027775
22. Serco SpA-led Consortium: Copernicus Sentinel Data Access Annual Report (2020). https://scihub.copernicus.eu/twiki/pub/SciHubWebPortal/AnnualReport2020/COPE-SERCO-RP-21-1141_-_Sentinel_Data_Access_Annual_Report_Y2020_final_v2.3.pdf
23. Tavares, P.A., Beltrão, N.E.S., Guimarães, U.S., Teodoro, A.C.: Integration of Sentinel-1 and Sentinel-2 for classification and LULC mapping in the urban area of Belém, eastern Brazilian Amazon. Sensors **19**(5) (2019). https://doi.org/10. 3390/s19051140
24. Zeil, P., Ourevitch, S., Debien, A., Pico, U.: Copernicus user uptake - Copernicus relays and the Copernicus academy. GI Forum J. Geogr. Inf. Sci. **5**, 253–259 (2017). https://doi.org/10.1553/giscience2017_01_s253

A Tool to Aid the Navigation in La Spezia Harbour (Italy)

M. Soldani$^{(\boxtimes)}$ (iD) and O. Faggioni

Istituto Nazionale di Geofisica e Vulcanologia, Via di Vigna Murata 605, 00143 Roma, Italy
{maurizio.soldani,osvaldo.faggioni}@ingv.it

Abstract. The knowledge of sea level in harbours is very important to manage port activities (safety of navigation, prevention of ship stranding, optimization of vessel loading, water quality control). In this article we describe the use of a software tool developed to help local authorities and working organizations to optimize navigation and avoid or manage hazardous situations due to sea level changes in port basins. This prototype application, starting from reading data coming from a monitoring station in La Spezia harbour (in North Western Italy), updates dynamically the port bathymetry based on sea level oscillations (measured in the past or real-time, or expected in the near future). Then, it detects potentially dangerous areas for a given ship moving in the basin at a certain time, by means of the idea of "virtual traffic lights": sea level variations are provided as parameters to the application that performs the updating of the bathymetric map and the subdivision of the harbour in allowed (green)/warning (yellow)/prohibited (red) areas for each ship, based on its draft. The tool can provide a useful support interface to competent authorities to avoid or manage critical situations by detecting hazardous areas for a given vessel at a given time.

Keywords: Coastal maritime transport · Port navigation safety · Harbour water management

1 Introduction

Sea level changes influence significantly the water management in harbours, e.g. ship navigation, maritime transport safety, dock performances, ship loading and mooring, seawater quality and pollution control. Then, being able to monitor and forecast sea level variations should be essential to plan the best time for a vessel to enter or leave a port, to decide its best route, to determine how much it can be loaded or in which dock it can berth, to prevent the risk of accidents, the consequent impact on the surrounding environment and economic damages, or to plan when refloat stranded vessels.

The software prototype application described in the following starts from monitoring or forecasting meteo-mareographic parameters in coastal areas, with the aim of updating port bathymetric maps depending on sea level variations, and then providing to port communities and decision makers a useful tool to optimize harbour water management and port operations or to prevent hazardous situations. In the following, we analyse its

© The Author(s) 2022
E. Borgogno-Mondino and P. Zamperlin (Eds.): ASITA 2022, CCIS 1651, pp. 89–101, 2022.
https://doi.org/10.1007/978-3-031-17439-1_6

use in La Spezia harbour (Eastern Ligurian Sea, Italy). It is important to note that the bathymetric map of a port must also be updated (by means of multibeam surveys) after changes in the harbour topography, e.g. as a results of dredging operations.

Sea level oscillations along Italian coastline consist mainly in astronomical tides, first of all the diurnal and semidiurnal components: they are caused by the Earth-Moon-Sun gravitational relationships, so they are periodic and predictable in advance everywhere through the harmonic analysis and tide charts [1].

Nevertheless, sea level changes in harbours also depend on meteorological tides, that are Newtonian adjustment of water mass due to atmospheric pressure unbalances over a sea basin (water level increases when the atmospheric pressure decreases and vice versa): this phenomenon is evaluated by performing a statistical analysis, whose purpose is to estimate the correlation between atmospheric pressure variations (cause inducing) and sea level changes (effect induced) and then to forecast future tides. In particular, a meteorological tide is a geodetic compensation caused by a variation of atmospheric loading over a free water surface: an atmospheric weight rise causes an outgoing seawater flux (low meteorological tide); a lowering of atmospheric loading, on the contrary, causes an incoming seawater flux (high meteorological tide). This phenomenon is influenced by many parameters (the topography of the harbour, the atmosphere dynamics over it, etc.) and then, unlike the astronomical tides, it cannot be described by a deterministic relationship: the change of sea level caused by atmospheric pressure is evaluated by means of the study of the cause - effect events (water level variations following atmospheric pressure changes) that happen in a given basin during a long period of time. After this statistical correlation (represented by the hydro-barometric transfer factor) has been estimated, it will be possible to estimate in advance meteorological tides based on the knowledge of atmospheric pressure changes [2–12].

Meteorological tides can play a fundamental role in contributing to sea level changes in Italian harbours, especially when they add up to the astronomical ones: over the past fifteen years, many unusual tidal fluctuations have been monitored in the Port of La Spezia; the maximum meteorological tide observed in this period was about 53 [cm].

Effects induced by wind or storm surges (not relevant in this place) were not considered in the present work.

2   The Software Application

The starting point of the software tool is the bathymetry of the harbour, also named static map since it has to be considered static until new multibeam surveys are carried out, after changes in the harbour topography (following dredging activities, seabed subsidence, accumulation of sediments, or coastal erosion). Figure 1 represents the georeferenced bathymetric map of the Gulf of La Spezia, that extends over an area of approximately 22 [km^2]. In the north-eastern area of the gulf there are cruise terminal and merchant port; the southern area is bounded by breakwater [13–26].

The harbour can be classified in three zones, by setting two depth levels, a lower and an upper threshold, that vary vessel by vessel based on their draft; the three areas are identified by as many colours: the red identifies zones forbidden for that ship (bottom depth less than the lower threshold, typically chosen equal to the ship draft), whereas the green represents deep or permitted areas for that vessel (bottom depth more than the upper threshold, in its turn greater than vessel draft: there is a great space between the vessel keel and the seafloor); lastly, the yellow represents shallow or warning areas (bottom depth between the lower and upper threshold: there is a small space between the ship keel and the sea bottom). This subdivision implements the idea of virtual traffic lights customized vessel by vessel, a useful interface to support decision makers to mitigate the risk arising from potentially dangerous circumstances:

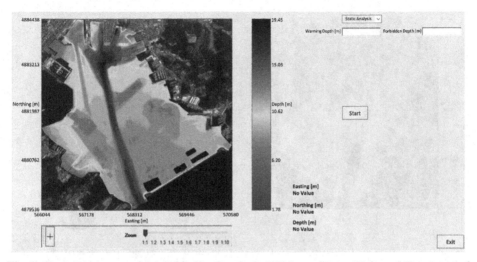

Fig. 1. Bathymetric map of the Gulf of La Spezia, in UTM coordinates (Universal Transverse of Mercator, Zone 32T); the sea depth is referred to IGM's 0 sea level (Italian Military Geographic Institute); data are kindly provided by Port Authority of La Spezia (now named Port System Authority of the Eastern Ligurian Sea).

For a vessel characterized by a draft of 11 [m], for instance, we can choose thresholds equal to 11 and 12.5 [m] respectively; the result is the partition of the bathymetric map reported in Fig. 2: so, for that vessel the zones with bottom depth values smaller than 11 [m] are considered prohibited (red), those where bottom depth values are between 11 and 12.5 [m] are classified warning areas (yellow), and those in which bottom depth values are more than 12.5 [m] are permitted areas (green). This represents the static analysis (the map remains the same as the time changes). Figure 3 shows the same bathymetry but partitioned by setting other threshold levels, for a vessel having a deeper draft than the earlier example (e.g. a Panamax cargo ship, whose draft is nearly 12 m): thresholds fixed at 12 and 13.5 [m] respectively cause the enlargement of the red (forbidden) areas and the reduction of the green (permitted) ones: the tool classifies as prohibited the areas with bottom depth less than 12 [m], warning zones those characterized by bottom depth values between 12 and 13.5 [m], and permitted zones those with bottom deeper than 12 [m]; of course, the greater the draft of the vessel, the wider the zone prohibited to it.

The software application is able to automatically update in real time the bathymetric map of the harbour by using sea level data acquired and transmitted by a meteomareographic station working in the port area. Moreover, as explained below, the software tool can start from atmospheric pressure values to evaluate expected sea level variations known as meteorological tides, that will be summed to the astronomical ones, periodic and known by means of tide charts, to estimate the forecasted sea level and finally the expected bathymetric map of the harbour.

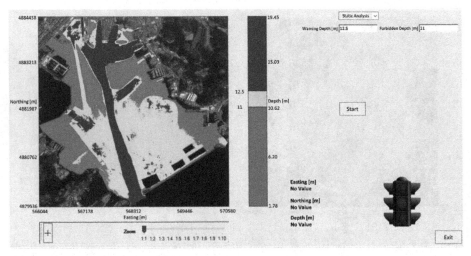

Fig. 2. Virtual traffic lights in the Gulf of La Spezia; thresholds equal to 11 and 12.5 [m].

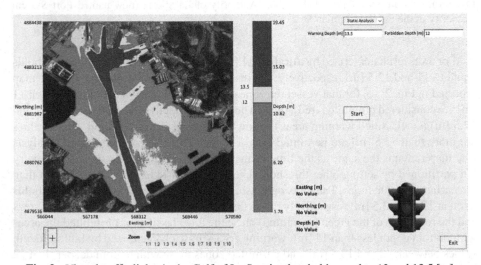

Fig. 3. Virtual traffic lights in the Gulf of La Spezia; thresholds equal to 12 and 13.5 [m].

3 Monitoring and Forecasting Tides in Harbours

Meteorological tides (briefly called "meteo-tides") are sea level oscillations related to atmospheric pressure changes over a coastal basin such as a port or a bay. These are due to Newtonian adaptations of the free water surface that re-balance the geodetic disequilibrium caused by atmosphere weight variations: a rise of atmospheric pressure causes a decrease in sea level (low meteorological tide) and vice versa (high meteorological tide). The phenomenon of meteo-tides is completely known in the open sea (the so-called "inverted barometer" effect: 1 [hPa] of atmospheric pressure variation induces about 1 [cm] of sea level change), but it needs further insights in coastal regions, where the coastline stops the horizontal movement of seawater mass and then enhances its vertical displacement. In addition to this, the relationship between atmospheric pressure and sea level (described by the so-called hydrobarometric transfer factor J_{ph}) is due to some characteristics of the considered basin (first of all its topography), so in the present work it has evaluated by means of a local monitoring and a statistical analysis of parameters involved. So, the knowledge of meteorological tides starts from the acquisition of atmospheric pressure and sea level in harbours; then, the following step is to evaluate the hydrobarometric transfer factor J_{ph} by studying all the events (sea level changes following atmospheric pressure variations) happened in a certain site along a given time interval (typically several years) [27–32].

To monitor port environmental parameters in the port of La Spezia, data coming from the measurement station belonging to ISPRA's[1] National Tidegauge Network are used. It includes instrumentation to acquire meteo-mareographic data (the most interesting for our study are the hydrometer to measure water level and the barometer to acquire atmospheric pressure). Data used in this article and various information about ISPRA's monitoring station in La Spezia harbour are available on the website https://www.mareografico.it/. In Fig. 4 are explained parameters observed in the port of La Spezia from 28 February to 4 March 2020; the date and the time are reported to UTC (Universal time Coordinates), hydrometer measurements to IGM's 0 level.

The changes over time of the sea level recorded are comprehensive of contributes resulting from different causes, first of all astronomical (mainly diurnal and semidiurnal) and meteorological tides; other short-term effects induced by wind or storm surges were not considered in the present work (events happened in the presence of wind were not taken into account). To avoid components other than those of meteorological origin (characterized by low frequencies), data are filtered properly: a Low Pass filtering removes spectral components related to astronomical tides, that are represented by dashed lines in Fig. 4: only slow fluctuations, due to to atmospheric pressure variations, survive the filtering (solid lines in Fig. 4); respect to the time interval from 28 February to 4 March, an atmospheric pressure fall Δp (cause) of 28.6 [hPa] produces a low frequency sea level increase Δh (height of high meteorological tide, effect) of about 53 [cm].

---

[1] Italian Institute for Environmental Protection and Research.

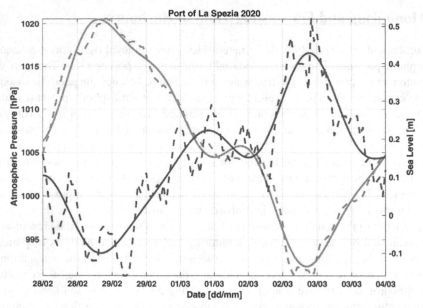

Fig. 4. Meteo-mareographic parameters acquired by ISPRA's monitoring station in the port of La Spezia from 28 February to 4 March 2020 (dashed lines) and their low frequency components (solid lines).

Then, for this event the hydrobarometric transfer factor J_{ph} [cm*hPa^{-1}] can be evaluated as indicated in Eq. 1:

$$J_{ph} = \Delta h / \Delta p \tag{1}$$

in this example a value of nearly 1.9 [cm*hPa^{-1}] is obtained, expressed in absolute value.

Similarly, for all the events occurred in the time interval of study, the gradient Δh of sea level and the variation Δp of atmospheric pressure are considered, and J_{ph} is recalculated. Thus a lot of couples (Δp, Δh) and corresponding estimations of J_{ph} are computed, one for every occurrence of the phenomenon in the period under consideration: as a first approximation, the average of J_{ph} values can be employed as a linear estimate of J_{ph} (the resulting error is acceptable for our purposes); a better representation could consider a non-linear (e.g. cubic) dependence of Δh from Δp, as shown in Fig. 5. The knowledge of the hydro-barometric transfer factor allows calculating, for a given basin, an expected variation of sea level Δh based on the measurement or forecasting of atmospheric pressure: simply multiply the future change Δp by the estimated J_{ph} factor and then change the sign, given that atmospheric pressure and sea level variations have opposite signs: if the first rises, the second falls and viceversa.

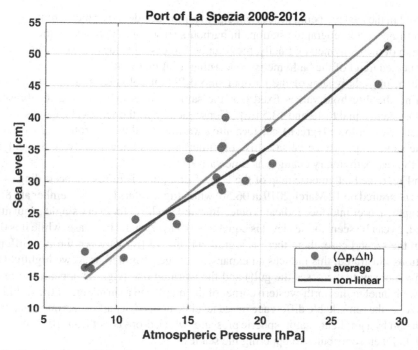

Fig. 5. Couples (Δp, Δh) for the events occurred in the port of La Spezia from 2008 to 2012 (red dots), linear (green line) and cubic (blue line) approximations. (Color figure online)

The estimation of J_{ph} is very useful in order to manage port activities: the effects of atmospheric pressure changes on sea level (and on water depth) can be applied to bathymetric maps in harbours to know in advance their evolution: a variation of atmospheric pressure can be turned, through J_{ph}, into an expected meteorological tide and then, by adding to it the expected astronomical tide, in a forecasted sea level and finally in a new bathymetry. In La Spezia harbour and, more in general, along Italian coastline, typical values found by means of a multi-year statistical analysis carried out for J_{ph} are often very larger (about twice) in comparison to the characteristic value 1 [cm*hPa^{-1}] of the offshore.

Furthermore, it is worth to highlight that it is needed to recalculate periodically the J_{ph} factor, especially following variations of the topography of the basin (due to dredging activities, coastal erosion, accumulation of sediments, seabed subsidence).

Anyway, a multi-decade statistics is necessary to assess the possible influence of long-term phenomena such as climate change on the hydrobarometric transfer factor.

4   Results

Sea level measurements are added to the initial seafloor depth to recalculate instant by instant the real bathymetry and update the so-called dynamic bathymetric map (it varies as time varies). Sea level values can be data recorded in an archive (if critical events that occurred in the past are being processed, e.g. to replay accidents) or measurements coming from meteo-mareographic stations in harbours (if we are interested in the real-time variation of the bathymetry); finally, they can be forecasted values (if we are estimating the expected trend of the bathymetry concerning a future event).

Then, the subdivision of the harbour into different coloured zones is updated by retaining the threshold values fixed (for the same ship assumed in Fig. 6, threshold levels are kept equal to 12 and 13.5 [m]). Consequently, as the sea level changes, a zone that before was allowed (green), can turn into a warning (yellow) or prohibited zone (red) for the same ship, or vice versa. This constitutes what is known as dynamic analysis, since the real bathymetry changes as time varies.

In Fig. 6 the bathymetric map of the Port of La Spezia is refreshed according to the values measured on 12 March 2019 at 06:50, while Fig. 7 refers to 23 November at 18:30; the graphical user interface indicates date, time and sea level for every single acquisition loaded: as can be seen, the sea level is equal to −0.41 [m] in the first case, while it is 0.72 [m] in the second case: then, there is a gradient of 1.13 [m] between the two different situations illustrated; this induces an expansion of the permitted area (we highlight the green waterway that crosses the gulf) and the warning one (e.g. the appearance of the yellow channel in the north-western corner of the map), and a shrinkage of the forbidden (red) zone; the remarkable difference in sea level is induced in part by astronomical tides and in part by a gradient of atmospheric pressure, which drops about from 1025 to 1001.5 [hPa] and then contributes to uppering the sea level.

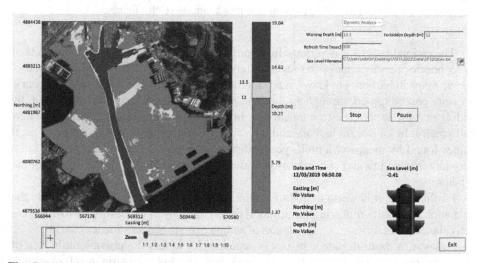

Fig. 6. Virtual traffic lights in the Gulf of La Spezia on 12 March 2019 at 06:50; thresholds equal to 12 and 13.5 [m]. (Color figure online)

Moreover, a particular of the harbor can be shown in more detail: for example, Figs. 8 and 9 show that the permitted area near the access to quays in the northern part of the gulf expands, and this is induced by the sea level increase of 1.13 [m]. In addition, moving mouse pointer over the gulf, the graphical interface displays the coordinates of its position and the corresponding depth instant by instant; finally, the traffic light indicates at any moment whether that position is prohibited, permitted or included in a warning zone, by turning on the appropriate light: keeping the pointer in a given place, we can observe how its state changes as time passes. In this example of comparison of two situations, the bottom depth in position Easting 567318, Northing 4883902 [m] indicated by the mouse pointer in the area between Garibaldi (in the upper left corner) and Fornelli (in the top middle) piers on the western part of the port changes from 11.38 to 12.51 [m], then the corresponding traffic light goes from red (forbidden position) to yellow (warning position) colour (lower threshold is fixed to 12 [m]).

Then, the graphical user interface achieves the idea of the so-called virtual traffic lights (subdivision in forbidden, warning or allowed zones) customized ship by ship, based on its draft: changing the sea level, a zone that before was red (prohibited), can turn into a yellow (warning) or green (permitted) zone for the same vessel, or vice versa; this prototype application is aimed at providing support to port operators in planning and optimizing coastal maritime transport (e.g. deciding when a ship can enter or leave a port or tracing its best route), vessel moorings and docking performances (e.g. to which dock a ship can access), vessel loading (e.g. determining the cargo of a ship at the departure port based on the expected tide at the destination), and maritime works (e.g. sizing breakwaters); above all, it can represent a useful tool to port communities (port authorities, coast guards, pilots, terminal operators) to improve coastal navigation safety, to avoid maritime accidents, to manage events occurred as vessel stranding, or to minimize environmental damages and economic losses.

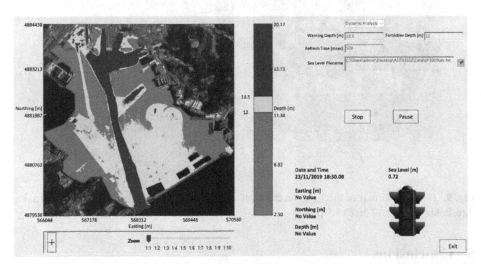

Fig. 7. Virtual traffic lights in the Gulf of La Spezia on 23 November 2019 at 18:30; thresholds equal to 12 and 13.5 [m].

In general, the utility of this software tool is that it can identify hazardous situations in specific positions, at particular moments, and for a certain vessel: in fact, the current state of virtual traffic lights relies on the location, on the current time, and on the thresholds selected that, in their turn, rely on the draft of the vessel taken into account.

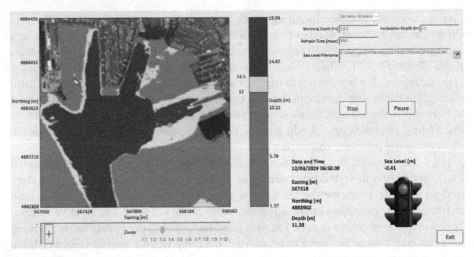

Fig. 8. Detail of virtual traffic lights in the Gulf of La Spezia on 12 March 2019 at 06:50; thresholds equal to 12 and 13.5 [m].

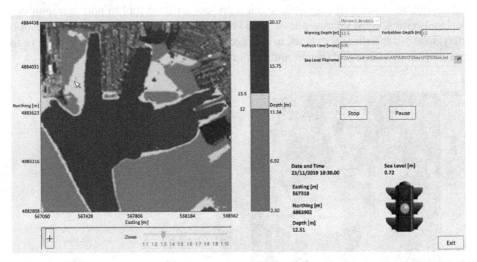

Fig. 9. Detail of virtual traffic lights in the Gulf of La Spezia on 23 November 2019 at 18:30; thresholds equal to 12 and 13.5 [m].

5   Conclusions

This work shows the usefulness of a prototype application developed to support port communities and decision makers (port authorities, coast guard, pilots) in order to mitigate risks induced by sea level oscillations and then to increase maritime safety in ports by identifying hazardous areas for a certain ship at a given instant. It is highlighted the importance of observing, processing and forecasting environmental parameters in harbours. The results of monitoring and analysing activities in La Spezia harbour (Eastern Ligurian Sea, Italy) are described.

Using this tool in the framework of harbour water management can be helpful to authorities in analysing a posteriori maritime accidents occurred in the past as well as to decision makers in optimizing port activities or planning them in advance, in particular:

- in improving effectiveness and safety of port navigation by determining, for a certain ship, the ideal route to be flown depending on its draft (to minimize the risk of stranding), or in which pier it would be better to berth, or the optimum instant when it should enter or leave a basin;
- in optimizing the cargo (how much a ship can be loaded in the departure port according to the expected tide at the destination port);
- in managing the refloating of stranded vessels (in case of accident occurred), in order to minimize the impact on marine environment and economic losses for the port community.

Moreover, forecasting tides in harbours may also be useful to optimize:

- the berthing of vessels (how much to pull the berths to avoid breaking ropes);
- the dimensioning of maritime works (e.g. outer dams, quays and piers) according to the highest tides expected;
- the marine water exchange in port areas and the quality control of coastal environment: evaluating the concentration of pollutants (solute) at a given time based on the actual volume of marine water (solvent) measured or forecasted.

In a hypothetical operational scenario, a display showing the dynamic bathymetry of the sea basin could be hosted in a command and control center managed by a local authority, that in this way would receive useful information to take the best decisions, with the aim of improving safety for the community working in harbours. The same tool could also run on board vessels, e.g. on mobile devices.

Virtual traffic lights are of course reliable as long as the parameters passed to the tool are, i.e. that the starting static bathymetry is still valid (otherwise a new map should be acquired by performing new multibeam surveys), that the forecasting of meteorological parameters and sea level are accurate, and that tide measurements carried out by a meteo-mareographic station operating in a given location are representative of the whole harbour; anyway, having more hydrometers spread over a harbour would permit a better spatial resolution in the dynamic updating of the bathymetric map by making available more sea level values, one for each subdomain into which the basin is divided.

Lastly, the application is able to include other phenomena, such as wind effect and storm surges (not relevant and therefore not considered in this work), which particularly in certain sites can be very important and thus should be passed as inputs to the sea level forecasting algorithm to enhance its effectiveness.

Acknowledgements. The authors wish to thank ISPRA for providing meteo-mareographic data acquired in La Spezia harbour and Port Authority of La Spezia (now named Port System Authority of the Eastern Ligurian Sea) for providing bathymetric data. They also thank Dr. D. Leoncini for his contribution in software applications development. These studies were possible thanks to funding from Port Authority of La Spezia and from European Union and Regional Government of Liguria (Italy) by means of Regional Plan of Innovative Actions - European Funds for the Regional Development.

Part of these activities was conducted when the first author was at OGS - National Institute of Oceanography and Applied Geophysics (Trieste, Italy).

Finally, the authors wish to thank the anonymous reviewer, whose comments and suggestions helped to improve this work.

References

1. Istituto Idrografico della Marina: Tavole di Marea 2022. Istituto Idrografico della Marina, Genoa, Italy (2021)
2. Bâki Iz, H.: The effect of regional sea level atmospheric pressure on sea level variations at globally distributed tide gauge stations with long records. J. Geod. Sci. **8**(1), 55–71 (2018)
3. Cabos, W., et al.: Impact of ocean-atmosphere coupling on regional climate: the Iberian Peninsula case. Clim. Dyn. **54**, 4441–4467 (2020)
4. Deser, C., Tomas, R.A., Sun, L.: The role of ocean-atmosphere coupling in the zonal-mean atmospheric response to arctic sea ice loss. J. Clim. **28**(6), 2168–2186 (2015)
5. Dickman, S.R.: Theoretical investigation of the oceanic inverted barometer response. J. Geophys. Res. Solid Earth **93**(B12), 14941–14946 (1988)
6. Fu, L.-L., Pihos, G.: Determining the response of sea level to atmospheric pressure forcing using TOPEX/POSEIDON data. J. Geophys. Res. **99**(C12), 24633–24642 (1994)
7. Garrett, C., Toulany, B.: Sea level variability due to meteorological forcing in the northeast Gulf of St. Lawrence. J. Geophys. Res. **87**(C3), 1968–1978 (1982)
8. Halliwell, G.R., Allen, J.S.: Large-scale sea level response to atmospheric forcing along the west coast of north America, summer 1973. J. Phys. Oceanogr. **14**(5), 864–886 (1984)
9. Merriam, J.B.: Atmospheric pressure and gravity. Geophys. J. Int. **109**(3), 488–500 (1992)
10. Tsimplis, M.N.: The response of sea level to atmospheric forcing in the mediterranean. J. Coastal Res. **11**(4), 1309–1321 (1995)
11. Willebrand, J., Philander, S.G.H., Pacanowski, R.C.: The oceanic response to large-scale atmospheric disturbances. J. Phys. Oceanogr. **10**(3), 411–429 (1980)
12. Wunsch, C., Stammer, D.: Atmospheric loading and the oceanic "inverted barometer" effect. Rev. Geophys. **35**(1), 79–107 (1997)
13. Bąk, A., Zalewski, P.: Determination of the waterway parameters as a component of safety management system. Appl. Sci. **11**(10), 4456 (2021)
14. Bartlett, D., Celliers, L. (eds.): Geoinformatics for Marine and Coastal Management, 1st edn. CRC Press, Boca Raton (2016)
15. Couper, A.D.: Environmental port management. Marit. Policy Manag. **19**(2), 165–170 (1992)
16. Giuffrida, N., Stojaković, M., Twrdy, E., Ignaccolo, M.: The importance of environmental factors in the planning of container terminals: the case study of the Port of Augusta. Appl. Sci. **11**(5), 2153 (2021)
17. Lam, S.Y.-W., Yip, T.L.: The role of geomatics engineering in establishing the marine information system for maritime management. Marit. Policy Manag. **35**(1), 53–60 (2008)
18. Meyers, S.D., Luther, M.E.: The impact of sea level rise on maritime navigation within a large, channelized estuary. Marit. Policy Manag. **47**(7), 920–936 (2020)

19. Nguyen, T.-H., Garrè, L., Amdahl, J., Leira, B.J.: Benchmark study on the assessment of ship damage conditions during stranding. Ships Offshore Struct. **7**(2), 197–213 (2012)
20. Nohheman, W.: Benefits of dredging through reduced tidal waiting. Marit. Policy Manag. **8**(1), 17–20 (1981)
21. Ogura, T., Inoue, T., Uchihira, N.: Prediction of arrival time of vessels considering future weather conditions. Appl. Sci. **11**(10), 4410 (2021)
22. Palikaris, A., Mavraeidopoulos, A.K.: Electronic navigational charts: international standards and map projections. J. Mari. Sci. Eng. **8**(4), 248 (2020)
23. Petraška, A., Čižiūnienė, K., Jarašūnienė, A., Maruschak, P., Prentkovskis, O.: Algorithm for the assessment of heavyweight and oversize cargo transportation routes. J. Bus. Econ. Manag. **18**(6), 1098–1114 (2017)
24. Vandermeulen, J.H.: Environmental trends of ports and harbours: implications for planning and management. Marit. Policy Manag. **23**(1), 55–66 (1996)
25. Vidmar, P., Perkovič, M., Gucma, L., Łazuga, K.: Risk assessment of moored and passing ships. Appl. Sci. **10**(19), 6825 (2020)
26. Weintrit, A.: Geoinformatics in shipping and marine transport. In: Mikulski, J. (ed.) TST 2016. CCIS, vol. 640, pp. 13–25. Springer, Cham (2016). https://doi.org/10.1007/978-3-319-49646-7_2
27. Faggioni, O.: Measurement and forecasting of port tide hydrostatic component in North Tyrrhenian Sea (Italy). Open J. Mar. Sci. **10**(2), 52–77 (2020)
28. Faggioni, O., et al.: The Newtonian approach in meteorological tide waves forecasting: preliminary observations in the East Ligurian harbours. Ann. Geophys. **49**(6), 1177–1187 (2006)
29. Faggioni, O., Soldani, M., Leoncini, D.A.: Metrological analysis of geopotential gravity field for harbor waterside management and water quality control. Int. J. Geophys. 2013 Spec. Issue Geophys. Methods Environ. Stud., 12 (2013)
30. Faggioni, O., et al.: Harbour water management for port structures and sea bottom design, coast proximity navigation management, water quality control. In: Proceedings of the 1st Mediterranean Days of Coastal and Port Engineering, Palermo, Italy. PIANC (2008)
31. Soldani, M.: The contribution of geomatics to increase safety and security in ports. Appl. Geomat., 12 (2021)
32. Soldani, M., Faggioni, O.: A system to improve port navigation safety and its use in Italian harbours. Appl. Sci. **11**(21), 10265, 31 (2021)

An Innovative Experimental Software for Geomatics Applications on the Environment and the Territory

Vincenzo Barrile[1](✉) , Francesco Cotroneo[2], Federica Iorio[2], and Giuliana Bilotta[1]

[1] Department of Civil, Energetic, Environmental and Material Engineering -DICEAM-
Geomatics Lab, Mediterranea University of Reggio Calabria, via Graziella, Feo di Vito,
89124 Reggio Calabria, RC, Italy
vincenzo.barrile@unirc.it
[2] Nophys srls, Via Maddaloni 74, 00177 Rome, RM, Italy

Abstract. In the field of extreme weather and climate events management and territorial protection, there is an increasing need for decision support tools that allow the creation of the most realistic virtual scenarios in time for prevention and the design of risk containment systems. This paper describes the operation of an atmospheric simulator capable of generating weather field outputs within a limited domain and with very high resolution. The simulator is technically characterized by the use of a bottom-up approach that does not use differential equations; in fact, the atmosphere is modelled by means of SPH (Smoothed-Particle Hydrodynamics) fluids, while the different atmospheric phenomena (convection, turbulence, pressure distribution), are output by the software as emergent properties of the single interactions between the SPH particles of the simulated atmosphere. On a practical level, it can be initialized with data that are inhomogeneous in quality and distribution (Radar, Sensors, Historical Surveys and data from forecast models) and used by personnel who have only GIS skills.

Keywords: Atmosphere simulator · Particle solver · Decision support models for medium and extreme events

1 Introduction

In this paper we illustrate the capabilities and implementation techniques of a limited area 3D HR-Scale (high resolution scale) atmospheric simulator.

The instrument, starting from very few inputs, provides in output (3D Cells) the wind, temperature, humidity, cloud cover, rain, and other atmospheric values related to cubic cells smaller than even 50 m. The temporal evolution of these values is provided in the short term, so it is not a NWP (Numerical Weather Prediction) [1], but then neither would it be the engine. The software was developed as part of a broader scientific collaboration on research topics related to the field of Geomatics between the Geomatics Laboratory of DICEAM and the company Nophys srls. The present work concerns the creation of an experimental software resulting from a specific scientific research collaboration aimed at implementing a suitable open software for research and application purposes that can be integrated with different research and application sectors. This software simulates the phenomenology of the Earth's atmosphere related to the weather context.

The main feature of this software is that it is implemented with a bottom-up approach, through the application of local microphysics. The numerical processing of the simulator is therefore not aimed at the numerical resolution of a priori defined differential equations, but to represent the state variation of thousands of particles interacting with each other, with the orographic domain and the characterization of the territory in terms of weather. More specifically, the software models the atmosphere through a special implementation of SPH fluids [2].

The fields of application are innumerable. Here are just a few. Increased resolution for climate models and weather data. Alternative energies: the experimental software indicates how and where to install wind and photovoltaic systems for maximum yield. Safety and Prevention, Scientific Research, Training, Base Engine for Weather models, Reports with 3D Animation, and much more.

2 The Particle Solver, Advantages of a Bottom-Up Approach

The experimental software is a simulator that reproduces the behaviour of the atmosphere with regard to typical weather variables. Its implementation makes use of a bottom-up approach, the atmosphere is modelled through SPH fluids.

Therefore, neither differential equations modelling (a priori) the different atmospheric phenomena, such as convection, turbulence, pressure distribution, are defined or solved [3]. These phenomena are output by the software as emergent properties of the individual interactions between all SPH particles in the "virtual" atmosphere simulated by the software.

It is useful before going into the mechanisms and algorithms to highlight two aspects:

1. The article makes broad comparisons with NWP software, as mentioned the simulator developed is not an NWP; therefore, it refers to the (intrinsic) atmospheric physics component of the latter.
2. The model output is considered valid when the evolution of the simulation has reached a certain stability and consolidates phenomenological patterns. Therefore, in this paper the time variable is understood in terms of simulation cycles (internal simulator iteration) and therefore has no correspondence with clock time.

This approach has many advantages in different application fields:

1. Local and inhomogeneous initialization. Model initialization can be performed with input data located anywhere in the simulation domain without the need for grid interpolation. This is necessary for numerical solvers of differential equations in classical NWPs.
2. Limited Area - Micro Areas. The simulator operates and provides valid outputs only in the area of interest. Classical numerical solvers require enormously larger

areas, due to the iterative dependence between the points discretizing the solution domain. The advantage is therefore linked to being able to provide initialization data (Sensors, Radar and others) sampled exclusively in the area being simulated, with enormous savings in resources and guaranteeing considerable autonomy even for small organizations or laboratories.

3. Computation with Inhomogeneous Data. The simulator is intrinsically tolerant to the presence of some punctual surveys for the initial conditions which occasionally report highly inaccurate or erroneous data. Data assimilation can be performed through several sources with different Quality, Quantity and Geographical Distribution; Radar input can alternate between areas with many stations and uncovered areas.

4. Commercial Hardware. The software requires the presence of HPC - GPU hardware of the type of workstations dedicated to gaming, in this sense the costs of the hardware are accessible and do not constitute a constraint to the use of the simulator.

5. Non-specialized users. There is no need for the operators who start and initialize the simulator to be atmospheric physicists, or mathematical modelers, or computer scientists. No special calibrations implying such skills are required. GIS and geomatics skills are required.

6. Microscale, i.e., the output of the weather fields (Temperature, Precipitation, Wind, Pressure) is discretized on contiguous three-dimensional cells of width (per side) of much less than 100 m. This is mainly a consequence of the aspects related to the possibility of operating on limited areas and using commercial hardware.

Peripheral Monitoring Authorities are the classical case where these features are fundamental. If they, for example, have the task of studying and predicting the possibility of flooding, they will probably want to equip themselves with a DSS (Decision Support System) consisting of hydrogeological software that needs realistic weather hypotheses as input and provided with high accuracy. The features of the software illustrated above, such as microscale output, low cost, and staff skills, are well suited to the needs set out in this example.

2.1 The Characteristics of the Particle Model

The basic idea is to schematize the atmosphere as a set of macro particles. These interact with their neighbours (proximity and adjacency interaction), and together have contextual and individual exchanges with the surrounding environment (orography, sea, lakes, urbanization, solar radiation).

The interactions and exchanges concern kinetic energy (collisions between particles, collisions with surfaces and mountain ranges, compression and expansion phenomena), thermal energy (heat exchanges between adjacent particles and between particles and different types of soil), and matter (quantity of vapour and aerosol transferred). Interactions can therefore be classified into two types: Newtonian interactions as far as SPH dynamics is concerned, and exchange interactions that alter the states of adjacent particles on the model of cellular automata.

It follows that the MICROPHYSICS of the atmosphere is now "translated" not into differential equations with a value in the whole domain (as for classical NPWs) [4], but into laws that regulate the interactions mentioned above, i.e. the interactions that the single particle experiences moment by moment with what surrounds it (other particles or the environment). In other words, the ensemble "behavioural" phenomenologies are now exclusively solutions, not 'model' constraints. Turbulence, winds and convective phenomena are no longer equations that close the system, they represent 'epiphenomena' (or rather emergent properties) of the said interactions. In other words, there is no need for aprioristic modelling of all the phenomena involved in atmospheric dynamics at the micro scale, since most of them are framed as forecast outputs of the model, without giving it or them any constraints whatsoever.

Proximity Cells. The particle model discretizes the atmosphere as represented in Fig. 1.

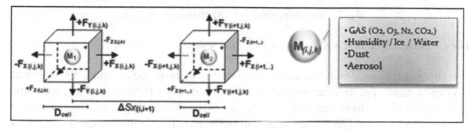

Fig. 1. Representation and discretization of the atmosphere.

There are three principles underlying this representative scheme:

- The particles are contained (in abstract) in the centre of cubes (Cells) of side *Dcell*, these are initially distributed, at rest, in a uniform way without solution of continuity to fill all the space, this discretization definitively marks the particles with the indices (i, j, k) according to the axes x, y, z (right-handed system).
- Each Particle can be idealized as an incompressible sphere inside which are stored the quantities of GAS, Humidity, Ice, Water and other elements foreseen for it at a given time (mainly Aerosol). These quantities and qualities define its Mass and its direct and indirect behaviour in the interchanges with the environment and other particles (radiation absorption, kinetic energy, etc.). Compressibility, on the other hand, is a property of the Cells, which is expressed when they eventually interpenetrate, or in other words we can say that the particles interact, from the mechanical point of view, in an elastic way.
- Each particle is subject to a force resulting from its energy state, or from the kinetic interaction with neighbouring particles, or with the surface and the orography.

Two Solvers, L1 and L2. While the solver of the NWP models is an Algebraic Recursive processor (discretization of differential equations and numerical solution) and therefore performs locally "elementary" activities (such as algebraic calculations) [5]; in the model proposed here instead there are two Solvers linked in feedback, and each of them processes tasks at a higher level, even if oriented to a Bottom-Up approach.

More precisely, the Solver consists of a two-level SIMULATOR, called L1 and L2, which translates into the particle representation of the atmosphere the phenomena of the troposphere and of the vertical exchange and mixing in the PLB (Planetary Boundary Layer), as shown in Fig. 2.

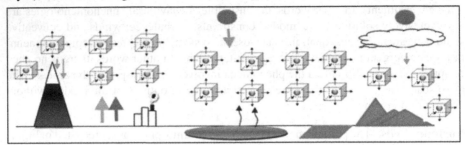

Fig. 2. Interchange and vertical mixing in the PLB.

The L1 Solver. The first Solver has mainly four tasks:

- It attributes physical and chemical state properties to the particles (and to the cells that inscribe them), i.e. the concentrations of the various gases (humidity of all) and particles (aerosols). This is done starting from the Microphysics applied to the simulation state in the previous prediction steps and of the exchanges with the environment; in fact L1 makes use of an orographic map characterizing the surface (mountains, hills, sea and similar).
- It assigns forces to the particles according to the energy state obtained from the interaction with radiation and "heat sinks" (e.g. glaciers, mountains, night terrain). Synthetically, always referring to Fig. 3, we have $F_{r,t}(i, j, k) = f(T, t, i, j, k)$, therefore we attribute a force at a given time t, which depends on T (temperature). Under specific conditions, the L1 solver can impose velocities and position fields that would not be imposed by standard evolution. The information about the three-dimensional array of forces is then passed to solver L2.
- Initialization: it is the responsibility of the first solver to associate the initial state to all particles, and to the environmental elements (terrain, cloud type, cloud thickness, solar radiation incidence, etc.), this initialization can be compared, with due distinction, to the data assimilation of the initial conditions for classical NWP models. The input can be given by real time data, such as radar, central units, public data and even NWP models. Or hypothetical values, taken from seasonal averages, historical archives, case studies, can be input. The former is mandatory in experimental model validation, the latter in DSS contexts or for validation by detecting specific and expected patterns.
- It divides the 3D domain into Macro-Clusters and provides for each of these the atomically referable forecast fields, i.e. the output values (temperature, rain, and so on). The output clusters also define the (three-dimensional) scale of the model. The parameters are generally square-based parallelepipeds (in the case study: 400 m × 400 m × 100 m).

The L2 Solver. The Second Solver is a Newtonian Simulator that operates on the values of Force, Mass, Viscosity, local density associated by the First Solver to the single particles. It is built around a software library for fluid modelling SPH (Smoothed Particle Hydrodynamics) [2].

The library and development environment are produced by Nvidia and the specific technology is called Nvidia Physx. Fluid modelling using the SPH approach is therefore also particle-based; however, it is oriented towards the realistic simulation of fluids or gases that develop within a few hundred metres (e.g. building virtual wind tunnels). The experimental software uses the Nvidia Physx engine, assigning values of the order of 70 m at rest (in our case study) to the intraparticle distances. It is natural that this last "inductive" step is governed by Solver L2 by setting appropriate parameters to the Nvidia Physx engine. Note that the distance between particles does not necessarily coincide with what is defined for the L1 clusters.

The Solver L2 then introduces in the simulation the forces attributed to the particles by L1, and so begins the dynamic evolution by PhysX with the rules of the SPH Fluids: therefore if for example there is a local interpenetration of the cells at time t (e.g. $\Delta Sx_{(i,i+1)} < D_{cell}$), the repulsion forces come into play as dictated by the parameters with which the fluid "Atmosphere" is represented: partial compressibility, friction, viscosity, mass. It is clear that this mechanism is intended to represent in the 3D domain the Winds (also with complex characterizations such as turbulence) and the variations of extremely localized Pressure (convective, ascending, etc.), and it is also clear that this mechanism is particularly effective with complex orographies, such as those of the Apennines where there is a sudden variation of altitude in a few kilometres, such situations, it is known, are hardly managed by the classic NWP.

Overall Architecture. The various software modules (and model) that make up the experimental software and their interactions are summarized in Fig. 3, that also summarizes the interaction between the two solvers shown above.

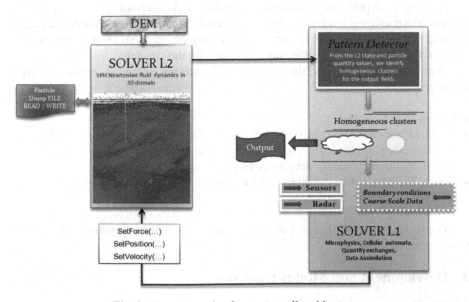

Fig. 3. Experimental software, overall architecture.

The main modules are the Solver L2 (Particle Newtonian Solver) and the Solver L1, connected through a feedback that is the way the software operates the simulation. The initialization of the system in Solver L2 involves the reading of an ASCII DEM which will constitute the orographic domain of the simulation, the particles will be positioned on the scene distributed in a uniform manner and evolving this configuration until a point of stability (the particles will thicken in the valleys and will be more rarefied on the mountainous reliefs).

The initial position of the particles can optionally be read from a previously saved dump file. This phase also includes the processing of the configuration file indicating some characteristic parameters of physical or behavioural nature to be associated to the particles (mass, viscosity, maximum speed, etc.), parameters that have been the object of the study phase for their calibration, a calibration that can be refined by anyone with statistical (or other) approaches useful to enhance them with adjustments related to the area of interest, so that the spatial-variant behaviour of the model, besides orography and latitude (and the like), is also due to this process.

At this point, the forecast simulation ORCHESTRATED by Solver L1 can begin. Focusing on the lower portion of the block in Fig. 3, it can be observed that Solver L1 processes the initial conditions provided by the measurements (sensors, radar) and transforms this information into directives that are provided to Solver L2, directives for assigning forces, velocities and positions to particles contained in specific spatial volumes (Clusters). After this, the L2 solver evolves by applying the directives for a certain parameterized time interval. At the end of the evolution the Solver L1 will be informed about the new state of the particles: Position, Velocity, Density and change of these compared to the previous state. Solver L1, who acts as orchestrator, associates the attributes provided by L2 with the particle, but also atmospheric state related characteristics such as humidity, temperature, and the like.

From the states provided by Solver L2, the Pattern Detector (part of L1) creates zones, clusters with homogeneous atmospheric characteristics (equal in size to the desired scale, or larger) identifying cloud cover, rain, humidity, average temperature, pressure, etc. The values referred to Clusters are the output provided by the simulator.

Continuing with feedback, the "bottom" of L1 has the following inputs (no longer initial conditions):

- Pattern Detector Clusters.
- Internal Phenomenological Conditions; such as the position of the sun, orography as seen from the point of view of atmospheric heat absorption, such as any maps showing lakes or pollutant sources, factories or maps of vegetation.
- Coarse Scale boundary conditions, at the boundaries of the domain only forcings of this type are required.

The processed output is again the directives for the new evolutionary step for L2, thus closing the feedback.

3   Development and Modus Operandi

3.1   Hardware and Software

The Nvidia PhysX library used for the L2 Newtonian solver is developed around the CUDA infrastructure, that is the basic library of all the Nvidia technologies designed for HPC (High Performance Computing), whose code is not executed on the usual CPU COREs, but on the hyper-parallel ones of the GPUs installed in the 3D-accelerated video cards; these cores are specialized to solve almost exclusively mathematical calculations, which allows a surprising number of them on a single chip (in the order of thousands).

Consequently, the dimensioning of the hardware for the production and development machine has taken this characteristic into account to a great extent, Fig. 4.

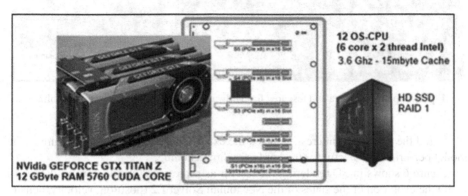

Fig. 4. Hardware dimensioned for experimental software in the case study.

So, we are in the presence of a workstation with 3 GPUs configured in SLI mode (a technology that allows the exchange of data between the three video cards without using the central PCIe bus) with a total of 17280 CUDA CORE and 36 GBytes of video memory, in addition to 12 CORE (6 x 2 th.) Intel CPUs dedicated CPU Intel I7-10810U and 16 GByte RAM (net of the host ecosystem) to the Solver L1.

This solution, despite the well over 8 TeraFLOPS developed has a market cost of a few thousand dollars. The sizing listed above was designed to cover a simulation area of 60 km × 60 km (case study presented here), obtaining stable output from the simulator, and considered valid, on average after 15 min.

Figure 5 reports the area to which the performance evaluation refers, and the experimental area taken into consideration, located between the centres of Catanzaro and Lamezia Terme, in Calabria. The application data carried out was acquired thanks to Remote Sensing techniques [6] (to build the 3D model, survey vegetation, water) and UAVs (Unmanned Aerial Vehicles), used with thermal imaging cameras. The choice of area was dictated by the particular orographic and climatic conditions. In fact, this is the narrowest point of the Italian peninsula, the one between two seas (Tyrrhenian Sea and Ionian Sea), and in a few kilometres one passes from the warmer coast to the cold Apennines and then back to the other warmer coast. In such conditions of abrupt altitude variation, Classical NWPs have more difficulty in such contexts. In fact, the output returned by the Classical NWP represents mean values over the cells discretizing the domain, which in this case are characterized by high variance.

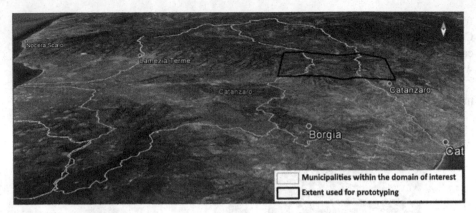

Fig. 5. Application area and test area for hardware dimensioning. (Color figure online)

In red the domain of interest, in black the extent used to have a first measure of the model performances useful for the hardware dimensioning.

Figure 6 shows in 3D rendering the test air as represented inside the simulator and in 3D the evolution of the states of the Newtonian Solver L2 (position, velocity, density etc.).

In more detail, Fig. 6 represents a single frame extracted from the 4-dimensional animation that the software GUI offers as output after the simulation run. In red is the orography imported from DEM raster, while the dots are the particles represented by the

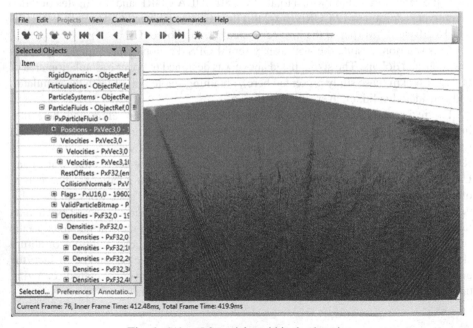

Fig. 6. Solver L2 particles within the domain.

atmosphere evolving over time according to the model (SPH, microphysics and local interchange of properties, as per Figs. 1 and 2).

In Fig. 7 two screenshots with small parts of the code.

(a)	(b)

Fig. 7. (a) Initialisation of solver L2 SPH. (b) Iteration in solver L1.

3.2 Validation

The validation operations used for the simulator input the historical data of the central unit provided by the Calabria Region (average density: 1 every 7 km) and radar (Spatial Resolution 1 km - Rain Field), for the boundary constraints the historical ECMWF (European Centre for Medium-Range Weather Forecasts) data were used. At this point it was necessary to verify whether typical recurrent atmospheric phenomena, with low variability, predicted in the literature in the contexts under investigation were found.

In particular, the phenomena investigated concerned:

- Orographic waves [7].
- Turbulence [8].
- Convective motions [9].
- Breezes: sea breezes (diurnal), land breezes (nocturnal) [10].
- Rainfall (expected intervals) [11].

All the phenomena indicated were "reproduced" by the simulator every time as expected by the literature for the specific initialization data, the characteristics of the territory (orography, sea, city, etc.) from the date to which the execution refers.

Minimal errors were found with validation on the same sensors. For the future, validation on meteorological fields distributed over the territory by means of IOT mobile stations and the use of UAVs, measuring certain temperature and pressure fields at altitude is planned; in the latter case both for a matter of convenience and for the 3D connotation of the model.

4 Conclusions

The simulator presented here is designed to support institutions, monitoring organizations, and designers in various fields in studying weather/atmospheric dynamics with very high resolution in limited areas. The displacements of air masses, the weather fields in general, are provided by following the orography of the territory. In other words, even in the presence of narrow reentrants, the simulator output provides an elaborated data on this land feature, and not as an average of an area where this reentrant is located.

The special bottom-up approach without the use of differential equations brings a number of advantages in terms of cost effectiveness (hardware, quantity and quality of data for initial conditions, specialization of personnel), accuracy and flexibility of use. The simulator can thus be used in a variety of fields to better characterize the response of specific areas to a wide range of weather conditions. Examples include the design of a wind farm, flood [12] or landslide prevention [13–15], agriculture, and even zoogeographical research, when it is necessary to map possible new habitats for species that are alien to an area (e.g. mosquitoes). In addition, the flexibility of the initialization data makes it easy to compare time series simulations in order to trace how climate change impacts on micro areas. Finally, it can be used as a special downscaling software.

The model has been extensively validated for the detection of expected patterns (from convective motions, to turbulence, to temperature distribution). It will soon undergo validation on values measured with the use of mobile stations and UAVs in the presence of interesting climatic situations. A variant of the software that works in NWP mode will be developed after this verification.

References

1. Bauer, P., Thorpe, A., Brunet, G.: The quiet revolution of numerical weather prediction. Nature **525**, 47–55 (2015). https://doi.org/10.1038/nature14956
2. Vacondio, R., et al.: Grand challenges for smoothed particle hydrodynamics numerical schemes. Comput. Part. Mech. **8**(3), 575–588 (2020). https://doi.org/10.1007/s40571-020-00354-1
3. Klemp, J.B., Dudhia, J., Hassiotis, A.D.: An upper gravity-wave absorbing layer for NWP applications. Mon. Weather Rev. **136**(10), 987–4004 (2008). https://doi.org/10.1175/200 8MWR2596.1
4. Wang, S., Zhang, K., van Beek, L.P.H., Tian, X., Bogaard, A.: Physically-based landslide prediction over a large region: scaling low-resolution hydrological model results for high-resolution slope stability assessment. Environ. Model. Softw. **124**, 104607 (2021). https://doi.org/10.1016/j.envsoft2019.104607
5. Brdar, S., Baldauf, M., Dedner, A., et al.: Comparison of dynamical cores for NWP models: comparison of COSMO and Dune. Theor. Comput. Fluid Dyn. **27**, 453–472 (2013). https://doi.org/10.1007/s00162-012-0264-z
6. Barrile, V., Bilotta, G.: An application of remote sensing: object-oriented analysis of Satellite data. In: The International Archives of the Photogrammetry, Remote Sensing and Spatial Information Sciences, vol. XXXVII, pp. 107–113 (2008)
7. Seo, J.M., Baik, J.J., Moon, S.: Orographic–convective flows, wave reflection, and gravity-wave momentum fluxes in a two-layer hydrostatic atmosphere. Tellus A Dyn. Meteorol. Oceanogr. **70**(1), 1–16 (2018). https://doi.org/10.1080/16000870.2018.1487223
8. Muñoz-Esparza, D., Sharman, R.D., Trier, S.B.: On the consequences of PBL scheme diffusion on UTLS wave and turbulence representation in high-resolution NWP models. Mon. Weather Rev. **148**(10), 4247–4265 (2020). https://doi.org/10.1175/MWR-D-20-0102.1
9. Emanuel, K.A.: Atmospheric Convection. Oxford University Press, New York (1994)
10. Haurwitz, B.: Comments on the sea-breeze circulation. J. Atmos. Sci. **4**(1), 1–8 (1947). https://doi.org/10.1175/1520-0469(1947)004<0001:COTSBC>2.0.CO;2

11. Sachidananda, M., Zrnić, D.S.: rain rate estimates from differential polarization measurements. J. Atmos. Ocean. Technol. **4**(4), 588–598 (1987). https://doi.org/10.1175/1520-042 6(1987)004<0588:RREFDP>2.0.CO;2

12. Barrile, V., Bilotta, G., Fotia, A.: Analysis of hydraulic risk territories: comparison between LIDAR and other different techniques for 3D modeling. WSEAS Trans. Environ. Dev. **14**, 45–52 (2018)

13. Barrile, V., Meduri, G.M., Bilotta, G.: Comparison between two methods for monitoring deformation with laser scanner. WSEAS Tran. Signal Process. **10**(1), 497–503 (2014)

14. Barrile, V., Meduri, G.M., Bilotta, G.: Laser scanner technology for complex surveying structures. WSEAS Trans. Signal Process. **7**(3), 65–74 (2011)

15. Barrile, V., Meduri, G.M., Bilotta, G.: Laser scanner surveying techniques aiming to the study and the spreading of recent architectural structures. In: Proceedings of the 2nd WSEAS International Conference on Engineering Mechanics, Structures and Engineering Geology, EMESEG 2009, pp. 25–28 (2009)

Linked (Open) Chorems: A Semantically Enriched Visual Representation

Pietro Battistoni[✉][iD], Monica Sebillo[iD], and Giuliana Vitiello[iD]

University of Salerno, 84084 Fisciano, SA, Italy
{pbattistoni,msebillo,gvitiello}@unisa.it

Abstract. The term *chorem* was initially introduced in 1986 by Brunet to visually represent geographic information by a set of spatial primitives. By focusing on specific features of interest and simplifying non-relevant aspects, a chorem can synthesize and depict territorial dynamics and strategies, such as connection path, propagation, and urban distribution. Since then, several approaches have been proposed to design maps of chorems and associate them with geographic information. However, the lack of a uniform approach to associate them with both a basic figure and a meaning, caused a proliferation of *ad hoc* solutions, sometimes failing in conveying the information they were meant to. The goal of the present paper is to describe an innovative approach to design and build chorems and maps of chorems, aimed at both improving their capability to represent dynamics and strategies and avoiding redundancies and inconsistencies in the meaning comprehension. To achieve this goal, a Web of data paradigm is followed and a three-level model is introduced, which starts from a paradigm that assembles concepts and their relationships, defines domain-specific concepts and completes itself in supporting the definition of individuals of a knowledge base. The whole building process of both chorems for domains of interest and individuals expressed as instances of chorems is supported by guidelines, which can be implemented through a whatever platform to build and populate ontologies.

Keywords: Geographic information · Visual representation · Ontologies · Knowledge bases

1 Introduction

The concept of *chorem* was first introduced in 1986 by the French geographer Brunet. By eliminating details not useful to the map comprehension, a chorem associated basic figures, from line to network, with essential dynamics and strategies, as shown in Fig. 1 [5]. The image illustrates the chorems introduced by Brunet along with their meaning.

Partly supported by MIUR PRIN 2017 grant number 2017JMHK4F 004.

E. Borgogno-Mondino and P. Zamperlin (Eds.): ASITA 2022, CCIS 1651, pp. 114–125, 2022.
https://doi.org/10.1007/978-3-031-17439-1_8

Since then, the concept has evolved over the years, and several approaches have been proposed for its design, although such a proliferation of *ad hoc* solutions sometimes caused failing in conveying the information they were meant to [1,2,10].

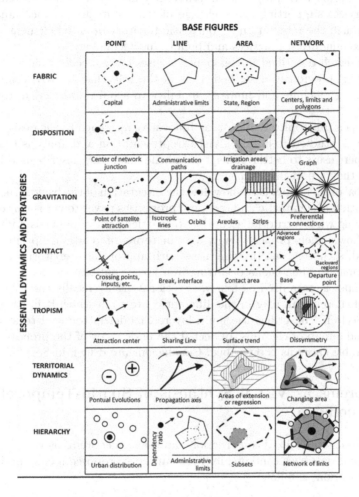

Fig. 1. Chorems designed by Brunet [5]

The potentiality of chorems was discussed by Laurini et al. in [7], where a list of the different roles that chorems may play is given. The authors state that chorems can be used to represent geographic knowledge, to visually summarize database contents and finally to underlie the creation of a novel entry system for geographic databases. Indeed, the vision that most authors share about the capability a chorem can express, relates its contribution in territorial valorization. A chorem can work as a *prosumer*, namely a collector of data deriving from multiple sources and, by processing it, a producer of actionable information (knowledge), useful to problem solving tasks.

Along this line, the research carried out at the Laboratory of Geographic Information Systems (University of Salerno) is addressed to investigate open and shared tools with properties of scalability and interoperability, capable to realize services supporting the exchange of know-how among local and global actors through the integration of four basic territory-oriented elements, namely content, communities, practices and policy, and technology.

The research described in this paper focuses on a specific theme within the wide context previously described, that is the role that *chorems* can play in strengthening machine and human capability to acquire knowledge from a territory.

To deepen this topic of interest, an innovative approach to the design and use of chorems is studied to obtain a visual representation and analysis tool, which allows expert users to better understand phenomena they describe and interpret dynamics they are involved in.

The goal of this paper is to show how the integration of the basic structure of a chorem with both syntactic and semantic properties paves towards this objective when dealing with territorial scenarios. In particular, the paper is addressed to describe how, when properly built also in terms of relationships in which it is involved, a chorem can provide users with appropriate territorial knowledge useful to analyse phenomena occurring in a given context.

The paper is organized as follows. Section 2 briefly recalls the role that the concept of chorem can play in the different contexts in which it has been investigated. Section 3 describes the multi-layered model introduced to structure a chorem and a map of chorems. In Sect. 4 the basic steps of the process useful to build sharable chorems is described. Conclusions are drawn in Sect. 5.

2   Chorems as Visual Synthesis of Spatio-Temporal Phenomena

To support a standardized construction and usage of chorems as visual syntheses of geographic database contents, in [8] the authors proposed a chorem definition and classification as follows:

- Geographic chorems,
- Phenomenal chorems and
- Annotation chorems.

Geographic chorems represent geographic data with associated simple geometries, such as points, lines, polygons, and objects made up of their combinations, such as networks. Phenomenal chorems describe spatio-temporal phenomena involving one or more geographic chorems, and, when useful, they can be further classified in Flow, Tropism, and Spatial Diffusion. A Flow chorem represents objects movement between geographic chorems. A Tropism chorem represents an homogeneous attractive or repulsive space, around a geographic chorem. A

Spatial Diffusion chorem represents a spatial progression or regression, from a geographic chorem along a given direction. Finally, an Annotation chorem represents map labels or remarks, useful to provide users with additional information about the map. It is worth to noting that a chorem can be built as a set of chorems, each contributing to its definition.

As for the chorem building, also in [8], the underlying structure of a chorem was introduced to manage the complex nature of geographic data and phenomena (Fig. 2). To this aim it visually integrates the iconic and the property components defined as follows. As for the former, the iconic representation assemblies a graphical component, corresponding to the visual representation, and a meaning, referring to the semantic component. In such a way, users can quickly perceive the meaning associated with data and use it properly. As for the property component of a chorem, it is divided into two parts, a type attribute specifying the category the chorem belongs to, namely geographic, phenomenal or annotation, and a source indicating where data could be retrieved.

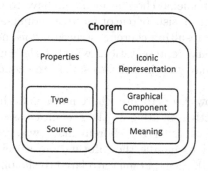

Fig. 2. The structure of chorems [8]

Following this line, in [6,8], a set of operators was introduced, both geographic and semantic, to derive spatial knowledge, useful to help domain experts face and get rapid and exhaustive responses in critical situations.

Based on the Ben Shneiderman's mantra and on Keim's adaptation to the Visual Analytics domain [9,11], applying these operators allows users to navigate a chorem map from an initial overview to a detail, as follows.

i) *Geographic Zoom*

This operation corresponds to the traditional map zooming (in/out) operator. When applied to a chorematic map, it acts exclusively on the visual aspect of the chorem, by changing the size of the visible details of the involved chorem elements, leaving them unchanged, also in terms of structure.

ii) *Semantic Zoom*

A semantic zoom (in/out) changes the type and meaning of information associated with chorems. When applied, it allows accessing to a different level of information, that is, it analyzes the chorem and its elements by (dis)aggregating and visualizing them in detail. In particular, when the operation is applied to geographical chorems, they are simply split up (resp., aggregated), by showing a new level of geographic data abstraction. The chorem structure is modified accordingly, by properly substituting the corresponding iconic representation component, both in terms of graphical component and meaning. When a semantic zoom is applied to a Phenomenal chorem, it is decomposed (resp., aggregated) along with the Geographic Chorems related to it. In this case, the chorem structure is differently modified. In fact, even if the output chorem still corresponds to the initial phenomenal chorem, its meaning changes, being referred to a different abstraction of the territory.

iii) *Geographic Filter*
This operation allows the user to select Phenomenal Chorems elements by using the graphical component of one or more Geographic Chorems elements as spatial filter. In this case, the condition corresponds to the territory of interest where phenomenal chorems elements have to be analyzed. The output of the operation consists of one or more phenomenal chorems that satisfy the condition. The resulting chorems structure does not change in terms of properties and iconic representation, whereas the number of phenomenal chorem elements may vary in order to satisfy the condition.

iv) *Semantic Filter*
This operation allows users to filter chorem elements that satisfy a particular condition, by directly operating on the semantics associated to them.
A recent usage of chorems and chorem maps was described in [4], where they are conceived to handle the information associated with the Urban Heat Islands (UHIs). Each parameter related to the phenomenon is properly modelled and processed in an environmental context.

Figure 3 shows the chorems associated with both the UHI phenomenon and each parameter contributing to its development, namely Urban Area, Urban Greenery, Urban Geometry and Albedo, represented themselves as chorems. The goal of the following Section is to enhance the expressiveness of chorems and make them machine-processable by associating them with (general-purpose) concepts and establishing relationships among them, according to the Semantic Web paradigm.

3   The Linked Chorems: From Data to Knowledge

Figure 4 depicts a data supply chain designed to derive knowledge from data. The red area contains all phases needed to obtain a Global Data Source. The green one collects phases and disciplines addressed to derive knowledge from data and exploit it for applications in different domains. The goal of integrating the chorem concept within this supply chain is to have an additional paradigm to enhance the capability of the built knowledge bases to express and represent each feature of the domain under investigation. Moreover, if semantics is an integral part of

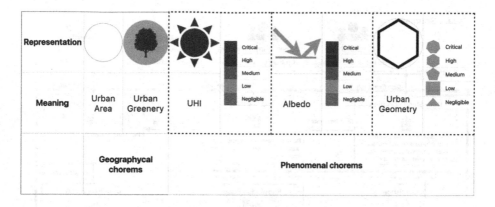

Fig. 3. Chorems for the UHI phenomenon [3]

the chorem structure, acquired from the initial step of the chorem modeling, such an approach results more effective, being machine processable.

Enriching the chorem definition with semantics is therefore fundamental and implies to act on the underlying schema as described in the following.

3.1 The Proposed Three-Layered Model

Each component of the chorem structure but the *Type*, is involved during this enhancement, namely the *Source* component, which assemblies several types of sources available to acquire and collect data; the *Meaning* component, which embeds the description of the content that a chorem is conceived to represent; the *Graphical Component*, which relates the icon used to depict the concept. The tasks required to achieve the goal are the following:

- modifying the *Source* component,
- extending the *Meaning* component,
- defining concepts that abstract each individual/item,
- establishing relationships between concepts and applying them to their individuals,
- applying constraints and rules.

These tasks have been performed at different levels. First, the general purpose definition of chorem has been modelled in terms of concepts and relationships according to the structure shown in Fig. 2. Such a definition can be used as a paradigm and can represent a standard approach to guarantee the goals proposed with the chorem introduction.

The association with a domain represents the second level. It is necessary to define classes of chorems, modelled according to the previous paradigm and specific of a given context. The example of Fig. 8 is useful for the specific Climate Change context of the Environment domain. Several other classes can be modelled within this domain, such as Marine and Land.

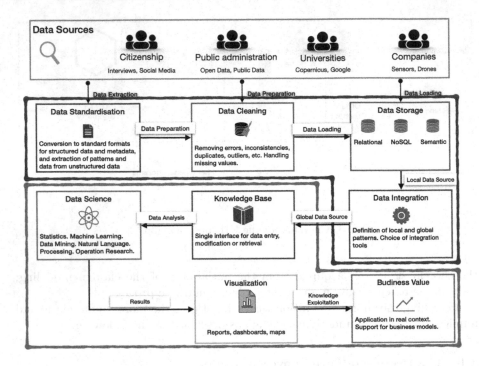

Fig. 4. Integration and analysis of data from multiple sources (Color figure online)

As for the *Source* component, to associate the chorem with a Global Data Source, an appropriate data integration method is first required for standardized and cleaned data, whose goal is to provide users with a unified, single view of data for subsequent data analysis processes and knowledge exploitation functions, as shown through the connection between the blue Data Storage and the purple Data Integration boxes of Fig. 4. The data integration method is in charge of producing a linked version of data in terms of Web-based resources (identified by Internationalized Resource Identifier (IRI)/Uniform Resource Identifier (URI)). Such a version is mandatory and can be expressed in different modalities, depending on the given source, such as OWL and SPARQL query to an endpoint.

As for the *Meaning* component, domain-specific concepts and semantic relationships between more general concepts are integrated, thus enriching the knowledge heritage that this component carries with it. Moreover, also this component can be used to describe how chorems can be composed by assembling other chorems.

Also the *Graphical Component* can benefit from such an improvement. Using collections of visual items, possibly standardized and accompanied by metadata, can contribute to associate a unique graphics with a given meaning, thus reducing multiple visual representations that differ slightly.

Finally, as for the third level, populating a knowledge base implies to create individuals, that is, chorems associated with location, values acquired from their sources, and a contextualized meaning.

For a preliminary vision of the ontology, only some classes are expanded in Fig. 5, namely Chorems and its components, Sources and its subclasses. UHI is represented as an individual of the Chorems class just to clarify its role within the whole schema.

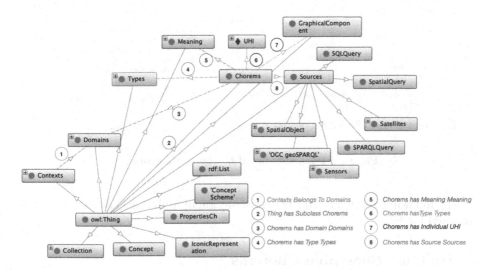

Fig. 5. Classes for the chorem description

As for the operations, establishing relationships at the second level implies that the *Meaning* component of a chorem contains the details useful to perform a *Semantic Zoom* or a *Semantic Filter*. As an example, by applying a semantic zoom-in to the UHI chorem, it is disaggregated according to the parameters depicted in Fig. 3. In particular, it discloses the involved chorems, namely Urban Area, Albedo, Urban Geometry and Urban Greenery.

Figures 6 show a portion of serialization, namely prefixes and object properties, and classes, based on the *turtle* syntax.

The schema explains concepts and relationships in terms of OWL-based triples. In particular, according to the ontological approach, concepts are subjects of triples expressed as URI/IRI, properties are predicates, while objects can be both concepts (i.e., URI/IRI) and literals.

When the resulting multi-layered model is adopted, populating the Chorems class with individuals means defining chorem instances by following a homogeneous approach, which prevents redundancies, inconsistencies and synonyms. Moreover, creating chorem instances according to this model implies populating a knowledge base on which further manipulations can be applied to derive new knowledge, such as thematic maps and a Linked Open Chorem version to be published on the Linked Open Data Cloud.

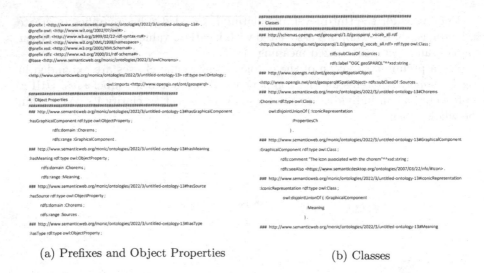

(a) Prefixes and Object Properties   (b) Classes

Fig. 6. Serialization based on the *turtle* syntax

The following Section details the construction of individuals according to the proposed model.

4   Building Shareable Chorems

The goal of information sharing and cooperative exploitation is to achieve a profitable combination of territorial knowledge and actionable intelligence. Chorems can contribute to this aim by improving users' experience while creating public value for services. Indeed, information flowing across individuals and the surrounding territory may be aggregated and transformed into knowledge to support decision-making procedures and ultimately delivered back to individuals in the form of services. Within this transformation, chorems can be used to convey users the right message and synthesize the salient properties of phenomena under investigation.

In the present Section, the construction of a chorem instance is illustrated, realized according to the OWL model previously introduced. Adopting this approach allows users to overcome the lack of uniformity in chorem building in terms of components, which caused a proliferation of homonyms and synonymies, i.e., the same representation for different meanings or different representations for the same meaning.

Although it may result crowded to be clear, Fig. 7 is included to show the most relevant part of the whole graph derived as visual representation of the ontology built in Protegé. All classes and most of relevant individuals defined and modelled according to the previous approach are located. It is worth to noting that some ontologies were imported, thus establishing connections with existing concepts and avoiding redundancies.

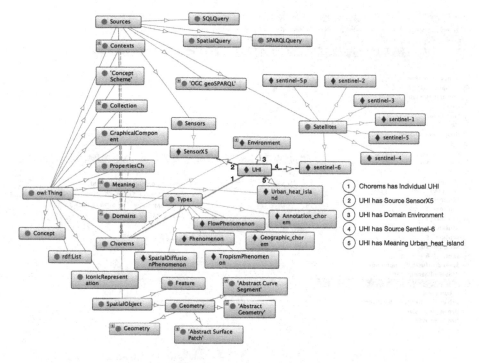

Fig. 7. Classes and individuals

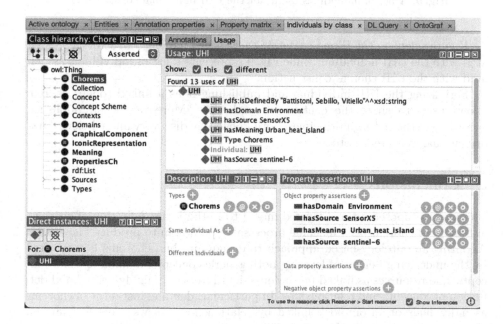

Fig. 8. Building the UHI chorem individual

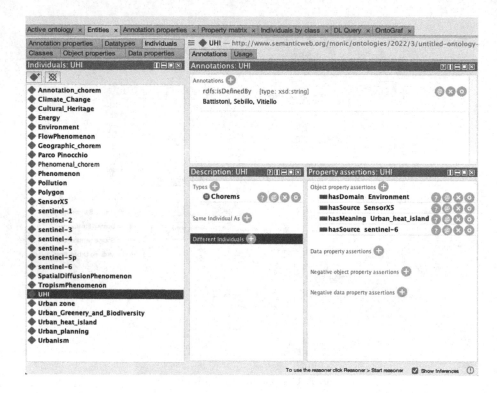

Fig. 9. A list of individuals useful for the UHI individual construction

Figure 8 depicts the frame containing all classes modelled in Protegé associated with the UHI individual, while Fig. 9 represents a list of individuals associated with the UHI chorem construction.

Serializing the UHI individual and publishing it as a linked (open) chorem allows users to share the content it synthesizes. Moreover, when published according to these design principles, both knowledge discovery and efficient data-driven analytics are boosted.

5   Conclusions

The paper proposed a three-layered model to re-think the definition of chorems and maps of chorems as a machine processable paradigm to produce knowledge. Adopting an ontology-based approach to design and buil chorems is motivated by the underlying benefit of layering both generic concepts, domain-specific concepts, and resources as linked but independent layers of a highly articulated definition of concepts and relationships. In particular, defining instances of chorems as individuals of an ontology linked by relationships, allows users focusing on objects and phenomena they study disregarding the need of guaranteeing consistency and avoiding redundancy.

Future work is addressed to the integration of this model in applications conceived for expert users and decision makers to experiment its possible extent on real case studies in different domains.

References

1. Arreghini, L.: La modélisation graphique dans la réalisation des atlas pour le développement. Les atlas pour le développement en coopération, pp. 1–10 (1995)
2. Batardy, C.: Le berry antique-de la carte au modèle-chorème. Revue archéologique du Centre de la France **43**, 253–258 (2005)
3. Battistoni, P., Grimaldi, M., Romano, M., Sebillo, M., Vitiello, G.: Interactive maps of chorems explaining urban contexts to align smart community's actors. In: Gervasi, O., Murgante, B., Misra, S., Garau, C., Blečić, I., Taniar, D., Apduhan, B.O., Rocha, A.M.A.C., Tarantino, E., Torre, C.M. (eds.) ICCSA 2021, Part V. LNCS, vol. 12953, pp. 549–564. Springer, Cham (2021). https://doi.org/10.1007/978-3-030-86976-2_37
4. Battistoni, P., Grimaldi, M., Sebillo, M., Vitiello, G.: Living labs and open innovation to support local development policies. In: Borgogno-Mondino, E., Zamperlin, P. (eds.) ASITA 2021. CCIS, vol. 1507, pp. 339–350. Springer, Cham (2022). https://doi.org/10.1007/978-3-030-94426-1_25
5. Brunet, R.: La carte-modèle et les chorèmes. Mappemonde (1986)
6. De Chiara, D., Del Fatto, V., Laurini, R., Sebillo, M., Vitiello, G.: A chorem-based approach for visually analyzing spatial data. J. Vis. Lang. Comput. **22**(3), 173–193 (2011)
7. Del Fatto, V., et al.: Potentialities of chorems as visual summaries of geographic databases contents. In: Qiu, G., Leung, C., Xue, X., Laurini, R. (eds.) VISUAL 2007. LNCS, vol. 4781, pp. 537–548. Springer, Heidelberg (2007). https://doi.org/10.1007/978-3-540-76414-4_52
8. Del Fatto, V., Laurini, R., Lopez, K., Sebillo, M., Vitiello, G.: A chorem-based approach for visually synthesizing complex phenomena. Inf. Visual. **7**(3–4), 253–264 (2008)
9. Keim, D.A., Mansmann, F., Schneidewind, J., Ziegler, H.: Challenges in visual data analysis. In: Tenth International Conference on Information Visualisation (IV 2006), pp. 9–16. IEEE (2006)
10. Patrick, C.: Modélisation graphique et chorèmes: la gestion des parcours collectifs à massaroca (brésil du nordeste). Mappemonde 62, June 2001
11. Shneiderman, B.: The eyes have it: a task by data type taxonomy for information visualizations. In: Proceedings of 1996 IEEE Symposium on Visual Languages, pp. 336–343 (1996). https://doi.org/10.1109/VL.1996.545307

Remote Sensing Course in Geography Online Education: A MOODLE Learning Materials Adaptation and Optimization Workflow

G. A. Di Carlo[1]($\boxtimes$) (iD), Pietro Boccardo[2] (iD), and V. Fissore[1] (iD)

[1] ITHACA Srl, Via P.C. Boggio 61, Turin, Italy
{guido.dicarlo,vanina.fissore}@ithacaweb.org
[2] DIST - Interuniversity Department of Regional and Urban Studies and Planning, Politecnico di Torino, Viale Mattioli 39, Turin, Italy
piero.boccardo@polito.it

Abstract. Learning management systems (LMS) have been evolving since the late 1990s as a category of specialized web-based software for educational content delivery and experience. LMS assumed pivotal importance in learning experiences due to the COVID-19 spread. In this software pool, MOODLE (Modular Object-Oriented Dynamic Learning Environment) is a seasoned open-source LMS framework that has been widely adopted by companies, schools, and the academic community. This work aims to set up the learning materials of the Remote Sensing course theoretical and practical modules of UNITO master's degree in Geography and Territorial Sciences, on the LMS MOODLE and to adapt it considering the multi-disciplinary approach typical of the Geographic domain. Thanks to inherent LMS features and different plugins available on the platform, some analytical approaches originally optimized for face-to-face didactics, are re-developed to optimize the ingestion, classification, and delivery of learning materials through the LMS, to facilitate comprehension and access to such materials by students in the Remote sensing course.

Keywords: Remote sensing education · Online learning · Learning management systems metadata · Keyword tagging · Ontology-based competency framework

1 Introduction

Out of necessity, the recent COVID-19 pandemic has forced educators and academia in general, to hastily move all their learning programs to an online environment with little time to plan and design an effective learning setup as the spread of the virus abruptly interrupted well-consolidated face-to-face learning environments [14]. The necessity for health safety resulted in a quick migration to online learning environments via Learning Management Systems, which typically allow students and instructors to exchange instructional materials, make class announcements, etc. This haste process has been recently referred to as emergency remote learning [6], which might add to the stigma

© The Author(s), under exclusive license to Springer Nature Switzerland AG 2022
E. Borgogno-Mondino and P. Zamperlin (Eds.): ASITA 2022, CCIS 1651, pp. 126–138, 2022.
https://doi.org/10.1007/978-3-031-17439-1_9

of online learning being a weaker substitute for classroom experiences, despite research showing different results [1, 15].

Lecture modalities consequently changed with professors recurring to teleconferencing tools to live-stream lectures to students. The recordings are generally made available for students to replay.

Like many others, the Remote Sensing course, part of UNITO master's degree in Geography and Territorial Sciences [3], had to be adapted to such a new remote learning method. The course, made of both theoretical and practical modules, permits to test the adaptability of these two teaching modalities, inevitably different due to their diverse nature, to the e-learning approach, by their incorporation and adaptation in MOODLE LMS platform.

Moreover, Geography, as an area of knowledge, is made of broadly different contents and sub-divisions that call, when taught in face-to-face mode, for broadly different teaching methods [13]. Due to such diversity and intrinsic interdisciplinary nature, Geography is deemed an optimal testing ground to adapt such diverse teachings in an online setting.

With these premises, this work aims to set up the Remote Sensing course learning materials, both considering theoretical and practical modules, on the LMS MOODLE platform, and to adapt it considering the specific and diverse characteristics of the Geographic domain. This last process is facilitated thanks to different plugins available on the platform. In this way, some analytical approaches are developed to permit the ingestion, classification, and delivery of learning materials, to facilitate the access to and the comprehension of such materials by students in the Remote sensing course.

This is done through a selection of tools and extensions available in MOODLE aimed at delivering and categorizing learning materials, and through the decomposition of available learning materials for the Remote Sensing course.

2 Material and Methods

2.1 Modular Object-Oriented Dynamic Learning Environment (MOODLE)

MOODLE is an open-source learning management system framework written in PHP scripting language and distributed under the GNU General Public License. It is one of the most adopted frameworks in the world, with more than 140 million users [12] that follows a standard three-layer architecture:

- User Interface: handling the interactions between the user and the PHP code.
- Libraries: specialised precompiled routines that are invokable by non-related processes.
- Databases: organised collections of data.
- Files: single files hosted in specialised folders in the framework.

A high-level schema of MOODLE's three-layer architecture is shown in Fig. 1.
In MOODLE, libraries are divided in:

- Core libraries, that handle basic features of the framework, such as roles, categories, courses, users and refer to data stored in either framework databases or files databases.

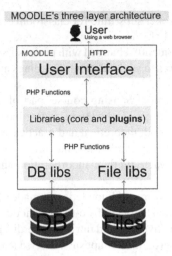

Fig. 1. Moodle three-layer architecture – adapted from https://www.slideshare.net/tjh1000/a-basic-introduciton-to-the-moodle-architecture-5442122

- Plugin libraries interact with core libraries, which are grouped in subsystems, and categorised according to the libraries area they refer to.

A plethora of tools is available in MOODLE to form courses and customize learning experiences, divided in two main categories:

- Resources are objects that contain files, text, images, or media and do not require any interaction or grading by the MOODLE libraries.
- Activities are objects that are programmed to require an interaction between the user and the MOODLE LMS.

For this work, a selection of features and plugins were first tested among the ones available in MOODLE and considered useful for students, in particular tools providing proper indexing and classification of materials aimed at enhancing their learning process [9]. Consequently, tags, competence frameworks and the H5P plugin [8] were selected, to develop and extend functionalities to the one available by default in MOODLE.

Concept Tagging and H5P Plugin
Concept tagging [4] is an interesting option for interactively marking keywords or key concepts in MOODLE. Tags in MOODLE are interactive elements that, when clicked, show all the resources the user has access to that belong to that specific tag. The built-in tag feature may function as a visual aid to categorize resources, connect data, and visualize it in a specialized tag cloud block. The most basic use of tagging is a form of metadata visible to the user as, for example, resource classification or thematic categorization tagged elements are visible when the element the tag is associated to, is navigated to.

The enhancement with added-value features of video resources can be achieved through the open-source, HTML5 based H5P plugin. Interactivity in videos can be added in the most basic form as content indexing, and interactive tools (like questions, text boxes, interruptions, and so forth) to be displayed during the video reproduction.

2.2 The Remote Sensing Course

The overall formative objectives of the Remote Sensing course, part of UNITO master's degree in Geography and Territorial Sciences [3], are described as follows: *Fundamentals of multispectral optical remote sensing aimed at the generation thematic maps in the environmental domain. The focus is on the free available image datasets having a middle geometric resolution, useful for investigations at the territorial and landscape scale.*

2.2.1 Learning Materials

Because of the COVID-19 pandemic, the face-to-face course was adapted to a pre-recorded format for the academic year 2019/2020. For this course, the materials were shared with students on a file hosting service folders tree containing:

- 1 video containing the logistics of the course.
- Lecture notes available in.pptx file format, in support to lecture videos.
- 14 videos containing lecture material, available as one file per lesson in the mp4 format, averaging 1,5 h per video, and ranging from the basic concepts of remote sensing to their application in passive sensors images' processing.
- 13 videos containing laboratory sessions, available as separate files in the m4a format averaging 1,5 h per video, where the use of ENVI software in the management of satellite imagery is step-by-step explained from the opening of the satellite images to the execution of an assisted image classification.
- 1 copy with a valid license of the ENVI 5.5 software (used in the laboratories).
- A collection of optical satellite images to be used with the ENVI software during the laboratory sessions, specifically:

  - Landsat-7 imagery at processing level "Precision and Terrain Correction" (L1TP) with separate band files (B1 to B8).
  - Landsat-8 imagery at processing level L1TP with separate files for each band (B1 to B11).
  - Sentinel-2 imagery at processing level 1C with separate band files (B02 to B12) at 10m and 20m resolution depending on the native resolution of the relevant spectral bands.

Students are expected to reproduce the proposed steps on a locally installed copy of the software and understand the outputs.

2.3 Course Format Setup in MOODLE

Learning materials, both for the theoretical and for the practical modules, were adapted to be suitable for MOODLE platform [11], which allows four course formats: "Weekly" format, "Topics" format, "Social" format, and "Single activity" format. A selection among course formats was done to better fit the Remote sensing course, which is split into two sub-courses, the theoretical one, and the laboratory, thus presenting two distinct designs.

Theoretical Course

After the choice of the course format, the learning materials for each obtained module (by thematically grouping the lectures, see Result section) have been built to achieve a specific setup.

Subsequently, to transpose the contents of the course in an online format, and to add potential layers of information, the styling of PowerPoint files was normalized and transcribed to a.txt file (plain text), to release the information from proprietary formats and print-optimized paging. The operation was performed through several steps:

- Text cleaning of repetitive chapter names.
- Removal of indentations.
- Standardization of headings.
- Addition of a place-mark string of non-alphanumeric characters to mark the break between topics.

Given the prosaic nature of text materials, they have been adapted to the LMS architecture through MOODLE default book tool.

At this point, the concept tagging with relevant key concepts was applied to rich-text materials, by developing a dedicated workflow (see Results section). The reference geomatic glossary "Trilingual Glossary of Remote Sensing" [2] was chosen as a source for keywords selection to be associated with tags. The glossary includes 892 terms in the Geomatics theoretical and technological fields up to 1995 in three languages (Italian, French, and English).

As regards the video lessons, a dedicated workflow was also defined (see Result section) to allow the best and most useful exploitation by students.

Practical Course

The course format was, first, chosen. After the subsequent practical modules' generation, the development of a specific setup was achieved and applied to each of the modules. As regard laboratory videos lecture, a specific workflow was also developed and applied to guarantee the best learning experience.

2.4   Hierarchical MOODLE Competency Framework for the Remote Sensing Course E-Learning Materials

An ontology of Geographic Information Science and Technology is currently being developed in the Earth Observation for GEOgraphical sciences framework (EO4GEO) in the form of the EO4GEO Book of Knowledge (BoK) [5]. Here, through a controlled vocabulary and agreed-upon terminology, knowledge in the domain of Geographic Information Science and Technology is represented through hierarchical and interconnected relationships [7] and the functionality of MOODLE is extended by creating a competency framework that is now a default feature in MOODLE [10].

Following this approach, a simple hierarchical MOODLE competency framework demo was also built from part of the EO4GEO BoK Geographic Information Science and Technology ontology, for the Remote Sensing course learning materials.

3 Results

3.1 Course Setup

Remote Sensing Theory

For the theoretical course, since it is made of pre-recorded learning materials, the setup in Topics format was chosen to have a thematic division of contents and corresponding learning objectives. By thematically grouping the lectures, giving additional context for each topic, 7 modules arise (Table 1).

Table 1. Theoretical Remote Sensing course classification into thematic areas

Lecture contents	Module name
Lecture 1 – Introduction (part II)	1 – Introduction to Remote Sensing
Lecture 2 – Electromagnetic radiation	2 – Remote sensing: Main Physical Laws
Lecture 3 – Radiation Laws	
Lecture 4 – Electromagnetic energy sources and interaction between EM energy and atmosphere	3 – Electromagnetic radiation and its interactions
Lecture 5 – Interactions between EM energy and surfaces (part I)	
Lecture 5b – Interactions between EM energy and surfaces (part II)	
Lecture 6 – Human vision	4 – Visual perception and colorimetry basics
Lecture 7 – Colorimetry	
Lecture 8 – Observation systems	5 – Satellites for Earth Observation
Lecture 9 – Digital sensors	
Lecture 10 – Photo-interpretation basics	6 – Image interpretation
Lecture 11 – Radiometric Image Processing	7 – Image processing
Lecture 12 – Geometric Image Processing	
Lecture 13 – Image classification	

Besides such modules, an initial section displayed on top of the course page was also added and contains an announcements channel (for important communications about the course), a forum (to share with the whole classroom discussions or questions that may arise from students), and an introductory video about the logistics of the course.

Moreover, a series of thematic modules regarding the following, are also present:

- An introductory page with clearly stated learning objectives of the module.
- Completely indexed video lectures.
- Corresponding lecture notes in the MOODLE book format.
- A set of self-assessment set of questions for each lecture, referring to the main topics of each lecture.
- A glossary, containing key definitions for the course.

Modules Content

The learning materials for each theoretical module have been built to achieve the setup shown in Fig. 2:

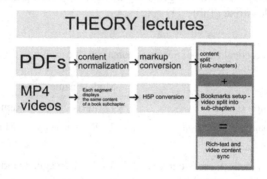

Fig. 2. Theory lectures in their media forms

To transpose the contents of the course in an online format and to add potential layers of information, the styling of PowerPoint files was normalized and transcribed to a.txt file (plain text). The results are one simple-text file for each lecture in which the contents are standardized for further processing.

Rich-text learning materials in the course have maintained their structure and flow but are divided into a chapter/sub-chapter interactive architecture, typical of e-books.

The prose nature of text materials has been adapted to the LMS architecture through MOODLE default book tool. For each lecture, one chapter is displayed on a single page, with relevant key concepts tagged as keywords at the bottom of each page. Key terms that are present in the glossary database for the course are dynamically hyper-linked in the book module. If the keyword is clicked on or passed on with a cursor, the relevant definition is displayed on top of the book text.

Concept Tagging in Rich-Text Materials and H5P Videos Content Indexing

Concept tagging with relevant key concepts was applied to rich-text materials, by developing the following workflow:

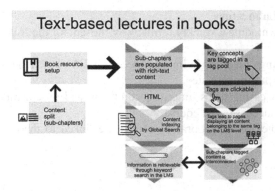

Fig. 3. Workflow for text-based lectures

Consequently, as shown in Fig. 3, each subchapter of the books' materials is manually tagged with relevant key concepts mentioned in the text. The topic of the lecture is not tagged.

Tags are a system-wide metadata system and provide an alternative way of browsing through learning materials. So, if other relevant materials in different courses are tagged with the same logic, the student can click on a tag and browse all learning materials that are relevant for that topic. If any tag is clicked, a page displays all the sub-chapters that display a specific key concept.

As regards the video lessons material, this was uploaded to the YouTube platform to be linkable from the MOODLE platform without significant use of CPU and server resources during simultaneous streaming by several users/students.

Ideally, videos in an LMS should be of reasonable length and with properly indexed contents. Videos available for this project were not indexed and in long-form (90 min on average). For this reason, content indexing was performed through H5P. The equivalent of YouTube timestamps is called bookmarks in H5P, and it allows the content creator to mark specific timestamps that are browsable through the video time bar. A list of bookmarks is also created, allowing for an interactive table of contents.

The following workflow has been developed and applied to video lectures:

1. Videos are uploaded on the YouTube platform.
2. An H5P activity module is created.
3. The video is named the same way as the YouTube counterpart, namely "Lecture n – Topic of the lecture"
4. The short description field is not filled because, in this case, the videos start with the title of the lecture, which is also introduced orally during the first few minutes. In all other cases, it is recommended to insert a short description of the topics.
5. Both "start with bookmarks menu open" and "show button for rewinding 10 s" are activated to increase browsing options.
6. On the "add interactions" panel, bookmarks have been added for all major topics in each video to segment the explanations into browsable chunks, so that an easier retrieval of pieces of information is achieved.

Remote Sensing Laboratory

For the Laboratory module a Weekly format was chosen, for the following reasons:

- to achieve learning objectives in image processing, ENVI must be correctly set up by all students as a preliminary step,
- some ENVI processing takes time to accomplish, and procrastination needs to be avoided for the success of the course,
- some of the topics of the laboratory course are linked to theoretical explanations (Table 2).

Table 2. Week activities of the laboratory course and their dependency on theoretical modules

Course week	Laboratory sessions	Dependency on theoretical courses modules
Week 1 – Introduction to ENVI	Lab 1 – Introduction to ENVI and image display	None
Week 2 – Colour management in satellite images	Lab 2 – Colour image and location tools Lab 3 – Colour mapping	Independent from theoretical modules
Week 3 – Histograms, scatter plots and ROIs	Lab 4 – Histograms and scatter plots Lab 5 – Regions of interest	Independent from theoretical modules
Week 4 – Radiometric processing	Lab 6 – Radiometric pre-processing Lab 7 – Band math, NDVI and Layer Stacking	Module 7
Week 5 – Geometric processing	Lab 8 – Geometric pre-processing Lab 9 – Digital filters	Module 7
Week 6 – Unsupervised classifications	Lab 10 – Unsupervised classification	Module 7
Week 7 – Supervised classification	Lab 11 – Supervised classification part I Lab 12 – Supervised classification part II	Module 7
Week 8 – Multitemporal analysis	Lab 13 – Multitemporal analysis	Module 7

Modules Content

The laboratory course also contains a separate section, displayed at the beginning of the course made of the following activities: an announcement channel (for important communications to students), a forum activity where students are encouraged to troubleshoot eventual software-related problems, and an initial page where relevant software (ENVI), Landsat imagery and related instructions are clearly stated.

A series of thematic modules follows where laboratory exercises are grouped in a series of consequential experiences. Each laboratory module is set up following the organization reported in Fig. 3. A "how-to" page, listing all sequences of inputs for the laboratory and relevant explanations; a page with learning objectives for the laboratory session; and the per-se laboratory in video form.

With a specific focus on the laboratory videos, these follow a standard approach to video lectures, where the professor talks about specific topics, while the videos display the appropriate lecture slide, which includes text, images, graphics, and charts. The overall goal of the laboratory is to perform a series of quantitative measurements to be carried out in ENVI Classic 5.5 on passive sensors' images, including supervised and unsupervised classifications and multi-temporal analysis.

The student is supposed to follow the progressive tutorials, reproduce the given steps in the ENVI software (which is available to the students) possibly during the duration of the video.

Laboratory videos are indexed as the ENVI steps to achieve processing steps and outputs. For laboratory videos, the following approach was developed as shown in Fig. 4.

A minimal setup for the laboratory videos, with one screen per student in mind, is made through the H5P plugin: since every video, aside from collateral explanations, is a step-by-step process explained to achieve specific functions in the software, the videos have been split into chapters, this time where timestamps are the singles instructions to be achieved in the video.

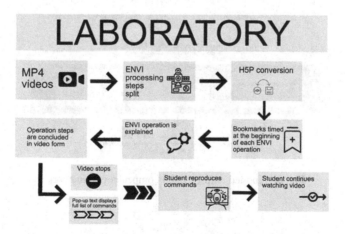

Fig. 4. Laboratory video lectures workflow

Moreover, at the end of each segment, the videos are programmed to stop playing until the command chain, that appears in the video in a text box, is clicked, causing the resuming of the laboratory. This measure is envisioned so that the student can perform the task in the ENVI software, and once it is performed, the student input allows the video to resume.

Some of the text boxes also envision a link to specific help resources form HARRIS (ENVI developer company) software. Through this simple procedure, no re-recording of lectures is necessary to achieve a categorised and ordered content which is, albeit virtually, split up into concise fragments.

3.2 Hierarchical MOODLE Competency Framework for the Remote Sensing Course E-Learning Materials

Moreover, a competency framework was created and set up by translating the ontology subdomains of knowledge into the competency framework sublevels. This provides when contents are linked to the related competency, a hierarchical classification of knowledge of content activities and resources.

For the specific work, the interest was in finding multiple ways to classify and connect educational content. Activities in the remote sensing theory and laboratory course are consequently marked, based on the lowest level the materials pertaining to.

For example, lecture 2 and lecture 3 both are marked with the Electromagnetic radiation domain. The competencies, or in this case the taxonomy level, is always visible by the students in a separate section of the course that is reachable by the main course menu giving additional context for the information they receive. Figure 5 sums up the applied ontology and competency frameworks approach.

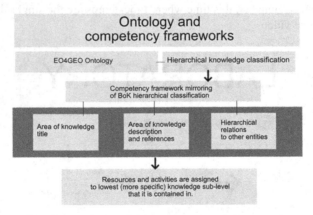

Fig. 5. Applied ontology and competency framework

4   Conclusions

This work developed a method to set up the Remote Sensing course learning materials on the LMS MOODLE platform and to adapt it considering the multi-disciplinary approach typical of the Geographic domain. The course, made of both theoretical and practical modules, permitted to test the adaptability of these two teaching modalities, inevitably different due to their diverse nature, to the e-learning approach. Their incorporation and adaptation on MOODLE were achieved thanks to the development of dedicated work-flows, and through the exploitation of different plugins available on the platform (i.e., concept tagging and H5P plugin), dedicated to facilitating and enriching the comprehension of text materials and videos lectures to students. Moreover, a classification of learning materials into the domain of knowledge of Geomatics was performed by building a hierarchical MOODLE competency framework demo, as part of a Geographic Information Science and Technology ontology.

The authors think that the achieved design of the modules and courses can be considered a preliminary and already adequate organization and categorization of modules, learning goals, and materials. Also, this type of thematic content subdivision offers a simple modularisation, which allows the learner to always separate and contextualize the course content into thematic categories, as well as explain the topic order.

Finally, the hierarchical ontology-based schema characterizing the learning objectives and areas of the specific domain of Geomatics, and the learning materials referring to such objectives, allows a punctual and browsable network of such materials to essential knowledge areas to be mastered by the students, taking care of the multi-disciplinary approach typical of the Geographic domain.

From this point of view, different courses or programmes that belong to the same domain, but different subdomains of knowledge become linked in case a student needs to find additional (authoritative) materials about a particular topic. Tags and competency frameworks allow a parallel browsing system explicitly connecting areas of knowledge, in a multidisciplinary setting such as geography, optimally working, in the proposed approach, if resources are openly available to students.

References

1. Balram, S.. Teaching and learning pedagogies in higher education geographic information science. In: Balram, S., Boxall, J. (eds.) GIScience Teaching and Learning Perspectives. AGIS, pp. 1–8. Springer, Cham (2019). https://doi.org/10.1007/978-3-030-06058-9_1
2. Brivio, P.A., Zani, G.: Glossario Trilingue di Telerilevamento. AIT edizioni, Milano (1995) http://www.irea.cnr.it/glossario/glossario.htm
3. Corso di Laurea Magistrale Interateneo in Geografia e Scienze Territoriali (LM-80). https://www.geografia.unito.it/do/corsi.pl/Show?_id=0xcq
4. Elmadani, M., Mathews, M., Mitrovic, A.: Concept Tagging in Moodle. University of Canterbury. Computer Science and Software Engineering (2012). https://ir.canterbury.ac.nz/handle/10092/7377
5. Eo4geo. http://www.eo4geo.eu/bok/
6. Hodges, C., Moore, S., Lockee, B., Trust, T., Bond, A.: The Difference Between Emergency Remote Teaching and Online Learning. Educase Review (2020) https://er.educause.edu/articles/2020/3/the-difference-between-emergency-remote-teaching-and-online-learning
7. Hofer, B., et al.: Complementing the European earth observation and geographic information body of knowledge with a business-oriented perspective'. Trans. GIS 24(3), 587–601 (2020). https://doi.org/10.1111/tgis.12628
8. Interactive Content - H5P Activity - MoodleDocs'. https://docs.moodle.org/37/en/Interactive_Content_-_H5P_activity. Accessed 6 Dec 2020
9. Mylonakis, M., Arapi, P., Pappas, N., Moumoutzis, N., Christodoulakis, S.: Metadata management and sharing in multimedia open learning environment (MOLE). In: García-Barriocanal,

E., Cebeci, Z., Okur, M.C., Öztürk, A. (eds.) MTSR 2011. CCIS, vol. 240, pp. 275–286. Springer, Heidelberg (2011). https://doi.org/10.1007/978-3-642-24731-6_29

10. MOODLE Competency Frameworks. https://docs.moodle.org/310/en/Competency_frameworks

11. MOODLE Course Formats. https://docs.moodle.org/310/en/Course_formats

12. Radoslava, K., Sabani, M., Kralev, V.: An analysis of some learning management systems. Int. J. Adv. Sci. Eng. Inf. Technol. **9**(4), 1190–1198 (2019). https://doi.org/10.18517/ijaseit.9.4.9437

13. Robinson, A.C., Kerski, J., Long, E.C., Luo, H., DiBiase, D., Lee, A.: Maps and the geospatial revolution: teaching a massive open online course (MOOC) in geography. J. Geogr. High. Educ. **39**(1), 65–82 (2015). https://doi.org/10.1080/03098265.2014.996850

14. Schultz, R.B., DeMers, M.N.: Transitioning from emergency remote learning to deep online learning experiences in geography education. J. Geogr. **119**(5), 142–146 (2020). https://doi.org/10.1080/00221341.2020.1813791

15. Schultz, R.B.: A critical examination of the teaching methodologies pertaining to distance learning in geographic education: andragogy in an adult online certificate program. Rev. Int. Geogr. Educ. Online **2**(1), 45–60 (2012). https://dergipark.org.tr/en/pub/rigeo/133636

Geo(big)data, GeoAnalytics, AI and Decision Support

Geo-Business Intelligence and Spatial Data Warehousing: A Railway Company Case Study

Mario Tartaglia[1] and Andrea Fiduccia[2](✉)

[1] Strategy Sustainability and Asset Management, FS Research Centre, Ferrovie dello Stato Italiane Spa, Stazione Santa Maria Novella Binario 2, 50123 Florence, Italy
m.tartaglia@fsitaliane.it

[2] Strategy Sustainability and Asset Management, FS Research Centre, Decision Support Models, Ferrovie dello Stato Italiane Spa, Piazza della Croce Rossa 1, 00161 Rome, Italy
a.fiduccia@fsitaliane.it

Abstract. The Italian Ferrovie dello Stato Group has adopted and continues its roadmap for the implementation of a Strategic Information Monitoring System (SIMS) aimed at supporting the strategic decision-making processes of the Holding Company FSI and the other FS Group companies and at "the collection, storing and processing of official Group data according to the Process of Supply and Management of Official Data of the FS Italiane Group".

The purpose of the SIMS is to support the collection and supply of data, information, and information tools through appropriate analysis tools and through the creation of a Data Warehouse. This Database Layer not only guarantees the segregation of data with respect to classification/confidentiality/sensitivity needs, but manages the historicization of data using, as a factor of relationship between the data, mainly geometric objects and geographical and spatial references of the territory (paradigm of the spatial database [1]). In this way it is possible to analyze phenomena of a territory through appropriate analysis tools, selecting the context and the topic of the analysis from time to time, in order to then be able to carry out simulations or monitoring of phenomena related to the business of the FS Group companies, or detect and evaluate potentials, needs, strengths, weaknesses, opportunities and threats.

Finally, SIMS allows to produce data and reports for systematic mandatory communications (e.g. statistical reports for the Italian National Statistical Program – PSN Programma Statistico Nazionale [2] - or other legal obligations), and non-systematic data communications, as well as to provide data and information agreed with the associations to which the companies of the FSI Group have joined.

Keywords: GeoBI · Spatial data warehouse · Knowledge management

1 Introduction

A group of companies has a huge data quantity stored both in company-specific systems and in process-specific systems. E.g. data about asset management are owned by the companies having in charge the infrastructures (rails, roads, etc.) or the rolling stocks

E. Borgogno-Mondino and P. Zamperlin (Eds.): ASITA 2022, CCIS 1651, pp. 141–155, 2022.
https://doi.org/10.1007/978-3-031-17439-1_10

(trains, cars, trucks, ...) but the data flow of the consolidation of balance sheet of the companies lies in their ERP (Enterprise Resource Planning) systems sending reports to the ERP of the Holding.

Some indicators seem to be the same, but the real meaning is process-related. Just to give an example, the infrastructure maintenance system and the traffic control system measure different lengths of the same transportation network.

In a not remote past, the reports for decision makers and the supply of data to institutions and associations were made through manual data extraction from several legacy systems and sending data sets to analysts through files attached to emails. The data were processed on the analysts' PCs with multiple tools (spreadsheets, personal databases, desktop GIS) and the reports were often created with presentation tools such as MS PowerPoint and sent to recipients via email.

The datasets used for the single report and the report itself were stored - often in an unstructured way - on the analysts' PCs. It was therefore very difficult, even after a short time, to trace the sources and the procedure followed for a report.

A request to update an already issued report implied having to re-run the entire workflow with related email exchanges.

Centralized data architectures make possible to avoid such problems and detect inconsistencies and low data quality [3, 4]. According to [5] the economic impact of a low data quality reaches tens of percent of the company's total costs: data can be considered as an economic asset [6].

Data warehouses and business intelligence are the two technical tools through which companies face the problem of having correct and high quality data for decision support and reporting to institutions, stakeholders, users and customers [7, 8].

The third foundation tool is a metadata framework [3, 9, 10].

2   System Architecture of SIMS

The SIMS is a system divided into components which provides for the complete coverage of the "data >> analysis >> information" life cycle. On the one hand, it provides for data processing processes, on the other software components allowing the use of the data and enabling the functional administration of the system.

The SIMS was developed by FS Technology, the ICT (Information and Communication Technologies) company of the Ferrovie dello Stato Italiane Group, starting from a highly articulated set of requirements prepared by the organizational structure FS Research Centre (FSR) of FS Holding.

The organizational structure FSR of FS Holding is in charge of the operational management of the system, data ingest and the preparation of reporting in its various forms (BI dashboard and WebGIS).

The SIMS users, both internal to the FS Italiane Group and external, appropriately authorized and profiled, access the SIMS through a Portal based on MS SharePoint technology. In the pages of the Portal, users can find multimedia documents, BI dashboards, and GIS representations inserted through custom web parts (Fig. 1).

Fig. 1. The homepage of the SIMS Portal of Ferrovie dello Stato Italiane Group.

The Portal provides a menu called "megamenu" for accessing a set of content classified by thematic areas plus an access menu to "dedicated" areas including WebGIS apps, the FS Mobility Lab document and newsletter system and areas for specific projects/thematic areas.

From the point of view of the data warehouse, the support to analysts and the production of BI, GeoBI and GIS/WebGIS reports, the SIMS is a 3-tier system (Fig. 2):

- Presentation tier - BI and WebGIS
- Application tier - application server BI (Tableau), WebGIS (Hexagon Geospatial technology) and ETL (FME Feature Manipulation Engine - Safe Software)
- Database tier – Oracle.

The users of the SIMS system are profiled so that they have access in consultation (and processing, where permitted) only to data for which they are authorized according to the policies of the data owners/data providers ("declaratory").

Data owners of FS Group data and FSR managers for the provisioning of data external to the FS Group (Institutional, Open or Commercial data) identify the specific policies for access to data ("declaratory"), with the aim of limiting the scope of visibility and specifying the conditions to be applied for the access to be allowed (for example, visibility of data only if aggregated).

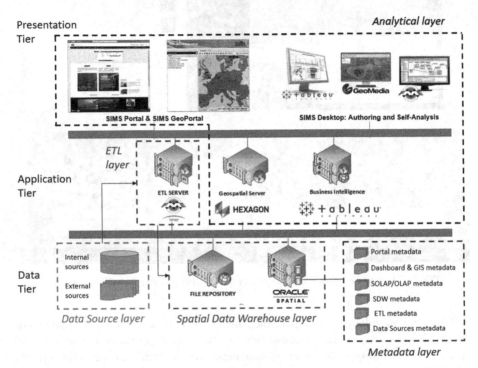

Fig. 2. The system architecture of SIMS.

It is important to point out that any access - in addition to those expressly specified in the declaratories - to the FS Group data is blocked both at the level of consultation of the SIMS Portal pages and at the level of specific contents of the pages (BI, GeoBI and GIS custom web parts) and at the level of the data shown by the custom web parts (a BI dashboard shows only the contents that the user is authorized to view). The same filtering mechanism is applied to any other client tools having a direct connection to the SIMS Database. The same restriction is implemented in compliance with the policies of commercial and institutional data providers.

A taxonomy of the content of SIMS Data Warehouse is shown in Fig. 3.

In the SIMS data warehouse the temporal extension of the data is managed through the mechanisms of historicization and versioning.

The term "historicization" of data means the presence within the database of the temporal component of the data. This historicization process can be managed at the table level (layer, feature class, information layer) or at the single record level:

- At the table level. When SIMS receives a new dataset, the ingestion flow puts a time marker on the data itself, which represents the moment from which the data is valid. The time marker can be calibrated to the needs of the data itself, for example it could represent the beginning of a certain event or the date of production of the data itself. When SIMS receives an update of a dataset, a time marker is associated to the information layer present in the system, a value starting from which the data is no longer valid, and a value corresponding to the time marker of entry into validity of the updated data.
- At the record level. At the record level, the principle is similar to that of historicization at the table level, with the advantage of being able to update even partially the dataset present through automatic or semi-automatic control workflows to identify the records to be updated.

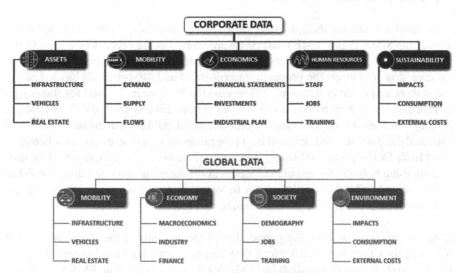

Fig. 3. Taxonomy of the content of SIMS data warehouse.

In SIMS it's used the "tuple timestamping" approach [11].

Some data flows are naturally subject to corrections over time (e.g. Gross Domestic Product), for others the correction may be necessary due to inaccuracy in the supply. The SIMS manages the corrections with the versioning mechanism: the corrected dataset replaces the one of the previous supply. The various versions are not deleted, but "labeled" and can be consulted in case of need.

3   From Data to Analyses

The data ingesting into the SIMS is managed via automated ETL procedures. The term PROCESSES defines these data acquisition, transformation and storing operations. The term FLOWS defines the formalized agreements between the data providers and FSR establishing the transmitted contents (dataset), the data structures (tables and attributes) and the frequency of supply (sending) of the datasets themselves.

Therefore, SIMS provides FSR with a platform allowing it to carry out analyses and data processing activities based on constantly updated, certified, unique, coherent, documented and geo-referenced data.

From this point of view, the platform is made up of various software components that perform the following macro-tasks:

● Population of the Data Waterhouse:

Data providers upload their datasets using a web interface hosted in a dedicated area of the SIMS Portal. FME (Safe Software) supports the process of ingesting the datasets uploaded by the providers and allowing to code the appropriate ETL logics for each flow and insert the processing result into the database. FME has a desktop component and a server component. The desktop component is used for the design of processes (workbench) that can be executed both directly from the PC where the desktop component is installed and, where authorized, published at the server level and executed there on-demand or based on a programming based on events or scheduled. GeoMedia Desktop suite (Hexagon Geospatial) supports the geographic data processing using both the feature classes stored at the database level and those available locally on PCs. The data produced can be stored in dedicated schemas, leaving the ETL component to populate the main database schema.

● Data analysis activities and the preparation of the contents of the Portal are carried out using the COTS software Tableau (Tableau Software) for the BI component, and GeoMedia (Hexagon Geospatial) and FME for the GIS component. FME was chosen because it is an ETL processor characterized by support for GIS data formats and by having an extensive set of functions for geospatial analyzes. FME allows FSR to perform server-side complex and time-consuming GIS workflows.

Both Tableau and Hexagon Geospatial GIS software desktop components are used not only for analysis purposes but also as authoring environments to publish respectively web Dashboards and WebGIS Apps/GIS webservices though their server components. Web Dashboards of Tableau and GIS webservices has to be inserted in the SIMS Portal using custom web parts. WebGIS Apps are self-consistent GIS Viewers hyperlinked in the SharePoint portal (Fig. 4).

Fig. 4. A WebGIS App of SIMS GeoPortal.

- The management of back office activities is delegated to a custom web application called "Calendar" integrated in MS SharePoint, which allows you to define activities, schedule them, assign them to specific operators, automate communications and activity flows and monitor their progress/completion/compliance.

4 Geospatial Dashboards: GeoBI vs WebGIS Apps

We adopt the following definitions:

Geo-Business Intelligence (or GeoBI, or "Geospatial-Business Intelligence" or "Geospatial-BI" [12]) – it *"is a collection of technologies that combines Geographic Information Systems (GIS) and Business Intelligence (BI) for evaluation of the results achieved, planning and decision-making"* [13].

Spatial Data Warehouse (SDW) – *"it is a subject-oriented, integrated, time variant, and non-volatile collection of spatial and nonspatial data in support of management's decision making process"* [14].

Geospatial Dashboard - it is *"a web-based interactive interface that is supported by a platform combining mapping, spatial analysis, and visualization with proven business intelligence tools"* [15].

Spatial OLAP (or SOLAP) – it is *"a visual platform built especially to support rapid and easy spatio-temporal analysis and exploration of huge volume of data. It follows a multidimensional approach that is available in cartographic displays, as well as in tabular and diagram displays"* [16, 17].

The concepts just outlined extend BI and its components - data warehouse, OLAP and dashboard - for the management of geographic information and its analytics and representations.

In the science of GIS, the integration of analytics, models, cartographic representations and indicators constitutes the peculiarity of the SDSS compared to "simple" GIS [18].

On the other hand, what characterizes a spatial dashboard is the presence of cartograms and indicators [15].

Both technologies, GIS and BI, have evolved from desktop or legacy client-server architectures into web platforms. The simple representation of GIS cartography through a web interface (Web Mapping) has expanded into WebGIS, a functionally richer platform [19], having a further evolution in the GeoWeb paradigm [20].

The spatial data warehouse can offer a data layer for both GeoBI dashboards, and WebGIS apps. However, an identical problem arises for the two fruition systems: the processing times of geospatial queries and analytics.

It is therefore necessary to proceed to a design phase of the materialization of the views that feed the user apps because spatial indexing cannot be sufficient for the SOLAP [14].

There are three factors to be analyzed to choose whether a feature class or an attribute table should be materialized [21]:

- the access frequency of the materialized view;
- the size of the materialized view;
- the benefit of the materialization of a feature class/view for other a feature classes/views and analytics.

Several algorithms are available for such an analysis [14, 21].

In SIMS we adopted an "a priori" analysis of the above first two factors and there is a systematic monitoring of the performances of Geo BI dashboard and GIS Apps to evaluate the third factor since there is a continuous growth of new dashboards and new data flows generating cross-flows analytics.

According to [15] geospatial dashboards can be categorized in:

- Operational Dashboards providing descriptive measurement of a territory using indicators based on original geospatial data and other geo-referenced data;
- Analytical Dashboards performing diagnostic analysis using geospatial analytics (e.g. geostatistics, spatial statistics, proximity analysis, map algebra);
- Strategical Dashboards offering predictive analysis using spatial models (e.g. Land Use/Land Cover Change CA [22]).

A very detailed analysis of the design issues of geospatial dashboards is reported in [23].

The typical geospatial dashboard is made up of several elements that must be coordinated and interactive with each other: one or more cartographic windows and data visualization elements (tables) and analytical representations of the same (pie charts, graphs of various types) according to the Coordinated Multiple View (CMV) model [24]. To actions on the map (e.g. the selection of one or more features) the coordinated elements respond by modifying their contents and vice versa.

The capability of modern BI software to generate CMV dashboards with a cartographic component without the need for programming has represented a strength compared to "traditional" WebGIS software.

Indeed, a careful design of the SDW component allows to obtain performing and functional GeoBI dashboards. We can consider the following two SIMS geospatial dashboards as an example. The first dashboards allows the multitemporal analysis of transportation modal share in EU Countries based on Eurostat (the statistical office of the European Union) data [25] (Fig. 5) and the second dashboard shows the evolution of road network in EU Countries based on EuroGeographics EuroGlobalMap data [26] (Fig. 6).

On the other hand, the cartographic component of BI software still offers poor functionality in terms of representable feature classes and does not offer spatial analysis functionality.

GIS vendors have responded with a new generation of platforms that complement WebGIS capabilities with the coordinated accessory elements of the CMV model: for example, HEXAGON Geospatial M.APP Enterprise [27] and ESRI ArcGIS Insights [28].

In an initial operational phase, we created in SIMS CMV dashboards with a simple cartographic component (using the BI Tableau platform) and GIS apps offering complex thematic representations (using HEXAGON Geospatial Server) (Fig. 4).

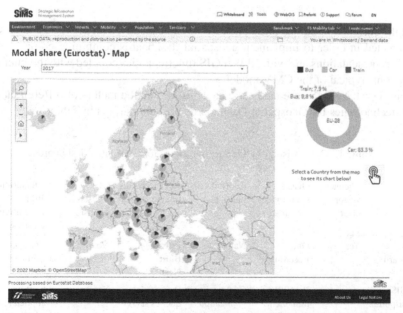

Fig. 5. An example of geospatial dashboard in SIMS Portal: multitemporal analysis of transportation modal share in EU Countries based on Eurostat (the statistical office of the European Union) data [25].

Fig. 6. An example of geospatial dashboard in SIMS Portal: evolution of road network in EU Countries based on EuroGeographics EuroGlobalMap data [26].

In the current operational phase, a Proof of Concept based on M.APP Enterprise has been created in order to implement geospatial dashboards combining complex cartographic representations and with all WebGIS functionalities coupled with the interactive components typical of the CMV model.

Based on the SIMS case study, the capabilities and the factors of differentiation of COTS technologies for Geospatial Dashboards are summarized in Table 1.

Table 1. Comparison of COTS technologies for Geospatial dashboards.

	Thematic vector layers	OGC webservices consumer	Coordinated multiple view	Advanced GIS functionalities	OGC webservices publisher	Integration with 3rd party systems/custom services
GeoBI dashboard	Yes	Only BaseMap	Native	Proximity Buffer Near	No	Custom application
WebGIS viewer/portal	Yes	WMS/WFS thin client	Custom application	Parametric queries server side	Yes	Custom application
WebGIS geospatial dashboard app	Yes	WMS/WFS thick client	Native	Full	Yes	Custom application

5   Self-service BI and Metadata

The prevailing operating mode of BI is made up of non-specialist users interacting with BI specialists and the IT department. Non-specialist users ask BI experts to develop dashboards for their needs. The IT department deals with data ingesting and optimization of the data warehouse [29]. It is a slow and expensive operating mode. An alternative, aimed at making non-specialist users autonomous is Self-Service BI (SSBI) [29, 30].

SSBI is defined as: *"The facilities within the BI environment which enable BI users to become more self-reliant and less dependent on the IT organization. These facilities focus on four main objectives: easier access to source data for reporting and analysis,*

Table 2. SSBI challenges. Based on [31].

Self-reliant user	Difficult to access and use data	Difficult to know available data sources
		Difficult to locate data
		Difficult to use data
		Different data sources
		Support is required to add data
	Low user skills	Limited competence level
		Difficult to interpret report content
		Limited general IT skills
	Difficult SSBI tools	Difficult to use SSBI tools
		Users create isolated solutions
		Give the right tools to the right user
Creating SSBI reports	Difficult to create and change content	Difficult to create SSBI reports
		Requires lots of time and manual work
		Difficult to change content
	Difficult to assure quality	Difficult to assure quality of reports
		Redundant reports exist
		No governance of SSBI reports
		Unsupported tools are used
SSBI education	No formal education	No formal educations are given
		Users forget how to use SSBI
		Not using SSBI after education
	Low interest in SSBI	Users do not see the benefits of SSBI
		Users have different technical backgrounds

easier and improved support for data analysis features, faster deployment options such as appliances and cloud computing, and simpler, customizable, and collaborative end-user interfaces" [30].

However, there are many difficulties in affirming the SSBI paradigm [31] (Table 2). Among the difficulties identified, the one relating to access and use of data is particularly blocking. BI solutions include metadata management, but that's not enough. In fact, what is missing is the explicit knowledge of the BI experts and the tacit knowledge of the process owners [3].

The SIMS aims at the development of the SSBI. Specific attention, therefore, was paid to the design of the metadata layer that describes the input datasets and flows, the ETL procedures, the structure of the SDW, the SOLAP/OLAP processes, dashboards and WebGIS apps. A first implementation exploited an extension of the RNDT Metadata model [32]. Following the development of the SIMS Portal based on MS SharePoint, a revision of the metadata layer has begun based on the DCAT-AP_IT standard [33]. Metadata layer now must also include the pages of the portal and the technical metadata relating to the web parts. The tacit knowledge is valued according to the principles of Data Governance by including the business owners in the technical process of managing the data flow [34] together with FSR dataflow managers.

6   Conclusions

In the context of a rapidly changing competitive scenario and a regulatory framework being harmonized at European level, the achievement of the strategic objectives of the FS Italiane Group is significantly influenced by the ability to respond accurately and quickly to the challenges the market presents.

A first benefit deriving from the SIMS to the Ferrovie dello Stato Italiane Group is the optimization of the resources generated by the automation of the data entry processes in the data warehouse, of the data analysis procedures and of the distribution of reports using dashboards, WebGIS and webservices (Table 3).

Table 3. Analysis of effort for a recurring report.

Phase	Without SDW-SOLAP-dashboard/GIS	Using SDW-SOLAP-dashboard/GIS	SDW-SOLAP-dashboard/GIS component
Data flow agreement	n.a.	Specification of the dataset structure Effort: x	
Input data analysis	Every dataset differs from the previous one Effort of an analyst: x	Design of the ETL workflow (only for the first dataset of the data flow) Effort: from x/4 to x Virtuous effect: library of reusable procedures	ETL, BI, GIS and DB Desktop Client

(continued)

Table 3. (*continued*)

Phase	Without SDW-SOLAP-dashboard/GIS	Using SDW-SOLAP-dashboard/GIS	SDW-SOLAP-dashboard/GIS component
Data normalization	Every dataset differs from the previous one thus it is needed a normalization effort Effort of an analyst: x	n.a.	
Data ingesting	The target data structure is a spreadsheet, a GIS file-based format or a local DB Effort of an analyst: x	Automated Data Ingesting (historicization/versioning) in the SDW No effort: only data processing time	ETL server
Analysis and reporting	Recurrent activity every time the dataset is updated using spreadsheet, local DB, GIS The final output is a pdf document or a ppt Effort of an analyst: from x to 10 * x	Only for the first dataset of the data flow: • Design of the GIS workflow and materialization of views Effort: from x/4 to x • Design of GeoBI dashboard/WeBGIS spatial dashboard effort: from x to 2 * x Every time the DWH is updated, the GeoBI dashboard/WeBGIS Spatial dashboard automatically updates	ETL desktop DB admin tools BI & GIS desktop authoring ETL, GeoBI, WebGIS server
Reports in one year (Hypothesis: 3 updates/year for each report)	N/3	N	

The second important benefit is related to the virtuous circuit of knowledge production. Using traditional business intelligence, the analytical potential is very rigid and it is necessary to turn to development teams very often, sometimes even to build a single chart or dashboard. With the SSBI approach adopted by the SIMS, each user will be able to freely carry out analyzes and create reports using all the data available, with the sole limitations of data protection for privacy and confidentiality reasons. The FS Group's strategic analysis activities are thus led to a collaborative paradigm that multiplies the potential and results.

References

1. Roddick, J.F., Lees, B.G.: Paradigms for spatial and spatio-temporal data mining. geographic data mining and knowledge discovery. In: Miller, H., Han, J. (eds.) Research Monographs in Geographic Information Systems. Taylor and Francis, London (2001)
2. Programma Statistico Nazionale (PSN). https://www.sistan.it/?id=52. Accessed 02 May 2022
3. Zelenka, M., Podaras, A.: Increasing the effectivity of business intelligence tools via amplified data knowledge. Stud. Inform. Control **30**(2), 67–77 (2021)
4. Xu, J.(D.), Benbasat, I., Cenfetelli, R.T.: Integrating service quality with system and information quality: an empirical test in the e-service context. MIS Q. **37**(3), 777–794 (2013)

5. Orr, K.: Data quality and systems theory. Commun. ACM **41**(2), 66–71 (1998)
6. Djerdjouri, M.: Data and Business Intelligence Systems for Competitive Advantage: prospects, challenges, and real-world applications. Mercados y Negocios **1**, 5–18 (2020)
7. Tavera Romero, C.A., Ortiz, J.H., Khalaf, O.I., Ríos Prado, A.: Business intelligence: business evolution after Industry 4.0. Sustainability **13**, 10026 (2021)
8. Negro, A.R., Mesia, R.: The Business Intelligence and its influence on decision making. J. Appl. Bus. Econ. **22**, 147–157 (2020)
9. Lawrenz, S., Sharma, P., Rausch, A.: The significant role of metadata for data marketplaces. In: International Conference on Dublin Core and Metadata Applications, pp. 95–101 (2019)
10. Zuiderwijk, A., Janssen, M., Susha, I.: Improving the speed and ease of open data use through metadata, interaction mechanisms, and quality indicators. J. Organ. Comput. Electron. Commer. **26**(1–2), 116–146 (2016)
11. Atay, C.: An attribute or tuple timestamping in bitemporal relational databases. Turk. J. Electr. Eng. Comput. Sci. **24**, 4305–4321 (2016). https://doi.org/10.3906/elk-1403-39
12. Julio, Y.F.H., Bernal, W.N.: Capítulo 14. Business intelligence using geo-location and computational intelligence: a systematic literature review. In: Canabal, J.D., Munoz Herdandez, H., Franco, D.P., Castillo Osorio, B. (eds.) Retos del sector Empresarial en el Proceso de Convergencia al marco normativo contable y de aseguramiento de la informacion financiera, Universidad del Sinu, Ediciones Unisinú, 193 (2018). ISBN: 978-958-8553-53-5
13. Trisnawarman, D.: Geospatial business intelligence (geobi) application for sales performance analysis. In: The 2018 International Conference on Information Technology, Engineering, Science, and its Applications. SSRN (2018)
14. Han, J., Stefanovic, N., Koperski, K.: Selective materialization: ancient method for spatial data cube construction. In: Proceedings of 1998 Pacic-Asia Conference on Knowledge Discovery and Data Mining (PAKDD 1998), Melbourne, Australia, April 1998
15. Jing, C., Du, M., Li, S., Liu, S.: Geospatial dashboards for monitoring smart city performance. Sustainability **11**, 5648 (2019). https://doi.org/10.3390/su11205648
16. Del Fatto, V., Bimonte, S., Hassan, A., Sebillo, M.: A preliminary study of metrics and methods for readable spatial OLAP maps: VGI4Bio case study. In: 22nd International Conference Information Visualisation (IV), pp. 303–308 (2018). https://doi.org/10.1109/iV.2018.00058
17. Bédard, Y., Merrett, T., Han, J.: Fundamentals of spatial data warehousing for geographic knowledge discovery. In: Geographic Data Mining and Knowledge Discovery, Chap. 3. Research Monographs in GIS, pp. 53–73. Taylor & Francis (2001)
18. Tang, W., et al.: A web-based spatial decision support system of wastewater surveillance for COVID-19 monitoring: a case study of a university campus. medRxiv 2021–12 (2022)
19. Kurbanov, O.: Applied GIS: using Open source Web GIS for serving public safety in Central Asia. In: GISCA 2015 Conference (2015)
20. Muki, H., Singleton, A., Parker, C.: Web mapping 2.0: the neogeography of the GeoWeb. Geogr. Compass **2**(6), 2011–2039 (2008). https://doi.org/10.1111/j.1749-8198.2008.00167.x
21. Harinarayan, V., Rajaraman, A., Ulman, J. D.: Implementing data cubes efficiently. In: Proc. 1996 ACM-SIGMOD International Conference on Management of Data, Montreal, Canada, pp. 205–216 (1996)
22. Fiduccia, A., Cattozzo, L., Filesi, L., Marotta, L., Gugliermetti, L.: A framework for sustainable land planning in ICZM: cellular automata simulation and landscape ecology metrics. In: Gervasi, O., et al. (eds.) ICCSA 2020. LNCS, vol. 12252, pp. 378–393. Springer, Cham (2020). https://doi.org/10.1007/978-3-030-58811-3_27
23. Rahman, A.: Designing a dashboard as geo-visual exploration tool for origin-destination data. The University of Twente, Enschede, The Netherlands (2017)
24. Roberts, J. C.: State of the art: coordinated & multiple views in exploratory visualization. In: Fifth International Conference on Coordinated and Multiple Views in Exploratory Visualization (CMV 2007), pp. 61–71 (2007). https://doi.org/10.1109/CMV.2007.20

25. Eurostat. https://ec.europa.eu/eurostat/web/main/home. Accessed 02 May 2022
26. EuroGlobalMap. https://www.mapsforeurope.org/datasets/euro-global-map. Accessed 02 May 2022
27. HEXAGON Geospatial M.APP Enterprise. https://www.hexagongeospatial.com/products/ mapp-portfolio/mapp-enterprise. Accessed 02 May 2022
28. ESRI ArcGIS Insights. https://www.esri.com/it-it/arcgis/products/insights-for-arcgis/ove rview. Accessed 02 May 2022
29. Alpar, P., Schulz, M.: Self-service business intelligence. Bus. Inf. Syst. Eng. **58**(2), 151–155 (2016). https://doi.org/10.1007/s12599-016-0424-6
30. Imhoff, C., White, C.: Self-service business intelligence. empowering users to generate insights. TDWI Best practices report, TWDI, Renton, WA. TDWI Research (2011)
31. Lennerholt, C., Van Laere, J., Söderström, E.: User-related challenges of self-service business intelligence. Inf. Syst. Manag. **38**(4), 309–323 (2021). https://doi.org/10.1080/10580530. 2020.1814458
32. Repertorio Nazionale Dati Territoriali, Archivio Documenti. https://geodati.gov.it/geoportale/ documenti. Accessed 02 May 2022
33. Agenzia per l'Italia Digitale, DCAT-AP_IT v1.1 – Profilo italiano di DCAT-AP. https://www. dati.gov.it/content/dcat-ap-it-v10-profilo-italiano-dcat-ap-0. Accessed 02 May 2022
34. Abraham, R., Schneider, J., vom Brocke, J.: Data governance: a conceptual framework, structured review, and research agenda. Int. J. Inf. Manag. **49**, 424–438 (2019). https://doi.org/10. 1016/j.ijinfomgt.2019.07.008

Constructing Dynamic Scenarios of Crime Risk Exposure. A Methodological Proposal Based on Geo-Social Media Data

Francesca Coppola$^{(\boxtimes)}$ (iD), Michele Grimaldi (iD), and Isidoro Fasolino (iD)

Department of Civil Engineering, University of Salerno, Via Giovanni Paolo II, n.132, 84084 Fisciano, SA, Italy
{fracoppola,migrimaldi,i.fasolino}@unisa.it

Abstract. The topic of urban security is at once a necessity and an important challenge for cities and metropolitan areas. The daily occurrence of predatory crimes or environmental and social incivility increase insecurity, both real and perceived by citizens, and fear of crime. The widespread fear is a social problem whose impacts on the city' s functioning and the economy of the whole urban structure are actual and measurable. Crime risk prevention plays a fundamental role in creating sustainable cities and communities, as confirmed by the Sustainable Development Goals (SDGs) of the 2030 Agenda, in particular SDG 11 [1]. The proposed research addresses the issue through a quantitative model of crime risk mapping. The latter is based on a spatially explicit *composite crime risk index*, IR_c [2] constructed as a function of three factor-maps: crime hazard (H_c), crime vulnerability (V_c) and crime exposure (E_c). In this paper, the focus is on E_c and on the possibility of constructing dynamic scenarios of crime exposure and crime risk using geo-social media data.

Keywords: Crime risk exposure · Geo-social media data · Urban planning

1 Introduction

The topic of urban security is at once a necessity and an important challenge for cities and metropolitan areas. Nowadays, very few urban realities can actually be said to be free of all forms of crime and its associated impacts. The daily occurrence of predatory crimes or environmental and social incivility rise actual risk, perceived insecurity and fear of crime [3–5]. The widespread fear is a social problem whose impacts on the city' s functioning and the economy of the whole urban structure are actual and measurable.

Crime risk prevention therefore plays a fundamental role in creating sustainable cities and communities, as do other social, economic and environmental actions and the prevention and mitigation of other types of risk [6–9]. This is evidenced by the topic's inclusion among the Sustainable Development Goals of the 2030 Agenda, in particular in SDG 11 and target 11.7 [1], and by some important International and European initiatives [2, 10, 11].

E. Borgogno-Mondino and P. Zamperlin (Eds.): ASITA 2022, CCIS 1651, pp. 156–165, 2022.
https://doi.org/10.1007/978-3-031-17439-1_11

The presence of people on the street and in public spaces, who can act as *eyes on the street* [12], plays a key role in environmental crime prevention strategies but can also provide increased targets for offenders [13–15] and needs to be carefully considered.

Nowadays, a powerful information source for social presence and activity in urban spaces are Social Media (Twitter, Facebook, Flickr, Instagram, TikTok, etc.). Although their advent is quite recent, they have now become part of every aspect of daily life. «While navigating through a city, no matter whether they follow their own interest or another obligation, social network users leave their mark on their exact routes and thus blur the distinction between their physical habits and virtual traces» [16, p. 2].

Geo-social media data, properly filtered and analysed, provide added value in several applications and research fields. Their versatility means that they are currently used: in the financial sector, to detect stock market trends [17]; in marketing operations, to detect users' preferences and wishes [18]; in the health sector, to identify epidemic illnesses or pandemic influenza outbreaks [19]; in the political field, to gather opinions and predict the outcome of future elections [20]; in the field of natural disasters, to develop early warning systems based on early user signals, such as for earthquakes [21]; in the study of natural environment values and how changes in ecosystems may affect visitation patterns for tourism and recreation purposes [22]; in predictive crime analysis, in combination with appropriate analytical techniques, and as a tool for *virtual informal surveillance* in police activities [16, 23, 24].

In particular, knowledge about how people concentrate in specific streets and/or public places and how they move within urban spaces at specific hours and/or day of week can be used to examine their exposure to crime risk. Predatory crimes, whether planned or unplanned, require specific environmental conditions to occur. For example, a car theft will be more easily carried out by the offender in the absence of people and, therefore, of both formal and informal control. On the contrary, crowded places are more exposed to pickpocketing or similar crimes [25, 26].

This is the focus of the present paper, which aims to deepen an ongoing research study which addresses the issue of urban security in terms of risk [3]. More precisely, crime risk is described through a spatially explicit *composite crime risk index*, IR_C [2], based on three factor-maps: crime hazard (H_C), crime vulnerability (V_C), and crime exposure (E_C). The paper focuses on E_C and on the possibility of constructing dynamic scenarios both of crime exposure and crime risk using geo-social media data.

2 Materials and Methods

2.1 Data Mining from Geo-Social Media

Social media are «a group of Internet-based applications that build on the ideo-logical and technological foundations of Web 2.0, and that allow the creation and exchange of User Generated Content» [27, p. 60]. They currently exist in many different forms, and their use mainly follows current trends. It is possible to differentiate them according to purpose and functionality. Some of them are micro-blogging services (e.g., Twitter), others allow for creating and sharing content exclusively as photos and videos (e.g., Instagram, Flickr, TikTok), and some others are in-between, allowing for both messaging and for creating and sharing content of various kinds (e.g., Facebook).

A geocode is associated to information shared with the network (text messages, photos, videos). This one uniquely identifies the geographical position of users when the contents are shared. To safeguard privacy, each user can disable geolocation, thus complicating the use of such data for spatial analysis.

Access to geo-social media data is allowed by creating *Application Programming Interfaces* (API). APIs are programming interfaces that enable, using appropriate software, libraries, etc., to interact with the software for which they are created, in this case the Social, in order to formulate data requests. The latter are generally of HTTP type, and are followed by responses typically saved in JSON structures which are a subset of *JavaScript's Object Notation*. The most widespread API typology in the specific field of interest is the *REpresentational State Transfer* (REST) [28]. These ones are based on a Client-Server communication protocol which, if properly implemented, allows data creation, reading, uploading and downloading. Data extraction requires an authentication type *Open Authorization* (OAuth) which can be of 1.0 or 2.0 type, according to specific needs. The access is regulated by specific and personal keys released when the App is created: key and secret key.

In order to provide a practical example of this, Twitter is mentioned. This one allows data extraction using REST and STREAMING APIs. The former allows programmatic access to read and write data, identifying via OAuth 1.0 or 2.0 authors and applications by which Tweets are published; the latter allow the display of Tweets in almost real time using push technology. The main API, within the REST type, is *Search API*. It allows to extract the most relevant tweets published in the last 7 days. In order to obtain a significant result, it is essential to set the search parameters correctly. Depending on specific needs, this can take the form of: basic search (by words, phrases or hashtags); by user; by specific filter; temporal; geolocalised; or based on sentiment analysis. As mentioned above, extracting data from Twitter is possible through the interaction of the APIs with software components using different programming languages. For example, the Pyton *tweepy, TwitterSearch, searchtweets, tweetkit* libraries or the R packages *twitteR, streamR, rtweet, academictwitteR* and others. Again, using specific plugin created for software GIS, such the *Qweetgis, twitter2qgis* or *SocialActivity* of QGIS. Among these, for example, R's rtweet package [29] allows data to be extracted and organised after creating a specific app and an appropriate access token. Subsequently, search parameters can be set using, for example, the *search_tweets* function. The last allows to extract data from Twitter's REST API for the last 6–9 days, with a maximum limit of 18,000 tweets every 15 min. In order to guarantee meaningful results, it is advisable to set the function's subject in a specific way (Fig. 1). According to the aims of this contribution, the fundamental parameter to be set is the *geolocation code*. This one allows to extract all tweets whose geo-referencing data are included within a radius established starting from the indicated geographical coordinates (latitude and longitude expressed in degrees). Alongside this, it is possible to specify: the search query, which can be made up of one or more words (which integrate or exclude each other by using logical operators such as AND and OR), hashtags, sentences or filters; the number of tweets to be extracted; the choice of including, or excluding, retweets; the language; the type of tweet, to be chosen among three types: popular, recent or mixed; the need or not to repeat, in an automated way, the search; and others.

```
#installing and opening the rtweet library
install.packages(rtweet)
library(rtweet)

#creating the access token
app_name <- "specify your app name"
API_key <- "insert API key"
API_secret_key <- "insert API secret key"

#creating the access token
app_name <- "specify your app name"
API_key <- "insert API key"
API_secret_key <- "insert API secret key"

APP_Twitter_token <- create_token(
  app = app_name,
  consumer_key = API_key,
  consumer_secret = API_secret_key
)

#define the search query
data_tweet <- search_tweets(q= Covid-19 AND greenpass,
  n = 18000,
  type = "recent",
  include_rts = TRUE,
  lang = "en",
  geocode = "latitude,longitude,radius",
  retryonratelimit = FALSE,
)
```

Fig. 1. An R script example for retrieving geo-social data from Twitter using rtweet package. Source: Authors' elaboration.

A further example is Facebook which allows geo-social data extraction using the REST *Graph* API, on which the functioning of the whole social network is based. Through the latter, it is possible to access all public data and, after the creation of an OAuth 2.0 access token, additional information. The extraction of geo-social data is possible by querying the system through *Graph API Explorer* or by using different programming languages. These include, for example, the *Rcurl* and *Rjson* R libraries and the *seolib* Python library.

Again, as in the previous case, extracting geo-social data from Flickr is possible through the interaction of APIs with software components using different programming languages. For example, the *flickrapi* Pyton library, the *FlickrAPI* R package or using specific plugin created for software GIS, such the *Flickr Medatada Downloader* or *flickr2qgis* of QGIS. In particular, software that allows geo-social data to be extracted for specific purposes includes the *Visitation: Recreation and Tourism* package of *InVEST*, used in the study of ecosystem services.

2.2 Dynamic Scenarios of Crime Risk Exposure ($E_{c,ti}$)

In the research, crime risk modelling follows the recommendations given by the European Commission on risk assessment and mapping. In particular, the complexity of the examined phenomenon is addressed by exploiting the territorial risk paradigm and by adopting a semi-quantitative approach based on composite indices [30–32].

The IR_c index [2] combines the main aspects involved in risk scenarios through the convolution of three risk factor-maps (H_c, V_c, E_c), each one described by specific spatial indicators:

$$IR_c = H_c \times V_c \times E_c = H_c \times D_c \tag{1}$$

in which D_c represent the crime impact and is obtained as a product of the two factor-maps: V_c and E_c. IR_c is spatialized in a crime risk map structured in five risk classes: very low risk (R1), low risk (R2), moderate risk (R3), high risk (R4), very high risk (R5) [2, 3]. The last are assigned by using the *Risk Matrix (RM) method* (Fig. 2). This method is based on the risk matrix, obtained as a combination of two factor-maps: hazard (H) and impact (D). Each cell of this matrix identifies a specific intensity class of the mapped phenomenon, by relating the intensities of both variables through the logical Boolean operator AND. For example, cell 11 symbolically identifies the combination of intensity level 1 of the hazard map and intensity level 1 of the impact map. This combination corresponds to a risk class R1, and so on.

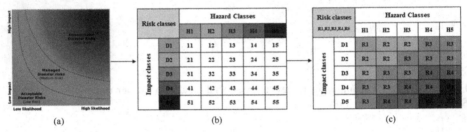

Fig. 2. RM method: a) Risk matrix template. Source: [31]; b, c) Matrix for risk-ranking in five classes (R1, R2, R3, R4, R5). Source: Authors' Elaboration.

Within the territorial approach used, each of risk factor-maps (H_c, V_c, E_c), can individually contribute to increasing or reducing crime risk. Consequently, it is possible to examine each of these separately to outline the most suitable strategies for reducing its critical levels and, as a result, minimising crime risk.

This study focuses in particular on E_c, in relation to which urban planning has an indirect control. In the research, crime exposure describes elements exposed to risk resulting from the occurrence or non-occurrence of a specific criminal event in a given area. E_c is modelled by focusing on person as the main victim of opportunity crimes and it is constructed as a combination of two spatial indicators: resident population, by census section (P_r) and attractors (P_a), each of which is a function of specific parameters [2, 3].

A sensitivity analysis of the IR_c construction model carried out in a previous study [2] showed that the currently E_c structure make it effective in describing crime risk exposure, but only in static form. Its basic variables do not make it possible to highlight the population's dynamic behaviour, nor the presence of *city users*, who are also exposed to crime risk.

People, both residents or not, move through the urban spaces at different hours of day, on different days of week, stopping and concentrating in certain places as intermediate steps or destinations. While travelling through urban spaces, social network users leave a footprint on their routes through the geo-spatial data associated with their posts.

Therefore, the aim of this study is to use geo-social media data to trace the daily and weekly travel routines and social habits of residents and city users. The intention is, then, to integrate this information into E_c for constructing dynamic scenarios of both exposure ($E_{c,ti}$, with i = 1, ..., n) and crime risk ($IR_{c,ti}$, with i = 1, ..., n), by using a parametric model specifically built as a Model Builder in a GIS environment: the *Crime Risk Map (CRM) model* [33].

More precisely, a new spatial variable with a dynamic nature is defined for this integration: *population moving at time t* ($P_{m,ti}$, with i = 1, ..., n). In it, time t can coincide with a specific time range of day (morning, afternoon, night) or with a specific day of week. Thus, E_c is constructed as a combination of three spatial indicators (Fig. 3):

$$E_{c,ti} = E_{c,ti}(P_r, P_a, P_{m,ti}) \qquad (2)$$

The introduction of time variable gives the IR_c index a dynamic character (Fig. 4):

$$IR_{c,ti} = H_c \times V_c \times E_{c,ti} = H_c \times D_{c,ti} \qquad (3)$$

In order to map E_c, it is necessary to first collect the information associated with its basic variables. P_r and P_a, as explained above, derive from a previous model, to which reference is made for detailed information about their construction [2, 3].

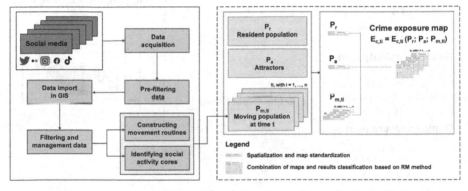

Fig. 3. Exposure maps construction scheme using geo-social media data. Source: Authors' elaboration.

The methodology of $P_{m,ti}$ construction consists of several steps (Fig. 3). The first of these is related to the acquisition of geo-social media data. According to the specific aims of this study, the focus is not on knowing the textual or graphic content of posted messages but on their geographical location. Therefore, the search is oriented towards extracting data related to a specific context, identified by its geographical coordinates (latitude and longitude) and related to certain time ranges of day, for all days of week. The second step requires a data pre-filtering process in order to restrict them exclusively to those containing the geospatial information of interest. Depending on the extraction method used, in the third step it may be necessary to convert the information into point type vector data to be managed in a GIS environment. Then, the next step involves a further process of filtering and organising data to trace the daily and weekly travel routines of people and to identify the intermediate and final stages of these movements, which are representative of social or work activities.

Once the basic variables have been defined, it is possible to construct dynamic crime exposure scenarios ($E_{c,ti}$) and, subsequently, crime risk scenarios ($IR_{c,ti}$) by implementing all the required steps in the CRM model [33]. The generic crime exposure scenario at time t_i is constructed by spatialising the three base variables (P_r, P_a, $P_{m,ti}$) through density analysis using *Kernel Density Estimation* (KDE) and, then, by implementing the *Standardization-Combination-Classification (S-C-C) method*. The latter is structured in three steps: the first standardizes the maps obtained from spatialization in a value range from 1 to 5. In this case, when standardizing the crime exposure base maps all the variable are considered directly proportional to E_c; the second step combines the standardized maps; finally, the third one interprets the combination results and according to the RM method assigns 5 criticality classes which, in this specific case, are crime exposure classes: very low exposure (E1), low exposure (E2), medium exposure (E3), high exposure (E4), very high exposure (E5). The highest intensity class corresponds to the highest concentration of all the variable involved and identify the most exposed values on which the attention should be focused.

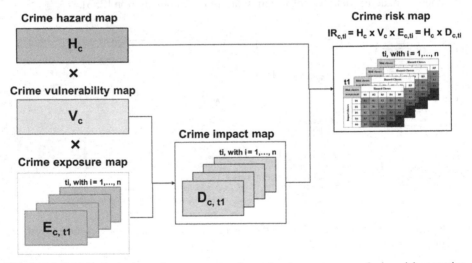

Fig. 4. Methodological scheme for constructing dynamic crime exposure and crime risk scenarios. Source: Authors' elaboration.

For each crime exposure scenario created, it is possible to construct the corresponding crime impact ($D_{c,ti}$) and crime risk scenarios ($IR_{c,ti}$). The advantage of constructing dynamic scenarios lies in the possibility of highlighting not only the areas but also the hours of day (and days of week) when crime risk conditions are most critical. Such a knowledge framework, used in the *ex ante* phase of the municipal urban Plan formation and/or in an *ex post* one, allows the decision-maker to outline suitable intervention strategies with energy and resource savings, and to monitor their results.

3 Discussion and Perspectives

The issue of urban security is of great importance for creating sustainable cities and communities. The contribution of urban planning to crime risk prevention is very important and should be considered as part of an integrated approach. Through appropriate urban planning choices, based on environmental prevention strategies, crime risk can be prevented and/or reduced. On the contrary, a lack of attention to the topic can lead to planning choices that may contribute to an increase in its critical levels [2, 34].

The work presented here is a small part of an ongoing research project aimed at exploring the topic of urban security and the urban planning contribution to safer urban spaces. The focus is on the crime exposure risk factor-map, whose dynamic nature is emphasised by using geo-social media data as an informative source to trace the travel routines and social habits of residents and city users. In detail, a model is outlined for constructing dynamic scenarios which are representative of crime exposure and crime risk conditions, in terms of surface extent and criticality levels, at different hours of day and different days of week.

The phenomenon examined is of great complexity. The effectiveness of strategies adopted requires an in-depth knowledge of the specific context and of all the variables, whether static or dynamic, that contribute to determining risk scenarios. Therefore, in a constructivist perspective [35], the model outlined is configured as a support tool for the decision-maker in outlining the most suitable strategies for prevention and mitigation of crime risk levels, and for monitoring the results.

The outlining of the proposed methodology requires a reflection on the actual possibility of its application to real case studies. Social networks are an extensive database currently used in various fields of research. Their additional value is, however, more or less powerful according to the aims for which the geo-social data are extracted and to the information to be derived from them. In the context of spatial analysis, on which this study focuses, a potentially critical element is represented by the need to obtain the geocodes associated with such data, not always available. For privacy protection, in fact, each user can choose to share or disable geolocation options associated with posted contents, making it more complex or impossible to track its location.

The methodology outlined will be applied to the case study of Milan, an urban reality examined in previous studies that have led to mapping its crime risk conditions [2, 3] and to examine crime vulnerability of its urban spaces at both urban and neighbourhood scales [2, 34, 36, 37]. Alongside this application, there are many development prospects for this research. These include: the introduction of additional variables in the crime exposure risk factor-map, such as age and gender; the use of geo-social media data both to map crime hazard and to map perceived risk and fear linked to the urban crimes under study by applying sentiment analysis.

References

1. European Union: Sustainable development in the European Union. Monitoring report on progress towards the SDGs in an EU context: 2021 edition. Office of the European Union, Luxembourg (2021). https://doi.org/10.2785/195273

2. Coppola, F.: Urbanistica e sicurezza. Un modello risk based per la prevenzione ambientale del rischio da criminalità. Ph.D. thesis, University of Salerno (2021)
3. Fasolino, I., Coppola, F., Grimaldi, M.: La sicurezza urbana degli insediamenti. Azioni e tecniche per il piano urbanistico. FrancoAngeli, Milano (2018)
4. Foster, S., Knuiman, M., Wood, L., Giles-Corti, B.: Suburban neighbourhood design: associations with fear of crime versus perceived crime risk. J. Environ. Psychol. 36, 112–117 (2013). https://doi.org/10.1016/j.jenvp.2013.07.015
5. Lorenc, T., et al.: Crime, fear of crime, environment, and mental health and wellbeing: mapping review of theories and causal pathways. Health Place 18(4), 757–765 (2012). https://doi.org/10.1016/j.healthplace.2012.04.001
6. Cozens, P.: Planning, crime and urban sustainability. WIT Trans. Ecol. Environ. 102, 187–196 (2007). https://doi.org/10.2495/SDP070181
7. Fasolino, I., Coppola, F., Grimaldi, M.: A model for urban planning control of the settlement efficiency. A case study. Archivio di Studi Urbani e Regionali, LI, 127(suppl.), 181–210 (2020). https://doi.org/10.3280/ASUR2020-127-S1010
8. Gerundo, R., Marra, A., Giacomaniello, O.: Environmental vulnerability to peripheralization risk in large area planning. Sustain. Mediterr. Constr. 14, 75–83 (2021)
9. Gerundo, R., Marra, A.: Landscapes at risk of peripheralization. A methodological framework for risk assessment to support regional planning strategies. Sustain. Mediterr. Constr. 5, 73–79 (2021)
10. United Nations Human Settlements Programme: Enhancing urban safety and security. Global report on human settlements 2007. Earthscan, London (2007). https://www.un.org/ruleoflaw/files/urbansafetyandsecurity.pdf. Accessed 14 Dec 2020
11. European Union: Action Plan. Urban Agenda Partnership. Security in Public Spaces (2020). https://ec.europa.eu/futurium/en/system/files/ged/final_action_plan_security_in_public_spaces.pdf. Accessed 02 Nov 2021
12. Jacobs, J.: The Death and Life of Great American Cities. Random House, New York (1961)
13. Cozens, P., Love, T.: A review and current status of crime prevention through environmental design (CPTED). J. Plan. Lit. 30, 393–412 (2015). https://doi.org/10.1177/0885412215595440
14. Crowe, T.D.: Crime Prevention Through Environmental Design, 3rd edn. Elsevier, Waltham (2013)
15. Newman, O.: Defensible Space. Mc Millan, New York (1972)
16. Bendler, J., Brandt, T., Wagner, S., Neumann, D.: Investigating crime-to-twitter relationships in urban environments – facilitating a virtual neighborhood watch. In: Proceedings of the European Conference on Information Systems (ECIS) 2014, Tel Aviv, 9–11 June 2014 (2014)
17. Bollena, J., Maoa, H., Zeng, X.: Twitter mood predicts the stock market. J. Comput. Sci. 2(1), 1–8 (2011). https://doi.org/10.1016/j.jocs.2010.12.007
18. Chamlertwat, W., Bhattarakosol, P., Rungkasiri, T., Haruechaiyasak, C.: Discovering consumer insight from twitter via sentiment analysis. J. Univ. Comput. Sci. 18, 973–992 (2012). https://doi.org/10.3217/jucs-018-08-0973
19. Lampos, V., De Bie, T., Cristianini, N.: Flu detector - tracking epidemics on Twitter. In: Balcázar, J.L., Bonchi, F., Gionis, A., Sebag, M. (eds.) ECML PKDD 2010. LNCS (LNAI), vol. 6323, pp. 599–602. Springer, Heidelberg (2010). https://doi.org/10.1007/978-3-642-15939-8_42
20. Boynton, B., Srinivasan, P., Mejova, Y.: GOP primary season on Twitter: "Popular" political sentiment in social media. In: WSDM 2013: Proceedings of the Sixth ACM International Conference on Web Search and Data Mining, pp. 517–526 (2013). https://doi.org/10.1145/2433396.2433463
21. Earle, P.S., Bowden, D.C., Guy, M.: Twitter earthquake detection: earthquake monitoring in a social world. Ann. Geophys. 54(6), 708–715 (2011). https://doi.org/10.4401/ag-5364

22. Wood, S.A., Guerry, A.D., Silver, J.M., Lacavo, M.: Using social media to quantify nature-based tourism and recreation. Sci. Rep. **3**, 2976 (2013). https://doi.org/10.1038/srep02976
23. Horsman, G., Ginty, K., Cranner, P.: Identifying offenders on Twitter: a law enforcement practitioner guide. Digit. Investig. **23**, 63–74 (2017). https://doi.org/10.1016/j.diin.2017.09.004
24. Ristea, A., Boni, M.A., Resch, B., Gerber, M.S., Leitner, M.: Spatial crime distribution and prediction for sporting events using social media. Int. J. Geogr. Inf. Sci. **34**, 1708–1739 (2020). https://doi.org/10.1080/13658816.2020.1719495
25. Bendler, J., Ratku, A., Neumann, D.: Crime mapping through geo-spatial social media activity. In: ICIS 2014, Thirty Fifth International Conference on Information Systems, Auckland (2014)
26. Hillier, B., Sahbaz, O.: Crime and urban design: an evidence-based approach. In: Coper, R., Evans, G., Boyko, C. (eds.) Designing Sustainable Cities, pp. 163–186. Wiley-Blackwell, Chichester (2009)
27. Kaplan, A.M., Haenlein, M.: Users of the world, unite! The challenges and opportunities of Social Media. Bus. Horiz. **53**, 59–68 (2010). https://doi.org/10.1016/j.bushor.2009.09.003
28. Fielding, R.T., Taylor, R.N.: Architectural styles and the design of network-based software architectures. Ph.D. dissertation, University of California, Irvine (2000)
29. Kearney, M.W.: rtweet: collecting and analyzing Twitter data. J. Open Source Softw. **4**(42), 1829 (2019). https://doi.org/10.21105/joss.01829
30. ECDC – European Centre for Disease Prevention and Control: Operational guidance on rapid risk assessment methodology. ECDC, Stockholm (2011). https://doi.org/10.2900/57509
31. European Commission: Commission Staff Working Paper Risk Assessment and Mapping Guidelines for Disaster Management; 21/12/2010, SEC (2010) 1626 final. European commission, Brussels (2010). https://ec.europa.eu/echo/files/about/COMM_PDF_SEC_2010_1626_F_staff_working_document_en.pdf. Accessed 12 Dec 2020
32. Poljansek, K., et al.: Recommendations for National Risk Assessment for Disaster Risk Management in EU. EUR 29557 EN. Publications Office of the European Union, Luxembourg (2019). https://doi.org/10.2760/084707
33. Coppola, F., Fasolino, I., Grimaldi, M., Sebillo, M.: A model to construct crime risk scenarios supporting Urban Planning choices. In: La Rosa, D., Privitera, R. (eds.) INPUT 2021. Lecture Notes in Civil Engineering, vol. 242, pp. 123–130. Springer, Cham (2022). https://doi.org/10.1007/978-3-030-96985-1_14
34. Coppola, F., Fasolino, I.: The axial analysis for defining neighborhoods' crime vulnerability. a methodological proposal. In: Gervasi, O., et al. (eds.) ICCSA 2021. LNCS, vol. 12958, pp. 457–473. Springer, Cham (2021). https://doi.org/10.1007/978-3-030-87016-4_34
35. Marques, S.C.R., Ferreira, F.A.F., Meidutė-Kavaliauskienė, I., Banaitis, A.: Classifying urban residential areas based on their exposure to crime: a constructivist approach. Sustain. Cities Soc. **39**, 418–429 (2018). https://doi.org/10.1016/j.scs.2018.03.005
36. Coppola, F., Fasolino, I., Grimaldi, M.: Measuring crime vulnerability at the neighbourhood scale. The case of Milan. Territorio **97**, 104–112 (2021). https://doi.org/10.3280/TR2021-097014
37. Coppola, F., Grimaldi, M., Fasolino, I.: A configurational approach for measuring the accessibility of place as an analysis tool for crime risk vulnerability. In: La Rosa, D., Privitera, R. (eds.) INPUT 2021. LNCE, vol. 146, pp. 501–509. Springer, Cham (2021). https://doi.org/10.1007/978-3-030-68824-0_54

A Methodology Based on GIS-BIM Integration to Evaluate Energy Efficiency at Urban Scale

Roberto Gerundo and Alessandra Marra[✉] [iD]

Department of Civil Engineering, University of Salerno, 84084 Fisciano, SA, Italy
{r.gerundo,almarra}@unisa.it

Abstract. Strengthening the energy efficiency of residential buildings brings numerous benefits, not only for the reduction of GHG emissions in urban areas, but also for the fight against energy poverty, which appears to be dramatically increasing. However, still little importance is attributed to efficiency on an urban scale, rather than on individual buildings, while an effective strategy is to start from the most energy-intensive neighbourhoods. The aim of this work is to propose a methodology for evaluating the energy efficiency of residential buildings on an urban scale, in the Italian geographical context, for urban planning purposes. To this end, in the absence of open data for the estimation of the buildings energy performance, a bottom-up approach is proposed that exploits the technological advances offered by GIS and BIM software, requesting input data normally available in urban planning processes. The proposed methodology is applied to the case study of Pagani, a municipality in Campania Region, Italy, showing the applicative potential of the proposed model in highly urbanized contexts, where facing the challenge of the energy transition is of absolute urgency.

Keywords: Energy efficiency · GIS&BIM · Urban planning

1 Introduction

The urban environment represents the life context of the majority of global population, but the concentration of anthropogenic activities makes cities greater consumers of energy. Therefore, the rise in climate-altering emissions and that of the local temperature seriously threaten the quality of life and, more in general, urban sustainability (Un-Habitat 2020). International agreements and agendas establish the need to introduce actions to achieve carbon neutrality, in order to combat the accentuation of climate change, also with specific reference to urban areas (UNFCCC 2015; UN 2015, 2017).

Looking in particular at the residential sector, according to the latest United Nations report on the subject, the energy demand of households is equal to 22% of the overall demand for the building sector, second only to that of transport (26%), resulting in the production of energy-related CO_2 emissions equal to 17% for residential land use and

All authors contributed to the design of the research and the definition of the methodology. A.M. prepared a draft manuscript and performed the applications. R.G. and A.M. revised the manuscript.

23% for transport. These data refer to 2019, the year before the pandemic, which saw a decrease in the overall energy requirement in the building sector, but an escalation in demand for the specific residential land use (UN 2021).

Improving the energy efficiency of residential buildings brings numerous benefits, not only for the reduction of GHG emissions, but also for the fight against energy poverty, which in Europe appears to be dramatically increasing (EU 2021).

With this awareness, the Italian Government has significantly incentivized energy efficiency measures for existing residential buildings with Law Decree 34/2020. However, still little importance is given to the efficiency improvement at urban scale, despite both scholars and international design companies have highlighted how it is possible to accelerate the energy transition by intervening on entire neighbourhoods or districts, rather than on individual buildings, in order to stress the impact and effectiveness of the actions undertaken (Paiho et al. 2019; C40Cities and ARUP 2021).

On the national scene, where over 60% of the building stock falls into the least efficient energy performance classes according to the 'SIAPE', the Italian cadastre of energy performance certificates (ENEA 2021), an effective strategy is to act as a priority on the most problematic urban areas under the energy consumption profile. So, the importance of municipal urban planning in defining remedial actions is understood, but taking this path requires the spatial knowledge of the most energy-intensive neighbourhoods. In the Italian geographical context, it is complex to find open-data relating to building energy performance certificates, as SIAPE only provides information on some Italian regions, mostly on a municipal basis, which is not adequate as spatial detail level for urban planning purposes. However, it is possible to make use of the technical-scientific literature, which offers multiple examples of residential consumption assessment, even if they are referable to two prevailing approaches: bottom-up, starting from data available at the same spatial level or at a more detailed scale; top down, based on the disaggregation of data referred to a less detailed level. Within the same bottom-up approach, statistical models are also distinguished from deterministic or engineering models (Kavgic et al. 2010; Gerundo et al. 2016; Torabi Moghadam et al. 2017).

In general, the bottom up approach is more suitable for the survey scale of municipal planning, as the disaggregation process typical of the top-down approach involves a high degree of uncertainty in the territorial distribution of energy consumption, which must be taken into account in the interpretation of the results obtained.

The most recent studies based on the bottom-up approach exploit the technological advances offered by GIS (Geographic Information System) software, also by simulating 3D city models, but still few works integrate the potential offered by the recent BIM (Building Information Modeling) software. Moreover, the problem of the time-consuming of this type of applications remains to be solved (Torabi Moghadam et al. 2018; Ferrando et al. 2020). The GIS-BIM integration is already recognized as a new approach to more effectively manage the complexity of urban processes (Grimaldi et al. 2022).

The aim of this work is to propose a methodology for estimating the energy performance of residential buildings on an urban scale, evaluated with a bottom-up methodological approach, easily implemented by taking advantage from the GIS-BIM integration. To this end, Sect. 2 below explains the proposed methodology, applied to the case study described in Sect. 3. The results of this application are presented and discussed in Sect. 4, while Sect. 5 reports the main conclusions of the study and future developments of the research.

2 Methodological Proposal

The methodology here illustrated consists in the estimation of the energy performance of the residential building stock in terms of heating and domestic hot water production, on a census basis. Operationally, this is possible starting from input data relating to different datasets, generally available in the ordinary town planning activity:

– Topographic database, from which to extract the thematic layer of the buildings present in the municipal area and the related attributes, with reference to the geometric characteristics of the spatial polygons constituting the buildings themselves;
– Urban land use map, a graphic elaboration of the Municipal Urban Plan, from which to derive the prevailing buildings use, information that makes it possible to isolate residential buildings from those mainly for productive use or for services;
– Census variables provided by ISTAT-National Institute of Statistics at census tract spatial level, containing different data on housing, including the age class of buildings.

Once the data collection and preparation has been carried out, the processing phase of such data can be launched.

First of all, it is necessary to associate the stock of residential buildings in each section to typical buildings, representative of the entire section, of which the annual energy consumption, expressed in kWh m^{-2}, is known, on the basis of the relevant literature.

More precisely, the reference buildings-types are those identified within the TABULA project, representative of the average construction and plant engineering characteristics of the Italian building stock, for which the global non-renewable energy performance index, $EP_{gl,nren}$, is known (Ballarini et al. 2014).

The association to a building-type can be carried out on the basis of the building form and the average age class per section, calculated in a GIS environment, according to a method already tested by the authors to support large area planning: the prevailing building typology can be assessed by crossing the information relating to the number of floors and the average shape ratio for each census section, where the prevailing shape ratio is calculated by dividing the average dispersing surface by the average heated volume (Marra 2020; Gerundo et al. 2021a, b).

In this work, data relating to the energy consumption of residential buildings, thus obtained, must be verified in relation to the specific characteristics of the municipal area from time to time assumed as case study, in order to make the proposed methodology more suitable for municipal urban planning purposes.

The study area, in fact, could have its own peculiarities, such that the parameters necessary for the implementation of the proposed method differ significantly from the national average, so that energy consumption, assessed on the basis of the technical literature referred to, could be overestimated or underestimated.

A verification of the results obtained can be carried out with the aid of a BIM software, which allows the modification of input parameters for estimating energy consumption, both with reference to the climatic zone and to the geometric, stratigraphic, technological and plant characteristics of the buildings. More precisely, among the commercial software available for this purpose, in this work it is proposed to use the TerMus software (ACCA Software SpA), for its moderate cost and, mainly, for its simplicity and speed of use.

This software primarily allows the definition of general building data in relation to its geographical and climatic location, its destination of use and the year of construction.

Subsequently, the software enables the modeling of the building for the purpose of energy calculation through two different modules: the "Energy Modeling" module, which permits the definition of the envelope, both vertical (walls, partitions, external cladding and any type of vertical closure) and horizontal (inter-floor or roof slabs) and the relative stratigraphy, as well as the external and internal fixtures; the "Architectural Modeling" module, which gives the insertion of additional objects such as walls, stairs and other elements useful for completing the geometric model. In addition, it is possible to specify further details regarding the type of heating or cooling system that may be present inside the building, as well as the energy sources used (electricity from the grid, natural gas, solar thermal or photovoltaic, etc.).

The definition of the model is followed by the energy calculation, which takes place according to the procedure indicated by the relevant legislation and is aimed at estimating the $EP_{gl,nren}$ index, depending on the building and the energy services present.

This value, identifying the energy consumption for the building-type representative of each section, can be used in place of the one known from the technical-scientific literature, as it is considered more representative of the territory in question.

At this stage, since the energy consumption for each census section is known, it is possible to associate the energy performance class on the basis of the threshold values set by Ministerial Decree of 26/06/2015, which establishes a total of 10 classes, from A4 to G.

The last step of the proposed methodology provides the visualization of the results obtained on a thematic map. To this end, output data of the analyses are incorporated in the original geodatabase, and associated to the census sections, in order to spatially map the energy performance classes (Fig. 1).

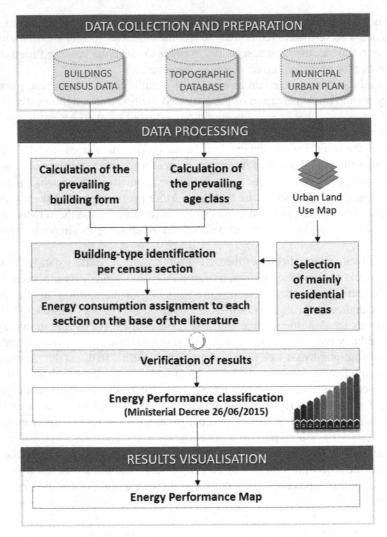

Fig. 1. Workflow of the proposed methodology.

3   Study Area

The methodology presented in this paper is applied to the case study of the Municipality of Pagani, sited in the province of Salerno, in Campania Region (Italy). Pagani is located in the so called 'Agro-Nocerino-Sarnese' conurbation, which is a highly urbanized and infrastructured area, where facing the challenge of the energy transition is of absolute urgency (Fig. 2). In the entire Salerno Province, it is the second municipality in terms of population density, with its 2933 inhabitants/km^2. Campania is one of the Italian regions for which the national cadastre of energy performance certificates does not provide public data, therefore the chosen case study is particularly suitable for effectively testing the proposed model.

40% of the buildings for mainly residential use are concentrated in the newly formed urban fabric and, for over 50%, in the rural area, characterized by a marked settlement spread. The housing stock in the historic center is equal to about 8% of the total, of which almost 3% is represented by recent buildings built on an historic urban fabric (Fig. 3). The expected prevailing reference buildings-types are represented by: single-family house and/or multi-family house in rural areas; apartment blocks in the recent urban fabric; multi-family house in the historic centre.

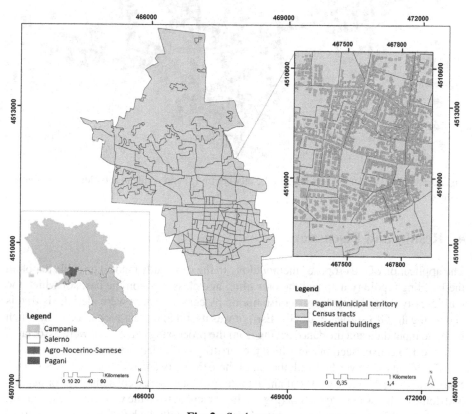

Fig. 2. Study area.

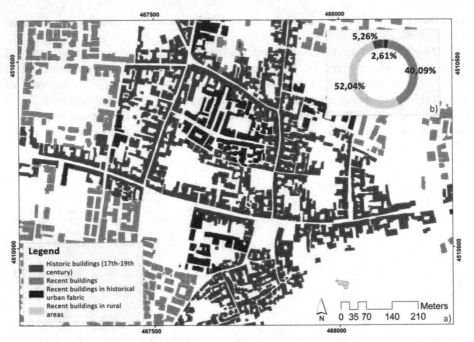

Fig. 3. Detail of residential buildings in the city centre (a) and residential buildings distribution in the entire municipal territory (b).

4 Results and Discussion

The application of the proposed methodology to the case study made it possible to obtain the building typology map and the prevailing age class map, on the basis of which the buildings-types and their energy consumption by census section were identified. To this end, using the GIS software ArcGis (Esri), it was useful to build a *geodatabase*, in which both the input data and the data deriving from the processing carried out were associated with the 125 census sections, in which the territory is divided.

The results were verified with the aid of the BIM software TerMus (ACCA Software Spa), obtaining different values of annual total primary energy consumption for heating and domestic hot water production (Fig. 4). In particular, from the verification carried out, we deduced that the energy consumptions associated with the building-types, identified on the basis of the technical-scientific literature, are overestimated for the case study (Tab. 1). From a series of simulations performed by varying the input parameters through the TerMus BIM Software, it was found that the overestimation mainly depends on the difference between the climatic area to which the Municipality of Pagani belongs (Zone C) and the average climatic area set in the selected literature (Zone E).

After recalibrating the energy consumption values for each census section, the final energy performance map was obtained, in which the threshold values of the various classes are set on the basis of the Ministerial Decree of 26/06/2015 (Fig. 5).

The results reached in the Energy Performance map reveal little variability in the classes identified according to current legislation, which only refer to the energy performance classes D, E, F and G, revealing a condition of high energy vulnerability. However, this result is in line with the national average, according to SIAPE data. It should also be noted that the classes shown are representative of the prevailing performance for each section, within which individual buildings with higher energy performance may be present, due to the recent energy efficiency measures encouraged by Law Decree 34/2020.

Compared to the methods based on bottom-up approaches already tested, recalled in the Introduction Section, the proposed method exploits the simplicity and effectiveness of the archetypal method of analysis, i.e. based on the identification of buildings-types valid for the entire national territory, but, at the same time, strengthens the results by recalibrating the evaluation parameters on the basis of the specificities of the territories examined from time to time.

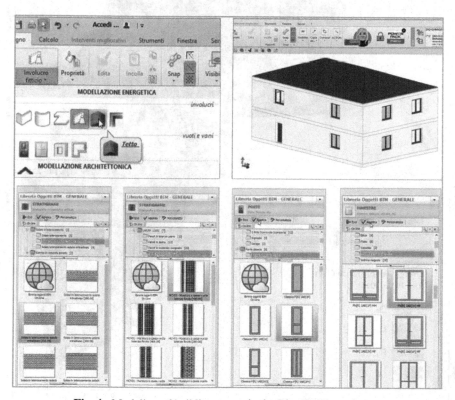

Fig. 4. Modeling of building-types in the Bim TerMus software.

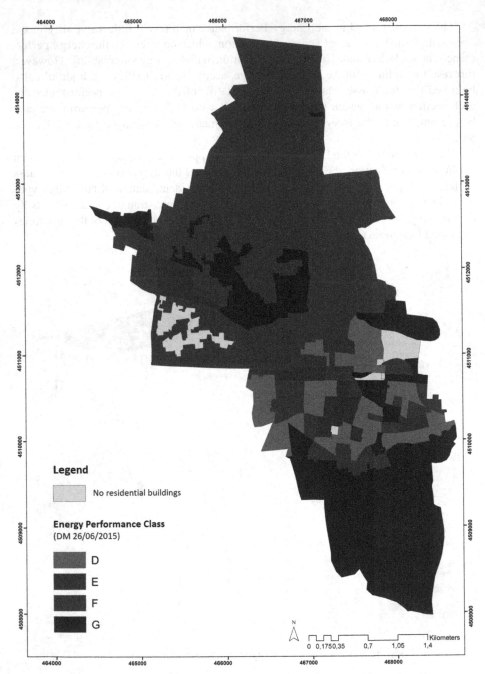

Fig. 5. Energy performance map of Pagani municipality.

Table 1. Comparison between the energy consumption values obtained for the case study.

Statistics	Annual energy consumption (kWh m^{-2})		Building-type
	Value calculated on the basis of the technical literature	Value calculated with the TerMus software	
Max	523,00	263,88	Single-family house (1961–1975)
Mean	307,47	123,85	Multi-family house (1946–1960)
Min	120,00	53,61	Apartment block (1976–1990)

5 Conclusion

The accentuation of climate change and the increase in energy poverty in urban areas raise the need to make the existing residential building stock more efficient, starting with the most critical areas from an energy point of view.

In the absence of open source data relating to the energy performance certificates of buildings, this work proposes a methodology to rapidly evaluate the energy efficiency of residential buildings, on a neighborhood scale, in highly urbanized contexts. Energy efficiency is estimated with an innovative bottom-up methodological approach, based on the GIS-BIM integration, which played an important role in the simplification and speed of application.

The map obtained by implementing the proposed methodology on a given municipal area supports the urban planning process regarding the location of the highest energy-consuming urban areas. In fact, in these areas it is possible to prioritize policies and interventions for the efficiency of the existing building stock at urban scale (Grimaldi et al. 2020; Grimaldi et al. 2019; Fasolino et al. 2020). Such actions can, for example, favour the development of Positive Energy Districts (Boeri et al. 2020), or of Energy Communities (Colombo et al. 2014; Boulanger et al. 2021), in order to accelerate the transition to renewable energy sources and reduce dependence on fossil fuels not available locally.

Future research could concern the application of the method presented in this study in urban areas belonging to territorial contexts different from the one examined: the transferability of this model is guaranteed by the availability of input data in ordinary planning processes.

References

UN-Habitat: World Cities Report 2020. The value of sustainable urbanization. United Nations (2021)

UNFCCC: The Paris agreement. In: Paris Climate Change Conference, COP 21 Paris, November 2015 (2015). https://unfccc.int/resource/docs/2015/cop21/eng/l09r01.pdf. Accessed 15 Mar 2022

UN-United Nations General Assembly: Transforming our world: The 2030 Agenda for Sustainable Development. A/RES/70/1. United Nations, New York (2015)

UN-United Nations General Assembly: New Urban Agenda. A/RES/71/256. United Nations, New York (2017). http://habitat3.org/wp-content/uploads/New-Urban-Agenda-GA-Adopted-68th-Plenary-N1646655-E.pdf. Accessed 15 Mar 2022

UN-United Nations Environment Programme: 2021 Global Status Report for Buildings and Construction: Towards a Zero-Emission, Efficient and Resilient Buildings and Construction Sector. United Nations, Nairobi (2021)

EU-European Commission: State of the Energy Union 2021 – Contributing to the European Green Deal and the Union's recovery. (2021). https://eur-lex.europa.eu/le-gal-content/EN/TXT/?uri=CELEX:52021DC0950&qid=1635753095014. Accessed 15 Mar 2022

Paiho, S., Ketomäki, J., Kannari, L., Häkkinen, T., Shemeikka, J.: A new procedure for assessing the energy-efficient refurbishment of buildings on district scale. Sustain. Cities Soc. **46**, 101454 (2019). https://doi.org/10.1016/j.scs.2019.101454

C40Cities and ARUP: Green and Thriving Neighbourhoods Guidebook (2021). https://www.arup.com/perspectives/publications/research/section/green-and-thriving-neighbourhoods. Accessed 15 Mar 2022

ENEA-National Agency for New Technologies, Energy and Sustainable Economic Development: Information System on Energy Performance Certificates-SIAPE (2021). https://siape.enea.it. Accessed 15 Mar 2022

Kavgic, M., Mavrogianni, A., Mumovic, D., Summerfield, A., Stevanovic, Z., Djurovic-Petrovic, M.: A review of bottom-up building stock models for energy consumption in the residential sector. Build. Environ. **45**, 1683–1697 (2010). https://doi.org/10.1016/j.buildenv.2010.01.021

Gerundo, R., Fasolino, I., Grimaldi, M.: ISUT model. a composite index to measure the sustainability of the urban transformation. In: Papa, R., Fistola, R. (eds.) Smart Energy in the Smart City. GET, pp. 117–130. Springer, Cham (2016). https://doi.org/10.1007/978-3-319-31157-9_7

Torabi Moghadam, S., Delmastro, C., Corgnati, S.P., Lombardi, P.: Urban energy planning procedure for sustainable development in the built environment: a review of available spatial approaches. J. Clean. Prod. **165**, 811–827 (2017). https://doi.org/10.1016/j.jclepro.2017.07.142

Torabi Moghadam, S., Coccolo, S., Mutani, G., Lombardi, P.: A new clustering and visualization method to evaluate urban energy planning scenarios. Cities **88**, 19–36 (2018). https://doi.org/10.31224/osf.io/b9znk

Ferrando, M., Causone, F., Hong, T., Chenc, Y.: Urban building energy modeling (UBEM) tools: a state-of-the-art review of bottom-up physics-based approaches. Sustain. Cities Soc. **62**, 102408 (2020)

Grimaldi, M., Giordano, C., Graziuso, G., Barba, S., Fasolino, I.: A GIS-BIM approach for the evaluation of urban transformations. A methodological proposal. WSEAS Trans. Environ. Dev. **18**, 247–254 (2022)

Ballarini, I., Corgnati, S.P., Corrado, V.: Use of reference buildings to assess the energy saving potentials of the residential building stock: the experience of TABULA project. Energy Policy **68**, 273–284 (2014). https://doi.org/10.1016/j.enpol.2014.01.027

Marra, A.: Peripheralization Risk in urban and metropolitan areas. A methodological proposal for the analysis and mitigation (Il Rischio di Periferizzazione nelle aree urbane e metropolitane. Una proposta metodologica per l'analisi e la mitigazione). Ph.D. thesis in Risk and Sustainability in Civil, Architectural and Environmental Engineering Systems, University of Salerno (2020)

Gerundo, R., Marra, A., Giacomaniello, O.: A methodology for analyzing the role of environmental vulnerability in urban and metropolitan-scale peripheralization processes. In: La Rosa, D., Privitera, R. (eds.) INPUT 2021. LNCE, vol. 146, pp. 459–468. Springer, Cham (2021a). https://doi.org/10.1007/978-3-030-68824-0_49

Gerundo, R., Marra, A., Giacomaniello, O.: Environmental vulnerability to peripheralization risk in large area planning. Sustain. Mediterr. Constr. **14**, 75–83 (2021b)

Grimaldi, M., Sebillo, M., Vitiello, G., Pellecchia, V.: Planning and managing the integrated water system: a spatial decision support system to analyze the infrastructure performances. Sustainability **12**(16), 6432 (2020). https://doi.org/10.3390/su12166432

Grimaldi, M., Sebillo, M., Vitiello, G., Pellecchia, V.: An ontology based approach for data model construction supporting the management and planning of the integrated water Service. In: Misra, S., et al. (eds.) ICCSA 2019. LNCS, vol. 11624, pp. 243–252. Springer, Cham (2019). https://doi.org/10.1007/978-3-030-24311-1_17

Fasolino, I., Coppola, F., Grimaldi, M.: A model for urban planning control of the settlement efficiency. A case study. Archivio di Studi Urbani e Regionali **127**, 181–210 (2020)

Boeri, A., Longo, D., Roversi, R., Turci, G.: POSITIVE ENERGY DISTRICTS: EUROPEAN RESEARCH AND PILOT PROJECTS focus on the Mediterranean area. Sustain. Mediterr. Constr. **12**, 22–27 (2020)

Colombo, G., Ferrero, F., Pirani, G., Vesco, A.: Planning local energy communities to develop low carbon urban and suburban areas. In: IEEE International Energy Conference (ENERGYCON), Dubrovnik, Croatia, 13–16 May 2014, pp. 1012–1018 (2014). https://doi.org/10.1109/ENERGYCON.2014.6850549

Boulanger, S.O.M., Massari, M., Longo, D., Turillazzi, B., Nucci, C.A.: Designing collaborative energy communities: a European overview. Energies **14**, 8226 (2021). https://doi.org/10.3390/en14248226

Smart Urban Waste Management System: The Case Study of Delft, Netherlands

Marika D'Agostini[✉], Simone Venturi, and Edoardo Vigo

GeoSmart Lab/Sis.Ter srl, Via Emilia 69 Imola, 40026 Bologna, Italy
sister@sis-ter.it

Abstract. Urban waste collection is a time-consuming and inefficient procedure for city municipalities. The loads on disposal units might differ by area, day or season. However, garbage trucks empty bins according to predefined routes and days, visiting bins that are often still not filled and increasing unnecessary expenses. This work aims to develop an urban waste collection management solution based on providing intelligence to garbage bins, using an IoT prototype with sensors. The Municipality of Delft (South Holland, Netherlands) is used as a case study. A grid-based approach is designed in order to estimate the Waste Stress Index and to identify 15 out of 1323 bins to be equipped with ultrasonic sensors able to read bins filling levels. The collected sensors data are used to predict future bins filling rates through a Convolutional Neural Network (CNN). Bins are then ranked according to their need to be emptied, and bins to be reached in each shift are selected solving a knapsack problem. To further reduce operational costs, the optimal set of routes for the fleet of garbage trucks are determined solving a graph-based asymmetric Vehicle Routing Problem (VRP). The optimized routes are then displayed both on a web-based Smart Waste Management Dashboard and on a mobile web app provided to waste collectors. As future work, 50 new sensors will be installed to further refine the predictions and increase the ranking accuracy. The CNN will be improved to support changes in garbage behaviour caused by events that take place in the municipality area.

Keywords: Smart city · Waste management · IoT · Artificial Intelligence (AI) · Convolutional Neural Network (CNN)

1 Introduction

One of the recent surveys conducted by the World Bank revealed that more than two billion metric tons of municipal solid waste are generated each year. It is estimated that the numbers would increase by 70% to 3.4 billion metric tons by 2050 [1]. These numbers raise concerns over city managers, who need to ensure effective waste collection and treatment to preserve public health and overall livability. Increasingly asked to shift from a linear to a circular economy, municipalities are then turning proactive and looking for smart technologies that address effective trash collection and management [2].

© The Author(s), under exclusive license to Springer Nature Switzerland AG 2022
E. Borgogno-Mondino and P. Zamperlin (Eds.): ASITA 2022, CCIS 1651, pp. 178–192, 2022.
https://doi.org/10.1007/978-3-031-17439-1_13

This work designed and implemented a solution based on the integration of Geographic Information Systems (GIS), Internet of Things (IoT), data access networks, graph optimization, Artificial Intelligence (AI), and machine learning in order to increase the efficiency of waste collection processes. The IoT integrated undifferentiated garbage bins, can measure fill levels and send trash volume data to a Smart Waste Management Dashboard through LPWAN technology (Sigfox). Using deep learning architectures and graph theory optimization techniques, data is processed to develop a dynamic and efficient waste collection management solution.

The proposed Smart Waste Management System was tested in the Municipality of Delft (South Holland, Netherlands) and proved to be an innovative solutions for smart cities to plan flexible and efficient urban waste collection schedules [3].

The remainder of this paper is organized as follows. This paper briefly presents the Smart Waste Management System components in Sect. 2. Next, the Municipality of Delft is used as a case study, and the adopted algorithms are described in Sect. 3. Case study results are discussed in Sect. 4. Finally, conclusions are provided in Sect. 5.

2 System Function and Components

The Smart Waste Management System consists of the Smart Waste Bins, the Smart Waste Management Dashboard, and the mobile web app.

Undifferentiated garbage volume data provided by sensors embedded in the waste bins are transmitted to the servers over the wireless network (LPWAN), and used to optimize and direct the municipality's waste collection process With this automated process, garbage collection teams are provided with new routes each day and trash bins are visited and cleared based on a data-driven approach, also ensuring that no full bins are left unmanaged. The results are a cleaner city with reduced maintenance costs and better-coordinated efforts.

2.1 Smart Waste Bin

The amount of waste is determined by the *BrighterBins* waste management ultrasonic sensors placed top-mount inside the bins [4]. Sensors detect the distance at which the first block of waste is located eight times a day. These measures are subsequently processed by the FIWARE components, together with bin dimensions, in order to obtain the percentages of filling. Specifically, FIWARE Context Broker is used to receive sensors data and process them according to the FIWARE Smart Data Model defined for *Smart Waste Management* [5]. Data are then stored on a PostgreSQL instance through a custom module that interfaces with Context Broker. An LPWAN (Sigfox) technology is used for the transmission of data from the sensors to the FIWARE node.

2.2   Smart Waste Management Dashboard

The Smart Waste Management Dashboard is a web-based platform through which authorities can configure, monitor and plan daily waste collection activities. The Dashboard displays real-time data about bins fill levels monitored by smart sensors (Fig. 1). All monitored bins can be seen on a digital map including last fill level measurement, the number of efficient emptying events, bin model, sensor model and sensor ID. Bins are visible on the map as green, yellow, orange or red according to their fill level. A panel on the left side shows the average fill level of the waste bins and which of these exceed a filling threshold of 80%. Moreover, the dashboard uses a Convolutional Neural Network (CNN) to predict when bins will be full [6]. Current states and predictions allow waste collection authorities to empty bins before overflow and to stop collecting half-empty ones. Through the Smart Waste Management Dashboard, it is also possible to plan optimal waste collection routes according to the capacities of the garbage trucks operating in each shift, create teams of waste collectors and assign them the determined routes.

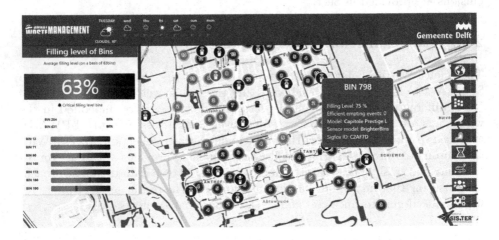

Fig. 1. Smart Waste Management Dashboard main interface

Database. Data collected from the smart waste bins are organized into a PostgresSQL database together with data related to the territory of the Delft municipality. The forecasts produced by the artificial intelligence algorithm are also stored in the database in order to evaluate the algorithm prediction accuracy. Finally, feedback on bins fill levels recorded by the waste collectors through the web app are collected and stored for further improvements of the algorithm performance.

Artificial Intelligence. Sensors data are used to predict future bins filling rates and the appropriate routes to be followed daily by the garbage collection team. The loads on disposal units might differ by day or season. Also, there are some city locations which need immediate cleaning compared to districts with less human interaction. Once AI is boosted into the system, routes are defined and optimized based on the timings and the corresponding need. Authorities are therefore equipped with a functional system able to reduce operational costs by eliminating unnecessary garbage collection trips and optimizing the garbage collection routes.

2.3 Mobile Web App

Waste collection professionals spend a lot of time outside and welcome anything that eases their job. This work includes the development of a mobile web app application, which is tailored to their specific needs and enables quick and convenient usage. Through the web app, waste collectors can view which bins need to be emptied and the routes to follow in order to optimize garbage collection. At each emptying stop, collectors can give feedback on the quality of the filling forecast and possibly report any bin problem (damage to the bin, damage to the sensor, area around the bin that needs to be cleaned, etc.). The web app interface is also characterized by a responsive skin, designed to minimize the interaction between the user and the interface itself. This choice allows providing a valuable information contribution to the operators, helping them in completing the garbage collection while receiving feedback on the bin waste and minimizing the boredom of the interaction.

3 Case Study

The case study was conducted using real GIS data of the streets and municipality-owned trash bins of the municipality of Delft, Netherlands. A total of 1323 bins are present in the city, divided into two collection areas (north and south Delft) as shown in Fig. 2. The following sections describe the models, assumptions and parameters necessary to implement the Smart Urban Waste Management System described above.

3.1 Bins Usage Modelling

A method based on an urban heterogeneity grid was adopted in order to build a dynamic system able to model the average frequency of weekly bins emptying in the city of Delft. This approach was already been experimented on several analyzes regarding urban phenomena, including urban obsolescence for the city of Bologna, Italy [7].

Using a 500-m^2 grid, a Waste Stress Index was calculated taking into consideration both population density and urban characteristics of the city, such as the presence of tourist attractions or periodic public events, the degree of

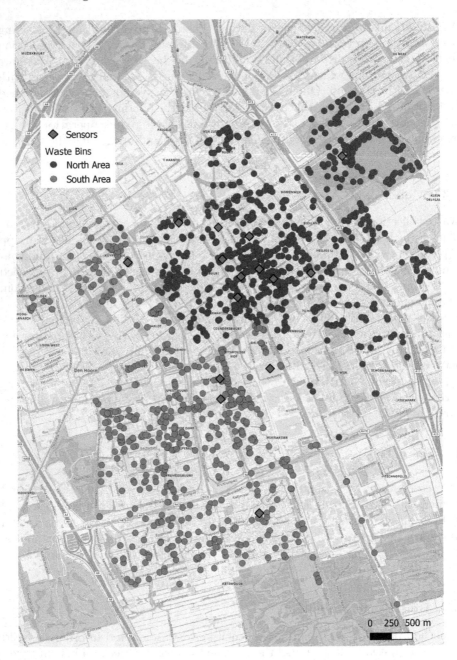

Fig. 2. Waste bins and sensors locations

urban heterogeneity, the analysis of roads and cycle flow. A full description of the urban heterogeneity grid realization can be found in [8].

High values of the Waste Stress Index define which quadrants took priority in the choice of the sensors installation areas. Also, a quality standard city division provided by the municipality (Delft Municipality CROW System) was considered for the selection of bins to be equipped with sensors able to accurately measure fill levels. Due to budget constraints, *BrighterBins* sensors have been installed only on 15 out of 1323 waste bins.

3.2   Waste Bins Fill Modelling

Data Cleaning. Several operations have been performed on time series coming from sensors in order to input them into the artificial neural network described in the next section.

First, sampling rate of sensors' measurements is variable and not equidistant. Eight fill level measurements per day are provided, temporally placed according to the need of the garbage collectors. The first four measurements are taken every three hours, from 4:30 to 13:30, while the other four are taken every two hours, between 15:30 and 21:30. It should also be stressed that measurements came from sensors subject to delays and variations in reporting times, so the aforementioned hours should be interpreted as a sort of average of the actual sampling times. Variability and irregular spacing of measurement times are undesirable properties for the correct training of an artificial neural network. Therefore, a resample of each time series was performed in order to group the measurements into three-hour bands and then consider the average value for each of them. With a single operation, we solved both the problem of variability and of equidistance between the measurements.

We also faced the problem of possible missing measurements. In fact, it is possible that one or more sensors at a certain point in time fail to communicate the measurement to the centralized manager, or that the latter fails to transmit it to the infrastructure responsible for processing and saving data to the database. The use of a resampling strategy has the side effect of creating instants without measurement, due to the actual frequency with which data are sampled. Therefore, we input missing data using linear interpolation. This method was chosen taking into consideration the equidistance measurements obtained with the resampling.

It was also necessary to take into account measurement errors, i.e. negative and inconsistent values. To solve these it was sufficient to mark them as absent values before resampling and interpolating the time series.

Finally, we took into consideration the possibility of malfunctioning sensors that a certain point in time stopping recording fill-level data. We implemented in the system the Granger causality test - a statistical hypothesis test used for determining whether a time series, stationary or not, is useful in forecasting another - between the available data of the faulty sensor and the data of the remaining functioning ones.

Granger causality test is based on two principles both satisfied by sensors data:

1. The cause happens prior to its effect.
2. The cause has unique information about the future values of its effect.

If a time series of a working sensor is found to Granger-cause the available measurements of the faulty one at some time lag, those values provide statistically significant information about future measurement values of the broken sensor. Therefore, the lagged measurement of the statistically significant time series is used to temporally estimate the missing values until the broken sensor is not replaced.

Data Preparation. Once data cleaning was completed, we adopted the Sliding Window method [9] in order to transform time series data into a proper format for a supervised learning problem. In particular, we chose a window width (or size of the sample) of two weeks for sensor measurements, in order to predict the eight next time steps (or labels), i.e. one full day of fill levels data.

Once all the sample-label pairs have been created by means of the Sliding Window technique, we shuffled them and generalized the prediction problem by putting the random-order pairs as input values for the neural network. Each shuffled time series X_i was then z-score normalized according to the formula

$$Z_i = \frac{(X_i - \mu)}{\sigma} \tag{1}$$

where μ is the mean of X_i and σ is the standard deviation of X_i. Since Convolutional Neural Networks (CNNs) better perform with z-score normalization, it was preferred over min-max scaling [10].

It should be noted that usually normalization is applied before the use of the Sliding Window technique [11]. We chose to reverse the order of the two operations since we were dealing with time series of different lengths. Applying the normalization in the first place, training, validation, and test data sets would have been defined for each time series separately and sets of the same type would have been merged together in order to estimate the normalization mean (μ) and standard deviation (σ). This procedure would have required non-uniform storage structures difficult to manage. Moreover, the presence of long time measurement lacks would have made it impossible to apply the Sliding Window technique uniformly, making it necessary to treat each sub-series of available data as distinct but, at the same time, considering all the sub-series as one in the definition of the training, validation, and test data sets. For these reasons, we decided to define these sets only after the application of the Sliding Window technique and to make the normalization according to the mean and standard deviation estimated from the training data set so formed.

Convolutional Neural Network (CNN). In recent years, deep learning techniques have outperformed traditional models in addressing time series forecasting problems. Therefore, we chose to adopt a deep Convolutional Neural Network (CNN) in order to predict future filling levels of waste bins equipped with sensors. CNNs are known to strike the best speed/accuracy trade-off for real-time applications, which makes them more suitable than recurrent approaches such as Long Short-Term Memory networks (LSTM) or Elman Recurrent Neural Networks (ERNNs) [10].

The architecture of the proposed deep CNN is shown in Fig. 3. The network receives the 56 measurements of the seven days preceding the one to be predicted as input (eight measurements per day), and it was trained using one year of measurements coming from 15 sensors, from 20 June 2020 to 21 June 2021. Assuming that the goal of training is to minimize the loss, we used the early-stopping callback in order to end the CNN training when a monitored metric (in this case, the loss on the validation set) stops improving. As a consequence, we also ensure the recovery of the best network weights. Moreover, network training was carried out with a patience parameter equal to 5–10% of the maximum number of training epochs.

In order to evaluate the performance of the CNN, we adopted three different metrics: the Mean Squared Error (MSE), the Mean Absolute Error (MAE) and the coefficient of determination (R^2).

The MSE corresponds to the prediction error per square:

$$MSE = \frac{1}{N} \sum_{i=1}^{N} (y_i - \hat{y}_i)^2 \tag{2}$$

where y_i are the real observed values, $\hat{y}_i$ are the predicted values, and N represents the series length. A low MSE value means that the predicted values are close to the real values, since squaring the prediction errors gives greater weight to larger differences between real measures and the forecast. For this reason, we considered it convenient to use this metric as the one that network tries to optimize during training in order to limit the presence of prediction outliers.

The MAE is defined as

$$MAE = \frac{1}{N} \sum_{i=1}^{N} |y_i - \hat{y}_i| \tag{3}$$

A small value for the MAE means that the estimated model is close to the real value. It also has the advantage of being easier to interpret and more robust, since it is less sensitive to extreme values than MSE.

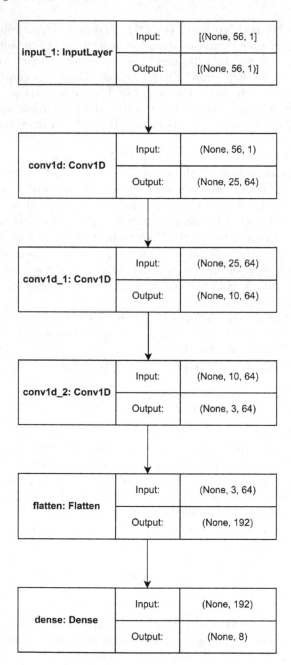

Fig. 3. Architecture of the proposed deep Convolutional Neural Network (CNN) for time series forecasting

The coefficient of determination R^2 is a metric able to evaluate the predictions quality with respect to a baseline that always predicts the mean time series value $\bar{y}$:

$$R^2 = 1 - \frac{\sum\limits_{i=1}^{N}(y_i - \hat{y}_i)^2}{\sum\limits_{i=1}^{N}(y_i - \bar{y})^2} \tag{4}$$

In the best case, where the forecast values exactly match the real observed values, we have $R^2 = 1$, while in a baseline model which always predicts $\bar{y}$ we have $R^2 = 0$.

3.3 Collection Modelling

The municipality of Delft is divided into two waste collection sectors (north and south of Delft) and the waste collection agency empties the bins in both areas during two collection shifts, one in the late morning and one in the late afternoon. This section describes how bins to be emptied are selected in each collection sector depending on the number and type of waste trucks available for each collection shift.

Bins Ranking. Once the fill levels for bins equipped with sensors are estimated using the CNN, fill levels of the garbage bins without sensors are estimated starting from the CNN predictions. Specifically, the difference between the Waste Stress Index of the quadrant in which they are located (see Sect. 3.1) and the most similar Waste Stress Index among the quadrants in which bins with sensors are located, is used as a proportional factor.

In order to select the bins to be reached on each garbage collection shift, a ranking of the bins is performed taking into consideration the future maximum fill level, the critical filling threshold, the distance from the collection starting point (i.e. the garbage trucks deposit), the distance from the collection endpoint (i.e. the waste dump), the time passed since the last emptying, the number of bins with a good rank in the neighbouring area (50 m radius). The highest-ranking bins would therefore be the ones with the greatest need to be emptied. In particular, the critical filling threshold is defined as the maximum percentage fill level that the municipality would like to maintain for a given waste bin. This value is derived by the area of the Delft Municipality CROW System - a city division into areas characterized by different quality levels - in which the bin is located: higher quality areas will have a critical threshold of 50% while lower quality areas a critical threshold of 80%. The calculation of the emptying rank is, therefore, performed in two stages. First, a temporary rank is calculated taking into consideration all the parameters except the ranking of the bins in a neighbour of 50 m. Second, the temporary rank of each bin is used to improve the rank of the bins around it. Each waste bin is thus associated with a value between 0 and 1: the higher the ranking value, the higher the need to be emptied. In order to correctly manage the importance of the bins emptying according to the critical threshold, we considered within the ranking function the ratio between the maximum future fill level and the critical threshold of each bin. This new ratio, together with the other aforementioned variables, is then normalized and weighed according to a set of parameters that can be changed in order to reflect seasonal variations in garbage behaviour. For example, in "Winter" set of parameters more weight is given to the number of bins with a good rank in the neighbouring area and to the future maximum filling level, while "Summer" set of parameters gives the same importance to all the variables used to calculate the rank.

Knapsack Problem. Once the bins ranking is completed, the bins that would actually be emptied have to be selected considering that the capacity of the waste trucks carrying out the task would be limited.

We decided to solve a knapsack problem [12] taking advantage of the *OR-Tools* Python library. Given a set of items (the bins), each with a weight (the volume of waste contained) and a value (the rank obtained in the previous step), it must be determined the items to include in a collection so that the total weight is less than or equal to a given limit (the capacity of the waste trucks) and the total value is as large as possible.

However, some problems have been encountered in the resolution of this combinatorial optimization problem. First of all, the purpose of solving a knapsack problem is to maximise the total value selected by keeping the total weight within the specified capacity. After the ranking phase, bins with a minimum waste volume still received a rank higher than zero. Therefore, the algorithm tended to include these bins in the solution despite their insignificant value and weight, since they were useful in increasing the total value of collected waste while still respecting the capacity limit. To avoid this behaviour, it has been decided to give only a limited number of bins, among those with a higher rank, as an input to the knapsack algorithm. Similarly to the previous problem, the Knapsack algorithm not always selected the first N bins with the best rank. Also, by limiting the number of considered bins, the algorithm tended to move its selection toward the bins of sufficiently high rank but of lower weight, rather than towards bins with a higher rank. This behaviour is correct and desirable but should be partially limited given the previous creation of a ranking that puts bins that would be in greater need of emptying in the top positions. It was therefore decided to use as bin value its own rank multiplied by its content volume, in order to obtain a more appropriate ranking selection.

3.4   Collection Route Creation

The municipality of Delft is divided into two waste collection sectors (north and south of Delft). Waste trucks operating in the two areas start their collection from two different depots and terminate the collection in a common location, the Delft's dump. The optimization of the set of routes for the fleet of garbage trucks takes into consideration the structure of the waste collection activity and, therefore, the algorithm described in this section must be intended as replicated with different starting points and bins involved for each of the two collection sectors.

Vehicle Routing Problem. The optimal set of routes for the fleet of garbage trucks was determined by solving a Vehicle Routing Problem (VRP) [13]. The Delft road network was described using a graph, where the arcs are roads and vertices are junctions between them. In particular, the arcs were considered either directed or undirected due to the possible presence of one-way streets or different costs in each direction. The original graph was then transformed into one where the locations of the bins, of the two depots (starting points of the collection shifts in the two sectors) and of the dump (common ending point of the collection shifts) are projected into the nearest arc creating new vertices. In this way, the vertices of the new graph are the bins, the depots, and the dump, while the arcs are the roads between them. The cost of each arc is the lowest cost between the two points in terms of distance on the original road network and the problem is accordingly solved as a shortest path problem [14]. This optimization takes into consideration road network characteristics and results in highly efficient routes to be followed by truck drivers, enhanced with a mobile app showing the generated routes.

4   Results

The average values of the MSE, MAE and R^2 obtained in the CNN training are shown in Table 1. The metrics were retrieved both for the time series and for the extrapolated maxima since the ultimate goal is to forecast the maximum fill levels of the waste bins. The average runs metrics are showed due to the randomness of the process, caused for example by data shuffling performed during data preparation.

Table 1. CNN training metrics

	MSE	MAE	R^2
Train metrics	0.0004	0.0157	0.9910
Train maximum metrics	0.0004	0.0149	0.9884

According to the experimental results, the CNN can provide reliable bins fill level forecasting with high prediction accuracy. This is due to the difference in the number of input steps (56 input steps, 8 steps per day for 7 days) compared to the steps to be predicted (8 steps). In fact, by having several days of measurements in input, the network is more easily able to recognize recurring patterns and average time series trends. Two examples of CNN predictions are shown in Fig. 4.

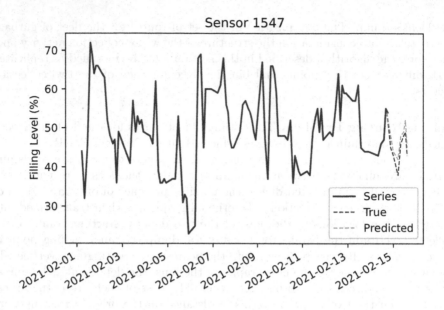

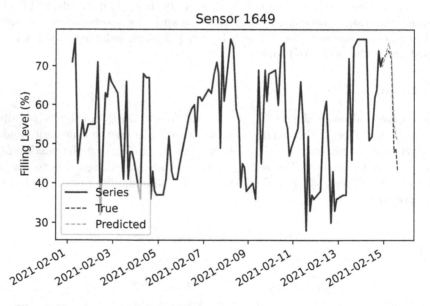

Fig. 4. Two examples of CNN forecasts for sensor 1547 and sensor 1649

5   Conclusions

The proposed Smart Waste Management System tested in the Municipality of Delft (South Holland, Netherlands), was proven to be an innovative solution in order to plan flexible and efficient urban waste collection schedules. Based on current bin fill levels and predictions of reaching full capacity, authorities are ready to respond and schedule waste collection reducing operational costs by eliminating unnecessary garbage collection trips and optimizing the garbage collection routes. Thus, this smart waste management solution makes the traditional waste collection more environment-friendly in each step, decreasing the carbon footprint.

The first phase of this work involved an in-depth analysis of the Delft municipality. Areas potentially more subject to intensive use of garbage bins was identified in order to select 15 undifferentiated waste bins to be equipped with ultrasonic sensors able to accurately measure garbage fill levels. A CNN with a fixed forecast slide window size of one week was then trained with the goal of learning garbage growth trends and predicting future garbage behaviour. As a further step, bins were ranked according to their need to be emptied. In order to select which bins to be reached in each shift, a knapsack problem was then solved defining the total capacity as the capacities of the garbage trucks operating in that shift, weights as the volume of waste, and values as the rank obtained by each bin. To further reduce operational costs, we also determined the optimal set of routes for the fleet of garbage trucks to traverse solving a graph-based VRP. The optimized routes are then made available to the collection authorities through a web-based Smart Waste Management Dashboard and displayed on a mobile web app provided to waste collectors.

As future work, it has been agreed with the municipality of Delft that 50 new sensors will be installed, increasing the number of monitored bins from 15 to 65. The addition of new sensors will improve the present model by providing more reliable data on filling levels and more variety and accuracy in sensorless bin references, resulting in a more reliable overall model. In addition, the new measurements will favour a more refined training of the CNN, further improving the accuracy of the predictions. We also plan to improve the CNN using auxiliary inputs for supporting changes in garbage behaviour by considering fluctuation factors caused by events that take place in the municipality area.

References

1. The World Bank Group: Solid Waste Management (2019). https://www.worldbank.org/en/topic/urbandevelopment/brief/solid-waste-management. Accessed 8 Feb 2022
2. Vicentini, F., et al.: Sensorized waste collection container for content estimation and collection optimization. Waste Manag. (2009). https://doi.org/10.1016/j.wasman.2008.10.017
3. Aithal, P.S.: Smart city waste management through ICT and IoT driven solution. Int. J. Appl. Eng. Manag. Lett. (IJAEML) 5(1), 51–65 (2021). https://doi.org/10.5281/zenodo.4739109

4. BrighterBins Homepage. https://www.brighterbins.com/. Accessed 3 Feb 2022
5. FIWARE Homepage. https://www.fiware.org/. Accessed 31 Jan 2022
6. Borovykh, A., Bohte, S., Oosterlee, C. W.: Conditional Time Series Forecasting with Convolutional Neural Networks. arXiv:1703.04691v5 [stat.ML] (2018). https://doi.org/10.48550/arXiv.1703.04691
7. Seravalli, A.: Urban Data per monitorare l'obsolescenza urbana - turismo e commercio nei centri storici. [Urban data for the monitoring of urban obsolescence - tourism and trade in the historic centers], In: Rapporto sulle città il governo debole delle economie urbane. Working Papers. Urban@it Online Journal 2/2018 (2018)
8. Seravalli, A., De Palma, I.: Modello dinamico per lo smart waste urbano: l'esperienza di Delft. [Dynamic model for the urban smart waste: the Delft experience]. In: ASITA Conference 2019 (12–14 November, Trieste, Italy). Acts of the Conference, pp. 955–961. http://atti.asita.it/ASITA2019/. Accessed 9 Feb 2022
9. Chia-Shang, J.C.: Time series segmentation: a sliding window approach. Inf. Sci. **85**(1–3), 147–173 (1995). https://doi.org/10.1016/0020-0255(95)00021-G
10. Lara-Benítez, P., Carranza-García, M., Riquelme, J.C.: An experimental review on deep learning architectures for time series forecasting. Int. J. Neural Syst. **31**(03), 2130001 (2021). https://doi.org/10.1142/S0129065721300011
11. Hota, H.S., Handa, R., Shrivas, A.K.: Time series data prediction using sliding window based RBF neural network. Int. J. Comput. Intell. Res. **13**(5), 1145–1156 (2017). ISSN 0973-1873
12. Kellerer, H., Pferschy, U., Pisinger, D.: Multiple knapsack problems. In: Kellerer, H., Pferschy, U., Pisinger, D. (eds.) Knapsack Problems, pp. 285–316. Springer, Heidelberg (2004). https://doi.org/10.1007/978-3-540-24777-7
13. Toth, P., Vigo, D.: The Vehicle Routing Problem. Monographs on Discrete Mathematics and Applications, vol. 9. Society for Industrial and Applied Mathematics, Philadelphia (2002)
14. Ahuja, R.K., Mehlhorn, K., Orlin, J., Tarjan, R.E.: Faster algorithms for the shortest path problem. J. ACM **37**(2), 213–223 (1990). https://doi.org/10.1145/77600.77615

Integration of LiDAR Data into a Regional Topographic Database for the Generation of a 3D City Model

Alessandro Di Benedetto and Margherita Fiani[✉]

Department of Civil Engineering, University of Salerno, Via Giovanni Paolo II, 132, 84084 Fisciano, SA, Italy
{adibenedetto,m.fiani}@unisa.it

Abstract. To analyze the resilience of road infrastructures to natural and anthropic hazards, the spatial and descriptive data provided by the Italian National Topographic Data Base (NTDB) and the 3D data coming from the LiDAR data of the *"Ministero dell'Ambiente e della Tutela del Territorio e del Mare"* (MATTM) can be used. The two datasets, having different nature, need to be properly joined. The aim of the work is the integration of the two datasets in a GIS environment for the 3D modelling of the anthropized territory and the optimization of the cartographic bases. On a test area, crossed by a network of linear infrastructures of great strategic importance and subjected to hydrogeological risk, an automated process has been implemented and tested in ArcGIS Desktop environment, to homogenize the data into the National Reference System. The planimetric component comes from the NTDB whereas the LiDAR data have been used to attribute the elevation to the extracted elements, to create the breaklines for a proper interpolation of the heights to build the Digital Terrain Model (DTM), to extract the height of the pitches of the buildings identified in the NTDB polygons, and finally to generate, filter and optimize the contour lines. The proposed workflow and the methodologies implemented also allowed the reconstruction of the volumes of each element involved (infrastructures and buildings) and to correct the altimetric aberrations present in the NTDB polygons.

Keywords: 3D model · National Topographic Data Base · LiDAR · Digital Terrain Models

1 Introduction

Land planning and management requires an accurate and rigorous knowledge of the area [1–3]. The complexity of urban or natural scenarios is an issue that is increasingly driving the use of a 3D approach over the traditional 2D approach [4].

3D vision technologies in recent years are becoming more and more popular, the 3D representation of the territory and the elements that feature it is a very debated issue in science and is very actual [5]. The demand comes from different sectors: from industry to government for state and local administrations [6]. 3D maps of the territory offer

© The Author(s) 2022
E. Borgogno-Mondino and P. Zamperlin (Eds.): ASITA 2022, CCIS 1651, pp. 193–208, 2022.
https://doi.org/10.1007/978-3-031-17439-1_14

significant advantages over a traditional 2D representation; the optimized and detailed three-dimensional representation of the territory, infrastructure and urban areas can be used for the analysis of morpho-evolutionary phenomena and for hydraulic analysis to assess the impact on anthropic activities, in addition to the provision of a higher quality visualization of information for planning applications [7, 8].

Three-dimensional reconstruction of land and anthropized territory requires the use of advanced and integrated processing techniques applied to many different types of geospatial data [9–11], which must be sourced by experienced users and involve quite significant investment, besides time consuming, especially if the areas to be modeled are large [12].

In recent years some government agencies have made available, free of charge, a few geospatial data. The resolution to make these data available arose to meet mainly public but also private needs. Among these are the LiDAR (Light Detection and Ranging) data acquired by aerial platform, high density data whose altimetric accuracy is on the order of the decimeter. The European Commission has recently published a report with the aim of disclosing all useful information on non-commercial LiDAR data made available by eighteen European Union countries, including Italy [13]. In Italy, LiDAR data have been acquired on behalf of the *"Ministero dell'Ambiente e della Tutela del Territorio e del Mare"* (MATTM) as part of the *"Piano Straordinario di Telerilevamento"* (PST-A) (Law 179 of 31/07/2002 art. 27) and are provided on demand [14].

The availability of data has led to a sudden increase in experimentation by both public and private entities for the development of new methods for the 3D modeling of the territory and the anthropic environment starting from data coming from remote sensing techniques [2, 15].

The methods proposed in the scientific community for the 3D reconstruction of the built environment can be grouped into two different macro-groups [11]: (i) methods that involve the integration of multiple data sources, typically both Airborne Laser Scanner (ALS) data and data acquired from 2D vector and raster cartography [16, 17]; (ii) methods that involve the use of only point clouds from ALS [18]. These latter methods are mainly constrained by the density of the point cloud, which mainly affects the extraction and vectorization of each single structure outlines. Differently, the methods based on the use of multiple data sources are more versatile and, in some respects, more accurate, since they are not influenced by the density of the LiDAR point cloud; the planimetric shape of the object is inferred directly from the 2D vector or raster cartographic information and subsequently extruded through the altimetric information coming from the data.

The methods based on the integration of different datasets for 3D modeling needs meeting strict requirements: the different spatial data, in addition to being framed in the same reference system, must also be processed to be aligned.

The main difficulties come up if the data are referred to different datums and there is no certain information about which is the reference datum and which is the target one; in these scenarios the error in the transformation may not result as acceptable [19]. These incongruences are mainly due to the different nature of the data, derived by means of different techniques, as well as their accuracy [20, 21].

Another example of open-source geo-spatial data are the National Topographic Data Base (NTDB) derived from a base cartography. The NTDB, produced by Public Administrations for the purposes of planning and land management according to the *Content Specifications of the Catalogue of Spatial Data* annexed to the *Ministerial Decree - November 10, 2011 "Technical rules for the definition of the specifications of the Geotopographic database content"*, follows the General Guidelines stated by the INSPIRE Directive (Directive 2007/2/EC of March 14, 2007).

A NTDB enables the structuring of spatial information into layers and classes linked topologically, this interaction should ensure a detailed and digital view of the territory [22]. At the beginning, NTDBs were designed for 2D use, also because there were no suitable tools (hardware and software) for modeling and managing 3D data, so the object-oriented approach and the extension to 3D has not been fully considered [9]. For up-to-date 3D models of the territory, data from different sources must be made congruent with each other and must be integrated. A very significant derivative application of NTDBs relevant to all countries that, like Italy, are affected by the occurrence of large areas subjected to high hydrogeological risk is their use for environmental protection, slope susceptibility analysis, risk assessment, and the resilience of road infrastructure to natural and anthropic effects [23, 24]. Since these aspects were generally not focused when NTDBs were originally developed, when they are used for these purposes the products may show some critical issues, not only in terms of accuracy inherent at the project scale, but also in relation to their reliability with respect to the reality of the territory.

Having this goal in mind, we have developed a procedure to implement the integration into a GIS environment of 2D and 3D data coming from two different sources and of different nature to model the 3D anthropized territory. The procedure was then applied on an area of great interest as it is strongly affected by hydrogeological phenomena that have a strong impact on the viability.

2 Test Area and Data

The area being considered, located in the municipality of Salerno (Fig. 1), is especially vulnerable in terms of hydrogeological risk and is characterized by the simultaneous presence of multiple transport infrastructures concentrated in an urban area of high socio-economic value.

The area analyzed belongs to the strip of land on the slopes of Monte San Liberatore, between Vietri sul Mare and Salerno, which represents a *Strategic Infrastructure Corridor* for the co-presence of stretches of major international infrastructure: the E45 freeway, the ex-state road SS18, the Naples-Salerno railway line, other minor roads (provincial and municipal) and the commercial port of Salerno. The E45 freeway from Salerno to Cava de' Tirreni is classified for various stretches at high and very high "*rischio frana*" and "*pericolosità da frana*" level in the basin planning in force. The peculiar morphological configuration, characterized by the rocky spur of San Liberatore and the presence of various altimetrically staggered infrastructural networks, makes it ideal for validating the methodology proposed.

On the test area, the available data are the LiDAR from MATTM and the NTDB derived from the "Numerical Regional Technical Cartography" at the scale 1:5,000. The

Fig. 1. Test area. (a) Location of the area; (b) Google Earth imagery of the area, the yellow polygon delimits the area being analyzed. (Color figure online)

large scale implies the need for periodic updating to monitor evolutionary dynamics within the area, otherwise the NTDB becomes less and less reliable.

The LiDAR data on the area were acquired on April 2013 using an Optech ALTM 3100 laser scanner by Optech, mounted on an aircraft flying at an altitude between 1,500 and 1,800 m height AGL (Above Ground Level). The direction of flight is parallel to the coastline, the maximum scan angle used is 25 deg and the scan frequency has been set equal to 100 kHz.

Detailed information about the acquisition and the dataset can be found in [25]. The LiDAR data were processed and filtered using TerraScan software from Terrasolid. The specifications of the data, as stated by the distributing authority, are as follows: point density greater than 1.5 points per square meter, planimetric accuracy (2σ) of 30 cm, altimetric accuracy (1σ) of 15 cm.

LiDAR data are processed at various levels:

XYZ: Point cloud (*.xyz). Each line in the text file contains ellipsoidal coordinates longitude and latitude (DD) and elevation (m), the value of intensity, a code that defines whether the point belongs to the ground (2, "ground") or not (1, "no ground"). Reference system: WGS84 (EPSG: 4979), ellipsoidal WGS84 height.

DSM First, DSM Last: Digital Surface Model, raster file format (*.asc), first-pulse and last-pulse respectively; GSD of 1 m inland and 2 m on the coast. 3D grid cells, planimetric size 10^{-5} DD. Reference system: EPSG: 4979.

DTM: Digital Terrain Model, raster file format (*.asc); GSD of 1 m inland and 2 m on the coast. 3D grid cells, planimetric size 10^{-5} DD. Reference system: EPSG: 4979. The DTM is derived by TIN interpolation of points classified as "ground".

Intensity: raster file format (*.asc) containing the reflection values of the laser beam. 2D grid cells (10^{-5} DD). Reference system: EPSG: 4326.

Analyses carried out on some NTDB strata have highlighted anomalies relating to the elevation component, on the polygons of the *"Immobili e Antropizzazioni"* layer, for the *"Opere delle infrastrutture di trasporto"* and *"Strade"* themes. The errors in elevation are presumably due to editing processes that are not appropriate for the 3D geometry: during the editing phases, to some vertices of the polygons of the roads, which overlap with other layers, for example the contour line layer, were attributed incorrect elevation values, as Figs. 2a–b shows.

For LiDAR, starting from the point cloud, given in geographic coordinates φ, λ, first a TIN was formed, a structure particularly suitable for representing complex landforms and highlighting orographic discontinuities, then this TIN was rasterized to have a matrix of cells more easily handled in common GIS software. The coordinate system φ, λ is not an isothermal coordinate system on the ellipsoid, so that an equal angular increment of latitude or longitude corresponds to an arc element of different length.

This affects the raster output, where bands formed by rectangular cells can be observed (Fig. 2c). The other problem related to DTMs is the poor rendering of areas in correspondence with infrastructures or certain geomorphological details, including areas modified by anthropic processes (slopes, roadways, etc.).

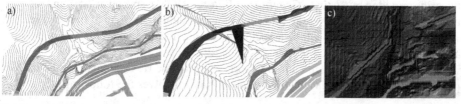

Fig. 2. a, b) NTDB: 3D excerpt view of polygons (theme *"Strade"*) overlaid on contour lines; c) LiDAR data from MATTM: DTM excerpt.

3   Methods

Since both input data do not meet the requirements of most experts and users of cartography - the DTM from LiDAR provided by the Ministry has some scaling, and some NTDB polygons have aberrations in the elevation component - to optimize the outputs and obtain a 3D representation of the territory and built environment giving an accurate rendering of geomorphological and anthropic features with their typical shape, an automated tool was implemented in ArcMap environment.

The process is implemented in Python using the ArcGIS library (ArcPy) and is based on the generation of a DTM and contour lines from the LiDAR data using planimetric information from the NTDB. The main steps of the process consist in: (i) homogenization of the different reference systems, (ii) extraction of the height from the LiDAR point cloud and attribution of the same to the 2D polygons implemented in the NTDB, (iii) generation of the DTM from the LiDAR data (iv), generation and filtering of the contour lines.

3.1 Homogenization of Coordinate Reference System

The files provided by the Ministry containing the LiDAR data (*.xyz) are imported into the GIS environment; the function implemented allows to import a single file or a set of files contained in a folder. The output consists of a file named *Point Features* (*.shp file), in the attributes *Table* the plano-altimetric coordinates are reported. Only the points associated with the "Ground" class (identified by scalar 2) are imported.

The next step is to associate the data with the correct datum. This is done using the *Define Projection* tool; for the planimetric coordinates it is EPSG: 4326. Since the reference systems of the input data are different from each other, coordinate/datum transformations that meet the nationally mandated specifications are required, also to enable interoperability between regions.

In Europe, so also in Italy, the system chosen is the ETRS89, realization ETRF2000 (epoch 2008.0), which is mandatory for the Public Administration, stated in the Ministerial Decree of November 10, 2011, as well as being specified in the European Directive INSPIRE (Technical Guidelines Annex I - D2.8.I.1). In Italy ETRF2000 is materialized by the RDN2008 (EPSG:6706).

To transform the coordinates of the LiDAR point cloud into ETRF00, we have used the grids provided by *"Istituto Geografico Militare"* (IGM), spaced at 7.50' in longitude and 5' in latitude. They cover the extension of an element of the map of Italy at a scale of 1:50,000. Each grid node will be associated with a corrective value for longitude ($\Delta\lambda$) and latitude ($\Delta\varphi$) contained in the *.GK2 file [26].

The algorithm implemented to transform the planimetric coordinate of the LiDAR point cloud into the ETRS89/ETRF00 (epoch 2008) involves the following steps:

1. Generation of two 6×6 grids (one for each coordinate) having 36 nodes with spacing 7.50' in longitude and 5' in latitude (DD). The coordinates of the origin of the grid (in the south-west node) are given in ETRS89/ETRF89 (input system);
2. Computation, through bilinear interpolation of the corrective values given in the *.GK2 file, of the corrections $\Delta\lambda_{Pi}$ and $\Delta\varphi_{Pi}$ to be assigned to the generic P_i point of the LiDAR cloud;
3. Conversion of $\Delta\lambda_{Pi}$ and $\Delta\varphi_{Pi}$ corrections from DMS into DD;
4. Application of $\Delta\lambda_{Pi}$ and $\Delta\varphi_{Pi}$ corrections to LiDAR point coordinates to accomplish the transformation into ETRF2000 (EPSG: 6706), according to the formula:

$$\lambda_{ETRF00} = \lambda_{ETRF89} + \Delta\lambda$$
$$\varphi_{ETRF00} = \varphi_{ETRF89} + \Delta\varphi$$

(1)

5. Conversion from geographic coordinates (EPSG:6706) into UTM/ETRF2000 map coordinates (EPSG:7792).

The *.GK2 file, in addition to the corrective parameters for the transformation of planimetric coordinates, also contains the values of the geoid undulation N (ITAL-GEO2005) to transform the heights from ellipsoidal h to orthometric H. The values, spaced at 2' DD in planimetry, are contained in the rows 267–406.

The conversion of the elevation values follows the following steps:

1. Creation of a grid with spacing 2' DD, made of 14 columns and 10 rows, the planimetric coordinates of the origin of the grid (in the south-west node) are given in ETRS89/ETRF89;
2. Bilinear interpolation of the undulation values, given at the grid nodes, to compute the value for each point in the LiDAR cloud;
3. Computation of orthometric heights H with the known formula:

$$H = h - N \tag{2}$$

3.2 3D Modeling of the Roads Within the NTDB

The next step is to create the 3D polygons of the roads, with a twofold purpose:

1. To correct the errors on the elevation values of the polygons for the themes "*Opere delle infrastrutture di trasporto*", "*Ferrovie*" and "*Strade*" in the NTDB;
2. To generate the 3D breaklines to correctly represent the roads, which are elements of discontinuity, in the DTM.

To this end, a specific procedure has been developed to extract altimetric values from the LiDAR point cloud and then attribute them to the 2D polygons of the roads within the NTDB. This will also provide a 3D modeling of the road system.

The process has been implemented in ArcMap environment, with some algorithms developed apart in MATLAB and Python, and it is based on the following steps:

1. Extraction from LiDAR data of points belonging to the road surface;
2. Extraction from NTDB of 2D polygons belonging to the layer "*Immobili e Antropizzazioni*" (Fig. 3);
3. Division of the polygons, along the longitudinal direction, into sub-polygons of assigned length; the length must be congruent with the resolution of the DTM to be produced;
4. Join process: a column is added to the polygon attributes table; the column will contain the average elevation values of the points within the sub-polygons;
5. Transformation of the 2D sub-polygons into 3D sub-polygons by attributing the elevation values contained within the attribute table, by running the tool *Feature to 3D By Attribute*.

The process of step #1 has been carried out using an algorithm implemented specifically for Mobile Laser Scanner (MLS) data [27], based on the extraction of *ground* points, belonging to the road surface, from the MLS trajectory. Unlike MLS data, in which it is possible to extract the trajectory given the scanning angle and the GPS time, in ALS data this input is not available, as the geometry and the point cloud acquisition method are different. Hence, the required information has been extracted from the NTDB; the layer related to the viability contains the polylines, at the axis of the carriageway, of the roads (Fig. 3, about urban and suburban roads). Here the polylines have been used as an alternative to the MLS trajectory for the application of the algorithm. The process requires as input the roadway polyline and the width of the sub-polygons.

Fig. 3. Polygons extracted from the NTDB on the test site: vertices of the polyline of the road network (blue points) overlapped by the polygons of the infrastructure one (purple polygons). (Color figure online)

3.3 3D Modeling of the Buildings Within the NTDB

The reconstruction of the 3D model is carried out by joining elementary volumes, means solid that are generated by the extrusion along the vertical of a surface, called the extrusion surface, up to a given height, called the extrusion height. Since the extrusion heights are absolute values, the direction of extrusion can be up or down.

The polygons of the buildings contained in the NTDB are lacking in altimetric values; therefore, they are used as a footprint for the extrusion process, that is based on the following steps:

1. Extraction of the 2D polygons relative to the *"Edificato"* theme of the *"Immobili e Antropizzazioni"* layer;
2. Selection of the LiDAR points within each polygon using the *Selection by Location* function;
3. Removal of the points belonging to the vertical walls of the buildings through the computation of the slope;
4. Selection of the points belonging to the single planes of the pitch by means of the aspect computation;
5. Semi-automatic generation of the pitch planes, through the implementation of the RANdom SAmple Consensus (RANSAC) algorithm, using the primitive *plane*;

6. Computation of the negative extrusion height (from the pitch towards the ground) for each interpolated plane by computing the difference in elevation between the DTM (average height of the site area) and the minimum height of the pitch plane.

The removal of the points belonging to the vertical walls is done by computing the slope on the TIN surface created from the points selected through the polygons of the buildings [28], the function used is *Surface Slope*. The function results in a polygonal feature, having the same structure as the mesh. To each polygon is associated the value of the slope, the slope is computed with respect to the horizontal plane. Only the points within the polygons which are associated with slope values lower than the chosen threshold will be extracted. The identification of the points belonging to the single pitch plane, in the case of hipped roofs, is done by computing the aspect on the TIN surface interpolated with the points resulting from the previous process, the function used is *Surface Aspect*. The function returns a polygonal feature, as for the Surface Slope function, with associated aspect values.

To have the number of classes equal to the number of slopes, a classification according to the Natural Breaks method has been carried out. The points belonging to each single class will be interpolated with the RANSAC algorithm proposed by [29], using the *plane* primitive.

3.4 DTM Construction

To better represent the land surface, we chose a TIN-type DTM rather than GRID one. To be effective, it must be assumed that the input data are free of outliers.

The implemented script creates the TIN with the Create TIN tool, which respects the Delaunay algorithm. The input data are the LiDAR point cloud (*.xyz) transformed into the reference system EPSG: 7792, with orthometric heights, limited to the *ground* class.

The tool allows the insertion of breaklines in the form of 3D polygonal surfaces; in our application we used as input the 3D polygons of the roads, obtained from the application of the processes detailed in Sect. 3.2.

After structuring the points into a TIN, the edge triangles were removed using the *Delineate TIN* tool. The last step of the process consists in the conversion of the 3D TIN into a two-dimensional image (raster), where each pixel is associated with an elevation value, performed by implementing the tool *TIN to Raster*. The cell size must be chosen according to the representation scale, which in turn must be congruent with the accuracy and density of the input data. The interpolation method used is linear; each triangle (face) belonging to the TIN identifies a plane in space, passing through the three vertices of the triangle itself. Using this interpolating plane, the elevation values of the corresponding raster cell are computed. Generally, as the resolution increases, the output raster will more accurately represent the TIN surface. Contour lines should represent small geomorphological details with their typical shape, making them immediately perceptible. This sometimes requires the enhancement of some terrain shapes, which are generally filtered and smoothed in standard processes [2].

The implemented algorithm is not limited to the generation of contour lines but includes a geometric filtering and smoothing process. The contour lines are generated from the raster DTM by applying the *Contour* function. New fields representing the geometric characteristics of each contour are added to the contour layer attribute table. For each individual contour line, the following are computed: (i) length; (ii) vertices coordinates.

Through the combination of the computed parameters and the height for each individual contour, the implemented algorithm removes/corrects all possible aberrations or elements that should not be present at a given representation scale. These include bull's eyes, altimetric inconsistencies, non-coincident edges, non-closed areas. The smoothing algorithm used is based on a local polynomial interpolation. The algorithm smooths the lines according to an assigned tolerance; the tolerance controls the maximum distance between the interpolated polyline and the spline vertex. The smaller the length, more detail will be preserved and the longer the processing time. The smoothing process was implemented using the *Smooth line* tool. The smoothing algorithm used is PAEK (Polynomial Approximation with Exponential Kernel).

4   Results

The accuracy of the coordinate transformation was checked by comparing our results with those resulting from the use of the official IGM conversion software (Verto3k). The average difference in the coordinates between 1,000 random samples was 0.3 mm $\pm$ 0.8 mm in East and $\pm$ 0.6 mm in North (Fig. 4) whereas for geographical coordinates the average differences was of the order of $1-10^{-8}$ DD. The differences are not significant, they are well below the accuracy of the LiDAR data, so the process can be deemed verified. As for the elevations, the comparison provided zero differences.

The construction of the breaklines corresponding to the roads was carried out by the extraction of the polygons relative to the "*Immobili e Antropizzazioni*" layer, only those relative to the themes of "*Strade*" and "*Ferrovie*" belonging to the domain level were selected (Fig. 5a).

The extraction of LiDAR points belonging to the road surface was made by applying the algorithm briefly described in Sect. 3.2 [27]. The *maxDistance* parameter was set equal to 0.25 m to account for the road cross slope while for the other parameters the defaults were used.

The polygons belonging to the domain layer were divided into sub-polygons of 0.5 m along the travel direction (Fig. 5b), less would not allow to contain enough points, due to the limited density of the LiDAR data. Each sub-polygon is associated with an elevation that is the average of those of the points, which are selected by a spatial join process. Therefore, each sub-polygon is horizontal and has that elevation value (Fig. 5c); such simplification is justified since the elevation differences between the center and the roadside, due to cross slopes, are lower than the accuracy of the elevation component of LiDAR data.

For the process of building extrusion, the 2D polygons related theme "*Edificato*" of the "*Immobili e Antropizzazioni*" layer were extracted. For each polygon, LiDAR points were selected (Fig. 5d), and they were then organized into TINs and the dihedral angle of each triangle face with respect to the horizontal plane was computed using the *Surface Slope* function. Triangle faces with an angle greater than 45 deg and their vertices were

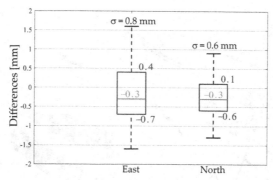

Fig. 4. BoxPlot of the differences between UTM coordinates from Verto3K and those resulting from the implemented process.

then deleted to remove all those points belonging to the vertical walls of buildings. The *Surface Aspect* function was applied to the remaining surfaces, and the values obtained were classified according to the *Natural Breaks* method. This type of classification allowed obtaining as many classes as the number of pitches. The pitch planes were constructed by RANSAC interpolation on the points belonging to the individual classes, using the single primitive *plane* (Fig. 5e).

The LiDAR point cloud transformed into EPSG: 7792, with orthometric heights, was run through spatial interpolation processes to generate the DTM. The TIN method was used, according to the Delaunay criterion and with the inclusion of breaklines derived from 3D infrastructure polygons. The variable size of the triangles results in a model with variable resolution. In addition, all edge triangles with a length greater than 30 m were deleted. Figure 6 shows the shaded relief maps of the DTM of the MATTM (Fig. 6a) and the one generated through the implemented process (Fig. 6b). In detail, in Fig. 6a it is possible to notice the poor rendering of the roadways, especially on the highway with staggered carriageways and on the shoulders of the viaducts.

In addition, it is also evident the scaling already discussed in Sect. 2. Figure 6b shows the DTM resulting from the optimization process in which it is possible to note a clear improvement in the definition of some geomorphological details, including areas modified by anthropic processes (slopes, roadways, etc.). The TIN is rasterized using a 20 cm pixel size. The effect of the scaling present in the MATTM data is absent, this is due to the interpolation being done in the cartographic system.

The contour lines are derived from the TIN raster with 1 m spacing. Figure 7 shows a comparison between contour lines derived from the DTM provided by the MATTM (Fig. 7a) and those derived from the optimization process implemented in GIS (Fig. 7b). The contour lines shown in Fig. 7a are featured by discontinuities, essentially related to the DTM interpolation and visible in the shaded relief map of Fig. 6a.

Aberrations have been removed with the automated filtering process, run by setting the tolerance value at 2 m because the tests carried out have proved the effectiveness of setting a tolerance equal to twice the equidistance so to enhance the landform without overly smoothing the edges.

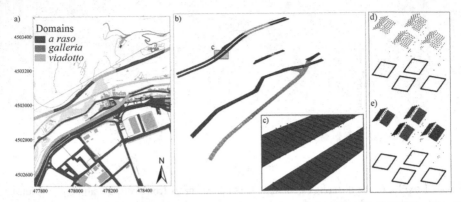

Fig. 5. Procedure for constructing breaklines. (a) Extraction of the infrastructures belonging to the domain *level*; (b) Perspective view of the polygons extracted with the infrastructure point cloud (blue points) overlaid; (c) Zoom-in of the 3D sub-polygons with the point cloud overlaid. d) LiDAR points extracted from 2D polygons of the NTDB; e) Pitch plans interpolated by RANSAC algorithm. (Color figure online)

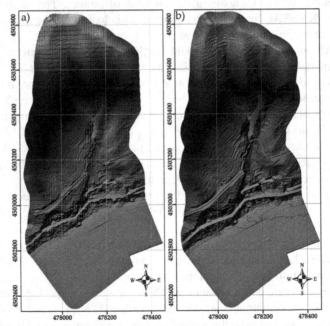

Fig. 6. Shaded relief maps of the test area. (a) DTM provided by the Ministry; (b) optimized DTM.

Figure 8 shows the 3D model in ArcScene environment, produced from extrusion of building and infrastructure polygons extracted from NTDB. The DTM was optimized using Breaklines.

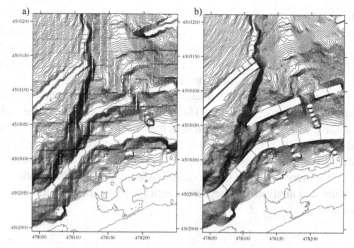

Fig. 7. Excerpt of contour maps with 1m spacing equidistance. (a) Contour lines from MATTM-provided DTM; (b) Contour lines from optimized DTM.

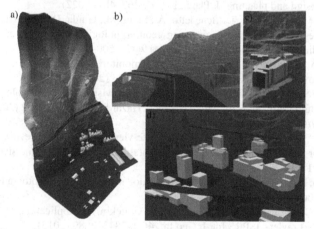

Fig. 8. a, b, c, d) perspective views of the 3D model of *"Vallone e Viadotto Olivieri"* created from NTDB-LiDAR integration.

5   Conclusions

The work highlights the benefits of an integrated use of regional NTDB and LiDAR data, through automatic procedures implemented using tools in ArcGIS Desktop environment. The integrated use of the two data sets (LiDAR and NTDB) requires data framed in the National Geodetic System and thus needs specific procedures for datum transformation and elevation homogenization.

The automated process allowed to optimize the DTM derived from LiDAR data, through correction and attribution of the altimetric component to the geometries contained in the NTDB, namely to the polygons of the roads, and to generate the 3D breaklines used in the DTM interpolation. The proposed methodology has also allowed to produce a DTM free of the aberrations present in the MATTM one.

The algorithm has been implemented in Python, using the libraries available in ArcMap. Some of the process for the identification of the pitch planes and for the generation of the polygons of the 3D buildings has been developed in a computing environment outside the GIS, given the complexity of the algorithms used and not included in the ArcMap libraries. The implemented methodology offers, moreover, an optimized and detailed 3D representation of the land, infrastructures, and urbanization, useful for the identification and analysis of morpho-evolutionary phenomena that may impact on human activities.

References

1. Abou Jaoude, G., Mumm, O., Carlow, V.M.: An overview of scenario approaches: a guide for urban design and planning. J. Plann. Lit. **37**, 467–487 (2022)
2. Barbarella, M., Cuomo, A., Di Benedetto, A., Fiani, M., Guida, D.: Topographic base maps from remote sensing data for engineering geomorphological modelling: an application on coastal mediterranean landscape. Geosciences **9**(12), 500–528 (2019)
3. Richiedei, A., Pezzagno, M.: Territorializing and monitoring of sustainable development goals in italy: an overview. Sustainability **14**(5), 3056–3075 (2022)
4. Li, N., Sun, N., Cao, C., Hou, S., Gong, Y.: Review on visualization technology in simulation training system for major natural disasters. Nat. Hazards **112**, 1851–1882 (2022). https://doi.org/10.1007/s11069-022-05277-z
5. Roberts, J.C., Butcher, P.W.S., Ritsos, P.D.: One view is not enough: review of and encouragement for multiple and alternative representations in 3D and immersive visualisation. Computers **11**(2), 20–42 (2022)
6. Remondino, F., El-Hakim, S.: Image-based 3D modelling: a review. Photogram. Rec. **21**(115), 269–291 (2006)
7. Biljecki, F., Stoter, J., Ledoux, H., Zlatanova, S., Çöltekin, A.: Applications of 3D city models: state of the art review. ISPRS Int. J. Geo Inf. **4**(4), 2842–2889 (2015)
8. Tao, W.: Interdisciplinary urban GIS for smart cities: advancements and opportunities. Geospat. Inf. Sci. **16**(1), 25–34 (2013)
9. Breunig, M., Zlatanova, S.: 3D geo-database research: retrospective and future directions. Comput. Geosci. **37**(7), 791–803 (2011)
10. Liu, X., Wang, X., Wright, G., Cheng, J.C.P., Li, X., Liu, R.: A State-of-the-art review on the integration of building information modeling (BIM) and geographic information system (GIS). ISPRS Int. J. Geo Inf. **6**(2), 53–73 (2017)
11. Zhu, L., Lehtomäki, M., Hyyppä, J., Puttonen, E., Krooks, A., Hyyppä, H.: Automated 3d scene reconstruction from open geospatial data sources: airborne laser scanning and a 2D topographic database. Remote Sens. **7**(6), 6710–6740 (2015)
12. Wulder, M.A., et al.: Lidar sampling for large-area forest characterization: a review. Remote Sens. Environ. **121**, 196–209 (2012)
13. European, C., Joint Research, C., Florio, P., Kakoulaki, G., Martinez, A.: Non-commercial Light Detection and Ranging (LiDAR) data in Europe. Publications Office (2021)

14. MATTM. http://www.pcn.minambiente.it/mattm/progetto-pst-dati-lidar/. Accessed 01 Mar 2022
15. Barbarella, M., Di Benedetto, A., Fiani, M.: Application of supervised machine learning technique on LiDAR data for monitoring coastal land evolution. Remote Sens. **13**(23), 4782–4802 (2021)
16. Brenner, C., Haala, N.: Rapid acquisition of virtual reality city models from multiple data sources. Int. Arch. Photogram. Remote Sens. **32**, 323–330 (1998)
17. Vosselman, G.: Fusion of laser scanning data, maps, and aerial photographs for building reconstruction. In: IEEE International Geoscience and Remote Sensing Symposium, vol. 1, pp. 85–88 (2002)
18. Vosselman, G.: Building reconstruction using planar faces in very high density height data. Int. Arch. Photogram. Remote Sens. **32**(3), 87–94 (1999)
19. Daniels, R.C.: Datum conversion issues with LIDAR spot elevation data. Photogramm. Eng. Remote Sens. **67**(6), 735–740 (2001)
20. Kim, Y., Kim, Y.: Improved classification accuracy based on the output-level fusion of high-resolution satellite images and airborne LiDAR data in urban area. IEEE Geosci. Remote Sens. Lett. **11**(3), 636–640 (2014)
21. Khanal, M., Hasan, M., Sterbentz, N., Johnson, R., Weatherly, J.: Accuracy comparison of aerial lidar, mobile-terrestrial Lidar, and UAV photogrammetric capture data elevations over different terrain types. Infrastructures **5**(8), 65–85 (2020)
22. Carrion, D., Maffeis, A., Migliaccio, F., Pinto, L.: Aspetti tecnici della progettazione di un database topografico multirisoluzione. In: Atti del Convegno Nazionale SIFET "Dal rilevamento fotogrammetrico ai data base topografici", 27–29 giugno 2007, pp. 195–200 (2007)
23. D'Aranno, P.J.V., Di Benedetto, A., Fiani, M., Marsella, M., Moriero, I., Palenzuela Baena, J.A.: An application of persistent scatterer interferometry (PSI) technique for infrastructure monitoring. Remote Sens. **13**(6), 1052–1074 (2021)
24. Budetta, P., Nappi, M., Santoro, S., Scalese, G.: DinSAR monitoring of the landslide activity affecting a stretch of motorway in the Campania region of Southern Italy Transp. Res. Procedia **45**, 285–292 (2020)
25. MATTM. http://www.pcn.minambiente.it/mattm/scheda-metadati. Accessed 01 Jan 2022
26. IGM. https://www.igmi.org/it/descrizione-prodotti/elementi-geodetici-1/prodotti-e-servizi-per-il-passaggio-tra-sistemi-geodetici-di-riferimento. Accessed 01 Jan 2022
27. De Blasiis, M.R., Di Benedetto, A., Fiani, M.: Mobile laser scanning data for the evaluation of pavement surface distress. Remote Sens. **12**(6), 942–966 (2020)
28. Gergelova, M.B., Labant, S., Kuzevic, S., Kuzevicova, Z., Pavolova, H.: Identification of roof surfaces from LiDAR cloud points by GIS tools: a case study of Lučenec, Slovakia. Sustainability **12**(17), 6847–6865 (2020)
29. Schnabel, R., Wahl, R., Klein, R.: Efficient RANSAC for point-cloud shape detection. Comput. Graph. Forum **26**(2), 214–226 (2007)

Agriculture and Forestry

Spectral Measures from Sentinel-2 Imagery vs Ground-Based Data from Rapidscan© Sensor: Performances on Winter Wheat

Alessandro Farbo[(✉)] ⓘ, Raffaele Meloni ⓘ, Massimo Blandino ⓘ, Filippo Sarvia ⓘ,
Amedeo Reyneri ⓘ, and Enrico Borgogno-Mondino ⓘ

Dipartimento di Scienze Agrarie, Forestali e Alimentari, Università degli Studi di Torino,
Torino, Italy
{alessandro.farbo,raffaele.meloni}@unito.it

Abstract. Precision agriculture can be supported by different instruments and sensors to monitor crops and adjust agronomic practices. Remote sensing and derived vegetation index are one of the main techniques that allows to derive related-vegetation information. In this work the Normalized Difference Vegetation Index (NDVI) and the Normalized Difference Red-Edge index (NDRE) derived by active handheld Rapidscan© (RS) and passive Sentinel-2 (S2) sensors were compared focusing on the wheat crop. To deal with different sensor wavebands centers, different S2 wavebands were considered and two different NDVI and four different NDRE derived by S2 data were computed. The comparison between RS and S2 was performed during three phenological stages of wheat: first node, flowering and milk. In each period, RS-derived indices were modelled to estimate the S2 ones. Results show that the best conversion models found was linear. In addition, a high correlation and R^2 (>0.7) coefficient was found, except during flowering stage. Results confirm the opportunity to scale data and related agronomic information from ground sensor to satellite improving decision support system in agriculture.

Keywords: Winter wheat · Vegetation indices · Proximal sensing · Remote sensing

1 Introduction

Remote sensing is a modern and enhanced tool, based on vegetation indices, which support crop management practices. It provides an accurate picture of crop status during growing season and highlights stresses [1]. Vegetation index (VI) application is becoming quite common due to its capability of investigating vegetation health and crop production. NDVI (Normalized Difference Vegetation Index) and NDRE (Normalized Difference Red-Edge index) are widespread vegetation indices (Vis) in agriculture [1]. Several studies [2, 3] show that these VIs are good predictors of active photosynthetic biomass and, therefore, grain yield and grain protein content (GPC).

E. Borgogno-Mondino and P. Zamperlin (Eds.): ASITA 2022, CCIS 1651, pp. 211–221, 2022.
https://doi.org/10.1007/978-3-031-17439-1_15

VIs are involved in nitrogen fertilizer management. They have the capability to estimate leaf N content indirectly, rapidly, intensively over space and time and they are quite inexpensive [4]. In this way, it is possible to adjust the nitrogen (N) fertilization rate [5] and to assess if an extra dose is necessary to improve GPC [6]. A more correct N management is extremely important to avoid environmental pollution and to increase farmers income [7]. Modulating farmer inputs (variable-rate application), according to the crop requirements and the field variability, is the precision agriculture (PA) main goal [8, 9]. Variable rate application is based on application maps, built on vegetation indices, to identify management zones characterized by homogeneous yield-limiting factors [10, 11]. In the Northern-Italy the presence of small fields suggests to consider and manage these fields as unitary zones.

Handheld active Rapidscan© (RS) sensors provide NDVI and NDRE indices able to track N status and yield estimations [12]. The main advantage of this instrument is the data collection quickness, easiness and daily repeatability. Furthermore, the active sensor overcomes the passive device sunlight calibration problems [13]. For this reason, scientific research usually relies on RS.

In recent years, the European Copernicus programme, with its main mission Sentinel-2 (S2), has provided free satellite images with high frequency and spectral resolution [14]. For this reason, S2 data are well known in literature for supporting the agricultural sector. In particular, its applications are quite different and include: crop production estimation [15], crop phenology monitoring [16, 17], crop damage assessment [18], land cover/use generation [19–21] and characterising ecosystems [22, 23]. Recently, S2 data opened new monitoring scenarios including the precision agriculture one [24, 25], even if its contribution is still being explored [26]. RS and S2's characteristics complement each other: the first can survey small areas (such as agronomic plots) while the second can investigate large areas at no costs and with no need for field surveys. Moreover, active optical sensors are not influenced by cloudiness while S2 data are strongly affected by weather conditions. Conducting trials on small plots and transferring the obtained results on a large scale thanks to satellites could be of great interest for PA applications [27]. The studies carried out so far have led to first interesting results, however, none of these involved RS and S2 comparisons about NDVI and NDRE [28, 29].

In this context, the TELECER project was set up. TELECER's aim is to apply remote sensing to improve cereals production and quality for advanced supply chains. The main objective is to make innovations for the agrotechnical management (irrigation, fertilization, defense) accessible to the cereal cooperatives of Piedmont (North-West of Italy) through the guidance offered by the satellite. It's possible to optimize the agronomic input and give information at harvest for the correct segregation of the product. Therefore, cultivations are valorized and more easily canalized from commodities to specialties with a specific use and transformation purpose.

2   Goals

This study aims to find the relations between spectral indices collected by two different instruments. Active proximal RS sensor and S2 multispectral measurements were compared. Subsequently, the best conversion models (CM) from RS proximal sensing to S2 remote sensing were analyzed. CM could be helpful in scaling small plots measurements and related agronomic information to a larger extent such as the one provided by S2 data.

3 Material and Methods

3.1 Study Area

Quality of crop monitoring by remote sensing is critically affected by observed field size in relation to ground sample distance (GSD) [30, 31]. Thus, 20 fields sizing more than 0.5 ha (having at least 10 S2 pixel @10m GSD) were identified as fields of interest (FOI). FOI are spread in the Piedmont lowlands (Fig. 1).

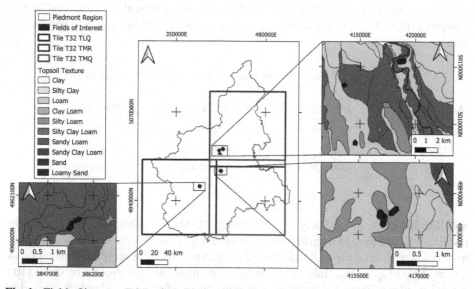

Fig. 1. Field of interest (FOI) within Piedmont Region (North-West Italy) are represented by red polygons. Sentinel-2 (S2) Tiles footprint is represented by red/blue/green squares. Soil texture (USDA Classification) is derived by Piedmont Region soil map (1:50000). (Reference System: WGS84/UTM 32N). (Color figure online)

Piedmont region is characterized by heterogeneous soils. Different soil textures are highlighted in Fig. 1. The plots in the south-west zone are the most fertile with loam texture with high water retention. In the north-east soils are typically sandy with low water retention and frequent water stress: those have the lowest fertility. Intermediate fertility is appreciable in the silty soils typical of the east zone: texture leads to a cold soil with frequent waterlogging.

3.2 Available Data

Proximal sensing RS Rapidscan© CS-45 (RS) (Holland Scientific, USA) is the proximal handheld active sensor used to scan wheat parcels. This device incorporates three bands measurement channels: Red (670 nm), Red-Edge (730 nm) and near infrared (NIR, 780 nm). In this way it is possible to calculate all VIs that include in their formula these bands. Particularly, NDVI and NDRE are automatically calculated by the sensor. This sensor has the ability to make height independent spectral reflectance measurements: it refers them as Pseudo Solar Reflectance (PSR) measurements. In this way spectral bands are scaled as Percentage and will not vary with sensor height above a target (www.hol landscientific.com).

Data acquisition was performed on previously define plot of 10 m long: along this space the sensor collects many reflectance values and averages the derived indices. A unique mean value is finally registered. The height of the sensor was maintained 1.5 m from the ground. In order to obtain more representative field data, ten measures were taken for each field and all averaged. During the growing season, three key moments have been selected to collect data in all fields: beginning of stem elongation (BBCH 31), flowering (BBCH 61) and medium milk ripening (BBCH 75) [32]. Table 1 shows when data were collected.

Table 1. Collected data timing in each area by using Rapidscan sensor (RS).

Area	BBCH 31	BBCH 61	BBCH 75
North-east	08/04/2021	14/05/2021	18/06/2021
South-east	08/04/2021	04/05/2021	10/06/2021
South-west	08/04/2021	04/05/2021	10/06/2021

Satellite Imagery. In this study three S2 tiles (T32TMR, T32TMQ and T32TLQ) were necessary according to FOI territorial distribution (Fig. 1). In order to test RS and S2 spectral consistency, six temporally closest S2 images per tile were acquired. Imagery was retrieved from Open Data Hub (https://scihub.copernicus.eu/) as Level 2A products (100 x 100 km^2 tiles calibrated at the bottom of atmosphere reflectance and orthoprojected in WGS84/UTM). S2 level 2A images are supplied along with a scene classification layer (SCL) providing information about cloudy, shadowy or faulty pixels. Therefore, only images with no unsuitable pixels on FOI were selected (Table 2). In Table 3 are reported S2 multispectral instrument (MSI) technical features.

Table 2. Acquisition date of the available Sentinel-2 (S2) images corresponding to the three phenological phases (BBCH) surveyed.

TILE	BBCH 31	BBCH 61	BBCH 75
T32TMR	06/04/2021	19/05/2021	18/06/2021
T32TMQ	06/04/2021	04/05/2021	18/06/2021
T32TLQ	06/04/2021	06/05/2021	13/06/2021

Table 3. Sentinel-2 (S2) MSI band technical features: central wavelength, band width and ground sample distance (GSD).

Spectral Band	Central wavelength (nm)	Band width (nm)	GSD (m)
B1 (Aerosol)	443	20	60
B2 (Blue)	490	65	10
B3 (Green)	560	35	10
B4 (Red)	665	30	10
B5 (Red edge 5)	705	15	20
B6 (Red edge 6)	740	15	20
B7 (Red edge 7)	783	20	20
B8 (Near infrared)	842	115	10
B8A (Near infrared plateau)	885	20	20
B9 (Water vapor)	945	20	60
B10 (Cirrus)	1380	30	60
B11 (Short wave infrared 1)	1610	90	20
B12 (Short wave infrared 2)	2019	180	20

3.3 Data Processing

Spectral Indices Processing. To assess the transferability of proximal RS measurements to a large-scale instrument such as S2, several VIs were generated. As already reported, RS spectral indices are processed using 3 bands (Red = 670 nm, Red-Edge = 730 nm and NIR = 780 nm) and the same was done with S2 data. It is common knowledge that the same spectral index computed with different wavelengths could lead to significantly different values and meanings [33, 34], therefore six S2 VIs (S2I) were

Table 4. Rapidscan (RS) and Sentinel-2 (S2) vegetation indices analyzed.

Spectral indices	RS	S2
NDVI	$NDVI = \frac{\rho 780 - \rho 670}{\rho 780 + \rho 670}$	$NDVI_{S2} = \frac{B8 - B4}{B8 + B4} = \frac{\rho 842 - \rho 665}{\rho 842 + \rho 665}$
		$NDVI^7_{S2} = \frac{B7 - B4}{B7 + B4} = \frac{\rho 783 - \rho 665}{\rho 783 + \rho 665}$
NDRE	$NDRE = \frac{\rho 780 - \rho 730}{\rho 780 + \rho 730}$	$NDRE5_{S2} = \frac{B8 - B5}{B8 + B5} = \frac{\rho 842 - \rho 705}{\rho 842 + \rho 705}$
		$NDRE5^7_{S2} = \frac{B7 - B5}{B7 + B5} = \frac{\rho 783 - \rho 705}{\rho 783 + \rho 705}$
		$NDRE6_{S2} = \frac{B8 - B6}{B8 + B6} = \frac{\rho 842 - \rho 740}{\rho 842 + \rho 740}$
		$NDRE6^7_{S2} = \frac{B7 - B6}{B7 + B6} = \frac{\rho 783 - \rho 740}{\rho 783 + \rho 740}$

ρ = reflectance (nm).

calculated to test their relationship with the two RS VIs (RSI) (Table 4). S2 VIs and the associated bands were chosen considering the wavelength similarity of the S2 and RS bands.

RSI measured in the field surveys were exported and converted into a vector layer. Subsequently the average for each FOI per survey date was calculated. S2's imagery processing implied a preliminary resampling (bilinear interpolation method) at 10 m for the 20 m GSD S2 bands (B5, B6 and B7). Resampling, S2I computations (according to the equations reported in Table 4) and FOI averages export were performed in SAGA GIS v. 8.1.1 (System For Automated Geoscientific Analyses). RS and S2 datasets were compared, in particular at each BBCH stage, RS and S2 comparison was firstly tested for equal means and equal distribution (T-test and F-test respectively) in order to test the hypothesis that the two SIs means and variances were not significantly different. Following, a first-order polynomial regression was calibrated for each of these based on the Eq. 1 as suggested by Gozdowski [28]:

$$S2I = a \cdot RSI + b \tag{1}$$

where a and b are the model coefficients estimated by ordinary least squares. Coefficient of determination and significance of each model were then calculated.

3.4 Results and Discussions

Rapidscan© vs Sentinel-2 NDVI. NDVI comparisons showed a common pattern, all T-tests revealed significant differences between indices while F-tests were always non-significant (Table 5).

NDRE T-test gave similar results to the NDVI ones, leading to significant results while F-test were found to be more unstable. In particular, all F-test were significant except the $NDRE5_{S2}$ and $NDRE5_{S2}^7$ for the BBCH 31, the $NDRE6_{S2}$ for the BBCH 61

Table 5. Rapidscan (RS) and Sentinel-2 S2 NDVI comparisons for different BBCH stages: T-test and F-test significance, R^2 and Linear model equation. (ns Not Significant, * Significant at $p < 0.05$, ** Significant at $p < 0.01$, *** Significant at $p < 0.001$)

Timing	NDVI comparison	T-test	F-test	R^2	Linear model eq
BBCH 31	$NDVI_{RS}$-$NDVI_{S2}$	***	ns	0.796	$y = 0.605x + 0.382$
	$NDVI_{RS}$-$NDVI_{S2}^7$	***	ns	0.779	$y = 0.642x + 0.344$
BBCH 61	$NDVI_{RS}$-$NDVI_{S2}$	***	ns	0.272	$y = 0.672x + 0.360$
	$NDVI_{RS}$-$NDVI_{S2}^7$	***	ns	0.264	$y = 0.635x + 0.346$
BBCH 75	$NDVI_{RS}$-$NDVI_{S2}$	*	ns	0.969	$y = 0.781x + 0.229$
	$NDVI_{RS}$-$NDVI_{S2}^7$	*	ns	0.961	$y = 0.787x + 0.221$
General	$NDVI_{RS}$-$NDVI_{S2}$	***	ns	0.937	$y = 0.791x + 0.247$
	$NDVI_{RS}$-$NDVI_{S2}^7$	***	ns	0.939	$y = 0.792x + 0.236$

and the $NDRE5_{S2}$ and $NDRE5_{S2}^7$ for the BBCH 75. F-test and more specifically the T-tests showed significant differences for RS and S2 VIs conducted comparisons, thus resulting in possible bias between indices.

Once the preliminary analyses had been carried out, the CM were developed for both NDVI and NDRE (Tables 5 and 6). It is worth to remind that the model coefficients are indicators of a possible bias between RSIs and S2Is: b indicates the model intercept while a is the model slope.

General model shows a highly significant correlation between NDVI collected by the two instruments ($R^2 > 0.93$). Looking at the specific growing stage, there is a weak relation at flowering stage (BBCH 61) resulting in a R^2 about 0.27. Concerning a and b coefficients, a common pattern between all CM is present. Specifically, b is always greater than 0 while a is minor than 1.

Comparing $NDRE_{RS}$ with those obtained from S2, a general good significant correlation is shown ($R^2 > 0.7$). However, CM goodness vary among growing stages: similarly to NDVIs CMs, a weaker correlation can be found at flowering stage (BBCH 61), with an R^2 about 0.4. Moreover, General CMs show notable differences between NDRE6 and $NDRE6^7$, resulting in a R^2 equal to 0.83 and 0.70 respectively.

Concerning a and b coefficients, two common patterns within CM are present: NDRE CMs change considering different bands. Specifically, in NDRE5 CMs b ranges between 0.15 and 0.25, while a is greater than 1.1. Conversely, in NDRE6 CMs b ranges between 0.02 and 0.06, while a is lower than 0.4. Concerning a, further differences can be noted in General CMs between NDRE6 and $NDRE6^7$ corresponding in a equal to 0.32 and 0.25 respectively. Finally, according to the above-mentioned results, $NDRE_{RS}$ appears to be more related to NDRE5 rather than NDRE6. High correlations between RS and S2, concerning NDVI and NDRE, were also found by Bonfil [35]. In particular, when proximal and remote sensing surveys occur within 4 days difference, the correlations were equal to 0.70 and 0.77 for NDVI and NDRE respectively.

The General CM were subsequently plotted to better understand the relation between S2 and RS VIs (Figs. 2, 3).

Figure 2 shows that S2 NDVIs seems to be underestimated by $NDVI_{RS}$ for poorly vegetated areas ($NDVI_{RS} < 0.6$) while a good correspondence was found for highly vegetated ones ($NDVI_{RS} > 0.6$). Similar results were found in literature comparing active and passive sensor. In particular Veverka compared VIs derived by RS and Micasense Red-Edge (MRE) and found an overestimation of MRE NDVI compared to low $NDVI_{RS}$ values [29]. Figure 3 shows that S2 NDRE5s appear to be underestimated by $NDRE_{RS}$, specifically the higher is the plots vegetation coverage the higher is the underestimation. Also in this case a similar underestimation was found by Veverka comparing $NDRE_{RS}$ and NDRE derived by MRE [29]. Contrary S2 NDRE6s seems to be overestimated by $NDRE_{RS}$ in highly vegetated areas, however a good correspondence was found in poorly vegetated ones.

Table 6. Rapiscan (RS) and Sentinel-2 (S2) NDRE comparisons for different BBCH stages: T-test and F-test significance, R^2 and Linear model equation. (ns Not Significant, * Significant at p < 0.05, ** Significant at p < 0.01, *** Significant at p < 0.001)

Timing	NDRE S2	T-test	F-test	R^2	Linear model eq
BBCH 31	$NDRE_{RS}$-$NDRE5_{S2}$	***	ns	0.772	y = 1.116x + 0.257
	$NDRE_{RS}$-$NDRE5_{S2}^7$	***	ns	0.749	y = 1.168x + 0.219
	$NDRE_{RS}$-$NDRE6_{S2}$	***	***	0.597	y = 0.333x + 0.054
	$NDRE_{RS}$-$NDRE6_{S2}^7$	***	***	0.770	y = 0.348x + 0.022
BBCH 61	$NDRE_{RS}$-$NDRE5_{S2}$	***	***	0.354	y = 1.124x + 0.253
	$NDRE_{RS}$-$NDRE5_{S2}^7$	***	*	0.344	y = 1.120x + 0.237
	$NDRE_{RS}$-$NDRE6_{S2}$	***	ns	0.468	y = 0.427x + 0.026
	$NDRE_{RS}$-$NDRE6_{S2}^7$	***	*	0.426	y = 0.359x + 0.022
BBCH 75	$NDRE_{RS}$-$NDRE5_{S2}$	***	ns	0.860	y = 1.336x + 0.159
	$NDRE_{RS}$-$NDRE5_{S2}^7$	***	ns	0.818	y = 1.314x + 0.155
	$NDRE_{RS}$-$NDRE6_{S2}$	**	***	0.862	y = 0.242x + 0.069
	$NDRE_{RS}$-$NDRE6_{S2}^7$	**	***	0.893	y = 0.196x + 0.068
General	$NDRE_{RS}$-$NDRE5_{S2}$	***	**	0.887	y = 1.388x + 0.171
	$NDRE_{RS}$-$NDRE5_{S2}^7$	***	**	0.881	y = 1.358x + 0.161
	$NDRE_{RS}$-$NDRE6_{S2}$	***	***	0.837	y = 0.319x + 0.059
	$NDRE_{RS}$-$NDRE6_{S2}^7$	***	***	0.702	y = 0.245x + 0.053

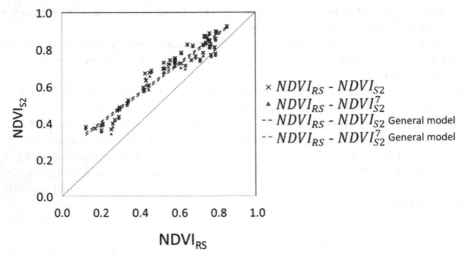

Fig. 2. RS and S2 CM for NDVI spectral indices following different bands. Linear general models are represented as dotted lines.

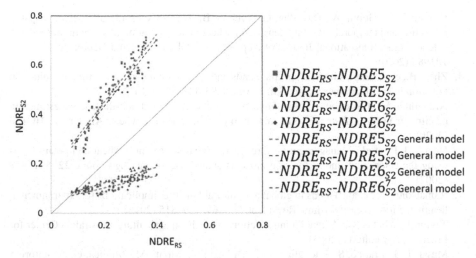

Fig. 3. RS and S2 CM for NDRE spectral indices following different bands. Linear general models are represented as dotted lines.

4 Conclusions

This study highlights the good correlation between RapidScan© and Sentinel-2 spectral indices despite different wavebands are considered. Particularly, it can be appreciable a good linear relation between indices with a constant dispersion around the mean independently from indices considered. Despite *a* and *b* coefficients differences, equations forecast S2 indices starting from RS in a valuable way. It means that S2 data are reliable and applicable to evaluate crops status although S2 measurements are affected by atmospheric conditions. Flowering stage indices comparison show lower correlation due to the highest land cover. Indeed, RS NDVIs of poorly vegetated plots are overestimated compared with S2 ones. Conversely, for high biomass areas, NDRE is underestimated by S2.

Numerous nitrogen application models (NAM) based on Rapidscan surveys have been developed [36, 37]. RS-S2 conversion models could be used to transfer the existent NAM to S2 data and therefore to extend the precision agriculture applications. These models could drive to interesting information useful for a proper and more sustainable management of crops. Future developments will be conducted in order to relate these deductions to the yields and over other crops pertaining the TELECER project like corn, barley and soybean.

References

1. Atzberger, C.: Advances in remote sensing of agriculture: Context description, existing operational monitoring systems and major information needs. Remote sensing. **5**, 949–981 (2013)
2. Vannoppen, A., et al.: Wheat yield estimation from NDVI and regional climate models in Latvia. Remote Sensing. **12**, 2206 (2020)

3. Durgun, Y.Ö., Gobin, A., Duveiller, G., Tychon, B.: A study on trade-offs between spatial resolution and temporal sampling density for wheat yield estimation using both thermal and calendar time. International Journal of Applied Earth Observation and Geoinformation. 86, 101988 (2020)
4. Zhao, B., et al.: Exploring new spectral bands and vegetation indices for estimating nitrogen nutrition index of summer maize. Eur. J. Agron. 93, 113–125 (2018)
5. Aranguren, M., Castellón, A., Aizpurua, A.: Crop sensor based non-destructive estimation of nitrogen nutritional status, yield, and grain protein content in wheat. Agriculture 10, 148 (2020)
6. Denuit, J.-P., et al.: Management of nitrogen fertilization of winter wheat and potato crops using the chlorophyll meter for crop nitrogen status assessment. Agronomie 22, 847–853 (2002)
7. Ramankutty, N., et al.: Trends in global agricultural land use: implications for environmental health and food security. Annu. Rev. Plant Biol. 69, 789–815 (2018)
8. Taylor, J., Whelan, B.: A general introduction to precision agriculture. Australian Center for Precision Agriculture. (2005)
9. Messina, G., Praticò, S., Badagliacca, G., Di Fazio, S., Monti, M., Modica, G.: Monitoring Onion Crop "Cipolla Rossa di Tropea Calabria IGP" Growth and Yield Response to Varying Nitrogen Fertilizer Application Rates Using UAV Imagery. Drones. 5, 61 (2021). https://doi.org/10.3390/drones5030061
10. Grisso, R.D., Alley, M.M., Thomason, W.E., Holshouser, D.L., Roberson, G.T.: Precision farming tools: variable-rate application. (2011)
11. Long, D.S., Carlson, G.R., DeGloria, S.D.: Quality of field management maps. In: Site-specific management for agricultural systems. pp. 251–271. Wiley Online Library (1995)
12. Bonfil, D.J.: Monitoring wheat fields by RapidScan: Accuracy and limitations. Adv. Anim. Biosci. 8, 333–337 (2017)
13. Li, F., et al.: Improving estimation of summer maize nitrogen status with red edge-based spectral vegetation indices. Field Crop Res 157, 111–123 (2014)
14. Delwart, S.: SENTINEL-2 User Handbook. European Space Agency. Available from: https://earth.esa.int/documents. esa. int/documents … (2015)
15. Parida, B.R., Kumar, A., Ranjan, A.K.: Crop Types Discrimination and Yield Prediction Using Sentinel-2 Data and AquaCrop Model in Hazaribagh District, Jharkhand. KN-Journal of Cartography and Geographic Information. 1–13 (2021).
16. Misra, G., Cawkwell, F., Wingler, A.: Status of phenological research using Sentinel-2 data: A review. Remote Sensing. 12, 2760 (2020)
17. Sarvia, F., De Petris, S., Borgogno-Mondino, E.: Mapping Ecological Focus Areas within the EU CAP Controls Framework by Copernicus Sentinel-2 Data. Agronomy 12, 406 (2022). https://doi.org/10.3390/agronomy12020406
18. F, S., S, D.P., E, B.-M.: Multi-scale remote sensing to support insurance policies in agriculture: from mid-term to instantaneous deductions. null. 57, 770–784 (2020). https://doi.org/10.1080/15481603.2020.1798600
19. Phiri, D., Simwanda, M., Salekin, S., R Nyirenda, V., Murayama, Y., Ranagalage, M.: Sentinel-2 Data for Land Cover/Use Mapping: A Review. Remote Sensing. 12, 2291 (2020)
20. Steinhausen, M.J., Wagner, P.D., Narasimhan, B., Waske, B.: Combining Sentinel-1 and Sentinel-2 data for improved land use and land cover mapping of monsoon regions. Int. J. Appl. Earth Obs. Geoinf. 73, 595–604 (2018)
21. Sarvia, F., De Petris, S., Ghilardi, F., Xausa, E., Cantamessa, G., Borgogno-Mondino, E.: The Importance of Agronomic Knowledge for Crop Detection by Sentinel-2 in the CAP Controls Framework: A Possible Rule-Based Classification Approach. Agronomy 12, 1228 (2022). https://doi.org/10.3390/agronomy12051228

22. Andrew, M.E., Wulder, M.A., Nelson, T.A.: Potential contributions of remote sensing to ecosystem service assessments. Prog. Phys. Geogr. **38**, 328–353 (2014)
23. Sarvia, F., De Petris, S., Borgogno-Mondino, E.: Exploring Climate Change Effects on Vegetation Phenology by MOD13Q1 Data: The Piemonte Region Case Study in the Period 2001–2019. Agronomy **11**, 555 (2021). https://doi.org/10.3390/agronomy11030555
24. Segarra, J., Buchaillot, M.L., Araus, J.L., Kefauver, S.C.: Remote sensing for precision agriculture: Sentinel-2 improved features and applications. Agronomy **10**, 641 (2020)
25. Mancini, A., Frontoni, E., Zingaretti, P.: Satellite and uav data for precision agriculture applications. In: 2019 International Conference on Unmanned Aircraft Systems (ICUAS). pp. 491–497. IEEE (2019)
26. Bukowiecki, J., Rose, T., Kage, H.: Sentinel-2 Data for Precision Agriculture?—A UAV-Based Assessment. Sensors. **21**, 2861 (2021)
27. Messina, G., Peña, J.M., Vizzari, M., Modica, G.: A Comparison of UAV and Satellites Multispectral Imagery in Monitoring Onion Crop. An Application in the 'Cipolla Rossa di Tropea' (Italy). Remote Sensing. 12, 3424 (2020). https://doi.org/10.3390/rs12203424
28. Gozdowski, D., et al.: Comparison of winter wheat NDVI data derived from Landsat 8 and active optical sensor at field scale. Remote Sensing Applications: Society and Environment. **20**, 100409 (2020)
29. Veverka, D., Chatterjee, A., Carlson, M.: Comparisons of sensors to predict spring wheat grain yield and protein content. Agron. J. **113**, 2091–2101 (2021)
30. Meier, J., Mauser, W., Hank, T., Bach, H.: Assessments on the impact of high-resolution-sensor pixel sizes for common agricultural policy and smart farming services in European regions. Comput. Electron. Agric. **169**, 105205 (2020)
31. Vajsová, B., Fasbender, D., Wirnhardt, C., Lemajic, S., Devos, W.: Assessing spatial limits of Sentinel-2 data on arable crops in the context of checks by monitoring. Remote Sensing. **12**, 2195 (2020)
32. Zadoks, J.C., Chang, T.T., Konzak, C.F.: A decimal code for the growth stages of cereals. Weed Res. **14**, 415–421 (1974)
33. Galvão, L.S., Vitorello, Í., Filho, R.A.: Effects of Band Positioning and Bandwidth on NDVI Measurements of Tropical Savannas. Remote Sens. Environ. **67**, 181–193 (1999). https://doi.org/10.1016/S0034-4257(98)00085-6
34. Mahlein, A.-K., et al.: Development of spectral indices for detecting and identifying plant diseases. Remote Sens. Environ. **128**, 21–30 (2013). https://doi.org/10.1016/j.rse.2012.09.019
35. Bonfil, D.J., Michael, Y., Shiff, S., Lensky, I.M.: Optimizing Top Dressing Nitrogen Fertilization Using VENμS and Sentinel-2 L1 Data. Remote Sensing. **13**, 3934 (2021). https://doi.org/10.3390/rs13193934
36. Aranguren, M., Castellón, A., Aizpurua, A.: Crop Sensor-Based In-Season Nitrogen Management of Wheat with Manure Application. Remote Sensing. **11**, 1094 (2019). https://doi.org/10.3390/rs11091094
37. Lu, J., et al.: Developing a Proximal Active Canopy Sensor-based Precision Nitrogen Management Strategy for High-Yielding Rice. Remote Sensing. **12**, 1440 (2020). https://doi.org/10.3390/rs12091440

Multi Crop Estimation of LAI from Sentinel-2 VIs with Parametric Regression Approach: Comparison of Performances and VIs Sensitivity

Margherita De Peppo[1]([✉]), Francesco Nutini[1], Gabriele Candiani[1],
Giorgio Ragaglini[2], Andrea Taramelli[3,4], Federico Filipponi[4], and Mirco Boschetti[1]

[1] Italian National Research Council, Institute for Electromagnetic Sensing of the Environment,
Via Bassini 15, 20133 Milan, Italy
{depeppo.m,nutini.f,candiani.g,boschetti.m}@irea.cnr.it
[2] Dipartimento di Scienze Agrarie e Ambientali-Produzione, Territorio,
Agroenergia, Università degli Studi di Milano, Via Celoria 2, 20133 Milano, Italy
giorgio.ragaglini@unimi.it
[3] Institute for Advanced Study of Pavia (IUSS), Palazzo del Broletto, Piazza della Vittoria 15,
27100 Pavia, Italy
andrea.taramelli@iusspavia.it
[4] Institute for Environmental Protection and Research (ISPRA), via Vitaliano Brancati 48,
00144 Rome, Italy
federico.filipponi@isprambiente.it

Abstract. Leaf Area Index (LAI) is a key variable for spatiotemporal modelling and analysis of several land surface processes. LAI can be successfully estimate by means of Vegetation Indices (VIs), retrieved from multispectral satellite images, however the different VIs show variable estimation uncertainty in relation to vegetation characteristics and soil background condition. In particular, VIs can show saturation behaviour at medium/high vegetation density. Thus, in this study we aimed at implementing parametric approach considering VIs belonging to three different classes computed on visible, red-edge and short-wave infrared spectral band combination provided by (multi spectral instrument) MSI sensor onboard Sentinel-2 satellites constellation. Results show that all VIs are generally well correlated to ground LAI, among the 11 tested ones EVI, NDI45 and NBR shows best results for the three considered categories.

Keywords: Parametric method · Sentinel-2 Vegetation Indices · Wheat · Maize · Sensitivity analysis

1 Introduction

Leaf Area Index (LAI) is a dimensionless variable, defined as the leaf area per unit ground surface area [1, 2]. It describes several canopy scale processes related to light interception and crop physiology (e.g. photosynthesis and respiration), as well as soil-plant relationships that affect evapotranspiration and nutrient use efficiency. Therefore,

E. Borgogno-Mondino and P. Zamperlin (Eds.): ASITA 2022, CCIS 1651, pp. 222–234, 2022.
https://doi.org/10.1007/978-3-031-17439-1_16

an accurate determination of LAI is a key for spatiotemporal modelling and analysing of several land surface processes related to agroecosystem dynamics [3, 4]. Several approaches based on remotely sensed data have been utilized for assessing LAI.

Among the methodologies parametric regression using Vegetation Indices (VIs) is the most widely used. In particular, VIs approach is based on the analysis of the relation between spectral data, combination of spectral bands and biophysical parameters.

However, the use of VIs poses several issues, which currently limit their application to local cases reducing a general exportability in other context differ from the ones where the relation has been generated. The major limitation of using vegetation indices is related to the saturation effect that occurs at certain vegetation densities, which results in a non-linear response of VIs to LAI variation. This effect is particularly evident for the well-known Normalised Different Vegetation Index (NDVI) when [5] computed with broad bands in red and near-infrared (NIR) portion of the electromagnetic spectrum [6]. In order to cope with saturation, many authors had focused on the linearization of VIs response to LAI by the development and the assessment of indices based on spectral bands or calculation procedure more suited to better discriminate the effect of chlorophyll and water content [7–9]. However, assuming a linear relation between VIs and LAI would imply also to assume a non-finite domain of the response variable and that reflectance depend on a oversimplified scheme, made by one or few variables at least. Thus, despite a proliferation of indices, an accurate estimation of LAI from satellite, based on empirical approaches, is still challenging because the analysis and the interpretation of land surface reflectance are influenced by the coexistence of uncertainty sources, varying differently in time and space [10–12]. The difficulty in measuring LAI by remote increases in heterogeneous scenes, such as mosaics of crops at different phenological stages or complex mixtures of woodlands and/or grasslands [13].

Thus, a diversified ground-LAI dataset, including different sources of variability, such as different crop types over different phenology stage (Genetics - G), under different soil and climatic seasons (Environment - E) and farming condition (Management - M) should be used in order to define a generalized regression function for LAI estimation in relation able to deal with G × E × M interaction [4]. In this context, the Sentinel-2 (S2) mission from European Commission implemented by the European Space Agency (ESA), designed to agroecosystem monitoring offers a great opportunity to improve remote sensing based techniques for LAI estimation [14]. With this purpose several authors have already evaluated a number of candidate spectral regions more suited to VIs formulation, considering different crop types and phenology stages [15, 16]. In particular, VIs based on visible (VIS) and red-edge (RE) spectral regions were evaluated sensible to green LAI (vegetative stages), while the short-wave infrared (SWIR) region was evaluated suited to senescent stages [17–19]. Past research, based on hyperspectral reflectance data showed that narrow bands VIS-based and RE-based VIs were able to accurately estimate LAI of different crops, maize, soybean, potato, and wheat, using a generalized regression function [12, 20]. Moreover, due to the strong absorption by chlorophyll pigments the VIS-based indices are less sensitive at ground-LAI values > 2–3 respect to the RE-based VIs [21], while the RE region due to lower absorption by chlorophyll is more sensitive at moderate-to-high ground-LAI values [22]. Delegido et al. [16], using simulated Sentinel-2 (S2) data, demonstrated that RE based VIs were more sensible to a wide range of ground-LAI values of different crop types than VIS-based indices. Xie et al., [13] using real S2 data indicated the RE-based VIs are suitable for LAI estimation of different crop types during the entire period of growth. However, the feasibly of S2-based VIs is still under investigation, and the contribution of different spectral regions should be further assessed in order to improve LAI estimation over a wide range of ground-LAI values, considering different crop types, phenology stages, soil condition and farm management systems [16, 23].

All this considered, the objective of this study was to exploit a data set of wide range of ground LAI (monthly measurements for two crops x two seasons × 3 farms) to analyse performances of different Sentinel-2 VIs computed with bands combination in the VIS, RE and SWIR region for the estimation of LAI in mixed-crop scenario. In order to achieve this, specific objectives were:

1) to evaluate and compare the accuracy of S2-based VIs for LAI estimation by exploiting parametric regression on different crops (winter wheat and maize) under different management conditions;

2) to assess the sensitivity of VIs to ground-LAI variation;

3) to assess influence of different crops on parametric relation.

2 Materials and Methods

2.1 Test Sites

The study sites were located in Pisa, Tuscany Region, Central Italy, on a flat area over 31,500 hectares, mainly dedicated to the cultivation of arable crops. The climate is Mediterranean with a mean annual precipitation of 907 mm and a mean annual temperature of 15 °C (long term average 1986–2016). According to land cover spatial information from the Tuscany regional authorities (http://dati.toscana.it/), in 2018–2019 two prevalent crop types were identified: (i) winter wheat (*Triticum aestivum L.*), among cold season cereals (ii) maize (*Zea mays L.*) among warm season crops. For the construction of the database three test sites have been identified, characterized by different soil and farm management conditions. The winter wheat and maize fields had an extension about 28 and 29 hectares respectively. Thus, ground-LAI of the two crops, during two growing seasons (2018 and 2019) have been measured in each site according to the following schedule: (i) from March to June for winter wheat, (ii) from July (late sowing) to August for maize.

2.2 Ground-LAI Measurements

Ground-LAI was measured for each crop in each site with a bi-weekly frequency by means of ceptometer SunScan Delta-t Canopy Analysis System (Delta-T Devices, Cambridge, UK). The ground-LAI measurements were collected from March to October in the 2018 and 2019 only on clear-sky days according to Sentinel-2 overpassing (at approximately 11:30 A.M. local time) with a maximum of 5 days' difference. In total 16 sampling date were scheduled for the sampling area. According to the VAlidation of Land European Remote Sensing Instruments (VALERI), the sampling strategy was based on Elementary Sampling Units (ESU) upscaling approach in order to capture the variability across the study area and within the field of each crop [24]. In total 192 samples were collected (4 ESU × 3 fields × 3 Farm × 16 time), 132 during the 2018 and 60 during the 2019 field campaign.

2.3 Sentinel-2 Data

The Copernicus Sentinel-2 (S2) is a satellite mission carrying the Multispectral Instrument (MSI) sensor with a high spatial resolution (10 m, 20 m and 60 m), high revisit capability (5 days with two satellites) and a moderately large band set (13 spectral bands) from the visible to short-wave infrared [25, 26]. The S2 Level 2A (L2A) images were downloaded from the Theia Land Data Centre, which provides time series of top canopy surface reflectance orthorectified and atmospherically corrected with MACCS-ATCOR Joint Algorithm (MAJA) [27]. A total of 16 cloud-free images, collected in correspondence of the in-situ monitoring period, were used to analyse the relationship between measured ground-LAI and VIs.

2.4 VIs Computation

Spectral reflectance data derived from Sentinel-2 were used to calculate 11 VIs, selected according to previous studies carried out on the two crop types considered in this work [13, 18, 19, 23, 28] (Table 1.).

Once the VIs were calculated, the centroid of each ESU was used to extract zonal statistics from raster images for each sampling time of S2 time series in order to couple the ground-LAI value and the VIs value. Only VIs values derived from images acquired within ±5 days from ground data collection were considered. As a result, a complete SQL database, of 192 records, of coupled ground-LAI and VIs values, was obtained for the three crops of each farm in the reference period March 2018 - October 2019.

2.5 Analysis of the Ground-LAI to VIs Relation

The relationship between ground-LAI and VIs was analysed by using: (i) linear, (ii) logarithmic and (iii) second order polynomial functions. In order to evaluate the performances of the parametric regression approach data were randomly divided in train (75%) and test (25%) dataset and functions performances were evaluated by the coefficient of determination (R^2), the Root Mean Square Error (RMSE) and the Mean Absolute Error (MAE). Furthermore, to evaluate the different VIs sensitivity to ground-LAI estimation the noise equivalent (NE) was calculated as Eq. 1.

$$NE\Delta ground - LAI = \frac{RMSE(VIvsgroundLAI)}{d(VI)/d(groundLAI)} \quad (1)$$

where d(VI)/d(ground-LAI) is the first derivative of the VI with respect to ground-LAI, and RMSE (VI vs. LAI) is the RMSE of the VI vs. ground-LAI relationship. All the statistical analysis was computed in R software. The NEΔground-LAI provides a measure of how well the VI responds to ground-LAI across its entire range of variation

Table 1. Vegetation Indices (VIs) evaluated in the study. The ρ represent reflectance of Sentinel-2.

VIs	Name	Formula	Reference
Visible			
EVI	Enhanced vegetation index	$2.5*(\rho842-\rho665)/(\rho842 + 6*\rho665-(7.5*\rho490) + 1)$	[29]
NDVI	Normalized difference vegetation index	$(\rho842-\rho665)/(\rho842 + \rho665)$	[5]
NIRv	Near-infrared reflectance of vegetation	$(\rho865-\rho665)/(\rho865 + \rho665) *\rho865$	[30]
NDVIgr		$(\rho842-\rho560)/(\rho842 + \rho560)$	
WDVI	Weighted difference vegetation index	$\rho865-\rho665*(\rho865/\rho665)$	[31]
Red-edge			
NDVIre1	NDVIRed-edge 1	$(\rho740-\rho705)/(\rho740 + \rho705)$	
NDVIre2	NDVIRed-edge 2	$(\rho783-\rho705)/(\rho783 + \rho705)$	
SeLI	Simple sentinel-2 LAI index	$(\rho865-\rho705)/(\rho865 + \rho705)$	[13]
NDI45	Normalized difference index	$(\rho705-\rho665)/(\rho705 + \rho665)$	[16]
SWIR			
NBR	Normalized burn ratio	$(\rho842-\rho2190)/(\rho842 + \rho2190)$	[32]
NDII	Normalized difference infrared index	$(\rho842-\rho1610)/(\rho842 + \rho1610)$	[33]

[34]. The NEΔground-LAI takes into the sensitivity of the VI to ground-LAI, thus providing a metric accounting for both the scattering of the points from the best-fit function and the slope of the best-fit function. In the end, to test the applicability of the identified regression models to estimate the ground-LAI over different crop type the analysis of covariance (ANCOVA) was performed. ANCOVA allows to identify if crop specific regression is significantly best performing than the mix-crop model hence indicating the capacity of the VI based regression model to be exploited across different cropping systems.

3 Results and Discussion

3.1 Ground-LAI Relation with VIs

For each VIs the best performing function was evaluated according the highest R^2 and the lowest errors (RMSE and MAE). In Table 1 are reported all the analyzed relationship between ground-LAI and VIs over the testing dataset. In general, for all the evaluated VIs, the linear model and the second order polynomial showed the best performances with $R^2 > 0.4$ and RMSE < 0.18. In particular, linear model showed a higher accuracy with

Table 2. Best-fit functions for the relationships between ground-LAI and vegetation indices (VIs) obtained over the validation dataset. The reported metrics were: (i) coefficient of determination (R^2) (ii) the Root Mean Square Error (RMSE) and (iii) the Mean Absolute Error (MAE). Model type: lm = linear; poly = second-order polynomial function and log = logarithmic

VIs	Model	a	b	c	R^2	MAE	RMSE
EVI	**lm**	**0.095**	**0.289**		**0.69**	**0.11**	**0.13**
EVI	log	0.228	0.355		0.63	0.1	0.12
EVI	poly	−0.031	0.272	0.095	0.66	0.1	0.13
WDVI	lm	0.04	0.23		0.48	0.06	0.07
WDVI	log	0.093	0.26		0.51	0.05	0.07
WDVI	**poly**	**−0.013**	**0.114**	**0.152**	**0.51**	**0.05**	**0.07**
NDVI	lm	0.128	0.359		0.5	0.13	0.16
NDVI	log	0.29	0.466		0.57	0.12	0.15
NDVI	**poly**	**−0.033**	**0.315**	**0.163**	**0.59**	**0.12**	**0.14**
NDVIgr	lm	0.125	−0.121		0.39	0.15	0.19
NDVIgr	log	0.267	−0.004		0.38	0.13	0.18
NDVIgr	**poly**	**−0.01**	**0.18**	**−0.179**	**0.4**	**0.15**	**0.18**
NIRv	**lm**	**0.061**	**0.098**		**0.51**	**0.06**	**0.08**
NIRv	log	0.142	0.147		0.5	0.06	0.08
NIRv	poly	−0.018	0.161	−0.008	0.5	0.06	0.08
SeLI	lm	0.12	0.249		0.38	0.14	0.18
SeLI	log	0.28	0.343		0.46	0.14	0.16
SeLI	**poly**	**−0.032**	**0.3**	**0.056**	**0.48**	**0.14**	**0.16**
NDVIre1	lm	0.132	0.298		0.56	0.12	0.15
NDVIre1	log	0.304	0.404		0.58	0.12	0.15
NDVIre1	**poly**	**−0.034**	**0.324**	**0.092**	**0.61**	**0.11**	**0.14**
NDVIre2	lm	0.123	0.374		0.62	0.14	0.16
NDVIre2	log	0.285	0.468		0.66	0.13	0.15
NDVIre2	**poly**	**−0.032**	**0.305**	**0.173**	**0.69**	**0.12**	**0.14**
NDI45	**lm**	**0.118**	**0.048**		**0.42**	**0.13**	**0.16**
NDI45	log	0.246	0.159		0.36	0.11	0.16
NDI45	poly	−0.009	0.165	−0.001	0.41	0.13	0.16
NBR	lm	0.13	0.202		0.55	0.14	0.16
NBR	log	0.295	0.309		0.67	0.11	0.13
NBR	poly	−0.034	0.322	−0.003	0.7	0.11	0.13

(*continued*)

Table 2. (*continued*)

VIs	Model	a	b	c	R^2	MAE	RMSE
NDII	lm	0.107	−0.007		0.59	0.11	0.13
NDII	log	0.248	0.079		0.63	0.1	0.12
NDII	poly	−0.03	0.275	−0.183	0.68	0.1	0.12

EVI, NIRv and NDI45 with R^2 of 0.69, 0.51 and 0.42 and RMSE of 0.13, 0.08 and 0.16 respectively. Similarly, [23] based on 108 ESU of the SPARC 2003 dataset, concluded that the linear model was the most suited regression function for estimating LAI values ($R^2 = 0.82$) exploiting a pool of various crops. Conversely for NDVI, WDVI, NDVIgr, SeLI, NDVIre1, NDVIre2, NDII and NBR the second order polynomial function showed the best performances with $R^2 > 0.4$ and RMSE < 0.18. These finding for the VIS and RE VI categories are in agreement with other study results [9]; The authors, using RapidEye sensors, demonstrated that when different crops (winter wheat, barley, alfalfa and maize) and vegetation stages are analysed together, relation between LAI and VIs is non-linear.

In addition, the comparison of the different fitting functions revealed that VIs with saturation behaviour at moderate/high LAI values (i.e. > 3) show polynomial function as best fitting.

3.2 VIs Sensitivity to Ground-LAI

Figure 1 shows NE Δ ground-LAI values of the best performing functions (linear and second-order polynomial) for VIS, RE and SWIR group of VIs. Because of first derivative of linear function is constant (slope), the NE values is constant across the range of ground-LAI variation. Therefore, results of linear function showed a shingly variation of NE values among all the VIs with the exception of WDVI that exhibited the highest NE values (the lowest sensitivity to LAI). Conversely, polynomial function showed that for all the VIs the NE values rapidly increase for ground-LAI > 2 m^2/m^2. By means NE analysis, several authors identified VIS and RE most appropriate regions to predict ground LAI below and above 2 respectively, and then suggested the use of composed VIs method for LAI estimation [12, 35]. However, in this study NE values, for both linear and polynomial functions, varying according to the different VIs without specific behavior in relation to spectral groups.

The ANCOVA test was performed in order to select the most accurate VIs for LAI prediction of different crop types. Thus, Fig. 2 reports the p-values of the ANCOVA test for all the evaluated VIs. Results showed that VIS based indices showed the lowest influence to crop type in the definition of the ground-LAI VIs relation. In particular, relation based on NIRv, EVI and WDVI are not significantly influenced by considered crop as demonstrated by a p-value of 0.12, 0.07 and 0.42 respectively. Conversely for the RE based indices only the NDI45 – LAI relation was uninfluenced by the crop type (p value of 0.52). Moreover, NBR (SWIR based VIs) showed a p value of 0.10 and thus was not influenced by crop type in ground-LAI predictions.

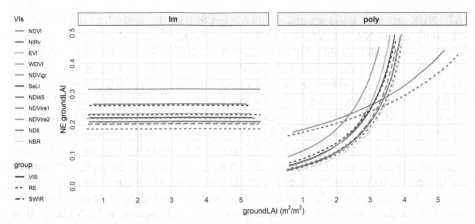

Fig. 1. Noise equivalent (NE) of the ground-LAI and VIs for linear function (lm) and second-order polynomial (poly) function. Different colours represent the VIs and line type the spectral regions (VIS, RE and SWIR).

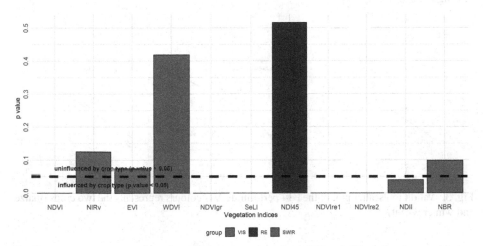

Fig. 2. Graphic representation of ANCOVA test values for the VIs – LAI relation by considering as factor crop types. Colour represents the spectral regions considered in VIs calculation. Dashed line shows the limit (p = 0.05) of statistical significance for evaluate the VIs influenced by crop factor.

4   Validation and Map Demonstration

Validation was performed on the best VIs for each category by considering regression performance (R^2 and MAE), sensitivity to LAI variation (NE) and (non)influence of crop typology (ANCOVA test). Results of validation for EVI, NDI45 and NBR are presented in Fig. 3, in general all the considered VIs can provide good LAI estimation with predictive capability ($R^2 > 0.6$ and RMSE < 0.8). The estimated LAI values, using the most suitable VIs and the most accurate function, revealed that linear model with EVI exhibited the highest correlation ($R^2 = 0.72$) and lowest error (RMSE =

0.67). NBR provided lower accuracy with respect to EVI ($R^2 = 0.67$ and RMSE 0.72). According to [13], SWIR band (S2-B12:2190 nm) can improve the LAI estimation when the regression model is calibrated on healthy crops, but it is inadequate when different conditions (phenological or water stress) were considered together. Among the three VIs, the less accurate performances were obtained by using the NDI45 with R^2 of 0.6 and RMSE of 0.78. This results was in contrast with findings of Frampton et al., [19] that identified the NDI45 the best performing VI for ground-LAI estimation over different crop types. An explanation of the different behaviour of NDI45 response according to the crop species could depend on the complex of factors affecting reflectance in relation to the covariation of soil coverage, canopy structure, water and chlorophyll content in the different growth stages [9]. Previous works have pointed out particular emphasis on chlorophyll content, whose level in the canopy significantly affect light absorbance by crop. In particular, Houborg et al., [36], analysing the LAI response to NDVI in relation to the chlorophyll content, evidenced that the decreasing of chlorophyll affects the shape of NDVI-LAI curve, lowering the saturation threshold of the index. Moreover, Xie et al., [9] evidenced that at same LAI values, leaf chlorophyll content may vary significantly among different crops.

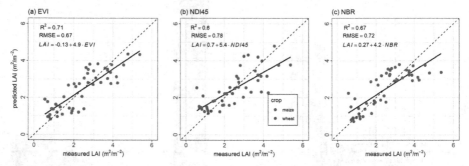

Fig. 3. Validation scatter plot of the best performing VIs colours represents the two crops (maize and winter wheat)

Figure 4 provides example of LAI maps obtained with the identified EVI – LAI relation for wheat (panel a, b and c) and maize (panel d, e and f). Values are in the expected range and changes according to crop growth. It is interesting to notice how the maps produced with S2 decametric data can provide useful information to highlight also within field variability, such data are in fact expected input also for precision farming management.

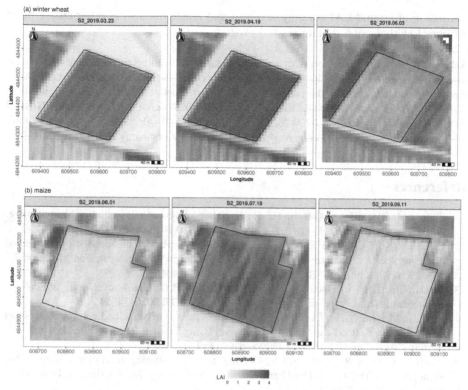

Fig. 4. Maps of estimated LAI with EVI based on linear function. In the figure above, from left to right are reported the wheat (a) stem elongation (BBCH 30), booting (BBCH 40) and maturity stages (BBCH 90) and in the figure below the emergence (BBCH 0), stem elongation (BBCH 30) and maturity (BBCH 90) of maize (b).

5 Conclusion

This study investigated performances of different S2 VIs computed with bands combination in the VIS, RE and SWIR region for the estimation of LAI in mixed-crop scenario by exploiting a dataset of wide range LAI values (two crops x two seasons x 3 farms). Results show that all S2-VIs are generally well correlated to ground LAI, among the 11 tested ones EVI, NDI45 and NBR shows best results for the three considered categories. Best parametric model was obtained with linear function, NE is below or comparable to the others one and ANCOVA tested revealed no significant influence of crop type. In fact, the identified VIs were evaluated crop type insensitive, thus may not require re-parameterization under different crop types. From the analyzed experimental data, EVI resulted the best one to be used to generate LAI product for mixed-crop scenario. The identification of VI – LAI relation insensitive to crop type may improve the predictability of LAI from a multi-crop patchiness scene. Moreover, EVI can exploit 10 m S2 bands hence producing products able to highlight within field spatial variability. Nevertheless, further studies are required to test the suitability of these VIs for the remote estimation of ground-LAI not only in wheat and maize but also in other crop type in different environmental conditions.

Acknowledgement. The authors wish to thank the staff from Scuola Superiore Sant'Anna for the filed trial management and ISPRA (Istituto Superiore per la Protezione e la Ricerca Ambientale) for their valuable support in the pre-processing stage of Sentinel-2 data. The study was part of the project E-Crops "TECNOLOGIE PER L'AGRICOLTURA DIGITALE SOSTENIBILE "(PON Ricerca e Innovazione 2014–2020 - Agrifood) and SOS-AP "SOluzioni Sostenibili per l'Agricoltura di Precisione in Lombardia" (FEASR funded by Lombardy PSR 2014–2021).

References

1. Chen, J.M., Black, T.A.: Measuring leaf area index on plant canopies with brach arquitecture. Agric. For. Meteorol. **57**, 1–12 (1991). https://doi.org/10.1016/0168-1923(91)90074-Z
2. Fassnacht, K.S., Gower, S.T., Norman, J.M., McMurtric, R.E.: A comparison of optical and direct methods for estimating foliage surface area index in forests. Agric. For. Meteorol. **71**, 183–207 (1994). https://doi.org/10.1016/0168-1923(94)90107-4
3. Bréda, N.J.J.: Leaf Area Index. In: Jørgensen, S.E., Fath, B.D., Eds., Encyclopedia of Ecology, Amsterdam, Netherlands, pp. 2148–2154 (2008) ISBN 9780080454054
4. Mao, H., Meng, J., Ji, F., Zhang, Q., Fang, H.: Comparison of Machine Learning Regression Algorithms for Cotton Leaf Area Index Retrieval Using Sentinel-2 Spectral Bands. Appl. Sci. **9**, 1459 (2019). https://doi.org/10.3390/app9071459
5. Rouse, J.W., Hass, R.H., Schell, J.A., Deering, D.W.: Monitoring vegetation systems in the great plains with ERTS. In: Third Earth Resources Technology Satellite (ERTS) Symposium. vol. 1, pp. 309–317 (1973)
6. Mutanga, O., Skidmore, A.K.: Narrow band vegetation indices overcome the saturation problem in biomass estimation. Int. J. Remote Sens. **25**, 3999–4014 (2004). https://doi.org/10.1080/01431160310001654923
7. Pasqualotto, N., Bolognesi, S.F., Belfiore, O., Delegido, J., D'Urso, G., Moreno, J.: Canopy chlorophyll content and LAI estimation from Sentinel-2: vegetation indices and Sentinel-2 Level-2A automatic products comparison. In: Proceedings of the Conference: IEEE International Workshop on Metrology for Agriculture and Forestry At: Portici, Naples. p. 7 (2019)
8. Verrelst, J., Rivera, J.P., van der Tol, C., Magnani, F., Mohammed, G., Moreno, J.: Global sensitivity analysis of the SCOPE model: what drives simulated canopy-leaving sun-induced fluorescence? Remote Sens. Environ. **166**, 8–21 (2015). https://doi.org/10.1016/j.rse.2015.06.002
9. Xie, Q., et al.: Vegetation indices combining the red and Red-edge spectral information for leaf area index retrieval. IEEE J. Sel. Top. Appl. Earth Obs. Remote Sens. **11**, 1482–1492 (2018). https://doi.org/10.1109/JSTARS.2018.2813281
10. Claverie, M., Vermote, E.F., Weiss, M., Baret, F., Hagolle, O., Demarez, V.: Validation of coarse spatial resolution LAI and FAPAR time series over cropland in southwest France. Remote Sens. Environ. **139**, 216–230 (2013). https://doi.org/10.1016/j.rse.2013.07.027
11. Ding, Y., et al.: Comparison of spatial sampling strategies for ground sampling and validation of MODIS LAI products. Int. J. Remote Sens. **35**, 7230–7244 (2014). https://doi.org/10.1080/01431161.2014.967889
12. Viña, A., Gitelson, A.A., Nguy-Robertson, A.L., Peng, Y.: Comparison of different vegetation indices for the remote assessment of green leaf area index of crops. Remote Sens. Environ. (2011). https://doi.org/10.1016/j.rse.2011.08.010

13. Pasqualotto, N., et al.: Retrieval of evapotranspiration from sentinel-2: comparison of vegetation indices, semi-empirical models and SNAP biophysical processor approach. Agronomy **9**, 663 (2019). https://doi.org/10.3390/agronomy9100663

14. Segarra, J., Buchaillot, M.L., Araus, J.L., Kefauver, S.C.: Remote sensing for precision agriculture: sentinel-2 improved features and applications. Agronomy **10**, 1–18 (2020). https://doi.org/10.3390/agronomy10050641

15. Delegido, J., Verrelst, J., Alonso, L., Moreno, J.: Evaluation of sentinel-2 red-edge bands for empirical estimation of green LAI and chlorophyll content. Sensors **11**, 7063–7081 (2011). https://doi.org/10.3390/s110707063

16. Delegido, J., Verrelst, J., Meza, C.M., Rivera, J.P., Alonso, L., Moreno, J.: A red-edge spectral index for remote sensing estimation of green LAI over agroecosystems. Eur. J. Agron. **46**, 42–52 (2013). https://doi.org/10.1016/j.eja.2012.12.001

17. Amin, E., Verrelst, J., Rivera-Caicedo, J.P., Pipia, L., Ruiz-Verdú, A., Moreno, J.: Prototyping Sentinel-2 green LAI and brown LAI products for cropland monitoring. Remote Sens. Environ. **255**, 112168 (2021) doi:https://doi.org/10.1016/j.rse.2020.112168

18. Delegido, J., Verrelst, J., Rivera, J.P., Ruiz-Verdú, A., Moreno, J.: Brown and green LAI mapping through spectral indices. Int. J. Appl. Earth Obs. Geoinf. **35**, 350–358 (2015). https://doi.org/10.1016/j.jag.2014.10.001

19. Frampton, W.J., Dash, J., Watmough, G., Milton, E.J.: Evaluating the capabilities of Sentinel-2 for quantitative estimation of biophysical variables in vegetation. ISPRS J. Photogram. Remote. Sens. **82**, 83–92 (2013). https://doi.org/10.1016/j.isprsjprs.2013.04.007

20. Kira, O., Nguy-Robertson, A.L., Arkebauer, T.J., Linker, R., Gitelson, A.A.: Informative spectral bands for remote green LAI estimation in C3 and C4 crops. Agric. For. Meteorol. **218–219**, 243–249 (2016). https://doi.org/10.1016/j.agrformet.2015.12.064

21. Haboudane, D., Miller, J.R., Pattey, E., Zarco-Tejada, P.J., Strachan, I.B.: Hyperspectral vegetation indices and novel algorithms for predicting green LAI of crop canopies: modeling and validation in the context of precision agriculture. Remote Sens. Environ. **90**, 337–352 (2004). https://doi.org/10.1016/j.rse.2003.12.013

22. Gitelson, A.A., Kaufman, Y.J., Merzlyak, M.N.: Use of a green channel in remote sensing of global vegetation from EOS-MODIS. Remote Sens. Environ. **58**, 289–298 (1996). https://doi.org/10.1016/S0034-4257(96)00072-7

23. Verrelst, J., et al.: Experimental Sentinel-2 LAI estimation using parametric, non-parametric and physical retrieval methods – a comparison. ISPRS J. Photogram. Remote. Sens. **108**, 260–272 (2015). https://doi.org/10.1016/j.isprsjprs.2015.04.013

24. Baret, F., et al.: VALERI : a network of sites and a methodology for the validation of medium spatial resolution land satellite products. Remote Sens. Environ. **76**, 36–39 (2005)

25. Drusch, M., et al.: Sentinel-2: ESA's Optical High-Resolution Mission for GMES Operational Services. Remote Sens. Environ. **120**, 25–36 (2012). https://doi.org/10.1016/j.rse.2011.11.026

26. Gascon, F., et al.: Copernicus sentinel-2A calibration and products validation status. Remote Sens. **8**, 1–78 (2017). https://doi.org/10.20944/PREPRINTS201610.0078.V1

27. Lonjou, V., et al.: MACCS-ATCOR joint algorithm (MAJA). Remote Sensing of Clouds and the Atmosphere XXI **10001**, 1000107 (2016). https://doi.org/10.1117/12.2240935

28. Herrmann, I., Pimstein, A., Karnieli, A., Cohen, Y., Alchanatis, V., Bonfil, D.J.: LAI assessment of wheat and potato crops by VENμS and Sentinel-2 bands. Remote Sens. Environ. **115**, 2141–2151 (2011). https://doi.org/10.1016/j.rse.2011.04.018

29. Huete, A.R., Didan, K., Miura, T., Rodriguez, E.P., Gao, X., Ferreira, L.G.: Overview of the radiometric and biophysical performance of the MODIS vegetation indices. Remote Sens. Environ. **26**, 195–213 (2002). https://doi.org/10.1080/0965156x.2013.836857

30. Badgley, G., Field, C.B., Berry, J.A.: Supplementary materials canopy near-infrared reflectance and terrestrial photosynthesis. Sci. Adv. **3**, 1602244 (2017). https://doi.org/10.1126/sciadv.1602244

31. Clevers, J.G.P.W.: Application of a weighted infrared-red vegetation index for estimating leaf area Index by correcting for soil moisture. Remote Sens. Environ. **29**, 25–37 (1989). https://doi.org/10.1016/0034-4257(89)90076-X

32. Key, C.H., Benson, N.C.: Measuring and remote sensing of burn severity: the CBI and NBR. In: Neuenschwander, L.F., Ryan, K.C., (eds) Proceedings Joint Fire Science Conference and Workshop Vol. II, University of Idaho and International Association of Wildland Fire, p. 284 (1999)

33. Gonsamo, A.: Normalized sensitivity measures for leaf area index estimation using three-band spectral vegetation indices. Int. J. Remote Sens. **32**, 2069–2080 (2011). https://doi.org/10.1080/01431161.2010.502153

34. Gitelson, A.A., Peng, Y., Huemmrich, K.F.: Relationship between fraction of radiation absorbed by photosynthesizing maize and soybean canopies and NDVI from remotely sensed data taken at close range and from MODIS 250m resolution data. Remote Sens. Environ. **147**, 108–120 (2014). https://doi.org/10.1016/j.rse.2014.02.014

35. Nguy-Robertson, A., Gitelson, A.A., Peng, Y., Viña, A., Arkebauer, T., Rundquist, D.: Green leaf area index estimation in maize and soybean: combining vegetation indices to achieve maximal sensitivity. Agron. J. **104**, 1336–1347 (2012). https://doi.org/10.2134/agronj2012.0065

36. Houborg, R., Boegh, E.: Mapping leaf chlorophyll and leaf area index using inverse and forward canopy reflectance modeling and SPOT reflectance data. Remote Sens. Environ. **112**, 186–202 (2008). https://doi.org/10.1016/j.rse.2007.04.012

Hyperspectral and LiDAR Data for the Prediction via Machine Learning of Tree Species, Volume and Biomass: A Contribution for Updating Forest Management Plans

Daniele Michelini[1] (ID), Michele Dalponte[2] (ID), Angelo Carriero[3] (ID), Erico Kutchartt[4] (ID), Salvatore Eugenio Pappalardo[1] (ID), Massimo De Marchi[1] (ID), and Francesco Pirotti[4,5(✉)] (ID)

[1] Master in GIScience and UAV, Department of Civil, Environmental and Architectural Engineering (ICEA), University of Padova, Via 8 Febbraio, 2, 35122 Padova, Italy
[2] Research and Innovation Centre, Fondazione Edmund Mach, via E. Mach 1, 38098 San Michele all'Adige, Italy
[3] Servizio Foreste - Provincia Autonoma di Trento, Via G.B. Trener, 3, 38121 Trento, TN, Italy
[4] TESAF Department, University of Padova, Viale dell'Università, 16, 35020 Legnaro, PD, Italy
francesco.pirotti@unipd.it
[5] CIRGEO Interdepartmental Research Center in Geomatics, University of Padova, Viale dell'Università, 16, 35020 Legnaro, PD, Italy

Abstract. This work intends to lay the foundations for identifying the prevailing forest types and the delineation of forest units within private forest inventories in the Autonomous Province of Trento (PAT), using currently available remote sensing solutions. In particular, data from LiDAR and hyperspectral surveys of 2014 made available by PAT were acquired and processed. Such studies are very important in the context of forest management scenarios. The method includes defining tree species ground-truth by outlining single tree crowns with polygons and labeling them. Successively two supervised machine learning classifiers, K-Nearest Neighborhood and Support Vector Machine (SVM) were used. The results show that, by setting specific hyperparameters, the SVM methodology gave the best results in classification of tree species. Biomass was estimated using canopy parameters and the Jucker equation for the above ground biomass (AGB) and that of Scrinzi for the tariff volume. Predicted values were compared with 11 field plots of fixed radius where volume and biomass were field-estimated in 2017. Results show significant coefficients of correlation: 0.94 for stem volume and 0.90 for total aboveground tree biomass.

Keywords: Species classification · Forest parameters · Tree-crowns · Remote sensing · Earth observation · Artificial intelligence

1 Introduction

The Autonomous Province of Trento (PAT, the acronym in Italian) has always had a strong forestry vocation, also given the large forest area that it manages: about 390,000

© The Author(s), under exclusive license to Springer Nature Switzerland AG 2022
E. Borgogno-Mondino and P. Zamperlin (Eds.): ASITA 2022, CCIS 1651, pp. 235–250, 2022.
https://doi.org/10.1007/978-3-031-17439-1_17

hectares, or 63% of its entire territory. Most of this area is publicly owned: together with the grazing areas they are part of the forest planning effort (about 397,000 hectares) and are managed in a timely and precise manner through the drafting of local area management plan (LAMP). A small portion of this area (about 77,000 hectares) is grouped into Forest Inventories, which are containers that aggregate small and fragmented private properties that have not had a LAMP since 1995. After 25 years it is necessary to understand what changes have taken place during this time lapse regarding tree species composition, stem volume and aboveground tree biomass distribution, which are information that are requested by PAT legislation [1].

To date, remote sensing technologies are increasingly used in the forestry sector, especially as a support during the back-office phase of field-based surveys. In the case of LAMP, these surveys are mainly used for determining the tree species compositions of the property and thus divide forest areas in forest units by identifying tree species composition and the prevailing height of the stands.

The operations of identifying and classifying the tree species compositions and estimating stem volume and aboveground tree biomass usually take place during the surveys in the field. The collection of information and the drafting of a LAMP therefore involves a substantial financial commitment and working hours in the field. In this work we test the hypothesis that remote sensing, in particular hyperspectral and LiDAR data, can reduce the effort in the field by predicting tree species composition and prevalent tree heights over the study area.

Among the remote sensing technologies mentioned, LiDAR is certainly the most used for predicting stem volume and aboveground tree biomass since the first experiments dating back to 1970. Nowadays LiDAR technology can represent a tool for making accurate measurements, allowing rapid data acquisition to the point of being integrated into the forest planning strategies of many countries [2, 3]. The classification of forest species is another aspect that highly relies on hyperspectral images that can be surveyed from airborne platforms, but also more recently unmanned airborne vehicles (UAVs). Hyperspectral data cubes have seen an increase in attention, driven by several scientific studies [4–6].

In various scenarios, hyperspectral sensors can provide data that have shown the possibility of discriminating many tree species with very high precision. Tropical habitats [4], and Mediterranean habitats [7] have shown to be able to distinguish up to 23 different tree species. Also noteworthy is the possibility of being able to discriminate different species of conifers using hyperspectral data [8, 9]; in these two investigations, six species of conifers were separated with 70–90% accuracy.

The aim of this specific work is (i) to test the use of hyperspectral data for the identification of the main tree species of Trentino; (ii) integrate LiDAR data into an automatic classification system in order to discriminate forest types and units; (iii) assess volume and biomass estimation from processing LiDAR data.

2   Materials and Methods

2.1   Study Area

The areas covered by this investigation are located in the southern part of PAT in Italy and consist of some forest parcels owned by private individuals, located in the municipalities of Calliano, Folgaria, Rovereto and Volano. The privately owned forest stands that do not reach an adequate size to be included in a LAMP are grouped in the inventories of the cadastral municipality in which they are located. These inventories are "management reservoirs" where stand and population information are summarized and, at the same time, where forest cuts made by the owners are communicated, by law, to the PAT Forest Service. The private inventories subject to this analysis are the following: Calliano III and Castelpietra in the Municipality of Calliano, Noriglio in the Municipality of Rovereto, Volano and Folgaria in the Municipalities of the same name (Fig. 1).

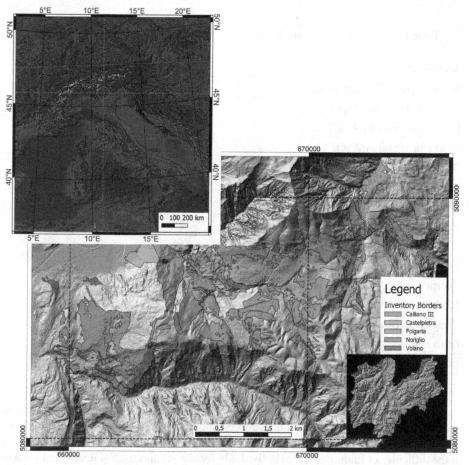

Fig. 1. Study area; in the top panel is the overall view with geographic coordinates and the bottom is a detail with coordinate reference system UTM-WGS84 zone 32.

The inventories of Castelpietra, Calliano III and Volano are located entirely in the drainage basin of the Rio Cavallo, while Folgaria is located between the latter, the Centa stream and the Lavarone interzone which, in part, overlooks the Astico stream; finally Noriglio is located between the Rio Cavallo and the Leno stream.

2.2 Surveys

The ground surveys consisted of identifying areas to use to train and test the model. These test areas are georeferenced points representing individual trees labeled with species name. Initially 253 trees were defined and geolocated by the PAT Forest Service. Subsequently they were integrated with more surveys in the field, expanding the number up to a total of 891. About 580 individuals (~65%) were used for training the model for species classification and biomass/model estimation and the rest ~35% for testing the model performance using accuracy metrics. Table 1 reports for each species the number for training and test samples.

Table 1. List of species and number for samples used for the training and test phases.

Species name	Training	Test
Norway spruce (*Picea abies* Karst.)	115	61
Silver fir (*Abies alba* Mill.)	53	24
Larch (*Larix decidua* Mill.)	78	43
Scots pine (*Pinus sylvestris L.*)	60	30
Black pine (*Pinus nigra* Arn.)	31	15
Beech (*Fagus sylvatica* L.)	71	39
Downy oak (*Quercus pubescens* Willd.)	17	8
Hop-hornbeam (*Ostrya carpinifolia* Scop.)	28	18
Manna ash (*Fraxinus ornus* L.)	14	9
European ash (*Fraxinus excelsior* L.)	12	7
Sycamore (*Acer pseudoplatanus* L.)	16	12
Birch (*Betula pendula* Roth)	10	10
Turkey oak (*Quercus cerris* L.)	3	2
Other conifers	12	5
Other broadleaves	60	28

The survey includes fifteen tree species which are not homogeneously distributed within the area. Some species are under-represented and some over-represented due both to the specialization of some species in certain ecological niches (*e.g.*, *Abies alba*), and to the difficulty of finding suitable individuals for the ground truth (intertwined foliage and rarity of the species). To compare the predicted biomass and volume, data deriving from private inventories made in 2017 by the PAT were used.

2.3   Remote Sensing Data

The PAT LiDAR data were acquired with the ALT M Gemini laser-scanning system (ALTM 3100 EA and LMS Q780) with an average point density of 10 pts/m^2. From this survey three products are available and were used in this investigation: the raw point cloud, the Digital Terrain Model (DTM) and the Canopy Height Model (CHM).

The hyperspectral survey was carried out with a CASI 1500 sensor from the Itres manufacturing company, capable of acquiring bands in the visible and near infrared (VNIR) range of the electromagnetic spectrum, from 0.38 to 1.05 μm with up to 288 spectral channels or bands, with a Field of View (FOV) of 40°. It is a pushbroom sensor with an across-track size of 1500 pixels. The survey campaign was carried out in fifteen days of flight that resulted in 268 strips that were processed to 39 batches of contiguous areas.

The mosaic process was carried out with the following steps: (i) radiometric calibration, (ii) mosaicking and normalization. Mosaicking the tiles was carried out using the R programming environment. Due to the excessive spectral noise, the first 7 bands and the last 8 bands were eliminated. The radiometric calibration was considered using a single strip as reference and all bands were analyzed, band by band. The mosaicking was carried out using the Mosaicking function of the ENVI® software and, in particular, without carrying out any further calibration. The last step was to normalize the data to reduce the differences in mosaic illumination and at the different times the strips were acquired. The normalization affected each pixel of the image based on the average of the spectral signature of the pixel itself:

$$x_{new} = \frac{x}{\frac{1}{N}\sum_{i=1}^{N} x_i} \tag{1}$$

where x is the value of the pixel to normalize, x_{new} is the value of the normalized pixel, x_i is the value of the pixel to normalize on the band i, and N is the number of image bands. ENVI® software was also used for normalization and in particular the sum data bands and band math operations.

2.4   Soil Morphology Analysis

The analysis of the local topography (elevation, slope and aspect) was essential to determine the prevailing forest type, for example the Altimontana xerica spruce forest. The height above sea level was calculated by analyzing the DTM and dividing it into altitude classes using the QGIS Raster calculator, while the slope and exposure were determined starting from the raster analysis tools of QGIS.

2.5   Delineation of Tree Crowns

The CHM is a raster image that represents the heights of the foliage. These images are extrapolated from LiDAR data or a normalized digital terrain surface model (nDSM) and are typically used in the forestry field to collect information useful for forest management [10, 11]. The CHM is also used as a basis for many important calculations, so its accuracy is of fundamental importance. An example of these applications is represented by the biomass estimation [12] and the specific composition [13], some authors have obtained good results starting from the extraction of the "model trees" from a CHM. Others, on the other hand, started from CHM for the delineation of stands [14] and for the identification of suitable habitats for fauna species [15].

In this work, starting from LiDAR data in LAS format, the CHM was extracted using the *lidR* library in R program. The function used is *grid_canopy* which is based on the *pitfree* algorithm. The process involves the creation of several triangulations at different heights from which different CHMs are extracted which are then combined to generate the final CHM [2]. The most recent LiDAR surveys have a density of points such as to allow the extraction of individual tree crowns (ITC) and there are numerous methods to do this [12, 16–19].

In this case study we opted for the *itcLiDAR* approach [12] inside the *itcSegment* library within the R environment. This library is able to extract the ITCs starting from a LAS file. This approach identifies the treetops within a raster CHM and from there defines the individual crowns around the highest point of the canopy. The same parameters were used throughout the survey area (Table 2).

Table 2. Parameters of the *itcLiDAR* algorithm used in this study.

Variable	Value	Variable	Value
resolution	0.5	TRESHSeed	0.55
MinSearchFilSize	3	minDIST	5
MaxSearchFilSize	7	maxDIST	40
TRESHCrown	0.6	HeightThreshold	2

Table 3. Parameters for equation for the main tree species (Eq. 4).

P.	Tree species						
	P. abies	*A. alba*	*L. decidua*	*F. sylvatica*	*P. silvestris*	*P. cembra*	*P. nigra*
a	0.000177	0.000163	0.000108	0.000055	0.000102	0.000188	0.000129
b	1.564254	1.706560	1.407756	1.942089	1.918184	1.613713	1.763086
c	1.051565	0.941905	1.341377	1.006420	0.830164	0.985266	0.938445
d_0	3.694650	3.694650	3.694650	4.009100	3.694650	3.694650	3.694650

2.6 Spectral Feature Selection

Numerous studies have reported that, with regard to the characterization of a forest stand, it is more important the position of the bands in the spectrum, with respect to the number of spectral bands [20, 21]. Some authors have reported how the classification of tree species is facilitated by using bands in the near infrared, subject to a lower amount of noise due to the atmospheric effects of the medium infrared [4, 22] and in the red bands [20, 23].

The hyperspectral survey used in this investigation is characterized by 122 bands distributed over all the visible and near infrared spectrum and thus for this reason, before moving on to the classification phase, a feature selection operation was performed. In this study, a feature selection method based on the Sequential Forward Floating Selection (SFFS) algorithm and the Jeffries-Matusita distance [24, 25] was used to identify the set of the suboptimal bands. Once the spectral bands to be used were identified, the actual classification was carried out.

2.7 Classifiers

In this study we used two non-parametric supervised machine learning classifiers: (1) K-Nearest Neighborhood and (2) Support Vector Machine (SVM).

The K-Nearest Neighborhood supervised non-parametric classification algorithm defines, starting from the training data, the average values of each class in the n-dimensional space defined by the input features. The result is an average of the classes with as many values as there are classes identified in the training data. The Euclidean distance of each pixel from the various centroids of the classes defined by the training areas is then calculated; finally, the pixels are attributed to the class whose centroid is placed at the minimum distance [26]. The SVM algorithm (supervised non-parametric classification algorithm) is based on the principle that the space of the starting features can be transformed into a higher-dimensional space, in which the classes are linearly separable. The transformation is performed using a Gaussian-type kernel function, the Radial Basis Function. As for the previous algorithm, the hyperspectral raster file, the ground truth vector file and the list of bands to be used were used. The raster has also been classified several times with different cost parameters C.

The starting data for the classification are the hyperspectral images, that are in raster stack format, and a polygonal vector file of the ground truths where each polygon geometry is labeled with the species and are used as training data and the list of bands to be used for the classification. The vector file of the truths on the ground was obtained starting from the file of the canopy polygons extracted by canopy delineation done in the previous step. The file was validated using ground surveys that geo-positioned trees with a Global Navigation Satellite System (GNSS) and assigned tree species on the ground. The point file was then brought into the QGIS environment, and a spatial join with the delineated ITCs polygons provides the species' information to the training and test ITCs.

2.8 Biomass and Volume Estimation Models

The biomass estimate was calculated starting from the LiDAR survey and in particular from the normalized LAS point cloud with which the crowns were extracted using the itcLiDAR R package; together with the extension of the tree canopy crowns, the package also reports the area and tree height for each of them. For the actual calculation, two equations were used that identify aboveground biomass (AGB) and volume. These were compared using the allometric Jucker equation [27] and the Scrinzi tariff volume equation [28]. Both equations are implemented inside the R libraries mentioned above. These two equations, as well as all existing allometric calculations, are based on the tree diameter as the basis for the volume estimate. Since this cannot be measured directly from the LiDAR survey, it was estimated using the equation identified by Jucker [27]. This equation takes into account, in addition to the height, also the diameter of the crown. In fact, although there is strong correlation between height and crown diameter, the relationship between these two variables varies greatly both within the species and as a function of climate and structure [29–32].

It should also be noted that, while taking these parameters into consideration, it is complex to identify a unique equation [29–36]. In most cases, trees grow very tall in order to capture as much light as possible until, once they reach the maximum height, they develop above all the diameter. Hence, a group of large individuals can have very different diameters. The relationship between crown size and diameter, on the other hand, tends to remain more constant over time as the stem of the plant must continue to grow to maintain stability and water supply [35, 37, 38], even after reaching the maximum height. For this reason, these two parameters are strongly correlated even in trees with large diameters [39].

AGB is a parameter strongly correlated to height and crown diameter (H × CD) which sees a great variation between functional groups, that is between gymnosperms and angiosperms. The most suitable equation identified, once taking into account the different relationships between angiosperms and gymnosperms, is the following:

$$AGB_{predicted} = (0.016 + \alpha_G) \times (H \times CD)^{(2.013 + \beta_G)} \times exp\left(\frac{0.204^2}{2}\right) \quad (2)$$

where α_G and β_G are functional group-dependent parameters representing the difference in scale constant α and scale exponent β between angiosperms and gymnosperms (gymnosperms: $\alpha_G = 0.093$ and $\beta_G = -0.223$; angiosperms: $\alpha_G = 0$ and $\beta_G = 0$). The Scrinzi tariff volume equation, on which the second estimation method is based, is as follows:

$$V = b_0 + b_1 G + b_2 GP_s + b_3 GP_s I_t + b_4 GP_s B_d \quad (3)$$

where G is the basal area per hectare, b_0, b_1, b_2, b_3 and b_4 are the regression coefficients, P_s is the stereometric potential index of the species, I_t is the tariff index, and B_d is the barycentric dimensional index.

The authors also developed the equation for estimating the volume of the tree trunk to be used in a double entry table:

$$V = a(d - d_0)^b \times h^c \quad (4)$$

where h is the total height of the plant and d the diameter at breast height while a, b, c and d_0 are parameters that depend on the different tree species and are reported in the table below (Table 3):

3   Results

3.1   Determination of the Species

From the feature selection process 35 bands of interest were identified for classification. Figure 2 shows an extract of the cartography resulting from three of the different classifications used:

a) K-Nearest Neighborhood
b) Support Vector Machine with all surveyed species;
c) Support Vector Machine with aggregations of species: we analyzed only the species that are subject to forest planning management (spruce, silver fir, larch, scots pine, black pine and beech) while the rest were grouped into three forest types (ornoo-ostrio-oak, maple-ash, other broad-leaved trees and other conifers).

The first visible evidence in Fig. 2 (panel A) is the presence of a gap that cuts the map obliquely; this is an area where in the hyperspectral images some bands had problems. These bands are variable and usually range from band 1 (0.39640 µm) to band 10 (0.43940 µm). In many analyzes, the bands of that range extracted from the feature selection have been manually eliminated (in this case we went from 35 to 28 bands). By eliminating these bands, the edge effect between one stripe and the next was also limited, as visible in the other two panels. The edge effect is due to the time elapsed between two stripes acquisitions, that sometimes is very long (a morning).

Panel C (Fig. 2) shows the result obtained by the SVM classifier with the parameter C set to 10, by carrying out a test based on the classification of only the most important species in Trentino and grouping the others into similar species. Table 4 shows the main accuracy metrics for the classifiers used. Accuracy is defined as the ratio of correct values (true positives) over the total number of values, and precision is defined as the ratio of correct values (true positives) over all values for a specific class, including false. The F-score measures the accuracy of the test that takes into account precision and recall (the number of true positives divided by the number of true positives plus false negatives).

The best results are those related to the classification carried out with SVM and its parameter C set to 10, both for the tree species being analyzed and for the other metrics identified. The classification accuracy of the most important species from the point of view of forest management range from 96% for black pine to 73% for beech; even firs (spruce: 85%, silver fir: 90%) performed well. Good precision (91%) was also obtained for the black pine. Lower performances resulted in the identification precision values of silver fir (55%), often confused with red fir. The F-score, on the other hand, goes from 48% for beech to 71% for black pine while most of the other species still reach a satisfactory score: spruce 70%, silver fir 62% and larch 65%.

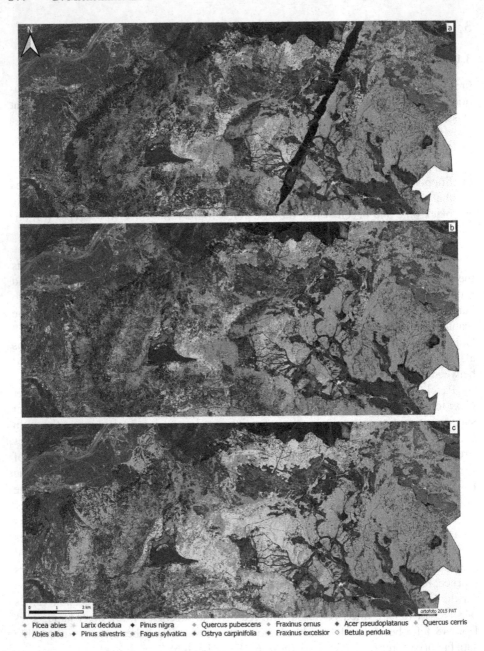

Picea abies ◆ Larix decidua ◆ Pinus nigra ◆ Quercus pubescens ◆ Fraxinus ornus ◆ Acer pseudoplatanus ◆ Quercus cerris
Abies alba ◆ Pinus silvestris ◆ Fagus sylvatica ◆ Ostrya carpinifolia ◆ Fraxinus excelsior ◇ Betula pendula

Fig. 2. Hyperspectral classification comparison: (a) K-Nearest Neighborhood; (b) SVM with all surveyed species; (c) SVM with aggregations of species.

Table 4. Accuracy metrics from test data sets. Acc. = accuracy, Prec. = Precision.

Species	K-means			SVM all species			SVM subset of species		
	Acc.	Prec.	F	Acc.	Prec.	F	Acc.	Prec.	F
P. abies	78%	64%	56%	85%	75%	70%	69%	53%	52%
A. alba	85%	44%	55%	90%	55%	62%	80%	39%	41%
L. decidua	76%	44%	50%	85%	59%	65%	65%	33%	42%
P. silvestris	78%	37%	42%	82%	42%	49%	73%	32%	32%
P. nigra	94%	63%	69%	96%	91%	71%	91%	60%	60%
F. sylvatica	74%	64%	49%	73%	51%	48%	65%	54%	47%
Q. pubescens	92%	17%	12%	95%	100%	44%	77%	0%	–
O. carpinifolia	85%	63%	45%	88%	73%	44%	70%	36%	32%
F. ornus	92%	–	–	93%	100%	12%	76%	7%	9%
F. excelsior	92%	0%	–	93%	25%	13%	89%	17%	12%
A. pseudoplatanus	90%	83%	34%	92%	83%	36%	88%	67%	31%
B. pendula	94%	–	–	94%	100%	33%	82%	15%	17%
Q. cerris	97%	40%	44%	99%	100%	67%	86%	11%	16%
Other conifers	99%	100%	67%	99%	100%	75%	97%	100%	33%
Other broadleaves	83%	68%	51%	84%	70%	55%	78%	61%	49%

3.2 Estimation of Volume and Above Ground Biomass

The above ground biomass and volume equations are species-specific, therefore each ITC that was delineated in the initial steps is labeled with a species using the results from the classification step. To do this the majority statistic within each single ITC is used over all classified pixels inside the ITC. The specific equation was then applied to each tree/canopy to calculate tree-based AGB and stem volume.

At the end of the process tree AGB/volume values, expressed in m^3 and a biomass value, expressed in kg, were aggregated for each area. The biomass represents the dendrometric biomass above ground (AGB). In order to verify these data, as reference data we used the fixed-area surveys that were carried out on behalf of the PAT on all private forests in Trentino. These are surveys on circular areas of 15 m radius where all tree individuals with a trunk diameter at breast height (DBH) greater than 7.5 cm have been measured for height and diameter and the Eqs. (2–4) used to calculate volume and AGB. The number of parcels that were used to compare ground-truth is relatively small (11) but provides a rigorous comparison. The eleven areas were also scattered and they are also at a great distance from each other and forest compositions are also quite different. This is also visible from the great heterogeneity of the quantities estimated and reported in Table 5.

Table 5. Biomass and volume results from observed ground truth values (Ob) and estimated predicted values (Pr) for volume (V) and above ground biomass (AGB).

Area		1	2	3	4	5	6	7	8	9	10	11
V (m^3)	Ob	3.00	3.33	57.87	21.32	15.41	12.22	14.53	25.09	18.42	6.74	20.51
	Pr	1.02	1.32	63.92	13.14	12.22	3.19	5.67	12.40	11.57	0.34	0.23
AGB (Mg)	Ob	1.84	1.99	26.95	11.82	7.49	6.10	7.24	12.76	9.21	4.04	12.25
	Pr	1.07	1.45	37.01	8.99	9.19	2.68	5.39	9.53	7.43	5.48	3.68

Finally, in Fig. 3, the scatter plots are shown which show a good correlation between the data, even if at times significantly different. This is also proved by the correlation coefficient (R): 0.94 for the stem volume and 0.90 for the aboveground tree biomass.

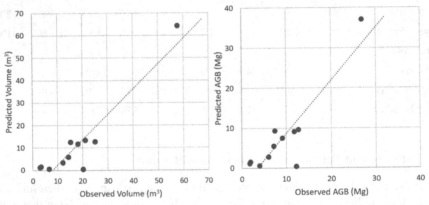

Fig. 3. Predicted vs. observed stem volume and aboveground biomass scatter plots respectively with R = 0.94 and R = 0.90.

4 Discussion and Conclusions

Comparing the classifiers used, SVM is by far the one that produces the most reliable results in this study. Other machine learning methods such as random forest have proven also to perform very well, with some advantages in many cases not only in forest environments [40–42]. Considering the distribution of the main species analyzed, Norway spruce is the one that reaches the best accuracy, notably thanks to the greater number of field samples used to train the model. The silver fir, dominant only in the area where the hyperspectral relief shows some defects, is very susceptible to false positives towards the spruce class, while maintaining a very high accuracy. Larch has a high number of false positives, which affects its accuracy and F-score. The determination of the Scots pine shows excellent results in Noriglio inventory area, while in the Folgaria area it is less efficient also with respect to the larch class. For the black pine, on the other hand, the classifier provides better results despite the fact that the number of ground-truths is not very high. As the beech tree is the most present and easiest to identify broadleaf tree, it appears to have numerous false negatives, especially regarding the analysis in the total area, which affects its accuracy.

The estimate of the tree biomass and the tariff volume is good despite the limited number of comparison areas and the parameters set for the determination of the foliage. A very important aspect to take into consideration is precisely the parameters with which the tree canopy crown of the plants were extracted. Given the extent of the area, we used parameters that would be general and adapt to different scenarios. It is reasonable to hypothesize that this brings higher errors than using site-specific parameters, in the estimated volume and biomass from LiDAR data.

The objective of this study was to outline the main features needed to identify the forest units of some Forest Inventories and to provide an overview of the biomass present starting from some remote sensing data available over PAT. The main conclusions that emerge from this work are:

(i)   the presence of a high point density LiDAR survey is fundamental for a good result of the processing [43]: the identification of the canopy height with as little error as possible allows not only the estimation of biomass and volumes but also a correct classification of the species - approaches like full-waveform metrics [44] can provide in some cases improvements, but are more complex to process;

(ii) among the two classifiers used only SVM gave optimal results; the survey carried out on an area that is too large generates excessive noise in the model due to a frequency difference in the incident and reflected electromagnetic waves, the same thing can be said in the case of surveys carried out with orthogonal streaks to the slopes and too distant in time;

(iii) among the species analyzed, the one that resulted easier to identify is certainly the spruce, probably also thanks to the widespread diffusion of this species; the choices of individual trees for the field data is fundamental and they cannot always be found in adequate numbers for all the species (*e.g.*, silver fir and hornbeam) or in optimal conditions (crowns intersected or subjected at the time of the hyperspectral survey).

Author Contributions. All authors contributed to the study conception and design. Michelini designed and carried out the methodology, and wrote the first draft of the paper. Dalponte and Carriero supported conception and data collection. Kutchartt carried out reviews and extensive editing. Pappalardo and De Marchi supervised the conceptual design and reviewed the paper. Pirotti reviewed the first draft and supervised the methodological approach. All authors commented on previous versions of the manuscript and have read and approved the final manuscript.

References

1. Provincia Autonoma di Trento: Le Foreste in Trentino. Tratto da Servizio Foreste e Fauna. https://forestefauna.provincia.tn.it/Foreste/Foreste-in-Trentino/Le-foreste-in-Trentino

2. Næsset, E.: Airborne laser scanning as a method in operational forest inventory: status of accuracy assessments accomplished in Scandinavia. Scand. J. For. Res. **22**, 433–442 (2007). https://doi.org/10.1080/02827580701672147
3. Woods, M., et al.: Operational implementation of a LiDAR inventory in Boreal Ontario. For. Chron. **87**, 512–528 (2011). https://doi.org/10.5558/tfc2011-050
4. Clark, M.L., Roberts, D.A., Clark, D.B.: Hyperspectral discrimination of tropical rain forest tree species at leaf to crown scales. Remote Sens. Environ. **96**, 375–398 (2005). https://doi.org/10.1016/j.rse.2005.03.009
5. Martin, M.E., Newman, S.D., Aber, J.D., Congalton, R.G.: Determining forest species composition using high spectral resolution remote sensing data. Remote Sens. Environ. **65**, 249–254 (1998). https://doi.org/10.1016/S0034-4257(98)00035-2
6. Thenkabail, P.S., Lyon, J.G., Huete, A.: Hyperspectral Remote Sensing of Vegetation. CRC Press, New York (2011). https://doi.org/10.1201/b11222
7. Dalponte, M., Bruzzone, L., Vescovo, L., Gianelle, D.: The role of spectral resolution and classifier complexity in the analysis of hyperspectral images of forest areas. Remote Sens. Environ. **113**, 2345–2355 (2009). https://doi.org/10.1016/j.rse.2009.06.013
8. Gong, P., Pu, R., Yu, B.: Conifer species recognition: an exploratory analysis of in situ hyperspectral data. Remote Sens. Environ. **62**, 189–200 (1997). https://doi.org/10.1016/S0034-425 7(97)00094-1
9. Yu, B., Ostland, M., Gong, P., Pu, R.: Penalized discriminant analysis of in situ hyperspectral data for conifer species recognition. IEEE Trans. Geosci. Remote Sens. **37**, 2569–2577 (1999). https://doi.org/10.1109/36.789651
10. Bortolot, Z.J., Wynne, R.H.: Estimating forest biomass using small footprint LiDAR data: an individual tree-based approach that incorporates training data. ISPRS J. Photogramm. Remote Sens. **59**, 342–360 (2005). https://doi.org/10.1016/j.isprsjprs.2005.07.001
11. Forzieri, G., Guarnieri, L., Vivoni, E.R., Castelli, F., Preti, F.: Multiple attribute decision making for individual tree detection using high-resolution laser scanning. For. Ecol. Manag. **258**, 2501–2510 (2009). https://doi.org/10.1016/j.foreco.2009.09.006
12. Dalponte, M., Coomes, D.A.: Tree-centric mapping of forest carbon density from airborne laser scanning and hyperspectral data. Methods Ecol. Evol. **7**, 1236–1245 (2016). https://doi.org/10.1111/2041-210X.12575
13. Hill, R.A., Thomson, A.G.: Mapping woodland species composition and structure using airborne spectral and LiDAR data. Int. J. Remote Sens. **26**, 3763–3779 (2005). https://doi.org/10.1080/01431160500114706
14. Mustonen, J., Packalén, P., Kangas, A.: Automatic segmentation of forest stands using a canopy height model and aerial photography. Scand. J. For. Res. **23**, 534–545 (2008). https://doi.org/10.1080/02827580802552446
15. Broughton, R.K., Hinsley, S.A., Bellamy, P.E., Hill, R.A., Rothery, P.: Marsh tip *Poecile palustris* territories in a British broad-leaved wood. Ibis **148**, 744–752 (2006). https://doi.org/10.1111/j.1474-919X.2006.00583.x
16. Hyyppä, J., Kelle, O., Lehikoinen, M., Inkinen, M.: A segmentation-based method to retrieve stem volume estimates from 3-D tree height models produced by laser scanners. IEEE Trans. Geosci. Remote Sens. **39**, 969–975 (2001). https://doi.org/10.1109/36.921414
17. Ferraz, A., et al.: 3-D mapping of a multi-layered Mediterranean forest using ALS data. Remote Sens. Environ. **121**, 210–223 (2012). https://doi.org/10.1016/j.rse.2012.01.020
18. Eysn, L., et al.: A benchmark of Lidar-based single tree detection methods using heterogeneous forest data from the alpine space. Forests **6**, 1721–1747 (2015). https://doi.org/10.3390/f6051721
19. Strîmbu, V.F., Strîmbu, B.M.: A graph-based segmentation algorithm for tree crown extraction using airborne LiDAR data. ISPRS J. Photogramm. Remote Sens. **104**, 30–43 (2015). https://doi.org/10.1016/j.isprsjprs.2015.01.018

20. Heikkinen, V., Tokola, T., Parkkinen, J., Korpela, I., Jääskeläinen, T.: Simulated multispectral imagery for tree species classification using support vector machines. IEEE Trans. Geosci. Remote Sens. **48**, 1355–1364 (2010). https://doi.org/10.1109/TGRS.2009.2032239

21. Dalponte, M., Bruzzone, L., Gianelle, D.: Tree species classification in the Southern Alps based on the fusion of very high geometrical resolution multispectral/hyperspectral images and LiDAR data. Remote Sens. Environ. **123**, 258–270 (2012). https://doi.org/10.1016/j.rse.2012.03.013

22. Jones, T.G., Coops, N.C., Sharma, T.: Assessing the utility of airborne hyperspectral and LiDAR data for species distribution mapping in the coastal Pacific Northwest, Canada. Remote Sens. Environ. **114**, 2841–2852 (2010). https://doi.org/10.1016/j.rse.2010.07.002

23. Cho, M.A., Skidmore, A.K.: A new technique for extracting the red edge position from hyperspectral data: the linear extrapolation method. Remote Sens. Environ. **101**, 181–193 (2006). https://doi.org/10.1016/j.rse.2005.12.011

24. Pudil, P., Novovičová, J., Kittler, J.: Floating search methods in feature selection. Pattern Recognit. Lett. **15**, 1119–1125 (1994). https://doi.org/10.1016/0167-8655(94)90127-9

25. Bruzzone, L., Roli, F., Serpico, S.B.: An extension of the Jeffreys-Matusita distance to multiclass cases for feature selection. IEEE Trans. Geosci. Remote Sens. **33**, 1318–1321 (1995). https://doi.org/10.1109/36.477187

26. Richards, J.A., Jia, X.: Remote Sensing Digital Image Analysis. Springer, Heidelberg (1999). https://doi.org/10.1007/978-3-662-03978-6

27. Jucker, T., et al.: Allometric equations for integrating remote sensing imagery into forest monitoring programmes. Glob. Change Biol. **23**, 177–190 (2017). https://doi.org/10.1111/gcb.13388

28. Scrinzi, G., Galvagni, D., Marzullo, L.: I nuovi modelli dendrometrici per la stima delle masse assestamentali in Provincia di Trento. Provincia Autonoma di Trento (2010)

29. Banin, L., et al.: What controls tropical forest architecture? Testing environmental, structural and floristic drivers. Glob. Ecol. Biogeogr. **21**, 1179–1190 (2012). https://doi.org/10.1111/j.1466-8238.2012.00778.x

30. Lines, E.R., Zavala, M.A., Purves, D.W., Coomes, D.A.: Predictable changes in aboveground allometry of trees along gradients of temperature, aridity and competition. Glob. Ecol. Biogeogr. **21**, 1017–1028 (2012). https://doi.org/10.1111/j.1466-8238.2011.00746.x

31. Hulshof, C.M., Swenson, N.G., Weiser, M.D.: Tree height-diameter allometry across the United States. Ecol. Evol. **56**, 1193–1204 (2015). https://doi.org/10.1002/ece3.1328

32. Jucker, T., Bouriaud, O., Coomes, D.A.: Crown plasticity enables trees to optimize canopy packing in mixed-species forests. Funct. Ecol. **29**, 1078–1086 (2015). https://doi.org/10.1111/1365-2435.12428

33. Muller-Landau, H.C., et al.: Testing metabolic ecology theory for allometric scaling of tree size, growth and mortality in tropical forest. Ecol. Lett. **9**, 575–588 (2006). https://doi.org/10.1111/j.1461-0248.2006.00904.x

34. Feldpausch, T.R., et al.: Tree height integrated into pantropical forest biomass estimates. Biogeosciences **9**, 3381–3403 (2012). https://doi.org/10.5194/bg-9-3381-2012

35. Iida, Y., et al.: Wood density explains architectural differentiation across 145 co-occurring tropical tree species. Funct. Ecol. **26**, 274–282 (2012). https://doi.org/10.1111/j.1365-2435.2011.01921.x

36. Chave, J., et al.: Improved allometric models to estimate the aboveground biomass of tropical trees. Glob. Change Biol. **20**, 3177–3190 (2015). https://doi.org/10.1111/gcb.12629

37. Sterck, F., Bongers, F.: Crown development in tropical rain forest trees: patterns with tree height and light availability. J. Ecol. **89**, 1–13 (2001). https://doi.org/10.1046/j.1365-2745.2001.00525.x

38. King, D.A., Clark, D.A.: Allometry of emergent tree species from saplings to above-canopy adults in a Costa Rican rain forest. J. Trop. Ecol. **27**, 573–579 (2011). https://doi.org/10.1017/S0266467411000319
39. Hemery, G.E., Savill, P.S., Pryor, S.N.: Applications of the crown diameter-stem diameter relationship for different species of broadleaved trees. For. Ecol. Manag. **215**, 285–294 (2005). https://doi.org/10.1016/j.foreco.2005.05.016
40. Tonion, F., Pirotti, F., Faina, G., Paltrinieri, D.: A machine learning approach to multispectral satellite derived bathymetry. ISPRS Ann. Photogramm. Remote Sens. Spat. Inf. Sci. **3**, 565–570 (2020). https://doi.org/10.5194/isprs-annals-V-3-2020-565-2020
41. Bernsteiner, H., et al.: Machine learning for classification of an eroding scarp surface using terrestrial photogrammetry with NIR and RGB imagery. ISPRS Ann. Photogramm. Remote Sens. Spat. Inf. Sci. **3**, 431–437 (2020). https://doi.org/10.5194/isprs-annals-V-3-2020-431-2020
42. Fernandez-Delgado, M., Cernadas, E., Barro, S., Amorim, D.: Do we need hundreds of classifiers to solve real world classification problems? J. Mach. Learn. Res. **15**, 3133–3181 (2014)
43. Pirotti, F., Kobal, M., Roussel, J.R.: A comparison of tree segmentation methods using very high density airborne laser scanner data. Int. Arch. Photogramm. Remote Sens. Spat. Inf. Sci. **XLII-2/W7**, 285–290 (2017). https://doi.org/10.5194/isprs-archives-XLII-2-W7-285-2017
44. Pirotti, F., Laurin, G., Vettore, A., Masiero, A., Valentini, R.: Small footprint full-waveform metrics contribution to the prediction of biomass in tropical forests. Remote Sens. **6**, 9576–9599 (2014). https://doi.org/10.3390/rs6109576

Forest Height Estimation Using Sentinel-1 Interferometry. A Phase Unwrapping-Free Method Based on Least Squares Adjustment

Samuele De Petris[1]($\boxtimes$) (ID), Giovanni Cuozzo[2] (ID), Claudia Notarnicola[2] (ID), and Enrico Borgogno-Mondino[1] (ID)

[1] Department of Agriculture, Forestry and Food Sciences, University of Torino, 10095 Grugliasco, TO, Italy
`{samuele.depetris,enrico.borgogno}@unito.it`
[2] Institute for Applied Remote Sensing, EURAC Research, Bolzano, BZ, Italy
`{giovanni.cuozzo,claudia.notarnicola}@eurac.edu`

Abstract. Forest height is a fundamental parameter in forestry. SAR interferometry (InSAR) has been widely used to retrieve digital elevation models (DEM), which are designed to provide a continuous representation of Earth topography, including forests. The ordinary InSAR framework requires a further phase unwrapping step in order to recover unambiguously the actual topography over the entire scene. The latter was proved to fail over vegetation due to low coherence values and therefore all algorithms tend to avoid these areas during the unwrapping, making InSAR-derived DEM over vegetation very unreliable. In this work, an alternate technique was coupled to least squares adjustment (LSA) with the aim of retrieving accurate forest heights avoiding phase unwrapping. It was computed entirely using free available Sentinel-1 data and SNAP ESA software. A mean absolute error equal to 2.6 m was found and it is consistent to the one estimated by LSA theoretical uncertainty. Preliminary outcomes suggest that proposed approach could be a valid alternative to retrieve forest height based on free data/software constituting an example of technological transfer of SAR technology into forest operative sector.

Keywords: Forest height · SAR · Interferometry · Least squares adjustment

1 Introduction

Forest height is a fundamental parameter in forestry. It is related to above ground biomass, timber volume [1] and canopy vertical structure [2]. Forest height is often measured using hypsometers with a precision of 1 m to 3 m during ground operations [3, 4]. Unfortunately, ground surveys take a long time and are expensive, so they are sparse across forested areas. Remote sensing, on the other hand, may cover this gap by giving continuous forest height estimates over large regions that are even more precise than ground measurements [5]. Space-based earth observation missions are well-suitable for forest needs, allowing a mapping and monitoring of large regions, as well as the early

E. Borgogno-Mondino and P. Zamperlin (Eds.): ASITA 2022, CCIS 1651, pp. 251–262, 2022.
https://doi.org/10.1007/978-3-031-17439-1_18

detection of changes and regular updating of forest attributes [6–9]. Synthetic aperture radar (SAR) is known to be sensitive to forest geometry characteristics, allowing data to be recorded in any weather state, even over equatorial/tropical ones where clouds are usually always present. SAR interferometry (InSAR) methodology has been widely used to retrieve digital elevation models (DEM), which are designed to provide a continuous representation of Earth topography, including forests.

In this context, satellite missions, such as the European Union's (EU) Copernicus Sentinels, are known to provide large amounts of data that may be used to support environmental research and land management. However, even if web-based services based on this data are becoming operational, technical transfer appears to be restricted at the moment [10–12]. SAR imaging, in the broader context of satellite open data, exhibits a significant limitation in terms of accessing operational services, due to the complex nature of data processing and data availability [13, 14]. The typical InSAR processing methodology includes a phase unwrapping step intended at unambiguously reconstructing the local topography, which is usually accomplished by processing the entire scene unitarily. This method has proven to be particularly ineffective over vegetation due to low coherence values; as a result, ordinary algorithms avoid these areas (or failed) during unwrapping [15, 16], making InSAR-derived DEMs exceedingly unreliable over vegetation [17]. Furtherly, ordinary unwrapping processing that InSAR software accomplishes, in the most of cases, hides the consciousness and an easy interpretability of results, making derived measures unreliable. In this paper, an alternative technique not been extensively explored in the literature [18–20], is discussed for generating more trustworthy and precise estimations of forest height using InSAR without phase unwrapping. This method changes the working paradigms moving from a mapping problem to a retrieval one based on the comparison between a forest pixel interferogram and a reference one closely located outside the forest.

In this work, the previous-mentioned approach was combined to least squares adjustment with the aim of retrieving accurate forest heights avoiding phase unwrapping. In order to facilitate the operational transfer of our deductions, proposed approach relays entirely on free available and accessible SAR open data and software (guaranteed cost-effective) with a special focus on the Copernicus Sentinel-1 (S1) mission.

2   Materials and Methods

2.1   Study Area

The area of interest (AOI) is called "Staffarda forest" and is located in the lowland part of Cuneo province (NW- Italy). AOI sizes about 4 km^2 (Fig. 1) and is characterized by the presence of Pedunculate oak-hornbeam forest [21]. In Italy, this type of forests has an high naturalistic values since it is one of the last remaining mixed floodplain forests in northern Italy and one of the most endangered ecosystems in Europe [22].

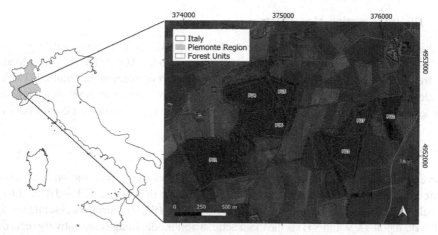

Fig. 1. AOI location and forest units (FUs). Google Satellite base map was adopted (WGS84 UTM32N reference frame).

2.2 Reference Data

The digital surface model (DSM) derived by an aerial photogrammetric survey (rDSM) was adopted to test the accuracy of proposed approach (Fig. 2). The aerial survey was performed in December 2019 by *Digisky s.r.l.* company. After the image block bundle adjustment [23], the photogrammetric point cloud was filtered and regularized into a gridded DSM with a ground sample distance (GSD) of 0.3 m having a plano-altimetric accuracy of 0.2 m. Moreover, a global navigation satellite system (GNSS) ground survey was performed to define forest units (FUs). FUs are forest areas having homogeneous vertical/horizontal structure and same expected silvicultural treatments adopted in forest planning [24]. A total of 7 FUs was acquired having a mean extension of about 15 ha.

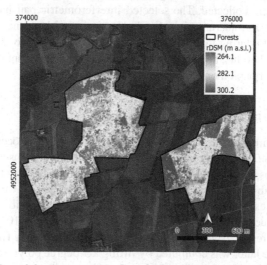

Fig. 2. rDSM (GSD = 0.3 m) over AOI. Google Satellite base map was adopted (WGS84 UTM32N reference frame).

2.3 Digital Elevation Model Data

In this work, the Piemonte region Digital Terrain Model (DTM) was used to geocode SAR-derived products and obtain elevation information for AOI. DTM was downloaded for free from Piemonte Geoportal (https://www.geoportale.piemonte.it/cms/). DTM has an elevation accuracy of about 0.6 m [25, 26] and was updated in 2009. It is provided already ortoprojected into WGS84 UTM 32N reference system with a GSD of 0.5 m.

2.4 Sentinel-1 Imagery

Currently, S1 is one of the largest space-borne mission giving free and open access to SAR data. The S1 mission is a two-satellite constellation that records C-band data (5.6 cm wavelength). Over land, the interferometric wide swath (IW) acquiring backscattered signal in dual pole (VV and VH) is the main acquisition mode. Images are natively recorded in SAR geometry (Range and Azimuth) and complex values (I/Q components). S1 mission is particularly suitable for a wide range of applications, including forest mapping, due to its medium-high spatial resolution and short revisit time (6 days). Furthermore, the European Space Agency (ESA) makes the free software SNAP (Sentinel Application Platform) available to users, allowing an easier and efficient use of Copernicus Program products [17, 27]. To preliminary test the proposed approach a single interferometric pair was selected and downloaded from Alaska Satellite Facility online tool [28]. Ordinarily, InSAR-derived DEM accuracy is higher for long baselines [29], nevertheless, this condition appears to fail over vegetation. In fact, longer baselines make coherence decreasing, thus negatively affecting forest height accuracy. Moreover, also temporal baseline could significantly affect interferogram reliability. Since forests are continuously changing, longer the temporal baseline, lower the associated coherence (temporal decorrelation) [17, 30]. Therefore, short temporal baseline and winter acquisitions are more suitable for forest height retrieval in temperate zone [31]. To take care about these issues, two S1 single look complex (SCL) IW images in ascending mode acquired on 20th and 26th December 2019 were collected. The selected interferometric pair has a perpendicular baseline of about 90 m guaranteeing the shorter temporal baseline available from S1 mission (i.e. 6 days) during the 2019 winter season over AOI. To avoid decorrelation errors due to rainfall events, no precipitation events were found from the meteorological data (https://www.arpa.piemonte.it/) in observed period.

2.5 Methodology and Data Processing

Interferogram Computation. The interferometric pair was pre-processed using the free software *SNAP vs 8.0* provided by ESA and according to common used processing chain [32]. The basic steps include TOPS Split, which reduces the SLC data to selected number of bursts within a sub-swath. Then, enhanced spectral diversity [33] were applied to refine the azimuth offset estimation and exploit a better fine coregistration provided by back geocoding. Subsequently, coherence estimates were mapped using 10×2 window (range and azimuth pixels respectively) and the interferogram was computed including flat-earth phase removal. The latter was computed by fitting a 5-degree polynomial involving 501 points distributed over interferogram. Using data from orbits state vectors and images metadata the flat-earth phase was then subtracted from the complex interferogram. After deburst, Goldstein filter was applied [34] using a window size of 3 × 3. Multilooking was also applied to the interferogram and coherence complex values [35] generating images having squared pixels sizing of about 30 × 30 m. Finally, the multilooked interferogram and coherence data were projected into WGS84/UTM 32N reference frame using DTM and Range Doppler terrain correction [36].

Interferometric Phase Modelling. The SAR interferometry technique is based on the image pairs processing acquired from multiple locations separated by distance known as a baseline (B). This criterion allows to recover topography via a simple geometric relationship [37]. The contribution to the interferometric phase provided by local topography is determined according to Eq. 1.

$$\frac{\partial \Delta \varphi}{\partial h} = \frac{4\pi \, Bn}{\lambda \, R \sin \theta} \tag{1}$$

where $\Delta \varphi$ is the interferometric phase; h is the target point elevation; λ is the radar wavelength; R is the sensor-target slant range; θ is the antenna off-nadiral angle (look angle) and Bn is the normal baseline length. Based on this relationship, the ordinary InSAR framework requires a further phase unwrapping step in order to recover unambiguously the actual topography over the entire scene. The latter was proved to fail over vegetation due to low coherence values and therefore all algorithms tend to avoid these areas during the unwrapping [15, 16] making InSAR-derived DEM over vegetation very unreliable [17]. An alternative approach, not widely explored in literature, to avoid phase unwrapping was proposed by [18–20]. This method changes the working paradigms moving from a mapping problem to a retrieval one involving, at least, one interferogram pixel from flat terrain close to forest and other over forest canopy. In principle, from Eq. 1, the elevation difference of a given point, $dh(x, y)$, corresponding to the interferometric phase difference at that point is given by Eq. 2. This approach is similar to a topographic levelling problem [38] where the surveyed variable is the heigh difference (dh) between two points (Eq. 2).

$$dh(x, y) = \omega \left[\Delta \varphi(x, y) - \Delta \varphi^{RP} \right] \tag{2}$$

where $\Delta \varphi(x, y)$ and $\Delta \varphi^{RP}$ are the target point (in this work a forest point) and reference point interferometric phases respectively; ω is the sensitivity of the topography to an interferometric phase variation and it is computed as the inverse of Eq. 1 as proposed by [37]. Subsequently, forest point absolute elevation, $h(x, y)$, can be obtained by adding dh to, at least, one reference point having known elevation (h^{RP} - Eq. 3).

$$h(x, y) = dh(x, y) + h^{RP} \tag{3}$$

It is worth to highlight that Eq. 2 not requires phase unwrapping (phase ambiguity term) only if the expected height difference is lower than height of ambiguity (*HOA*) of the interferometer [19, 39]. Since in this work HOA (deduced by SNAP metadata) is equal to 161.2 m, phase ambiguity term can be neglected because temperate forest heights do not commonly exceed 60 m [2] and no significant terrain variation exists in AOI.

Forest Height Retrieval Using Least Squares Adjustment. In this work, the paradigm in Eq. 3 was applied to flattened interferogram-derived measures and solved by a least squares adjustment (LSA) approach. LSA is a statistical tool commonly adopted to contemporarily solve levelling network and estimate the corrections to be given to the height difference measurements in order to make them all congruent to each other and satisfy the geometrical relations existing between them. In levelling network problem dh differences should be theoretically equal to 0. Unfortunately, in real levelling loop it does not happen due to measurement errors. Especially in interferometry, phase measures over vegetation are affected by many limitations mainly due to noise induced by canopy volume and signal decorrelation. This unneglectable noise deeply affects dh resulting from Eq. 2 application. All systematic errors like orbital-related ones, flattening residuals and atmospheric delays can be mathematically removed by considering height differences between neighboring interferogram pixels. In fact, measure differencing is expected to reasonably remove these errors assuming that they occur similarly for close points [40] (in this work interferogram pixels are at most 2 km apart). Nevertheless, LSA can mitigates the accidental observational errors component [41, 42] by share it according to defined weights across the system of equations of Eq. 4.

$$\hat{\beta} = (A^T\,W\,A)^{-1} \cdot (A^T\,W\,L) \tag{4}$$

where $\hat{\beta}$ is a column vector containing the elevations of the target points, $h(x, y)$ (in m a.s.l.); A is the design matrix; W is the weights matrix; L is the observations vector. Starting from flattened interferogram, the average interferometric phase value ($\mu_{\Delta\varphi}$) was computed for each FU and its uncertainty estimated by applying the variance propagation law to the average operator assuming pixels having different uncertainty (Eq. 5).

$$\sigma_{\mu_{\Delta\varphi}} = \sqrt{\frac{\sum_{i=1}^{n}\sigma_{\Delta\varphi(x,y)}^2}{n^2}} \tag{5}$$

where n is the number of interferogram pixels for each FU; $\sigma_{\Delta\varphi(x,y)}$ is the uncertainty of interferometric phase pixel. $\sigma_{\Delta\varphi(x,y)}$ was deeply proved [18, 29, 43] to be related to local coherence magnitude and can be properly computed using Eq. 6.

$$\sigma_{\Delta\varphi(x,y)} = \frac{1}{\sqrt{2NL}}\frac{\sqrt{1 - |\gamma(x,y)|^2}}{|\gamma(x,y)|} \tag{6}$$

where NL is the multilooking factor i.e. the number of pixels used to compute the complex multilooked interferogram (in this work set = 20); $|\gamma(x, y)|$ is the local coherence magnitude. To fix the datum above so that $\hat{\beta}$ can be computed, observations having known elevation are required in the LSA system. These were derived by photointerpreting some ground flat areas (GFAs) on coherence map. GFA was delineated as polygon layer searching for highly coherence patches ($\gamma > 0.8$) representing ground level having no significant vegetation cover. Built-up areas were excluded from GFA delineation by simultaneously checking their presence on the available Google Earth true colour orthophoto updated in 2019. The mean DTM and interferometric phase values were computed and assigned to GFA centroids (hereafter called reference points - RPs). A total of 7 GFA (and RP) were selected in AOI. Concerning LSA, **L** was defined as vector containing $n \cdot (n - 1)/2$ height differences computed by Eq. 2 and involving $\mu_{\Delta\varphi}$, RP phases and ω. The latter was computed as $HOA/2\pi$, where HOA was obtained by image pair metadata available in SNAP. Additionally, RP elevations were added to **L** to fix the datum. To take in to account the uncertainty of each observation in the LSA system, **W** elements were defined as the inverse of $\sigma_{\mu_{\Delta\varphi}}$ containing $\mu_{\Delta\varphi}$ (Eq. 7), while a value of 100 was assigned for constraining observations involving RP. The latter value was preventively set to 100 to give a high weight to RP elevations observations constraints.

$$W = \begin{bmatrix} 100 & 0 & \cdots & 0 & 0 & \cdots & \cdots & \cdots & 0 \\ 0 & 100 & 0 & 0 & 0 & \cdots & \cdots & \cdots & 0 \\ \vdots & \ddots & \ddots & \vdots & 0 & \cdots & \cdots & \cdots & 0 \\ 0 & \cdots & 0 & 100 & 0 & \cdots & \cdots & \cdots & 0 \\ 0 & \cdots & \cdots & \cdots & \delta_{i,j} & 0 & \cdots & \cdots & 0 \\ 0 & \cdots & \cdots & \cdots & 0 & \vdots & \ddots & \vdots & \vdots \\ 0 & \cdots & \cdots & \cdots & 0 & \cdots & \cdots & \cdots & \delta_{i,j} \end{bmatrix} \tag{7}$$

where $\delta_{i,j} = \frac{1}{\sigma_{\mu_{\Delta\varphi}}}$. Once $\widehat{\beta}$ was estimated, the uncertainty of each $h(x, y)$, $\sigma_{\widehat{\beta i}}$, can be estimated according to Eq. 8.

$$\sigma_{\widehat{\beta i}} = \sqrt{\mathbf{C}_{\boldsymbol{\beta\beta}}ii} \tag{8}$$

where $\mathbf{C}_{\boldsymbol{\beta\beta}}ii$ are the diagonal elements of $\mathbf{C}_{\boldsymbol{\beta\beta}}$. The latter is the variance-covariance matrix of the parameters computed according to Eq. 9.

$$\mathbf{C}_{\boldsymbol{\beta\beta}} = \frac{\varepsilon^t W \varepsilon}{m-n} \cdot (A^T W A)^{-1} \tag{9}$$

where ε is the LSA residuals vector; m is the number of equations in LSA (in this work 91, i.e. $14 \times 13/2$) and n is the number of unknowns (in this work equal to 14 $h(x, y)$).

Validation. To test the accuracy of elevation estimates over forest, a validation set based on rDSM was generated. In particular, the mean $(\overline{rDSM})$ and standard deviation (σ_{rDSM}) values were computed for each FUs. Finally, the mean absolute error (MAE) [44] was computed comparing only forest $h(x, y)$ estimates of $\widehat{\beta}$ and $\overline{rDSM}$. To test the presence of a significant bias in the proposed approach, normality of errors was assessed by *Shapiro-Wilk* test [45] and the *t-test* was used to assess zero-mean condition of errors [46].

3   Results and Discussions

3.1   Interferogram Computation

After the pre-processing in SNAP, the multilooked flattened interferogram and coherence maps were generated (Fig. 3) and subsequently managed by ordinary GIS tool.

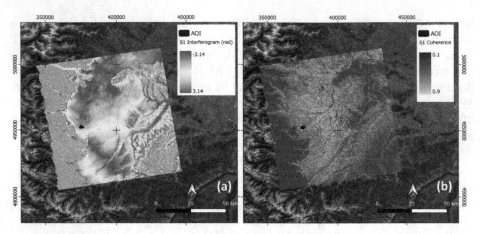

Fig. 3. (a) Multilooked flattened Interferogram; (b) multilooked coherence map (WGS84 UTM32N reference frame).

3.2   Forest Height Retrieval Using Least Squares Adjustment

Staring from coherence map, GFAs and RPs were generated (Fig. 4). Using a self-developed routine in *R software vs 3.0.0*, the LSA approach was implemented and performed involving $\mu_{\Delta\varphi}$, RP interferometric phases and ω. The latter was used as gain factor that allows to convert the interferometric phase difference into height difference (Eq. 2). It was computed as $HOA/2\pi$ and found equal to 25.65. To fix the datum RP elevation values were also included in the LSA.

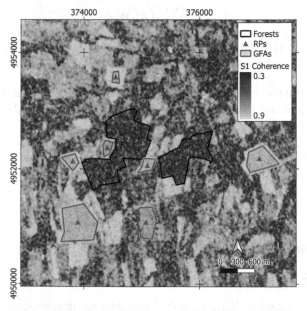

Fig. 4. Coherence map, GFAs and RPs location in AOI (WGS84 UTM32N reference frame).

3.3 Validation

FU heights, $h(x, y)$, were finally estimated by LSA and compared to $\overline{rDSM}$. Results were reported in Fig. 5. A MAE of 2.63 m was found. It is worth to remind that such accuracy is consistent with the one obtainable from ordinary ground survey based on hypsometers [4, 5] highlighting how such an approach is an effective tool that allows to give an height estimate with a density greater and greater than ordinary one based on ground surveys. It can be noted that in general, errors seldom exceed 3 m. *Shapiro-Wilk* test proved that errors are normally distributed ($W = 0.90$, *p-value* $= 0.33$). No significant bias was detected by *t-test* ($t = 0.87$, *p-value* $= 0.41$). These results suggest that the proposed approach is not affected by systematic errors; conversely a white noise like error component is present. Moreover, $\sigma_{\hat{\beta}}$ average value was 2.19 m proving that LSA theoretical uncertainty was consistent to the MAE found by comparing results to an external validation set. Finally, considering the FU σ_{rDSM}, no significant differences exist between rDSM and InSAR-LSA estimates.

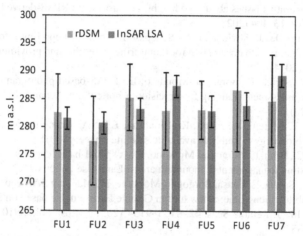

Fig. 5. Comparison between reference FU forest heights and estimated ones. Error bars are for rDSM are σ_{rDSM}, while error bars of InSAR LSA derived heights are $\sigma_{\hat{\beta}}$.

4 Conclusions

In this work, LSA was applied to S1 InSAR data to retrieve forest height over AOI. Results proved that LSA using a weights matrix involving theoretical uncertainties of interferometric phases generates estimates having a MAE of 2.6 m. No significant bias was found and the uncertainty of estimates was consistent with MAE, suggesting that no need of validation set should be necessary to test the accuracy. Unfortunately, these preliminary results were explored over a single study area and using a single winter interferometric pair. Future developments will be expected to test the robustness of such approach over different forests and involving many image pairs. Nevertheless, preliminary outcomes suggest that proposed approach could be a valid alternative to retrieve forest height based on free SAR data and open software. These features make this method a first prototype of technological transfer of SAR technology into forest operative sector for supporting in cheaper way forest management.

References

1. Segura, M., Kanninen, M.: Allometric models for tree volume and total aboveground biomass in a tropical humid forest in Costa Rica 1. Biotropica J. Biol. Conserv. **37**, pp. 2–8 (2005)
2. Hao, Z., Zhang, J., Song, B., Ye, J., Li, B.: Vertical structure and spatial associations of dominant tree species in an old-growth temperate forest. For. Ecol. Manag. **252**, 1–11 (2007)
3. Larsen, D.R., Hann, D.W., Stearns-Smith, S.C.: Accuracy and precision of the tangent method of measuring tree height. West. J. Appl. For. **2**, 26–28 (1987)
4. Bragg, D.C.: Accurately measuring the height of (real) forest trees. J. For. **112**, 51–54 (2014). https://doi.org/10.5849/jof.13-065
5. De Petris, S., Berretti, R., Sarvia, F., Borgogno Mondino, E.: When a definition makes the difference: operative issues about tree height measures from RPAS-derived CHMs. iForest-Biogeosci. For. **13**, 404 (2020)
6. Hüttich, C., Eberle, J., Shvidenko, A., Schepaschenko, D.: Supporting a forest observation system for Siberia: earth observation for monitoring, assessing and providing forest resource information (2014)
7. De Petris, S., Sarvia, F., Borgogno-Mondino, E.: RPAS-based photogrammetry to support tree stability assessment: longing for precision arboriculture. Urban For. Urban Green. **55**, 126862 (2020)
8. Vacchiano, G., Berretti, R., Motta, R., Mondino, E.B.: Assessing the availability of forest biomass for bioenergy by publicly available satellite imagery (2018)
9. Accastello, C., Brun, F., Borgogno-Mondino, E.: A spatial-based decision support system for wood harvesting management in mountain areas. Land Use Policy **67**, 277–287 (2017)
10. De Petris, S., Sarvia, F., Orusa, Borgogno-Mondino, E.: Mapping SAR geometric distortions and their stability along time: a new tool in Google Earth Engine based on Sentinel-1 image time series. Int. J. Remote Sens. **42**, 9135–9154 (2021). https://doi.org/10.1080/01431161. 2021.1992035
11. De Petris, S., Sarvia, F., Borgogno-Mondino, E.: Multi-temporal mapping of flood damage to crops using sentinel-1 imagery: a case study of the Sesia River (October 2020). Remote Sens. Lett. **12**, 459–469 (2021). https://doi.org/10.1080/2150704X.2021.1890262
12. Sarvia, F., De Petris, S., Borgogno-Mondino, E.: Multi-scale remote sensing to support insurance policies in agriculture: from mid-term to instantaneous deductions. GISci. Remote Sens. **57**, 770–784 (2020). https://doi.org/10.1080/15481603.2020.1798600
13. Reiche, J., et al.: Combining satellite data for better tropical forest monitoring. Nat. Clim. Change **6**, 120–122 (2016)
14. Vollrath, A., Mullissa, A., Reiche, J.: Angular-based radiometric slope correction for Sentinel-1 on Google earth engine. Remote Sens. **12**, 1867 (2020)
15. Goldstein, R.M., Zebker, H.A., Werner, C.L.: Satellite radar interferometry: two-dimensional phase unwrapping. Radio Sci. **23**, 713–720 (1988)
16. Chen, C.W., Zebker, H.A.: Phase unwrapping for large SAR interferograms: statistical segmentation and generalized network models. IEEE Trans. Geosci. Remote Sens. **40**, 1709–1719 (2002)
17. Braun, A.: Retrieval of digital elevation models from Sentinel-1 radar data–open applications, techniques, and limitations. Open Geosci. **13**, 532–569 (2021)

18. Hagberg, J.O., Ulander, L.M., Askne, J.: Repeat-pass SAR interferometry over forested terrain. IEEE Trans. Geosci. Remote Sens. **33**, 331–340 (1995)
19. Santoro, M., Askne, J., Dammert, P.B.: Tree height influence on ERS interferometric phase in boreal forest. IEEE Trans. Geosci. Remote Sens. **43**, 207–217 (2005)
20. Romero-Puig, N., Lopez-Sanchez, J.M.: A review of crop height retrieval using InSAR strategies: techniques and challenges. IEEE J. Sel. Top. Appl. Earth Obs. Remote Sens. (2021)
21. EEA: European forest types (2006)
22. Chianucci, F., et al.: Relationships between overstory and understory structure and diversity in semi-natural mixed floodplain forests at Bosco Fontana (Italy). iForest-Biogeosci. For. **9**, 919 (2016)
23. Capolupo, A., Saponaro, M., Borgogno Mondino, E., Tarantino, E.: Combining interior orientation variables to predict the accuracy of Rpas-Sfm 3D models. Remote Sens. **12**, 2674 (2020)
24. IPLA: Indicazioni Tecnico-Metodologiche Per La Redazione Dei Piani Forestali Aziendali – PFA (2009). http://www.regione.piemonte.it/foreste/images/files/pian_gest/dwd/nuova_legge/Indirizzi_PFA_2016_AllegatoA.pdf
25. Borgogno Mondino, E., Fissore, V., Lessio, A., Motta, R.: Are the new gridded DSM/DTMs of the Piemonte Region (Italy) proper for forestry? A fast and simple approach for a posteriori metric assessment. iForest Biogeosci. For. **9**, 901–909 (2016). https://doi.org/10.3832/ifor1992-009
26. Borgogno Mondino, E., Fissore, V., Falkowski, M.J., Palik, B.: How far can we trust forestry estimates from low-density LiDAR acquisitions? The Cutfoot Sioux experimental forest (MN, USA) case study. Int. J. Remote Sens. **41**, 4551–4569 (2020)
27. Veci, L.: SENTINEL-1 Toolbox SAR Basics Tutorial. ARRAY Systems Computing, Inc. and European Space Agency, Paris, France (2015)
28. ASF: ASF baseline tool. https://baseline.asf.alaska.edu
29. Ferretti, A., Monti-Guarnieri, A.V., Prati, C.M., Rocca, F., Massonnet, D.: INSAR Principles B. ESA Publications (2007)
30. Santoro, M., Shvidenko, A., McCallum, I., Askne, J., Schmullius, C.. Properties of ERS-1/2 coherence in the Siberian boreal forest and implications for stem volume retrieval. Remote Sens. Environ. **106**, 154–172 (2007)
31. Askne, J., Santoro, M.: Multitemporal repeat pass SAR interferometry of boreal forests. IEEE Trans. Geosci. Remote Sens. **43**, 1219–1228 (2005)
32. Grandin, R.: Interferometric processing of SLC Sentinel-1 TOPS data. In: FRINGE 2015: Advances in the Science and Applications of SAR Interferometry and Sentinel-1 InSAR Workshop, Frascati, Italy, 23–27 March 2015 (2015)
33. Yagüe-Martínez, N., et al.: Interferometric processing of Sentinel-1 TOPS data. IEEE Trans. Geosci. Remote Sens. **54**, 2220–2234 (2016)
34. Goldstein, R.M., Werner, C.L.: Radar interferogram filtering for geophysical applications. Geophys. Res. Lett. **25**, 4035–4038 (1998)
35. Huang, Y., Van Genderen, J.L.: Comparison of several multi-look processing procedures in INSAR processing for ERS-1&2 tandem mode. In: ERS SAR Interferometry, p. 215 (1997)
36. Schreier, G.: SAR geocoding: data and systems. Wichmann (1993)
37. Richards, J.A.: Remote Sensing with Imaging Radar. Springer, Heidelberg (2009). https://doi.org/10.1007/978-3-642-02020-9
38. Clancy, J.: Site Surveying and Levelling. Routledge, Milton Park (2013)
39. Soja, M.J., Persson, H., Ulander, L.M.: Estimation of forest height and canopy density from a single InSAR correlation coefficient. IEEE Geosci. Remote Sens. Lett. **12**, 646–650 (2014)
40. Hanssen, R.F.: Radar Interferometry: Data Interpretation and Error Analysis. Springer, Dordrecht (2001). https://doi.org/10.1007/0-306-47633-9

41. Ebong, M.B.: Weights for least-squares adjustments of levelling networks. Surv. Rev. **29**, 175–180 (1987)
42. Schwarz, C.R.: The trouble with constrained adjustments. Surv. Land Inf. Syst. **54**, 202–209 (1994)
43. Pepe, A., Calò, F.: A review of interferometric synthetic aperture RADAR (InSAR) multi-track approaches for the retrieval of Earth's surface displacements. Appl. Sci. **7**, 1264 (2017)
44. Willmott, C.J., Matsuura, K.: Advantages of the mean absolute error (MAE) over the root mean square error (RMSE) in assessing average model performance. Clim. Res. **30**, 79–82 (2005)
45. Shapiro, S.S., Wilk, M.B.: An analysis of variance test for normality (complete samples). Biometrika **52**, 591–611 (1965)
46. Ross, A., Willson, V.L.: One-sample T-test. In: Basic and Advanced Statistical Tests, pp. 9–12. Brill Sense (2017)

Low Density ALS Data to Support Forest Management Plans: The Alta Val Di Susa Forestry Consortium (NW Italy) Case Study

E. Ilardi[1]([✉]) [iD], V. Fissore[1] [iD], R. Berretti[2] [iD], A. Dotta[3], P. Boccardo[4] [iD],
and E. Borgogno-Mondino[2] [iD]

[1] ITHACA - Information Technology for Humanitarian Assistance Cooperation and Action,
Turin, Italy
{elisa.ilardi,vanina.fissore}@ithacaweb.org
[2] Department of Agricultural, Forest and Food Sciences, University of Torino, Turin, Italy
{roberta.berretti,enrico.borgogno}@unito.it
[3] Val Di Susa Forestry Consortium, Susa, Italy
[4] DIST - Interuniversity Department of Regional and Urban Studies and Planning,
Politecnico of Turin, Turin, Italy
piero.boccardo@polito.it

Abstract. LiDAR systems are evolving very rapidly. In recent years, in fact, the forest sector is largely taking advantage of such evolving progress. Aerial LiDAR (ALS) capability of collecting large amounts of data can directly influence the cost of ordinary in-field forest measurements. A great availability of freely accessible LiDAR data archives from public institutions, often obtained for different purposes than the forestry one, can, however, enormously contribute to forests management. The present study, based on pre-processed and freely available LiDAR-derived DTM and DSM from the Piemonte Region (NW Italy), is a further demonstration that forest planning can be valuable supported by this type of data, that proved to be able to support Forest Settlement Plans redaction. In this study, an estimate (and mapping) of the main forest structural parameters over a test area was achieved with an accuracy consistent with the one ordinarily required by planners when reviewing/setting up a new forest management plan. Moreover, this work proved that free official open data coupled with the current availability of free advanced software for data processing can make this technology easily transferrable to professionals and territory managers.

Keywords: Aerial LiDAR · CHM · DTM · DSM · Forest estimates

1 Introduction

Aerial Laser Scanning (ALS) is a high-resolution active remote sensing technique aimed at positioning points in space [8, 16, 26]. This technique represents an efficient survey technology to measure efficiently the territory, making possible its modelling [17, 20].

When working over forested areas, ALS pulses can partially penetrate tree canopies reaching their intermediate parts and, also, the ground, thus generating different sources

E. Borgogno-Mondino and P. Zamperlin (Eds.): ASITA 2022, CCIS 1651, pp. 263–274, 2022.
https://doi.org/10.1007/978-3-031-17439-1_19

of pulses reflection [10, 11, 18]. Number of penetrating pulses depends on species, structure and density of population [9].

In multi-pulses ALS systems, many reflections of the same emitted beam return to the receiver at different consequent times [7]. This phenomenon permits to get robust estimates of the main forest parameters [2, 12, 22], making such technology particularly suitable also for large and/or difficultly accessible areas. These features make ALS useful for forest inventories that, presently, rely on ground surveys including a limited number of sampling plots that are assumed to be statistically representative of the whole forest [14, 24, 28]. Field surveys are known to be highly time consuming and expensive [19] and their representativeness not always confirmed. ALS data can certainly improve deductions making possible to give more reliable estimates over large areas. This cannot however occur without ground data, whose importance remains unchanged despite the new task they account for. They are in fact called to calibrate and validate deductions from ALS [1, 21]. In other words, the most promising role that ALS data are expected to play is that of a 'robust generalizing tool' (over the whole forest) of a small number of locally operated measures achieved by plots [4].

Some limits are also known, mainly related to the unitary cost of ALS acquisitions that are particularly high when areas of interest are small [13, 15]. This limit can be somehow overcome by exploiting as much as possible ALS data collected for other purposes (urban planning, hydro-geological, civil protection etc…), admitting some compromises between costs and optimal requirements in terms of resolution, accuracy, time of acquisition [5, 25, 27].

In this study, DTMs (Digital Terrain Model) and DSMs (Digital Surface Model) available for free from the Cartographic Office of the Piemonte Region (North Western Italy), natively not designed to be used in the forest sector, were used to test their consistency with requirements for forest inventories.

2   Material and Methods

2.1   Study Area

Test site is in the municipality of Gravere, Susa Valley, NW Italian Alps, that is part of the Val di Susa and Val Sangone Mountain Community. The area is populated by pure coniferous, pure broad-leaved and mixed forest of conifers and broad-leaved. Main forest types in the area are Larici-cembretum at high altitude, and chestnut at lower altitudes. This diversified situation made possible to test eventual dependencies of forest estimates accuracy from different forest categories.

The study area is ordinarily managed by the Alta Val Di Susa Forestry Consortium (FC) and the property is of the municipality of Gravere. FC manages about 17809 ha of forest distributed over 14 municipalities.

As far as altitude is concerned, the municipality of Gravere ranges between about 600 and 2700 m a.s.l.. Plots were located out of the urbanized area, thus exploring an altitude range of 900–2000 m a.s.l.

2.2   Available Data

DTM and DSM. It is worth to remind that the specific goal of this work was to evaluate the potentialities in main forest parameter estimation from ready-to-use data. Accordingly, DTMs and DSMs obtained for free from the Piemonte Region Geoportal were used. This dataset was generated from an ALS dataset obtained during the ICE photogrammetric aerial acquisition covering the entire Piemonte Region in the period 2009–2011 [23]. Available DTM/DSM were used as-they-were, i.e. already pre-processed (filtered, classified, and regularized) and forming a raster data having a grid size of 5 m. Reference system is WGS84 UTM 32N. Declared precision is ±0.30 and ±0.60 m for 'ordinary' (open field) and 'reduced' (forest, urban) accuracy areas, respectively. In the study area nominal precision of DTM/DSM can be cautionary assumed equal to 0.60 m.

Ground Data. Thirty circular plots (radius = 15 m, area = about 707 m^2) were surveyed in the area between September and October 2016 and used as 'ground truth'.

Plots positions were chosen to ensure a good representativeness of local forest situation. Plots georeferencing was achieved by surveying the plot center by a Trimble Juno 3D - NEI GNSS (Global Navigation Satellite System). GNSS acquisition was operated with a time of recording >10 min with 5 s epochs. This made possible to operate a post-processing step for code differential correction that resulted in a final accuracy of 0.83 m @ CE95.

For each plot, the following measures were done: a) visual estimate of the percentage of foliage coverage; b) structure type (chronological class) of forest as indicated in the Regional 'Forestry Plan for the forest'; c) tree diameters (greater than 7.5 cm); d) tree heights over 1.30 m; e) forest type, according to the 'Tipi forestali del Piemonte – Metodologia e guida per l'identificazione' guide [6].

It should be noted that the time gap between ALS-derived measures (2009–2011) and the ground surveys (2016) is about 5–7 years; eventual discrepancies, especially in young stands, where tree height and volume increment (more evident for broadleaves) could have occurred, are therefore possible.

2.3   Diametric Curves Calibration from Ground Data

According to the ground-surveyed forest parameters (heights and diameters), correspondent diametric curves were calibrated for the most representative species in the area and the correspondent errors, computed. For the main tree species, diametric curves were assumed to be well modelled by Eq. 1, that is the one required when working with ALS dataset, where the direct available measure is tree height.

$$D^G = \gamma \cdot e^{\delta \cdot H^G} \tag{1}$$

where γ and δ are the model parameters to be estimated by Ordinary Least Squares (OLS). D^G and H^G the ground surveyed diameter and height values, respectively.

2.4   Forest Parameters Estimates from CHM

Refining and Calibrating CHM-Derived Estimates. Forest measures from ALS were computed with reference to the CHM (Canopy Height Model) obtained by grid differencing of the available DSMs and DTMs. CHM is a raster representation that, in forest areas, maps heights of trees with respect to the ground level.

CHM heights values lower than 4 m were masked out and excluded from successive analyses, since retained mainly related to renovation, shrubs, and scrubland (not of interest for this study). CHM was therefore oversampled, by bilinear resampling, to obtain a new grid with a step size of 2 m, trying to geometrically (horizontally) refine data analysis and smooth height variations related to abrupt variations of local canopy geometry.

Ground measures were operated at tree level, permitting species-specific calibration of dendrometric curves (Eq. 1). Nevertheless, all comparisons with CHM-derived measures were operated at plot level; consequently, some synthetic statistics were computed for the plots. Plot areas were defined as a buffer generated around its center with a radius of 15 m, thus generating circular polygons useful to compute the following statistics: (i) for ground data: average, maximum and minimum tree height (H^G_{mean}, H^G_{max}, H^G_{min}, m); average tree diameter (D^G_{mean}, cm); tree height (σ^G_h) and diameter (σ^G_d) standard deviations; (ii) for CHM-derived measures: minimum (H^L_{min}), maximum (H^L_{max}), mean (H^L_{mean}) tree height and the correspondent standard deviation (σ^L_h).

Uncertainty of height estimates from CHM was measured as MAE (Mean Absolute Error, [4]), as reported in Eq. 2.

$$MAE = \frac{1}{n} \sum_{i=1}^{n} |f_i - y_i| \tag{2}$$

where f_i is the predicted (CHM-derived) value, y_i is the ground correspondent value and n the number of observations (n. plots).

A high inconsistency between H^L_{mean} and H^G_{mean} was found (see Results section). This deprecable situation suggested that a systematic error (bias) was affecting CHM-derived data, making desirable a further assessment aimed at testing this hypothesis. Jointly considering H^G_{mean}, H^G_{min}, H^G_{max} and the correspondent H^L_{mean}, H^L_{min}, H^L_{max}, the Pearson's correlation coefficient was computed. Since a significant correlation was found ($r = 0.71$ @$p < 0.001$), a linear regression was calibrated (see Results section) and applied to minimize bias affecting CHM-derived height measures. New de-biased tree height ($\widehat{H^L}$) were therefore obtained according to Eq. 3.

$$H^G = \widehat{H^L} = \gamma \cdot H^L + \delta \tag{3}$$

where $\widehat{H^L}$ the de-biased CHM-derived tree height, H^L is the original CHM-derived tree height (plot mean, minimum and maximum were jointly considered while calibrating the model), and H^G is the ground surveyed tree height.

$\widehat{H^L}$ values were then used to estimate the correspondent average diameter at plot level using the calibrated per-species diametric models (Eq. 1). The proper diametric model for each plot was selected considering the local dominant species as mapped in the available PFT map. Diameter estimations from CHM within plots were then compared with the ground surveyed ones and the correspondent MAE computed.

Mapping Tree Height and Diameter in the Forest Stand. To generalize results over the whole forest, a vector graticule with a step size of 30 m × 30 m was generated to ensure a local estimates of forest parameters consistent with ground plot size. It is worth to remind that circular plots area size is 707 m^2, while square grid cell area is slightly higher (900 m^2). Ordinary GIS zonal statistics were used to assign to each cell of the graticule the local average tree height (H^L) from CHM. H^L was de-biased according to Eq. 3 as previously calibrated with reference to ground measures. The dominant local tree species was also mapped for all the graticule elements assuming it corresponding to the dominant one reported in the available map of Forest Types (PFT - Piani Forestali Territoriali). This made possible to estimate at grid cell level the local diameter entering the proper diametric curve (Eq. 1) with the de-biased tree height value ($\widehat{H^L}$). This step permitted to map the average height and diameter that can be locally found in the forest stand.

Estimating Tree Density. To get an estimate of tree density from CHM, the Local Maxima operator (Local Minima and Maxima tool) available from SAGA GIS (v. 8.1.1) was used [12]. This last oversees finding those pixels of CHM that could be candidate to represent the very top of a single tree. CHM-derived estimates proved to be poorly consistent with tree density values from ground measures, suggesting that a further aligning processing step was again needed.

To make up for this non-negligible gap, tree density values of plots from CHM (Φ^L) and ground surveys (Φ^G) were firstly aligned by normalization according to Eq. 4, obtaining a new local estimate of Φ^L ($\widehat{\Phi^L}$). This was separately achieved for broadleaves (B) and conifers (C).

$$\widehat{\Phi^L} = \frac{\Phi^L}{\overline{\Phi^L}} \cdot \overline{\Phi^G} \tag{4}$$

where $\overline{\Phi^L}$ and $\overline{\Phi^G}$ are the maximum tree density values from CHM and ground plots, respectively.

Remaining differences in tree density were then modelled according to Eq. 5 (B) and 6 (C):

$$\Delta\Phi_B = \left(\Phi^G - \widehat{\Phi^L}\right)_B = \alpha_B \cdot \left(\widehat{\Phi^L}\right)_B + \beta_B \tag{5}$$

$$\Delta\Phi_C = \left(\Phi^G - \widehat{\Phi^L}\right)_C = \alpha_C \cdot \left(\widehat{\Phi^L}\right)_C + \beta_C \tag{6}$$

where α and β are the coefficients of the 1st order polynomial relating $\Delta\Phi_B$ and $\Delta\Phi_C$ with $\widehat{\Phi^L}$. The new tree density estimates from CHM ($\widehat{\Phi^L}'$) were therefore separately derived for B and C according to Eqs. 7 and 8.

$$\widehat{\Phi^L}' = \widehat{\Phi^L} + \Delta\Phi_B \tag{7}$$

$$\widehat{\Phi^{L'}} = \widehat{\Phi^L} + \Delta\Phi_C \qquad\qquad (8)$$

3   Results

3.1   Summarizing Ground Data

Plot average values of the main dendrometric parameters were obtained. As regard to height values, H_{mean} ranged between 13 m and 26 m, relative standard deviation from 2.33 m to 9.37 m, and dominant height ranged between 21 m and 33 m. Considering diameter values, D_{mean} ranged between 18 cm and 48 cm, relative standard deviation from 3.57 cm to 19.83 cm.

3.2   Calibration of Dendrometric Curves from Ground Data

Tree height and diameters from ground were used to calibrate the species-specific diametric curves (Eq. 1) needed to get an estimate of tree diameters once tree height is known. Coefficients of diametric curves and correspondent MAE values are reported in Table 1. MAE values from models were assumed as reference to compare the one affecting estimates from CHM. Mean MAE value (averaged along all tree species) was found to be about 2.32 m and 4.11 cm for height and diameter estimates, respectively.

Table 1. Parameters of the calibrated diametric (Eq. 1) models. MAE is the Mean Absolute Error affecting estimates by models.

Species	N. of trees	Diametric curve coefficients		
		γ	δ	MAE (cm)
White fir	44	8.0827	0.0658	5.58
Maple	1111	6.4199	0.0607	3.92
Birch	22	9.7374	0.0532	4.56
Beech	96	7.4941	0.0600	5.61
Ash tree	198	9.1644	0.0308	3.95
Larch	359	12.5620	0.0466	6.32
Tilia	75	4.8818	0.0758	3.48
Maple-ash-tilia	384	5.9046	0.0673	3.54
Other conifers	16	11.5860	0.0500	1.55
Other broad-leaved trees	44	5.91	0.07	2.12
Chestnut	95	5.45	0.08	4.56

3.3 Refining and Calibrating CHM-Derived Estimates

Using the above mentioned 30 m × 30 m vector graticule, zonal statistics were computed from CHM (namely, H^L_{min}, H^L_{max}, H^L_{mean}, H^L_{std}) and aligned to ground estimates by Eq. 3, whose parameters were calibrated by OLS by relating CHM-derived tree height measures with ground ones (Fig. 1). Gain and offset of the calibrated 1st order polynomial model were found to be equal to 1.1599 and 3.9911, respectively.

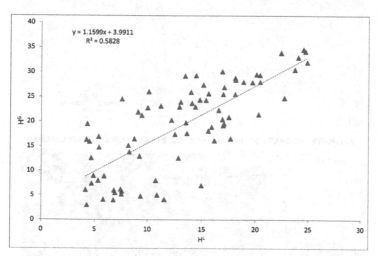

Fig. 1. Scatterplot relating ground and CHM-derived tree height measures (averaged at plot level). A 1st order polynomial was calibrated and applied to de-bias CHM-derived measures equally for all the tree species.

After application of Eq. 3, MAE values affecting CHM-derived tree height measures (average height in the plot) decreased from 7.19 m (native measures) to 4.71 m (corrected measures, $\widehat{H^L}$), corresponding to 23,6% of error compared with ground measures. De-biased $\widehat{H^L}$ tree height measures, at plots, were used to get the local estimate of the correspondent diameters using the proper per-species dendrometric model (Eq. 1, coefficient in Table 1). CHM-derived diameter estimates and ground measures were compared and the correspondent MAE computed. It resulted equal to 7.85 cm, corresponding to 23,1% of error compared to ground measures.

De-biased height and diameter mean estimations were then computed over the whole study area with reference to the vector graticule taking care of the local forest type as previously mapped with reference to PFT. Relative maps are reported in Fig. 2.

Estimating Tree Density. Local tree density from CHM was obtained with reference to the local maxima approach. Comparing counts from CHM with the correspondent ones from ground measures (in the surveyed plots), a significant underestimation was found. An average tree density of 36 trees/ha was estimated from CHM (Φ L) against 1429 trees/ha detected at the ground Φ(G). This can be related to the geometric resolution of CHM (5 m) whose size depends on the point density of the native point clouds that

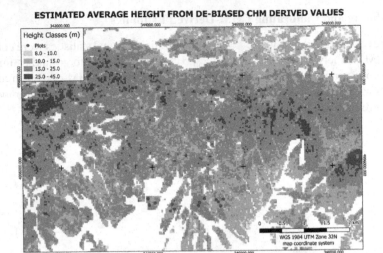

Fig. 2. Maps of averaged height (above) and diameter (below) estimations from de-biased CHM values, given for the whole forest stand. Classes were defined accordingly to the computed histograms for height and diameter values. Plots locations are given in red color. (Color figure online)

DTM and DSM were obtained from. This was averagely 0.5 points/m^2 [3] suggesting a limited capability of this type of data of detecting dominated layers and separating crowns in dense canopy. To account for this not negligible problem, Eq. 4 was initially used to rescale CHM-derived estimates using the following values: $\overline{\Phi^L} = 1429$, $\overline{\Phi^G} = 36$. New and more consistent estimates ($\widehat{\Phi^L}$) were obtained for both B and C. To further refine them, the difference $\Delta\Phi = \Phi^G - \widehat{\Phi^L}$ was computed at plot level and modelled by regression (Eqs. 5–8) against $\widehat{\Phi^L}$. Modelling was achieved separately for broadleaves and conifers. Coefficient estimates, coefficient of determination (R2) and p-value are reported in Table 2.

Table 2. Regression model coefficients, separately estimated for Broadleaves and Conifers.

Tree category	Gain (α)	Offset (β)	R^2	p-value
Broadleaves	−1.1946	876.62	0.532	<0.001
Conifers	−1.0074	275.27	0.888	<0.001

New estimates of tree density from CHM ($\widehat{\Phi^L}'$) were obtained and the mean percent error, affecting $\widehat{\Phi^L}'$, computed. It proved to be 30.8% and 23.9% for B and C, respectively. The major uncertainty in broadleaves density estimation from CHM can be related to their crown shape - that appears to present a less well-defined tip – and on forest stands that in general are denser than those of conifers. Also, we have to keep in mind that obtained results surely suffer the temporal difference between the LiDAR acquisition and ground survey (5–7 years), during which vegetation dynamics, also due to forest management abandonment, are increased causing differences in the type and structure of vegetation composition.

According to this approach, de-biased tree density estimates were computed over the whole study area and the correspondent density map created (Fig. 3).

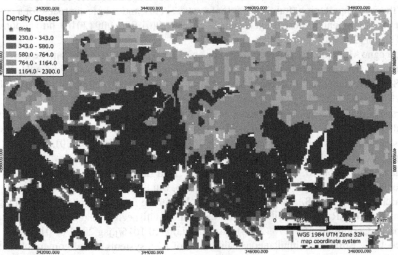

Fig. 3. Tree density map as estimated by the model with reference to CHM-derived (refined) measures. Red points are plots locations. (Color figure online)

4   Conclusions

This work highlighted that the use of low-resolution LiDAR derived data, not natively designed for forest applications, permitted to obtain estimations only at plot level, driving to a reasonable description and quantification of the main silvicultural metrics for wider forest stands, also helping in the application of eventual management policies. Further developments of this work could be the estimation of Volume parameters from LiDAR CHM values, and their subsequent comparison with Volume estimations obtained from height and diameter values collected on the ground.

Moreover, this work presented a simple method to investigate and model the presence of error bias affecting the adopted LiDAR derived data, from which improved LiDAR derived estimations can be obtained.

Finally, the work is a further demonstration that this type of data can efficiently support forest planning, proving that free official open data coupled with the current availability of free advanced software for data processing can make this technology easily transferrable to professionals and territory managers.

References

1. Armston, J.D., Denham, R.J., Danaher, T.J., Scarth, P.F., Moffiet, T.N.: Prediction and validation of foliage projective cover from Landsat-5 TM and Landsat-7 ETM+ imagery. J. Appl. Remote Sens. 3(1), 033540 (2009). https://doi.org/10.1117/1.3216031
2. Bolton, D.K., White, J.C., Wulder, M.A., Coops, N.C., Hermosilla, T., Yuan, X.: Updating stand-level forest inventories using airborne laser scanning and Landsat time series data. Int. J. Appl. Earth Observ. Geoinf. 66, 174–183 (2018). https://doi.org/10.1016/j.jag.2017.11.016
3. Borgogno Mondino, E., Fissore, V., Lessio, A., Motta, R.: Are the new gridded DSM/DTMs of the Piemonte Region (Italy) proper for forestry? A fast and simple approach for a posteriori metric assessment. iForest-Biogeosciences Forestry 9(6), 901–909 (2016). https://doi.org/10.3832/ifor1992-009
4. Borgogno Mondino, E., Fissore, V., Falkowski, M.J., Palik, B.: How far can we trust forestry estimates from low-density LiDAR acquisitions? The Cutfoot Sioux experimental forest (MN, USA) case study. Int. J. Remote Sens. 41, 4549–4567 (2020). https://doi.org/10.1080/01431161.2020.1723173
5. Brandtberg, T., Warner, T.A., Landenberger, R.E., McGraw, J.B.: Detection and analysis of individual leaf-off tree crowns in small footprint, high sampling density lidar data from the eastern deciduous forest in North America. Remote Sens. Environ. 85(30), 290–303 (2003). https://doi.org/10.1016/S0034-4257(03)00008-7
6. Camerano, P., Gottero, F., Terzuolo, P.G., Varese, P.: IPLA S.p.a.–Tipi forestali del Piemonte – Metodologia e guida per l'identificazione. p. 216, Blu Edizioni, Torino (2008)
7. García, M., Saatchi, S., Ustin, S., Balzter, H.: Modelling forest canopy height by integrating airborne LiDAR samples with satellite Radar and multispectral imagery. Int. J. Appl. Earth Observ. Geoinf. 66, 159–173 (2018). https://doi.org/10.1016/j.jag.2017.11.017
8. Hebel, M., Stilla, U.: Simultaneous calibration of ALS systems and alignment of multiview LiDAR scans of urban areas. IEEE Trans. Geosci. Remote Sens. 50(6), 2364–2379 (2012). https://doi.org/10.1109/TGRS.2011.2171974
9. Hill, R.A., Thomson, A.G.: Mapping woodland species composition and structure using airborne spectral and LiDAR data. Int. J. Remote Sens. 26(17), 3763–3779 (2011). https://doi.org/10.1080/01431160500114706

10. Huising, E.J., Pereira, L.M.G.: Errors and accuracy estimates of laser data acquired by various laser scanning systems for topographic applications. ISPRS J. Photogramm. Remote. Sens. **53**(5), 245–261 (1998). https://doi.org/10.1016/S0924-2716(98)00013-6

11. James, J.A., Watson, D.G., Hansen, W.F.: Using LiDAR data to map gullies and headwater streams under forest canopy: South Carolina, USA. CATENA **71**(1), 132–144 (2007). https://doi.org/10.1016/j.catena.2006.10.010

12. Kayitakire, F., Hamel, C., Defourny, P.: Retrieving forest structure variables based on image texture analysis and IKONOS-2 imagery. Remote Sens. Environ. **102**(3–4), 390–401 (2006). https://doi.org/10.1016/j.rse.2006.02.022

13. Ke, Y., Quackenbush, L.J., Im, J.H.: Synergistic use of QuickBird multispectral imagery and LIDAR data for object-based forest species classification. Remote Sens. Environ. **114**(6), 1141–1154 (2010). https://doi.org/10.1016/j.rse.2010.01.002

14. Kershaw, J.A., Ducey, M.J., Beers, T.W., Husch, B.: Forest Mensuration, 5th edn. Wiley Blackwell, Hoboken (2007)

15. Lefsky, M.A., Cohen, W.B., Parker, G.G., Harding, D.J.: Lidar Remote Sensing for Ecosystem Studies: Lidar, an emerging remote sensing technology that directly measures the three-dimensional distribution of plant canopies, can accurately estimate vegetation structural attributes and should be of particular interest to forest, landscape, and global ecologists. Bioscience **52**(1), 19–30 (2002). https://doi.org/10.1641/0006-3568(2002)052[0019:LRSFES]2.0.CO;2

16. Mallet, C., Bretar, F.: Full-waveform topographic lidar: state-of-the-art. ISPRS J. Photogramm. Remote. Sens. **64**(1), 1–16 (2009). https://doi.org/10.1016/j.isprsjprs.2008.09.007

17. Maltamo, M., Mustonen, K., Hyyppä, J., Pitkänen, J., Yu, X.: The accuracy of estimating individual tree variables with airborne laser scanning in a boreal nature reserve. Can. J. For. Res. **34**(9), 1791–1801 (2004). https://doi.org/10.1139/x04-05

18. Montaghi, A., Corona, P., Dalponte, M., Gianelle, D., Chirici, G., Olsson, H.: Airborne laser scanning of forest resources: an overview of research in Italy as a commentary case study. Int. J. Appl. Earth Obs. Geoinf. **23**, 288–300 (2013). https://doi.org/10.1016/j.jag.2012.10.002

19. Mura, M., et al.: Exploiting the capabilities of the Sentinel-2 multi spectral instrument for predicting growing stock volume in forest ecosystems. Int. J. Appl. Earth Observ. Geoinf. **66**, 126–134 (2018). https://doi.org/10.1016/j.jag.2017.11.013

20. Næsset, E.: Estimating timber volume of forest stands using airborne laser scanner data. Remote Sens. Environ. **61**(2), 246–253 (1997). https://doi.org/10.1016/S0034-4257(97)00041-2

21. Næsset, E., et al.: Mapping and estimating forest area and aboveground biomass in miombo woodlands in Tanzania using data from airborne laser scanning, TanDEM-X, RapidEye, and global forest maps: a comparison of estimated precision. Remote Sens. Environ. **175**, 282–300 (2016). https://doi.org/10.1016/j.rse.2016.01.006

22. Pacala, S.W., Canham, D.C., Saponara, J., Silander, J.A., Kobe, R.K., Ribbens, E.: Forest models defined by field measurements: estimation. Error Anal. Dyn. Ecol. Monographs **6**(1), 1–43 (1996). https://doi.org/10.2307/2963479

23. Regione Piemonte, Geoportale Regione Piemonte (Piedmont Region Geoportal). http://www.geoportale.piemonte.it/cms/servizi/servizi-di-scarico. Accessed 28 Feb 2022

24. Stone, C., Mohammed, C.: Application of remote sensing technologies for assessing planted forests damaged by insect pests and fungal pathogens: a review. Curr. For. Rep. **3**(2), 75–92 (2017). https://doi.org/10.1007/s40725-017-0056

25. Swatantran, A., Tang, H., Barrett, T., DeCola, P., Dubayah, R.: Rapid, high-resolution forest structure and terrain mapping over large areas using single photon lidar. Sci. Rep. **6**(1), 28277 (2016). https://doi.org/10.1038/srep28277

26. Wagner, W., Hollaus, M., Briese, C., Ducic, V.: 3D vegetation mapping using small-footprint full-waveform airborne laser scanners. Int. J. Remote Sens. **29**(5), 1433–1452 (2008). https://doi.org/10.1080/01431160701736398

27. White, J.C., Wulder, M.A., Vastaranta, M., Coops, N.C., Pitt, D., Woods, M.: The utility of image-based point clouds for forest inventory: a comparison with airborne laser scanning. Forests **4**(3), 518–536 (2013). https://doi.org/10.3390/f4030518

28. Wulder, M.A., Bater, C.W., Coops, N.C., Hilker, T., White, J.C.: The role of LiDAR in sustainable forest management. For. Chron. **84**(6), 807–826 (2008). https://doi.org/10.5558/tfc84807-6

An Open-Source Approach to Modelling and Analysing a Tree Detected with a Mobile Laser Scanner

Giulio Donati Sarti[1] (ID), Mauro Busa[2], Gabriele Garnero[1](✉) (ID), Andrea Magnani[2] (ID), and Ivano Rossato[2]

[1] Interuniversity Department of Regional and Urban Studies and Planning (DIST), Politecnico and University of Turin, Viale Mattioli 39, 10125 Turin, Italy
`{giulio.donati,gabriele.garnero}@polito.it`
[2] Corintea Soc. Coop., Via Sansovino 243/35, 10151 Turin, Italy
`{m.busa,a.magnani,i.rossato}@corintea.it`

Abstract. For many applications, in both forestry and urban environments, knowledge of the biometric parameters of trees is essential. In this sense the use of the Quantitative Structure Models (QSMs), generated from Terrestrial Laser Scanners (TLSs), to recreate the structure of trees has increased in recent years. However, the utilisation of TLS has two main limitations which can be summarised as follows: (i) very long acquisition time and (ii) limited portability. The use of Mobile Laser Scanners (MLSs) with Simultaneous Localization and Mapping (SLAM) technology can overcome these kinds of limitations, allowing both complex environments to be detected in a short time and surveys to be made possible in impervious areas. Therefore, in this research we illustrate a workflow based on an open-source software to model and analyse a tree using the data produced by a MLS. In addition, the model of the same tree is also generated on the basis of the TLS-derived point cloud, in order to evaluate the differences. The process of modelling the tree, starting from the MLS data, leads to the creation of a model that fits the original point cloud very well, with an average distance from it of 0.30 cm. However, it was not always possible, especially in the summit parts, to reconstruct the tree structure. In addition, it was noted that, due to the noisiness of the source cloud, this model also tends to overestimate the diameter and, consequently, the biomass of the tree. In order to reduce this overestimation, a corrective factor will be identified in the future. Our study confirms that open-source software-based reconstruction of a tree model from an MLS-derived point cloud is possible. With the help of this method, it is possible to extract numerous biometric and structural information about several trees in a short time. Such information can help to carry out fast broad-scale analyses, such as assessing plant growth, or provide basic information for the development of automatic pruning technologies.

Keywords: LiDAR · SLAM · Quantitative structure models · Tree reconstruction

© The Author(s), under exclusive license to Springer Nature Switzerland AG 2022
E. Borgogno-Mondino and P. Zamperlin (Eds.): ASITA 2022, CCIS 1651, pp. 275–286, 2022.
https://doi.org/10.1007/978-3-031-17439-1_20

1 Introduction

Knowing the biometric information of trees such as Above Ground Biomass (AGB), Diameter at Breast Height (DBH) and branch size distribution is essential in many contexts, both in forestry and urban environments.

Forest ecosystems are fundamental to biodiversity and the Earth's biogeochemical system [1]. Indeed, forests and woodlands play a key role in mitigating climate change, being the earth's largest carbon sink. In this sense, knowing their current state is fundamental to many aspects of forest management, making it possible to describe their structure and quantify their resources.

In urban environments, on the other hand, the presence of trees provides several key ecosystem services such as: reduction of rainwater runoff, removal of pollutants and some heavy metals from rainwater, carbon capture and reduction of heat islands [2]. In addition, the presence of plants in cities contributes to psychological well-being, reducing the stress of urban living [3]. However, with the increased frequency of extreme weather events, due to climate change, the probability and therefore the risk of trees falling has increased, leading to personal injury or damage to private and public property. Measuring the physical structure of trees is particularly useful for managing urban green spaces to ensure the safety of people and transport.

For these reasons estimating these parameters is therefore more relevant than ever. However, doing these measurements manually is time-consuming (even days), inaccurate and sometimes requires destructive tree sampling (e.g. biomass estimation) [4]. In recent years, the use of Terrestrial Laser Scanners (TLSs) to detect natural features has increased giving the possibility to achieve an accuracy and completeness of data that is not achievable with manual measurements. The use of these active sensors allows the acquisition of three-dimensional (3D) geometric data of a tree by measuring the time it takes for each laser pulse to return to the sensor. The first studies describing TLS applications on trees were performed with the aim of measuring the diameter of trunks and branches [5, 6]. Other studies have focused on 3D modelling of tree stem, estimating attributes that cannot be measured using conventional methods (e.g. stem volume) [7, 8]. Subsequently, various models were developed for the complete modelling of a tree [9–11]. Later, new methods were defined to determine the attributes of a tree in a very detailed manner (e.g. volume distribution in the various parts of the tree, bifurcation frequency and branching angles) [12, 13]. The latter methods, to derive highly detailed information from Light Detection and Ranging (LiDAR) sensors, are called Quantitative Structure Models (QSMs) and are used to describe the woody structure above the ground with a series of topologically oriented cylinders [14]. QSMs are able to reconstruct 99% of the tree structure with millimetre-accurate cylinder positioning relative to the point cloud [15, 16] and to estimate the AGB with an average accuracy above 90% compared to reference volumes [17].

These studies have focused on extrapolating biometric information from TLS-derived data. However, TLSs have two main limitations: (i) the high acquisition time which makes it difficult to detect a large area and (ii) the volume and weight of the equipment which makes portability limited. The use of Mobile Laser Scanners (MLSs) with technology can overcome these limitations, allowing both complex environments to be detected in a short time and surveys to be made possible in impervious areas. On the other hand, the accuracy of the detection decreases compared to the TLSs. Some studies involving the generation of QSMs from MLS data have shown that it is possible to accurately identify both stem and first-order branches [18, 19]. However, these studies investigated tree modelling based only on the potential of proprietary software.

The aim of this study is to illustrate a workflow entirely focused on open-source software for the generation and analysis of QSMs. In doing so, the differences between the QSM generated on the basis of data collected with the MLS and with the TLS will be analysed from the point of view of: (i) biometric information, (ii) fitting between the QSM and the original point cloud and (iii) distance between the two QSMs.

2   Materials and Methods

2.1   Data Acquisition and Pre-Processing

The survey was conducted in February 2022 in the Valentino Park, Turin, Italy (45° 03′ 18.0″ N; 7° 41′ 08.7″ E). The tree chosen for the study is located near the "Borgo Medievale" and the instrumentation used for this survey are a TLS Trimble SX10 and an MLS Gexcel Heron LITE Color (see Fig. 1).

Fig. 1. (a) The scanned tree (b) the TLS and (c) the MLS.

The Trimble SX10 is equipped with: (i) a laser scanner, (ii) an electronic distance measurement unit, (iii) three RGB cameras and (iv) a tablet control unit. Further information on the TLS model used can be found in Table 1.

The Gexcel Heron Lite Color is composed of: (i) a Velodyne Puck LITE LiDAR sensor, (ii) a XSens MTI Inertial Measurement Unit, (iii) a RGB panoramic camera and (iv) a tablet control unit. For other technical specifications please refer to Table 1.

Table 1. Specifications of the laser scanners used in the study.

Parameter	Trimble SX10	Gexcel heron LITE color
Scanning rate	26 600 points/s	300 000 points/s
Accuracy	2.5 mm at 100 m	~3 cm
Resolution	6.25 mm at 50 m	~2 cm
Laser wavelength	1 550 nm	903 nm
Vertical field of view	300° or 45°	30°
Horizontal field of view	360° or 90°	360°
Laser max range	600 m	80–100 m

For the TLS survey, three scans were made to obtain as complete a coverage of the tree as possible. The acquisition time was around 15 min. Scans were recorded using *Trimble RealWorks* software and exported as LAS file (Fig. 2).

Fig. 2. (a) The point cloud generated by the MLS and (b) by the TLS.

The MLS, for this survey, was used with the capture head attached to the telescopic pole and hand-held at an angle of 45°. In the study area the survey was carried out taking care to form closed-loop path circles by walking around the element of interest to have as complete a result as possible and to improve the final global accuracy. The time to scan the tree was about 1 min. The raw data were then processed with the *HERON Desktop* software. The three steps that are performed in the software are the following: (i) *Odometer*, for the reconstruction of the sensor trajectory, (ii) *Create maps*, to divide the entire survey into local maps, and (iii) *Global Optimization*, aimed to register the local maps. At the end of the process, the point cloud was imported into Reconstructor to be saved as a LAS file. The point cloud derived from the SLAM laser scanner is very noisy, so *CloudCompare*'s *Noise Filter* tool was used (Fig. 2).

The point clouds were then visually compared in order to check for discrepancies (Fig. 3). The clouds correctly overlapped, especially in the section up to four metres above the ground. As you move further away from the ground, the density of the MLS point cloud decreases. The TLS cloud, on the other hand, correctly represents the tree in its entirety.

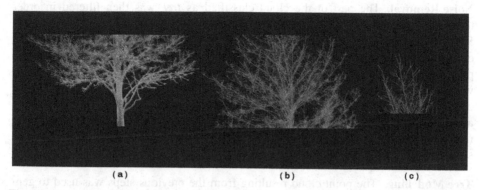

Fig. 3. Overlapping of the two point clouds (in red the one derived from the TLS and in green the one from the MLS) in the section (**a**) from the ground to 4 m, (**b**) from 4 m to 6 m and (**c**) from 6 m to the summit. (Color figure online)

2.2 Generation of the Quantitative Structure Models

The entire process for the realisation of the QSM was carried out within *Computree*, an open-source platform for processing point clouds obtained with LiDAR sensors or photogrammetry in forestry contexts. Within the platform, the *SimpleForest* plugin [16, 20, 21] was used for modelling QSMs.

The workflow used for the generation of QSMs is divided into three macro-stages: (i) tree segmentation, (ii) noise removal and (iii) tree modelling. The parameters chosen for each process step are the same for both TLS- and MLS-derived data and aim to keep as much geometric information as possible.

Tree Segmentation. After importing the cloud with the *CT_Reader_LAS* step, the tree portion of the cloud was separated from the ground cloud. To do this the *SF_StepGroundFilter* tool was used, which calculates the normal of each point and then determines the angle between the normal and the z-axis. If the angle is smaller than the user-defined threshold value, the point is classified as *ground*, otherwise as *noise*. As the result of the automatic ground classification also contains tree points, it was essential to use the *ONF_StepClassifyGround* tool. With this step, points that are further than 30 cm from the point with the minimum z-coordinate are removed from the ground class. These points, together with the points classified as *noise* in the previous step, represent the tree and are therefore merged with the *ONF_StepMergeClouds* tool. The *SF_StepEuclideanClusteringFilter* tool was then used to eliminate the remaining ground points classified as *tree*.

As there are additional points of the ground that are classified as *tree*, the *SF_StepEuclideanClusteringFilter* tool has been used to remove them. The tool divided the cloud into clusters of points generated with a search radius of 10 cm and only the largest cluster was stored as output [22]. After this stage, the cloud is then segmented into two classes: *ground* and *tree*.

Noise Removal. The part of the cloud classified as *tree* was then filtered in order to remove both outliers and noise. Initially the outliers were removed with the *SF_StepStatisticalOutlierRemoval* tool. The tool calculates the average distance between each point and the two nearest points. Points that are further than the total average distance plus three times the standard deviation are removed. The *SF_RadiusOutlierFilterStep* was then used to remove the noise from the point cloud. The instrument calculates, for each point, the number of points located at a distance of less than 5 cm and, if they are less than 3, the specific point has been considered as noise. The result of the noise removal stage is a cloud where the noise has been reduced while still keeping the tree structure as complete as possible.

Tree Modelling. The point cloud resulting from the previous steps was used to generate the tree model. The first operation carried out is to recreate the branches of the tree by placing topologically ordered cylinders in the point cloud with the function *SF_StepSpherefollowingBasic*. First the cloud was downscaled with a voxel size of 1 cm. Then the tool generated a series of spheres from the base of the stem to the top of the branches. In order to do this, a 25 cm section of the lowest part of the stem is first processed, then approximated to a circle, which in turn is transformed into a 3D sphere. The points that are close from the sphere are used to generate a number n of clusters, each representing a section of the tree. Each cluster of points is approximated by a circle, using the Center of Mass (CoM) method, and the procedure is repeated until no more points are found close to the spheres. The centre point and radius of each sphere determine the start/end point and radius of the cylinder. In the present case, the parameters related to the sphere generation were identified with the auto-parameter search, in which the default values are multiplied by factors and each obtained model is compared with the input point cloud. The parameters that create a model that differs least from the point cloud, using the Second Momentum Order MSAC method, were chosen. The *SF_StepQSMMedianFilter* tool was then applied to the generated QSM in order to adjust the radius of the cylinders that were over- or under-estimated. To do this, the average radius of the cylinders before and after each cylinder is calculated. If the cylinder radius differs by more than 15% from the average radius, it is replaced by the average radius. The resulting QSM was used to segment the point cloud with the *SF_StepSegmentTreeCloudFromQSM* tool. The purpose of this step is to divide the filtered point cloud into two clusters, based on the growth length value of the nearest cylinder. The first cluster contains the stem and the main branches while the second contains the smaller branches [20]. The derived point cloud was then used within the *SF_StepSphereFollowingAdvanced* tool to produce a higher quality QSM. The resulting model was then filtered with the *SF_StepQSMMedianFilter* tool and, subsequently, the *SF_StepReversePipeModelCorrection* tool was used to correct over- or under-estimated cylinders by examining the entire model. Outliers are corrected on the basis of pipe model theory, according to which the cross-sectional area of a branch before a junction is equal to the sum of the cross-sectional areas of all child branches [23]. Each cylinder of the model is then analysed and corrected with the *SF_StepQSMRefitCylinders* tool. In this way, the filtered point cloud was used to correct the characteristics of the cylinders that constitute the model. Lastly, the QSM was exported with the *SF_StepExportQSMList* tool. The resulting QSM derived from the MLS point cloud (QSM$_{MLS}$) and the QSM derived from the TLS point cloud (QSM$_{TLS}$) are shown in Fig. 4

(a)   (b)

Fig. 4. The resulting (a) QSM$_{MLS}$ and the (b) QSM$_{TLS}$. In red the stem. (Color figure online)

3 Results

Both QSMs were then analysed in order to assess the differences. The analyses performed can be divided into three categories: (i) biometric information analysis of the QSMs (ii) Cloud-to-Mesh analysis and (iii) Mesh-to-Mesh analysis. These analyses were carried out using the statistical analysis language *R*, through the software *RStudio*, and using the software *CloudCompare*.

Biometric Information Analysis. To extrapolate the biometric information from the QSMs, some functions defined in the *R aRchi* package [24] were used.

The first analysis carried out was the average branch angle for each branching order with the *BranchAngle()* function. A greater angle indicates a more horizontal average branch orientation. The mean branch angle divided by branch order is shown in Table 2.

Table 2. Mean branch angle values.

Branch order	QSM$_{TLS}$ branch angle	QSM$_{MLS}$ branch angle	Difference of QSM$_{MLS}$ from QSM$_{TLS}$
1st	14.03°	17.05°	+3.02°
2nd	56.65°	61.33°	+4.68°
3rd to 5th	68.90°	74.99°	+6.06°

The amount of biomass per branch order was then calculated with the *TreeBiomass()* function, assuming a wood density of 550 kg/m^3 (Table 3).

Table 3. Tree biomass values.

Branch order	QSM$_{TLS}$ biomass	QSM$_{MLS}$ biomass	Difference of QSM$_{MLS}$ from QSM$_{TLS}$
Stem	90.07 kg	107.38 kg	+17.31 kg
1st	50.82 kg	65.12 kg	+14.30 kg
2nd to 5th	32.01 kg	26.78 kg	−5.23 kg
Total	172.89 kg	199.26 kg	+26.37 kg

Next, *CloudCompare* was used to measure the difference in stem diameter between the two QSMs. Stem measurements at some significant heights are shown in Table 4.

Table 4. Stem diameter values.

Height from ground	QSM$_{TLS}$ diameter	QSM$_{MLS}$ diameter	Difference of QSM$_{MLS}$ from QSM$_{TLS}$
0.50 m	25.22 cm	29.86 cm	+3.64 cm
1.30 m	25.24 cm	27.26 cm	+2.02 cm
2.00 m	19.14 cm	22.56 cm	+3.42 cm
3.00 m	15.03 cm	17.10 cm	+2.07 cm

Cloud-to-Mesh Analysis. In this step, the distance between the original point cloud and the QSM was measured, in order to see how closely the two models match the distribution of the point clouds.

The two filtered point clouds detected by the MLS and the TLS were imported into *CloudCompare*, together with the corresponding QSM. Since the mesh of the QSMs is composed of sparse vertices, it was converted into a sampled point cloud with a density of 10 000 pts/m^2. The generated cloud was used instead of the QSM mesh within the *Compute cloud/cloud distance* tool. In the analysis the role of reference was referred to the point cloud detected by the laser scanners and subsequently filtered in *Computree*. The results of the Cloud-to-Mesh analysis are shown in Fig. 5. The QSM$_{MLS}$ has a mean distance from the original point cloud of 0.30 cm and a maximum distance of 11.73 cm. The standard deviation is 1.55 cm. The QSM$_{TLS}$, on the other hand, has an average distance from the original point cloud of 0.50 cm and a maximum distance of 16.80 cm. The standard deviation is 2.00 cm.

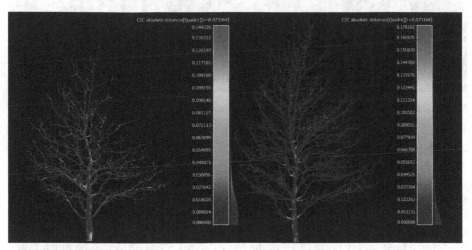

Fig. 5. Distribution of the distance between the QSMs and the point cloud generated by (**a**) the MLS and (**b**) the TLS.

Mesh-to-Mesh Analysis. The last analysis carried out concerns the difference between the mesh of the QSM$_{TLS}$ and that derived from the QSM$_{MLS}$ with the purpose of checking how much the two generated models differ.

As in the previous analysis, the two QSMs meshes were converted into a point cloud with a density of 10 000 pts/m^2. The two final point clouds were then analysed with *CloudCompare*'s *Compute cloud/cloud distance* tool. The point cloud generated by the QSM$_{TLS}$ sampling is used as a reference. The distance distributions between the models are shown in Fig. 6. The QSM$_{MLS}$ deviates on average 13.00 cm from the QSM$_{TLS}$ with a mean square deviation of 12.20 cm. The maximum distance between the two models is 1.25 m and is found in some fifth-order branch tips.

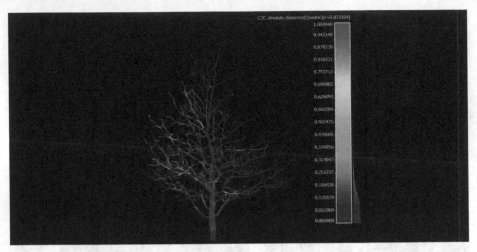

Fig. 6. Distribution of the distance between the QSM_{MLS} and the QSM_{TLS}.

4 Discussion

In this work was illustrated a workflow, based on open-source software, to model and subsequently analyse the structure of a tree starting from a point cloud detected with a laser scanner using SLAM technology. In doing so, the differences between the QSM_{MLS} and QSM_{TLS} were also analysed.

From a field survey point of view, the use of an MLS has proven to be much faster, allowing the tree to be detected in 1 min compared to 15 min required with the TLS. From our other experiences we found that the manual measurement of trees in a park of about 1.5 ha takes about 12 h, as opposed to 17 min with an MLS. In addition, the use of MLS is also more practical, especially using the backpack configuration, which can be crucial in some cases.

We first generated the two QSMs using the tools provided by the *Compu-tree*'s *SimpleForest* plugin, confirming their stability in both QSM_{MLS} and QSM_{TLS} reconstruction.

We then extrapolated the biometric information from the two models. Analysing this information, it appears that the QSM_{MLS} tends to significantly overestimate the biomass, by approximately 26 kg, which can be explained by the noise in the MLS cloud. On the other hand, the angle and diameter information of the stem and branches are more similar between the two models. In particular, the average angle of the first-order branches is overestimated by 3° in the QSM_{MLS}, and that of the second-order branches by about 5°. The stem diameter at the significant height of 1.30 m is overestimated by 2 cm in the QSM_{MLS}, a value consistent with the accuracy of the MLS used and with the results obtained by Bienert et al. [18].

The second test, in which we compared the distance of the QSMs from the initial point cloud, shows that both models approximate the cloud very well. Specifically, the QSM_{MLS} reports an average distance from the original point cloud of 0.30 cm, which is less than the average distance recorded by the QSM_{TLS} of 0.50 cm. The QSM_{MLS} also presents larger distances in the smaller branches where, on the other hand, the QSM$_{TLS}$ fits the source data better. In general, in both models it was seen that the bifurcations of the branches from the stem are the points where a greater distance from the original point cloud occurs.

Finally, we compared the two QSMs with a Mesh-to-Mesh analysis. Similar to the results obtained by Zhang et al. [19], ours also show that the models are very similar especially with regard to the stem and main branches. The lower order branches show a greater distance between the two models. However, the reconstruction of these branches is more error-prone and therefore more likely.

5 Conclusions

In this paper we presented the results obtained in modelling a tree, using open-source software, from a point cloud detected by a laser scanner equipped with SLAM technology.

The tools provided by the *Computree*'s *SimpleForest* plugin proved to be stable also for reconstructing the QSM from a point cloud created by an MLS, with an average distance between the QSM$_{MLS}$ and the point cloud of 0.30 cm. However, the use of this type of laser scanner resulted in a partial reconstruction of the tree model. This result can be attributed both to the lower accuracy of the instrument and to the difficulty of generating a cloud with a homogeneous density for the whole tree. Nevertheless, the portion of the QSM$_{MLS}$ that we were able to reconstruct is similar to the QSM$_{TLS}$; in particular, the reconstruction of the stem path and first-order branches. Yet due to the high noise in the source cloud, the model generated from the MLS data tends to overestimate the diameter and, consequently, the biomass of the tree.

This workflow makes it possible to derive the structure of trees in large and hardly accessible areas, with much faster and more affordable instrumentation than TLSs. The generated model can be used for many applications such as: biometric parameter extraction, growth assessment, information base automated pruning applications, etc. In future, applying this kind of comparative analysis to a larger number of trees with different scenarios can be useful to highlight the differences between the QSM$_{MLS}$ and QSM$_{TLS}$ and to assess the possibility of applying corrective factors to the extracted biometric information.

References

1. Shvidenko, A., et al.: Chapter 21 forest and woodland systems coordinating lead, pp. 585–621 (2006)
2. Livesley, S.J., McPherson, E.G., Calfapietra, C.: The urban forest and ecosystem services: impact on urban water, heat, and pollution cycles at the tree, street, and city scale. J. Environ. Qual. **45**, 119–124 (2016). https://doi.org/10.2134/jeq2015.11.0567
3. Ulrich, R.S., Parsons, R.: Influences of passive experiences with plants on individual well-being and health. In: Relf, D. (ed.) The Role of Horticulture in Human Wellbeing and Social Development: A National Symposium, pp. 93–105. TimberPress, Portland (1992)
4. Calders, K., et al.: Nondestructive estimates of above-ground biomass using terrestrial laser scanning. Methods Ecol. Evol. **6**, 198–208 (2015). https://doi.org/10.1111/2041-210X.12301

5. Simonse, M., Aschoff, T., Spiecker, H., Thies, M.: Automatic determination of forest inventory parameters using terrestrial laser scanning, pp. 252–258 (2003)
6. Aschoff, T., Spiecker, H.: Algorithms for the automatic detection of trees in laser scanner data. Int. Arch. Photogramm. Remote Sens. Spat. Inf. Sci. **36**, 71–75 (2004)
7. Pfeifer, N., Winterhalder, D.: Modelling of tree cross sections from terrestrial laser scanning data with free-form curves. Int. Arch. Photogramm. Remote Sens. Spat. Inf. Sci. **36**, 76–81 (2004)
8. Thies, M., Pfeifer, N., Winterhalder, D., Gorte, B.G.: Three-dimensional reconstruction of stems for assessment of taper, sweep and lean based on laser scanning of standing trees. Scand. J. For. Res. **19**(6), 571–581 (2004). https://doi.org/10.1080/02827580410019562
9. Binney, J., Sukhatme, G.S.: 3D tree reconstruction from laser range data. In: Proceedings - IEEE International Conference on Robotics and Automation, pp. 1321–1326 (2009). https://doi.org/10.1109/ROBOT.2009.5152684
10. Côté, J.F., Widlowski, J.L., Fournier, R.A., Verstraete, M.M.: The structural and radiative consistency of three-dimensional tree reconstructions from terrestrial lidar. Remote Sens. Environ. **113**(5), 1067–1081 (2009). https://doi.org/10.1016/j.rse.2009.01.017
11. Rutzinger, M., Pratihast, A.K., Oude Elberink, S.J., Vosselman, G.: Tree modelling from mobile laser scanning data-sets. Photogram. Rec. **26**(135), 361–372 (2011). https://doi.org/10.1111/j.1477-9730.2011.00635.x
12. Raumonen, P., et al.: Fast automatic precision tree models from terrestrial laser scanner data. Remote Sens. **5**(2), 491–520 (2013). https://doi.org/10.3390/rs5020491
13. Hackenberg, J., Wassenberg, M., Spiecker, H., Sun, D.: Non destructive method for biomass prediction combining TLS derived tree volume and wood density. Forests **6**(4), 1274–1300 (2015). https://doi.org/10.3390/f6041274
14. Raumonen, P., Casella, E., Calders, K., Murphy, S., Åkerblom, M., Kaasalainen, M.: Massive-scale tree modelling from TLS data. IISPRS Ann. Photogramm. Remote Sens. Spatial Inf. Sci. **II-3/W4**, 189–196 (2015). https://doi.org/10.5194/isprsannals-II-3-W4-189-2015
15. Hackenberg, J., Morhart, C., Sheppard, J., Spiecker, H., Disney, M.: Highly accurate tree models derived from terrestrial laser scan data: a method description. Forests **5**(5), 1069–1105 (2014). https://doi.org/10.3390/f5051069
16. Hackenberg, J., Spiecker, H., Calders, K., Disney, M., Raumonen, P.: SimpleTree—an efficient open source tool to build tree models from TLS clouds. Forests **6**(11), 4245–4294 (2015). https://doi.org/10.3390/f6114245
17. Kunz, M., et al.: Comparison of wood volume estimates of young trees from terrestrial laser scan data. iForest **10**, 451–458 (2017)
18. Bienert, A., Georgi, L., Kunz, M., Maas, H.G., Von Oheimb, G.: Comparison and combination of mobile and terrestrial laser scanning for natural forest inventories. Forests **9**, 395 (2018). https://doi.org/10.3390/f9070395
19. Zhang, C., et al.: Apple tree branch information extraction from terrestrial laser scanning and backpack-LiDAR. Remote Sens. **12**, 3592 (2020). https://doi.org/10.3390/rs12213592
20. Hackenberg, J.: The Simple Forest Handbook. A User Guide for QSM Building. Hoboken, Wiley (2019)
21. Hackenberg J., Calders K., Miro D., Raumonen P., Piboule, A., Disney, M.: SimpleForest-a comprehensive tool for 3D reconstruction of trees from forest plot point clouds (2021). https://doi.org/10.1101/2021.07.29.454344
22. Rusu, R.B., Cousins, S.: 3D is here: point cloud library (PCL). In: IEEE International Conference on Robotics and Automation, Shanghai, pp. 1–4 (2011). https://doi.org/10.1109/ICRA.2011.5980567
23. Shinozaki, K., Yoda, K., Hozumi, K., Kira, T.: A quantitative analysis of plant form-the pipe model theory: I. Basic analyses. Jpn. J. Ecol. **14**(3), 97–105 (1964)
24. aRchi. https://cran.r-project.org/web/packages/aRchi/aRchi.pdf. Accessed 24 Mar 2022

Cultural Heritage and Landscape Analysis

Potential Contributions of Geomatics to Garden Design, Landscape Planning and Plant Disease Management

B. Drusi[1] , M. Devecchi[1,3] , S. De Petris[1(✉)] , D. Bertetti[2] , M. Anibaldi[1],
W. Gaino[1] , A. Virano[1] , M. L. Gullino[2] , and E. Borgogno-Mondino[1,3]

[1] DISAFA, University of Torino, Largo Paolo Braccini 2, 10095 Grugliasco, Italy
samuele.depetris@unito.it
[2] AGROINNOVA, University of Torino, Largo Braccini 2, 10095 Grugliasco, Italy
[3] Centro Studi Per Lo Sviluppo Rurale Della Collina C/O DISAFA, University of Torino, Largo
Braccini 2, 10095 Grugliasco & c/o ASTISS, Area Fabrizio De Andrè, 14100 Asti, Grugliasco,
Italy

Abstract. The cross-disciplinary approach provided in this work has been applied
on a case study located in the province of Alessandria, within the 'cultural landscape' of Lower Monferrato, (Piemonte, NW Italy). From a methodological point
of view, a comparison was achieved between the native design of the garden (dated
back to the end of the sixties) and the actual one, as it developed along the time. For
that purpose, a UAV-based survey was operated to define the present situation. A
true color orthomosaic and a Digital Surface Model were derived and used for the
comparison that occurred in a GIS environment. A botanical and phytopathological
field survey was coupled to the UAV acquisition and a cross-reading analysis with
historical sources (maps) achieved. As extensively documented in this essay, the
interpretative tools provided by Geomatics made possible to quantify and locate
the differences affecting the realization of the project and qualifying the present
situation in terms of botanic content and phytopathological features. Some concerns were also provided about the potentiality that vegetation offers in protecting
the private garden from external looks through some visibility analyses. A GIS
project was finally structured to host all the obtained information, making possible
a more effective management of the garden and improving consciousness in its
evolution, aiming at the generation of scenarios useful for supporting conservation, planning and management choices and preventing the cancellation of such a
valuable heritage over time.

Keywords: Garden design · Plant disease management · GIS · UAV ·
Photogrammetry

1 Introduction

Each historical garden, even when recently planted, is configured as 'an architectural
and plant composition' which has got a public interest from a historical or artistic point

E. Borgogno-Mondino and P. Zamperlin (Eds.): ASITA 2022, CCIS 1651, pp. 289–303, 2022.
https://doi.org/10.1007/978-3-031-17439-1_21

of view; as such it is regarded as a monument (Paris, *Convention for the Protection of Cultural Heritage*, 1978). Furthermore, the 1981 Florence Charter defines the historical garden as a palimpsest, as well as a 'limited, perishable, unrepeatable *unicum*' (ICOMOS-IFLA, 1981). Unlike paintings or sculpture or buildings, a garden grows up, its appearance changes. Just a very few gardens can be left alone, while in most cases a mere skeleton of the original garden still remain after a few years of neglect. Within the garden, in fact, the plant element is constantly changing both through the changing seasons and in the biological cycle that is specific to each plant. The appearance of the garden thus results from a continuous balance, between the development and deterioration of nature and the desire for art and artifice, in the frame of the cyclical course of the seasons. Likewise, an historically layered garden could be compared to a musical composition being repeated over time with infinite variations on the theme, but always remaining the musical piece originally composed. 'Nature acts like an artist and performs the piece in real time' [1]. Garden restoration thus risks to override nature performance. Being living, growing things, gardens undergo an even greater change than ordinary static objects and monuments. Gardens tend to expand their sizes over time, whereas objects tend to shrink due to decay and entropy. Furthermore, Salwa analyzes the impact of two different approaches to garden restoration: the 'idealistic' theory, which treats gardens as cultural objects similar to other artworks and requires the restoration of an originally designed form, and the 'materialistic' theory, which emphasizes the conservation of the vegetative processes of the gardens [2]. Restoration actually deals with material, but this material is also material over time, in continuous evolution, and therefore requires an understanding and intervention criteria recognizing both materiality and temporality. If – as for the historic garden – the material is different, time behavior is different, but the cognitive approach and the intervention methods can be referred to Brandi's theory, according to which 'only the material of the artwork is restored' and 'restoration must aim at restoring the potential unity of the artwork, provided that that is possible both without committing an artistic or historical forgery and without erasing all traces of the crossing of the artwork over time' [3]. On the basis of the above, preserving and enhancing over time a historical garden in a high-value landscape involves an integrated planning of interventions at the cross-disciplinary levels of agronomic practices, phytopathological plant recovery and landscaping. The management of fungal and bacterial pathogens that threaten the survival and/or the aesthetic value of herbaceous species, shrubs and trees represents one of the most important aspect to preserve the plant heritage and the maintenance of the original project design of parks and gardens. The spread of pathogens on tree species as *Calocedrus decurrens* F., *Carpinus betulus* L., *Cedrus atlantica* M. and *Cupressus sempervirens* L. that are very common in the park under study could compromize the current compositional harmony. Monitoring the phytosanitary situation and evolution is carried out with the purpose of detecting the presence of foci of infection or the possible entry of new pathogens, permitting to provide, as soon as possible, the diagnosis and the strategy to contain their spread, with particular attention to the innovative approaches for disease management with low environmental impact. Monitoring activities have to be repeated one or more times a year, at scheduled intervals, according to the emerging problems. In this compound, the availability of botanical and photogrammetric surveys reproducing the current state of the park provides a very useful tool to locate the diseased specimens on the map with ease and precision.

2   Materials and Methods

2.1   Study Area

The beauty and originality of the Monferrato (NW Italy - Fig. 1) agricultural landscape derives from the orderly succession of vine rows, from the territory frame according both to geometric modules, regularly repeated from one hill to another, and to peculiar designs, due to the careful hydraulic-agricultural arrangements of the slopes, such as *'girapoggio'*, *'cavalcapoggio'* and *'rittochino'* [4]. From this point of view, the wine-growing landscape of Monferrato acquires an important memory value and a testimony quality of the ancient relationship between man and nature in a continuous reinterpretation of territory potentialities. It follows that agricultural landscapes denoting a balanced human intervention on natural components still represent elements of marked characterization of the territory [5]. Lower Monferrato *'cultural'* landscapes offer a spectacular backdrop to the case study selected within the present cross-disciplinary research, precisely dealing with a private historical garden in Cerrina Monferrato (province of Alessandria), Piemonte.

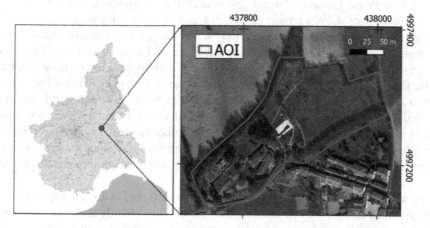

Fig. 1. AOI location (reference frame is ETRS89 UTM32N).

On behalf of Renèe Poncet, in 1969 the Parisian landscaper Jean-Pierre Combier was commissioned with the design of a majestic landscape-style garden, which however was never fully carried out. The project plans and the historical documents preserved by the owners show that the original vegetation layout was in fact entrusted to the Fantino plant nursery in Castiglione Torinese, while the design plans of the villa with its surroundings due to the architect Giorgio Giovannetti from Torino and date back to 1966. As far as the current owners remember, the greenhouse was built by the end of the 1970s, while its heating system was renovated in the nineties. In 1998, or a little later, an indoor game room was added, located on the ground floor under the north-facing terrace. The complete modernization of the electrical system of both the villa and the park dates back to the early 2000s. Around the end of the nineties, a vintage carousel from 1950s was placed on the tennis court area, that has no longer been used since the seventies. Such carousel was recently sold due to its fair conservative condition at an auction in Paris and therefore on the former tennis court area a space to be redesigned currently remains. Between 2018 and 2019 some interventions became necessary in the aim of inserting micropiles, respectively in two diverse structural sections of the house which were subject to ground movements. As regards the general garden layout, since the beginning countless small changes have occurred, including: the ultimate position of the pool; the building of several cemented terraced footpaths from 1990 onwards; the contemporary creation of a structured area in front of the kitchen; the planting of a new orchard in the late 1990s, followed by two further interventions there between 2016 and 2019. The swimming pool was rebuilt around 2005 through maintaining the original frame and replacing the tiling instead, including the external flooring; meanwhile, a dressing room with a shower and the footpath connecting to the pool have been created.

2.2 Available data

Original Garden Design. The main historical source of the expected garden design is the aforementioned '*projet de aménagement*' dating back to 1969 by the French landscaper Jean-Pierre Combier. Such 1:250 masterplan incorporates some key elements of the almost coeval 1966 project plan by the architect Giovannetti, consisting of five design drawings representing both the villa and the garden layout through plans, vertical sections and elevation views at 1:100 and 1:200 scales, beside of several A2 additional design plans outlining landscaping, earthworks or architectural interventions. Furthermore, the garden original vegetation layout by the nurseryman Fantino just consists of two A2 design sketches of the villa surroundings to the west and south, which are undated (although probably dating back to the 1980s), unsigned and without any indication of scale, drawn in pencil and connoted by a rather elementary graphic expression. Nevertheless, there is no evidence as regards the original design of the garden eastern portion, because no graphical documents providing details about the vegetation design to the east beyond the manor house are available.

From a methodological point of view, the aforementioned historical documents have been provided to the research team by the Poncet-Negro family since the first survey and shortly supplied in raster format by large format scanner. Subsequently, historical sources have been georeferenced through GIS tools and thus compared with the current orthomosaic survey. The comparison was achieved through both an on-screen photointerpretation and a cross-reading analysis of written documents, included information related to the designed and actual botanic conditions. In addition, an accurate phytopathological survey was also conducted. In the aim of better 'rendering' and visualizing the original design of the garden, the 1969 Combier's masterplan was properly 'dressed' in an image processing environment (Adobe Photoshop v. 22.1) Therefore, a watercolor drawing of the garden project was obtained from the raster copy, in the aim of highlighting the original design criteria. Compared to the original masterplan, such rendering in fact provides a colourful interpretation of the plantation arrangements envisaged by the Parisian landscape designer, including plants of relatively low height in combination with shrubs and herbaceous perennials and combining species of different colours and life-cycle, with a variety of foliage and/or flowerings.

Auxiliary Geographical Data. A DTM (Digital Terrain Model) having a grid size of 5 m and a height accuracy of $\pm$ 0.6 m [6] was obtained from the Piemonte Region Official Geoportal (DTM ICE 2009–2011) and used for deriving by grid differencing the Canopy Height Model of the garden.

2.3 Data Collection

The survey involved 3 types of expertises: one related to the photogrammetric acquisition and data processing, one concerning plant pathology and one concerning botany. All of them required that field data were properly georeferenced. For this task a GNSS Leica GX1200 receiver was used and operated in VRS-NRTK (Virtual Reference Station –Network Real Time Kinematic) mode supported by the Interregional Piemonte-Lombardia SPIN3-GNSS service (https://www.spingnss.it/). The average 3D-positional error was 0.03 m and the selected reference system was the ETRS89 UTM32N. Ellipsoidal height from GNSS survey was converted into the correspondent geoidic one using the ITALGEO05 local geoid model [7].

Photogrammetric Survey. A UAV (unmanned aerial vehicle)-based photogrammetric survey was operated on 26th October 2021 (h: 12 AM). A *DJI Mavic Pro* quadcopter was used. The integrated RGB camera (12.35 MP CMOS) has a focal length of 4.73 mm and a physical pixel size of 1.57 μm. Flying height above ground level (AGL) was set equal to 80 m, thus determining an average baseline of about 15 m. One-hundred eighty-nine images (about 4.5 Mb per image) were acquired having a GSD (Ground Sampling Distance) of about 0.026 m. Forward and side overlap were set equal to 80% and 70%, respectively. Five coded panels, sizing about 50 $\times$ 50 cm were positioned and surveyed by GNSS (see above) at the ground during the flight to be used as ground control points (GCPs).

Phytopathological and Botanic Surveys. A preliminary phytopathological survey was carried out on 26th October 2021, paying attention to trees, shrubs and herbs, with particular focus on the most widespread species. Observations were intended to record symptoms and signs related to the presence of fungi, oomycetes and bacteria on leaves, branches, stems etc. A structured form was used to collect information at plant level. Symptoms and signs were photographed and positioned through GNSS (see above). In the event that the only observations in the field were not able to identify the causal agent of the disease, one or more samples (whole plant or portions of affected tissue) were collected for more accurate laboratory analysis. The production of picnidia, acervuli, conidiophores, conidia and spores was investigated on a stereoscopic microscope (Leica M165 C) and/or on optical microscope (Leica DM 2500). Where needed, isolations were carried out from affected tissues using universal or selective media to observe on the microscope the morphological features of the isolates grown *in vitro*.

The preliminary botanic survey operated on 26th October 2021 was integrated with a new one occurred on 3rd May 2022 with the aim of completing eventual lacks of information and validating the UAV-derived one, with special concerns about plant counting and crown size as mapped from the Canopy Height Model (CHM). Only plant individuals having a height greater than 1.5 m were examined and positioned by GNSS (see above). The correspondent nomenclature was assigned based on the taxonomy edited on the Portal to the Flora of Italy (http:/dryades.units.it/floritaly) and integrated with the one from The Plant List one (http://www.theplantlist.org/) and the following macro-categories assigned to each specimen: 'Trees' or 'Shrubs'; 'Deciduous' or 'Evergreen species'; 'Plants mainly grown for ornamental and landscape purposes' or 'Plants primarily grown for fruit production'.

Each plant has been recorded in a database containing biometric data obtained from both the geomatic processing and the field surveys. According to Gullino [8] the individual can be associated with a sheet containing the following information: botanical name; representative picture of a specimen presents in the garden; botanical family name; main botanical characteristics of the species; longevity of the species; historical and cultural importance; reasons of interest (botanical, position of the specimen, invasive species or species' rarity); the ornamental features.

A preliminary analysis of ecosystem services was also achieved and, when possible, the S-AQI – i.e. a species-specific index of suitability to air quality improvement proposed by Sicard [9] and already applied by Battisti [10] – was associated to the recognized species.

Original Design Plans of the Garden. According to the rather coeval design plan by Giovannetti, the invariant features of the historic garden design – i.e. the 45° inclined position of the sheltered entrance; the course of the driveway that curves in a semicircle to the right and runs parallel to the municipal road, creating an extensive flowerbed designed in detail; the peculiar shape of the two-branched roof of the villa; the tennis court located to the north-west, the quadrangular swimming pool further down to the north-east, in the perspective of the Monferrato hills, and the *heather* greenhouse to the south-east attached to the house– were already plainly outlined in the 1969 garden layout by Jean-Pierre Combier (Fig. 2) and such core elements remain substantially unchanged through the diachronic comparison between Giovannetti's project (1966), the 1969 masterplan, Fantino's plant layout (approx. Late 1970s) up to the current situation. Furthermore, landscaping criteria were clearly expressed: Combier decided to insert relatively small trees in association with shrubs and perennial herbaceous plants, probably in the aim of not limiting the garden views from the villa, nor hindering the perspective of the hilly Monferrato landscape from both the house and the garden.

The garden layout by the Parisian landscaper included a first rock garden, in the form of an almost triangular flowerbed, in front of the house sleeping area designed by arch. Giovannetti, probably planted with succulents, rhododendrons and azaleas. A second tiered 'rocaille' was also planned along the slope to the east, beyond the service courtyard, divided by paved stairs connecting the villa to the pool. In front of the sleeping area, between the two wings of the manor house, Combier provided for the aforementioned enclosed rock garden and a mixed plant group, consisting of three birches (*Betula* L.), three specimens of *Carpinus piramidalis* L. and four specimens of *Pinus Griffithii* J. along a Japanese-step paved walkway. Not even the vegetable garden (*'potager'*) designed further east, between the north fence of the property and the aforementioned gravel road, was finally built. Across the eastern portion of the property, Combier had provided for a landscape-style garden served by winding Japanese-step paved and stone stepped paths crisscrossing the lawn through groves and clusters of trees and shrubs. In the eastern area of the garden, the landscaper had finally designed the above-mentioned terraced rock garden along the slope, beside of a scenic viewpoint (sort of a *belvedere*) at the driveway top and a stepped paved walkway uphill. However, instead of such landscaping solutions, the owner Poncet made different arrangements with the gardener Fantino, as it is documented by some handwritten notes in pencil on the masterplan anastatic copy.

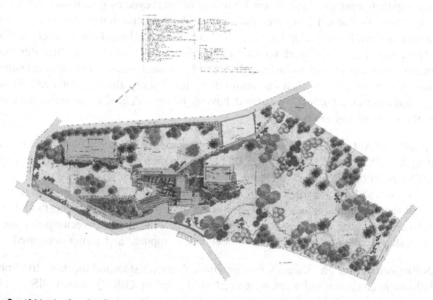

Fig. 2. *'L'Amis des Jardins et de la Maison – Jean-Pierre Combier paysagiste/ Jardin de Mr Giorgio Negro et Mme Renèe Poncet/ Projet d'Aménagement/ Jardin sis á Monferrato (Italie), echelle: 4 mm p m, 20 février 1969'* (scan from anastatic copy of the original floor plan "dressed" with Adobe Photoshop 2022).

2.4   Data Processing

Image Block Bundle Adjustment. Image Bundle adjustment was performed by *Agisoft PhotoScan vs 1.2.4* software (AGS) and the correspondent dense point cloud (PPC) generated. PPC was filtered and regularized using LAStools [11] in order to create a Digital Surface Model (DSM) with a grid size of 0.12 m. Finally, a true color ortho-mosaic (TCOM) having a GSD of 0.05 m (corresponding to a nominal map scale of 1:250) was generated. Since an operative approach and technology transfer were proposed, leave one out (LOO) procedure [12] was adopted to test bundle adjustment accuracy using the previously mentioned 5 GCPs without requiring additional survey. Therefore, height and planar RMSE (Root Mean Square Error) accuracy were computed.

Mapping Garden Elements. The local Canopy Height Model (CHM) was computed by grid differencing between the UAV-derived DSM and the regional DTM providing a raster map of objects height above the ground level. DSM proved to be not spatially coherent with the regional DTM showing a significant bias. This was minimized comparing 20 manually selected points referring about the ground level from both DSM and DTM. A linear model was calibrated and applied to the DTM making the two layers spatially consistent and proper for CHM generation. Improvement of spatial coherence was quantified by comparing the mean absolute error (MAE) before and after correction. Assuming that vegetation higher than 1.5 m was not surveyed by botanists, CHM pixels having a height value < 1.5 m were masked out and a segmentation process run to recognize tree crowns. In particular, the watershed algorithm [13] available in *SAGA GIS vs. 8.0* (local maxima; join method: seed to saddle difference = 1 m) was applied. Resulting segments were analyzed by ordinary GIS tool to compute: (i) CHM minimum/maximum values or each patch; (ii) patch maximum diameter. Finally, the polygon centroid was computed and a circular buffer generated, having the radius equal to the one of the circle with the same area of the polygon.

Planned and Actual Garden Discrepancy Assessment. The 1969 design plan (nominal scale 1:250) was digitalized @ 600 dpi. Resulting image was georeferenced by a 1st order polynomial using 6 reference points (house corners, man-made objects) surveyed by GNSS (see above). The original garden plan and TCOM were used to map, through vector editing, garden cover types like grass, paved surfaces, tennis field, buildings in order to generate the garden "land use" map. For all edited vector polygons, at the investigated dates, the correspondent area was computed and values compared.

GIS Project Definition. Data about vegetation characteristics and location, from phytopathological surveys and maps were organized within a GIS (Quantum GIS v. 3.22) project that is intended for future garden management. After having assigned a proper symbology to layers, phytopathological and botanic information from the collection forms and images were hyperlinked to the correspondent vectorized features. Hyperlink is useful for a holistic management of garden allowing an effective comprehension of its past and current characteristics, through a spatial representation that could address future interventions. Some of this information from the form can eventually been archived as attributes associated to correspondent vector layer.

Visibility Assessment. Visibility analyses is used to assess the perception about the spatial distribution of features in the landscape by analyzing the line of sight between two points involving a digital elevation model [14]. This kind of analysis can support planners/managers' choices concerning the effects on human perception of a given opera (e.g. vegetation cover removal or new planting, buildings). The most common viewshed analysis is the binary viewshed analysis. The output is a raster mapping the local degree of visibility from one or more viewpoints. If more viewpoints are involved, the final map reports number of points that the considered pixel can be seen from. In this work, the generated DSM was processed by the viewshed analysis tool available in *QGIS vs 3.22* using 12 viewpoints located on roads external and surrounding the garden, to assess the capability of vegetation of protecting the garden itself from unwilled sights.

3   Results and Discussions

Image Block Bundle Adjustment. Accuracy assessment of the image block bundle adjustment (LOO-based) provided an horizontal $RMSE_{xy}$ equal to 0.1 m and a vertical $RMSE_z$ equal to 0.2 m. The correspondent PPC was computed by AGS, filtered by LASTools (less than 0.0009% points were filtered out) and finally regularized with a GSD = 0.12 m (Fig. 3) to generate the correspondent DSM. TCOM was computed setting a GSD = 0.05 m.

Fig. 3. Photogrammetric-derived orthomosaic (GSD = 0.05 m) (reference frames is ETRS89 UTM32N).

Mapping Garden Elements. CHM was computed by differencing from DSM and the available (and de-biased) regional DTM. De-biasing proved to improve MAE (affecting the Z value) from 1.38 m to 0.88 m. The latter is consistent with the DTM nominal accuracy. With reference to CHM, masking out all values < 1.5 m, a watershed segmentation was run to automatically detect tree/shrubs crowns. The average crown radius was then estimated and mapped (Fig. 4), making possible some reasonings about management treatments as pruning and irrigating. In fact, segments (polygons) representing crowns can be qualified with other metrics, like local minimum/maximum values, maximum diameter, average radius, useful for supporting a quantitative management of the garden itself.

Phytopathological and Botanic Assessment. On 26th October 2021, an outbreak of infection was detected on some plants of common hornbeam (*Carpinus betulus*) growing in two points inside the park. Affected plants showed conspicuous decays, subcortical

Fig. 4. Trees/shrubs crown derived by CHM segmentation (reference frames is ETRS89 UTM32N).

discoloration and small cankers on stems, producing orange stromatic masses, one or few mm in size. These signs and symptoms led to the presence of *Naemospora* sp., subsequently re-identified as *Anthostoma decipiens* [15]. At the moment, *Endothiella* sp. That is frequently associated with *A. decipiens* on common hornbeam [16] has not been detected in the park. Moreover, some plants of stone pine (*Pinus pinea*) located near the house showed holes in the lower part of the trunk, probably caused by the great spotted woodpecker bird (*Dendrocopos major*), hunting for subcortical insect larvae. In this case, is conceivable the presence of the beetle *Melanophila cyanea* (Syn.: *Phaenops cyanea*, Buprestidae family), a xylophage insect causing subcortical tunnels [19]. As far as local botany is concerned, a total of 71 different plant species were identified in the garden and 82 different taxa (including cultivars and botanical varieties) were recognized. Local vegetation characterization is summarized in Table 1. At first glance, the average S-AQI value is 4.85.

Table 1. Distribution of vegetation categories within the garden (actual situation)

	Total	Trees	Shrubs	Deciduous Plants	Evergreen Plants	Ornamental Plants	Fruits Plants
Number of taxa	82	53	29	55	27	70	12
Percentage	100%	65%	35%	67%	33%	85%	15%
Number of individuals	436	301	135	271	165	390	46
Percentage	100%	69%	31%	62%	38%	89%	11%

Garden Visibility Assessment. The visibility scenario (Fig. 5) proved that the majority of garden is not visible from outside the propriety highlighting how tree and shrubs can provide a good view isolation. High visibility is present only at the garden main entrance while all along the garden limits the visibility is lower. Unfortunately, such analysis is affected by some limitations, like the one related to the fact that DSM cannot provide information about crown porosity and/or tree structure, possibly determining an overestimation of protection. In fact, especially for taller trees, the canopy is placed up to 5 m thus allowing visibility through the trees themselves.

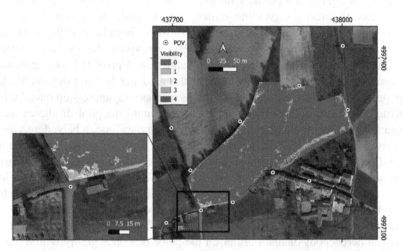

Fig. 5. Scenario concerning the garden visibility from outside the propriety (reference frames is ETRS89 UTM32N).

Planned and Actual Garden Discrepancy Assessment. According to Giovannetti's design plan, the 1969 garden layout specifically reproduces the plan of the villa roof including the terrace and the balconies on the north-west side, with the heather green-house and the service courtyard to the north-east, as well as the swimming pool located to the north-east and the tennis court in the north-west corner of the garden. Furthermore, as regards the infrastructural route, both the external perimeter of the property and the five-meter wide gravel driveway to the garage remain substantially unchanged through the diachronic comparison between Giovannetti's project (1966), Combier's 1969 garden design and the current survey. Through the reading of the orthomosaic elaborated in the context of this study, today a very different garden layout characterizes both the portion of the garden in front of the entrance to the villa, and the remaining area of the park beyond the facade to the east, between the attached greenhouse, the swimming pool to the north, the hornbeam alley to the south and the eastern border of the property towards the hills in the distance. In fact, there is no evidence of the original garden design related to the green spaces surrounding and exceeding the greenhouse and the pool towards the east and north-east, therefore it is impossible to make any diachronic comparison between the historical documents and the current survey as for such part of the garden. Moreover, if we exclude the still permanent core elements of the original garden design – i.e. the 45° inclined position of the entrance to the park; the driveway route curving to the right, running parallel with the *'chemin vicinal'* and cutting out an extensive flowerbed; the peculiar shape of the two-branched roof of the villa; the tennis court located to the north-west, the quadrangular pool further down and the greenhouse attached to the house, both to the east –, the current garden layout significantly differs from the original design plans. An earlier example among others: in comparison to both Giovannetti's and Fantino's project as well as to the actual survey, the oblong flowerbed running along the southern enclosure wall appears visibly tapered and with a sacrificed surface and that is perhaps due to a transcription error by Combier, who probably neglected to directly survey the garden. The original design as it was conceived by Jean-Pierre Combier thus appears mostly lost today, both beyond the house eastern front and in the garden portion to the south-west overlooking the driveway to the villa. Where on the western front of the villa Giovannetti had provided for a ground floor porch simply overlooking a main courtyard, the gardener Fantino designed a fenced lawn populated with trees, groves and shrubs, as well as a Japanese-step paved walkway connecting the driveway, the dining and guest areas until the pool. In the eastern area of the garden, instead of a terraced rock garden along the slope, a belvedere viewpoint at the driveway top and the stepped paved walkway uphill, nowadays the greenhouse faces a hillock characterized by a lawn parterre centered on a globular topiary laurel tree (*Laurus nobilis* L.) and radially divided by six Luserna-stone paved walkways rejoining two stepped paths to the pool. In front of the parterre, a luxuriant wisteria flanks a hexagonal gazebo and furnishes the hillock top; an arch covered with climbing roses joins the wisteria creating a sort of backdrop towards the gazebo; just behind it, a mixed border of perennial herbaceous plants. Further on the slope descends gently with a tree-lined lawn bordered by a curved stabilized gravel road, to the north joining the path that leads to the orchard, to the south instead the hornbeam row on the property southern border.

Based on the findings of this work, the 1970s landscaping criteria applied of associating deciduous and evergreen species and alternating different chromatic hues of foliage or flowers over the seasons, substantially still persist today.

Table 2. Discrepancy assessment between Actual garden and Original garden plan land use types (Actual-planned).

Cover type	Actual garden (m^2)	Original garden plan (m^2)	Discrepancy (m^2)
Tennis	0.0	624.5	-624.5
Buildings	854.5	725.0	129.4
Paved trails	3343.7	3454.1	-110.4
Grass	26139.6	25513.9	625.8
Total	30337.8	30317.4	20.4

Garden cover types defined by photointrepretation from TCOM (actual garden) and from the original garden plans (Fig. 6) were used to compare areas corresponding to the different land use categories (Table 2). It can be noted that actual garden is greater than

20 m^2 with respect to the planned one and the tennis field is not present. About 130 m^2 of building were added in a later period. Moreover, 110 m^2 of planned paved trails were not created.

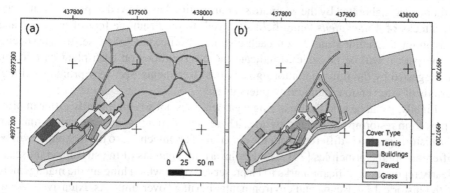

Fig. 6. (a) Garden land use types according to plan; (b) Garden cover types according to actual garden (reference frames is ETRS89 UTM32N).

4   Conclusions

The methodological approach applied within the present multidisciplinary research aims at assessing historical, compositional, botanical and management features at one time. A further and more in-depth quantification of further ecosystem services offered by individual components of the vegetation or by the vegetation as a whole will be possible by using surveyed biometric parameters and land use data. Software suites such as I-Tree and Invest are used for the assessment of ecosystem services provided by vegetation [9, 17, 18]. As regards landscaping assessments, the diachronic reading of the investigated garden textures up to its current layout clearly shows that its design deliberately combines woody plants, being arranged singly or in groups, with shrubs and perennial herbaceous species also shaped as mixed borders. In particular, the choice of mainly inserting plants of relatively low height in association with shrubs and perennial herbaceous species is probably motivated by the intent not to limit the views of the park from the villa, nor of the garden from the various viewpoints of the garden itself, nor to obstruct the perspective of the hilly Monferrato landscape from both the house and the garden. The first and second size specimens now present in the park, either grouped together or, more rarely, isolated, are therefore concentrated in a few places, deliberately exposing large areas of lawn to full sunshine. At the moment, the presence of *Anthostoma decipiens* on *Carpinus betulus* is the most relevant finding in the Cerrina park. The pathogen has been detected on a few plants, however it is necessary to act rapidly, removing the affected specimens that have to be get out of the park and burned. The cutting tools are one of the main vehicles for spreading the pathogen, then they have to be disinfected. Because of the large number of common hornbeams growing in the park, it is absolutely necessary to avoid the spread of the fungus that can cause very dangerous epidemics and significantly modify the park's tree composition [16]. In the case of *Pinus pinea*, the presence of *Melanophila cyanea* should be confirmed by examining the conformation of subcortical zigzag galleries [20]. However, *M. cyanea* usually attacks already decaying trees. The current survey orthomosaic elaborated by the geomatics' contribution has allowed to precisely indicate the attacks of *A. decipiens* being field surveyed, to eradicate the foci of infection and to monitor the future situation on each common hornbeam. Likewise, for all species of the park it will be possible to indicate the interventions on each plant carried out or suggested by the future monitoring activities: treatments, recovery pruning, felling, periods of intervention, monitoring intervals etc.

Finally, it can be said that restoring a garden does not so significantly differ in principles from restoring any other artworks. There is no doubt that the constituent material of a historic garden is different from the material of architecture, so the technique will be different, not the principles [20]. The key invariant elements of the stratified landscape clearly represent significant marks to be preserved upon which hinging the management of the historical-landscape and environmental heritage over time. As extensively documented in this work, the interpretative tools provided by Geomatics – through advanced techniques of overlay, visibility analysis, data processing – significantly improve garden consciousness therefore supporting conservation, planning and management choices and preventing the cancellation of such a valuable heritage over time.

Acknowledgement. The garden described was developed and cared for years by Renèe Poncet. The Authors are much thankful to Mme Poncet's memory, as well as to her family.

References

1. Salwa, M.: The Garden as a Performance. Estetika: The European Journal of Aesthetics. **51**, 42–61 (2014)
2. Capdevila-Werning, R., Spaid, S.: What's so authentic about restoration? Aesthetic Investigations (2019)
3. Brandi, C.: Theory of Restoration (trad. Cynthia Rockwell; rev. Dorothy Bell; cur. Giuseppe Basile). Firenze, Nardini (2005)
4. Accati, E., Bordone, R., Devecchi, M.: Il giardino storico nell'Astigiano e nel Monferrato (1999)
5. Scazzosi, L.: Rural landscape as heritage: reasons for and implications of principles concerning rural landscapes as heritage ICOMOS-IFLA 2017. Built Heritage **2**, 39–52 (2018)
6. Borgogno Mondino, E., Fissore, V., Lessio, A., Motta, R.: Are the new gridded DSM/DTMs of the Piemonte Region (Italy) proper for forestry? a fast and simple approach for a posteriori metric assessment. iForest - Biogeosciences and Forestry. **9**, 901–909 (2016). https://doi.org/10.3832/ifor1992-009
7. Barzaghi, R., Betti, B., Carrion, D., Gentile, G., Maseroli, R., Sacerdote, F.: Orthometric correction and normal heights for Italian levelling network: a case study. Applied Geomatics **6**(1), 17–25 (2014)
8. Gullino, P., Pomatto, E., Gaino, W., Devecchi, M., Larcher, F.: New challenges for historic gardens' restoration: a holistic approach for the royal park of moncalieri castle (turin metropolitan area, Italy). Sustainability **12**, 10067 (2020)

9. Sicard, P., et al.: Should we see urban trees as effective solutions to reduce increasing ozone levels in cities? Environ. Pollut. **243**, 163–176 (2018)
10. Battisti, L., Pomatto, E., Larcher, F.: Assessment and mapping green areas ecosystem services and socio-demographic characteristics in Turin neighborhoods (Italy). Forests **11**, 25 (2019)
11. Isenburg, M.: LAStools-efficient tools for LiDAR processing (2012). http://www.cs. unc.edu/~isenburg/lastools/ Accessed 9 Oct 2012
12. Brovelli, M.A., Crespi, M., Fratarcangeli, F., Giannone, F., Realini, E.: Accuracy assessment of high-resolution satellite imagery orientation by leave-one-out method. ISPRS J. Photogramm. Remote. Sens. **63**, 427–440 (2008)
13. Huang, H., Li, X., Chen, C.: Individual tree crown detection and delineation from very-high-resolution UAV images based on bias field and marker-controlled watershed segmentation algorithms. IEEE J. Selected Topics in Applied Earth Observations Remote Sensing **11**, 2253–2262 (2018)
14. Gillings, M., Wheatley, D.: GIS-based visibility analysis. In: Archaeological Spatial Analysis, pp. 313–332. Routledge (2020)
15. Rocchi, F., Quaroni, S., Sardi, P., Saracchi, M.: Studies on *Anthostoma decipiens* involved in *Carpinus betulus* decline. Journal of Plant Pathology. 637–644 (2010)
16. Saracchi, M., Rocchi, F., Quaroni, S.: Further Studies on the Etiological Agents of Carpinus Betulus Decline (2008)
17. Mexia, T., et al.: Ecosystem services: Urban parks under a magnifying glass. Environ. Res. **160**, 469–478 (2018)
18. Nowak, D.J.: Understanding i-tree: summary of programs and methods. General Technical Report NRS-200. Madison, WI: US Department of Agriculture, Forest Service, Northern Research Station. pp. 1–100 (2020)
19. Nierhaus-Wunderwald, D., Forster, B.: Coleotteri corticicoli sui pini. Istituto federale di ricerca WSL (2000)
20. Goetcheus, C., Mitchell, N.: The Venice Charter and cultural landscapes: evolution of heritage concepts and conservation over time. Change Over Time. **4**, 338–357 (2014)

Landscape Services and Their Impact on the Well-Being of Local Actors Through Participatory Mapping. A Case-Study in the Inner Areas of Northern Apennines, Piedmont

Rebekka Dossche[1(✉)], Antonella Primi[1], and Alessandro Valle[2]

[1] University of Genoa, 16126 Genoa, Italy
rebekka.dossche@unige.it
[2] Srl. EtaCarinae, Milan, Italy

Abstract. Landscape Services assessments provide opportunities for regional and local landscape planning since they offer a good overview of public values and perceptions of people on their landscapes. This study presents a spatial pattern analysis of public perception of an Inner Area in Piedmont, Italy. The Landscape Services were used as a framework on which a participatory mapping survey was constructed. To describe the spatial distribution and intensity of the landscape services, a Kernel density analysis on the point layers was executed. Together with a nearest-neighbour (NN) analysis, this contribution explores the distribution of the Landscape Services and their relation with the personal well-being. These aspects should be included in future projects aiming at the rural development of Inner Areas as it gives a good overview of what is used, valued, and considered by the local community.

Keywords: Participatory mapping · Landscape services · Inner areas

1 Introduction

Inner Areas in Italy mostly correspond to mountain rural landscapes, representing a (hi)story of man-maintained agro-silvo-pastoral systems, with a high balance between human management, restrictive environmental conditions and biological diversity. Such landscapes underwent a destabilization because of a large land abandonment and depopulation since the second half of the 20th century and the conversion of productive rural to remote low-fertility areas. Currently, few or no planning processes are executed in those Inner Areas, as if they do not have any future. However, people still live, work and visit those landscapes, generating public values and perceptions.

Paragraphs 1, 2.2, 2.4, 3 and 4 were written by R. Dossche. Paragraphs 2.1 and 2.3 by A. Primi. A. Valle elaborated the cartographic analysis

E. Borgogno-Mondino and P. Zamperlin (Eds.): ASITA 2022, CCIS 1651, pp. 304–316, 2022.
https://doi.org/10.1007/978-3-031-17439-1_22

In Italy remote areas are described and classified based on a measurement of distance to the closest service center. The National Strategy for Inner Areas (SNAI) identifies Inner Areas as being affected by depopulation, high rates of demographic ageing, different degrees and forms of inequalities in the provision of services and infrastructures, and geographical marginality (Vendemmia et al., 2021). The indicators with which the classification was constructed included the accessibility to basic urban opportunities and rights, in this case mobility, health and education. The resulting classification identifies three types of Inner Areas: intermediate, peripheral and ultra-peripheral area (Lucatelli, 2015; De Rossi 2019). Municipalities that are not considered Inner Areas and provide a full range of services are nominated 'Poles'. The areas located between the Poles and the Inner Areas, are considered 'Belt' areas. This classification is the starting point for the regional organisation of 'project areas' who receive EU-funds for development and planning strategies in Inner Area landscapes.

Nonetheless the classification is very interesting, as it does not include any demographic information (Dossche 2021) nor it does consider the valorisation of local actors of their landscape. In literature, public participation studies are increasingly considered a necessary part of effective landscape planning. Through public participation, residents communicate values, ideas and needs they believe should be considered during decision-making processes (Creighton, 2005; Rawluk et al., 2017). Contemporarily, public stakeholders are rarely consulted, and geospatial approaches to identifying public values are almost entirely absent from planning and development processes.

The consideration of the perceptual aspect is intrinsically related with the role of human beings within the landscape: they are not just seen as factors who have a positive or negative impact on nature (as in the conventional ecological approach), but are seen as an integral part of the landscape. In accordance to a transdisciplinary and integrated concept of landscape, literature has proposed the concept of 'landscape services' over 'ecosystem services' (MEA 2005) to enable the inclusion of both natural and cultural aspects, to take into consideration the spatial patterns, but also the involvement of stakeholders, especially in the context of local collaborative landscape planning (Temorshuizen and Opdam, 2009; Vallés-Planells et al., 2014).

This study aims to spatially identify public perceptions of the landscapes people live in. This will be done by linking public participatory mapping with the landscape services (LS) framework. LS focus on «the balance between the material and immaterial benefits of landscape perceived by local communities; between well-being gains derived from nature and from the interaction of nature with humans; and between the vertical and horizontal relations of landscape» (Vallés-Planells et al., 2014, p. 44). This study raises and answers the following research question: Where do residents spatially localize both the Landscape Services (provisioning and cultural) and Landscape Values and how do they improve their well-being?

2 Data and Methods

2.1 Study Area

The research was carried out in the southeastern part of the province of Alessandria, Region of Piedmont. The 30 municipalities of the research area are all considered mountain municipalities and are member of three Mountain Municipality Unions (Unione Terre Alte, Unione Curone-Grue-Ossona, Unione Borbera-Spinti). The research area contains four main valleys (Curone, Grue, Ossona, Borbera and Spinti) and two territorial areas (Valli Curone-Grue-Ossona, Val Borbera-Spinti). The whole surface contains a mixed geomorphology, including mountain tops until 1700 masl (Monte Ebro and Monte Chiappo) to hilly areas of around 243 masl (Vignole Borbera) in the lower parts. The landscape was historically dominated by pasture land, vineyards, chestnut plantations, coppice woodland, arable land and largely populated villages within an agro-silvo-pastoral system. Land abandonment induced an extensification process and resulted in a diverse landscape where agriculture is still present but clearly in decline.

The 30 municipalities have in total 14.698 inhabitants (1st of January 2020) and occupies 549,05 km^2. The highest populated municipality is Stazzano (2387 inhabitants) and the smallest is Carrega Ligure (85 inhabitants). In general, the population density of the whole research area is 26,77 inhabitants/km^2, with Carrega Ligure the lowest one (1,54), and Vignole Borbera the highest one (238,27).

In 2010, 34% (186,31km^2) of the territory is occupied for agricultural use, of which 31% for both cultivations and woodland and 25% for meadows and grasslands. Tourism is increasingly important thanks to a local economy associated with high environmental values, but also eno-gastronomic products (salami, wine, cheese).

2.2 Typology of Landscape Services

Based on a detailed content analysis of the research area (Dossche et al., 2016; Dossche, 2016; Dossche 2021), the focus of this analysis is based on a selection of different types of landscape services (LS), i.e. the provisioning and cultural services (Table 2). At the end of the survey, the respondents were generally asked about what locations had a specific landscape value (aesthetic, spiritual-religious, historical-cultural, natural-environmental, and personal). We focused our questions on how respondents valued the LS as individuals, rather than as members of a community. Thus, we asked people to associate their answers with their own well-being.

The interview questions slightly depended on the type of landscape service interrogated. For the Provisioning Services and a part of the Cultural Services, the respondents were asked the type of product and the frequency of visiting the located place. For another part of the Cultural Services, the respondents were asked how much time it took them to get there. This because those Cultural Services (health, educational and infrastructural services) are also seen as the parameters of remote areas classification (SNAI 2014) at a national level.

2.3 Data Collection

A participatory mapping survey was conducted from March until May 2021 through a web-based PPGIS within the digital Community Engagement Platform Maptionnaire (www.maptionnaire.com). Due to Covid-19 restrictions the survey was designed to be self-administered, including an instruction-video, and therefore filled in without the help of a facilitator. The survey started with mapping as point data the informants' home residence and work locations and subsequently the landscape services categorised under 1) provisioning services, 2) cultural services and 3) landscape values (Table 2). The informants could map a maximum of five places for every service indicator and a maximum of three for the landscape values. The background map was a satellite image provided by Maptionnaire with an overlay shape file including the administrative boundaries (province and municipalities) of the research area.

After each mapped item a pop-up window opened to collect subsequent data, such as the relation of the mapped point with the personal well-being of the respondent (Bieling et al., 2014) through a Likert scale ranging from 0 (strongly negative) to 5 (strongly positive).

The survey was shared by the stakeholders and their networks. The participants were expected to live in or know the research area, so it was expected that they would be personally positively or negatively affected. The final number of respondents who finished the whole survey was 175, while 556 different individuals started it. The level of difficulty and the length of the survey were considered as elimination aspects. Therefore, for the individual indicator questions the analysis was based on the number of respondents per question. The descriptive analysis and the Chi-square analysis were based on the 175 final responses.

2.4 Data Analysis

All mapped points using Maptionnaire software were digitalized and imported into a GIS system (QGIS 3.16 Hannover). After summarizing descriptive statistics, including the number of LS points mapped on our study area and the number of respondents who mentioned each LS as important, we used a Chi-square test to identify significant differences regarding the numbers of respondents with various socio-demographic characteristics who identified the various LS as important. We then used spatial analysis to interpret the distribution of mapped LS points with reference to the villages.

Kernel Density Analysis

To describe the spatial distribution and intensity of the LS, we elaborated a method that is largely used for participatory ecosystem services mapping, namely a Kernel density analysis on the point layers (Silverman, 2018; Brown and Fagerholm, 2015; Xu et al., 2020). The Kernel density calculates a smoothly curved circular surface of point density for each point, summing the values in a raster grid cell, thus facilitating an explicit visualisation of the spatial clustering for the mapped LS. The Kernel density estimation that we calculated had an output cell size of 5 pixels and a 2000 m search radius. The result of the spatial distribution is found in the Kernel density heat maps. Since there is the possibility that the respondents value certain LS as less or more important, we also weighted the mapped LS points by tracking the number of respondents who valued each kind of LS as 'important for their well-being'. This data is presented in our weighted Kernel density heat maps.

Table 1. Spatial clustering of individual services through NN analysis

	All points	Residence	Work
Number of points	1145	346	279
Z-Score	-94,5	-26,7	-25,8
NN index	0,1	0,3	0,2

	Provisioning services (6)					
	Food (4)				Craftsmanship (2)	
	Farm products	Harvested Products	Own cultivation	Own production	Craft products	Own production
Number of points	530	138	134	73	191	26
Z-Score	-36,2	-13,3	-11,9	-9	-18,89	-5,6
NN index	0,2	0,4	0,5	0,5	0,29	0,4

	Cultural Services (6)					
	Educational services	Health services	Transport services	Touristic services	Outdoor activities	Social interaction
Number of points	88	241	69	168	314	229
Z-Score	-13,8	-24,5	-10,3	-17,2	-24,4	-22
NN index	0,2	0,2	0,4	0,3	0,3	0,2

	Landscape Values (5)				
	Aesthetic value	Spiritual-Religious value	Historical-cultural value	Natural-environmental value	Personal value
Number of points	274	98	184	202	77
Z-Score	-19,9	-13,7	-18,4	-17,2	-7,8
NN index	0,4	0,3	0,3	0,4	0,5

Nearest Neighbour Statistics

Secondly, we performed a nearest-neighbour (NN) analysis to explore clustering or random distribution of the mapped LS points (Ebdon, 1985; Plieninger et al., 2018). The spatial distribution of points related to each kind of Landscape Service is shown as a ratio. Significant Z-scores indicate how many standard deviations from the mean the ratio value (p-score) is. Where the ratio is lower than 1 (p < 0,001) Landscape Service points on the layer are spatially clustered; a ratio greater than 1 (p > 0,001) indicates spatial dispersion. Small p-values combined with a very high z-score indicate statistically significant spatial clustering, in combination with a very low z-score, it means dispersion.

3 Results

3.1 Respondent Characteristics and LS Values

The majority of the respondents lived and worked in the municipality of Costa Vescovato which is due to the researchers' dense network with the local community. We had 175 completed surveys with an equally representation of both genders (52% male, 44% female, 4% preferred not to respond the question – Table 1). The educational degree in the area is 47% of university degree (first cycle) and 37% high school degree. 12% of the respondents have a master or doctoral degree, while 5% has a medium school degree. These degrees do not correspond with the ISTAT data, which is an indicator of the fact that the survey was rather high level and probably too difficult for a large part of the population. This also returns in the gender and age division. Only 13% of the over 65 population has responded the survey, of which only 3% are women.

Table 2. Overview of number and type of respondents of the online survey

	18–24	25–39	40–65	> 65	No response	Total
Male	2%	12%	27%	10%	1%	**52%**
Female	1%	12%	28%	3%	0%	**44%**
Preferred not to answer	1%	1%	1%	0%	2%	**4%**
Total	**3%**	**25%**	**56%**	**13%**	**3%**	**100%**

Self-estimated knowledge of the area was claimed extremely good (74%) or quite good (21%) while only 6% indicating poor knowledge of the area. Those who had a residential relationship to the area tend to estimate their knowledge higher compared to those who worked or had moved out of the area (Chi^2(42), df 27, p-value 0,03).

3.2 Spatial Distribution of Mapped Services

Generally, the landscape services are not equally assigned across the research area, as shown in the heat map of the spatial distribution of all mapped Landscape Services points (Fig. 1). The values for individual Landscape services were not randomly distributed. All of them statistically showed significant spatial clustering (p > 0.001, nearest neighbour ratios: 0,18–0,46, z-scores: −36,20 to −7,78) (Table 2). The highest spatial intensity is represented by the darkest colours and is located in the city center of Tortona, in the villages of Costa Vescovato, Volpedo and San Sebastiano. Other high-spatial-intensity areas featured settlements, historical sites, public spaces, water bodies. All kinds of LS showed statistically significant spatial clustering (p 0.001, nearest neighbour ratios: 0,18–0.47; z-scores: −36,20 to −5,58) (Table 2).

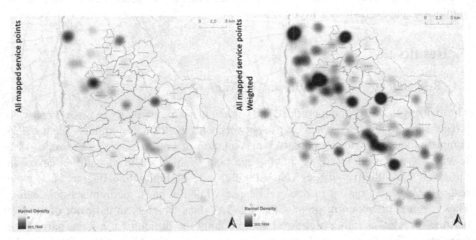

Fig. 1. Kerned density heat maps of the spatial distribution of all mapped Landscape Services (left: not weighted; right: weighted by the number of respondents who valued each Service as important)

Compared with other LS, the locations of selling farm products were rather dispersed across the whole study area (p < 0.001, z-score: −36,20), although a high density is seen near the agricultural cooperative Valli Unite in Costa Vescovato. Also, the health services, the outdoor activities and the social interaction locations have a very low z-score (between −24,45 and −22,04).

The most clustered LS (z-scores between −9,01 and −5,08) are the locations were respondents indicated their place of production and/or transformation of both alimentary and non-alimentary products. Here as well, the cooperative Valli Unite was largely indicated being a place where a lot of people live and work. But even the personal landscape values are largely clustered around rural centers and also more peripheric areas of mountain tops (Monte Ebro).

The Provisioning Services (Fig. 2a and 2b) were mostly located in closeby villages and around axes of connection. The indicated selling points are mostly small-scale initiatives like on-farm shops, local groceries and weekly markets. The harvest points have a larger dispersion, but are mostly located in the surroundings of the houses. The craftman products are located in the city of Tortona, and the villages of Costa Vescovato, San Sebastiano Curone and Cabella Ligure.

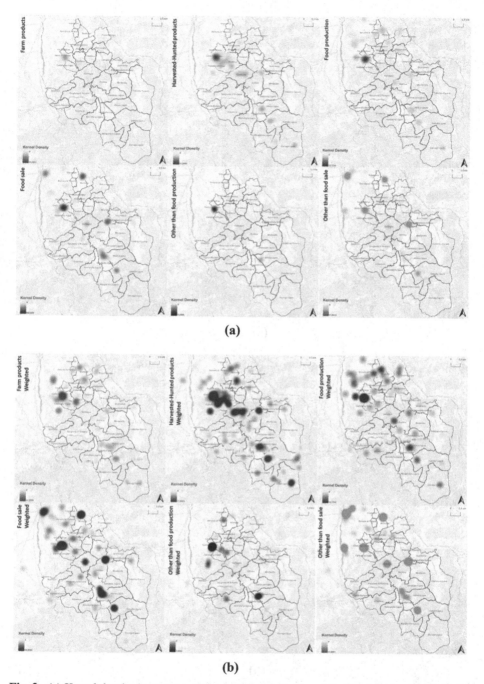

(a)

(b)

Fig. 2. (a) Kernel density heat maps of the spatial distribution of the Provisioning Services. (b) Heat maps of the spatial distribution weighted by the number of respondents who valued each Provisioning Service as important

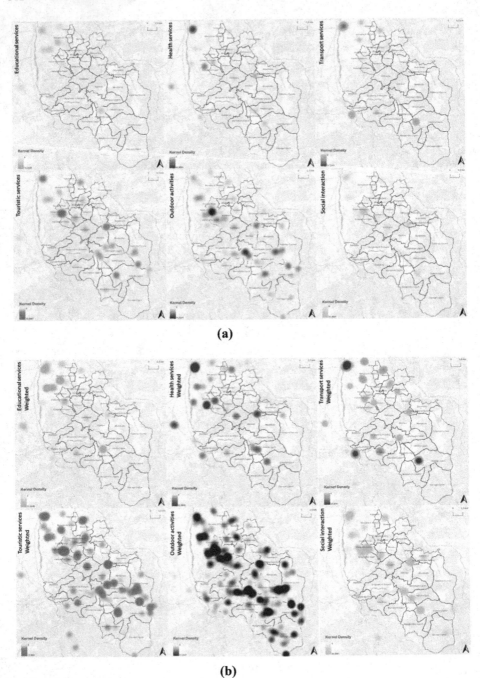

Fig. 3. (a) Kernel density heat maps of the spatial distribution of the Cultural Services. (b) Heat maps of the spatial distribution weighted by the number of respondents who valued each Cultural Service as important

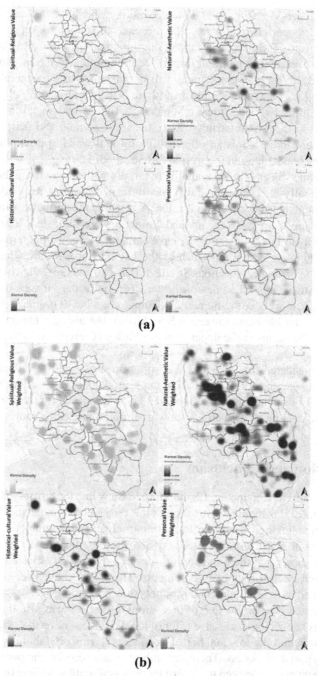

Fig. 4. (a) Kernel density heat maps of the spatial distribution of the Landscape Values. (b) Heat maps of the spatial distribution weighted by the number of respondents who valued each Landscape Value as important

The cultural services (Fig. 3a and 3b) educational, health and transport are mostly located in the less peripherical areas. The presence of schools is very clearly located in Costa Vescovato, Tortona, Sarezzano, Villaromagnano, Carbonara, San Sebastiano and Rocchetta Ligure. The public transport locations indicate the bus stops and train stations. The health services correspond with the presence of the general practitioners or the pharmacies. In the more remote areas there is a clear absence of all of those three services. The cultural services tourism, outdoor activities and social interaction show more diffusion in the whole territory. Also, the more remote and peripheric areas of the territory were indicated as an offer for hiking and walking possibilities, but also mountainbiking and bathing in the river at the Strette di Pertuso.

The landscape values (Fig. 4a and 4b) are largely widespread throughout the whole territory. Especially the aesthethic value was indicated by most respondents, but also the environmental and historic-cultural value. As regards the aesthetic value the villages of San Sebastiano Curone, Garbagna and Volpedo were indicated, together with the Torri di San Alosio in Castellania. The environmental value of the territory is mostly related with mountain or hill tops such as the Mount Ebro, Mount Chiappo and San Vito, but also the geological locations Strette di Pertuso, and the Calanchi of the Ossona Valley. The historic-cultural values of the territory lie in the villages of Volpedo and San Sebastiano, as well as the numerous Roman churches (i.e. *pievi*) throughout the whole territory, the Medieval towers of San Alosio, but also the historic pasturelands and chestnut cultivations in the upper Borbera Valley (Carrega, Mongiardino, Cabella, Cantalupo).

We also considered the impact of the importance ascribed to different LS by the residents. Those weighted heat maps show the spatial distribution of each LS weighted by the number of respondents who valued that LS as important for their own well-being (Fig. 2). These heat maps of each LS show a similar, but clearer pattern of the spatial distribution.

4 Discussion and Conclusion

In this study we used participatory LS mapping to show that the territory is still valorised largely by its local stakeholders, even though it is considered remote and depressed. The study shows that linking LS assessment with participatory mapping can contribute to a better inventory of what a territory offers, but also the identification of potential conflicts.

The study shows that the provisioning services are spatially clustered in the lower part of the territory and around the settlements. The results show a very dense mapping of the selling and buying of local rural products (n = 530) being cheese, salami and wine the most indicated. The production of provisioning services was also tightly clustered. The territory is known for its elevated offer of local products, nevertheless, the clustering of its production and the low number of producers (farms or elaboration of products) indicate a territorial weakness. Therefore, a higher attention on the possibility and the support to create places devoted to the production, elaboration, selling of local products (for example farms, local shops, markets ...) should be considered. Especially since those locations indicate a very high importance for the well-being of the respondents. This corresponds with the fact that the territory has an active offer of local products, and that local actors consider those products fundamental for the identity of their territory.

Cultural services such as outdoor activities, social interaction and touristic activities, show a high distribution and low clustering. This demonstrates an active territory with a large variety of cultural services. Respondents indicated them as highly important for their well-being. The cultural services such as educational, health and transport services on the other hand are very much clustered and show less difference when weighted with their personal well-being. The absence of those landscape services, being also the parameters for the SNAI-financing, confirm the biggest weakness of the territory for local actors.

When it comes to landscape values, personally important places indicate a large clustering since "sense of place" is where people psychologically respond to their environments, and find it therefore important. The highest distribution is found for the landscape values, where especially the environmental-natural value is noted. This value (n = 202) shows a big difference when the weight of importance for the respondents' well-being is considered. This corresponds with other literature (Xu et al., 2020; Zube, 1987) where the way people perceive and use the LS is related to their experiences and their thinking, feeling and acting in those sites. The analysis of the personal well-being generally highlights a higher spread of indicated locations within the territory than their concentration in city centers or rural settlements.

We performed a public participation LS mapping in order to indicate not only the spatial distribution of the LS used, perceived and valued, but also the weight those locations have on the personal well-being of the local stakeholders. We found that the services generally are much more representative when weighted with the respondents' personal well-being. The landscape is valued largely and shows a high importance of provisioning and cultural services. We therefore want to underline the importance of financing institutions to look not only at the basic cultural services (education, health and transport), but also to consider the large amount of services and values in the aim of seeing the landscape potential. By creating a territory overlay with the positive perceptions, we identified which areas local administrators and planners would be well advised to emphasize in order to meet the needs of the local stakeholders. Thus, this participatory mapping approach can be understood as a way to improve both landscape development and planning. In this case, the analysis can even be used as input for project proposals for funding (i.e. SNAI, PNRR). This bottom-up analysis can be understood as a way to improve current development strategies of Inner Areas.

References

Bieling, C., Plieninger, T., Pirker, H., Vogl, C.R.: Linkages between landscapes and human well-being: an empirical exploration with short interviews. Ecol. Econ. **105**, 19–30 (2014)

Brown, G., Fagerholm, N.: Empirical PPGIS/PGIS mapping of ecosystem services: a review and evaluation. Ecosyst. Serv. **13**, 119–133 (2015)

Creighton, J.L.: The Public Participation Handbook: Making better Decisions Through Citizen Involvement. John Wiley & Sons (2005)

De Rossi, A.: Riabitare l'Italia: le aree interne tra abbandoni e riconquiste. Donzelli editore (2019)

Dossche, R., Rogge, E., Van Eetvelde, V.: Detecting people's and landscape's identity in a changing mountain landscape. An example from the northern Apennines. Landscape Res. **41**(8), 934–949 (2016)

Dossche, R.: Towards a sustainable rural mountain landscape. Exploring the (hi)stories of Val Borbera (northern Apennines, Italy). PhD-Thesis, University of Genoa, Genoa, Italy (2016)

Dossche, R.: Is shrinking really a bad thing? XXXIII Congresso Geografico Italiano, Geografie in Movimento – Moving Geographies, 8 - 13 settembre 2021 – Padova (2021)

Ebdon, D.: Statistics in Geography Second Edition: A Practical Approach. Blackwell Publishing, Malden, MA (1985)

Lucatelli, S.: La strategia nazionale, il riconoscimento delle aree interne. Territorio (2015)

MEa, M.E.A.: Ecosystems and Human Well-Being: Synthesis. Island, Washington, DC (2005)

Plieninger, T., et al.: Identifying and assessing the potential for conflict between landscape values and development preferences on the Faroe Islands. Global Environmental Change **52**, 162–180 (2018)

Rawluk, A., Ford, R.M., Neolaka, F.L., Williams, K.J.: Public values for integration in natural disaster management and planning: a case study from Victoria, Australia. J. Environ. Manage. **185**, 11–20 (2017)

Silverman, B.W.: Density Estimation for Statistics and Data Analysis. Routledge (2018)

Temorshuizen, J.W., Opdam, P.: Landscape services as a bridge between landscape ecology and sustainable development. Landscape Ecol. **24**(8), 1037–1052 (2009)

Vallés-Planells, M., Galiana, F., Van Eetvelde, V.: A classification of landscape services to support local landscape planning. Ecology and Society **19**(1) (2014)

Vendemmia, B., Pucci, P., Beria, P.: An institutional periphery in discussion. rethinking the inner areas in Italy. Applied Geography, **135**, 102537 (2021)

Xu, H., Zhao, G., Fagerholm, N., Primdahl, J., Plieninger, T.: Participatory mapping of cultural ecosystem services for landscape corridor planning: a case study of the Silk Roads corridor in Zhangye, China. J. Environ. Manage. **264**, 110458 (2020)

Zube, E.H.: Perceived land use patterns and landscape values. Landscape Ecol. **1**(1), 37–45 (1987)

Techniques and Survey for 3D Modeling of Touristic Caves: Valdemino Case

Isabella Nicole Pisoni[(✉)] [iD], Alberto Cina [iD], Nives Grasso [iD], and Paolo Maschio [iD]

DIATI - Department of Environmental, Land and Infrastructure Engineering, Politecnico di Torino, Corso Duca degli Abruzzi 24, 10129 Torino, Italy
{isabella.pisoni,alberto.cina,nives.grasso,
paolo.maschio}@polito.it

Abstract. Nowadays, touristic caves are a relevant topic among topographical and geological studies. Modern techniques allow to elaborate 3D models with high accuracy and precision. Anyway, underground surveys are always delicate to perform, due to narrow and difficult to reach environments. In this paper, we show a case study, "Valdemino" cave, that involved the utilization of different point cloud acquisition methods: UAV, TLS, SLAM. The first purpose was to obtain 3D models of outdoor and indoor environments with a medium and high accuracy. These models were used to calculate the thickness of the rock between surface and cave's roof and will be used for further studies, taking part in the PRIN 2017 project, concerning the impact of the tourist on show caves. The second purpose was to discuss about the feasibility and precision of the different survey methods, when studying a cave. The results showed how SLAM technology is enough accurate for speleological purposes, if compared with the more accurate TLS method. It is precise, maneuverable, easy to use and it allowed to get into environments that TLS can't reach, such as non-touristic areas.

Keywords: SLAM technology · Touristic cave · UAV acquisition · LiDAR technology · Underground survey · 3D modeling

1 Introduction

In the last decades, a particular attention has been raised on touristic caves and the impact of human presence on the equilibrium of these delicate environments [1–4]. The contribute of geomatics has become really significant, with the implementation of various 3D mapping methods [5–8]. 3D modeling can be used for a lot of different purposes that range from tourism to risks assessment.

Terrestrial laser scanners (TLS) have been widely used to map outdoor environments and even caves [9], but underground and indoor surveys are a critical case, since instruments whose acquisitions are realized with marker surveyed by GNSS (Global Navigation Satellite System) and total station, such as TLS, are hard to use, due to difficult operating conditions [10]. That's why it is necessary to use them together with topographical instruments, that measure angles and distances, for example total stations

E. Borgogno-Mondino and P. Zamperlin (Eds.): ASITA 2022, CCIS 1651, pp. 317–328, 2022.
https://doi.org/10.1007/978-3-031-17439-1_23

[11]. This way, a geodetic traverse is built and TLS are placed over points with known coordinates. Anyway, it happens that underground areas are not easily accessible and therefore not suitable for TLS. In these cases, some other instruments can be used, starting from SLAM (Simultaneous Localization And Mapping) based portable instruments, for example [5, 6, 12]. They are equipped with Distance Measuring Instruments (DMI), profilers, Inertial Measurement Units (IMU) and sometimes with camera sensors. They are portable, maneuverable and they can be placed on a backpack or handheld. They don't need to be constantly geo-referenced during acquisition, because point clouds are built over trajectories calculated by algorithms based on image navigation integrated with IMU [13, 14].

In this paper we show a case study, "Valdemino Cave" in Borgio Verezzi, where we have studied and compared some geomatic techniques in very difficult and extreme environment. The purpose is to give support and analysis of environmental sustainability of touristic caves.

We adopted two different approaches for data acquisition. The first one consisted in using a Teledyne Optech Polaris (a TLS) and a total station, the second one using a KAARTA Stencil 2 (SLAM technology based). For indoor surveys, in fact, there is often the need to compare and integrate different systems to get more complete data and to verify the precision of each technique with respect to the others [12, 15]. In this case study, we used TLS method as reference for the other one.

Evaluating the impact of the tourist in show caves means also studying the impact of urbanization around the cave's territory. The cave has to be considered as what it is: cavity underground, lying among urbanized areas, maybe with houses or that are going to host new buildings in the immediate future. In fact, one of the main purposes of this study is to investigate the thickness of the rock lying upon the cave's roof.

Modern photogrammetry techniques are a consolidated technique in many fields of environmental monitoring and surveys [16–19]. For our study, an unmanned aerial vehicle (UAV) DJI Phantom 4 aircraft was used to carry a camera in order to acquire images of the outside area surrounding the cave. Images have been later elaborated to get a 3D model of the surface and a digital elevation model (DEM). The photogrammetric model has been integrated with 3D underground model. We analyzed the accuracy of photogrammetric flight 3D model and Stencil 2 with respect to a traditional LiDAR (Light Detection And Ranging).

The products we obtained from this study consist in: dense clouds, orthomosaic images and DEM images.

1.1 Case Study

The Valdemino cave is situated on Borgio Verezzi territory, in Liguria region (Italy). Coordinates of the entrance: latitude 44°09′45" N, longitude 8°18′15" E. It's around 500 m distant from the sea and its elevation is a few meters above sea level, starting from 30 m at the entrance and lowering up to 2 m in correspondence to the last room.

Our study is part of the PRIN 2017 project about the impact of the tourist on show caves: "Progetto PRIN 2017: SHOWCAVE: a multidisciplinary research project to study, classify and mitigate the environmental impact in tourist caves".

2   Materials and Methods

This research is based on four essential parts: UAV based data acquisition with a DJI Phantom 4 aircraft for 3D terrain model, terrestrial laser scanner (TLS) and portable laser scanner LiDAR (PLS) data acquisition, data processing, DEMs and 3D models realization and analysis.

TLS acquisition was carried out after topographical measurements to build a geodetic traverse. In discussion we analyze and compare results and accuracy of different techniques.

2.1   UAV Based Data Acquisition and Processing

The very first step was to realize a manual flight embracing an area approximatively corresponding to the extension of the underground cave (about 5,5 ha). For this purpose, a DJI Phantom 4 aircraft was used, equipped with a GNSS receiver able to acquire RTK (Real Time Kinematic) corrections; the fix ambiguity phase allowed centimetric accuracy. Coordinates acquired belong to the projection centers, with centimetric accuracy, used for geo-localization and 3D model elaboration. On the drone, a gimbal camera, whose specifics are reported in Table 1, was placed. This camera can be oriented in different directions with different angles, up to 90°. Moreover, five markers were placed and detected their position with RTK GNSS (accuracy of a few cm). Three hundred-ninety-six nadir pictures were taken during the flight.

Table 1. Camera parameters.

Camera model	Ground resolution GSD	Focal length	Pixel size	Average height from the ground	Average scale
FC6310R 12 MP × 1″ sensor	1.32 cm/pix	8.8 mm	2.4 × 2.4 μm	48 m	5400

Data processing was realized through proprietary software AgiSoft Metashape [20]. For this study, we decided to try three different geo-localization approaches to estimate the variations in calibration parameters and distortion plot, involved in photos alignment and camera optimization. In the three different approaches we tried different combinations of GCPs (Ground Control Point), and CPs (Check Points), always using all the PCs (projection center) we had. We used the three approaches to evaluate the differences between the different solutions and to evaluate the importance of GCPs in the accuracy and estimation of the camera calibration. In Table 2 a resume of the three different cases.

After that, we elaborated different products: dense cloud, tiled model, orthomosaic, DEM. A particular attention was dedicated to DEM. Since one of the main aims of this study is to investigate the thickness of the rock lying between the surface and the roof of the cave, we actually needed a DTM. For this purpose, a classification was

Table 2. GCPs, CPs and PCs utilisation in the three different cases.

Case	GCP	CP	PC
1	5	0	396
2	1	4	396
3	0	5	396

realized. This procedure consisted in taking the dense cloud, selecting the groups of points corresponding to trees or houses by manually drawing polygonal contours around those elements and assigning them to two different classes, in this case respectively *trees* (green) and *buildings* (red). All the other points remained into class *ground*, as default. From here, we built a mesh using ground points only, obtaining a DTM. In Fig. 1, the classification is shown.

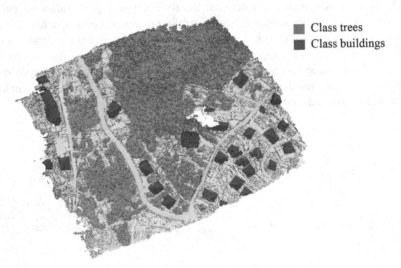

■ Class trees
■ Class buildings

Fig. 1. Manual classification of dense cloud's points.

2.2 TLS Methodology, Acquisition and Processing

We used a Teledyne Optech Polaris (see Fig. 2a) for the acquisition of the reference point cloud of the indoor of the cave. This instrument is equipped with integrated sensors, such as internal L1 GNSS, inclination compensator, compass, camera controls and with external camera imaging system, a Nikon with a resolution of 24 MPx. It has a really wide acquisition range (up to 2000 m) and a high resolution (up to 1 mm at 33 m). The acquisition field of view is adjustable and reaches 360° [21]. Its specifics make it suitable for all kinds of environments but can have some limitation for caves, for example, due to the narrow indoor spaces.

The Polaris laser scanner allows to acquire point clouds directly georeferenced from a station point and an orientation point, starting from three points outside the cave and we built a geodetic traverse using a total station Leica MS50. With this method, we managed to place some points with extrapolated coordinates inside the cave, for a total of fifteen points, that have been used to place the Polaris for acquisition, directly georeferencing with targets on known points.

Data processing was realized using proprietary software Polaris ATLAScan [22]. We had fifteen separate directly georeferenced point clouds to be imported and elaborated, one for each scan. It was necessary to operate alignment; the majority of the clouds were already correctly oriented in space, since geo-referenced, but two appeared to be inclined with respect to the horizontal and needed to be corrected. When every scan was processed, we merged all the point clouds in a single one and colorized it, using internal camera pictures.

In the end, we exported a DEM, to have the elevation of the roof of the cave (the highest points detected during acquisition with TLS). DEM's resolution is 5 cm/pix.

2.3   SLAM Methodology, Acquisition and Processing

Slam method was applied using a KAARTA Stencil 2 (Fig. 2b). This instrument is composed by a Velodyne VLP-16, a MEMS (Micro Electronic Mechanical System) inertial platform and a feature tracker camera, connected to a processor Intel Core i7. The measuring procedure puts together LiDAR point acquisition and information from the feature tracker system, estimating motion where instrument is held.

This method is particularly suitable for caves because it allows to acquire points in small and narrow environments, since the instrument range goes from 10 cm up to 100 m, and it doesn't necessarily need a GNSS positioning (even if it can be integrated with). In fact, the instrument registers translational and rotational movement, registering a point cloud based on the trajectory of acquisition. Data processing integrates motion estimation, laser point acquisition and speed information to register acquired points in a local reference system. Then, with a mapping algorithm, similar geometric features are detected, to recognize coincident points in the point cloud [23].

KAARTA Stencil 2 is a relatively small and light instrument; it can be transported by hand or placed on a backpack. In this case study, we at first put it on a small handheld pole and then on a small backpack, in order to move easily inside the cave.

We performed several loop closed acquisitions. A first one covered the whole touristic path. We started and ended at the main entrance of the cave. The other acquisitions were taken along the non-touristic areas, considering the same room inside the cave as reference for starting point and ending point. In fact, we have placed particular attention to start and end at the same point, in order to operate loop closure and recognize later, during data elaboration, common areas in different acquisitions. Lastly, it was really important to have a minimum overlap between two or more scans, to allow post-processing registration activity.

A specific tool allows to simulate the acquisition process with a lower speed, changing some parameters characterizing the surveyed scene, to improve the trajectory estimation and the point cloud registration. Then, we performed loop closure for each acquisition. This allowed to force the overlap of the initial point with the ending point and it's really important because sometimes the inertial-odometry system fails in registering correctly angles and directions, making the trajectory deviate from the real one, causing a shift between starting point and ending point, that should be the same [24].

After having all the scans cleaned and given a correct trajectory, we had to assign them coordinates. For this task, we used an open source software: Cloud Compare [25]. It has a specific tool that allows to align and orientate a point cloud using another one as reference, taking common points between the two. So, we imported the point cloud from ATLAScan software (that, for practical reasons we are going to call Polaris Cloud from now on) to be the reference. Fifteen common points between the two clouds were used, all of them with a residual error < 1 m. After registration, we performed the algorithm called Iterative Closest Point (ICP) that allows an even more precise registration of the two models [26], to optimize the result. The final global error after ICP was 43 cm. In the end, we calculated the distance cloud-to-cloud, between Polaris Cloud and the Cloud registered with Stencil 2 acquired in touristic path. We remind that we used Polaris Cloud as a reference, to evaluate the accuracy of Stencil 2 acquisition method.

Once we had assigned coordinates to the main cloud (the touristic path), we could merge it with the other point clouds, non-touristic areas, using the align tool and merging all the clouds as one (that we'll call KAARTA Cloud).

a)   b)

Fig. 2. a) Teledyne Optec Polaris. b). KAARTA Stencil 2.

3 Obtained Results

3.1 UAV Modeling

The first important result involves camera calibration and the role of the GCP. As said previously, three different cases were analyzed. For each case, camera calibration parameters and the distortion plot were analyzed (see Table 2). We expected to get at least a small difference between the three cases, since we thought that placing GCPs would have had an important influence on the geo-localization. The difference both in the calibration parameters and in the distortion plot of the three separate cases was actually really small. As an example, some calibration parameters in the three different cases are reported in

Table 3. Camera internal orientation and distortion coefficients.

Case	F [pixel]	Cx [pixel]	Cy [pixel]	K1	K2	K3
1	3628.78 ± 0.11	−2.39 ± 0.09	5.87 ± 0.09	0.006 ± 7.2E-5	−0.05 ± 3.5E-4	0.09 ± 6.6E-4
2	3631.99 ± 0.10	−2.94 ± 0.05	5.79 ± 0.10	0.006 ± 2.7E-5	−0.05 ± 1.2E-4	0.09 ± 2.3E-4
3	3634.15 ± 0.15	−3.41 ± 0.06	3.83 ± 0.14	0.006 ± 2.7E-5	−0.05 ± 1.2E-4	0.09 ± 2.3E-4

Table 3: we consider only the contribution of the radial distortion (coefficients K). The tangential distortion was negligible.

We plotted two curves representing the difference between distortion plots (Fig. 3).

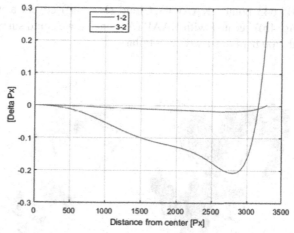

Fig. 3. Curves representing the difference between distortion plots of case 1 and case 2 (blue) and between distortion plots of case 3 and case 2 (red). Color figure online.

Taking case 2 as reference, we can observe that case 3 (0 GCP) and case 2 (1 GCP) have a difference almost equal to zero. On the contrary, case 1 (5 GCP) and case 2 have distortion plots that reach a difference of 0.3 Px.

Lastly, the final RMSE (root mean square deviation) for each case is pretty low (<10 cm), absolutely adequate for our purpose. Comparing the three cases, we could see how markers weren't strictly necessary, since the precision of geo-localization is guaranteed even with only the image acquisition centers: RTK projection centers.

If the camera calibration parameter and distortion plot of the three cases happened to be really similar in the three cases (showed in Table 3), a difference in the final RMSE (of GCPs, CPs and PCs) was observed. In Table 4 a resume.

GCPs appear not to be strictly necessary, since we obtained a centimetric accuracy even without them. Anyway, we noticed how the presence of even one GCP (case 2) decrease systematic effects obtained with only PCs (case 3); in fact, residuals on CPs get halved (8.7 ➔ 4.8 cm).

Table 4. Total 3D RMSE (cm) of residuals.

Case	GCP	CP	PC
1	2.2	–	1.6
2	6.2	4.8	2.9
3	–	8.7	2.1

3.2 Point Cloud Comparison

We had three different point clouds: drone photogrammetric model, 215.550.150 points, LiDAR Polaris Cloud (see Fig. 4a)), 150.158.080 points and KAARTA Cloud (see Fig. 4a)), 170.045.643 points. KAARTA Cloud (Fig. 4a)) covers a wider area than Polaris Cloud (Fig. 4b)) because with KAARTA Stencil 2 we could survey in part of the non-touristic path, too hard to survey with Polaris.

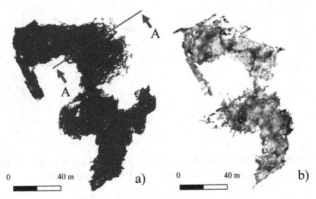

Fig. 4. a) and b) top view of Polaris Cloud (4a) and top view of KAARTA Cloud (4b).

When overlapping the point clouds, we observed that the RMSE after the alignment and the ICP is 0.43 m, that is acceptable for the speleological purpose of our study. Next step was to compare the external area and the cave, from now on using KAARTA Cloud. With Cloud Compare tools, we took some sections to examine the thickness of the rock along the area, that corresponds to the distance between surface cloud and KAARTA Cloud (example in Fig. 5).

Moreover, we imported the DTM from ATLAScan and the DTM from Metashape in QGIS [27], with a resolution of 5 cm/pix. With a difference between the second and the first, we obtained another DTM: thickness of the rock (see Fig. 6b)). On this DTM we could visualize the geodetic traverse built inside the cave, with its ellipses of error with 95% of probability (see Fig. 6a)).

Fig. 5. Section A-A of the surface and the cave in correspondence of the first room. The red line shows the area where the thickness of the rock is the smallest.

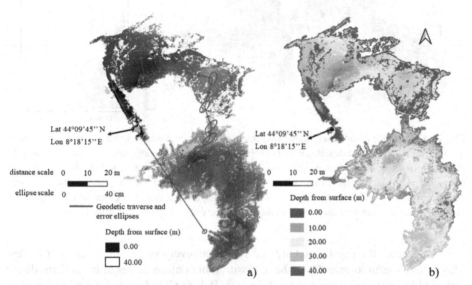

Fig. 6. a). DTM: difference between the classified DTM of the surface and the DTM of the cave, greyscale, with geodetic traverse and error ellipses, enhanced dimension by factor 50. b) DTM: difference between the classified DTM of the surface and the DTM of the cave, colorscale.

4   Discussion

4.1   Point Cloud

We said that the RMSE after KAARTA Cloud to Polaris Cloud registration is 0.43 m. In Fig. 7b) is shown the gaussian curve (in grey color) related to the distance between Polaris Cloud and KAARTA Cloud (colored histogram) in one particular selection of area (see Fig. 7a)), where the majority of the points see an average distance cloud-to-cloud lower than 24 cm. So, for our purposes, SLAM method can for sure be a valid substitute for static LiDAR technology, comporting a saving of time and a higher flexibility to move inside narrow environments. In Fig. 4a) and b), we can see how KAARTA Cloud has actually some parts more than Polaris Cloud. That's because with KAARTA Stencil 2 we managed to address more narrow environments, in addition to the touristic path. That made KAARTA Cloud more complete.

From the DTM showed in Fig. 6a), we could identify one particular critical point, that corresponds to the first big room of the cave and that can be seen also in section represented in Fig. 4. Here, the thickness of the rock appears to be less than 5 m; this has to be considered in case there is the need to build in correspondence of the area. The deepest roof point of the cave is approximatively at 21 m depth.

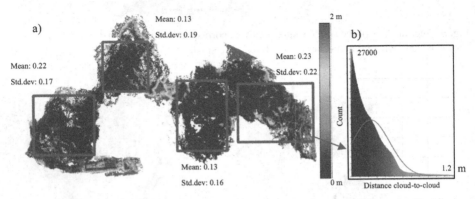

Fig. 7. a). Distance cloud-to-cloud in the entire area. Some captions were taken to verify the mean distance and the standard deviation. b). Histogram (coloured) and gaussian curve representing the distribution of absolute distance cloud-to-cloud between points belonging to KAARTA Cloud and points belonging to Polaris Cloud in one section of the entire area. On the x-axis: cloud-to-cloud distance, on the y-axis, count of points with a corresponding distance cloud-to-cloud. We can generally estimate the accuracy as a weighted average of the 4 cases: it results 17 ± 3 cm.

Lastly, since the point cloud are geo-localized, every single point has coordinates. This is very useful to investigate the disposition of conformations of interest inside the cave and in particular the water level. In fact, Polaris Cloud is so detailed and precise that shows the presence of water in some of the rooms of the cave. Even if laser scanner doesn't actually work for water (the signal is not reflected), some light blue color is detected, together with the presence of a clear horizontal line where the surface of the cave seems to be cut, that corresponds to water level.

5   Conclusions

In this case study, two different laser scanner acquisition techniques have been compared. Teledyne Optec Polaris, a TLS and KAARTA Stencil 2, a SLAM technology-based laser scanner. Both the techniques appeared to be precise and correct enough for the purpose of building a 3D model of the cave but SLAM technology resulted to be more practical and more suitable to map really narrow environments, where TLS can't reach. In fact, it allowed to register a wider area of the cave, including also non-touristic paths, without the need of a GNSS localization during acquisition. Moreover, while TLS acquisition took two days to be concluded, with KAARTA Stencil 2 we needed just a few hours to complete our tour. Anyway, Teledyne Optec Polaris for sure was useful to determine the accuracy of KAARTA Stencil 2 acquisition and processing.

The 3D models obtained are so accurate, that could be implemented as a virtual reproduction of the indoor area of the cave. The accuracy can be estimated from the comparison with respect to the reference cloud (Polaris) and is equal to 17 cm.

Then, thanks to 3D modeling of the surface, through UAV based method, we managed to get an approximation of the thickness of the rock lying between the surface and the roof of the cave, comparing two different DEMs.

Fundings and Acknowledgments. Progetto PRIN 2017: SHOWCAVE: a multidisciplinary research project to study, classify and mitigate the environmental impact in tourist caves.

Particular thanks to Professors Bartolomeo Vigna and Engineer Valentina Balestra. Special thanks also to Professors Marco Isaia and Rossana Bellopede, coordinators of the project PRIN 2017.

References

1. Calaforra, J.M., et al.: Environmental control for determining human impact and permanent visitor capacity in a potential show cave before tourist use. Environ. Conserv. **30**(2), 160–167 (2003)
2. Constantin, S., et al.: Monitoring human impact in show caves. A study of four Romanian caves. Sustainability **13**(4), 1619 (2021)
3. Mulec, J.: Human impact on underground cultural and natural heritage sites, biological parameters of monitoring and remediation actions for insensitive surfaces: case of Slovenian show caves. J. Nat. Conserv. **22**(2), 132–141 (2014)
4. Balestra, V., et al.: Study of the environmental impact in show caves: a multidisciplinary research. Geoingegneria Ambientale e Mineraria, Anno LVIII, n. II-III, dicembre **163–164**, 24–35 (2021). https://doi.org/10.19199/2021.163-164.1121-9041.024
5. Daniele, G., et al.: Survey solutions for 3D acquisition and representation of artificial and natural caves. Appl. Sci. **11**(14), 6482 (2021)
6. Sammartano, G., Spanò, A.: Point clouds by SLAMbased mobile mapping systems: accuracy and geometric content validation in multisensor survey and stand-alone acquisition. Appl. Geomatics **10**(4), 317–339 (2018)
7. De Waele, J., Fabbri, S., Santagata, T., Chiarini, V., Columbu, A., Pisani, L.: Geomorphological and speleogenetical observations using terrestrial laser scanning and 3D photogrammetry in a gypsum cave (Emilia Romagna, N. Italy). Geomorphology **319**, 47–61 (2018)
8. Weinmann, M.: Reconstruction and Analysis of 3D Scenes. Springer, Cham (2016). https://doi.org/10.1007/978-3-319-29246-5
9. Mohammed Oludare, I., Pradhan, B.: A decade of modern cave surveying with terrestrial laser scanning: a review of sensors, method and application development. Int. J. Speleol. **45**, 8 (2016)
10. Kang, Z., Yang, J., Yang, Z., Cheng, S.: A review of techniques for 3d reconstruction of indoor environments. ISPRS Int. J. Geo-Inf. **9**, 330 (2020)
11. Keller, F., Sternberg, H.: Multi-sensor platform for indoor mobile mapping: system calibration and using a total station for indoor applications. Remote Sens. **5**(11), 5805–5824 (2013)
12. Lagüela, S., Dorado, I., Gesto, M., Arias, P., González-Aguilera, D., Lorenzo, H.: Behavior analysis of novel wearable indoor mapping system based on 3D-SLAM. Sensors **18**, 766 (2018)

13. Dissanayake, M.G., Newman, P., Clark, S., Durrant-Whyte, H.F., Csorba, M.: A solution to the simultaneous localization and map building (SLAM) problem. IEEE Trans. Robot. Autom. **17**(3), 229–241 (2001)
14. Zhang, J., Singh, S.: Laser–visual–inertial odometry and mapping with high robustness and low drift. J. Field. Robot. **35**(8), 1242–1264 (2018)
15. Chiabrando, F., Della Colletta, C., Sammartano, G., Spanò, A., Spreafico, A.: Torino 1911 project: a contribution of a slam-based survey to extensive 3D heritage modeling. Int. Arch. Photogrammetry. Remote. Sens. Spat. Inf. Sci. **XLII-2**, 225–234 (2018). https://doi.org/10.5194/isprs-archives-XLII-2-225-2018
16. Elena, B., et al.: Precision agriculture workflow, from data collection to data management using FOSS tools: an application in northern Italy vineyard. ISPRS Int. J. Geo. Inf. **10**(4), 236 (2021)
17. Marco, P., et al.: Multi-temporal study of BELVEDERE glacier for hydrologic hazard monitoring and water resource estimation using UAV: tests and first results. IN:EGU General Assembly Conference Abstracts (2016)
18. Piras, M., Di Pietra, V., Visintini, D.: 3D modeling of industrial heritage building using COTSs system: test, limits and performances. Int. Arch. Photogrammetry. Remote Sens. Spat. Inf. Sci. **42**, 281 (2017)
19. Nex, F., Remondino, F.: UAV for 3D mapping applications: a review. Appl. Geomatics **6**(1), 1–15 (2013). https://doi.org/10.1007/s12518-013-0120-x
20. Agisoft Metashape Professional. www.agisoft.com. Version 1.8.2 build 14127 (64 bit) (2022)
21. Teledyneoptec Homepage. www.teledyneoptech.com/en/products/static-3d-survey/polaris/. Accessed 11 Mar 2021
22. Teledyne Optec, 2021, ATLAScan Version 1.2.10
23. Kaarta, Kaarta, Instructions for Stencil® (2018)
24. Williams, B., Cummins, M., Neira, J., Newman, P., Reid, I., Tardós, J.: A comparison of loop closing techniques in monocular SLAM. Robot. Auton. Syst. **57**, 1188–1197 (2009)
25. Cloud Compare. www.cloudcompare.org. 2022, Version 2.11.3 (Anoia)
26. Dabove, P., Grasso, N., Piras, M.: Smartphone-based photogrammetry for the 3D modeling of a geomorphological structure. Appl. Sci. **9**(18), 3884 (2019)
27. QGIS GNU General Public License. www.gnu.org. 2022, Version 3.16.1-Hannover

A Comprehensive Understanding of Machine Learning and Deep Learning Methods for 3D Architectural Cultural Heritage Point Cloud Semantic Segmentation

Yuwei Cao[1] , Simone Teruggi[2(✉)] , Francesco Fassi[2] , and Marco Scaioni[1]

[1] Department of Architecture, Built Environment and Construction Engineering, Politecnico di Milano, Via Ponzio 31, 20133 Milan, Italy
{yuwei.cao,marco.scaioni}@polimi.it
[2] 3D Survey Group, ABC Department., Politecnico di Milano, Via Ponzio 31, 20133 Milan, Italy
{simone.teruggi,francesco.fassi}@polimi.it

Abstract. As a result of the development of Artificial Intelligence (AI) techniques, in recent years, machine learning (ML) and deep learning (DL) approaches have been widely used to semantically enrich 3D architectural cultural heritage (ACH) point clouds. While existing approaches for analyzing and interpreting point clouds continue to improve, the generalizability of pre-trained ML and DL methods to various types of historic buildings remains uncertain. In this context, a comprehensive understanding of both methodologies can enable us to make more effective use of AI techniques in the ACH domain (e.g., data exploitation, model definition, analysis, and preservation). This work presents and compares two very different approaches for the 3D ACH semantic segmentation task. Specifically, we train and test a ML method based on the Random Forest (RF) classifier on the point cloud of three chapels part of the "Sacromonte Calvario di Domodossola" and on the two test scenes of the ArCH dataset. Then, we employ dynamic graph convolutional neural network (DGCNN) as our DL method, training on the ArCH dataset and testing on both the two unseen test scenes of the ArCH dataset and on the "Sacrimonti" chapel point clouds. We provide empirical experiments to illustrate the efficiency of applying ML and DL methodologies to ACH point clouds. Following that, the advantages and limitations of these two approaches are evaluated through a systematic study of the classification results.

Keywords: Machine learning · Deep learning · Architectural heritage · 3D point cloud · Classification

1 Introduction

Recent advances in 3D point cloud representation have facilitated the development of new applications such as heritage information digitalization [1]. However, even the most powerful 3D laser scanners available today may produce physically accurate but semantically meaningless 3D representations. Machine Learning (ML) and Deep Learning (DL)

© The Author(s), under exclusive license to Springer Nature Switzerland AG 2022
E. Borgogno-Mondino and P. Zamperlin (Eds.): ASITA 2022, CCIS 1651, pp. 329–341, 2022.
https://doi.org/10.1007/978-3-031-17439-1_24

techniques for extracting semantic information from 3D point clouds have emerged and applied in a variety of applications, including construction engineering [2], building modeling [3], energy estimation [4], and cultural heritage [5].

Despite substantial advances in the existing methods for analyzing point clouds, applying ML and DL approaches to the semantic segmentation of architectural cultural heritage (ACH) remains challenging due to their complexity and uniqueness. More specifically, hand-crafted geometric features such as anisotropy, planarity, linearity, sphericity, and verticality are required for ML-based approaches [6, 7], which may raise concerns about the generalization of ML methods to other ACH datasets. On the other hand, DL-based methods can automatically learn features from input point clouds and classify each point in an end-to-end manner. However, their success is based on the presumption that annotated data is constantly available and covers a wide range of samples. What remains unknown is the generalizability of the pre-trained machine learning and deep learning methodologies to various types of architectural heritage.

Certain challenges have been described by Grilli et al. [8], while their focus is on evaluating the generalization of ML-based techniques. In this context, a comprehensive understanding of both approaches is critical for optimizing the use of AI techniques on ACH (e.g., data usage, analysis, and conservation). This paper aims to compare the generalization capabilities and limitations of ML-based and DL-based approaches for the semantic segmentation task of 3D ACH. Specifically, we employ a supervised ML Random Forest (RF) classification method described in the work presented by Grilli et al. [7] as our ML-based approach. Then we employ Dynamic Graph Convolutional Neural Network (DGCNN) [9] as the DL-based method, which automatically derives classification results from input point clouds.

The ML method and the DL approach are trained and tested on i) the test scene part of the Architectural Cultural Heritage (ArCH) dataset [10] and ii) point clouds from three different chapels part of the "Sacromonte Calvario di Domodossola" complex [11]. To assess its generalization, the DL-based technique is trained solely on the training split of the ArCH dataset and then evaluated on both the test split of the ArCH and "Sacrimonti" datasets. The classification results of this approach are compared to those of the supervised ML approach. The advantages and limitations of these two methodologies are then compared through a systematic study of the results. The contribution of our research can be summarized in the following points:

- In the ML-based method, satisfactory classification results are reached by training specific RF classifiers for each dataset that require minimal manual annotations and previously computed covariance features.
- Without manually annotating the "Sacrimonti" dataset, the DL-based classification algorithm delivers competitive performance in cross-dataset point clouds.
- We conducted empirical experiments to gain a comprehensively understand of how pre-trained ML and DL methods perform on distinct types of 3D ACH point clouds.

2 Related Works

Contemporary survey techniques can collect the geometrical representation of ACH in the form of point clouds models. At the same time, to maximize the exploitation of acquired measurements, the huge volume of data necessitates a semantic interpretation at a high Level-of-Details (LoDs). Machine learning (ML) and deep learning (DL) methods for 3D point cloud analysis are constantly being developed and enhanced, the state-of-the-art approaches for determining the feasibility of ML and DL methods applied to ACH point clouds are discussed in this part. These approaches are reviewed from two perspectives: i) ML-based methods, and ii) DL-based methods.

2.1 ML-Based Method

Semantic categories are learned from a dataset of manually annotated data using supervised machine learning techniques such as support vector machines [12], naive Bayes [13], and random forests [14]. The semantic categorization is then disseminated across the full dataset using the trained model. In most cases, providing a substantial amount of annotated data to train the model is not required. Traditional approaches, on the other hand, often use a set of hand-crafted form descriptors as feature vectors to learn the categorization pattern. Local surface patches, spin pictures, intrinsic shape signatures, and heat kernel signatures are among the descriptors listed by Griffiths and Boehm [15]. To accomplish classification, a 2.5D technique uses features and labels from 2D photos and projects them onto 3D models. Grilli et al. [16] presented a classification method that uses 2D data as input ("texture-based" approach). For the test scenarios under investigation, optimized models, orthoimages, and UV maps were developed. They classified the items using orthoimages or UV maps first and then projected the 2D classification findings onto the 3D objects.

Only during the last few years have AI techniques that work directly on the 3D CH point model appeared. In supervised machine learning, the algorithms use certain manually annotated parts of the datasets as inputs, as well as hand-crafted features (such as geometric and/or radiometric qualities), to learn patterns that are then projected throughout the whole dataset. Grilli et al. [7] proposed a classification method that works directly on point clouds, using geometric characteristics to train a Random Forest (RF) classifier. The approach iteratively extracts the most important aspects based on a set of geometric properties that are tightly tied to the dimensions of architectural elements. In [8], the same author confirmed the ability to generalize the categorization model across various architectural settings.

Teruggi et al. [5] suggested an MLMR technique based on the approach described by Grilli et al. The full resolution dataset is subsampled, and large macro-elements are categorized using a low-resolution version of the point model and a particular RF classifier. The output is then back interpolated on a higher resolution point cloud to subdivide components that require great geometric precision. Using the full resolution dataset, the algorithm iterates up to the categorization of single high detail architectural elements. Each step in this approach necessitates training a specific RF model, but only a small amount of labelled data is required, and the training and classification speed has proven to be effective. It divides the data into sub-classes in a hierarchical manner as the geometric features rise. When compared to non-hierarchical categorization, this technique was shown to be more computationally efficient and allowed for more accuracy in the case of complex datasets.

2.2 DL-Based Method

Qi et al. presented PointNet [17], a ground-breaking approach that operates directly on point clouds and employs the shared Multilayer Perceptrons (MLPs) to learn high-dimensional features for each point separately. This approach has been extended in numerous ways to extract local information from a point cloud [9, 18].

For instance, the Dynamic Graph Convolutional Neural Network (DGCNN) improves segmentation efficiency by constructing graphs with point correlations encoded in graph edges [9]. In the CH domain, Pierdicca [19] proposed using DGCNN [9] for the point cloud segmentation of the Architectural Cultural Heritage (ArCH) dataset [10]. DGCNN-Mod [19] improves the performance of classification by including radiometric (HSV value) and normal information. By integrating spectral information and hand-crafted geometric features, DGCNN-Mod + 3Dfeat [20] combines the positive aspects of both ML and DL for semantic segmentation of point clouds in the field of CH. Their work demonstrated the promise of deep learning approaches for segmentation tasks. Unsupervised learning technologies have been developed in this domain to address the absence of labeled data. By faithfully reconstructing the input original point cloud, an autoencoder (AE) is trained to learn a compressed representation from unlabeled data [21]. Among them, DGCNN is utilized as their backbone due to its robustness when applied to point clouds of different scales.

In general, learning to generate powerful and robust representations from inhomogeneous point clouds, particularly ACH point clouds with complex geometric patterns, remains a challenge. We compare the ML-based and DL-based methods using two different ACH datasets to achieve a compressive understanding of the generalizability of both methods in the CH point cloud semantic segmentation task to enable us to make more effective use of AI techniques in the ACH domain.

3 Method

3.1 ML Method

In this work, we present a supervised ML classifier based on the work presented by Grilli et al. [7].

The RF classifier does not need a significant amount of manually annotated data to classify the final dataset, but it requires as input significative geometrical features able to highlight the discontinuities between elements.

These features highlight the structure of the point cloud in the point neighbourhood of a certain radius which is directly dependent on elements dimensions.

Following the reasoning behind the work presented in [5, 7 and 9] in addition to taking the z coordinate of the point into account, the following geometric covariance features (Fig. 1) are computed for radii from 0.05 m to 0.4 m with an increment of 0.05 m: i) anisotropy, ii) planarity, iii) linearity, iv) surface variation, v) sphericity, vi) verticality.

The classification process encompasses different steps: i) extraction of geometric features based on the covariance matrix for the whole dataset; ii) manual segmentation of a portion of the dataset to be used as training set and evaluation set; iii) training the RF classifier; iv) input the dataset to be classified together with computed covariance features to the trained model to obtain the final prediction (Fig. 2).

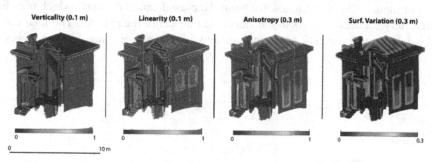

Fig. 1. Examples of computed covariance features on Chapel 3 of "Sacrimonti" dataset. The number inside the parentheses indicates the radius of the searching neighborhood.

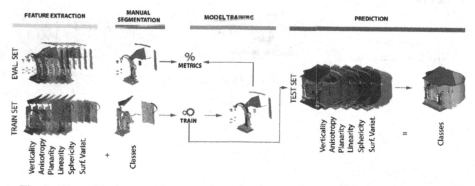

Fig. 2. The architecture of the used ML-based point cloud semantic segmentation method.

3.2 DGCNN-Based DL Network

We employ DGCNN [9] as our DL-based approach for ACH point cloud semantic segmentation. As shown in Fig. 3, the input of the encoder of the network is N coordinates (x, y, z) and their features – RGB color and normalized coordinates (r, g, b, nx, ny, nz) of ACH point clouds. Graphs are constructed using input points and their k-nearest-neighbors as nodes and the connections of nodes as edges. The local and global geometric features are extracted by utilizing shared multilayer perceptron (MLP). Then, the edge features are aggregated by a local max-pooling operation on the extracted features. Additionally, by dynamically constructing graphs in each layer and stacking three Edge-Conv layers, the receptive field is enlarged, and information is aggregated across many receptive fields. The intermediate outputs are learned discriminative representations, a 1,024-dimensional "codeword", and three 64-dimensional edge features. To semantically segment input ACH point clouds, we build the classification network, which uses four shared fully connected layers to transform the outputs of the encoder. The final output of the downstream semantic segmentation network is per-point classification scores.

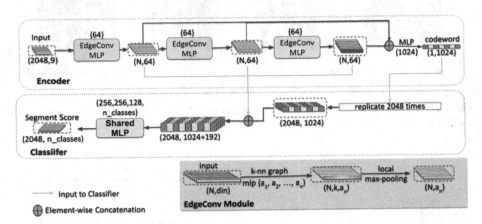

Fig. 3. The architecture of DGCNN-based DL network.

4 Experiment

4.1 Datasets

Arch Dataset. The architectural cultural heritage (arch) dataset [10] includes 17 annotated indoor and outdoor scenes. we employ the 15 labelled scenes as training data of the dl-based method. moreover, two unseen scenes ("a smg portico" and "b smv chapel 27to35") are used as test data in both our dl-based approach and ml-based method to validate the generalizability across different types of ach.

"SACROmonte calvario di domodossola". It is a roman catholic complex (piedmont, italy) that is part of piedmont and lombardy's nine "sacri monti" and has been on the unesco world heritage list since 2003. The structure has a sanctuary and fifteen chapels each with sculptures and murals depicting the stages of the "via crucis" [11]. The site has been surveyed during the summer school "laboratory of places – isprs workshop" [22] organized by the 3d survey group of the department of architecture, built environment and construction engineer of politecnico di milano. Chapel n.3, 6 and 7 taken into consideration for this work have been measured using a terrestrial laser scanner (leica rtc360/leica c10) and uav photogrammetry (chapel n.3: avg. Resolution 5 mm for 14,294,406 points; chapel n.6: avg resolution 1 cm for 10,352,825 points; chapel n. 7: avg res 5 mm for 17,816,051 points).

4.2 Experiment Settings

ML-Based Method. The classification conducted in the following experiment leverage the RF classifier present in the Scikit-learn Python library (version 1.0.2). Following the experiment performed in [5] and in [7] the number of the decision trees and the number of variables to be selected and tested for the best split when growing the trees as been set to 100 and "None" respectively. This allows creating the forest trees. From each tree, a prediction is obtained, and the best solution is selected through voting among all. Specific RF classifiers have been trained for each chapel part of the "Sacrimonti" dataset and the two scenes extracted from the ArCH dataset (A_SMG_portico and B_SMV_chapel_27to35). Figure 4 report an example of the training sets (manually annotated portions) that have been used to train the model for the chapels of "Sacromonte Calvario di Domodossola".

Dl-Based method. We chose a block size of 1×1 square-meter area for dividing each ach scene into blocks along the horizontal direction as training input. In addition, the points in each block are sampled into a uniform number of 2,048. The setup of the neighbor size and hidden layers in our encoder follows that of dgcnn [9]. We have used adam as our optimizer, with a learning rate of 0.01, batch size of 4, and training epochs of 200. A 0.5 probability dropout is used in the last fully connected layer.

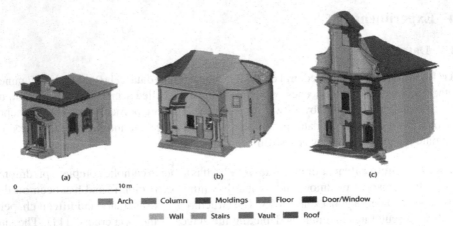

Fig. 4. Training set for (a) Chapel 3, (b) Chapel 6, (c) Chapel 7 of the sacrimonti dataset.

4.3   Results

The overall performance of the two approaches is reported in Table 1 and it is evaluated in terms of overall accuracy (OA), weighted precision, weighted recall, and weighted F1-score as explained in [23]. Weighted metrics have been used to take into account the unbalanced number of samples belonging to the different classes.

Results of ML-based method are strictly dependent on the quality of the geometric features computed on the point cloud and fed to the RF classifier. Errors are concentrated in those parts of the point cloud where the point cloud is particularly noisy (resulting in bad features computations). Furthermore, elements in different classes that present similar geometric characteristics are easily confused.

The ML-based approach proved successful in the classification of the considered scenes. The OA reaches up to 0.97 for Chapel 6, with the lower result on the "B_SMV_chapel_27to35" coming from the ArCH dataset.

In the case of the DL-based approach, the model gets 0.678 and 0.749 of OA on the unseen and varied types of scenes (portico and chapel) of the ArCH dataset. When we use the "Sacrimonti" point clouds to cross-test our approach, we get 0.738, 0.761, and 0.628 in term of OA on Chapel 3, Chapel 6, and Chapel 7, respectively.

The qualitative results of the classification are shown in Figs. 5, 6, 7. We can see that both the ML-based and DL-based methods generate acceptable results, with the second one having some difficulties in recognizing classes such as columns and moldings.

Table 1. Classification metrics. "Scene_A" and "Scene_B" denote "A_SMG_portico" and "B_SMV_chapel_27to35", respectively.

Method	Test scene	OA	W Precision	W. Recall	W. F1-score
ML-based	Scene_A	0.937	0.939	0.937	0.937
	Scene_B	0.874	0.867	0.874	0.867
	Chapel_3	0.948	0.943	0.948	0.944
	Chapel_6	0.976	0.98	0.976	0.977
	Chapel_7	0.912	0.911	0.912	0.908
DL-based	Scene_A	0.678	0.697	0.678	0.645
	Scene_B	0.749	0.721	0.749	0.705
	Chapel_3	0.738	0.717	0.738	0.669
	Chapel_6	0.761	0.746	0.761	0.732
	Chapel_7	0.628	0.575	0.628	0.544

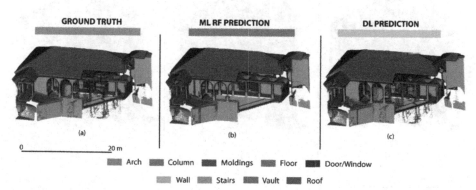

Fig. 5. Qualitative results of ML-based and DL-based approach for the ArCH dataset "B_SMV_chapel_27to35" (a) ground truth, (b) ML-RF prediction and (c) DL prediction.

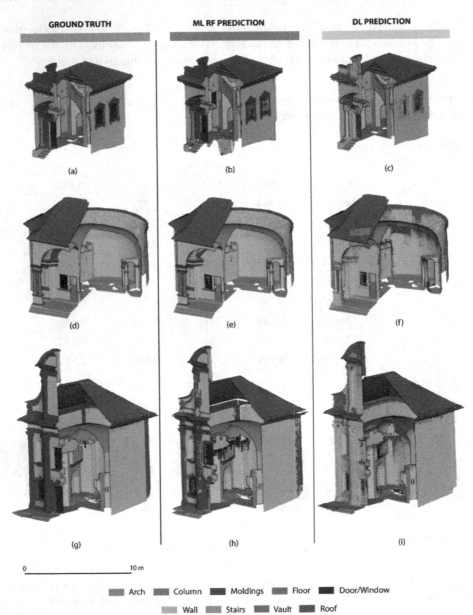

Fig. 6. Qualitative results of ML-based and DL-based approach for the "Sacrimonti" dataset. Chapel 3 (a) ground truth, (b) ML-RF prediction and (c) DL prediction. Chapel 6 (d) ground truth, (e) ML-RF prediction and (f) DL prediction. Chapel 7 (g) ground truth, (h) ML-RF prediction and (i) DL prediction.

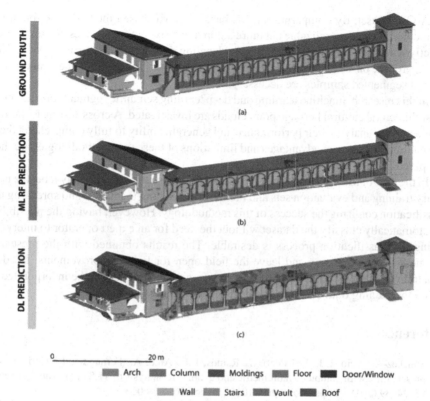

Fig. 7. Qualitative results of ML-based and DL-based approach for the ArCH dataset "A_SMG_portico" (a) ground truth, (b) ML-RF prediction and (c) DL prediction.

5 Discussion and Conclusions

We observed a difference in the DL-based method in performance between "B_SMV_chapel_27to35" and "A_SMG_portico" (0.749 *vs.* 0.678) in Table 1. Due to the fact that the ArCH dataset has five chapel scenes but only one portico scene, the portico type performs worse than the chapel type. To help us understand the generalization of the DL-based method on a dataset that has never been seen for testing, we also provide the results of testing on a cross dataset – "Sacrimonti" point clouds that consist of three chapels. Equivalent results are produced on Chapel_3 and Chapel_6 to the "B_SMV_chapel_27to35" result, while some decline happened on Chapel_7.

We can quickly assess the reliability of the two methods by comparing the results of directly testing on unseen scenes of the ArCH dataset using the DL method against using the ML approach that was trained and tested on the test scenes of the ArCH dataset. Compared to the ML method, we found that the performance of the DL method is lower (see Table 1). The results demonstrate the performance of the DL method is highly dependent on the amount and diversity of training data, as the performance on chapels is closer to that of the ML method. Furthermore, to validate the DL approach generalization, in addition, tests on the "Sacrimonti" chapels used the model trained on the ArCH dataset. By comparing the DL-based and ML-based methods, we found the DL method is less generalizable but more automatic at extracting features and test scenes directly without the requirement of manual labeling during the classification phase. The ML approach, on the contrary, requires specific training for each test case and a few manual segmented samples are necessary.

In this research, machine learning and deep learning semantic segmentation methods for architectural cultural heritage point clouds are investigated. A cross-testing technique is presented to analyze their performance and generalizability to fully comprehend these two methodologies. The advantages and limitations of these two methodologies are then compared.

In the case of ML-based methods, the short amount of time to manually label the necessary training and evaluation sets and the speed of training the model and spreading the classification confirms the success of this methodology. However, having the possibility to automatically classify the dataset without the need for an expert operator to intervene during the classification process is desirable. The results obtained with the presented DL method are promising and leave the field open for future improvements. In addition, transfer learning techniques such as pre-training techniques can be incorporated to enrich the training data diversity and enhance the generalizability.

References

1. Sánchez-Aparicio, L.J., Del Pozo, S., Ramos, L.F., Arce, A., Fernandes, F.: Heritage site preservation with combined radiometric and geometric analysis of TLS data. Autom. Constr. **85**, 24–39 (2018). https://doi.org/10.1016/j.autcon.2017.09.023
2. Bosché, F.: Automated recognition of 3D CAD model objects in laser scans and calculation of as-built dimensions for dimensional compliance control in construction. Adv. Eng. Inform. **24**(1), 107–118 (2010). https://doi.org/10.1016/j.aei.2009.08.006
3. Czerniawski, T., Leite, F.: Automated digital modeling of existing buildings: a review of visual object recognition methods. Autom. Constr. **113**, 103131 (2020). https://doi.org/10. 1016/j.autcon.2020.103131
4. Ham, Y., Golparvar-Fard, M.: Three-dimensional thermography-based method for cost-benefit analysis of energy efficiency building envelope retrofits. J. Comput. Civ. Eng. **29**, B4014009 (2015). https://doi.org/10.1061/(ASCE)CP.1943-5487.0000406
5. Teruggi, S., Grilli, E., Russo, M., Fassi, F., Remondino, F.: A hierarchical machine learning approach for multi-level and multi-resolution 3D point cloud classification. Remote Sens. **12**(16), 2598 (2020). https://doi.org/10.3390/rs12162598
6. Weinmann, M., Jutzi, B., Mallet, C., Weinmann, M.: Geometric features and their relevance for 3D point cloud classification. ISPRS Ann. Photogramm. Remote Sens. Spatial Inf. Sci., IV-1/W1, 157–164 (2017).https://doi.org/10.5194/isprs-annals-IV-1-W1-157-2017
7. Grilli, E., Farella, E. M., Torresani, A., Remondino, F.: Geometric features analysis for the classification of cultural heritage point clouds. Int. Arch. Photogramm. Remote Sens. Spatial Inf. Sci. XLII-2/W15, 541–548 (2019). https://doi.org/10.5194/isprs-archives-XLII-2-W15-541-2019
8. Grilli, E., Remondino, F.: Machine learning generalization across different 3D architectural heritage. ISPRS Int. J. Geo-Inf. **9**, 379 (2020). https://doi.org/10.3390/ijgi9060379
9. Wang, Y., Sun, Y., Liu, Z., Sarma, S.E., Bronstein, M.M., Solomon, J.M.: Dynamic graph CNN for learning on point clouds. ACM Trans. Graph. Tog. **38**, 1–12 (2019). https://doi.org/ 10.1145/3326362

10. Matrone, F., et al.: A benchmark for large-scale heritage point cloud semantic segmentation. Int. Arch. Photogramm. Remote Sens. Spatial Inf. Sci. XLIII-B2-2020, 1419–1426 (2020). https://doi.org/10.5194/isprs-archives-XLIII-B2-2020-1419-2020

11. Tommasi, C., Fiorillo, F., Jiménez Fernández-Palacios, B., Achille, C.: Access and web-sharing of 3D digital documentation of environmental and architectural heritage. Int. Arch. Photogramm. Remote Sens. Spatial Inf. Sci. XLII-2/W9, 707–714 (2019). https://doi.org/10.5194/isprs-archives-XLII-2-W9-707-2019

12. Mathias, M., Martinovic, A., Weissenberg, J., Haegler, S., Van Gool, L.: Automatic architectural style recognition. In: Int. Arch. Photogramm. Remote Sens. Spatial Inf. Sci., XXXVIII-5-W16, 171–176 (2011). https://doi.org/10.5194/isprsarchivesXXXVIII-5-W16-171-2011

13. Ho, T.K.: Random decision forests. In: 3rd International Conference on Document Analysis and Recognition, vol. 1, pp. 278–282. IEEE, Montreal, QC, Canada (1995). https://doi.org/10.1109/ICDAR.1995.598994

14. Breiman, L.: Random forests. Mach. Learn. **45**, 5–32 (2001). https://doi.org/10.1023/A:1010933404324

15. Griffiths, D., Boehm, J.: A review on deep learning techniques for 3D sensed data classification. Remote Sens. **11**, 1499 (2019). https://doi.org/10.3390/rs11121499

16. Grilli, E., Dininno, D., Petrucci, G., Remondino, F.: From 2D to 3D supervised segmentation and classification for cultural heritage applications. Int. Arch. Photogramm. Remote Sens. Spatial Inf. Sci. XLII-2, 399–406 (2018). https://doi.org/10.5194/isprs-archives-XLII-2-399-2018

17. Qi, C.R., Su, H., Mo, K., Guibas, L.J.: PointNet: Deep learning on point sets for 3D classification and segmentation. In: IEEE/CVF Conference on Computer Vision and Pattern Recognition, pp. 652–660. IEEE, Honolulu, HI, USA (2017). https://doi.org/10.48550/arXiv.1612.00593

18. Thomas, H., Qi, C.R., Deschaud, J.E., Marcotegui, B., Goulette, F., Guibas, L.J.: KPConv: Flexible and deformable convolution for point clouds. In: IEEE/CVF International Conference on Computer Vision, pp. 6411–6420. IEEE, Seoul, South Korea (2019). https://doi.org/10.48550/arXiv.1904.08889

19. Pierdicca, R., et al.: Point cloud semantic segmentation using a deep learning framework for cultural heritage. Remote Sens. **12**, 1005 (2020). https://doi.org/10.3390/rs12061005

20. Matrone, F., Grilli, E., Martini, M., Paolanti, M., Pierdicca, R., Remondino, F.: Comparing machine and deep learning methods for large 3D heritage semantic segmentation. ISPRS Int. J. Geo-Inf. **9**, 535 (2020). https://doi.org/10.3390/ijgi9090535

21. Cao, Y., Scaioni, M.: 3DLEB-Net: Label-efficient deep learning-based semantic segmentation of building point clouds at LoD3 level. Appl. Sci. **11**, 8996 (2021). https://doi.org/10.3390/app11198996

22. Achille, C., Fassi, F., Mandelli, A., Fiorillo, F.: Surveying cultural heritage: summer school for conservation activities. Appl. Geomatics **10**(4), 579–592 (2018). https://doi.org/10.1007/s12518-018-0225-3

23. Goutte, C., Gaussier, E.: A probabilistic interpretation of precision, recall and F-score, with implication for evaluation. In: Losada, D.E., Fernández-Luna, J.M. (eds.) Advances in Information Retrieval. Lecture Notes in Computer Science, vol. 3408, pp. 345–359. Springer, Heidelberg (2005). https://doi.org/10.1007/978-3-540-31865-1_25

ARMENTIS: Abruzzo Region's Management of an Enhanced Tratturi Information System

Francesco Zullo(✉) ⓘ, Chiara Cattani, Cristina Montaldi ⓘ, and Gianni Di Pietro

Department of Civil - Construction-Architectural and Environmental Engineering, University of L'Aquila, L'Aquila, Italy
francesco.zullo@univaq.it, {cristina.montaldi, gianni.dipietro}@graduate.univaq.it

Abstract. *Tratturi,* intended as the ancient routes along which transhumance was practiced, are today paths of considerable landscape interest [1–3] as well as historical and environmental heritage [4, 5] as also valued by the different regulations that today protect them as national cultural heritage as well as intangible heritage of humanity (UNESCO) [6]. Despite these forms of protection, the original path has undergone several anthropic transformations that intensified between the 50s and 80s of the last century and that have profoundly modified the original layout to make it unrecognizable in some parts. Nevertheless, this heritage is today the subject of several projects aimed at the enhancement and recovery of both the tracks and the villages crossed by these, by assigning them the task of possible drivers of economic development, particularly for the internal areas of the country [7–10]. This work, therefore, focuses on four of the Abruzzo region's tratturi, with a dual objective. On the one hand, the aim is to analyze the urban transformations in the recent past and on the other hand to implement an updated information system of this regional heritage. The latter makes it possible not only the awareness of the site current state of conservation but also of the system of constraints and the existing urban planning previsions. A system of this nature makes it possible to check, in real-time, any discrepancies with the plan forecasts and proves to be an indispensable tool for the management of this important heritage.

Keywords: Urban planning · Transhumance · Decision support system

1 Introduction

The "Regi tratturi" are an important living monument in the territories of the central-southern Apennines. They are linked to the economic productions and social structures that have supported the local development since protohistoric times, long before the Roman age and the Middle Ages, a period in which, however, these ancient routes represented one of the main economic and fiscal lines for the different dominations that reigned in these places [11]. Flocks of thousands of sheep - in 1475 there were about one million [12] and 5 and a half million in the XVII century - from the inland areas of the region reached the winter pastures of the *Tavoliere di Puglia* through the great

Abruzzo's tratturi including those of L'Aquila - Foggia (*Tratturo Magno*), Lanciano - Cupello, Celano - Foggia, Centurelle - Montesecco object of this study. From a regulatory point of view, tratturi have been the object of several national laws. The first was issued on December 20, 1908 Law no. 746 "On the regime of the tratturi of Tavoliere di Puglia", while in 1939 tratturi have been declared of archeological interest. In 1977 tratturi's administrative functions were transferred from the State to the Regions. Fundamental for tratturi's management is the Decree of the Ministry for Cultural and Environmental Heritage (D.M. 20 March 1980) which prescribes that any intervention in these areas is subject to authorization by the local Superintendence. This law introduces the Piano Quadro Tratturo (P.Q.T.). This plan, predisposed by the municipalities and approved by the archeological Superintendence, surrounds tratturi's areas to distinguish build-up areas from those that have conserved their original characteristics. In 2000 tratturi become inalienable goods of archeological interest and four years later the "Code of Cultural Heritage and Landscape" prohibits any action of transformation.

The Abruzzo Region transposed the national laws and issued some acts on the subject. Among the most recent there is law no. 134/1998 that intervene on the inalienability of the tratturi and defines the calculus method of soil's prices. In 2012 the guidelines specifies that for soils defined by P.Q.T. as agricultural and not compromised the citizens can ask only the regional concession, while soils defined as compromised and not recoverable, are instead under the requirements of the urban plan, but anyway, they are subject to the archaeological constraint.

Aspects such as the terrain morphology, urban growth and the current level of the anthropization of tratturi, play a role of primary importance in the implementation, not only of protection policies but also for actions aimed at enhancing these important routes. Today the management of this path is difficult also because of the absence of an updated information system that can be used by both the regional offices for issuing concessions and the Superintendence that must control and authorize the transformations of soil that characterizes tratturi's routes. The main goal of this work is to achieve integrated management of the regional tratturi's system by the setting up a territorial information system to provide information on both transformation processes that have generated the actual urban, infrastructural and environmental asset through the integration of the P.Q.T. and the updated framework of concessions.

2   Study Area

The Abruzzo region is crossed by several and important tratturi. Those under consideration are: L'Aquila-Foggia Tratturo or *Tratturo Magno* (about 140 km in the Abruzzo region), Centurelle – Montesecco Tratturo (155 km), Celano – Foggia Tratturo (75 km) ed Lanciano – Cupello Tratturo (35 km). These routes together reach a length of more than 400 km and are characterized by average width of 100 m. The geography of Abruzzo's tratturi is shown in Fig. 1. This network covers a surface of about 38 km² and concerns the territory of 87 of the 305 Abruzzo's municipalities.

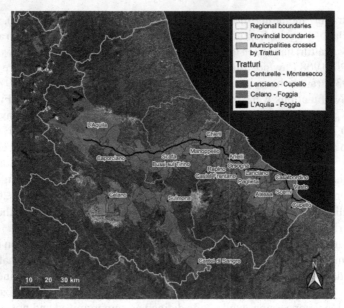

Fig. 1. Abruzzo's tratturi geography

The altitude of the tratturi routes is variable. The one that reaches the highest altitude is Celano-Foggia, which overcome 1400 m in the Rivisondoli-Roccaraso municipalities. L'Aquila-Foggia tratturo reaches instead the sea level along the Adriatic coast from Torino di Sangro to San Salvo.

From the point of view of environmental protection, only a few of the 58 Natura 2000 sites of Abruzzo concern these routes. Specifically, the highest coverage of the network sites is measured along the Celano-Foggia tratturo, which is crossed by Sirente-Velino Regional Park and Maiella National Park. Different is the situation for Magno and Lanciano - Cupello tratturi. The first runs through the southern areas of the Gran Sasso and Monti della Laga National Park while the second one intercepts in its routes a single Natura 2000 site.

3   Materials and Methods

This work used data from several sources. Specifically, the tratturi routes come from the acquisition of cadastral cartography (about mid-20s) of the different routes available in the Abruzzo Region [13]. The data about buildings were found in the website of the National Civil Protection [14], the attribution of the realization period of buildings has been made through specific overlay operations with urbanization data. In particular, they come from the digital transposition of IGM cartography through the interpretation of symbology related to built-up/urbanized areas. The considered chrono-section are 1956, 1980 (nominal scale 1:25,000). For 1997, regional land use data was used (nominal scale 1:10,000). The built-up area is the surfaces covered by buildings and identifiable through the ground projection of the perimeter of the latter. Instead, the urbanized area is the one intended for urban functions, with the replacement or maintenance of the natural soil. This type of area includes parts of built-up land and those intended for ancillary functions of the settlement, such as public and private gardens, sports facilities, unpaved roads and other service areas. Suburban roads are excluded from the calculation. For the historical reconstruction of the build-up areas pattern, a specific Kernel Density analysis has been made. This kind of analysis is a non-parametric method of estimating the density of a random variable and allows to consider possible interaction phenomena as this can weigh more the objects close to each other than the distant ones. The bandwidth is a function of the investigated phenomenon, the extent of the study area and the reference scale [15–17]. Some urban research uses a bandwidth of 300 m [18] o 400 m [19, 20] up to a few kilometers for larger territories. Starting from these considerations, several simulations were carried out with different values of the bandwidth before the most suitable value was found. In this specific case the value of 2000 m was set, while the cell size of the resulting raster is equal to 50 m/pixel. The effects of urbanization were studied through indicators engineering techniques. Specifically, the following indexes were used:

Urban Density – UD

$$UD = \frac{urban\ areas}{reference\ surface}[\%] \tag{1}$$

Urban Dispersion Index – UDI

$$UDI = \frac{nr.\ urban\ nuclei}{reference\ surface}\left[\frac{nr.}{km^2}\right] \tag{2}$$

The UD index allows the evaluation of the degree of urbanization of each segment of the tratturo while the UDI index provides indications about the number of urbanized nuclei present for each km^2 of the reference area. These indexes, analyzed in a diachronic key, allow to reconstruct the urban evolution along these ancient routes.

4   Results

The diagram in Fig. 2 shows the buildings and urban areas evolution for the four analyses tratturi as a function of time and highlights the main laws on the issue. What emerges is a substantial growth of both built-up and urbanized areas for all 4 routes analyzed even if in different periods. Specifically, for Lanciano-Cupello tratturo the highest growth of urban areas is concentrated in the period from 1980 to 1997 while for L'Aquila-Foggia and Celano-Foggia tratturi, the highest growth is pointed out at the end of the last century. It is important to highlight that already in 1997, in all routes, the UD exceeded the current national value of 7% [21].

Among all, the one under greater transformation is Lanciano-Cupello tratturo, that in 1997 reached UD of 15% value about five-time higher than the current regional one (5%). Currently, the higher urban density is found along L'Aquila-Foggia tratturo (17,4%) followed by Lanciano-Cupello (15,2%), Celano-Foggia (12,7%) and Centurelle-Montesecco (11%). It is necessary to highlight that morphology has had an important role in these dynamics. Where the tratturo crossed places at higher altitudes, the processes of urbanization have been less intense while tratturi in flatter areas in most cases have lost their native functions. These routes, in their paths, cross some inhabited centers but are also adjacent to important regional industrial areas (i.e. Centurelle-Montesecco tratturo in Atessa municipalities passes near the industrial area of Val di Sangro) Also, this aspect has an important role to influence processes of a settlement nature. The changes in the values of the urban dispersion index (UDI), shows as in almost all cases, that the urbanization has occurred in dispersed form with the formation of new residential areas often consisting of a small number of buildings in areas previously used for agricultural purposes. The growth in aggregate continuity occurred along those areas where the tratturi, as mentioned, crosses the urban centers of some municipalities such as Lanciano (Lanciano - Cupello) or the town of Orsogna (Centurelle-Montesecco).

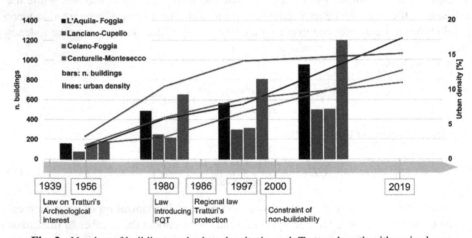

Fig. 2. Number of buildings and urban density in each Tratturo's path with major laws

It was examined if the approval of P.Q.T. has had any effect on the speed of urbanization. Specifically, it results that the speed of soil consumption has not decreased after the approval of the plans, actually, in almost all cases the speed has grown progressively regardless of the presence of the plans. Furthermore, in 2000, by national law, the constraint of non-buildability for the tratturi soils was imposed. However, it turns out that between 1997 and 2019 the conversion speed not only did not reach zero value, but even grew in most cases, a symptom of a reduced cogency of plans. The growth pattern of the built-up area was analyzed with the Kernel Density Estimation. The results are reported in Fig. 3.

1956

2019

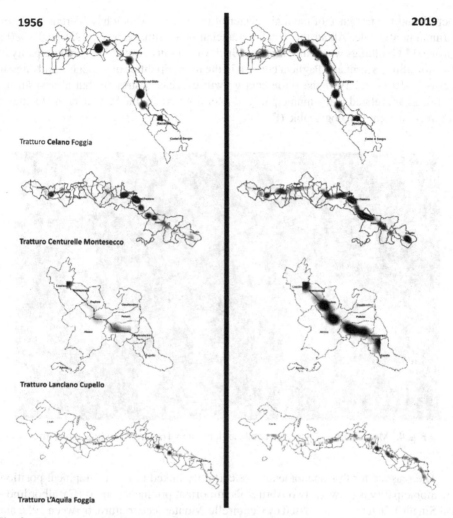

Fig. 3. Diachronic scheme based on the built-up surface along the municipalities of the Tratturi different chrono-sections by the Kernel Density. The darker the tones, the greater the built-up area during the period under consideration.

Along L'Aquila-Foggia tratturo, between 1956 and 1980 the main transformations took place with a greater concentration along the section from Arielli to Vasto. The intensity of the transformative processes drops strongly in the following period, where the only important variations are found in the municipality of L'Aquila and along the territory between Casalbordino and Vasto. About the current condition, there are greater increases in the sector between Chieti and Vasto while the settlement processes in the municipalities of L'Aquila are lower. In the Celano-Foggia tratturo the situation is different. In the first analyzed period, the buildings are concentrated more in specific areas, instead today, it is evident the strong diffusion of the urbanization along the whole tratturo, particularly in the sector between the municipalities of Raiano and Sulmona, where the morphological factors and the presence of the main center of the Peligna valley have certainly played a fundamental role. About the Tratturo Lanciano-Cupello, between 1956 and 1980 a further 173 buildings were built, most of which were concentrated in the municipality of Casalbordino, Scerni and Paglieta but also in the municipalities of Lanciano and Atessa. Between 1980 and 1997 the settlement growth decreased strongly but almost all the buildings are related to the municipality of Scerni where, in the San Giacomo hamlet, a comb settlement is recognizable (Fig. 4).

Fig. 4. Municipality of Scerni, a comb settlement in Tratturo-San Giacomo district.

The reasons for this phenomenon are certainly linked to its geographical position, the municipality is between two Abruzzo's important productive areas (Casalbordino – Val Sinello). In territories crossed by Centurelle-Montesecco tratturo, between 1956 and 1980 there are deep transformations: 47 ha of soil were urbanized with the construction of about 500 new buildings located in most in Atessa and Castel Frentano municipalities. In the following years, there is a strong linearization of the settlement along the routes in the municipality of Orsogna, Castel Frentano e Atessa. Moreover, in the municipalities of Bussi sul Tirino, Castiglione a Casauria, Scafa and Manoppello it is found an intense edification that in previous periods had not been detected. Today the most urbanized area is the one between the municipality of Rapino and Atessa.

5   Discussion and Conclusion

Tratturi are a cultural-historical and environmental heritage. They represent the place of transit of the flocks during transhumance. This activity took place until the 70s of the last century and was recently declared by UNESCO as an Intangible Cultural Heritage of Humanity on the basis of a transnational candidacy presented by Italy, Austria and

Greece (2019) [6]. The study carried out concerned some of the main Abruzzo's tratturi, covering an area of 38 km² and a linear extension of about 400 km. It results that, despite the strong testimonial value, these ancient routes have been subjected to strong urban transformations. As already mentioned, various regulatory provisions have been issued at the national and regional level both to protect the tratturi and to regulate the eligible interventions. With the Ministerial Decree on 1983, December 22, also tratturi of Abruzzo become of archaeological interest, and for this reason, the municipalities crossed by tratturi must write and update the P.Q.T. To the present day, as is shown in Fig. 5, only 46 of 87 municipalities have a plan in force. The first writing of this plan has taken place, in almost all the municipalities, between the 80s and 90s. On average, the plans were updated approximately every three years and almost half of the municipalities carried out at least two updates P.Q.T.

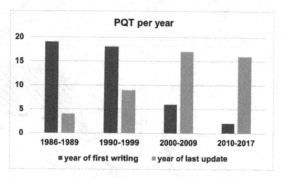

Fig. 5. P.Q.T.'s years of first and last update

This work highlighted that, despite these numerous regulatory measures, the effects of urban changes, which in some cases have been totally transformed parts of the territory, have not been completely contained. The case history of urban transformations is broad (i.e. the passage of important roads such as the highway A14 in the municipalities of Vasto and San Salvo and in other cases the construction of important industrial complexes as, for example, the industrial area of Bazzano-Paganica in the municipality of L'Aquila). It is certain that, the absence or the delay in the approval of P.Q.T. has had consequences on the transformation of the soil, but we must not forget the numerous ex-post requests received by the Archeological Superintendence relating to the acquisition of these areas by private citizens. It is important to remember that, in Italy, between the 80s and the first years of 2000, have been approved three building-amnesty, therefore some of these interventions may have been the results of these forms of ex-post legitimacy. Nowadays, one of the problems that the regulatory Authorities deal with is mainly linked to the absence of an effective and efficient system for the monitoring of transformative processes in these areas. The numerous P.Q.T., written over the years, are in most cases in paper format, for this reason, it is difficult or expensive (georeferencing processes and digitization of the zoning plan) to integrate them into the GIS environment. The systematization of all the P.Q.T. in force today with the data shown in this work, would allow the implementation of a territorial information system aimed at the management and control of the tratturi routes. In this way, it would be possible to reconstruct, for each building that has non-compliant characteristics with the requirements of the zoning plans, its history in order to verify its legitimacy (Fig. 6).

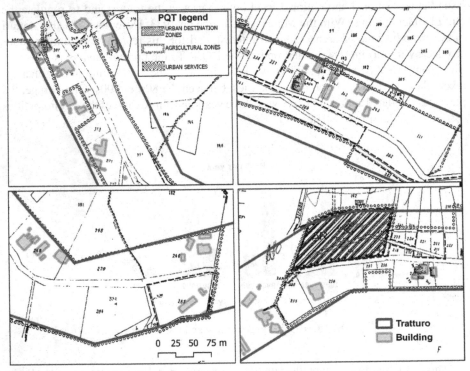

Fig. 6. Example of overlapping a P.Q.T. with the existing buildings and the Tratturo. The transparency of the buildings' layer allows seeing the divergence from the requirements of the plan.

In addition, this information system would be enriched by the system, already created by the Abruzzo Region, relating to the concessions that private individuals have in place on the tratturi. Management and monitoring are essential to assess the conservation status of these archaeological heritages, identify their potential as a tourist attraction and encourage the economic revival that could act as a growth driver for the communities that today live in these territories.

Acknowledgements. We would like to thank the Forests and Parks Service and Tratturi Office of the Abruzzo Region for successful cooperation. We also thank the anonymous reviewers who have critically examined the work and suggested many additions that have undoubtedly improved it in its understanding.

References

1. Minotti, M., Giancola, C., Di Marzio, P., Di Martino, P.: Land use dynamics of drove roads: The case of tratturo castel di Sangro-Lucera (Molise, Italy). Land 7(1), 3 (2018)
2. Sidiropoulou, A., et al.: Landscape pattern changes in response to transhumance abandonment on Mountain Vermio (North Greece). Sustainability 7 15652–15673 (2015)
3. Cazzani, A., Boriani, M.: The Role of Historic Roads to Preserve and Valorize the Landscape. In: Pileri, P., Moscarelli, R. (eds.) Cycling & Walking for Regional Development. Research for Development, pp. 85–103. Springer, Cham (2021). https://doi.org/10.1007/978-3-030-44003-9_8
4. Oteros-Rozas, E., et al.: Traditional ecological knowledge among transhumant pastoralists in Mediterranean Spain. Ecol. Soc. 18(3), 33 (2013)
5. D'Ottavio, P., et al.: Methods and approaches used for assessing ecosystem services provided by grazing systems. Options, 51 (2016)
6. UNESCO. https://www.unesco.it/it/ItaliaNellUnesco/Detail/820, Accessed 22 Mar 2022
7. Gaeta, L., Curci. F.: Prospettive di recupero della transumanza e dei percorsi tratturali nell'Italia meridionale. In: XXI conferenza nazionale della Società Italiana degli Urbanisti. Planum Publisher (2019)
8. Fistola, R., La Rocca, R.A.: Slow mobility and cultural tourism. Walking on historical paths. In: Papa, R., Fistola, R., Gargiulo, C. (eds.) Smart planning: sustainability and mobility in the age of change. GET, pp. 301–322. Springer, Cham (2018). https://doi.org/10.1007/978-3-319-77682-8_18
9. Meini, M., Di Felice, G., Petrella, M.: Geotourism perspectives for transhumance routes. analysis, requalification and virtual tools for the geoconservation management of the drove roads in Southern Italy. Geosciences 8(10), 368 (2018)
10. Mastronardi, L., Giannelli, A., Romagnoli, L.: Detecting the land use of ancient transhumance routes (Tratturi) and their potential for Italian inner areas' growth. Land Use Policy 109, 105695 (2021)
11. Staffa, A.R.: La transumanza in Abruzzo fra tarda antichità e medioevo. Eur. J. Post-Classical Archaeol. 10, 401–441 (2020)
12. Violante, F.: Agricoltura e allevamento transumante nella Puglia medievale: osservazioni sul governo della mobilità rurale. Mélanges de l'École française de Rome - Antiquité, 128(2), 329–340 (2016)
13. Zullo, F., Marucci, A., Falasca, F., Fiorini, L.: Tecniche per l'informatizzazione del patrimonio armentizio tratturale della regione Abruzzo. Atti Asita Academy (2021)
14. Dipartimento di protezione civile. https://rischi.protezionecivile.gov.it/it/approfondimento/dataset-nazionale-degli-aggregati-strutturali-italiani/
15. Murgante, B., Borruso, G.: Analyzing migration phenomena with spatial autocorrelation techniques. In: Murgante, B., et al. (eds.) Computational Science and Its Applications – ICCSA 2012. Lecture Notes in Computer Science, vol. 7334, pp. 670–685. Springer, Heidelberg (2012). https://doi.org/10.1007/978-3-642-31075-1_50
16. Borruso, G.: Network density estimation: a GIS approach for analysing point patterns in a network space. Trans. GIS 12, 377–402 (2008)
17. Danese, M., Lazzari, M., Murgante, B.: Kernel density estimation methods for a geostatistical approach in seismic risk analysis: The case study of potenza Hilltop Town (Southern Italy). In: Gervasi, O., Murgante, B., Laganà, A., Taniar, D., Mun, Y., Gavrilova, M.L. (eds.) Computational Science and Its Applications – ICCSA 2008. Lecture Notes in Computer Science, vol. 5072, pp. 415–429. Springer, Heidelberg (2008). https://doi.org/10.1007/978-3-540-69839-5_31

18. Thurstain-Goodwin M., Unwin D.J.: Defining and delimiting the central areas of towns for statistical modelling using continuous surface representations. Trans. GIS **4**, 305–317 (2000)
19. Borruso G.: Il ruolo della cartografia nella definizione del Central Business District. Prime note per un approccio metodologico. Bollettino dell'associazione italiana di cartografia. vol. 126–127–128, pp. 271–287 (2006)
20. Battaglia F., Borruso G., Porceddu A.: Sistemi Informativi Territoriali e analisi spaziale per l'analisi dei valori immobiliari. Un caso applicato alla città di Swindon (UK). Territorio Italia n. 1/2012: 27–40 (2012)
21. Munafò, M. (a cura di): Consumo di suolo, dinamiche territoriali e servizi ecosistemici. Edizione 2021. Report SNPA 22/21(2021)

Environmental Monitoring and Analysis

Rapid Seismic Risk Assessment of Bridges Using UAV Aerial Photogrammetric Survey

Vincenzo Barrile[1](✉) , Gabriele Candela[1] , Cristoforo Demartino[2] ,
Giorgio Monti[3] , Ernesto Bernardo[1] , and Giuliana Bilotta[1]

[1] Mediterranea University of Reggio Calabria, 89128 Reggio Calabria, Italy
vincenzo.barrile@unirc.it
[2] Zhejiang University-University of Illinois Institute, Haining, Zhejiang, China
[3] Department of Structural Engineering and Geotechnics, University Sapienza of Rome,
Rome, Italy

Abstract. In this paper a framework for the rapid seismic risk assessment of
bridges using aerial surveys using Unmanned Aerial Systems is presented. The
acquisition process to obtain data for the photogrammetric 3d reconstruction and
the procedure for the automatic extraction of the visible variables using computer
vision are described. The extracted features are combined with standardized structural information to obtain the structure's capacity model and perform a seismic
risk assessment. A case study of a highway simple supported bridge is presented
to validate the 3d model reconstruction and the results of the structural analysis.

Keywords: UAV survey · Infrastructure surveying · 3d reconstruction · Point
cloud classification · Bridge structural analysis

1 Introduction

Infrastructures have great environmental and economic impacts on territories, providing
essential services, and increases economic productivity and employment. Infrastructure
maintenance and risk mitigation is a research field in Civil Engineering with growing
importance. Nowadays developed countries have to deal with deterioration of a large
infrastructure stock that exceeded the design working life (usually around 50–100 years)
and/or with inadequate or missing maintenance. Beam bridges are the simplest structural
forms for bridge spans supported by an abutment or pier at each end. In the following,
this study will focus on this specific typology given the large stock. For this structural
typology, the seismic damages are mainly concentrated at the bearings and piers. In the
first case, relative displacements between the deck and the pier at the bearings can lead
to the collapse due to the loss of support. In the latter, the pier can fail for inadequate
flexural ductility and/or shear resistance. Additional damages can be also observed at
the foundations and/or abutments. However, in the following, these mechanisms will be
disregarded and attention will be paid only on the first two. Different techniques were
developed during the years to assess the conditions of bridges.

© The Author(s), under exclusive license to Springer Nature Switzerland AG 2022
E. Borgogno-Mondino and P. Zamperlin (Eds.): ASITA 2022, CCIS 1651, pp. 355–367, 2022.
https://doi.org/10.1007/978-3-031-17439-1_26

Recently, the availability of low-cost sensors made photogrammetric techniques cheap and fast compared with traditional techniques [1].

There are many methods for doing structural analysis (LIDAR, other methods), we propose a method of rapid seismic assessment using UAVs. With UAVs we build the 3D model, with innovative technology we extract the characteristic parameters of the bridge, then a structural analysis, using these parameters as well, is done to calculate the fragility curve. The use of Unmanned Aerial Vehicles (UAVs) in Civil Engineering is gaining interest and the possible applications are also growing very rapidly [2]. Accordingly, the visible geometric characteristics of a bridge can be extracted from a photographic survey performed using UAVs [3]. However, although the capabilities of performing photographic survey using UAVs and accurately reconstruct the 3D geometry of a bridge was recently demonstrated by different authors, a framework for the rapid seismic risk assessment of bridges using input data retried from UAV aerial photogrammetric survey is still missing [4, 5]. To this extent, UAV can potentially play a key role in the seismic risk assessment of infrastructures. This rapid assessment is crucial for the identification of the elements with the largest risk in the network and to optimize the resources for performing high-LOD seismic risk analysis on specific elements [6–8]. In this context, this study aims at presenting a framework for the rapid seismic risk assessment of bridges [9–11] using the UAV aerial photogrammetric survey (Fig. 1).

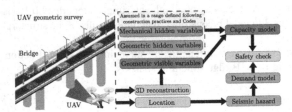

Fig. 1. General workflow for the rapid seismic risk assessment of bridges using UAV aerial photogrammetric survey.

The framework presented herein is focusing on the specific case of multispan RC simply supported beam bridge although extensions are possible. An archetype simply supported beam bridge is presented and the main variables defining the mechanical behavior are identified. The variables are divided in visible and hidden ones with reference to the capability of the UAV aerial photogrammetric survey to detect them. The framework is applied to a RC simply supported beam bridges case study that is the Annunziata highway viaduct in Italy. The case study demonstrates the applicability of the methods proving a real testbed for the procedure. Besides, the measurements obtained from the UAV-3D reconstruction are cross-validated using the measurements obtained using traditional laser scanner.

2   General Framework

2.1   Archetype Multispan Simply Supported Beam Bridge

This study focuses on multispan RC simply supported beam bridges. The proposed archetype model follows the common layouts and modeling approaches for highway multispan RC simply supported beam bridges adopted in the literature.

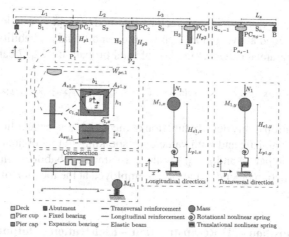

Fig. 2. Archetype multispan simply supported beam bridge: geometrical and mechanical variables and mechanical model.

The transverse reinforcements are usually placed in the form of rectangular, spiral or circular stirrups. The stirrups are defined in terms of A_{sw} that is the area of shear reinforcement within length s. The amount of transverse reinforcements is defined in a non-dimensional form as the shear reinforcement ratio. There are visible and non-visible variables; for these, that are known to structural engineers, and the structural analysis please refer to the references. With the aim of understanding the input variables involved in the rapid seismic risk assessment, the conceptual division of the input variables into visible (observable) and hidden (non-observable) is useful. The observability of a variable is related to the possibility to be measured during the UAV survey (see Sect. 2.2), which is considered the only direct source of information in this study. Furthermore, it is convenient to classify the variables into geometrical variables, representing the geometry and details of the bridge, and mechanical variables which define the nonlinear mechanical response of the bridge. The mechanical variables are always hidden to the UAV survey while the some of the geometrical ones are in some cases hidden and other visible. For instance, the hollow parts (c_x and c_y in Fig. 2) and the reinforcement layouts are hidden while the pier cross-section shape and size (h and b in Fig. 2) are visible. Additionally, some variables are dependent on input variables. For instance, the mass is a dependent variable which is function of visible variables (h and b in Fig. 2) and hidden variables (c_x and c_y in Fig. 2).

Henceforth, the following four groups of variables are considered: (i) visible geometric variables, x_{gv}; (ii) hidden geometric variables, x_{gh}; (iii) hidden mechanical variables, x_{mh}; (iv) dependent variables, x_d. Accordingly, the capacity model of the bridge (see Case Study) can be expressed as:

$$c = \int_{-\infty}^{\infty} PC(c|\mathbf{x})d\mathbf{x} \tag{1}$$

where $\mathbf{x} = [x_{gv}, x_{gh}, x_{mh}, x_d]$ T is the vector contained the input variables factorize in the four groups described above and PC (c|x) is the conditional probability of the capacity given the input parameters. Using the law of total probability, Eq. 7 can be written as:

$$c = \int_{-\infty}^{\infty} P_C(c|\mathbf{x}) \cdot p(\mathbf{x}_{gv}) \cdot p(\mathbf{x}_{gh}) \cdot p(\mathbf{x}_{mh}) \cdot [p(\mathbf{x}_d|\mathbf{x}_{gv}, \mathbf{x}_{gh}, \mathbf{x}_{mh}) \cdot p(\mathbf{x}_{gv}) \cdot p(\mathbf{x}_{gh}) \cdot p(\mathbf{x}_{mh})] \, d\mathbf{x} \tag{2}$$

where $p(\bullet)$ is the probability density function of the variable $\bullet$. In the following, $p(x_{gv})$ will be assumed deterministic and with value corresponding to that obtained from the UAV survey (2.2) while $p(x_{gh})$ and $p(x_{mh})$ will be assumed probabilistic in a range defined following construction practices and Codes employed at the location of the bridge at the construction time.

2.2   UAV: Acquisition - 3D Reconstruction – Elaboration - Output

The workflow for the UAV aerial survey of multispan RC simply supported beam bridges is described in Fig. 3. Three main phases are defined: (a) set-up of the survey and data acquisition; (b) data optimization, 3D reconstruction and classification; (c) extraction of the defined geometrical features, and creation of as-built and geometrical model (visible variables). In the following, the three steps will be described.

Fig. 3. Workflow for UAV photogrammetric survey of multispan RC simply supported beam bridges.

For the acquisition, the design of the survey plan requires: (i) analysis of the structure and surrounding area to be acquired and (ii) definition of the UAV type and sensors to be used. A preliminary analysis of the area should be conducted to consider multiple factors such as: the complexity of the environment and structure visibility (e.g., Presence of obstacles/vegetation around the structure), the area accessibility to identify the take-off and landing point, flight restriction according to local regulations (e.g., presence of no-fly zones, maximum allowed flying height, etc.). The choice of the UAV and payload/sensor must be conducted to optimize time and costs of the tasks, according to the mission needs. in this study, commercial small multi-rotor drones with a high-resolution photographic sensor are employed. This UAV type is selected because of their hovering capability and move along the three directions. In this context, the goal is to acquire the 3d full bridge geometry with a centimetric accuracy. The flight plan is controlled using a waypoint navigation that allows the UAV to fly following a series of waypoint in the space creating a defined route. A virtual fence area (bounding box in which the UAV can move) is defined to guarantee flight safety, respect of flight regulation avoiding distraction for road users and interruption of traffic, and availability of the GPS signal. The virtual fence area bounds a no-flight zone defined as the volume under the bridge deck with added an extrusion orthogonal to the deck axis at a safe distance, D_s, see Fig. 4. The no-flight zone is considered as the extruded volume at a safe distance, D_s, from the ground and obstacles. $D_s = 5$ m is suggested in the real application. To capture the object from different angles according to photogrammetric principles, a series of semicircular routes around $C\alpha$, executed at different heights and tilt angles are adopted (Fig. 4). The Points of Interest (POIs) are located on the vertical symmetry plan of the bridge. In the following, the elevations will be referred to the deck height.

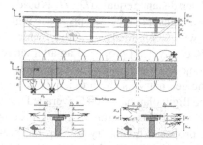

Fig. 4. Semi-circular path for bridge survey.

The centimetric accuracy is guaranteed with a certain Ground Sampling Distance, (GSD) and images overlap (OV) during the survey. The GSD is defined as the ratio between the measure of the real object to the pixel size. The overlap represents the percentage of the object covered in two consecutive frames depending on the distance of the center of two consecutive shoots. In this study, a GSD equal to 1 cm/pixel is adopted/used. Having the required GSD, the flight distance D from the object is calculated as:

$$D = GSD \cdot FL \cdot \frac{im_d}{S_d} \quad (3)$$

where FL is the focal length, im_d/S_d is the ratio of the image diagonal to the sensor diagonal.

In the horizontal direction, the semicircular paths (Fig. 4) are defined by the radius, R, the distance between two POIs, D_p, and the angular location, α. The radius R of the semicircular path is calculated to guarantee a distance equal to D from the POIs for $\alpha = 90°$:

$$R = D - D_s - D_b \qquad D_p = \frac{(R + D_s) \cdot S_w}{FL} \cdot (1 - OV) \quad (4)$$

where D_b is half width deck. D_p is related to the overlap between two perpendicular with respect to deck $\alpha = 90°$ images nearest to the camera $(R + D_s)$ of consecutive POIs. An overlap of 30% between two POIs is suggested. Finally, α has been bounded in the range $10° \le \alpha \le 170°$ and maximum rotation between two images has been limited to $20°$ [12]. In this way, the overlap is improved since the camera captures the same POI from different angles, α. S w is the sensor width.

In the vertical direction, three different types of mission (A, B, C) are defined according to the camera tilt angle γ (Fig. 4). Missions A have a positive tilt angle, γ, and is used to acquire the upper part of the deck at a quote H γ A, and the terrain respecting the safety height, D_s, at a quote $H_{\gamma A}$ from the ground level. Mission C has a positive tilt angle, γ, and is used to acquire the lower part of the deck at a quote $H_{\gamma C}$. H_γ is used to calculate the height of the A and C missions:

$$H_\gamma = (R + D_s + D_b) \cdot tan\,\gamma \qquad H_v = \frac{(R + D_s \cdot S_h)}{FL} \cdot (1 - OV) \qquad (5)$$

Missions B have a zero-tilt angle (horizontal). B missions are executed at different heights from the deck level to guarantee a certain overlap, until the reaching of the no-flight zone with a vertical step distance equal to D_s. H_v is used to calculate the height of the different B missions, with S_h sensor height. The proposed flight plan is able to reconstruct 3D full bridge geometry with a centimetric accuracy, which is consider adequate with the scope of this study. Recently, [12] proposed an alternative framework for the UAV survey aiming at similar objectives of this study. The proposed procedure is based on the detailed knowledge of the geometry, or the pre-acquisition with a preliminary manual flight. Then, an automated flight plan based on Coverage Path Planning (CPP) is used to find and plan a path that cover all the structure in a complex environment with obstacles. However, the procedure proposed herein try to skip the pre-acquisition part and the automated flight below the deck. Finally, the use Ground Control Point (GCP) with a GNSS survey on the deck level is necessary to obtain a scaled oriented and geolocalized model and recommended to improve accuracy of the 3D reconstruction (reduction of the distortions).

The flight plan proposed herein is a general suggested scheme for the UAV aerial photogrammetric survey considering the general characteristics of simply supported bridges. However, for specific bridges, it is required a case-by-case design of the survey eventually requiring variation of the proposed plan and/or integrating in manual mode.

The acquired data (frame from video or images) have to be preliminary optimized before the 3D reconstruction, to highlight details and maximize the number of key points for each image. The following images parameters have to be optimized: white balance to obtain a neutral tone, exposition to cancel the over and under exposure zone, contrast, light and shadow, clarity as a measure of the localized contrast, vividness to act only on less saturated colors.

Subsequently the obtained geo-localized images are used as input for the generation of the 3d geo-referenced point cloud through a standard Structure from Motion - Multi-View Stereo (SfM – MVS) workflow.

The obtained 3D point must be split to identify and classify the terrain and the different structural sub-systems part of the bridge (such as a pier, pier cap, deck and cable). Methodologies for semantic segmentation of point cloud actually under research, are based on different approach. The presented methodology an image based method, performed applying image instance segmentation using convolutional neural network (CNN) on each image of the dataset, transferring the information on the 3d point cloud. Instance segmentation is performed using Mask-RCNN architecture (Convolutional Neural Network) that enable the creation of a pixel-wise mask to segment complex objects and shape from images: the model is trained to perform structure recognition and subsequently split the different structural part. The quality and precision of the segmentation and classification strictly rely on the accuracy of the trained model in order to fit at the pixel-wise level the masks around the structure needed. The overall workflow for 3d reconstruction from images, including the image classification and segmentation, is synthesized in Fig. 5. The output of this process, thanks to the application of the 2d masks on the 3d model, is a classified measurable 3D point cloud of the object.

As output, the creation of a solid mesh starting from the 3D point cloud is performed using the Poisson surface reconstruction obtaining the mesh of the different structural object starting from the classified point cloud. The extraction of the visible geometry from the obtained segmented 3D model is performed using a semi-automated methodology. A bounding box outside the single mesh element is used to extract the shape from the different parts and automatically export the data into a dedicated application. The creation of the simplified geometry for the Archetype model of the bridge is performed using Rhinoceros and Grasshopper (McNeel, North America). Through a simple user interface and the definition of two cut-plane XY and YZ according to the structure resistant section the user can move and select the section to extract the data (Fig. 5). Initially the mesh is discretized and automatically oriented the dominant axis according to z-axis. The bounding box, as volumetric element around the object, is created to intersect cut-plan inside the box and the object. Subsequently the cut-planes are set-up in XY and YZ. The user can define the position of the cutting plan in % compared with height, offset distance from cutting plane and a total number of cutting plane. Finally, the closed polyline that defines the perimeter is extracted. A preventive verification of the planarity and closure of the polyline is executed. If the polyline is not close, the algorithm will approximate the closure. Geometrical feature confirmed by the user are then automatically uploaded on the archetype model for the structural analysis.

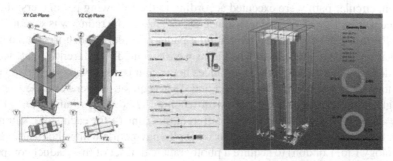

Fig. 5. Workflow for point cloud 3d reconstruction and classification from UAV aerial survey.

3 Case Study

3.1 Viaduct Description

The case study was performed on a double (one bridge per each direction) highway bridge in Italy (Fig. 6). The viaduct name, location and the specific information are anonymized to focus on the scope of the work, validate the results of the presented methodology. The viaduct analyzed was designed around 1970 and constructed in 1980 upon a river, represents a common topology of a simply supported, beam viaduct with 9 short-spans of 27 m, and a total length of 254 m. The curvature radius is 150 m, and the medium height of the bridge is 25 m a.g.l.

Fig. 6. General view of the viaduct from the North-East side.   **Fig. 7.** Deck and piers details

The viaduct deck is composed of a standard module of 29 m with 4 beams and 3 crosses in pre-stressed RC beams. The two decks are sustained by a couple of piers with a common foundation (Fig. 7). Piers are made of a rectangular section of 2,50 m × 1,60 m and pier cap dimensions are 8 m × 3 m. The height of the piers ranges from 16 to 26 m. The bridge is composed by 66 elements in total.

3.2 UAV Aerial Photogrammetric Survey and 3D Reconstruction

The survey realized with the proposed methodology to acquire the viaduct geometry, was executed July 2020 with cloudy weather to avoid direct sunlight and overexposed photos. The aerial survey was performed using a commercial quadrotor, DJI (DJI, Shenzen, China) Mavic 2 Pro. This portable UAV has a build-in GPS used both way-point navigation and dataset geotaging. To achieve a $GDS \leq 1$ for the 3D model reconstruction, the maximum flight distance (both perpendicular and vertical) was set $D = 30$ m. The semicircular path were executed according to the following parameters: the safety distance was set $D_s = 5$ m, bridge distance $D_b = 8$ m and the radius was set equal to R = 17 m. The distance between two semicircular paths, considering an horizontal overlap of 30% was set equal to $D_p = 23$ m. The flights were executed at different height, according to the defined parameters: vertical distances between missions were set with an overlap equal to 60% as $H_v = 8$ m. The terrain and deck acquisition were executed set-up the tilt angle of the camera as $\gamma = 35°$ with resulting $H_{\gamma A} = 22$ m and $\gamma = -10°$ with $H_{\gamma C} = 5$ m. With these parameters 8 different missions (4 for each side), summarized in Fig. 8 were planned and executed in waypoint navigation using litchi software (VC Technology Ltd, London) to acquire a photographic dataset of the viaduct composed of 1398 photos (13.2 GB of data).

To georeferencing and scale the 3d model a GNSS survey with Leica Viva CS15, was executed acquiring 6 points in accessible location, distributed on the plan to create a topographic reference for the model.

Fig. 8. Missions path details.

The dataset elaboration was executed using Agisoft Metashape (Agisoft LLC, Russia) based on the described SFM-MVS reconstruction algorithm: the results obtained from the process are visualized in (Fig. 9).

Fig. 9. Camera position and point cloud reconstruction.

The point cloud classification was obtained using the image segmentation of each image of the entire dataset. The training dataset of 15 images was used to train the neural network (Fig. 10) applying defined label to separate the structural component in each images.

Fig. 10. Training dataset label for image segmentation.

3.3 Validation of the 3D Reconstruction

To validate the survey results obtained using UAV aerial photogrammetry, a 3D laser scanner survey of the analyzed viaduct was executed. The obtained results were compared to demonstrate the precision and validity of the proposed aerial survey methodology for geometrical survey. The Terrestrial Laser Scanner (TLS) survey was executed using Faro Focus 3D (FARO Technologies, Lake Mary, Florida, USA), a 3D laser scan with built-in Gps & Glonass receiver for geo-localization, with a maximum range of 120 m. The scanner accuracy is given as 2 mm at 25 m. In total 15 different scans were executed from various accessible position around the structure (Fig. 11). Each scan took about 5 to 7 min to complete the acquisition with a rate of 1 million pts/sec. The scan alignment was executed automatically and manually on the proprietary software Faro Scene, to obtain a 3D point cloud of the surveyed scene made of 267 million points (Fig. 11).

Fig. 11. Scan points (a) and point cloud from laser scanner (b).

The laserscanner point cloud was used as reference model for the comparison and validation of the photogrammetric UAV point cloud, using Cloud Compare (open source software under GPL license), a tool for point cloud analysis and metrics.

The point cloud was cleaned to remove noise point and vegetation at the base of the pier using noise filter, and the alignment was also performed using the fine registration tool. The metric comparison was localized on a single pier in order to calculate the mean distance cloud 2 cloud (C2C) and the standard deviation (RMS) between the two model. The lidar point cloud was used as reference for the UAV cloud. The mean distance was equal to 0.2308 m while the Std deviation was equal to 0.3226 m. The results, shown in figure (Fig. 12) validate the obtained results in terms of centimeter accuracy of the UAV survey.

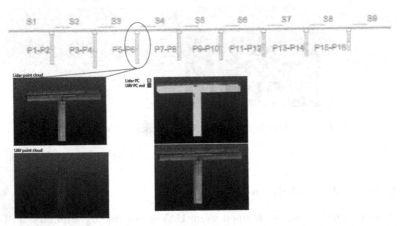

Fig. 12. Laserscanner and UAV point cloud comparison.

3.4 Seismic assessment

The seismic assessment to obtain the fragility curves was conducted using a procedure based on a demand model, a capacity model, a check.

Please refer to the literature for more details on the terms mentioned.

The described procedure is applied on 4 different bridge piers.

Our seismic assessment has a Demand model, that can be assumed that the hazard curve is linear in log-log coordinates:

$$H(im) = k_0 im^{-k_1} = k_0 \exp(-k_1 \ln im) \tag{6}$$

where $k_1 > 0$ is the slope of the hazard function in log–log coordinates, and $k_0 > 0$ is the annual rate of exceedance of $im = 1$.

Our seismic assessment has a Capacity model, given a pier of height L and made up of n_p equal elements in parallel, having cross-section with moment of inertia I and made of concrete with elastic modulus E_{cm}.

$$D_{\chi LS} = Q \cdot \frac{L}{L_e} \left[min(M_{\chi LS}, V_R L_e) \cdot \frac{1}{K \cdot L_e} + <\phi v_{R,\chi LS} - \phi_{DLS} > \mathcal{L}^2 \right] \tag{7}$$

$M_{\chi LS}$ is the base section moment capacity at the χ LS, V_r is the shear capacity, ϕ_{DLS} is the curvature at the DLS, and y, $\phi VR\chi LS$ is the curvature capacity at the χLS accounting for possible attainment of shear capacity, given as:

$$\phi_{Vr\chi LS} = min \left(\phi_{\chi LS}, \phi_{(x-1)LS} + \frac{<V_R L_C - M_{(x-1)LS}>}{K_{S,\chi LS}} \right) (x = D, L, C) \tag{8}$$

where $\phi_{\chi LS}$ is the curvature capacity at the χ LS, without accounting for possible attainment of the shear capacity, and the Sectional Stiffness $K_{S,\chi LS}$ at the χ LS is:

$$K_{S,\chi LS} \frac{M_{\chi LS} - M_{(x-1)LS}}{\phi_{\chi LS} - \phi_{(x-1)LS}} (x = D, L, C) \tag{9}$$

In the above equations, it is intended that for $x = D$, all quantities relevant to $(x-1)$ are zero. For the Check, the mean annual failure probability, λ_{LS} of a system corresponding to a specified performance level (limit state) due to a certain hazard is given as follows:

$$\lambda_{LS} = P[C_{LS}(x) - D_{LS}(x, im) < 0] \tag{10}$$

Capacity and demand are expressed in the form of Engineering Demand Parameters (EDPs), which are structural response quantities used to estimate damage to structural and nonstructural components and systems.

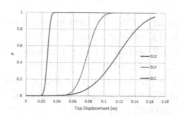

Fig. 13. Damage assessment.

The Total Probability Rule can be used in the fragility function (probability for a certain LS that the demand is exceeding the corresponding capacity) defined as the exceedence probability conditioned on the intensity measure.

The results are shown in Fig. 13 and calculated according to Italian laws and verified for the limit states.

4 Conclusions

The results achieved make it possible to frame the type of survey and complexity as a function of the geometry, the level of detail to be achieved, the number of structural elements and the location (environment within which one operates).

The image classification techniques developed with the application of neural networks have also made it possible to semantically segment the structural components first in the images themselves and then with the transfer method in three-dimensional space in the form of a point cloud. This information can then be consulted in the three-dimensional model in the form of a triangular mesh and can be inspected for individual elements. The expeditious workflow thus elaborated in its entirety has evident advantages in terms of acquisition times and costs compared to traditional geomatic survey methods and allows a rapid visualization and sharing of data. These data were used as inputs in simplified structural models for obtaining typological fragility curves, to directly link the visible variables (acquired through UAV) and the health status of the structure.

Further in-depth research is developed in the integration of lidar systems with SLAM (Simultaneous Localization And Mapping) functions and dedicated payloads in the data acquisition and processing workflow, optimization of routes and flight trajectories for the identification of the flight plan optimal taking into account the surrounding environment and the complexity of the structure to be acquired. The possibility of quickly identifying the deteriorations and the structural parts necessary for maintenance based on the structural type can also be explored using the machine learning tools applied to the images, having available a large visual database of acquired data.

Acknowledgments. ReLUIS 2019–2021 project, research line 4, is acknowledged for the financial support given to the present research. This work has been partially supported by the Zhejiang University/University of Illinois at Urbana-Champaign Institute.

References

1. Fiore, A., et.al.: Seismic safety of the Calabria hospitals and road networks. Int. J. Math. Models Methods Appl. Sci. **13**, 141–148 (2019)
2. Greenwood, W.W., Lynch, J.P., Zekkos, D.: Applications of UAVs in civil infrastructure. J. Infrastruct. Syst. **25**(2), 04019002 (2019)
3. Jung, H.J., Lee, J.H., Yoon, S., Kim, I.H.: Bridge inspection and condition assessment using unmanned aerial vehicles (UAVs): major challenges and solutions from a practical perspective. Smart Struct. Syst. **24**(5), 669–681 (2019)
4. Kilanitis, I., Sextos, A.: Integrated seismic risk and resilience assessment of roadway networks in earthquake prone areas. Bull. Earthq. Eng. **17**(1), 181–210 (2018)
5. Li, Y., Dong, Y., Frangopol, D.M., Gautam, D.: Long-term resilience and loss assessment of highway bridges under multiple natural hazards. Struct. Infrastruct. Eng. **16**, 1–16 (2020)
6. Liu, L., Zong, Z., Gao, C., Yuan, S., Lou, F.: Experimental and numerical study of CFRP protective RC piers under contact explosion. Compos. Struct. **234**, 111658 (2020)
7. Barrile, V., Bernardo, E., Fotia, A., Candela, G., Bilotta, G.: Road safety: road degradation survey through images by UAV. WSEAS Trans. Environ. Develop. **16**, 649–659 (2020)

8. Marmo, F., et al.: On the form of the Musmeci's bridge over the Basento river. Eng. Struct. **191**, 658–673 (2019)

9. Morgenthal, G., et al.: Framework for automated UAS-based structural condition assessment of bridges. Autom. Constr. **97**, 77–95 (2019)

10. Pan, Y., Dong, Y., Wang, D., Chen, A., Ye, Z.: Three-dimensional reconstruction of structural surface model of heritage bridges using UAV-based photogrammetric point clouds. Remote Sens. **11**(10), 1204 (2019)

11. Spencer B.F. Jr., Hoskere, V., Narazaki, Y.: Advances in computer vision-based civil infrastructure inspection and monitoring. Engineering (2019)

12. Barrile, V., Bernardo, E., Candela, G., Bilotta, G., Modafferi, A., Fotia, A.: Road infrastructure heritage: from scan to InfraBIM. WSEAS Trans. Environ. Dev. **16**, 633–642 (2020). https://doi.org/10.37394/232015.2020.16.65

Machine Learning Approaches for Coastline Extraction from Sentinel-2 Images: K-Means and K-Nearest Neighbour Algorithms in Comparison

Emanuele Alcaras[ID], Pier Paolo Amoroso[ID], Francesco Giuseppe Figliomeni[ID], Claudio Parente[✉][ID], and Andrea Vallario[ID]

DIST - Department of Science and Technology, Parthenope University of Naples, Centro Direzionale, Isola C4, 80143 Naples, Italy
{emanuele.alcaras,pierpaolo.amoroso,
francescogiuseppe.figliomeni,claudio.parente,
andrea.vallario}@uniparthenope.it

Abstract. In the last decades, machine learning techniques have increasingly spread to many application fields of remote sensing and, more recently, have also involved the extraction of the coastline from satellite images. The presence of different machine learning algorithms as well as the availability of different types of remote sensing data, make it necessary to further investigate in order to identify methodological solutions for providing accurate results. This article aims to compare two alternative and typical methodological approaches of machine learning, one unsupervised, the other supervised, represented respectively by the K-Means (KM) and K-Nearest Neighbour (KNN) algorithms. The experiments are conducted on Sentinel-2 satellite images, limited to the bands with the highest geometric resolution (10 m). The dataset includes also the image resulting from the application of the Normalized Different Water Index (NDWI), which is particularly effective for distinguishing water/non-water. The coastline obtained by manual vectorization on the Sentinel-2 RGB composition is the term of comparison for evaluating the result accuracy. The Distributed Ratio Index (DRI) is applied for this purpose. The use of training sites with the KNN method allows to obtain a more reliable classification in the presence of multiple spectral bands. On the contrary, using only the NDWI layer the KM method produces better results, demonstrating how in this case the land-sea distinction is clearer and the automatic clustering, as it is not affected by human error that accompanies the detection of the training sites, is more reliable.

Keywords: Coastline extraction · Machine learning · K-Means · K-Nearest Neighbour · Sentinel-2 · Accuracy evaluation

1 Introduction

Coastal environment is often subject to changes due to several phenomena such as subsidence [1], erosion [2], floods [3] and nourishment [4]. The causes can be just

E. Borgogno-Mondino and P. Zamperlin (Eds.): ASITA 2022, CCIS 1651, pp. 368–379, 2022.
https://doi.org/10.1007/978-3-031-17439-1_27

as many, such as proximity to river deltas [5], anthropic activities [6], marine [7] or geological phenomena [8], climate change [9], etc. Due to these changes, the position of the coastline is often variable over time and geomatics is suitable for measuring these variations [10]. There are different geomatics techniques for identifying the coastline: GNSS survey [11], UAV survey [12], SAR [13], LiDAR [14], aerial photogrammetry [15], and optical satellite [16]. Remote sensing techniques that rely on optical sensor are among the most widespread, being used both for the identification of the instantaneous coastline [17] and to evaluate the evolution of the coastline over time [18]. There are many techniques that can be used in remote sensing to identify the dividing line between water and soil, these are often based on the use of indices such as the Normalized Difference Vegetation Index (NDVI) [19] and the Normalized Difference Water Index (NDWI) [20]. Recently [21] proposed an adaptive threshold determination technique on NDWI, [22] used an experimental algorithm for image analysis, called J-Net, [23] developed the Coastal Extraction Tool within the ModelBuilder extension of ArcGIS 10.1 software.

It is therefore evident that the attention of the scientific community is shifting toward techniques that allow to extract the coastline automatically with good accuracy. For this reason, in this work two machine learning techniques are tested in order to identify the separation between land and sea: the K-Means (KM) and the K-Nearest Neighbour (KNN) algorithms. In particular, the experiments are carried out on Sentinel-2 images with a geometric resolution of 10 m. The algorithms are applied on the initial images (Blue, Green, Red and Near Infrared bands), as well as on the NDWI and on a combination of the latter with the 4 selected bands. The operations are carried out using the software free and open source: QGIS - version 3.16 [24].

2 Data and Methods

The Copernicus Sentinel-2 mission is based on a constellation of two identical satellites in the same orbit, phased at 180° to each other. Each satellite can acquire optical images with 13 multispectral bands. The launch of Sentinel-2A was on 23 June 2015, while for the Sentinel-2B was on 7 March 2017 [25]. The visible and the near-infrared (NIR) bands have a spatial resolution of 10 m, the infrared bands have 20 m spatial resolution, and the other bands have 60 m. Sentinel-2 services a wide range of applications related to Earth's land and coastal water [26]. The characteristics of Sentinel-2A satellite sensor, named MultiSpectral Instrument (MSI) which products are used in this article, are reported in Table 1.

The study area analysed in this article extends from the coastline of Acciaroli (Campania, Italy) to Diamante (Calabria, Italy) in the Tyrrhenian Sea. This region, located in the south of Italy, presents the coast running mostly in the north-west to south-east direction. The northern coast appears to be mainly high and rocky and shaken banks [27]. The central area regards the Gulf of Policastro and generally presents sandy beaches [28]. The Calabrian coasts, in the south, appear initially jagged, for the most part high, rocky and steep [29]. In order to ensure a high degree of classification accuracy, it is imperative that the scene be free of cloud cover and/or haze [30] as well as captured in calm sea conditions. For this reason, we select, in the Copernicus Open Access Hub database, a

Sentinel-2A imagery acquired on September 24ᵗʰ 2021 capable of guaranteeing all the requirements listed above.

As reported in Fig. 1, the study area is included in the following UTM/WGS84 zone 33N coordinates: $E_1 = 499,980$ m; $E_2 = 575,980$ m; $N_1 = 4,390,200$ m; $N_2 = 4,453,200$ m.

Table 1. Characteristics of Sentinel-2A MultiSpectral Instrument (MSI) Bands used in this study.

Bands	Central Wavelength (nm)	Resolution (m)
B2 - Blue	490	10
B3 - Green	560	
B4 - Red	665	
B8 - NIR	842	

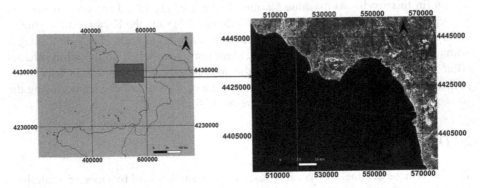

Fig. 1. Localization of the study area in the Tyrrhenian Sea in UTM/WGS84 plane coordinates (EPSG: 32633).

The main characteristics of the algorithms applied in this work are described below. Particularly, the Sect. 2.1 presents the Normalized Different Water Index (NDWI) that is applied using Green and NIR Sentinel-2 bands. Section 2.2 illustrates the machine learning approaches, focusing on how K-Means and K-Nearest Neighbours work. Section 2.3 introduces the index used for accuracy tests, the Distributed Ratio Index (DRI).

2.1 NDWI

Normalized Different Water Index (NDWI) derived from satellite images is commonly and successfully utilized in surface water body detection and mapping [31]. This index was introduced using the green and near infrared spectral bands of Landsat TM [32]. As water bodies strongly absorb light in visible to infrared electromagnetic spectrum, NDWI uses green and near infrared bands to highlight water bodies. It is sensitive to built-up land and can result in over-estimation of water bodies. The visible green wavelengths maximize the typical reflectance of the water surface. The near infrared wavelengths (NIR) maximize the high reflectance of terrestrial vegetation and soil features, while minimizing the low reflectance of water features. The NDWI is expressed as follows [20]:

$$NDWI = \frac{Green - NIR}{Green + NIR} \tag{1}$$

It presents a range of variability between $[-1, 1]$, where the higher values denote the water surface, as shown in Fig. 2.

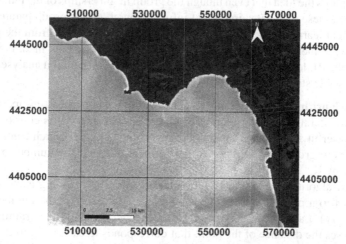

Fig. 2. NDWI obtained from the Sentinel-2A images in the study area (UTM/WGS 84 plane coordinates)

2.2 Machine Learning

Machine learning (ML) is an important research field of artificial intelligence that assists computers in modelling based on experiences and accurately predicting future events [33]. Therefore, the ML is a set of techniques, which helps in dealing with vast data in the most intelligent way to derive actionable insights. ML has been applied in many sciences like computer vision, economics, data mining, bioinformatics, and other areas. This widespread diffusion is due to the fact that it significantly reduces computational costs and shortens development [34]. ML methods can help process a wide range of remote sensing datasets and determine the relationship between components such as the reflectance continuum and features of interest; these methods are robust in processing spectral and ground truth measurements against noise and uncertainties [35]. With the increasing availability of datasets describing the coasts, it is reasonable to speculate that ML will become more useful and widespread in coastal applications in the future [36].

The ML can be divided into four categories: supervised learning, unsupervised learning, semi-supervised learning and Reinforcement Learning [37, 38]. Unsupervised learning is utilized in clustering problems [39]. It is used to train models where target is not set and the goal of the machine is to find the natural categories. In other terms, algorithms find meaningful patterns in datasets or sort data into groups [40]. In supervised learning, the training data are divided into labelled categories, such as samples, and the goal of the machine is to learn how to assign labels to data outside the training set [41]. Semi-supervised learning is placed between the previous two. It is an approach to machine learning that combines a small quantity of labelled data with a large quantity of unlabelled data during training. In many situations, too much time is spent to choose the label, since the skills of an experienced human are required. Therefore, using a few labels, it exploits the idea that even though the group memberships of the unlabelled data are unknown, these data carry important information about the group parameters [42]. Reinforcement learning (RL) aims at using observations collected from the interaction with the environment. It continuously learns from the environment in an iterative way. In the trial, the RL learns from its experiences of the ambience until it analyses the entire range of possible states [43].

K-Means Algorithm The K-Means (KM) algorithm is a numerical, unsupervised, non-deterministic, iterative method usable for image classification. It is considered one of the most powerful and popular data mining algorithms in the research community [44] and attempts to group similar items in the form of clusters; the number of groups is represented by K.

The KM algorithm accomplishes the classification by mapping each pixel in the input dataset to a point in the n-dimensional space (where n is the number of bands of the imagery). Each cluster has a centre (mean) and during model training, the KM algorithm uses the distance of the point that corresponds to each pixel in the dataset to the cluster centres as the basis for clustering. The user chooses the number of clusters (k) to create. The method randomly chooses K observations in the input dataset as cluster centres (means). This is the procedure initialization and requires setting K {m(k)} to random values. The method proceeds by alternating between two steps [45]:

1. Assignment step;
2. Update step.

The first step assigns each observation to the cluster with the nearest mean (centroid). To determine the distance between each pixel and the cluster centre, the Euclidean distance is generally used. Each cluster $S_i^{(t)}$ is generated in compliance with the following relationship:

$$S_i^{(t)} = \left\{ x_p : \|x_p - m_i^{(t)}\|^2 \leq \|x_p - m_j^{(t)}\|^2 \forall j, 1 \leq j \leq k \right\} \tag{2}$$

where:s

x_p is the single pixel of the image; m_i is the centroid of the i-cluster; m_j is the centroid of each of the remaining clusters.

When all the pixels are included in some clusters, an early grouping is done. The second step recalculates the average of early formed clusters, so new centroid for each i-cluster is determined. The process stops when nothing changes from one-step to next, that is there are no more variations in terms of allocation of centres and cluster boundaries.

The resulting classes will be indicative of the natural spectral clusters present in the data [46]. However, there always exists a difficult problem in the KM algorithm and its extensions, because they are affected by initializations and require a given number of clusters a priori [47]. In this article we fix k = 2 since we want to determine two clusters that correspond to the classes that the coastline separates: water/no water.

K-Nearest Neighbour Algorithm The K-Nearest Neighbour (KNN) algorithm is the simplest supervised machine learning algorithm that can be used to resolve classification problems. It was first developed by Fix and Hodges in 1951 [48] and expanded by Cover and Hart [49].

The KNN assigns a category to unlabelled observations in the dataset by comparing them to the observations in the labelled samples that absolve to the function of training dataset [50]. Similarly, to KM, this algorithm maps each pixel in the input dataset to a point in the n-dimensional space, but in this case classifies it by distance from the samples in the training set, also represented by points in the same space. For the calculation of the distance, different criteria can be adopted: the Euclidean distance or the Manhattan distance, are main examples.

KNN is a simple but effective method for classification [51], since it is easy to implement, requires few parameters to set and is also versatile. The major drawback is that it gets significantly slower as the number of training sites and the volume of data increase [52]. In the KNN algorithm the configuration of parameter K is fundamental. In fact, if K is too small, the pixel is assigned based on the closest few samples. If K is too large, the pixel is ranked in the largest category in the training sites; furthermore, the computational cost of the algorithm increases because the distance calculation is a very expensive operation in terms of resources and time [53].

2.3 Accuracy Tests

In this study, each achieved coastline is compared with the reference one, obtained by direct vectorization of the RGB composition by visual analysis. In particular, 6 coastlines are compared with the reference one:

Coastline obtained by applying the KM on the NDWI index (KM1);
Coastline obtained by applying the KM on the R + G + B + NIR (KM2);
Coastline obtained by applying the KM on the R + G + B + NIR + NDWI (KM3);
Coastline obtained by applying the KNN on the NDWI Index (KNN1);
Coastline obtained by applying the KNN on the R + G + B + NIR (KNN2);
Coastline obtained by applying the KNN on the R + G + B + NIR + NDWI (KNN3).

To carried out the accuracy test, the Distributed Ratio Index (DRI) is applied. DRI can be considered as an enhancement of Ratio Index (RI). Developed by Maglione et al. [54], the RI considers the deviation between the two coastlines. In particular, if the overlap does not happen perfectly, polygons are generated. This index is given by the ratio between the sum of the areas of the polygons (A) and the length of the coastline chosen as reference (L):

$$RI = \frac{A}{L} \qquad (3)$$

RI represent the average of the shifts between the two coastlines: the lower the shift, the better the quality.

DRI was introduced by [55] to overcome the limits of RI that is a unique value and does not provide other parameters (i.e. the standard deviation, the minimum and maximum values of the shifts between the two compared lines), so the analysis of the level of accuracy remains incomplete. DRI requires that the area of each polygon generated by the non-perfect overlay between the two compared features, is divided by the length of the effective coastline on which it develops. In this way, several values of DRI are obtained, as many as polygons generated by the intersection between the manually achieved coastline and the extracted one. Those values are considered as residuals and statistical parameters are extracted from them as accuracy indicators.

3 Results and Discussion

Table 2 shows the statistics of DRI obtained for the resulting coastlines.

Table 2. Statistical values of DRI for the extracted coastlines.

Method	Mean (m)	St.Dev. (m)	RMSE (m)	Min (m)	Max (m)
KM1	2.295	1.542	2.764	0.000	14.610
KM2	4.106	4.660	6.210	0.000	64.278
KM3	4.013	3.967	5.643	0.000	44.536
KNN1	2.576	2.082	3.312	0.000	22.332
KNN2	3.453	4.014	5.295	0.000	41.229
KNN3	2.938	2.917	4.140	0.000	34.425

DRI values are expressed in meters as that they can be compared with the spatial unit of the pixel, i.e. 10 m, for establishing the accuracy of the automatically extracted coastline, as reported in the literature. The results show a better performance of the KNN compared to the KM when using the visible and infrared bands, confirming the effectiveness of the training sites. By adding the NDWI layer to the aforementioned bands, the extracted coastline has a higher accuracy, but it is not the absolute best among the cases compared. In fact, KM and KNN provide the best results when applied to the NDWI layer alone. Contrary to what happens in other cases, for applications conducted on the single NDWI band, the unsupervised approach provides more accurate results in accordance with a previous study [56]. In fact, the mean value of the shift between the resulting coastline and the exact one is 2.295 m for KM1 (2.576 m for KNN1) with RMSE equal to 2.764 m (3.312 m for KNN1).

The Histogram of the NDWI reported in Fig. 3 highlights the reason of the good performance of the KM1 application: the distribution of pixel values remarks the capability of this index to distinguish water from everything else, so two classes are clearly evident. It is certainly difficult (if not impossible) to make a choice of training sites capable of identifying the threshold values to correctly classify the pixels as water or no-water. KM obviously performs this task because it is trained on all the data that actually have different characteristics for the two classes. By introducing other data, like the other bands, the distinction is no longer so evident and the training sites become more effective.

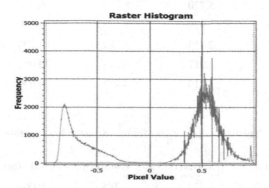

Fig. 3. NDWI histogram.

The best performing classification in two classes (water/no-water) resulting from KM applied to the NDWI map, is shown in Fig. 4.

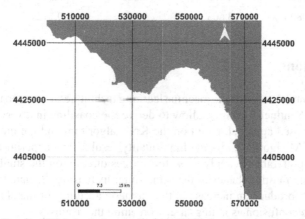

Fig. 4. Result of KM clustering applied to NDWI (land is grey, water is white).

In order to evaluate the method performance related to morphological aspects, samples of high coastline (HCS) as well as low coastline (LCS) are analysed in terms of accurate detection. HCS and LCS both extend for about 6 km. Tables 3 and 4 shows respectively the statistics of DRI obtained for the high and low coastline samples.

DRI statistics confirm the better performance of NDWI used standalone (KM1 and KNN1). Particularly, K-means based methods (KM1, KM2 and KM3) supply more accurate results on LCS rather than HCS.

On the other hand, the KNN algorithm in two out of three cases is better in HCS (KNN 1 and KNN 2). However, the differences are very low (a few centimetres).

Table 3. Statistical values of DRI for the extracted high coastline samples.

Method	Mean (m)	St.Dev. (m)	RMSE (m)	Min (m)	Max (m)
KM1	2.373	1.706	2.923	0.000	10.190
KM2	5.706	5.770	8.115	0.079	22.145
KM3	5.353	5.379	7.589	0.079	21.525
KNN1	2.917	2.419	3.789	0.000	12.043
KNN2	3.799	4.917	6.213	0.051	32.032
KNN3	3.310	3.710	4.972	0.040	32.733

Table 4. Statistical values of DRI for the extracted low coastline samples.

Method	Mean (m)	St.Dev. (m)	RMSE (m)	Min (m)	Max (m)
KM1	2.365	1.470	2.785	0.000	8.656
KM2	3.375	1.897	3.871	0.103	9.291
KM3	3.366	1.869	3.850	0.103	8.591
KNN1	2.354	1.659	4.137	0.067	7.715
KNN2	3.848	4.163	5.669	0.297	15.946
KNN3	3.806	3.603	5.241	0.112	14.068

4   Conclusions

This article demonstrates that the machine learning techniques applied to the NDWI map resulting from Sentinel-2 images, allow to derive the coastline in a very accurate way. Both the supervised approach based on the KNN algorithm and the unsupervised one based on the KM algorithm provide high quality results. The experiments carried out show that it is preferable to apply these techniques directly on the single NDWI layer rather than using multiple bands at the same time: increasing the data to be processed does not always produce an increase in the thematic accuracy of the classification, but it can introduce confusion as in this case, worsening the results.

Although the supervised approach is usually preferable to the unsupervised one as it supports the classification with a model based on samples of the considered classes, the experiments carried out show a better performance of the KM compared to the KNN when both are applied to the NDWI map. This is due to the capability of the NDWI to distinguish the two categories considered, namely water and non-water, that take on very different values: automatic clustering is certainly reliable and better than the classification based on training sites since those are affected by the human error of identification and selection.

Finally, distinguishing between low and high coastline, NDWI used standalone (KM1 and KNN1) supplies the best performance. In addition, the results of unsupervised approaches using KM1, KM2 and KM3 are more accurate on LCS rather than HCS.

References

1. Bitelli, G., et.al.: Radar interferometry-based mapping of the present land subsidence along the low-lying northern Adriatic coast of Italy. In: Land Subsidence, Associated Hazards and the Role of Natural Resources Development, Proceedings of EISOLS, **339**, 279–286 (2010)
2. De Sanjosé Blasco, J.J., Serrano-Cañadas, E., Sánchez-Fernández, M., Gómez-Lende, M., Redweik, P.: Application of multiple geomatic techniques for coastline retreat analysis: The case of Gerra Beach (Cantabrian Coast, Spain). Remote Sens. **12**(21), 3669 (2020)
3. Zong, Y., Tooley, M.J.: A historical record of coastal floods in Britain: frequencies and associated storm tracks. Nat. Hazards **29**(1), 13–36 (2003)
4. Pepe, G., Coutu, G.: Beach morphology change study using ArcGIS spatial analyst. Middle States Geogr. **41**, 91–97 (2008)
5. Fabris, M.: Monitoring the coastal changes of the Po River Delta (Northern Italy) since 1911 using archival cartography, multi-temporal aerial photogrammetry and LiDAR data: implications for coastline changes in 2100 AD. Remote Sens. **13**(3), 529 (2021)
6. Pagán, J.I., Aragonés, L., Tenza-Abril, A.J., Pallarés, P.: The influence of anthropic actions on the evolution of an urban beach: case study of Marineta Cassiana beach. Spain. Sci. Total Environ. **559**, 242–255 (2016)
7. Ferrando, I., et al.: Coastal modification in relation to sea storm effects: application of 3D remote sensing survey in Sanremo Marina (Liguria, NW Italy). Water **13**(8), 1040 (2021)
8. De Groot, T.A.: Climate shifts and coastal changes in a geological perspective. A contribution to integrated coastal zone management. Geol. en mijnbouw **77**(3), 351–361 (1998)
9. Nicholls, R.J., Lowe, J.A.: Benefits of mitigation of climate change for coastal areas. Glob. Environ. Chang. **14**(3), 229–244 (2004)
10. George, S.L., et al.: A multi-data geospatial approach for understanding flood risk in the coastal plains of Tamil Nadu. India. Earth **3**(1), 383–400 (2022)
11. Mendonça, F.J.B., Gonçalves, R.M., Awange, J., Silva, L.M.D., Gregório, M.D.N.: Temporal shoreline series analysis using GNSS. Bol. de Ciênc. Geodésicas **20**, 701–719 (2014)
12. Zanutta, A., Lambertini, A., Vittuari, L.: UAV photogrammetry and ground surveys as a mapping tool for quickly monitoring shoreline and beach changes. J. Mar. Sci Eng. **8**(1), 52 (2020)
13. Baselice, F., Ferraioli, G.: Unsupervised coastal line extraction from SAR images. IEEE Geosci. Remote Sens. Lett. **10**(6), 1350–1354 (2013)
14. Aguilar, F.J., et al.: Preliminary results on high accuracy estimation of shoreline change rate based on coastal elevation models. Int. Arch. Photogramm. Remote Sens. Spat. Inf. Sci, **33**, 986–991 (2010)
15. Fabris, M.: Coastline evolution of the Po River Delta (Italy) by archival multi-temporal digital photogrammetry. Geomat. Nat. Haz. Risk **10**(1), 1007–1027 (2019)
16. Alcaras, E., Errico, A., Falchi, U., Parente, C., Vallario, A.: Coastline extraction from optical satellite imagery and accuracy evaluation. In: Parente, C., Troisi, S., Vettore, A. (eds.) R3GEO 2019. CCIS, vol. 1246, pp. 336–349. Springer, Cham (2020). https://doi.org/10.1007/978-3-030-62800-0_26
17. Dominici, D., Zollini, S., Alicandro, M., Della Torre, F., Buscema, P.M., Baiocchi, V.: High resolution satellite images for instantaneous shoreline extraction using new enhancement algorithms. Geosci. **9**(3), 123 (2019)
18. Giannini, M.B., Maglione, P., Parente, C., Santamaria, R.: Cartography and remote sensing for coastal erosion analysis. WIT Trans. Ecol. Environ. **149**, 65–76 (2011)
19. Rouse, J.W., Haas, R.H., Schell, J.A., Deering, D.W.: Monitoring vegetation systems in the Great Plains with ERTS. NASA Spec. Publ. **351**, 309 (1974)

20. McFeeters, S.K.: The use of the Normalized Difference Water Index (NDWI) in the delineation of open water features. Int. J. Remote Sens. **17**(7), 1425–1432 (1996)
21. Dai, C., Howat, I.M., Larour, E., Husby, E.: Coastline extraction from repeat high resolution satellite imagery. Remote Sens. Environ. **229**, 260–270 (2019)
22. Zollini, S., Alicandro, M., Cuevas-González, M., Baiocchi, V., Dominici, D., Buscema, P.M.: Shoreline extraction based on an active connection matrix (ACM) image enhancement strategy. J. Mar. Sci. Eng. **8**(1), 9 (2020)
23. Domazetović, F., Šiljeg, A., Marić, I., Faričić, J., Vassilakis, E., Panđa, L.: Automated coastline extraction using the very high resolution WorldView (WV) satellite imagery and developed Coastline Extraction Tool (CET). Appl. Sci. **11**(20), 9482 (2021)
24. QGIS. https://www.qgis.org/en/site/about/index.html. Accessed 05 Apr 2022
25. ESA - Observing the Earth, Copernicus, Sentinel-2. https://www.esa.int/Applications/Observing_the_Earth/Copernicus/Sentinel-2. Accessed 05 Apr 2022
26. SENTINEL-2 User Handbook, ESA (2015). https://sentinels.copernicus.eu/documents/247904/685211/Sentinel2_User_Handbook. Accessed 05 Apr 2022
27. Alcaras, E., Parente, C., Vallario, A.: The importance of the coordinate transformation process in using heterogeneous data in coastal and marine geographic information system. J. Marine Sci. Eng. **8**(9), 708 (2020)
28. Valente, R., Stamatopoulos, L., Donadio, C.: Environmental design criteria through geoindicators for two Mediterranean coastlands. CSE-City Saf. Energy **2**, 63–76 (2014)
29. Salvo, F., Romita, T., De Ruggiero, M., Tavano, D.: Residential tourism and real estate appraisal. Valori e Valutazioni, (25) (2020)
30. Abdelhady, H.U., Troy, C.D., Habib, A., Manish: A simple, fully automated shoreline detection algorithm for high-resolution multi-spectral imagery. Remote Sens. **14**(3), 557 (2022)
31. Özelkan, E.: Water body detection analysis using NDWI indices derived from landsat-8 OLI. Pol. J. Environ. Stud. **29**(2), 1759–1769 (2020)
32. Xu, H.: Modification of normalised difference water index (NDWI) to enhance open water features in remotely sensed imagery. Int. J. Remote Sens **27**(14), 3025–3033 (2006)
33. Dogan, A., Birant, D.: Machine learning and data mining in manufacturing. Expert Syst. Appl. **166**, 114060 (2021)
34. Wei, J., et.al.: Machine learning in materials science. InfoMat, **1**(3), 338–358 (2019)
35. Shirmard, H., Farahbakhsh, E., Müller, R.D., Chandra, R.: A review of machine learning in processing remote sensing data for mineral exploration. Remote Sens. Environ. **268**, 112750 (2022)
36. Beuzen, T., Splinter, K.: Machine learning and coastal processes. In: Sandy beach morphodynamics, pp. 689–710. Elsevier (2020)
37. Parvin, H., Alinejad-Rokny, H., Minaei-Bidgoli, B., Parvin, S.: A new classifier ensemble methodology based on subspace learning. J. Exp. Theor. Artif. Intell. **25**(2), 227–250 (2013)
38. Minaei-Bidgoli, B., Asadi, M., Parvin, H.: An ensemble based approach for feature selection. In: Iliadis, L., Jayne, C. (eds.) Engineering Applications of Neural Networks, pp. 240–246. Springer, Heidelberg (2011) https://doi.org/10.1007/978-3-642-23957-1_27
39. Abu Khurma, R., Aljarah, I.: A review of multiobjective evolutionary algorithms for data clustering problems. Evol. Data Clust. Alg. Appl. 177–199 (2021)
40. Algren, M., Fisher, W., Landis, A.E.: Machine learning in life cycle assessment. In: Data Science Applied to Sustainability Analysis, pp. 167–190. Elsevier (2021)
41. Alcaras, E., Amoroso, P.P., Parente, C., Prezioso, G.: Remotely sensed image fast classification and smart thematic map production. Int. Arch. Photogrammetry, Remote Sens. Spat. Inf. Sci. **46**, 43–50 (2021)
42. Zhu, X.J.: Semi-supervised learning literature survey, University of Wisconsin (2005)

43. Botvinick, M., Ritter, S., Wang, J.X., Kurth-Nelson, Z., Blundell, C., Hassabis, D.: Reinforcement learning, fast and slow. Trends Cogn. Sci. **23**(5), 408–422 (2019)
44. Ahmed, M., Seraj, R., Islam, S.M.S.: The k-means algorithm: a comprehensive survey and performance evaluation. Electronics **9**(8), 1295 (2020)
45. MacKay, D.: An example inference task: clustering. Inform. Theo. Inference Learn. Alg. **20**, 284–292 (2003)
46. Nazeer, K.A.A., Sebastian, M.P.: Improving the accuracy and efficiency of the k-means clustering algorithm. In: Proceeding of the World Congress on Engineering, 1, London, July 2009
47. Sinaga, K.P., Yang, M.S.: Unsupervised K-means clustering algorithm. IEEE Access **8**, 80716–80727 (2020)
48. Fix, E., Hodges, J.L.: Discriminatory analysis, nonparametric discrimination: Consistency properties. Technical Report 4, USAF School of Aviation Medicine, Randolph Field (1951)
49. Cover, T., Hart, P.: Nearest neighbor pattern classification. IEEE Trans. Inf. Theory **13**(1), 21–27 (1967)
50. Zhang, Z.: Introduction to machine learning: k-nearest neighbors. Ann. Translational Med. **4**(11) (2016)
51. Guo, G., Wang, H., Bell, D., Bi, Y., Greer, K.: KNN model-based approach in classification. In: Meersman, R., Tari, Z., Schmidt, D.C. (eds.) OTM 2003. LNCS, vol. 2888, pp. 986–996. Springer, Heidelberg (2003). https://doi.org/10.1007/978-3-540-39964-3_62
52. Amra, I.A.A., Maghari, A.Y.: Students performance prediction using KNN and Naïve Bayesian. In: 2017 8th International Conference on Information Technology (ICIT), pp. 909–913. IEEE, May 2017
53. Bajpai, D., He, L.: Evaluating KNN performance on WESAD dataset. In: 2020 12th International Conference on Computational Intelligence and Communication Networks (CICN), pp. 60–62. IEEE (2020)
54. Maglione, P., Parente, C., Vallario, A.: Coastline extraction using high resolution WorldView-2 satellite imagery. Eur. J. Remote Sens. **47**(1), 685–699 (2014)
55. Alcaras, E., Falchi, U., Parente, C., Vallario, A.: Accuracy evaluation for coastline extraction from Pléiades imagery based on NDWI and IHS pan-sharpening application. Appl. Geomatics, 1–11 (2022)
56. Alcaras, E., Amoroso, P.P., Baiocchi, V., Falchi, U., Parente, C.: Unsupervised classification based approach for coastline extraction from Sentinel-2 imagery. In: 2021 International Workshop on Metrology for the Sea; Learning to Measure Sea Health Parameters (MetroSea), pp. 423–427. IEEE, October 2021

Preliminary Spatiotemporal Analysis of Mortality in Northern Italy During COVID-19 First Wave

Stefania Bertazzon[✉], Isabelle Couloigner, and Alison Hanes

University of Calgary, Calgary, AB T2N 1N4, Canada
bertazzs@ucalgary.ca

Abstract. We present a large-scale spatiotemporal analysis of excess mortality (EM) in the first COVID-19 epidemic wave in Lombardy and Veneto. Spatial statistics show that EM is spatially heterogenous in both regions. Global spatiotemporal correlation identifies EM trends that differ across regions during the epi-curve peak, but are uniform in early and late stages. Local spatiotemporal correlation identifies EM hotspots, coldspots, and transition zones. Identifying process dynamics and local features, spatiotemporal correlation can support epidemic surveillance.

Keywords: Spatio-temporal diffusion · Bivariate Moran I · COVID-19 mortality

1 Introduction

Spatial analysis, in conjunction with GIS tools, may provide a valid approach for the interpretation of the spatial and spatiotemporal processes associated with the COVID-19 pandemic [1]. It is well known that Italy was, chronologically, the first western country to be hit by the epidemic[1], which, in early 2020, affected predominantly northern Italy. The first two outbreaks were recorded, independently, on February 21 in Codogno, Lombardy, and in Vo', Veneto [3]. Contagion and mortality exhibited very different trajectories in those two regions that were first hit.

Compared with regions that were hit later, as well as with subsequent pandemic waves, the first wave took place in Lombardy and Veneto in a context of relative unpreparedness, where it can be hypothesized that a greater role was played by pre-existing local factors, including socioeconomic and environmental factors, along with the location of health care facilities, local industrial and urban patterns, transportation networks and commuter flows, as well as air pollution and prevailing winds. For these reasons, a comparison of the spatiotemporal patterns of contagion and mortality in the two regions may provide useful information for management and prevention of potential new epidemic waves. Indeed, the pandemic outcomes were very different in the two regions, especially in terms of mortality; therefore, this study aims to identify potential local

---

[1] The definition of SARS-COV-2 changed from epidemic to pandemic on March 11, 2020, i.e., during the time analyzed by this study [2]; therefore, both terms are used in the paper.

E. Borgogno-Mondino and P. Zamperlin (Eds.): ASITA 2022, CCIS 1651, pp. 380–391, 2022.
https://doi.org/10.1007/978-3-031-17439-1_28

conditions, including socioeconomic, environmental, and transportation, that may have favoured or inhibited contagion and mortality in the two regions.

2   Methods

2.1   Study Area and Timeline

The two regions where the first epidemic outbreaks were recorded, i.e., Lombardy and Veneto, are contiguous, and some descriptive analyses presented in this study consider them as a single area (Figs. 2 and 3). The land surface of Lombardy is 1.5 times larger than Veneto's (23,861 km^2 vs. 18,345 km^2) and its population consists of almost 10 million[2], that is, just over double that of Veneto; its population density is 428 persons per square kilometer, vs. 268 for Veneto. Moreover, the territory of Lombardy is divided into 1506 municipalities (*comuni*), with an average surface of 15.85 km^2 and an average population of 6618. Conversely, the territory of Veneto consists of 563 municipalities, with an average surface of 32.58 km^2 and an average population of 8666[3]. Both regions comprise lowlands (47% in Lombardy, 56% in Veneto), hills (12% in Lombardy, 15% in Veneto) and mountain areas (41% in Lombardy, 29% in Veneto); only Veneto has a seacoast [4].

   The temporal definition of the first epidemic wave used in this study was obtained combining the epidemic wave, drawn from data issued by Protezione Civile [5], with the sequence of SARS-COV-2 emergency health acts [6], as shown in Fig. 1.

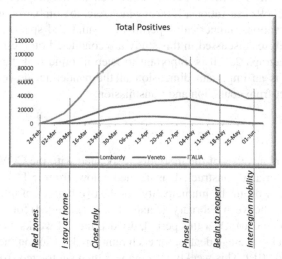

Fig. 1. National and regional epidemiological curves and SARS-COV-2 emergency health acts.

Based on these sources, the first wave is defined as the time interval between February 21 (first recorded cases) and May 18 (first re-openings). This period is divided into

---

[2] According to ISTAT data, referred to 1 January 2020.

[3] The municipal borders are visible in Fig. 5.

weeks, referred to their Fridays, as epidemiologic data were recapped weekly for health planning measures every Friday [5]. An extra week was added at the tail as a buffer. With these adjustments, the timeline of this study is defined as the 14 weeks beginning on Saturday, February 22, and ending on Friday, May 29. Figure 1 shows the national epidemic curve, as well as the epi curves of the two regions of interest, although they appear somewhat flattened by the numerically larger national values. Whereas the Veneto curve is substantially consistent with the national one, the Lombardy curve appears to reach its peak later, and to decline more slowly than the others.

2.2 Data

Throughout the pandemic, the *Protezione Civile* has released daily a rich set of data on several epidemiological variables, plotted in Fig. 1. However, all of these data were released at the regional level; that is, for 21 spatial units, with the only exception being the case count data, which were released provincially; that is, for 108 spatial units [5]. Unfortunately, for the two regions under scrutiny, these data would provide a very limited sample, consisting, at most, of 19 provincial-level observations (i.e., 12 for Lombardy and 7 for Veneto): too small a sample for a proper spatial analysis.

More recently, the National Statistics Institute, ISTAT, has begun the publication of mortality data at the municipal level; that is, on almost 8,000 spatial units, for the period between 2011 and 2022 [7]. As stated by ISTAT [7] and consistently with epidemiological literature [8], these data can serve as an indicator of the portion of the overall mortality that can be ascribed to COVID-19. For our study area, the municipal level data provide a spatial sample of 2069 observations, 1506 of which refer to Lombardy, and 563 to Veneto. This set of observations, numerically, permits a spatial and spatiotemporal analysis; therefore, the analyses discussed in this study are conducted on these data, elaborated as defined in paragraph 2.3. It is important to keep in mind that these data represent mortality, which is an important dimension of the pandemic; however, it remains a dimension distinct from contagion and transmission.

2.3 Methods

The spatiotemporal analysis of the mortality associated with the COVID-19 pandemic is analyzed on a variable constructed, as defined below, from ISTAT data [7]. Starting from the list of daily deaths by municipality, for the two regions of interest, we selected the deaths recorded between February 22 and May 29 (included) for each year between 2015 and 2020 (included). Over this period, divided into 14 weeks (see paragraph 2.1), we calculated weekly average deaths, for each municipality, during the five-year period between 2015 and 2019. This weekly average was then subtracted from the number of deaths recorded in the corresponding week of 2020 for each municipality. This difference was divided by the population residing in that municipality on January 1, 2020, and multiplied by 100 000, as described by Eq. 1.

$$WEM_{k(2020)} = \frac{\left(WM_{2020} - \frac{\sum_{y=2015}^{2019} WM_{yk}}{5} \right)}{Pop_{Jan2020}} \times 100\,000 \qquad (1)$$

In the equation, WEM denotes weekly excess mortality and WM weekly mortality; k denotes weeks (1–14); y denotes years (2015–2019); PopJan2020 is the 2020 population. Kernel density [9], was used as a smoothing technique, to aid visualizing clusters of excess mortality. It was computed in ArcGIS Pro 2.8 using default parameters.

The spatiotemporal analysis was conducted on a bivariate spatial autocorrelation index Moran's I [10]. The standard [univariate] spatial autocorrelation index [11] is computed for a spatial process, defined by the attribute x on a set of point locations i of a spatial sample. It measures the self-similarity of the attribute over short distances; that is, it compares the value of the attribute x at location i with the value of the same attribute at location j, provided that locations i and j are deemed contiguous according to the given contiguity definition, as described by Eq. 2.

$$I = \left(\frac{n}{\sum_{i=1}^{n} \sum_{j=1}^{n} w_{ij}} \right) \left(\frac{\sum_{i=1}^{n} \sum_{j=1}^{n} w_{ij}(x_i - \mu_x)(x_j - \mu_x)}{\sum_{i=1}^{n}(x_i - \mu_x)^2} \right) \qquad (2)$$

In Eq. 2, I is Moran's spatial autocorrelation index [11], n is the sample size; i and j are any pair of spatial points, i.e., locations of the sample; x_i is the value of attribute x at location i; μ_x is the sample average of the attribute values; and w_{ij} defines the contiguity (i.e., proximity) between i and j, where $w_{ij} = 0$ for any i not contiguous to j and for $i = j$. Moran's I index is defined in the interval $[-1 \leq I \leq 1]$ and represents negative spatial autocorrelation in the interval $[-1 \leq I < 0]$, positive in the interval $[0 < I \leq 1]$, and null for $I = 0$. In this study, the spatial process of interest can be thought of as the excess mortality (attribute x) measured in the centroids (points i) of the municipal territories (polygons) of the two regions under scrutiny [11].

The bivariate Moran's I index is defined similarly to the univariate index [10], with the main difference being that the latter compares the values of two attributes, x and y, at contiguous locations i and j, according to Eq. 3. As it compares two processes, this index measures similarity, as opposed to self-similarity, and will be referred to as a spatial correlation, as opposed to spatial autocorrelation index.

$$I = \left(\frac{n}{\sum_{i=1}^{n} \sum_{j=1}^{n} w_{ij}} \right) \left(\frac{\sum_{i=1}^{n} \sum_{j=1}^{n} w_{ij}(x_i - \mu_x)(y_j - \mu_y)}{\sum_{i=1}^{n}(x_i - \mu_x)(y_i - \mu_y)} \right) \qquad (3)$$

The notation in Eq. 3 is the same as in Eq. 2, though Eq. 3 contains also the second attribute, y. The interval of variation and the interpretation of the index remain unchanged. Unlike the univariate index, the bivariate index does not compare the similarity across different realizations of a single spatial process (represented by attribute x); instead, it compares the similarity across the realizations of two spatial processes (represented by attributes x and y) at contiguous locations (i and j).

In this study, the first spatial process is the excess mortality in the week k (represented by attribute x), and the second one is the excess mortality in week $k + 1$ (represented by attribute y) within the given spatial interval, i.e., *neighbourhood* of spatial contiguity. The index thus measures the similarity between excess mortality in a given week and excess mortality in the following week within a defined neighbourhood of contiguous municipalities. Clearly, the two processes, x and y, are, indeed, different temporal realizations of a single process, considered over a given temporal lag (in this case, a week).

For this reason, conceptually the bivariate spatial correlation index measures the self-similarity of the process over space and time; therefore, in this study we refer to it as a spatiotemporal correlation index.

Of the spatiotemporal correlation index, we will calculate both the global and the local version for each region. Local indices of spatial association [12] are mathematically equivalent to the global ones, defined above, but they are calculated locally, yielding one value for each sampled location. Local indices are mathematically related to global ones, as the sum of local indices is proportional to the global index [12].

Inferential statistics are applied to the correlation results, to assess the difference between the two regional trends. While the t test [13] is generally used in these cases, here we use the non-parametric Mann-Whitney-Wilcoxon (M-W-W) test [14], which does not require the normality assumption, assessed by the Shapiro-Wilks test [15].

3   Results

3.1   Spatial Distribution of Excess Mortality in Lombardy and Veneto

The sequence of maps in Fig. 2 represents the excess mortality by municipality during the first pandemic wave in Lombardy and Veneto. The maps further show the first epidemic outbreaks; that is, Codogno (Lodi) in Lombardy and Vo' (Padua) in Veneto. We could render this spatial process more effectively through an animation of the 14 maps, each one depicting one week; however, for this traditional static representation on paper, we selected alternate weeks, starting from the first until the 11th week.

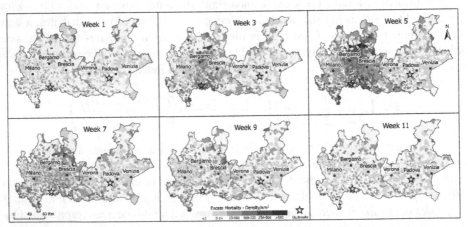

Fig. 2. Excess mortality in Lombardy and Veneto during the first pandemic wave: weeks 1, 3, 5, 7, 9, and 11.

It can be observed that during the initial and final stages of the epidemic wave (weeks 1 and 11) the excess mortality is mostly negative or null in both regions. Positive and large values are observed in most of Lombardy especially between the third and the seventh week, whereas in Veneto values continue to remain largely null or negative throughout the whole period. Indeed, as observed by [8], the expected value of excess mortality in 2020, compared to the 2015–2019 average, should have been negative, owing to the decreasing trend over the previous five years, although this expectation was altered by the pandemic. Throughout the 14 weeks, excess mortality, in both regions, exhibits a heterogeneous spatial distribution, characterized by the simultaneous presence of positive and even large values along with negative and null values in neighbouring municipalities.

3.2 Excess Mortality Clusters Visualized by Kernel Density Analysis

The maps in Fig. 3 show the spatiotemporal evolution of excess mortality clusters. A spatial cluster signals a local intensification of a given spatial process, indicating that the process is not characterized by a random spatial distribution. In this study, it is important to reiterate that these clusters show local intensifications of excess mortality, which shall not be confused with epidemic clusters, outbreaks, or contagion trajectories. The visualization obtained through a simple kernel density analysis is not used as an analytical tool, but is rather used solely to illustrate, descriptively, the spatial expansion of the excess mortality, aiding the identification of homogeneous clusters, which are hard to discern in Fig. 2. Again, in this case, we selected alternate weeks for the static representation; however, in order to provide a more complete picture of the process, we selected the even weeks, that were excluded from Fig. 2.

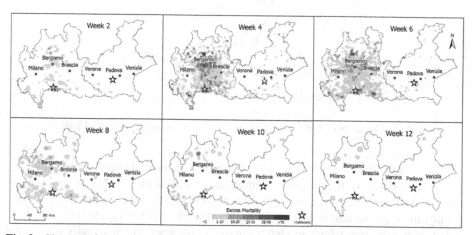

Fig. 3. Clusters of excess mortality in Lombardy and Veneto during the first pandemic wave, visualized through kernel density analysis: weeks 2, 4, 6, 8, 10, and 12.

This visualization, like the previous one, shows a notable difference between the two regions, particularly during the central weeks of the pandemic wave. In Lombardy, clusters appear to be closer to one another and, as the weeks progress, they tend to expand and converge, forming larger clusters. Conversely, in Veneto, clusters vary in intensity and distance, yet they are fewer in the initial stages, and they remain distinct from each other, never converging over the entire period.

3.3 Spatio-Temporal Correlation Analysis

Figure 4 illustrates the global spatiotemporal correlation calculated, for each region, by the global bivariate Moran's I. The spatial interval, or neighbourhood, is defined as the five nearest neighbours. We also defined a 5-nearest-neighbour buffer along the perimeter of the study area, using the contiguous Regions, in order to contain potential distortions in the peripheral areas, i.e., the so-called edge effects [16]. Clearly, the buffer could not be defined along the international borders and the seacoast.

The index reaches maximum values just under 0.20 for Lombardy and 0.10 for Veneto, exhibiting similar trends in the two regions except with a week delay for Veneto. In Veneto the index starts with negative values between the first and second weeks, increases gradually through the fourth week, then increases more sharply between the fourth and fifth weeks, when it peaks just below 0.10. It remains almost constant through the fifth and sixth weeks, then declines sharply through the seventh and eighth weeks, followed by low oscillating values.

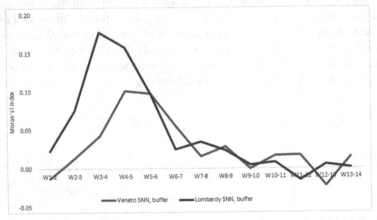

Fig. 4. Global spatiotemporal correlation analysis: bivariate Moran's I index.

The Lombardy trend is similar to the Veneto one in its general traits; however, it exhibits differences that might be important for health monitoring and prevention policies. As early as between the first and second week, the index is positive and rises sharply, its slope increasing as early as the third week, when it rapidly peaks at 0.18, then it starts a descent, which accelerates in the fourth week and practically ends in the sixth-seventh week, followed by a series of low and oscillating values.

The sequence of maps in Fig. 5 illustrates local spatiotemporal correlation at the municipal scale, computed by the local version of the bivariate spatial correlation Moran's I index, and corresponding to the global indices presented in Fig. 4. For the local index we used the same spatial neighbourhood and corresponding buffer defined and employed for the global index. Unlike the maps presented in Fig. 2 and Fig. 3 (which are snapshots), these maps present an index that compares two consecutive weeks. For this figure, based on the results presented in Fig. 4, we chose to show the correlation across the first seven weeks of the pandemic wave as they present a greater interest.

The municipalities colored in grey exhibit non-significant spatiotemporal correlation; those colored in dark red exhibit significant positive correlation across high values of excess mortality (high-high); and those colored in dark blue exhibit significant positive correlation across low values of excess mortality (low-low). The municipalities colored in light red and light blue exhibit significant negative correlation, that is, contiguous municipalities exhibit alternating high and low values: the light red represents a high value in the first week of the comparison in proximity to a low value in the second week (high-low); conversely, the light blue represents a low value in the first week followed by a high value in the following week (low-high).

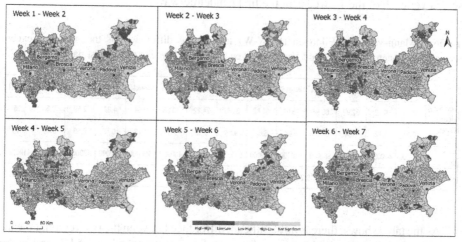

Fig. 5. Local spatiotemporal correlation analysis through local bivariate Moran's I index: weeks 1–2, 2–3, 3–4, 4–5, 5–6, and 6–7.

The latter areas (negative correlation, i.e., light red and light blue) may represent transition zones, with the light blue indicating a tendency to an intensification of excess mortality, and the light red indicating a tendency to a decrease. In any event, these are significant correlations; that is, the statistical difference across values is significant, as opposed to the grey polygons, where the difference across values is not significant.

The local analysis complements the global one, illustrating in detail the correlation in the various parts of the study area, in contrast with the concise curves of the global indices (Fig. 4). In Lombardy, significant *high-high* correlation is observed initially in the south-west and northern portions (weeks 1–2 and 2–3); it then intensifies, extending to a central portion of the region, oriented north-south (weeks 3–4 and 4–5); it then retreats toward the north and south peripheral areas (weeks 5–6 and 6–7). Areas of *low-low* correlation, as well as transition areas (*high-low* and *low-high*) persist in the north and south margins throughout the whole period. In Veneto, the observed spatiotemporal correlation is mostly non-significant, along with areas of *low-low* correlation, particularly in the north and north-west mountain areas in the early weeks, and in the southern lowland in the final weeks. Transition areas (*low-high* and *high-low*) are almost exclusively in the northern portion. Only very few areas of *high-high* correlation appear in the first week (corresponding to the Vo' outbreak) and over the weeks 3–4 and 4–5 in the northern portion. As noted, the buffer could not be applied to national borders, i.e., the northern mountain zones of both regions (more extensive in Lombardy), nor to the Veneto seacoast. Therefore, correlation in these zones may be impacted by edge effects. Significant correlation (*high-high*) is observed along the south and southwest borders of Lombardy; likewise, significant correlation (*low-low* and negative) is observed along northwest and northeast borders of Veneto. Interestingly, no significant correlation is observed along the Lombardy - Veneto border.

Finally, Table 1 presents the M-W-W test [14], which assesses the hypothesis that, on average, the excess mortality of Lombardy differs from that of Veneto, at the municipal scale over each of the 14 weeks of the first pandemic wave.

Table 1. Mann-Whitney-Wilcoxon (M-W-W) test of the difference of the mean of excess mortality between Lombardy and Veneto over each of the 14 weeks of the first pandemic wave.

	Week1	Week2	Week3	Week4	Week5	Week6	Week7	Week8	Week9	Week10	Week11	Week12	Week13	Week14
Lombardy Mean	0.46	9.62	32.92	66.96	78.02	54.82	30.67	24.22	13.88	9.54	4.37	2.59	-0.68	1.35
Veneto Mean	-0.37	1.77	0.64	7.93	6.98	6.67	9.24	6.20	2.75	1.73	-0.73	0.59	0.08	-0.19
M-W-W test	410000	440000	540000	580000	620000	600000	520000	490000	460000	450000	440000	420000	410000	410000
p-value	0.30	0.20	2.00E-16	2.00E-16	2.00E-16	2.00E-16	2.00E-16	4.00E-09	2.00E-03	0.05	0.30	1.00	0.30	0.40

As the table shows, there is no significant difference between the two regional means (p-value > 0.05) in the initial stages of the pandemic wave (weeks 1 and 2) and in the final ones (10th and following weeks), whereas their difference is statistically significant (p-value < 0.05) between the third and the ninth weeks.

4   Discussion

Owing to its large-scale analytical tools, the spatial and spatiotemporal analysis of excess mortality in the first SARS-COV-2 pandemic wave in Lombardy and Veneto allows for the identification of less-known aspects of the spatiotemporal process. The descriptive analysis portrays a locally heterogeneous pattern of excess mortality that is common to both regions. The Mann-Whitney-Wilcoxon test confirms the similarity of these patterns, but only in the tail ends of the pandemic wave. Indeed, during the initial (and, less so, in the latest) weeks, the mortality pattern portrays conditions of relative normality. This, in turn, suggests a relative homogeneity of the socioeconomic, environmental, and logistic spatial patterns of the two regions. Conversely, the significant difference in mortality outcomes during the central pandemic phases may be associated with contingent situations, such as differing responses of the regional health care systems to the health emergency [17, 18]. Moreover, different characteristics of individual regions may have affected the mortality outcomes, by amplifying or reducing the effects of health policies, for example with respect to centralized vs. diffused locational pattern of health care services and facilities.

The descriptive analysis also shows that the heterogeneity of excess mortality was, in both regions, more pronounced during the tail phases of the pandemic wave. This phenomenon could be associated with other processes, of varying local intensity, such as the demographics, pollution, or health care accessibility [19, 20]. These processes may be mediated by a measurable spatial process: population density, which tends to be greater in Lombardy, along with the urban and residential density. This said, municipalities of eastern Lombardy exhibit relatively large surfaces, not unlike those of neighbouring Veneto, potentially related to widespread agriculture in both regions. Interestingly, even though the peak of excess mortality in Lombardy occurred near the Veneto border, no Lombardy clusters have expanded into Veneto. Conversely, the smallest Lombardy municipalities tend to be located in the western part of the region. This may suggest that the higher urban density, along with its associated greater connectivity, may constitute a risk factor under epidemic conditions, which would suggest intensifying epidemic prevention and surveillance in densely urbanized areas [21, 22]. In addition, it shall be noted that the Lombardy mortality received paramount international attention, just because it was chronologically the first, while it has been argued that its magnitude was not greater than comparable metropolitan areas [23].

Global spatiotemporal correlation allowed for identifying a consistent trend of excess mortality, though with different local features, in the two regions; this trend can be described through four distinct phases: 1) spatiotemporal correlation initially low and rapidly growing; 2) high and stable correlation for a short period; 3) rapid descent; 4) slow and inconstant descent leading to a return to initial values. Important differences between the two regions lie in the slope of the curves and transition points between phases [24]. Owing to its ability to identifying such patterns, the combination of global and local spatiotemporal correlation can provide valid decision support tools, particularly if applied to real-time data [25].

The correlation analysis (both global and local) rests on the definition of a spatial neighbourhood. In this study, several neighbourhoods were experimented with [26]. The neighbourhood discussed in this paper suggests that urban connectivity extends over five contiguous municipalities. Importantly, this parameter was calibrated for the entire study area, whereas local regional or provincial analyses are likely to yield different results [27]. Local spatiotemporal correlation identifies clusters of *high-high* vs. *low-low* mortality, referred to as hotspots vs. coldspots. Despite the drastic difference between these local situations, both constitute positive correlation, equally contributing to the global index. This observation cautions against simplistic comparisons of global indices across regions, suggesting that such analyses be complemented by local analyses [28]. This is apparent in our study, where the Lombardy global index appears to be largely formed by *high-high* positive correlation, in contrast with the Veneto index, predominantly formed by *low-low* positive correlation. Further to the importance of large-scale local analysis, these considerations point to the importance of significant negative correlations, namely the *low-high* clusters that may signal the imminent development of *high-high* clusters. These situations can easily be detected by spatial analysis, leading to better epidemic preparedness and monitoring.

5 Conclusion

This paper analyzed, at large scale, the mortality experienced in the first COVID-19 pandemic wave by Lombardy and Veneto: the study is relevant because these were the first western regions to be hit; therefore, transmission and mortality took place in a context of relative unpreparedness to the public health emergency. The mortality in excess of the previous 5-year average exhibits a heterogeneous pattern in both regions, which suggests further multivariate analyses of potentially phenomena, such as demographics, pollution, urban density, productive activities, and health care services.

Global spatiotemporal correlation allows an analysis of the temporal trend of excess mortality in its general traits, as well as its regional features. Indeed, both regions exhibit uniform features in the initial and final phases of the pandemic wave, but divergent patterns in the central phases. This may suggest substantially consistent background conditions, which would normally be associated with uniform mortality outcomes; however, in the most acute pandemic phases, regional and local differences may have amplified or decreased the efficacy of public health measures, impacting epidemic and mortality outcomes. Urban and residential density may be among these factors, which would lead to flagging high-density areas for greater epidemiological risk, that may be potentially targeted by local prevention and surveillance public health policies. The spatiotemporal correlation analysis also identified local thickening (clusters) of high excess mortality. Even though our analyses were conducted after-the-fact on consolidated ISTAT data, this method may permit timely identification and monitoring of developing epidemic and mortality clusters, pending the availability of timely, if not real-time, data.

This study, however preliminary, illustrates the potential of large-scale spatiotemporal analytical methods in understanding spatiotemporal epidemic processes, potentially providing useful information to support public health policy decisions, especially at the local level, tailored to the specific needs of different regions and territories.

References

1. Rosenkrantz, L., Schuurman, N., Bell, N., Amram, O.: The need for GIScience in mapping COVID-19. Health Place **67**, 102389 (2021)
2. https://www.who.int/emergencies/diseases/novel-coronavirus-2019/interactive-timeline#event-72. Visited 25 Mar 2022
3. Remuzzi, A., Remuzzi, G.: COVID-19 and Italy: what next? Lancet **395**(10231), 1225–1228 (2020)
4. https://www.istat.it/it/informazioni-territoriali-e-cartografiche. Visited 24 Mar 2022
5. https://github.com/pcm-dpc/COVID-19. Visited 24 Mar 2022
6. https://www.gazzettaufficiale.it/attiAssociati/1/?areaNode=12. Visited 24 Mar 2022
7. https://www.istat.it/it/archivio/240401. Visited 24 Mar 2022
8. Gibertoni, D., et al.: Patterns of COVID-19 related excess mortality in the municipalities of Northern Italy during the first wave of the pandemic. Health Place **67**, 102508 (2021)
9. https://pro.arcgis.com/en/pro-app/2.8/tool-reference/spatial-analyst/how-kernel-density-works.htm. Visited 24 Mar 2022
10. Anselin, L.: An introduction to spatial autocorrelation analysis with GeoDa. Spatial Analysis Laboratory, University of Illinois, Champagne-Urbana, Illinois (2003)
11. Anselin, L.: Spatial Econometric. Methods and Models. Kluwer, New York (1988)

12. Anselin, L.: Local indicators of spatial association – LISA. Geogr. Anal. **27**, 93–115 (1995)
13. Burt, J., Barber, G., Rigby, D.L.: Elementary Statistics for Geographers. Guilford Press, New York (2009)
14. Bauer, D.F.: Constructing confidence sets using rank statistics. J. Am. Stat. Assoc. **67**(339), 687–690 (1972)
15. Royston, J.P.: Algorithm AS 181: The W test for normality. J. Roy. Stat. Soc. Ser. C (Appl. Stat.) **31**(2), 176–180 (1982)
16. Griffith, D.A.: Correcting for edge effects in spatial statistical analyses. In: Advanced Spatial Statistics, pp. 175–199. Springer, Dordrecht (1988). https://doi.org/10.1007/978-94-009-275 8-2_7
17. Bourdin, S., Jeanne, L., Nadou, F., Noiret, G.: Does lockdown work? A spatial analysis of the spread and concentration of Covid-19 in Italy. Reg. Stud. **55**(7), 1182–1193 (2021)
18. Lai, A., et al.: Phylogeography and genomic epidemiology of SARS-CoV-2 in Italy and Europe with newly characterized Italian genomes between February-June 2020. Sci. Rep. **12**(1), 1–12 (2022)
19. Tchicaya, A., Lorentz, N., Leduc, K., de Lanchy, G.: COVID-19 mortality with regard to healthcare services availability, health risks, and socio-spatial factors at department level in France: a spatial cross-sectional analysis. PLoS ONE **16**(9), e0256857 (2021)
20. Ji, Y., Ma, Z., Peppelenbosch, M.P., Pan, Q.: Potential association between COVID-19 mortality and health-care resource availability. Lancet Glob. Health **8**(4), e480 (2020)
21. Benedetti, R., Piersimoni, F., Pignataro, G., Vidoli, F.: Identification of spatially constrained homogeneous clusters of COVID-19 transmission in Italy. Reg. Sci. Policy Pract. **12**(6), 1169–1187 (2020)
22. Maietti, E., Golinelli, D., Fantini, M.P.: COVID-19 in Italy: did the virus run on an ancient Roman road? J. Public Health **30**(4), 1041–1043 (2022). https://doi.org/10.1007/s10389-020-01377-x
23. Signorelli, C., et al.: The spread of COVID-19 in six western metropolitan regions: a false myth on the excess of mortality in Lombardy and the defense of the city of Milan. Acta Bio Medica: Atenei Parmensis **91**(2), 23 (2020)
24. Michelozzi, P., et al.: Temporal dynamics in total excess mortality and COVID-19 deaths in Italian cities. BMC Public Health **20**(1), 1–8 (2020)
25. Parvin, F., Ali, S.A., Hashmi, S.N.I., Ahmad, A.: Spatial prediction and mapping of the COVID-19 hotspot in India using geostatistical technique. Spat. Inf. Res. **29**(4), 479–494 (2021). https://doi.org/10.1007/s41324-020-00375-1
26. Bertazzon, S.: L'analisi spaziale: la geografia che… conta. Nuove Geografie. Strumenti di lavoro, n. 11111.7, Milano, FrancoAngeli (2022)
27. Ghosh, P., Cartone, A.: A spatio-temporal analysis of COVID-19 outbreak in Italy. Reg. Sci. Policy Pract. **12**(6), 1047–1062 (2020)
28. Fatima, M., Arshad, S., Butt, I., Arshad, S.: Geospatial clustering and hotspot detection of covid-19 incidence in 2020: a global analysis. Int. J. Geospatial Environ. Res. **8**(1), 4 (2021)

Multi-platform, Multi-scale and Multi-temporal 4D Glacier Monitoring. The Rutor Glacier Case Study

Myrta Maria Macelloni[1] ⓘ, Elisabetta Corte[1(✉)] ⓘ, Andrea Ajmar[3] ⓘ,
Alberto Cina[1] ⓘ, Fabio Giulio Tonolo[2] ⓘ, Paolo Felice Maschio[1] ⓘ,
and Isabella Nicole Pisoni[1] ⓘ

[1] DIATI – Department of Environmental, Land and Infrastructure Engineering,
Politecnico di Torino, Corso Duca degli Abruzzi 24, 10129 Torino, Italy
`{myrta.macelloni,elisabetta.corte}@polito.it`
[2] DAD – Department of Architecture and Design, Politecnico di Torino,
Viale Pier Andrea Mattioli 39, 10125 Torino, Italy
[3] DIST - Interuniversity Department of Regional and Urban Studies and Planning,
Politecnico di Torino, Viale Pier Andrea Mattioli 39, 10125 Torino, Italy

Abstract. At present most alpine glaciers are not in equilibrium with the current climate, as a result they are undergoing a dramatic mass loss. Monitoring glacial variations is crucial to assess the consequences of climate change on the territory. In this work different geomatics techniques are exploited to measure and monitor the Rutor glacier over the years. In this study two different techniques were adopted to generate 3 digital surface models (DSMs): aerial and satellite photogrammetry. Two photogrammetric aerial surveys were carried out: at the end of the hydrological year 2019/20 and at the end of the following hydrological year. Additionally, a very high-resolution satellite stereo pair, acquired by the Pléiades-1A platform in 2017, was processed to assess whether satellite images can be applied to extract the 3D surface of the Rutor glacier. In order to evaluate the Rutor glacier mass-balance throughout the years several reference points were positioned and measured before the 2021 aerial flight. Thanks to the presence of the materialized points the 2021 model is considered as the 'Reference Model' against which subsequent models can be compared for glacier analysis. This model was validated by means of a comparison with the authoritative Regional DSM based on LiDAR surveys. In alpine glaciers, the positioning of artificial square cross target in time invariant areas is crucial to enable a multitemporal 4D analysis. The use of very high-resolution satellite imagery allows large areas to be mapped in 3D, but with lower accuracies proportionally decreasing with respect to slope and exposure.

Keywords: Aerial photogrammetric survey · Satellite · Photogrammetry · 3D · Glacier monitoring · Multi-temporal

© The Author(s) 2022
E. Borgogno-Mondino and P. Zamperlin (Eds.): ASITA 2022, CCIS 1651, pp. 392–404, 2022.
https://doi.org/10.1007/978-3-031-17439-1_29

1 Introduction

Alpine areas are one of the most affected by climate change. Alpine glaciers recession has remarkable consequences on the water supply of the valley floor sectors, on the production of hydroelectric energy and on the agricultural productivity of the downstream areas [1, 2]. Hence monitoring glacial variations enable the analysis of climate change impact and the assessment of its effects on the territory.

Remote sensing techniques have always been used to investigate glaciers. Satellite images allow the study of glaciers without requiring direct in situ measurements (depending on the positional accuracy requirements), furthermore these can cover extremely wide areas (in the range of hundreds of km^2, including several glaciers) and long archive time-series are potentially available. Nowadays satellite images are widely used in cryosphere studies. Satellite images have been successfully used to study glaciers kinematics and dynamics [3, 4]. However, despite the very high level of detail (with a spatial resolution up to 30 cm) the vertical accuracy may still be limiting for some applications.

Satellite images drawbacks can be overcome with Manned or Unmanned Aerial Vehicles (UAVs) photogrammetry. Aerial photogrammetry allows very high-resolution images (up to few centimeters) to be acquired over areas with limited accessibility. Manned aerial flights are more expensive but, unlike UAVs, they allow to survey much wider areas without requiring a team to be deployed in the field. The acquired very high-resolution imagery can be used to build high resolution 3D point clouds, Digital Surface Models (DSMs) and orthophotos exploiting Structure-from-Motion (SfM) and Multi-View Stereo (MVS) algorithms [5, 6]. These products have been widely employed for applications such as: river flow velocity and discharge estimation [7, 8], mapping hazard related to glacier collapse [9], glacier dynamics [10, 11].

Rutor glacier mass-balance has been monitored since 2004 by ARPA Valle d'Aosta and Fondazione Montagna Sicura. At first, mass-balance measurements were achieved only through direct in situ measurement [12]. Since 2020, with the cooperation of the Glacier Lab of Politecnico di Torino, field work has been integrated with aerial and drone photogrammetry.

To investigate the yearly evolution two photogrammetric manned flights were performed over the Rutor glacier, the first at the end of the hydrological year 2019/20 and the second at the end of the following hydrological year. Moreover, a very high-resolution satellite stereo-pair from the Pléiades constellation was used to assess the feasibility of a satellite-based monitoring. Considering the extent of the monitored areas, UAV photogrammetry is not discussed in this manuscript.

1.1 Case Study

Rutor glacier is Valle D'Aosta's third largest glacier and is one of the most representative due to its geographical position, morphological and glaciological characteristics [12]. It is located at the head of the Dora valley in La Thuile, in north-western Italy, next to the French-Italian border. The Rutor glacier has a surface area of 8,4 km^2 and its longest flow line is 4,68 km long. The glacier descends from its top elevation of 3486 m a.m.s.l. up to the front at 2540 m a.m.s.l. alternating sloping areas with more flat zones. The accumulation zone of Rutor is formed by two large main circuses confined by rocky ridges and divided by the Vedettes du Rutor. The ablation zone is formed by three tongues, the lowest altitude is reached by the orographic right one.

Rutor glacier has been the object of several studies [13–15] and its mass-balance has been monitored since 2004 by ARPA Valle d'Aosta and Fondazione Montagna Sicura: their analysis confirms that from 2004/05 to 2011/12 the net mass balance has always been negative while for the two hydrological years 2012/13 and 2013/14 mass accumulation exceeded mass loss [12].

2 Materials and Methods

In this study different digital photogrammetry techniques were used. The processed remotely sensed imagery were acquired from a camera carried on a light aircraft and from the Pléiades satellite constellation. The adopted cartographic reference system is ETRF2000 UTM 32 N (EPSG: 6707), while the elevation component refers to the ITALGEO2005 geoid model. When required, datum conversion have been carried out using VERTO IGM transformation approach [16].

2.1 Photogrammetric Flight

Two photogrammetric flights were carried out to survey the Rutor glacier on 30 September 2020 and 13 September 2021. The flights were commissioned to DigiSky, which is a Turin-based EASA certified company. Both flights required about an hour to survey the entire glacier surface, as shown in Fig. 1 [17].

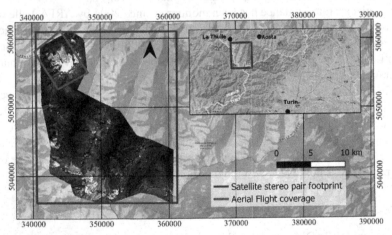

Fig. 1. Satellite (orthophoto and blue rectangle) and aerial 2021 (red rectangle) covered area. Coordinate System: ETRF2000 UTM32N (Color figure online)

The aircraft used to carry out the photogrammetric flights was equipped with a global navigation satellite system (GNSS) antenna, an inertial measurement unit (IMU) with low accuracy and a PhaseOne camera. The PhaseOne camera model is the iXM-RS150F and was installed under the right wing of the aircraft. This is a medium format camera with a focal length of 50 mm, a sensor size of 40 mm × 53.5 mm and a resolution of 151.3 MP [18].

2.2 Satellite Imagery

ARPA Valle D'Aosta shared with the Glacier Lab of Politecnico di Torino a Pléiades stereo pair acquired on 20/08/2017 at 10:34 UTC characterized by off-nadir angles of ±8° leading to a real GSD of 0,71 m (delivered products are resampled at 0,5 m by the satellite data provider). The sensor installed on the satellite constellation covers the visible and the Near-Infrared (NIR) spectral bands with a spatial resolution of 0,7 m (panchromatic spectral band) and 2,8 m (multispectral spectral bands). The swath field of view is 20 km in nadiral position [19]. The covered surface is 268,468 km^2 in the Aosta Valley region (Fig. 1) close to the borders among Aosta Valley, Piedmont, and France, with different mountainous areas, the Gran Paradiso area and the Rutor glacier.

2.3 Control Points and Measurement Campaigns

Before the second aerial flight, a set of 30 reference points was positioned and measured with artificial square cross targets, measured by means of GNSS surveys. The first survey purpose was to position the targets on the glacier and to determine their position.

Since the purpose of this project is to evaluate the Rutor glacier mass-balance throughout the years and not its displacement, the targets on the glacier were placed on stable areas along the moraines and the rocky ridges, aiming to use these targets as invariant reference points also for future photogrammetric flights. We considered as stable areas the rocky ridges bordering the glacier and the proglacial area, assuming that these are time invariant zones.

To determine the 3D coordinates of the targets, a master station was installed in the barycentric reference point of the glacier and the coordinates of the targets were obtained in Real Time Kinematic (RTK) mode. When internet connectivity is available, HxGN SmartNet GNSS RTK Network was used as Virtual Reference Station (VRS) techniques. Since the points were placed after the first flight, the model of the 30 September 2020 was co-registered to the 2021 model with 18 Ground Control Points (GCPs). The coordinates of these points were extracted from the 2021 model. Among all the 30 measured points, 12 were used as Ground Control Points (GCPs) to orient the photogrammetric flight carried out in 2021 (6 placed on the glacier area and 6 on the proglacial area, Fig. 2a). In addition, the IGM95 (Istituto Geografico Militare) point placed on the Testa del Rutor was used as a GCP for the 2020 and 2021 models.

To build the 3D model from the stereo satellite imagery, 6 GCPs were extracted automatically from the orthophoto obtained from the processing of the aerial survey carried out in 2021 with a Ground Sample Distance (GSD) of 50 cm and a planar accuracy of 9 cm. The height of these GCPs was derived from the 2021 aerial DSM.

To determine the accuracy of the 2020 aerial model with respect to the 2021 one, 10 Independent Check Points (ICP) were used. To check the accuracy of the satellite imagery model, only 2 stereo CPs were selected on the reference 2021 aerial orthoimagery due to the challenging identification of homologues points.

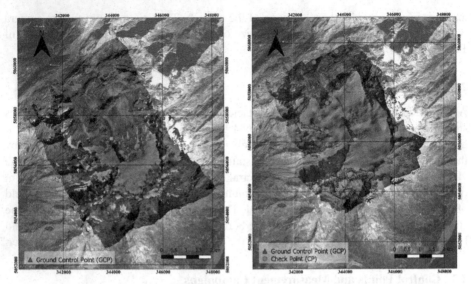

Fig. 2. a) GCP distribution for the 2021 aerial survey; b) GCP and CP distribution for the 2020 aerial survey

2.4 Reference Cartographic Data

In order to determine the accuracy of the DSM obtained from the 2021 aerial survey, a DSM produced in 2008 by Valle d'Aosta was used as reference. This DSM is derived from LIDAR surveys and has a spatial resolution of 2 m. The reference system of the model is ED50/UTM zone 32N (EPSG: 23032). Since the reference system of the 2021 model is ETRF2000, the required Datum conversion was carried out with the Italian ConveRgo software and VERTO approach [16].

2.5 Data Processing

Aerial Photogrammetry. The images acquired during the photogrammetric flights were processed using AgiSoft Metashape Professional v 1.8.1.

After the images were imported and aligned, the markers were manually identified linking the relevant 3D coordinates. The dense point cloud (generated with high resolution settings) is composed by 3.338.453.261 points for the 2021 model and 1.871.761.605 points for the 2020 model. The number of points of the dense cloud of the two models is proportional to the area of the surveys. Once the dense cloud and the mesh were generated, the cartographic products were extracted.

The 2021 model is considered as the 'Reference Model' against which subsequent models can be compared for glacier retreat and melting considerations. To further validate the 2021 model, a comparison with the 2008 LIDAR DSM [18] was carried out.

Satellite Photogrammetry. The Pléiades satellite stereo pair was processed using Geomatica Banff software 2019 edition. The adopted model is the Rational Function Model,

RFM (or RPC, Rational Polynomial Coefficients), a non-parametric math-based model that relates ground 3D coordinates to image 2D coordinates.

After a preliminary pansharpening step (producing a new multispectral dataset at the spatial resolution of the panchromatic band), the satellite stereopair orientation was carried out by automatically identifying reference points from the aerial orthomosaic and the related DSM (to be used both as GCP and CP) and tie points (TPs) (Fig. 3). The automatic identification was manually cross-checked by means of visual interpretation. After the model calculation, the epipolar images are generated and the Digital Surface Model (DSM) and the two orthophotos are extracted. The 3D positional accuracy was estimated on both GCP and CP, as shown in Tables 1 and 2.

Glacier 4D monitoring.   Multitemporal DSMs describing the glacier surface allow the glacial mass ablation between two dates to be calculated. In this study four different DSM were used to assess the elevation differences (as well as to evaluate the accuracy of the aerial and satellite surface models in the stable areas).

Lidar (2008) vs Aerial (2021).   As mentioned previously, the 2021 aerial model is considered the reference dataset since it was oriented exploiting the artificial targets positioned before the aerial survey. To assess the accuracy and validate the 2021 aerial model, a comparison with the authoritative Regional LIDAR DSM was carried out, as described in Sect. 2.2. The two DSMs are subtracted in a GIS environment to calculate the differences and evaluate the accuracy on the selected time-invariant areas. The difference between the two DSMs on the glacier area provides an estimation of the glacier mass changes.

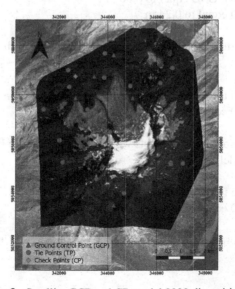

Fig. 3. Satellite GCP and CP model 2020 disposition

Aerial (2020) vs Aerial (2021). The same procedure was applied to subtract the 2021 Aerial DSM from the 2020 Aerial DSM to compare invariant zones and glacier melt in one year. To properly interpret the results, it has to be highlighted that 2020 aerial imagery is characterised by an extensive snow coverage, as clearly visible in the orthophoto.

Satellite (2017) vs Aerial (2021). As far as satellite photogrammetry is concerned, the comparison was carried out between the 2017 Satellite DSM and the 2021 Aerial DSM.

A first qualitative analysis of the elevation differences highlighted that the elevation accuracy seems to be related to the slope. To quantitatively confirm this hypothesis, the elevation differences have been grouped in 5 different slope ranges and the accuracy metrics have been recalculated accordingly (Table 3). Adopting the same approach, the analysis was carried out considering 8 DSM aspect classes (mountainside azimuth) to understand if the illumination condition as well as the relative position of the satellite, with respect to the main orientation of the glacier valley, could impact on the accuracy of the satellite stereo-pair processing (Table 4). The slope and aspect analysis were carried out only on stable areas.

3 Results

3.1 Cartographic Products: Orthophoto and DSM

The following cartographic products were obtained from the Digisky 2021 flight model:

- an Orthophoto with a GSD equal to 0.06 m
- a DSM with a GSD equal to 0.24 m

The following cartographic products were obtained from the Digisky 2020 flight model:

- an Orthophoto with a GSD equal to 0.07 m
- a DSM with a GSD equal to 0.14 m

The following cartographic products were obtained from the Pléiades 2017 satellite photogrammetric model:

- 2 Orthophotos (one for each image of the stereo pair) with a GSD equal to 0.50 m
- a DSM with a GSD equal to 0.50 m.

The residual errors [cm] on GCPs and CPs are shown in Table 1 and Table 2 respectively :

Table 1. Residual errors on GCPs.

Model	N. Points	RMSE X [cm]	RMSE Y [cm]	RMSE Z [cm]
Aerial 2021	13	4,6	2,7	5,5
Aerial 2020	18	24,9	13,7	7,9
Plèiades 2017	6	5,5	15,5	43,5

Table 2. Residual errors on CPs.

Model	N. Points	RMSE X [cm]	RMSE Y [cm]	RMSE Z [cm]
Aerial 2020	10	18,0	18,3	26,2
Plèiades 2017	2	12,4	0,8	0,8

Table 3. Statistics related to slope range (stable areas).

Slope range	Count (pixel)	Mean [m]	Standard deviation [m]
$S < 18°$	4.631.745	−2.89	3.88
$18° < S < 36°$	8.574.643	−2.26	6.00
$36° < S < 54°$	5.625.899	−1.41	7.58
$54° < S < 72°$	2.087.941	0.75	9.86
$S > 72°$	544.735	5.13	12.47

3.2 DSM Comparisons

Lidar (2008) vs Aerial (2021). Considering that the Geoportal DSM is based on airborne LIDAR, as expected, the average difference is about −0.24 m and the standard deviation is 0.42 m on stable areas around the glacier area (Fig. 4A).

Aerial (2020) vs Aerial (2021). The average difference between the DSMs on the stable areas around the lakes area is equal to about 0.09 m and the standard deviation is 0.11 m. The glacier melt estimation highlights the difference of snow ablation between the upper part and the lower part: the east forehead thickness loss is around 4 m/year, 2 m/year on the west forehead and 3–4 m/year on the central forehead (Fig. 4B).

Satellite (2017) vs Aerial (2021). Similarly to studies based on other glaciers, although the morphology of the glaciers is different, the altimetric accuracy seems to decrease with the slope's increase [3]. For selected slope classes on stable areas, the difference between the Satellite and aerial DSM was assessed, and the relevant statistics were calculated (Table 3).

The mean value of difference between the two DSM increases significantly between the slope classes, but more significant is the increase in the standard deviation from 3.8 m to over 12 m for the steepest parts. As a general result, it can be highlighted that the DSM obtained from the satellite images tend to smooth the elevation differences with respect to the reference DSM.

The same approach was adopted to investigate the possible relation between elevation accuracy and terrain aspect, i.e. a thematic map showing the azimuth of the terrain.

There is a clear correlation between the satellite DSM residuals and the terrain aspect, due to possible impact of illumination condition during the stereopair acquisition.

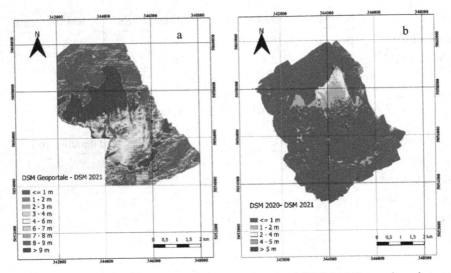

Fig. 4. a) Comparisons between GEOPORTALE VDA and aerial DSM; b) Comparisons between 2020 and 2021 DSM

Moreover, the relation between vertical accuracy and terrain aspect can be also due to the relative satellite/mountainside position, which leads to occluded areas in the stereoscopic pair. It is important to underline that the vast majority of the analysed areas are facing South, making the interpretation of the results less robust.

Table 4. Statistics related to exposure range (stable areas).

Exposure Range	Direction	Count	Mean [m]	Standard Deviation [m]
$-22.5° < E < 22.5°$	North	7.000.022	−5.09	4.76
$22.5° < E < 67.5°$	North-East	969.933	−3.26	5.51

(continued)

Table 4. (*continued*)

Exposure Range	Direction	Count	Mean [m]	Standard Deviation [m]
$67.5° < E < 112.5°$	East	470.927	−1.98	6.22
$112.5° < E < 157.5°$	South-East	1.027.201	−0.87	6.49
$157.5° < E < 202.5°$	South	9.087.075	1.1.54	7.70
$202.5° < E < 247.5°$	South-West	1.352.347	−2.21	5.28
$247.5° < E < 292.5°$	West	700.060	−3.10	4.92
$292.5° < E < 337.5°$	North-West	1.436.766	−3.95	4.58

4 Discussion and Conclusion

In this work, photogrammetric approaches based on imagery acquired from aerial and satellite platforms were adopted for a multi-temporal 3D monitoring of the Rutor glacier. For our purposes the positioning and measuring of artificial square cross targets had a crucial role on the analysis. The accuracy of the models depends strongly on the availability of reference points with known 3D accuracy that can be easily pinpointed on the acquired imagery. In glacier environments is really hard to identify points that are stable over time and that can be recognised in different years due to the rapid landscape changes. Moreover, snowfalls can hide the more stable areas surrounding the glacier preventing the identification of the same points in multi-temporal acquisitions. Indeed, this was the case of the 2020 model. Due to the snow coverage on the accumulation area of the Rutor glacier, the search of points along the glacier upper part was a challenging task.

The use of very high-resolution satellite imagery is a theoretically shorter process than processing aerial images and enables much wider areas to be covered, but it presents some disadvantages that have not been fully solved. From the elevation variations perspective, although the measurements are consistent with other analyses, the accuracy is lower with a clear influence of both terrain slope and aspect. Additionally, although rocky areas are considered to be stable over time, these could include areas subject to landslides or partial changes over time. Nevertheless, it is still effective in identifying relevant (> ±5 m) elevation changes and consequently hot spots were to focus more detailed surveys. In planar terms, the satellite orthoimages allow the retreat of the glacial fronts to be assessed and a comparison with other products to be carried out. In fact, the Rutor front was delineated using the orthophotos obtained from: Digisky and UAV flights models, Pléiades photogrammetric model and the Geoportale VdA [20] (Fig. 5). Further analyses are planned to evaluate the expected improvements when using 30 cm satellite stereopairs.

The relative orientation of the terrain aspect with respect to the satellite azimuth has an impact on the 3D accuracy and therefore is a limitation in the use of satellite imagery in glacier monitoring. The influence of terrain aspect could be overcome by combining targeted drone surveys in areas characterised by lower accuracy or, where possible, by

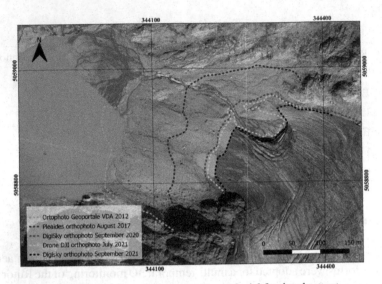

Fig. 5. Multitemporal analysis of east glacial forehead retreat.

choosing the optimal azimuth among the available archive satellite images covering the area under investigation.

The availability of DSM with an elevation accuracy of few centimeters enable to estimate the ablation rate, that for the Rutor case study is as average 4 m/year on the east glacial forehead, 2 m/year on the west forehead and in the range from 3 to 4 m/year on the central forehead. This outcome is consistent with the results of the comparison with the 2008 Geoportal LIDAR DSM that estimates the melting of the east front up to 60 m in 13 years. This is also possible considering the different amount of snow melted per year and the consideration of 2020 as a year of less melting of the Aosta Valley glaciers. (ARPA VDA mass balances preliminary results).

The strong dependence of elevation precision from terrain slope and aspect suggest to carefully evaluate the use of satellite photogrammetry with actual GSD larger than 0.5 m for monitoring glaciers with centimetric accuracy, mainly depending on of glaciers morphology and orientation. Although the validation of the model on stable areas did not lead to the expected results, the gentle slope of the glacier allows us to qualitatively estimate the mass melted as about 20 m in the period 2017–2021 on the front, a figure consistent with those of other comparisons. The work carried out can be further developed, collaborating with ARPA Valle D'Aosta for increasingly accurate and multidisciplinary glacier 4D monitoring. In addition, another group of experts carried out geophysics and hydrological surveys not addressed in this work during the summer campaigns. The integration of these data in the 3D model would enable a complete analysis of the evolution of the glacial environment.

References

1. Beniston, M., et al.: The European mountain cryosphere: a review of its current state, trends, and future challenges. Cryosphere **12**, 759–794 (2018)

2. Gobiet, A., Kotlarski, S., Beniston, M., Heinrich, G., Rajczak, J., Stoffel, M.: 21st century climate change in the European Alps-A review. Sci. Total Environ. **493**, 1138–1151 (2014)
3. Giulio Tonolo, F., Cina, A., Manzino, A., Fronteddu, M.: 3D glacier mapping by means of satellite stereo images: the belvedere glacier case study in the Italian alps. Int. Arch. Photogrammetry Remote Sens. Spat. Inf. Sci. ISPRS Arch. **43**, 1073–1079 (2020)
4. Fieber, K.D., Mills, J.P., Miller, P.E., Clarke, L., Ireland, L., Fox, A.J.: Rigorous 3D change determination in Antarctic Peninsula glaciers from stereo WorldView-2 and archival aerial imagery. Remote Sens. Environ. **205**, 18–31 (2018)
5. Westoby, M.J., Brasington, J., Glasser, N.F., Hambrey, M.J., Reynolds, J.M.: "Structure-from-Motion" photogrammetry: a low-cost, effective tool for geoscience applications. Geomorphology **179**, 300–314 (2012)
6. Seitz, S.M., Curless, B., Diebel, J., Scharstein, D., Szeliski, R.: A comparison and evaluation of multi-view stereo reconstruction algorithms. In: Proceedings of the IEEE Computer Society Conference on Computer Vision and Pattern Recognition, vol. 1, pp. 519–526 (2006)
7. Detert, M., Johnson, E.D., Weitbrecht, V.: Proof-of-concept for low-cost and non-contact synoptic airborne river flow measurements. Int. J. Remote Sens. **38**, 2780–2807 (2017)
8. Ioli, F., Pinto, L., Passoni, D., Nova, V., Detert, M.: Evaluation of airborne image velocimetry approaches using low-cost UAVs in riverine environments. In: International Archives of the Photogrammetry, Remote Sensing and Spatial Information Sciences - ISPRS Archives. pp. 597–604. International Society for Photogrammetry and Remote Sensing (2020)
9. Fugazza, D., et al.: Combination of UAV and terrestrial photogrammetry to assess rapid glacier evolution and map glacier hazards. Nat. Hazard. **18**, 1055–1071 (2018)
10. Ioli, F., et al.: Mid-term monitoring of glacier's variations with UAVs: The example of the belvedere glacier. Remote Sens. **14**, 1–19 (2022)
11. Geissler, J., Mayer, C., Jubanski, J., Münzer, U., Siegert, F.: Analyzing glacier retreat and mass balances using aerial and UAV photogrammetry in the Ötztal Alps, Austria (2021)
12. Attività glaciologiche - Fondazione Montagna sicura - Rutor Intro. http://app.fondazion emontagnasicura.org/multimedia/crgv/default.asp?principale=32&indice=32_33_91&sez ione=90. Accessed 23 May 2022
13. Badino, F., et al.: 8800 years of high-altitude vegetation and climate history at the Rutor Glacier forefield, Italian Alps. Evidence of middle Holocene timberline rise and glacier contraction. Quat. Sci. Rev. **185**, 41–68 (2018)
14. Strigaro, D., Moretti, M., Mattavelli, M., Frigerio, I., de Amicis, M., Maggi, V.: A GRASS GIS module to obtain an estimation of glacier behavior under climate change: a pilot study on Italian glacier. Comput. Geosci. **94**, 68–76 (2016)
15. Villa, F., Tamburini, A., Sironi, S., Maggi, V.: Volume decrease of Rutor Glacier (Western Italian Alps) since little ice age: a quantitative approach combining GPR, GPS and cartography EPICA-European Project for Ice Coring in Antarctica View project POLLiCE View project (2008)
16. Software VERTO2k E VERTO3k—IGM E-Commerce Site. https://www.igmi.org/en/descri zione-prodotti/elementi-geodetici-1/software-verto-2k-3k. Accessed 23 May 2022
17. Avionic System Design Services - Digisky. https://www.digisky.it/. Accessed 20 May 2022
18. High Resolution Aerial Imagery & Photography Cameras - Phase One. https://geospatial.pha seone.com/cameras/ixm-rs150f/. Accessed 23 May 2022
19. Pleiades - eoPortal Directory - Satellite Missions. https://earth.esa.int/web/eoportal/satellite-missions/p/pleiades. Accessed 20 May 2022
20. Geoportale SCT - Dati territoriali Regione Valle d'Aosta. https://geoportale.regione.vda.it/. Accessed 20 May 2022

SAR and Multispectral Data Contribution to the Monitoring of Wetland Ecosystems Vulnerable to Climate Change

Marco Dubbini(✉) ⓘ, Michaela De Giglio ⓘ, and Chiara Salvatori

Department of History, Cultures, Civilization (DiSCi)-Geography Section,
University of Bologna, Via Guerrazzi 20, 40125 Bologna, Italy
marco.dubbini@unibo.it

Abstract. Wetlands ecosystems support a significant percentage of the world's biodiversity and also provide a number of ecological services, such as carbon sequestration. These fragile ecosystems need to be monitored over time in order to better understand the ecological dynamics and changes within. The study areas are the marshland of the Ostiglia and Busatello marshes. Thus, geographic and climatic aspects have been investigated in order to better explain the dynamics of this ecosystem. The aims of this study were: (i) the evaluation of satellite instruments and methods for monitoring the health state of wetland ecosystems and the impacts of Climate Change; (ii) the investigation of seasonal dynamics of this wetland. The temperature, precipitation and humidity trends have been analyzed from 2016 to 2021. Time series of spectral indices (NDVI, NDMI and NMDI) and backscatter (VV and VH) have been extracted in order to analyze the trends of seasonal variation. To better understand the backscatter variation, the correlation between spectral indices and backscatter have been computed.

Keywords: Wetlands · Remote sensing · Climate change · SAR · Multispectral

1 Introduction: Wetlands and Climate Change

The term "wetland" refers to a region of the world that is wet, where are present both features of aquatic and terrestrial ecosystems. The wetland biome has a various nature, because are included all the "areas of marsh, fen, peat land, or water, whether natural or artificial, permanent or temporary, with water that is static or flowing, fresh, brackish or salt, including areas of marine water the depth of which at low tide do not exceed 6 m" [1]. Several factors, such as climate, soil and topography influence the shape, size and structure of the different wetland types [2].

According to the last report of the Intergovernmental Panel on Climate Change (IPCC, 2021), the solution to limit these climate changes would be the

---

The original version of this chapter was revised: The first-last name order has been reversed for all authors. The correction to this chapter is available at
https://doi.org/10.1007/978-3-031-17439-1_34

E. Borgogno-Mondino and P. Zamperlin (Eds.): ASITA 2022, CCIS 1651, pp. 405–417, 2022.
https://doi.org/10.1007/978-3-031-17439-1_30

reduction of carbon dioxide emissions (CO_2) [3]. The report estimates that in the next decades, if the greenhouse gas emissions won't be seriously reduced, the global temperatures will rise above 1.5 °C and the number of extreme climatic events will increase significantly [4].

Due to the variety of wetland types all over the world, some negative effects may be "customized" [5]. The ecological and hydrological impacts of Climate Change among wetland ecosystems depend on the wetland's dependency on the water supply. The effects of Climate Change are also affecting the waterfowl, because the changes in temperature and precipitation is altering their aquatic habitat [6].

Wetlands, when restored and not under disturbance, are considered important *carbon sinks*, because they store carbon and therefore help to mitigate the consequence of Climate Change. Wetland vegetation is a key element when studying wetlands, because they take up carbon via photosynthesis and build plant biomass, that accumulates in the soil as peat [7]. If damaged or drained, wetlands become a major source of greenhouse gas emissions thus releasing carbon to the atmosphere in form of the greenhouse gasses such as CO_2 (carbon dioxide) and CH_4 (methane). Their release is mainly caused by human disturbance, particularly by drainage, and is leading to the loss of all the carbon stored in the wetlands that accumulated over centuries [8–10].

The *Ramsar Convention on Wetlands of International Importance Especially as Waterfowl Habitat* is an international treaty signed in Ramsar (Iran) in 1971 [11]. The mission behind this treaty is *"the conservation and wise use of all wetlands through local and national actions and international cooperation, as a contribution towards achieving sustainable development throughout the world"* [12]. The convention also recognizes the value of wetlands for many ecosystem services, such as Climate Change effects mitigation and for maintenance of biodiversity [13].

2   Study Area: The Ostiglia and Busatello Marshes

The Ostiglia marshes are located at the south-eastern Lombardy cover an area of 123 hectares, of which circa 40 hectares are marshland an the remaining part is arable land, forest and wet meadows and it's situated on the border with the Veneto region, where the Busatello Oasis is located [14] (Fig. 1).

The vegetation cover of the Ostiglia and Busatello wetlands is principally composed of reeds and sedges. The *reedbed* has a type of vegetation characterized by the prevailing presence of the reeds *Phragmites australis*, a graminaceous plant that grows with its roots in the inundated soil, in fact, this type of vegetation grows along the Busatello river. The *sedgebed* has a hygrophilous prairie mainly composed by different types sedges, such as *Carex elata* and *Carex riparia* [15, 16].

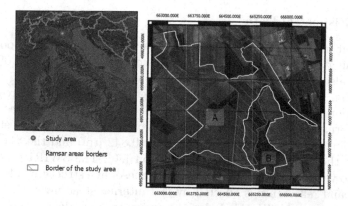

Fig. 1. A: Busatello Oasis; **B**: Ostiglia Marsh. **SR**: UTM ED50 Zone 32N

3   Materials and Methods

For this research have been collected thermo-pluviometric, Multispectral and SAR data from fall 2016 to fall 2021. The development of the methodology is based on the use of Multispectral data (Sentinel-2), SAR data (Sentinel-1), and thermo-pluviometric data, from which have been retrieved time series of specific spectral indices and, subsequently, correlated to better define the backscatter information.

3.1   Thermopluviometric Analysis

The thermo-pluviometric data were retrieved from the Ostiglia meteorological station and were collected daily over a period from 2016 to 2021. The data were presented in form of a CSV file containing the day of the acquisition, the minimum and maximum temperature, total precipitation, and minimum and maximum air humidity. The output was set to show daily thermos-pluviometric data for a single month. The mean temperature, mean humidity and total precipitations have been calculated from the starting data. The humidity is a fundamental factor that could define ecosystem and the animal and plant species can thrive in it [17].

The mean annual temperature and the total annual precipitation have been computed to evaluate the climatic changes from 2016 to 2021. To evaluate the yearly aridity, the Aridity index of De Martonne [18] has been computed, using the following formula:

$$I_{DM} = \frac{P}{T + 10} \tag{1}$$

P is the total annual precipitation and T is the mean annual temperature. The Index values ranges explain the classification of the climate, from Semi-Arid (lower values) to Very-Humid (higher values) [18,19].

3.2   Multispectral Data

Due to their unavailability, the Sentinel-2 data were retrieved form Google Earth Engine, using an algorithm that resample the data with a resolution of 30 m per pixel and also apply a cloud mask. Were downloaded a total of 60 Sentinel-2 images, from the which were computed, using QuantumGis, the three Spectral Indices reported below, thus obtaining a total of 180 Spectral Indices images.

The Normalized Difference Moisture Index describes the water stress level in vegetation. This index uses the NIR (cwl: 0.842 μm) and the SWIR1 band to present the moisture content in vegetation [20]. The SWIR1 reflectance is sensitive to vegetation water content and the mesophyll structure of leaves while the NIR band reflectance is affected by leaf internal structure and the relative dry matter content. With this index the accuracy in retrieving the vegetation water content result improved [21]. The index is computed as follows:

$$NDMI = \frac{NIR - SWIR1}{NIR + SWIR1} \tag{2}$$

The Normalized Multi-Band Drought Index is used to monitor potential drought conditions in soil and vegetation [22]. The Near Infrared and the two Short Waves Infrared bands were chosen due to their spectral response to variations in vegetation and soil moisture. The index does not use a single liquid water absorption band, but uses the difference between the two liquid-water absorption (SWIR1 and SWIR2, respectively 1610 and 2190 nm) [23] as a reason of water sensitivity in vegetation and soil [24]. The index is computed as follow:

$$NMDI = \frac{NIR - (SWIR1 - SWIR2)}{NIR + (SWIR1 - SWIR2)} \tag{3}$$

NMDI values <0.6 are associated to wet soil conditions; higher values of this index are associated to *dry soil conditions*.

The Normalized Difference Vegetation Index is the most common index used to describe the vigor of vegetation and its health state. This index exploits the spectral response of vegetation in the Red and NIR spectral bands. Healthy vegetation only reflect circa 10% of the radiation received in the spectral region of red and reflects over 40% of the radiation received in the spectral region of near infrared [25,26]. The index is computed as follows:

$$NDVI = \frac{NIR - RED}{NIR + RED} \tag{4}$$

The Spectral Indices values were sampled using 20 point per class area and their mean value was computed.

3.3   SAR Data

The Sentinel-1 SAR data were collected from Alaska Satellite Facility Data search (ASF). For the pre-processing the software SNAP (SeNtinel Application

Platform) has been used. The satellite sensor operating in C-Band is not able to penetrate the vegetation canopy, so the interaction is limited to the leaves and the other elements that compose the canopy structure [27].

Due to the massive amount of data, the pre-processing has been automatized using the SNAP Graph Builder and the Batch Processing. The data chosen were the SLC (Single-Look Complex), in order to retrieve the GRD data. The steps are reported in Fig. 2. The SLC data were chosen as an experiment for performing a polarimetric decomposition, to evaluate the different scattering contributions, but the result is that Sentinel-1 data does not allow to obtain optimal results.

The σ^0 values (in both VH and VV polarization) have been extracted and backscatter time-series created.

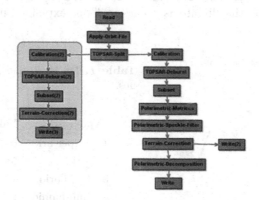

Fig. 2. In this workflow, the part evidenced in orange shows the processing steps to i) retrieve a GRD data from a SLC one and ii) their pre-processing steps.

In order to distinguish the characteristics of the different target on the ground is necessary to understand the different scattering mechanism that occur when the microwaves interact with these target within the wetland area. *Specular reflection* occurs if the radar pulse hits a smooth, flat surface, so the energy is scattered away in a specular direction. These areas will appear very dark in the radar image as no energy (or extremely little amounts) return to the sensor. Examples of smooth surfaces in wetlands are water bodies. *Surface scattering* occurs when the microwave hits a rough, heterogeneous surface. Parts of this energy is scattered back to the sensor but some is dissipated away. *Volume scattering* occurs when the radar pulse penetrates into the vegetation and tree canopy [28]. The signal is scattered various times in multiple directions inside this three-dimensional structure, before parts of it are eventually returned to the sensor but tilted of 90°. Volume scattering is the main source of VH backscatter [29,30]. The backscatter intensity also depends on *dielectric* properties [31]. With changes in soil moisture or vegetation water content it is possible to observe significant variations in radar reflectivity [32]. The amount of water stored in vegetation influence the backscatter of a radar signal, as it affects the propagation and absorption of electromagnetic energy [33]. With the rising of water content, the penetration of the radar signal through the canopy decrease. On the contrary, drier vegetation will present lower backscatter values [34].

4   Results and Discussion

4.1   Climate

The years with lower total annual precipitation are 2017 with 503.6 mm and 2021 with 505.8 mm. The De Martonne aridity index computed using the mean annual temperature and the total annual precipitation - from 2016 to 2021 - reported that the most arid years are 2017 and 2021. from 2019 the index dropped from 33 to 20, classifying the climate as *"semi-arid"*, as explained in Table 1 (Fig. 3).

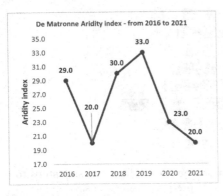

Fig. 3. De Martonne Aridity index from 2016 to 2021.

Table 1. De Martonne Aridity index values.

Type	Values
1 - Hyper arid	$0 \leq I_{DM} \leq 5$
2 - Arid	$5 \leq I_{DM} \leq 15$
3 - Semi-arid	$15 \leq I_{DM} \leq 20$
4 - Sub-humid	$20 \leq I_{DM} \leq 30$
5 - Humid/wet	$30 \leq I_{DM} \leq 60$
6 - Very wet	$I_{DM} > 60$

4.2   Multispectral Data Analysis

The pattern of NDVI, NDMI and NMDI time series has been analyzed from fall 2016 to fall 2021. The NDVI index sensitivity to vegetation growth dynamics shows values higher than 0, with 0 considered non vegetated area, such as water basins. NDVI values over 0.4 are considered healthy vegetation and values. Values in range 0.2–0.4 are considered less vegetated area or non-healthy vegetation [35]. Lower values of NDVI and NDMI shows a seasonal trend, with higher values during leaf-on season and lower values during leaf-off season. The classes analyzed for NDVI and NDMI are *arable land, marsh* and *meadow*. The trends relative to year 2018 are reported in Fig. 4.

Taking as example the 2018 NDVI data it is possible to notice the seasonal trend of the index. The highest values are registered in June and July, with NDVI values that reach 0.8. The NDVI trend of the meadow class shows values similar to the previous classes, but with a low peak of 0.1 in March 25th, the day

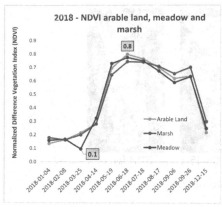

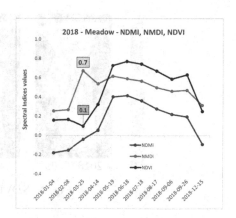

Fig. 4. NDVI seasonal trend of the *Arable Land, Marsh* and *Meadow* areas.

Fig. 5. Spectral indices values of the *Meadow* area SI. The arson took place in 2018-03-25.

after the fire, classifying the burned area as "naked soil", thus demonstrating that there is no vegetation (Fig. 5).

The Spectral Indices maps are reported below and their values are explained by the legend (Figs. 6 and 7).

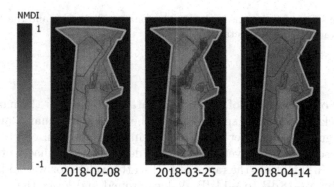

Fig. 6. NMDI map of 2018.

4.3   Time-Series Decomposition

The graph in Fig. 8 obtained by decomposing the time series of the De Martonne index and the NDMI (both with central moving average with a time window of 3 months) highlights how the two data have a good correlation on the trend of the phenomenon. The annual variability of the two indices confirm the trend.

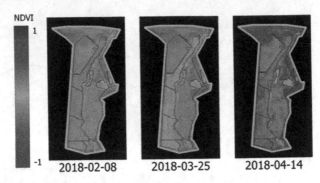

Fig. 7. NDVI map of 2018.

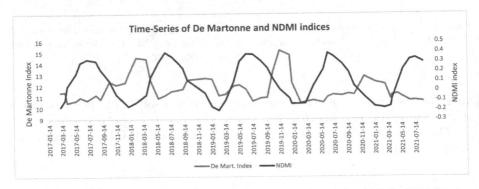

Fig. 8. Time series of variations in the De Martonne aridity index and the NDMI index relating to water stress in vegetation.

4.4 SAR

The results of the analysis of GRD SAR data are related to the monthly variation of backscatter over a specific class. The arable land, marsh and meadow classes are analyzed together due to their similar vegetation cover. The variation of backscatter values over these classes depend on the phases of vegetation growth [36]. In this study the range of backscatter values for wetland vegetation class vary from $-18\,\mathrm{dB}$ to $-14\,\mathrm{dB}$. Values around and lower than $-20\,\mathrm{dB}$ are associated with the presence of water.

Lower backscatter values in the area dominated by wetland vegetation are in the leaf-off season, when the vegetation cover became less dense and shows the water below the vegetation canopy. In the leaf-on season the backscatter values rises reaching values around $-16\,\mathrm{dB}$. For the classes characterized by wetland vegetation the VH backscatter variation has been reported in a graph that show the trend of variation of these values. VH polarization has been chosen for vegetation analysis because the random and complex structure of the vegetation canopy depolarizes the signal. The VV backscatter has been analysed for the wet meadow class, because of its sensitivity to water content in the soil. As the water content in soil rises, the VV backscatter values rise too [37].

In 2018, the trend of VH backscatter for the marsh and the meadow classes follow the trend explained before. The backscatter values reported in Fig. 9 describe the backscatter trend of vegetation. For the arable land class the values show a slightly different trend. This could be explained by the annual winter fire-weeding practice that removes old reeds [38], leaving bare soil until the next growth of vegetation, that for this class happens to start in March and peaks in April.

The VV backscatter trend has been extracted for 2018 and compared to the monthly total precipitation. Higher VV backscatter values are registered in the periods characterized by higher precipitations level (Fig. 10).

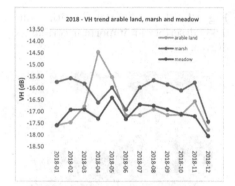

Fig. 9. VH backscatter values for the marsh, meadow and arable land classes relative to the year 2018.

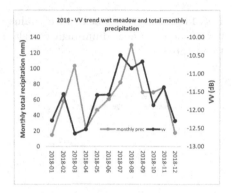

Fig. 10. VV backscatter values and total monthly precipitation for the wet meadow class. Relative to the year 2018.

Based on the study of Kaplan and Avdan (2018) a correlation between NDVI and VH backscatter has been found [36]. 2017 has been chosen as the ideal year to search for correlation due to monthly correspondence between multispectral and SAR data. The scatterplot has been computed using the VH backscatter values and the NDVI values of the arable land class. As a first experiment, a scatterplot between NDMI and VH backscatter values has been computed. The last scatterplot of the experiment has been computed using the VV backscatter values and the NMDI values of the wet meadow, to understand if there is a correlation between moisture content in soil and VV backscatter. The negative correlation is explained by the values interpretation of the NMDI index. Higher values of NMDI are associated to *"dry soil condition"*. When the soil moisture increase, the index value decrease (Figs. 11, 12, 13 and 14).

The different scattering mechanisms are displayed in different color: Water bodies appear black to the specular scattering; Surface scattering is displayed in shades of pink; Volume scattering of vegetation is displayed in green (Fig. 15).

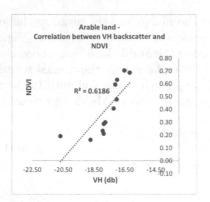

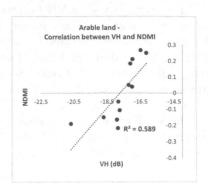

Fig. 11. The R^2 index with value 0.6186 describe a medium-high correlation degree.

Fig. 12. The R^2 index with value 0.589 describes an important correlation degree.

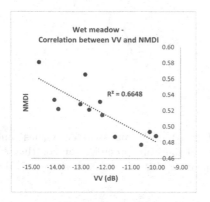

Fig. 13. The R^2 index with value 0.6648 describes a high correlation degree.

Fig. 14. The *Wet meadow* in the Ostiglia Marshes.

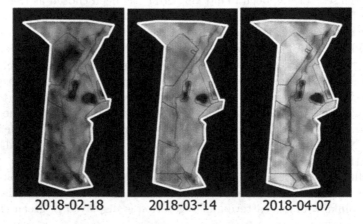

Fig. 15. RGB map of SAR data. R: VV, G: VH, B: VV-VH. (Color figure online)

5   Conclusions

The main objective of this work is to show the contribution of SAR and Multispectral data to the monitoring of wetland ecosystems vulnerable to Climate Change.

The preliminary thermo-pluviometric analysis carried out has shown important variation in precipitation regime over the last three years. The level of precipitation decreased causing drought in the area that led to the unbridled arson in the meadow area in the Busatello Oasis.

The spectral indices derived from Sentinel-2 Multispectral data retrieved in the same period of the fire have shown variation from their seasonal trend. Lower values of NDVI and NDMI described a situation of poor vegetation cover and high water stress. Higher values of NMDI have shown the burned area, where the soil beneath the vegetation is dry. The time series decomposition shows how good correlation on the trend of the phenomenon of aridity, thus the trend is confirmed.

The study of the VH and VV backscatter response of vegetation and soils provides fundamental information on the growth phases of vegetation, and the relative water content.

An important correlation has been found between VH backscatter and the spectral indices NDVI and NDMI, because are strongly related to the density of vegetation, its structure and its water content. Another important correlation has been found between the VV backscatter response and the NMDI, due to their sensitivity to soil surfaces and water content.

References

1. Matthews, G.V.T.: The Ramsar Convention on Wetlands: its history and development. Ramsar Convention Bureau, March 1993
2. Keddy, P.A.: Wetland Ecology: Principles and Conservation (2010)
3. Lahn, B.: Changing climate change: the carbon budget and the modifying-work of the IPCC. Soc. Stud. Sci. **51**(1), 3–27 (2021)
4. Erwin, K.L.: Wetlands and global climate change: the role of wetland restoration in a changing world. Wetlands Ecol. Manage. **17**(1), 71–84 (2009)
5. Burkett, V., Kusler, J.: Climate change: potential impacts and interactions in wetlands of the United States. JAWRA J. Am. Water Resour. Assoc. **36**(2), 313–320 (2000)
6. Winter, T.C.: The vulnerability of wetlands to climate change: a hydrologic landscape perspective. JAWRA J. Am. Water Resour. Assoc. **36**(2), 305–311 (2000)
7. Fennessy, M.S., Jacobs, A.D., Kentula, M.E.: An evaluation of rapid methods for assessing the ecological condition of wetlands. Wetlands **27**(3), 543–560 (2007)
8. Kayranli, B., Scholz, M., Mustafa, A., Hedmark, Å.: Carbon storage and fluxes within freshwater wetlands: a critical review. Wetlands **30**(1), 111–124 (2010)
9. Dawson, T.P., Berry, P.M., Kampa, E.: Climate change impacts on freshwater wetland habitats. J. Nat. Conserv. **11**(1), 25–30 (2003)
10. Temmink, R.J., et al.: Recovering wetland biogeomorphic feedbacks to restore the world's biotic carbon hotspots. Science **376**(6593), eabn1479 (2022)

11. Gardner, R.C., Davidson, N.C.: The Ramsar convention. In: LePage, B. (eds.) Wetlands, pp. 189–203. Springer, Dordrecht (2011). https://doi.org/10.1007/978-94-007-0551-7_11

12. Finlayson, C.M., Davidson, N., Pritchard, D., Milton, G.R., MacKay, H.: The Ramsar Convention and ecosystem-based approaches to the wise use and sustainable development of wetlands. J. Int. Wildlife Law Policy 14(3–4), 176–198 (2011)

13. Lovejoy, T.E.: Climate change and biodiversity (2006)

14. Cuizzi, D., et al.: Gestione delle zone umide e conservazione attiva degli habitat e delle specie di interesse comunitario. Il progetto LIFE-Natura 2000/IT7161 delle Paludi di Ostiglia (2005)

15. Franchini, D.A.: Il pirodiserbo come tecnica di gestione nella Riserva Naturale Regionale "Paludi di Ostiglia": influenza su flora e fauna. Atti Convegno "Zone umide d'acqua dolce, Tecniche e strategie di gestione della vegetazione palustre", Regione Lombardia e Comune di Ostiglia. Quad. Ris. Nat. Paludi di Ostiglia, vol. 1, pp. 59–70 (2000)

16. Franchini, D.A., Franchini, C.: Molluschi d'acqua dolce nelle torbe del Busatello: ricerche stratigrafiche. Bollettino malacologico 32, 11–18 (1996)

17. Hartmann, D.L.: Global physical climatology (2015)

18. Pellicone, G., Caloiero, T., Guagliardi, I.: The De Martonne aridity index in Calabria (Southern Italy). J. Maps 15(2), 788–796 (2019)

19. Meng, M., Ni, J., Zhang, Z.G.: Aridity index and its applications in geo-ecological study. Chin. J. Plant Ecol. 28(6), 853 (2004)

20. Jahangir, M.H., Arast, M.: Remote sensing products for predicting actual evapotranspiration and water stress footprints under different land cover. J. Clean. Prod. 266, 121818 (2020)

21. Gao, B.C.: NDWI-a normalized difference water index for remote sensing of vegetation liquid water from space. Remote Sens. Environ. 58(3), 257–266 (1996)

22. de Oliveira Santos, R., et al.: NMDI application for monitoring different vegetation covers in the Atlantic Forest biome, Brazil. Weather Clim. Extremes 33, 100329 (2021)

23. Phiri, D., Simwanda, M., Salekin, S., Nyirenda, V.R., Murayama, Y., Ranagalage, M.: Sentinel-2 data for land cover/use mapping: a review. Remote Sens. 12(14), 2291 (2020)

24. Wang, L., Qu, J.J.: NMDI: a normalized multi-band drought index for monitoring soil and vegetation moisture with satellite remote sensing. Geophys. Res. Lett. 34, L20405 (2007). https://doi.org/10.1029/2007GL031021

25. Brivio, P., Lechi-Lechi, G., Zilioli, E.: Principi e metodi di telerilevamento (2006)

26. Carlson, T.N., Ripley, D.A.: On the relation between NDVI, fractional vegetation cover, and leaf area index. Remote Sens. Environ. 62(3), 241–252 (1997)

27. Baghdadi, N., Bernier, M., Gauthier, R., Neeson, I.: Evaluation of C-band SAR data for wetlands mapping. Int. J. Remote Sens. 22(1), 71–88 (2001)

28. Satalino, G., Balenzano, A., Mattia, F., Davidson, M.W.: C-band SAR data for mapping crops dominated by surface or volume scattering. IEEE Geosci. Remote Sens. Lett. 11(2), 384–388 (2013)

29. Meyer, F.: Spaceborne Synthetic Aperture Radar: Principles, data access, and basic processing techniques. Synthetic Aperture Radar (SAR) Handbook: Comprehensive Methodologies for Forest Monitoring and Biomass Estimation, pp. 21–64 (2019)

30. Yamaguchi, Y., Moriyama, T., Ishido, M., Yamada, H.: Four-component scattering model for polarimetric SAR image decomposition. IEEE Trans. Geosci. Remote Sens. 43(8), 1699–1706 (2005)

31. Steele-Dunne, S.C., Friesen, J., Van De Giesen, N.: Using diurnal variation in backscatter to detect vegetation water stress. IEEE Trans. Geosci. Remote Sens. **50**(7), 2618–2629 (2012)
32. Hobbs, S., Ang, W., Seynat, C.: Wind and rain effects on SAR backscatter from crops. Eur. Space Agency-Publ.-ESA SP **441**, 185–190 (1998)
33. Wagner, W.: Soil moisture retrieval from ERS scatterometer data, vol. 49. Inst. für Photogrammetrie u. Fernerkundung d. Techn. Univ (1998)
34. Esch, S.: Determination of Soil Moisture and Vegetation Parameters from Space-borne C-Band SAR on Agricultural Areas (2018)
35. Meneses-Tovar, C.L.: NDVI as indicator of degradation. Unasylva **62**(238), 39–46 (2011)
36. Kaplan, G., Avdan, U.: Monthly analysis of wetlands dynamics using remote sensing data. ISPRS Int. J. Geo-Inf. **7**(10), 411 (2018)
37. van Emmerik, T., Steele-Dunne, S.C., Judge, J., van de Giesen, N.: Impact of diurnal variation in vegetation water content on radar backscatter from maize during water stress. IEEE Trans. Geosci. Remote Sens. **53**(7), 3855–3869 (2015)
38. Fracasso, G.: L'impatto del pirodiserbo sulla comunitá ornitica del canneto. Atti Convegno Zone umide d'acqua dolce-Tecniche e strategie di gestione della vegetazione palustre-Quaderni Riserva Naturale Paludi di Ostiglia **1**, 71–80 (2000)

Sustainable Development and Climate Change

How to Combine Spatial Data for Ecosystem Services Mapping? A GIS-MCDA Approach and Its Application in Tuscany, Italy

Massimo Rovai[1] (iD), Francesco Monacci[2], and Tommaso Trinchetti[1]([envelope]) (iD)

[1] Department of Civil and Industrial Engineering (DICI), University of Pisa, Pisa, Italy
massimo.rovai@unipi.it, tommaso.trinchetti@ing.unipi.it
[2] Department of Agricultural, Food and Agro-Environmental Sciences (DAFE),
University of Pisa, Pisa, Italy

Abstract. Agricultural and forest areas produce sets or bundles of ecosystem services (ESs) key to human well-being and quality of life. The impacts of the processes of urban development and abandonment of cultivated land require policies and governance measures for promoting integrated and mutually beneficial relationships between urban and rural areas, by properly managing the capacity of the latter to produce ESs. For this purpose, an accurate mapping of ESs is essential. In some regions, many spatial data that provide useful indicators for assessing the ESs supply are available, and it is interesting to develop methods to organize and combine them. We propose a method for mapping and bundling the capacity of agricultural and forest areas to supply five ESs, based on the processing of open-source territorial data through GIS and Multi-Criteria Decision Analysis (MCDA), and tailored for Tuscany Region (Italy). This method attempt to combine a Land Use and Land Cover map with other data, e.g., on crops, pedology, ecosystems properties and conditions, hydrogeological instability, climate, to obtain a comprehensive ESs assessment. The regional database of crops provides very useful information for ESs assessment but contains inconsistencies which must be corrected for it to be used. We present a case-study that shows the potentiality of the method for advancing research on ESs mapping, even if it needs to be further refined and tested.

Keywords: Geographic AHP · Ecosystem services bundles · Tuscany

1 Introduction

Land use changes are the factors with the highest impacts on biodiversity and ecosystems worldwide [1]. In Europe, the analysis of land use changes highlights two main trends: urban development and abandonment of cultivated land [2]. The former causes the loss and fragmentation of fertile peri-urban agricultural areas, a limited food sovereignty and an increasing dependence on imports [3]. Abandonment of cultivated land, both close to cities, due to increased real estate value, and in more remote areas, less profitable, is associated to agricultural intensification in most productive areas, nearby or in other

E. Borgogno-Mondino and P. Zamperlin (Eds.): ASITA 2022, CCIS 1651, pp. 421–436, 2022.
https://doi.org/10.1007/978-3-031-17439-1_31

regions of the world [4]. Together these processes result in threats to the ecosystems and should be considered as incorrect and unbalanced land management types [5].

In Italy, as in many other regions of Europe, land use changes generate a profound divergence between highly populated and urbanized lowlands and coastal areas, and rural hills and mountains. The former are overexploited areas where productive activities, intensive agriculture, and environmental impacts are condensed. The latter are often neglected, sparsely populated or abandoned, less productive areas, where forests, parks and reserves, and biodiversity are concentrated.

Sustainable social, economic, and environmental development requires the reconstruction and maintenance of mutually beneficial relationships between urban and rural areas to improve quality of life in both, through a mitigation of the impacts of the former, and an efficient use of the natural resources of the latter.

The concept of ecosystem services (ESs) is used to refer to the contributions of ecosystem structure, functions, or processes, to human well-being. It was proposed in the late 1990s and widespread in 2005 by the Millennium Ecosystem Assessment [6]. Since then, it has increasingly shown the potential to inform policy and decision making, on different scales and in many sectors, e.g., natural resources management, territorial governance, nature conservation and restoration, landscape planning.

Research has identified the potential of agriculture and forestry to produce a variety of ESs that support human well-being and quality of life, both in urban [7] and rural areas [8]. The management of ESs, and the design of strategies and measures to promote equilibrium and integration between urban, peri-urban, and rural areas, is getting an increasing interest in political debates.

Availability of spatially explicit information is considered particularly important for the design and implementation of plans and policies for ESs management. In last twenty years, research on ESs assessment has significantly increased and many approaches and methods for ESs mapping have been developed [9]. In many cases, when primary data are not available, proxy data are used, especially Land Use and Land Cover (LULC) maps and other remote sensing data [10]. In many studies, the capacity of different areas of a territory to produce ESs is described in relative terms, rather than through a quantitative assessment. For example, a widely used method assigns scores to each land cover class based on expert judgment [11].

However, some concerns emerge about the correctness or accuracy of describing the complex ecosystem functions and processes that produce the ESs only based on the land cover [12]. Regarding this issue, there is a need to investigate, for territorial contexts where additional spatial data are available, how to combine those data with the LULC maps, to obtain a better assessment of the capacity of land to produce ESs.

In recent years, research has also attempted to analyze the relationships between the ESs. Since a land system has the potential to simultaneously produce multiple ESs, understanding their relationships is essential for adapting policies and governance not to each of them individually but to a set of them, according to an integrate approach. This approach helps to avoid trade-offs and enhance synergies among the ESs [13].

Mapping ESs co-occurrence or association is made possible by a methodology based on cluster analysis, that allows to characterize a territory with ESs bundles repeated in space and time and gives a first indication on their relationships [14]. Many different approaches to ESs bundling have been developed, which vary for ESs considered, assessment methods, scale, and resolution [15].

We propose a method for mapping and bundling five ESs produced by agricultural and forest areas. It uses open-source territorial data, the Analytic Hierarchy Process (AHP) technique, and the software QGis 3.24. It is tested on the Val di Nievole and Val d'Arno Inferiore, i.e., a specific area located in the north-central part of the Tuscany Region (Italy), and one of the twenty homogeneous areas called "Ambiti Paesaggistici" (Landscape Areas) identified by the main regional planning tool, the "Piano di Indirizzo Territoriale con valenza di Piano Paesaggistico Regionale" (PIT-PPR).

In Sect. 2, after a brief description of the study area, we explain the AHP technique and illustrate the hierarchical trees designed for its application, the used data, and the processing procedure followed for ESs mapping and bundling. In particular, we describe the details of the elaborations implemented on the ARTEA ("Azienda Regionale Toscana per le Erogazioni in Agricoltura") Database, which contains data on regional crops, for correcting the inconsistencies it presents. Section 3 contains the results, and Sect. 4 the concluding discussion.

2 Methodology

2.1 The Study Area

Tuscany is one of the twenty administrative regions of Italy and is in the central-western part of the country (Fig. 1). The PIT-PPR has classified the regional territory into twenty Landscape Areas according to their historical-identity, rural, ecosystemic, and hydro-geomorphological characteristics, as well as to their socio-economic characteristics and to the characteristics of their settlement and infrastructural systems.

Being the supply of ESs ensured by the complexity of ecosystems and influenced by natural processes which, in turn, depend more on biophysical characteristics than on administrative divisions, in our analysis Landscape Areas are considered the most appropriate territorial scale for ESs mapping.

The proposed method allows to create maps for all the twenty Landscape Areas of Tuscany and to make comparisons, but here we describe the case-study of the Val di Nievole and Val d'Arno Inferiore Landscape Area (Fig. 1).

The territory of Val di Nievole and Val d'Arno Inferiore is in the north-central part of Tuscany and has an extension of approx. 782 km2, almost equally subdivided between the provinces of Firenze (35.9%), Pistoia (34%), and Pisa (30.1%).

It is bordered to the east by the Firenze-Prato-Pistoia Landscape Area, to the south by that of Val d'Elsa, to the west by those of Piana Livorno-Pisa-Pontedera and Lucchesia, and to the nord by that of Garfagnana e Val di Lima.

It comprises 22 municipalities, of which 6 are in the province of Florence, 11 in the province of Pistoia, and 5 in the province of Pisa, and has a population of about 317.500 inhabitants (119.000 in the province of Florence, 118.500 and 80.000 in those of Pistoia and Pisa, respectively).

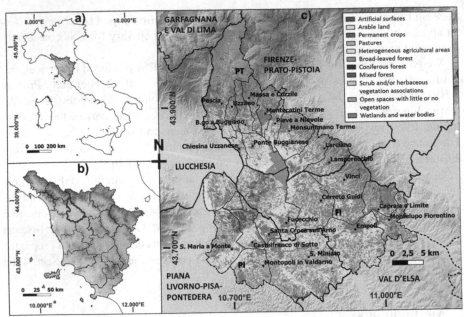

Fig 1. a) Tuscany's location. b) Tuscany's Landscape Areas (dotted black lines) and study area's location (blue line). c) Study area's land cover distribution. Solid black lines indicate municipal boundaries, dotted black lines indicate Landscape Areas boundaries, red lines indicate provincial boundaries (PT = Pistoia, FI = Firenze, PI = Pisa). National boundaries from ISTAT; regional, provincial and municipal boundaries from Tuscany Region; Landscape Areas boundaries from Tuscany PIT-PPR cartography. (Color figure online)

This territory includes very heterogeneous landscapes: is crossed by two alluvial plains in the east-west and north-south direction; surrounded by hills to the east, south and west; and crowned by the Apennine mountains to the north.

In 2019, land cover distribution was the following: artificial surfaces, 17.5%; agricultural areas, 50%; natural and semi-natural areas, 30%; wetlands, 1.6%; water bodies, 0,9%.

The plains host both the largest arable lands, characterized by progressive simplification, and wetlands and water bodies of high ecological value: the Arno River, the Fucecchio Marshs, and a dense hydrographic network. At the same time, the plains are affected by an intense development of dispersed urban areas, and soil sealing is the main critical factor there, threatening agricultural areas and water ecosystems.

The hills maintain a denser settlement system and a complex and articulated agrarian mesh. They are characterized by distinct cultivations: mainly olive groves or vineyards, sometimes associated with arable lands or forests. The mountains are dominated by forests. In both hills and mountains, the main critical factors are the abandonment of cultivated land and re-naturalization.

2.2 The Elaborations on the ARTEA Database

ARTEA is the regional agency of Tuscany that authorizes and controls the EU aid requested by farms. Farmers must submit the Graphic Cultivation Plans (GCPs) of their farms in digital format, indicating the spatialized cadastral references of the cultivated parcels, the crops, the Ecological Focus Areas (EFAs), as well as the cultivation method (i.e., conventional, organic or in conversion).

Every year ARTEA makes the GCPs of all Tuscan farms available in an anonymous form. These data are a very interesting information base on regional agriculture but contain a very high number of topological errors (invalid geometries, overlaps, duplicates), which may prevent their processing. The database is indeed created essentially for controlling the cultivation plans of farms, but it could be used, for example, to develop territorial analyses on the potential benefits and impacts of agricultural activities. In our opinion, it provides useful information for assessing both provisioning and regulating ESs but, to be used, it is necessary to correct the errors it contains.

A repair procedure is applied, which involves recreating the polygons that define the cultivated parcels and transferring the attributes of the starting data to the newly created elements (errors are so numerous that it is impossible to use standard geometries repair tools). Firstly, the damaged polygons are transformed into both points and lines. Points retain the attributes of the starting polygons, while lines are used to create new polygons with the same boundaries but without topological errors. Secondly, from the newly created polygons, which are very fragmented, those that do not contain one of the created points are selected and merged to the adjacent ones. Finally, the attributes retained by the points are transferred back to the created polygons.

The GCPs of the years from 2016 to 2020 are used. Each of them is repaired and only two fields are maintained in the attribute table and used as indicators: the crops and the cultivation method.

In the period 2016–2020, a very high number of crops were cultivated in Tuscany making it necessary a reclassification by homogeneous groups. Three different classifications of crops are created, according to the crop destination, to the crop type, and to the length of crop cycle.

The GCPs are then overlaid on the LULC maps of Tuscany (scale 1:10,000) for the years 2016 and 2019, to differentiate the agricultural and forest areas managed by professional farms (the areas corresponding to the GPCs) and those where hobby or residual agriculture is practiced. Firstly, agricultural and forest areas corresponding to class 2 of the first Corine Land Cover (CLC) level, class 31 of the second CLC level, and classes 321 and 324 of the third CLC level, are exported from the LULC maps of the years 2016 and 2019. Then, the GCPs of the years 2016/2017 are overlaid on these elements of the LULC map of 2016, while the GCPs of the years 2018/2020 on those of the LULC map of 2019. This allows to identify the type of activity performed in different areas during this five years period (classified as non-professional, professional conventional, or professional organic), and to deepen the knowledge of the cultivation activities in the areas managed by professional farms.

Furthermore, the ARTEA Database provide a map of the cadastral parcels considered as EFAs, for example terraces, hedges, rows of trees, groves, buffer strips. This data is used for the assessment of the regulating ESs, as explained in the following paragraph.

2.3 The Analytic Hierarchy Process

The chosen multi-criteria decision analysis (MCDA) technique for ESs mapping is the AHP. In MCDA a set of criteria are identified to compare and evaluate different alternatives for ordering them on a scale of relative relevance [16]. The possibility of evaluating alternatives both qualitatively and quantitatively, and with the unit of measure most suited to what the criteria describe, makes MCDA particularly effective in addressing the complex and transdisciplinary problems of territorial planning [17].

With the AHP technique is possible to simplify a complex decision-making problem, such as ESs mapping addressed in this paper, into a hierarchical tree of four levels: goal; criteria and sub-criteria; attributes; and alternatives [18]. When integrating this technique with GIS, alternatives are the single spatial units of a map, i.e., polygons of a vector file or pixels of a raster file [19]. Attributes are used to describe the values that alternatives can assume from the available data, for each criterion or sub-criterion. Criteria are characters or properties considered relevant to the goal, which, in our case, is the assessment of the capacity of the territory to produce the specific ES mapped.

Weights are assigned to each element of the hierarchical tree, to define the relevance with respect to the elements of the higher level, by using a matrix of pairwise comparisons. The hierarchical tree is finally reassembled according to the weights assigned to each element, and a general ordering of the alternatives on a relative scale with dimensionless values is obtained [18]. Thanks to this technique, it is possible to assign to each spatial unit a value that express its capacity to produce a certain ES, based on the integration of information obtained from the heterogeneous available data.

2.4 The Design of the Hierarchical Trees for ESs Assessment

Five ESs are mapped, with reference to the Common International Classification of Ecosystem Services (CICES), developed by the European Environment Agency (EEA). The CICES currently describes 72 ESs, of which 44 depend on the biotic components of the ecosystems and 28 on their abiotic characteristics. It is organized in a hierarchical structure of four levels. At the highest level are three broad categories of ESs: provisioning, regulating and cultural. The three lower levels of the hierarchy make the description of the ESs increasingly detailed and specific. Each ESs is assigned a unique four-digit code, and it is possible to aggregate them in different ways, according to the thematic and spatial scale of the analysis [20].

Four provisioning ESs and six regulating ESs are selected from the CICES for our analysis. The selected provisioning ESs cover the main nutritional, non-nutritional materials, and energetic outputs from agricultural and forest ecosystems. They are aggregated in a single ES. The selected regulating ESs cover some of the ways in which the same ecosystems contribute to mediate or moderate the physical, chemical, and biological conditions of the environment. Two pairs of them are aggregated in two single ESs. Regulating ESs are essential to ensure the stability and continuity of provisioning services, as well as human health, safety, and comfort.

The five mapped ESs, as derived from the CICES, are:

- provisioning of food (1.1.1.1), fibers and other materials (1.1.1.2), plants for energy (1.1.1.3), and reared animals (1.1.3.1), aggregated into a single service,

- erosion control (2.2.1.1) and attenuation of mass movements (2.2.1.2), aggregated into a single service,
- hydrological cycle and water flows regulation (2.2.1.3),
- maintenance of habitats (2.2.2.3),
- weathering processes (2.2.4.1) and decomposition processes (2.2.4.2) for soil quality, aggregated into a single service.

Five hierarchical trees are created for the mapping of each ES considering two aspects: on the one hand, the potential of ecosystems, by combining some criteria that evaluate the properties and conditions of soils and ecosystems; and on the other hand, the human contributions in the production of ESs, by combining other criteria that evaluate the human management (in the period 2016–2020). For example, the capacity of a spatial unit to supply the provisioning service is considered to depend on the characteristics of the soil (potential) but also on whether that land is cultivated or not (management).

The proposed method aims to map the capacity of each area of a territory to supply the five ESs on a relative scale from 0 to 10. Spatial units are compared and evaluated for each considered criterion according to the attributes they assume from the available open-source data.

Provisioning. The hierarchical tree designed for mapping provisioning service considers: a criterion for assessing soil potential, namely the *Land Capability Classification (LCC)*; and two criteria for assessing human management, namely *crop destination* and *type of activity*.

The *LCC* expresses soil potential for agricultural use on a scale of eight classes. Used *LCC* of soils of Tuscany comes from the regional Pedological Database.

Crop destination and *type of activity* are evaluated by using the overlay of the GCPs on the LULC maps. Crops, reclassified into 21 categories according to their main destination, are not evaluated based on their productivity but on a judgment of relative relevance among them. Crops for food are compared according to the following three types of value: economic, caloric, and health value. Crops for fibers and materials and crops for various destinations are compared according to economic and caloric values; crops for fodder for reared animals are compared only according to caloric value.

Soil Quality. The hierarchical tree designed for mapping soil quality service considers three criteria for assessing soil potential, namely their *physical, chemical,* and *hydraulic properties,* and three criteria for assessing human management, namely *crop type, type of activity,* and *EFAs.*

Considered soil *physical properties* are *texture, skeleton,* and *depth.* Considered soil *chemical properties* are *fertility, organic matter,* and *salinity.* Considered soil *hydraulic properties* are *available water capacity, water content, saturated hydraulic conductivity,* and *internal drainage.* All data on soils properties come from the Pedological Database of Tuscany.

Crop type and *type of activity* are evaluated by using the overlay of the GCPs on the LULC maps. Crops are reclassified into 6 categories and compared for their contribution to this service in terms of crop type. The *EFAs* are taken from the ARTEA Database and evaluated for their ability to contribute to soil structure and fertility at increasing distances.

Erosion and Mass Movements Control. The hierarchical tree designed for mapping erosion and mass movements control service considers two criteria for assessing land potential to avoid or resist these processes, namely soil *physical properties* and its *vulnerability*, and four criteria for assessing human management, namely *length of crop cycle*, *type of activity*, *EFAs*, and *hydrogeological constraint*.

Considered soil *physical properties* are *slope, hydrologic group*, and *texture*. Soil *vulnerability* is assessed considering *potential surface erosion, landslide hazard*, and *actual landslides*. *Slope* is calculated from the regional Orographic DTM. Data on soil *hydrologic group*, *texture*, and *potential surface erosion* come from the Pedological Database of Tuscany. The map of *landslide hazard* is supplied by Italian Higher Institute for Protection and Environmental Research (ISPRA), while *actual landslides* are taken from the regional Landslides Database.

Length of crop cycle and *type of activity* are evaluated by using the overlay of the GCPs on the LULC maps. Crops are reclassified into 6 categories and compared for their contribution to this service in terms of length of crop cycle. The *EFAs* are evaluated for their ability to contribute to soil protection at increasing distances. The map of the areas subject to hydrogeological constraint, provided by Tuscany Region, identifies areas protected pursuant to RD 3267/23.

Water Flows Regulation. The hierarchical tree designed for mapping water flows regulation service considers four criteria for assessing soil potential to retain water and favor its infiltration, namely soil *moisture*, soil *hydraulic* and *physical properties*, and soil *distance from surface waters*, and three criteria for assessing human management, namely *length of crop cycle*, *type of activity*, and *EFAs*.

Soil *moisture* is assessed considering *water shortage risk*, and *annual average precipitation*. *Distance from surface waters* is assessed considering the configuration of the *hydrographic network*, and the *hydraulic hazard*. Data on soil *water shortage risk* come from the Pedological Database of Tuscany, while the map of *annual average precipitation* (for the period 1995–2014) is provided by the regional Environmental Monitoring and Modeling Laboratory (LaMMA). The map of *hydrographic network* is taken from the PIT-PPR cartography, while the map of *hydraulic hazard* is supplied by ISPRA. Soil *hydraulic properties* are assessed as for soil quality service, while soil *physical properties* are assessed as for erosion and mass movements control service.

Crops (in terms of *length of crop cycle*) and *EFAs* are evaluated for their ability to contribute to water retention and infiltration.

Maintenance of Habitats. The hierarchical tree designed for mapping maintenance of habitats service considers three criteria for assessing habitats potential, namely their *ecological value*, their *vulnerability*, and the structure of the regional *ecological network*, and four criteria for assessing human management, namely *crop type*, *type of activity*, *EFAs*, and *protected areas*.

Vulnerability of habitats is assessed considering *ecological sensitivity* and *anthropogenic pressure*. Data on *ecological value*, *ecological sensitivity* and *anthropogenic pressure* are taken from the ISPRA Nature Map of Tuscany. The map of the regional *ecological network* comes from the PIT-PPR cartography, and it is evaluated according to its structural elements, i.e., different components of forest and agricultural ecosystems, and to its functional elements, i.e., components with high value or criticality.

Crops (in terms of *crop type*) and *EFAs* are evaluated for their ability to contribute to habitat quality. Maps of *protected areas* provided by Tuscany Region identify the borders of national and local parks and reserves.

2.5 The Process for ESs Mapping and Bundling

The assignment of weights to criteria, sub-criteria, and attributes in the AHP, like in many other MCDA techniques, can involve the participation of citizens, stakeholders, and experts. In this first analysis, weights are assigned by authors using a simpler paired comparison technique than that originally proposed by Saaty for the AHP. The Saaty's fundamental scale makes use of nine values (from 1 to 9) to define the relative relevance of the various elements of the hierarchical tree [18]. With the simpler paired comparison technique, only three values are used: 0, 0,5 and 1. The value 1 is given to the most relevant element, 0 to the less relevant one, and 0,5 is given to both when they are thought to have the same relevance.

For example, Table 1 shows how weights are assigned to the three criteria of the hierarchical tree designed for mapping the provisioning service, by using a matrix of pairwise comparisons. In this case, *LCC* is considered more relevant than *crop destination* and *type of activity* for defining the capacity of the different areas of the territory for the provisioning service. *Crop destination* is considered more relevant than *type of activity*. A *fictive indicator* is added to prevent one of the criteria from obtaining a zero weight.

The weights assigned in the same way to the attributes that the spatial units can assume for these criteria are shown in Table 2.

Table 1. Matrix of pairwise comparison for the assignment of weights to the criteria of the hierarchical tree designed for mapping the provisioning service.

	LCC	Crop destination	Type of activity	*Fictive indicator*	Total Scores	Weights
LCC	/	1	1	1	3	0.500
Crop destination	0	/	1	1	2	0.333
Type of activity	0	0	/	1	1	0.167
Fictive indicator	0	0	0	/	0	0.000
Tot.					6	1.000

After weights are assigned to the attributes, they are transferred to the spatial units (polygons) of all the used maps, for each criterion or sub-criterion of the five hierarchical trees created, in a new field of their attribute table. All maps are then converted into

Table 2. Weights assigned to the attributes of the criteria of the hierarchical tree designed for mapping the provisioning service.

Criteria	Attributes	Weights
LCC	Class I	1.000
	Class II	0.875
	Class III	0.750
	Class IV	0.625
	Class V	0.500
	Class VI	0.375
	Class VII	0.250
	Class VIII	0.125
Crop destination	*Crops for food*	
	Fruit trees and berry plantations	1.000
	Horticulturals	0.920
	Cereals	0.880
	Leguminous	0.800
	Vineyards	0.760
	Olive groves	0.680
	Crops for various destination	
	Arable crops	0.750
	Greenhouses	0.750
	Heterogeneous areas	0.300
	Crops for fodder for reared animals	
	Cereals for fodder	0.500
	Leguminous for fodder	0.417
	Fodder	0.333
	Pastures	0.250
	Grasslands	0.167
	Fallow land	0.083
	Crops for fibers and materials	
	Nurseries	0.250
	Arboriculture	0.219
	Forests	0.219
	Oleaginous	0.219

(*continued*)

Table 2. (*continued*)

Criteria	Attributes	Weights
	Ornamentals	0.219
	Officinals	0.187
Type of activity	Professional organic	1.000
	Professional conventional	0.875
	Non-professional	0.375

raster format, choosing as attributes for the pixels the weights contained in the new fields created. Because the overlay of GCPs on LULC maps generates some small and fragmented polygons, whose information should not be lost, maps are converted into raster format setting the highest resolution compatible with the need for an efficient processing, that is 3×3 m.

The maps obtained from the overlay of GCPs on LULC maps are converted into raster format for the weights assigned to the crops according to the three different classifications created. In all three cases, as well as in the case of the type of activity, the maps for the years from 2016 to 2020 are separately converted into raster format, and then the average value of the weights taken by the pixels for the five years is calculated.

When all the maps are converted into raster format, map algebra operations allow to easily recompose the hierarchical trees, multiplying maps by weights assigned to criteria and sub-criteria, and adding them at each level of the trees. Thus, five raster maps containing the general ordering of spatial units (pixels) according to their capacity to supply the ESs considered are obtained. The five raster maps have high resolution, but are very fragmented, due to the imperfections of the original GCPs and the effects of their overlay on LULC maps.

Therefore, a vector grid of hexagonal polygons, with an area of approx. 1 ha, is created to ascribe the values obtained for the five ESs to spatial units that homogeneously cover the territory, and that collect the values of capacity for all the ESs. This grid is much greater than raster maps resolution, but comparable with the average dimensions of GCPs and LULC maps elements.

To each vector polygon of the grid, the average value of pixels contained within it is assigned, for each of the five raster maps of the ESs. These values are then normalized between 0 and 10, in a new field of the attribute table. The normalized values are used for characterizing the territory according to the capacity of different areas to supply the five ESs. These values are also used for the cluster analysis, performed by the Attribute Based Clustering plug-in for QGis, selecting K-Means method and testing quality of results when using 4, 5, 6, or 7 clusters.

The algorithm groups a few isolated polygons in each cluster, which may limit the good visibility of the results. For this reason, the polygons of each cluster with area less than 5 ha are selected and merged with the neighboring polygons with the largest common boundary. Finally, the averages of the values of capacity for the five ESs obtained by the polygons grouped in each cluster are calculated.

3 Results

3.1 ESs Maps

The proposed method makes it possible to obtain five maps that subdivide the analyzed territory into areas with different capacity to supply the considered ESs, on a relative scale from 0 to 10 (Fig. 2).

The capacity to supply the provisioning service appears mainly located in the plains, as well as in the eastern hills. It is lower in the mountains and in the hills to the west and south.

The capacity to supply the erosion and mass movements control service shows a rather homogeneous distribution. It is slightly higher in the western hills and in the plains, and slightly lower in the mountains and in the hills to the east and south.

The capacity to supply the soil quality service is higher in the mountains and in the hills to the east, south, and west, while it is lower in the plains.

The capacity to supply the water flows regulation service appears higher in the mountains, as well as in the western and south-western hills. The plains and the other hills show a lower capacity to supply this service.

The capacity to supply the habitat maintenance service is concentrated in the mountains, in the hills to the west and to the south, in the areas surrounding the Fucecchio Marshs, and on the ridge of the hills to the east. It is limited in the plains.

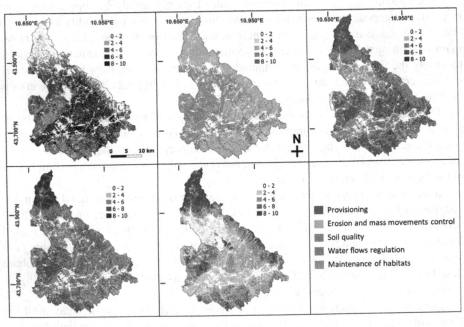

Fig. 2. ESs maps.

3.2 ESs Bundles

Based on the five ESs maps obtained, cluster analysis allows to identify areas that are more homogeneous in terms of capacity to supply different bundles of the considered ESs.

When using 4 clusters, a relevant distinction between two bundles disappears, while when using 6 or 7 clusters, bundles very similar to each other are created. A number of 5 clusters proves to be in this case the one that best allows to subdivide and characterize the territory.

The territory is thus characterized according to five ESs bundles that synthesize the capacity of different areas to supply different combinations of the five mapped ESs (Fig. 3).

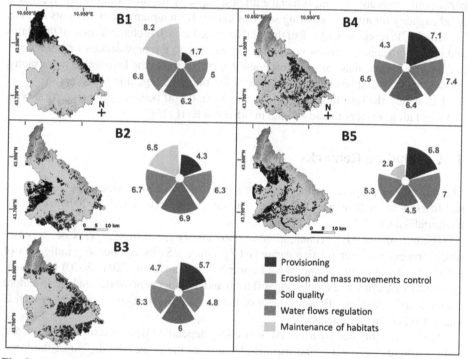

Fig. 3. ESs bundles. Dark areas indicate bundles' location, circular barplots indicate average values of ESs supply capacity (graphs created with ggplot2 package in R 4.1.2).

Bundle B1 represents 20.5% of the total area of the analyzed territory. It is characteristic for the Apennine mountains and the ridge of the eastern hills, mainly covered by forests. It has a very high capacity for maintenance of habitats service, but an almost absent capacity for provisioning service. It also shows good capacity for water flows regulation and soil quality services, but it has a low capacity for erosion and mass movement control service.

Bundle B2 represents 15.3% of the total area of the analyzed territory. It is mainly located in the hills to the west, a protected area covered by forests (the Cerbaie Plateau), and to the south, typical mosaics of forests and agricultural areas. It has a very good and balanced capacity for all the considered ESs, even if its capacity for maintenance of habitat service is lower than that of bundle B1 and its capacity for provisioning service is lower than those of other bundles.

Bundle B3 represents 23.4% of the total analyzed area. It is mainly located in the hills to the east and south-east, which are multifunctional territories where permanent crops, arable land, and agroforestry areas are mixed. It shows a balanced capacity for all the ESs, but lower than that of bundle B2 for every ESs except for the provisioning service. Especially its capacity for erosion and mass movement control and water flow regulation services is very low.

Bundle B4 represents 17.1% of the total analyzed area. It collects areas of the eastern part of the plains, and of the foot of the eastern hills, where both arable lands and permanent crops are present. It has the highest capacity for provisioning service, and a good capacity for all the regulating services except for maintenance of habitats service.

Bundle B5 represents 23.8% of the total analyzed area. It is characteristic of the plains and has a high capacity for provisioning service, due to the prevalence of arable lands, and for erosion and mass movements control service, due to the favourable topography. On the other hand, it has the lowest capacity for the other regulating services.

Ultimately, the resulting ESs bundles show a trade-off between provisioning service and regulating services already found in other contexts [15].

4   Concluding Remarks

The method we propose for mapping the supply of five ESs produced by agricultural and forest areas in Tuscany Region is a first attempt to combine LULC maps with other territorial data.

The use of the AHP technique allows to classify the different areas of the case-study territory for their relative capacity to produce ESs by considering indicators of both ecosystem properties and human contributions in recent (2016–2020) land management. Organizing and combining different and heterogeneous data can lead to a more comprehensive and specific assessment of the ESs supply, than considering only LULC maps or other single indicators.

The results obtained by using AHP strongly depend on designed hierarchical trees, and on weights assigned to the various elements of the trees. The design of the trees, influenced by data availability, is the most rigid part of the method, while the assignment of weights is the most adjustable and questionable part, as it requires data interpretation. The method is configured as a flexible tool, open to participation of experts and stakeholders, which is fundamental to make the ESs assessment more accurate, and to develop scenario analyses, according to different preferences.

The results obtained with weights assigned according to authors personal judgment show that the method has potentiality for advancing research on ESs mapping, even if it needs to be further refined and tested.

Cluster analysis allows to identify homogeneous areas in terms of capacity to supply different ESs bundles. This can deepen the knowledge of the capacity of a territory to produce different combinations of ESs in different locations. Highlighting strengths and criticalities, ESs bundles maps can provide useful indications for territorial strategies and policies. However, bundles give only an initial knowledge of the relationships among ESs, and further research is needed to understand the factors that determine their association, with the aim of helping to focus strategies and measures not just on some isolated ESs, but on a set of them [14].

In conclusion, the proposed method allows for very interesting results, but also has room for improvement. Firstly, it is necessary to widen the set of considered ESs, e.g., including the cultural services of agricultural and forest areas. Secondly, is to be explored how to evaluate ESs by separately analyzing, on one side, ecosystems potential (intrinsic characteristics) and, on the other, the role played on it by human activities (management features), to verify the effects of different management practices. Furthermore, it could be interesting to map ESs bundles on other scales (both larger or smaller), for identifying different configurations of the relationships between ESs, and to verify the effect of spatial resolution on ESs assessment and bundling, for identifying the best compromise between effectiveness and costs of the analysis. Finally, it is necessary to open a further front of research on data and methods for evaluating also the ESs demand, with the aim of defining territorial balances between the ESs supply and demand.

References

1. IPBES: Summary for policymakers of the global assessment report on biodiversity and ecosystem services. IPBES secretariat, Bonn (2019). https://doi.org/10.5281/ZENODO.565 7041
2. EEA: Land and soil in Europe. Signals, 2443–7557 (2019). https://doi.org/10.2800/779710
3. Bueno-Suárez, C., Coq-Huelva, D.: Sustaining what is unsustainable: a review of urban sprawl and urban socio-environmental policies in North America and Western Europe. Sustainability 12(11) (2020). https://doi.org/10.3390/su12114445
4. van der Zanden, E.H., Verburg, P.H., Schulp, C.J.E., Verkerk, P.J.: Trade-offs of European agricultural abandonment. Land Use Policy 62, 290–301 (2017). https://doi.org/10.1016/j.lan dusepol.2017.01.003
5. Stoate, C., et al.: Ecological impacts of early 21st century agricultural change in Europe - a review. J. Environ. Manag. 91(1), 22–46 (2009). https://doi.org/10.1016/j.jenvman.2009. 07.005
6. Costanza, R., et al.: Twenty years of ecosystem services: how far have we come and how far do we still need to go? Ecosyst. Serv. 28, 1–16 (2017). https://doi.org/10.1016/j.ecoser.2017. 09.008
7. La Rosa, D., Barbarossa, L., Privitera, R., Martinico, F.: Agriculture and the city: a method for sustainable planning of new forms of agriculture in urban contexts. Land Use Policy 41, 290–303 (2014). https://doi.org/10.1016/j.landusepol.2014.06.014
8. Ricart, S., Kirk, N., Ribas, A.: Ecosystem services and multifunctional agriculture: unravelling informal stakeholders' perceptions and water governance in three European irrigation systems. Environ. Policy Gov. 29(1), 23–34 (2019). https://doi.org/10.1002/eet.1831
9. Burkhard, B., Maes, J. (Eds.): Mapping Ecosystem Services. Pensoft Publishers, Sofia (2017). https://doi.org/10.3897/ab.e12837
10. Eigenbrod, F., et al.: The impact of proxy-based methods on mapping the distribution of ecosystem services. J. Appl. Ecol. 47(2), 377–385 (2010). https://doi.org/10.1111/j.1365-2664.2010.01777.x

11. Campagne, C.S., Roche, P., Müller, F., Burkhard, B.: Ten years of ecosystem services matrix: review of a (r)evolution. One Ecosystem (5) (2020). https://doi.org/10.3897/oneeco.5.e51103
12. Agostini, D., Lucchesi, F., Monacci, F., Nardini, F., Rovai, M., Zetti, I.: Land consumption, ecosystem services and urban planning policies: preliminary results of research undertaken in the Tuscany Region. Int. J. Environ. Sci. Sustain. Dev. 6(1), 24 (2021). https://doi.org/10.21625/essd.v6i1.789
13. Lee, H., Lautenbach, S.: A quantitative review of relationships between ecosystem services. Ecol. Ind. 66, 340–351 (2016). https://doi.org/10.1016/j.ecolind.2016.02.004
14. Spake, R., et al.: Unpacking ecosystem service bundles: towards predictive mapping of synergies and trade-offs between ecosystem services. Glob. Environ. Chang. 47, 37–50 (2017). https://doi.org/10.1016/j.gloenvcha.2017.08.004
15. Saidi, N., Spray, C.: Ecosystem services bundles: challenges and opportunities for implementation and further research. Environ. Res. Lett. 13(11), (2018). https://doi.org/10.1088/1748-9326/aae5e0
16. Greene, R., Devillers, R., Luther, J.E., Eddy, B.G.: GIS-based multiple-criteria decision analysis. Geogr. Compass 5(6), 412–432 (2011). https://doi.org/10.1111/j.1749-8198.2011.00431.x
17. Rovai, M., Andreoli, M.: Integrating AHP and GIS techniques for rural landscape and agricultural activities planning. In: Berbel, J., Bournaris, T., Manos, B., Matsatsinis, N., Viaggi, D. (eds.) Multicriteria Analysis in Agriculture. MCDM, pp. 69–98. Springer, Cham (2018). https://doi.org/10.1007/978-3-319-76929-5_3
18. Saaty, T.L.: The modern science of multicriteria decision making and its practical applications: the AHP/ANP approach. Oper. Res. 61(5), 1101–1118 (2013). https://doi.org/10.1287/opre.2013.1197
19. Mosadeghi, R., Warnken, J., Tomlinson, R., Mirfenderesk, H.: Comparison of Fuzzy-AHP and AHP in a spatial multi-criteria decision making model for urban land-use planning. Comput. Environ. Urban Syst. 49, 54–65 (2015). https://doi.org/10.1016/j.compenvurbsys.2014.10.001
20. Haines-Young, R., Potschin, M.: Common International Classification of Ecosystem Services (CICES) V5.1. Guidance on the Application of the Revised Structure. Fabis Consulting Ltd (2018). https://cices.eu/content/uploads/sites/8/2018/01/Guidance-V51-01012018.pdf

A Model for Considering the Crossed Effects of Plans in the Strategic Environmental Assessment

Valentina Adinolfi[✉] [iD], Michele Grimaldi [iD], Vincenzo Naddeo [iD], and Isidoro Fasolino [iD]

University of Salerno, Baronissi, Italy
{vadinolfi,migrimaldi,vnaddeo,i.fasolino}@unisa.it

Abstract. The variety and number of urban and territorial plans, general and sectoral, present in the Italian regulatory framework, requires a systematized recognition of the same for the purpose of a conscious and exhaustive consideration within the environmental report, as a technical elaboration foreseen in the context the strategic environmental assessment procedure (SEA) of plans and programs, where the significant effects that the implementation of the plan or program could have on the environment are identified, described and evaluated, as well as reasonable alternatives in light of the objectives and territorial scope of the plan or program. The SEA, in turn, is intended as an evaluation of the plan because it integrates the process by pursuing the objective of environmental sustainability of the plan's forecasts. Furthermore, since human actions are the main cause of climate change, spatial and urban planning can play a key role in opposition to it increasingly recognized. The aim of this work is to propose an operational tool useful for verifying which other plans, in addition to the one for which the SEA is conducted, operating in the same area concerned, should be considered in order to evaluate their possible effects on the environmental components.

Keywords: Strategic Environmental Assessment (SEA) · Plans · Environmental effects

1 Introduction

With the term Planning System, we mean to refer to a conventional conceptual scheme that allows to frame more easily the main characters of any plan that has to do with urban and territorial planning.

The current system of urban and territorial planning in Italy derives from the sedimentation over time of a series of tools, with a sectoral and / or general content, of intervention at the territorial and, or, local scale, introduced by a respective relevant number of norms [3, 4, 22, 37].

Supplementary Information The online version contains supplementary material available at https://doi.org/10.1007/978-3-031-17439-1_32.

The Italian urban planning system provides for a hierarchical organization where local plans must take into account the requirements of higher-level plans.

Considering the effects of a plan on the environment, starting from the 1970s it is time to realize that environmental resources, even those apparently inexhaustible, are limited and constitute a precious value for our community.

The concept of development sustainability is therefore based mainly on the awareness that resources are not inexhaustible; the individuals who inhabit (or interact with) an ecosystem have two ways of relating to it: by extracting from the ecosystem resources that can be renewable or non-renewable and by introducing into the ecosystem waste deriving from their activities and which come from the ecosystem decomposed and reabsorbed, in a very different time depending on the biodegradability of the waste. The timing of human interventions must, therefore, be in a balanced relationship with the time of natural processes, both of the rhythms of regeneration of renewable raw materials or of ecosystems and of waste decomposition processes.

Considering the issue of sustainability, the Agenda 2030 is an action programme for people, planet and prosperity. It provides a common basis for defining goals to build an environmentally, socially and economically sustainable world.

In this perspective, the Strategic Environmental Assessment (SEA) of plans is an important instrument to achieve the sustainability goals. However, given the remarkable variety of urban planning tools in the Italian urban planning system, it is crucial to verify the crossed effects of plans in the SEA process.

The aim of this work is to propose an operational tool useful for verifying which other plans, in addition to the one for which the SEA is conducted, operating in the same area concerned, should be considered in order to evaluate their possible effects on the environmental components. So, a specific matrix was developed, in order to have a useful tool to verify the relevant plans to be considered, in a sustainable design perspective, in compliance with the 2030 Agenda.

After a brief overview of the relevant literature, the methodology used in the construction of the matrix is described, together with its results and possible future developments.

2   Materials and Methods

2.1   The Planning System in Italy

Planning consists of a series of rules, forms and methods, applied to a spatial context of different dimensions, for the government (use, protection and transformation) of the territory [16, 17]. These rules are applied to a defined territory or to areas of the territory that may consist of individual municipalities or portions of them, or from several municipalities up to covering provinces and regions or the entire national territory. Urban and territorial planning can be framed with reference to three fundamental aspects: levels, subjects and instruments [15, 21]. All plans and programs are subject to the Strategic Environmental Assessment (SEA): it is a systematic process for assessing the environmental consequences of proposed policies, plans and programs in order to ensure that they are fully included and adequately considered, right from the earliest appropriate stages of the decision-making process, on a par with economic and social considerations [14, 32].

The objective of the SEA is to ensure a high level of environmental protection by pursuing sustainable development of the city and the area through:

- the integration of environmental considerations, through an Environmental Report when drawing up plans and programs and before their approval, in order to promote sustainable development;
- consideration of the environmental effects of the strategic actions proposed in terms of urban, territorial and environmental forecasts in the plan or program;
- timely knowledge of the consequences of large-scale actions;
- the identification of the best practicable alternative from an environmental point of view;
- guarantee, through participation, the sharing of objectives and plan or program choices, also in order to improve decision-making processes;
- verify, by monitoring, the environmental effects of the implementation of the plan or program.

In general, it can be affirmed that all plans, general and sectoral, by their nature, being conceived as instruments aimed at improving the living conditions of settled communities, provide for actions which, in principle, should only produce positive effects on the environmental components concerned.

The general objectives of territorial and urban planning, in fact, are the following:

- promotion of the rational use and orderly development of the urban and suburban territory;
- safeguarding the safety of human settlements from hydrogeological, seismic and natural risk factors in general;
- protection of the physical integrity and cultural identity of the territory and landscape through the enhancement of landscape-environmental and historical-cultural resources, the conservation of ecosystems, the redevelopment of existing settlement fabrics and the recovery of compromised sites;
- regulation of the physical and functional transformations of the territory and of the systems of mobility of goods and people;
- improvement of infrastructure and livability of built-up areas;
- development of economic activities through transformation interventions compatible with the needs of safeguarding natural, landscape-environmental, agro-forestry-pastoral and historical-cultural resources [15, 20, 21, 41, 42].

In the plans, in reality, certain choices, despite positively pursuing precise purposes, can produce negative effects on some environmental components, sometimes even not easily predetermined.

2.2 Methodology Addressed

Following a detailed analysis of the technical prerogatives relating to each plan and how the latter affects the environmental components taken into consideration, giving rise to a direct or indirect impact, depending on the case, a matrix was built. The methodology considered verifies how the plan considered produces direct or indirect impacts.

Two tables are defined in advance, the objective of which is to scan the plans according to their nature: the first one defines the reference regulatory framework of the plan, the person entrusted with the training, the level on which the tool operates and finally, its nature, whether of development, management and / or recovery; the second one is intended as a compendium of the objectives and actions of the individual plans, with particular regard to the areas of conservation, protection and defense, thus establishing whether a plan can adapt to one or more objectives considered, supported by the SEA process. The last step was the one that saw the construction of a plan-environmental component matrix capable of identifying potentially significant direct impacts. Through the construction of the environmental plans-components matrix, it is possible to obtain a checklist to verify, depending on the plan and the territory for which the SEA is being carried out, which other plans, if applicable in that specific area of interest, it is necessary to consider with reference to the single environmental component examined. The checklist technique is chosen because of its simplicity and communicative capacity, as well as the possibility of updating and improving certain information and integrating information elements whenever necessary. In particular, the environmental components considered below are air; waterfall; soil; vegetation flora and fauna; ecosystems; landscape; socio-economic; health; noise and vibrations; radiation. In the matrix of plans and environmental components, the elements for which it is believed that the single plan produces a direct impact on the environmental component concerned are valued.

For all the empty elements of the matrix, the impact is assumed to be indirect. For each instrument, according to the possible actions envisaged by it, the environmental components potentially affected by some effects are determined. The following conditions may occur impact that may require specific mitigation and compensation measures; generally positive impact, as it is the specific mission of the plan itself; impact tendentially not determinable a priori in terms of positivity or negativity of the effects. The potentially positive impacts identify the possibility that the action considered may result in benefits on the environmental components. In general, it is assumed that the actions contribute both to the protection and enhancement of existing resources and to the promotion of sustainable development processes.

The potentially null impacts refer to those actions that, in some cases, do not affect the thematic area under consideration, while in other cases, they are such as not to affect the state of the environment.

The potentially negative impacts make explicit the negative externalities that the action considered, while having a positive purpose, could determine and the implications of which must be considered with attention and caution.

The methodology well fits within the action program of the United Nation (UN), "Transforming our world, the 2030 Agenda for Sustainable Development".

The agenda consists of 17 "Sustainable Development Goals", SDGs, framed within a broader action program of 169 targets or Goals, associated with them, to be achieved in the environmental and economic fields, social and institutional by 2030.

The objectives are characterized by a global validity, they see all countries involved, considering the economic, social and ecological spheres, having as a common purpose also that of mitigating climate change.

In particular, the Goal 11 is projected into the definition of an inclusive, safe, long-lasting, and sustainable city, increasing inclusive planning and the capacity for participatory planning and management of human settlement (UN, 2015).

3   Results

The matrix obtained contains the various plans and the relative environmental impacts that each plan generates on the environment. The following are the relative environmental components taken into account for the construction of this matrix (Table 1).

Certain plans (regional plan for the rehabilitation and protection of air quality, atmospheric depollution plan) have as their main objective the rehabilitation and maintenance of air quality, for which a direct positive effect is expected.

Plans with a generally negative impact are, on the other hand, energy plans, waste disposal plans, transport, traffic, mobility and parking plans, regional plans for extractive activities, regulatory plans for industrial development areas.

Improving air quality consists in reducing the emissions of pollutants into the atmosphere from point, linear and diffuse sources, also using renewable energy sources, reducing the negative per capita environmental impact of cities, in particular with regard to air quality and waste management (Goal 11, Subgoal 11.6).

Some plans have as their main objective precisely the rehabilitation and maintenance of water quality (regional water rehabilitation plan, water protection plan), for which, also in this case, a direct positive effect is expected. The aim is to ensure the availability and sustainable management of water, improving its quality by reducing pollution (Goal 6, Subgoals 6.3).

In particular, the optimal territorial area plan has the task of promoting sustainable water use based on long-term management.

Other plans (general plan for the defense of the sea and coasts, hydrographic basin plan, territorial plan of the park (or reserve), management plan of the protected area), still have the purpose of protecting aquatic ecosystems, the marine environment and the wetlands that directly depend on them, in order to ensure their ecological function, also to safeguard and develop the potential uses of water.

Finally, some plans, on the other hand, have contents whose effects are potentially negative on the quality of the water; for them it is necessary to envisage actions aimed at curbing and eliminating pollution, through specific rules of planning tools aimed at stopping or gradually eliminating discharges, emissions and losses of dangerous substances.

All the general plans and almost all the sector plans imply, in different forms and intensities, a physical modification of the territory to which they apply.

Some plans, such as the hydrographic basin plan, have the task of preventing risks and defending the soil from hydrogeological instability phenomena in order to guarantee permanent and homogeneous environmental conditions. Others instead (plan for the rehabilitation of areas at environmental risk, plan for the reclamation of polluted sites) have the task of contrasting the phenomena of soil contamination, reducing their release into air, water and soil in order to minimize their negative effects on human health and the environment (Goal 12, Subgoal 12.4). Containment of land consumption is no longer just an enunciation of a cultural and political principle, but, in recent years, has translated into operating methods that are increasingly present in the contents and technical standards of general and sector planning tools (Fig. 1).

N.	Acronym	Denomination	Air	Waterfall	Soil	Vegetation and Fauna	Ecosystems	Landscape	Heath	Noise and vibration	Radiations
1	PTR	Regional territorial plan			X	P /X	P	P			
2	Ptcp	Territorial provincial coordination plan			X	P /X	P	P			
3	PTAM	Territorial plan of the metropolitan area			X	P /X	P /X	P /X			
4	Prg /PUC	General land use plan / Municipal town planning plan	P /X	P /X	P /X	P/X	P /X	P/X	P/X	P /X	
5	Pgdmc	General plan for the defense of the sea and coasts		P	P	P	P	P /X			
6	PdiB	Hydrographic basin plan		P	P		P	P	P		

Legend
X = Impact that may require specific mitigation and compensation measures;
P = Tendentially positive impact;
P /X = Possible impact tends not to be determinable a priori

Fig. 1. Plan components matrix, Authors' elaboration (supplementary materials)

A series of plans with an environmental content (general plan for the defense of the sea and coasts, territorial landscape plan / landscape plan, territorial plan of the park or reserve management plan of the protected area, socio-economic development program of the mountain community, wildlife plan and hunting) should give rise to generally positive impacts, as the relative contents are characterized by the presence of specific protection systems.

The effect of the general plans on this component is linked to the contents of these in terms of development forecasts, so the possible impact is generally not determinable a priori. The purpose is to protect, restore and promote sustainable use of the terrestrial ecosystem, counteract desertification, stop land degradation, stop the loss of biological diversity, getting urgent measures to reduce habitat degradation (Goal 15, Subgoals 15.2–15.5).

In general, it is a question of promoting and supporting strategies, interventions, and actions, to be included in the regulatory provisions of the plans, aimed at preventing at source, mitigating or compensating for the negative impacts on biological diversity connected to the carrying out of anthropic processes and economic activities.

Various plans with environmental content (general plan for the defense of the sea and coasts, hydrographic basin plan, territorial landscape plan / landscape plan, territorial plan of the park or reserve, management plan of the protected area, regional plan for the rehabilitation of waters and water protection plan, socio-economic development program of the mountain community, wildlife and hunting plan) should give rise to generally positive impacts, as they are full of contents based on protection, conservation, protection and the integration of ecosystem and biodiversity values into national and local planning, in the development processes, in the strategies of poverty alleviation (Goal 15, Subgoal 15.9).

The general territorial plans (regional territorial plan and provincial territorial coordination plan) also present contents traditionally moved from the point of view of the contents of environmental protection. Conversely, potentially negative effects can potentially derive from the contents of the regional plans for extractive activities and the like: also in this case, for these plans, it is a question of promoting and supporting strategies, interventions, techniques and technologies to prevent, mitigate or compensate the negative impacts on ecosystems connected to the carrying out of anthropic processes and economic activities.

The general plans, especially territorial ones (regional territorial plan and territorial plan for provincial coordination), have contents that are increasingly sensitive to the theme of the landscape. The identity and the recognizability of the landscape are an essential element of the quality of the places. A fundamental rule is attributed to the landscape increasing individual and social well-being and raising the quality of life of populations, but also protecting, restoring and promoting a sustainable use of the terrestrial ecosystem, stopping the desertification, land degradation, and the loss of biological diversity (Goal 15).

Tendentially negative effects can potentially derive from the contents of transport and traffic plans, regulatory plans for industrial development areas, regional plans for extractive activities, energy plans, antennae plans and port regulatory plans. For these plans it is necessary to include in the relevant technical standards the contents of protection, conservation and enhancement of the landscape-cultural heritage, on the one hand, and the recovery of decaying elements, on the other.

By their nature, all plans have as their objective the development, management or rehabilitation of the existing in order to pursue better social and economic conditions of the settled communities, in this sense, therefore, the impact is always to be understood as direct and generally positive, the plans encourage lasting economic growth, inclusive and sustainable, full employment and productive (Goal 8).

In the field of waste, the plans must aim at: developing the prevention, reduction of the quantity and dangerousness of the waste produced, also in order to guarantee its disposal in conditions of environmental safety; increase separate collection for the purpose of maximizing the recovery of materials and energy from waste and the residual use of landfilling; maximize the interception of illegally disposed waste streams; increase self-sufficiency in the management of special waste and reduce its export; guarantee the sustainability of the waste cycle, minimizing the environmental, social and economic impact of waste production and management.

In the energy field, the plans must aim to achieve: a minimum level of general energy mix that comes from safe low-carbon sources; greater efficiency and development of renewable sources.

In general, the plans, through their forecasts, are required to reduce the percentage of the population exposed to various types of pollution, reducing the impacts of hazardous chemicals on the environment and, in particular, on human health.

Safeguarding health constitutes the main objective of specific plans, such as: the rehabilitation of areas at environmental risk and the remediation of polluted sites, water rehabilitation and water protection, rehabilitation and protection of air quality and atmospheric depollution, acoustic zoning and acoustic sanitation and the antenna plan, urban waste disposal and waste management; these plans include, among their actions, specific interventions to deal with potential noxious emissions and to remove situations of degradation and danger to health, looking for the healthiness (Goals 7–11-12).

Conversely, negative effects can potentially derive from the contents of transport and traffic plans, regulatory plans for industrial development areas, regional plans for extractive activities and energy plans. The river basin plan and the civil protection plans are generally considered positive, more precisely for the safety of people against natural and territorial risks.

The specific objective of some specialized plans (acoustic zoning plan and consequent acoustic remediation plan) is to maintain a high level of attention to the quality of life in the municipal area while allowing for the development of production activities, creating sustainable settlements (Goal 11).

The interaction between noise planning and urban planning entails the need for a process of progressive coordination between the new roles and competences of the local government bodies in terms of noise impact that starts and goes alongside the state of the settlements and the scenarios development defined by the urban planning instruments in force. Tendentially negative effects can potentially derive from the contents of transport and traffic plans, regulatory plans for industrial development areas, regional plans for extractive activities and energy plans. In any case, the objectives and priorities of the actions for the protection of noise pollution are to be achieved with the noise abatement plans which, not surprisingly, obligatorily integrate municipal urban planning. In addition to the noise remediation plan, the remediation plans for areas at environmental risk and the remediation of polluted sites also include, among their actions, specific interventions to deal with potential noise and vibration emissions.

Some tools, such as the urban waste disposal plan, the waste management plan, the remediation plan for areas at environmental risk and the remediation plan for polluted sites, include among their actions specific interventions to deal with potential emissions of radiation. The antenna plan deals with the localization of mobile telephone systems and the monitoring of electric, magnetic and electromagnetic fields as well as providing for methods of control of potentially polluting emissions to protect public health (Goals 11–12).

4 Summary Evaluation and Perspectives

Urban and territorial plans are the tools that the subjects of planning use to organize a territory in physical and functional terms, in general or for specific aspects, with a view to improving the living conditions of the established community. All plans are subject to SEA, in order to consider all possible significant impacts on the environment.

In this work, through the construction of a matrix of plans-environmental components, we propose to create a checklist to verify, depending on the plan and the territory for which the SEA is being carried out, which other plans, if applicable on that specific territory concerned, it is necessary to consider with reference to the single environmental component examined.

There is an excessive fragmentation of sector instruments and, moreover, many of their contents, often of an environmental nature, must, more effectively, be integrated within the general urban and territorial planning instruments.

Generally, the technical standards for the implementation of the individual plans must provide for mitigation contents, compensation for negative effects associated with actions that involve the introduction of elements strictly connected with the systems on which the plan is called upon to intervene.

These are measures to be specifically envisaged to prevent, reduce and compensate for possible negative effects that emerged during the identification of the impacts.

In order to optimize and mitigate the pressure of the settlement system on the natural environment and to improve the quality of the urban environment and recognized landscape values, the general and superordinate sectoral planning outlines some project objectives and guidelines, as a reference for subordinate planning, in particular municipal, aimed at limiting the consumption of resources, at maintaining natural and historical-cultural morphologies (constitutive, typological elements, of typical construction materials), at rebalancing and mitigating the negative impacts of anthropic activity, at strengthening infrastructures and of the environmental ecological endowments that contribute to improving the quality of the urban environment.

In planning, sectoral and non-sectoral, this quality is measured through assessments that include the negative effects of disturbance (noise, pollution, congestion, etc.), the positive ones (environment, public space, social harmonization, etc.) and those of large infrastructural works (ports, airports, etc.) as opportunities to regenerate the spaces of the city and, ultimately, to bring about greater social well-being.

Given the number of plans provided by law, having a reference framework of the possible operating instruments, certainly to be specified for the individual national realities, appears to be of evident utility and susceptible of progressive refinement in a perspective aimed at making environmental assessment procedures of plans and programs increasingly efficient.

446   V. Adinolfi et al.

References

1. Ameen R.F.M., Mourshed, M., Li, H.: A critical review of environmental assessment tools for sustainable urban design, review article. Environ. Impact Assess. Rev. **55**, 110–125, 55 (2015)
2. Avarello, P.: Il piano comunale. Evoluzione e tendenze, Il Sole24Ore, Milano (2000)
3. Barbieri, C.A.: I sistemi di pianificazione e i piani. In: Properzi, P. (eds.) "Rapporto dal Territorio 2010". INU Edizioni, Roma (2011)
4. Barbieri, C.A.: Sistemi e processi di pianificazione. In: Properzi, P.L. (eds.) "Rapporto dal Territorio 2005". INU Edizioni, Roma (2006)
5. Bruton, M., Nicholson Hutchinson, D.: Local planning in practice **5**(1), 452, pp. 156–157. Land Use Policy, London (1987)
6. Bryson, J.M., Einsweiler, R.C.: Strategic Planning: Threats and Opportunities for Planners. Planners Press, American Planning Association, Chicago (1988)
7. Cabanillas, F.J.J., Aliseda, J.M., Gutiérrez Gallego, J.A., Jeong, J.S.: Comparison of regional planning strategies: countywide general plans in USA and territorial plans in Spain, original research article. Land Use Policy **30**(1), 758–773 (2013)
8. Cajot, S., Peter, M., Bahu, J.-M., Koch, A., Maréchal, F.: Energy planning in the urban context: challenges and perspectives, original research article. Energy Procedia **78**, 3366–3371 (2015)
9. Cities **6**(4), 355–356 (1989)
10. Colavitti, A.M., Usai, N., Bonfiglioli, S.: Urban Planning in Italy: The Future Urban General Plan and Governance. Eur. Plann. Stud. **21**(2), 167–186 (2013)
11. Dallhammer, E., Gaugitsch, R., Neugebauer, W., Böhme, K.: Spatial planning and governance within EU policies and legislation and their relevance to the New Urban Agenda, European Union (2018)
12. Debrie, J., Raimbault, N.: The port–city relationships in two European inland ports: a geographical perspective on urban governance, original research article, Cities **50**, 180–187 (2016)
13. Delmastro, C., Lavagno, E., Schranz, L.: Underground urbanism: Master Plans and Sectorial Plans, original research article. Tunn. Undergr. Space Technol. Elsevier **55**, 103–111 (2016)
14. Faludi, A.: A turning point in the development of European spatial planning? The 'Territorial Agenda of the European Union' and the 'First Action Programme', original research article, Prog. Plann. **71**(1), 1–42 (2009)
15. Hall, P.: Planning: millennial retrospect and prospect, original research article. Prog. Plann. **57**(3–4), 263–284 (2002)
16. Healey, P.: Local Plans in British Land Use Planning, pp. 19–43, British Land Policy and Land Use Planning (1983)
17. Healey P.: Planning Theory: the good city and its governance, International Encyclopedia of the Social & Behavioral Sciences (2nd edn), pp. 202–207 (2015)
18. Hickman, R., Hall, P., Banister, D.: Planning more for sustainable mobility, original research article. J. Transport Geogr.**33**, 210–219 (2013)
19. Hurlimann, A.C., March, A.P.: The role of spatial planning in adapting to climate change. WIREs Clim. Change **3**(5), 379–488 (2012)
20. Huxley, M.: Planning, Urban, International Encyclopedia of Human Geography, pp. 193–198 (2009)
21. Lord, A., Tewdwr-Jones, M.: Regional Planning, International Encyclopedia of the Social & Behavioral Sciences (2nd edn.), pp. 129–133 (2015)
22. Mattogno, C.: Il sistema della pianificazione territoriale e urbanistica in alcuni paesi europei. In: Salustri, S. (eds.) La città complessa dall'approccio radicale a quello riformista, Francoangeli, Milano (1994)

23. Mirakyan, A., De Guio, R.: Integrated energy planning in cities and territories: areview of methods and tools, review article. Renew. Sustain. Energy Rev. **22**, 289–297 (2013)
24. Ognjenović, S., Zafirovski, Z., Vatin, N.: Planning of the Traffic System in Urban Environments, Original research article. Procedia Eng. **117**, 574–579 (2015)
25. Ogrin, D.: Landscape architecture and its articulation into landscape planning and landscape design, original research article. Landscape Urban Plann. **30**(3), 131–137 (1994)
26. Oregi, X., Roth, E., Alsema, E.A., Ginkel, M., Struik, D.: Use of ICT tools for integration of energy in urban planning projects, original research article. Energy Procedia **83**, 157–166 (2015)
27. Panagopoulos, T., González Duque, J.A., Bostenaru Dan, M.: Urban planning with respect to environmental quality and human well-being, original research article, part A, Environmental Pollution, vol. 208, pp. 137–144. Elsevier (2016)
28. Pilone, E., Mussini, P., Demichela, M., Camuncoli, G.: Municipal emergency plans in Italy: requirements and drawbacks, review article. Saf. Sci. **85**, 163–170 (2016)
29. Pourebrahim, S., Hadipour, M., Bin, M.M.: Integration of spatial suitability analysis for land use planning in coastal areas; case of Kuala Langat District. Selangor, Malaysia, original research article. Landscape Urban Plann. **101**(1), 84–97 (2011)
30. Properzi, P. (eds.) Rapporto dal territorio 2007. INU Edizioni, Roma (2008)
31. Ran, J., Nedovic-Budic, Z.: Integrating spatial planning and flood risk management: a new conceptual framework for the spatially integrated policy infrastructure, original research article. Comput. Environ. Urban Syst. **57**, 68–79 (2016)
32. Richardson, T.: Environmental assessment and planning theory: four short stories about power, multiple rationality, and ethics, original research article. Environ. Impact Assess. Rev. **25**(4), 341–365 (2005)
33. Romano, B., Zullo, F., Marucci, A., Fiorini, L.: Vintage urban planning in Italy: land management with the tools of the mid-twentieth century. Sustainability **10**, 4125 (2018)
34. Shafie, F.A., Omar, D., Karuppannan, S.: Environmental health impact assessment and urban planning, original research article. Procedia Soc. Behav. Sci. **85**, 82–91 (2013)
35. Steadie, S.M., Dellaert, N.P., Nuijten, W., Van Woensel, T., Raouti, R.: Multimodal freight transportation planning: aliterature review, original research article. Eur. J. Oper. Res. **233**(1), 1–15 (2016)
36. Still, B.G., May, A.D., Bristow, A.L.: The assessment of transport impacts on land use: practical uses in strategic planning, original research article. Transport Policy **6**(2), 83–98 (1999)
37. Talia, M.: La pianificazione del territorio. Conoscenze, politiche, procedure, e strumenti per il governo delle trasformazioni insediative, Il Sole24Ore, Milano (2003)
38. Wild, C., Narath, M.: Evaluating and planning ICUs: methods and approaches to differentiate between need and demand, original research article. Health Policy **71**(3), 289–301 (2005)
39. Wood, G., Whyatt, D., Stevens, C.: Towards the integration of urban planning and biodiversity conservation through collaboration, original research article. Environ. Technol. Innov. **4**, 218–226 (2015)
40. Zhang, T.: Urban Planning in China. Int. Encyclopedia Soc. Behav. Sci. 2nd edn, pp. 869–881 (2015)
41. Gerundo, R., Grimaldi, M., Marra, A.: A methodology hazard-based for the mitigation of the radon risk in the urban planning, UPLanD. J. Urban Plann. Landscape Environment. Des. **1**(1), 27–38 (2016)
42. Gerundo, R., Marra, A.: Landscapes at risk of peripheralization. A methodological framework for risk assessment to support regional planning strategies. Sustain. Mediterr. Constr. **5**, 73–79 (2021)

Soft Mobility in Mountain Areas: Methodological Approach and GIS Analysis for the Fruition of the Forts System in Genoa (Italy)

Federica Bisi, Ilaria Ferrando$^{(\boxtimes)}$ ⓘ, Francesca Pirlone ⓘ, and Bianca Federici ⓘ

Department of Civil, Chemical and Environmental Engineering (DICCA), University of Genoa, Via Montallegro 1, 16145 Genoa, Italy
ilaria.ferrando@edu.unige.it

Abstract. From 2014, the European Commission established guidelines for drafting the SUMP (Sustainable Urban Mobility Plan), defined as "a strategic plan to meet the varied mobility demand of people and businesses in urban and peri-urban areas in order to improve the quality of life in cities". More recently, BiciPlans were introduced as mandatory for municipalities over 100,000 inhabitants to reduce car travel in favor of bicycles, both for daily needs and for tourist and recreational activities. Since there is no legislation regulating bicycle and pedestrian paths outside urban areas, and more specifically in the mountains, a methodology to identify their characteristics is here described. It takes into account accessibility by public transport, interconnection with other routes, services available along or close to the routes, historical and natural value of the itineraries and the classification of mountain trails carried out by the Italian Alpine Club (CAI). The methodology, implemented in the free and open source QGIS, leads to the identification of four classes of paths: tourist level, good, very good and high technical capacity. Its application to the Genoa Forts system, due to their historical and architectural value, highlights its applicability and usefulness in supporting the fruition of the area under study. Finally, a webGIS allows the proposal to be shared with local government technicians and end users.

Keywords: Soft mobility · Mountain paths · GIS

1 Introduction

Sustainable mobility has gained increasing attention in local, national, and international environmental policies, as it is considered an effective resource to face pollution and the effects of climate change. Soft mobility, being by its nature non-motorized, meets the requirements of sustainability to the maximum and it contributes to the development of new forms of tourism aimed at the rediscovery of naturalistic and historical-cultural resources in the territory.

Even the *Piano Nazionale Ripresa Resilienza* (PNRR, National Recovery and Resilience Plan) [1], approved at European level on 13 July 2021, under *Mission 2:*

Green Revolution and Ecological Transition, provides a strong allocation of resources for the Renewable Energy, Hydrogen, Grid and Sustainable Mobility component. In Italy, where road transport contributes to the total GHG emissions to the extent of 23% [2], a proposal for a Piano di Transizione Ecologica (PTE, Plan for Ecological Transition) reports sustainable mobility among the objectives of environmental policies [3].

The impact of cycling network expansions was analyzed also from the health point of view [4]. In that context, the cycling network length increase was correlated to the public health and the advantages in terms of ecological (reduction of air and noise pollution, decrease of greenhouse gas emissions and constrain in the loss of natural outdoor environments) and economic consequences. What clearly emerged is the need of well-designed and safe cycling infrastructures to facilitate the shift to cycling [5]. Moreover, the realization of safe cycling paths represents a key goal for the transition sustainable mobility. Indeed, in case the reliance on cycling is limited, it is due to insufficiently developed cycle paths and the lack of basic safety standards, mainly related to the perceived danger for traffic, intersections and discontinuities [6]. The same perceived danger, together with unsafe pedestrian crossings and uncomfortable paths, discourages walking as well [7]. Concluding, safer and wider pedestrian and cycling paths are the most important aspects to promote sustainable mobility, especially among car and public transport users. Indeed, the incompleteness and the unsafety of pedestrian and cycling networks reduce the satisfaction of all the users, also the potential ones [8, 9].

During 2020 and 2021, the whole world faced exceptional difficulties due to the COVID-19 sanitary emergency. Cities and local governments have deployed creative and unprecedented responses to the pandemic, such as the exponential increase in cycling and walking routes, initiating a process of improving urban mobility in the direction of environmental sustainability combined with local economic growth and quality of life in cities [10].

In this context, taking advantage of the strong interdisciplinary nature of urban planning disciplines, of the growing amount of freely accessible geographical data, and of the capacity of the GIS (Geographic Information System) environment to manage, visualize and analyze geospatial data, a detailed analysis of soft and sustainable mobility is carried out, so to find a methodology for the creation of cycle/pedestrian routes in sub-urban mountain areas, since there is no regulation governing them.

Based on the classification of mountain trails carried out by the Italian Alpine Club (CAI), the geometrical characteristics of cycle and pedestrian paths and other parameters, like accessibility, interconnection and services, are analyzed. Then, the commonly available vector data relative to mountain paths are integrated with the parameters derived by DTM analysis in GIS, to classify them with regard to the degree of difficulty.

Then the identified methodology, implemented in the free and open source QGIS [11], is applied to the territory of the Forts system in Genoa (Italy), due to their historical and architectural value. Moreover, the city of Genoa has recently given a special impetus to soft mobility, with the creation of new cycle routes in the city centers. An in-depth analysis of the territory is performed, and then the Rete Escursionistica Ligure (REL, Ligurian hiking network) and the network of pedestrian paths, available on the Geoportals of the Liguria Region [12] and the Municipality of Genoa [13], are classified. Finally, a webGIS page is created so to share the results with local government technicians and to support the fruition of the study area by end users [14].

The paper is organized as follows: the topic of soft and sustainable mobility, the SUMP (Sustainable Urban Mobility Plan), and BiciPlan are introduced in Sect. 2; the evaluation criteria for defining mountain bike and pedestrian routes are defined in Sect. 3; the case study of the Forts system in Genoa is described in Sect. 4; Sect. 5 is dedicated to illustrate the GIS analysis of the case study; finally, the conclusions are reported in Sect. 6.

2   Soft and Sustainable Mobility

In 1987, the World Commission on Environment and Development gave the first definition of sustainable development, in the Brundtland Report, referring to the three fundamental dimensions of human lives, i.e., society, economy and environment, from which social, economic and ecological sustainability develop accordingly [15]. The application of the concept of sustainable development to the transport system introduces the topic of sustainable mobility, i.e., an ideal transport system, both for people and goods, that meets travel needs without negative consequences for the environment, ensuring a good quality of life. Europe is driving the evolution of mobility through emission standards and policy documents. For some years now, European legislation has been focusing on transport emission problems, intervening through Directives and Regulations on fuel quality, emission standards, fueling infrastructure and energy sources [16-19]. In accordance with European regulations, the member states, including Italy, are carrying out strategies and tools. Sustainable mobility must meet some criteria, for example: enable safe, economically viable and socially acceptable access to people, places goods and services; meet the needs of different groups in society and of different generations; use renewable resources at a level below their rate of regeneration and non-renewable resources at a level below the rates of development of renewable substitutes; promote community education and participation in transport decisions.

Soft mobility, being by its nature non-motorized, meets the requirements of sustainability to the maximum and it contributes to the development of new forms of tourism aimed at the rediscovery of naturalistic and historical-cultural resources in the territory.

Soft mobility is based on three essential components: weak users (pedestrians, cyclists, people with limited mobility abilities), specific means of transport (walking, bicycles, animal traction, water and other means of transport), and adequate infrastructures (greenways, cycle routes/lanes, secondary roads where vehicle traffic is encouraged to moderate its speed, limited speed zones, pedestrian routes, …).

Soft mobility (bicycles, scooters, etc.) is a great alternative to focus on, especially in cities where it is "uncomfortable" to travel on foot but perfectly accessible by bicycle. It will therefore be necessary to identify protected routes for bicycles, which may be able to use the corridors of the local public transport [20].

In 2014, the European Commission's Directorate for Mobility and Transport established guidelines for the drafting of the SUMP, defining it as "a strategic plan that aims to meet the varied mobility demand of people and businesses in urban and peri-urban areas, to improve the quality of life in cities. The SUMP complements other existing planning instruments and follows principles of integration, participation, monitoring and evaluation" [21]. SUMPs must focus on the integration of all "movements" within the city (and the term "movement" also includes pedestrian movements) in terms of sustainability (environmental, energy, socio-economic).

European legislation mainly focuses on improving the quality of fuel, on the differentiation of energy sources used in the transport sector, on the improvement of emission standards, and on the promotion of good practices [22, 23].

To promote a soft mobility, in particular cycling in urban and metropolitan areas, it is necessary to introduce the BiciPlan (Urban Cycling Mobility Plans). The aim of these plans is to reduce car travel in favor of the use of bicycles, especially in city centers, both for daily needs and for tourist and recreational activities. Table 1 contains BiciPlan macro-objectives and relative indicators. BiciPlans are sector plans of the SUMP and are therefore also to be understood as mandatory for municipalities and associations of municipalities with populations over 100,000 inhabitants not included in metropolitan cities.

Table 1. BiciPlan macro-objectives and indicators.

Macro-objective	Indicator	Unit of measure
Modal rebalancing of mobility	% increase of bicycle paths	Dimensionless
Significant decrease of accidents with deaths and injuries among weak users	Road fatality/injury rate	Deaths/inhabitants
Reduction of mobility costs	Motorization rate	Cars/inhabitants

3 A New Methodology for Mountain Cycle and Walking Routes

A cycle/pedestrian path is a path reserved for pedestrians and bicycles, where motorized traffic is excluded. There are different types of cycle path: considering path position and the construction types. Regarding the path position, the pedestrian/cycle paths can be grouped in urban and extra-urban paths. Instead, in terms of the types of construction, the following classes are defined: own-site (running in parallel to motorized roads and separated by curbs, pavements or barriers), optical/logical separation (indicated only by vertical and horizontal markings, without physical separation), adjacent to pavements (the cycle lane is separated from the pedestrian flow by a continuous white stripe with an optional colored background), promiscuous (pedestrians and cyclists share a common infrastructure, while maintaining a good degree of protection from motorized traffic).

Checklists can be drawn up to assess the quality of a bicycle/pedestrian path, so to build a systematic procedure for inspections following the improvement of the detected criticalities. The main characteristics to be checked are:

− accessibility: the main poles of attraction (e.g., schools, health services) should be mapped and the presence of accessible paths should be assessed. Furthermore, to be considered accessible, a cycle-pedestrian route must comply with the "Design for All" principles, i.e., make the use of cycle-pedestrian routes accessible to all, i.e., avoiding architectural barriers;

– degree of safety, accident rate, risk perception: a route is safe when it runs on roads with low traffic, is homogeneous (i.e., the road hasn't significant changes in traffic type and volume), has no danger spots and conveys a sense of security;
– continuity: a route is continuous if it directly connects two points and is capillary;
– signposting: when designing a cycle route, special attention should be paid to road signs, which provide users with rules of behavior, other information about the route, and are aimed at improving its safety and usability;
– geometrical and constructional characteristics: section width, curvature radius, visibility distance and longitudinal slope have to be checked.

If precise rules regulate the construction and use of cycle paths on the plain or valley floor, this is not the case for similar routes in other environments. At present, in Italy there are no rules limiting the passage of bicycles on paths. Based on the classification of mountain trails carried out by the CAI, an attempt was made to find a series of evaluation criteria for mountain bike and pedestrian routes:

– identification of the departure and arrival points of the excursions bearing in mind their accessibility also by public transport;
– access to mountain huts, alpine pastures and high-altitude accommodation within a few kilometers from the trails;
– historical and natural value of the itineraries, to preserve elements of knowledge and representativeness of the historical substance, not only of the road network, but also of the human and natural landscape of the crossed areas;
– connection with other existing path networks;
– ability to carry out regular maintenance to guarantee the viability over time;
– documentation on the development and condition of the existing network;
– offering interconnected routes, preparatory to the future creation of longer routes.

Moreover, CAI provides a classification of the routes, distinguishing between those which are exclusively for excursionist and those which are cyclable. The evaluation carried out in the following analysis concerns the routes in their entirety, i.e., considering them as "mountain cycle/pedestrian routes", for which a mediation of the characteristics provided by the CAI has been carried out. With regard to the degree of difficulty, the routes were distinguished as follows:

– T (Tourist): routes on small roads, mule tracks or easy paths, with clearly marked routes that do not pose uncertainties or orientation problems. Slight slope (<3%) routes that can be used by families with children either by bike or on foot;
– BC (Good technical ability): routes that typically take place on paths or on passing traces of various terrain (pastures, debris, scree), usually with signposts. They require a certain sense of orientation as well as some experience and knowledge of the mountainous terrain. Moderate slope (3–8%), routes suitable for families on foot and for medium-trained cyclists;

- OC (Very good technical ability): routes that are generally signposted but that imply an ability to move along paths or tracks on impervious and treacherous terrain. High slope (8–20%), recommended for moderately fit hikers and very fit cyclists or those with electric bikes;
- EC (High technical ability): equipped routes or via ferrata where the use of self-belaying devices (harnesses, dissipators, carabiners, lanyards) and personal protective equipment (helmet, gloves) is necessary. For cycle-hikers, routes that require trial-type techniques due to the presence of steps and obstacles in continuous succession. Very high slope (>20%).

4 Case Study: Genoa and Its Forts System

The metropolitan territory of Genoa covers an area of about 240 km^2 and has a morphologically complex and difficult structure. It is characterized by a coastal strip with an average gradient of 25% and bordered by mountain slopes with an average altitude of more than 600 m above sea level. In addition, the inland valleys have typically mountainous characteristics and penetration into them is often complex with the main roads concentrated in very restricted areas.

In this context the development of cycling has historically had to face a series of criticalities and obstacles, mainly related to the complexity of the orographic and urban configuration of the metropolitan territory. The criticalities of the current cycling system can therefore be summarized in the following points: orography, road network structure and congestion, lacking integration between transport modes, coexistence of different road users, lacking culture of "soft mobility", scarcity of service facilities and equipment.

The regulatory tool used for the promotion and encouragement of cycling is the BiciPlan, a sector plan provided for and coordinated by the SUMP, approved on 31 July 2019 by the Metropolitan City of Genoa [24]. In the post-COVID period, following a growth in the use of green mobility, the city of Genoa has been attentive to the issue of sustainable mobility, as it has built 30 km of emergency cycle lanes and new cycle lanes are planned in various parts of the city that better respect the issue of safety for users. Some parts of the city have been included in the BiciPlan of Genoa, others, such as the Forts System, are not yet included.

The nineteenth-century Forts are one of the symbols of the city of Genoa. These massive stone constructions, positioned at the top of inland hills, are in stark contrast to the typically Mediterranean landscape of the nearby Riviera or the metropolitan landscape of streets and houses, which penetrate down to the slopes of the heights. The hills on which the Forts stand are still wild, with large areas of greenery, scattered, low trees and no less than 70 species of diurnal butterflies, representing almost a quarter of those found in Italy.

Genoa Forts system comprises a significant number of fortifications, classified according to two systems, the central and the eastern, separated by the Bisagno stream valley. The central system is constituted by the Forts Castellaccio, Sperone, Puin, Fratello Maggiore (demolished), Fratello Minore, Diamante, Begato, Tenaglia, Crocetta, Belvedere (ruins), and the Towers Specola, Granarolo and Granara. Whereas Forts San Giuliano, San Martino, Santa Tecla, Richelieu, Monteratti, Quezzi and Quezzi Tower constitute the eastern system. The Central System of Forts is the most reinforced by connections with the city, due to the proximity of the 17th century city walls of Genoa. The Forts cover an area of approximately 900 hectares with a horseshoe-shaped route that starts in the city center and returns after crossing uninhabited hills. Genoa Forts system is currently the longest walled enclosure in Europe and the second longest in the world after the Great Wall of China. Figure 1 reports the position of Forts (green stars) with the Liguria hiking network and the cycle paths, in white and purple, respectively.

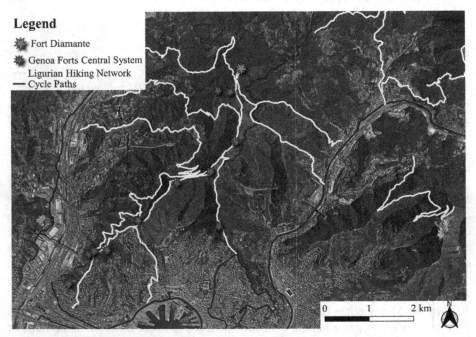

Fig. 1. Genoa Forts positions (green and yellow stars) on the orthophoto provided by Liguria Region geoportal. The white and purple lines represent the ligurian hiking network and the cycle paths, respectively (Color figure online).

The redevelopment of Genoa Fort system is part of a long-term plan structured in several successive phases that envisage the recovery of the city fortifications by exploiting the architectural and scenic potential offered by the entire fortified system. The recovery includes the creation of guided tours, leisure areas, event spaces, commercial and tourist reuse compatible with the cultural and landscape value of the places with the aim of ensuring the best use and public enjoyment of these structures [25].

To understand the importance of encouraging the creation and improvement of cycling and walking routes in that area, that is a resource for both tourists and the inhabitants of the municipality, a SWOT (Strengths, Weaknesses, Opportunities and Threats) analysis was performed, as follows:

– Strengths: landscape and historical value, existing connections, proximity to the city center, tourist interest;

- Weaknesses: need of securing and restoring part of the structures, degradation and abandonment, lacking knowledge, accessibility;
- Opportunities: enhancement process, financing from European funds, creation of cycle-pedestrian route;
- Threats: collapse and infiltration, property ownership.

5   GIS analysis of the Case Study

The main steps of the GIS analysis of the path networks in the Forts area, and the classification of difficulty as proposed in Sect. 3, are here described. Moreover, the evaluation criteria proposed in Sect. 3 are applied to identify the accessibility to the Fort Diamante and the supplementary services along these paths, as a more detailed case study.

5.1   Analysis and Classification of Path Networks

The two main digital path networks, the REL and the cycle paths, are considered and analyzed to understand the typology and quality of the descriptive data stored in the attribute tables (database) associated to the vectorial geometries. The description of REL is fundamental to understand if a path can be transitable by bicycle. Unfortunately, the description of road regards only the type of surface (asphalt/concrete, natural, pavement/sandstone), and the information on presence of stairs or other obstacles that cannot be climbed by bicycle is not available. Also, the information about the state of the bottom (friable or compact) and the width of the path are lacking. The type of cycling site allows to evaluate the quality and safety of the route. Most of the routes in the Municipality of Genoa are declared as own cycle lanes, but the routes in the area of interest are of promiscuous type, either motorized or pedestrian.

The REL and the cycle paths were compared according to some geometrical characteristics, properly calculated in GIS environment and inserted in the attributes table of each analyzed network:

- sinuosity, i.e. the ratio between the curvilinear length and the distance (straight line) between the extreme points of the road; for both networks, this dimensionless index is not excessively high, except in some local section (Fig. 2a);
- absolute slope, i.e. the degree of steepness or inclination of a road or section of a route; it was calculated using GRASS GIS; no distinction was made between downhill and uphill sections; the slope varies between 0 and 45% (Fig. 2b);
- absolute height difference: computed as the gradient multiplied by the length of the individual sections; no distinction is made between downhill and uphill sections (Fig. 2c).

Hence, the rules to classify the difficulty of paths in four categories (touristic, good, very good and high technical ability) in function of the slope, as suggested by the CAI guidelines and described in Sect. 3, were applied to both networks. Difficulty was calculated for each individual digitalized reach of the networks, dividing the single path in multiple short and heterogeneous ones (Fig. 2d).

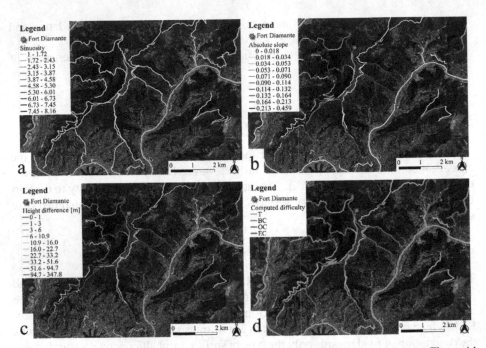

Fig. 2. Sinuosity (a), absolute slope (b) and absolute height difference (c, in m) maps. Figure 4d represents the difficulty classification of REL and cycle paths according to CAI guidelines.

5.2 Analysis of Paths to Fort Diamante

The evaluation criteria, proposed in Sect. 3, are analyzed to identify the accessibility to the Fort Diamante and the additional services needed along these routes, as a more detailed case study. The criteria are:

- identification of departure and arrival points and their accessibility: funicular, bus and train stops, the Youth Hostel and parking areas were selected (Fig. 3);
- access to mountain huts, alpine pastures and accommodation at high altitude within a few kilometers of the trails: only reception and refreshment services are present;
- connection with other existing path networks;
- ability to carry out regular maintenance and collect information on the state of the network: these two points are analyzed together because only after maintenance that guarantees the practicability of the paths, the necessary information can be obtained;
- search for interconnected routes, preparatory to the future creation of longer routes: the cycle path and the REL have numerous connection points, which could lead to the creation of longer distance cycle and pedestrian routes. However, data concerning the networks are not detailed enough (e.g., there is not sufficient information about the state of the ground surface and the width of the path), so it is not possible to make an objective assessment of the feasibility of connecting the two networks.

Five different routes were considered, as described below and represented in Fig. 4.

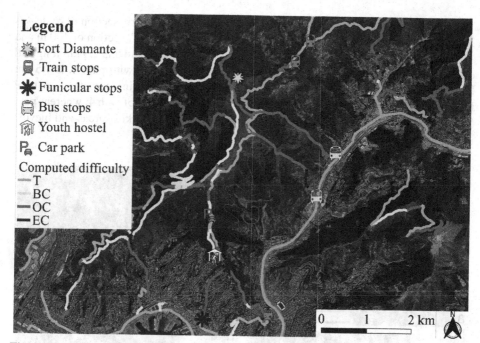

Fig. 3. Position of starting points of analyzed paths to the Fort Diamante and networks with the different difficulty classification.

Route 1 is about 5 km long and is mostly of tourist "T" difficulty grade, except for a section of almost 600 m that falls under category "BC" and a 1.5 km section of category "OC" for which the gradient of the sections is between 8 and 20%. This corresponds to 60% "T", 12% "BC" and 27% "OC" of the entire length. Whereas a pedestrian may consider the route of average difficulty, a cyclist may consider its difficulty depending on his/her abilities. To meet all requirements, possible bicycle parking areas have been positioned at the two blue points, which are 800 m apart. In this way the cyclist can either stop and resume the route for the more difficult section or put the bike in the parking areas and continue on foot.

Route 2 is almost 4 km long, mostly requires good technical skills. The "BC" sections have a total length of 2.4 km, then there is a "T" section of 400 m and two "OC" sections of a total of 900 m, corresponding to 9% "T", 60% "BC" and 31% "OC" of the total length. Also in this case, points for rest areas and bicycle stations are present (marked in light blue).

Route 3 can be reached from the city center by taking the train. Depending on the starting train station, the total length can be either 4 km or 4.6 km. The 600 m separating the two train stations fall in category "T". Regardless the starting point in the route, there are "OC" category sections with a total length of 2 km, so that the route is distributed in 50% of the total length falling in "T" category and the remaining 50% in "OC" category. The rest areas and bicycle stations can be the same as for route 1.

Routes 4 and 5 are considered together because they both start from the same area reachable by bus, have a similar degree of difficulty and share many portions of the track.

The starting points of the two routes are about 1 km apart. The first section of route 4 is 3 km long and is mainly in the "OC" category, except for an "EC" section of 400 m and "T" sections with a total length of 300 m. The first section of route 5 is 2.5 km long and entirely in the "OC" category. The second section, in common with path 4, is 1.5 km long and falls entirely in "OC" category. This leads to the following percentage of total length falling in each category 7% "T", 84% "OC" and 9% "EC" of path 4; whereas path 5 is 100% in "OC" category. Also in this case, the points for parking areas and bicycle stations are marked in light blue.

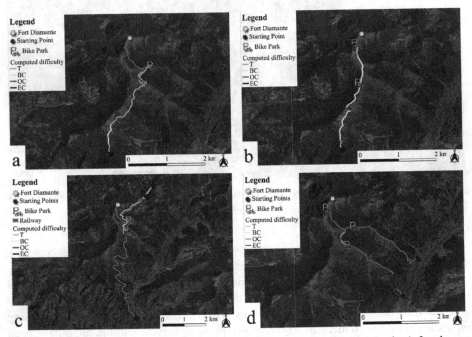

Fig. 4. Paths to Fort Diamante (yellow star). Figures 4a–4c correspond to paths 1–3, whereas paths 4 and 5 are reported together in Fig. 4d (Color figure online).

5.3   Final Assessment of Route Planning Criteria

The accessibility, continuity, connection of routes and geometric characteristics seems adequate, while the safety level and signposting are not. The introduction of the following improvement suggestions will help to meet all criteria.

The safety level of a route is high when suitable lighting and paving are guaranteed. Obviously, since these are mountain routes, artificial lighting cannot be guaranteed but, in order to achieve an adequate level of safety, it is advisable to use the routes at times when there is good natural lighting, for example in winter from 9 am to 4 pm and in summer from 8 am to 7 pm. Considering the pavement, it will be necessary to carry out the appropriate maintenance work to ensure bicycle transit, especially in the case of natural friable surfaces.

Regarding signposting, it would be useful to install vertical signposting providing information on the level of difficulty of the route to be covered and possible alternatives for reaching the destination.

6 Conclusions

The present project analyzed soft mobility with particular attention to bicycle and pedestrian mobility in the suburban area, with an in-depth study, in a GIS environment, of the territory of the Forts of Genoa, in consideration of the new projects of landscape and architectural enhancement that the local administration intends to carry out soon.

The topic of cycle and pedestrian paths was addressed analyzing their characteristics and the quality standards required for their construction. Since there is no legislation regulating them, an attempt was made to find a methodology for the creation of cycle and pedestrian routes outside urban areas, and more specifically in the mountains. Evaluation criteria and rules to classify the difficulty of each path were proposed.

The Fort system in Genoa was then analyzed from both a morphological and a regulatory point of view in the field of sustainable mobility, for their historical and architectural value. The proposed rules and criteria were applied to the case study, defining a methodology for processing the data in a GIS environment. The suitable for cycling and pedestrian activity and the difficulty level of the existing Ligurian hiking network (REL) and of the network of pedestrian paths were evaluated.

It can be noted that the accessibility, continuity, connection of the paths and geometric characteristics are adequate, while the degree of safety and signposting seem not. The level of safety of a route is high when suitable lighting and paving are guaranteed. Obviously, since these are mountain trails, artificial lighting cannot be guaranteed but, to reach an adequate level of safety, it is advisable to walk during daylight hours with adequate natural lighting. Regarding the pavement, appropriate maintenance work should be planned to ensure bicycle transit, especially in the case of natural friable surfaces. About signposting, it is suggested to install vertical signs providing information about the level of difficulty of the route to be covered and possible alternatives to reach the destination. Therefore, all criteria identified in the approach could be fulfilled in the analyzed case study.

In conclusion, it is hoped that the Sustainable Urban Mobility Plan (SUMP) of the Genoa Metropolitan City, which already contains a scenario of sustainable mobility and regeneration of the urban environment, will take up the findings of this work and translate them into concrete practices for the full realization of the objectives aimed at the integration of soft mobility with other mobility systems and the development of cycle/pedestrian routes in those suburban areas of historical and tourist interest in the city.

To share the results of the case study with local government technicians and end users, the qgis2web plugin was used to generate a web map.

References

1. PNRR, national recovery and resilience plan. https://www.governo.it/sites/governo.it/files/PNRR.pdf. Accessed 25 Mar 2022
2. Italian greenhouse gas inventory 1990–2017. National Inventory Report 2019. https://www.isprambiente.gov.it/it/pubblicazioni/rapporti/italian-greenhouse-gas-inventory-1990-2017.-national-inventory-report-2019. Accessed 25 Mar 2022
3. PTE, Plan for ecological transition. https://www.ambientesicurezzaweb.it/piano-per-la-transizione-ecologica-approvata-la-proposta/. Accessed 25 Mar 2022
4. Mueller, N., et al.: Health impact assessment of cycling network expansions in European cities. Prev. Med. **109**, 62–70 (2018). https://doi.org/10.1016/j.ypmed.2017.12.011
5. Mertens, L., et al.: Differences in environmental preferences towards cycling for transport among adults: a latent class analysis. BMC Public Health **16**, 1 (2016). https://doi.org/10.1186/s12889-016-3471-5
6. Wałdykowski P., Adamczyk J., Dorotkiewicz M.: Sustainable urban transport − why a fast investment in a complete cycling network is most profitable for a city. Sustainability **14**, 119 (2022). https://doi.org/10.3390/su14010119
7. Dėdelė A., Miškinytė A.: Promoting sustainable mobility: a perspective from car and public transport users. Int. J. Environ. Res. Public Health **18** (2021) https://doi.org/10.3390/ijerph18094715
8. Tolley, R.: The Greening of Urban Transport: Planning for Walking and Cycling in Western Cities. Wiley, Hoboken (1997)
9. Modesto, A., Kamenečki, M., Tomić Reljić, D.: Application of suitability modeling in establishing a new bicycle–pedestrian path: the case of the abandoned Kanfanar–Rovinj railway in Istria. Land **10** (2021) https://doi.org/10.3390/land10060600
10. Spadaro I., Pirlone F.: Sustainable urban mobility plan and health security. Sustainability **13**(8), (2021). https://doi.org/10.3390/su13084403
11. QGIS. https://www.qgis.org. Accessed 25 Mar 2022
12. Liguria Region geoportal. https://geoportal.regione.liguria.it. Accessed 25 Mar 2022
13. Geoportal of the genoa municipality. https://geoportale.comune.genova.it/. Accessed 25 Mar 2022
14. Web map of the present project. http://www3.dicca.unige.it/geomatica/FortiGenova/index.html. Accessed 25 Mar 2022
15. World Commission on Environment and Development of United Nations: Brundtland Report (1987)
16. European commission: the future development of the common transport policy: a global approach to the construction of a community framework for sustainable mobility, White Paper (1992)
17. European commission: European transport policy for 2010: time to decide, White Paper (2001)
18. European commission: towards a new culture for urban mobility, Green Paper (2007)
19. European commission: roadmap to a single European transport area - towards a competitive and resource efficient transport system, White Paper (2011)
20. Campisi, T., Basbas, S., Skoufas, A., Akgün, N., Ticali, D., Tesoriere, G.: The impact of COVID-19 pandemic on the resilience of sustainable mobility in Sicily. Sustainability **12** (2020). https://doi.org/10.3390/su12218829
21. European commission: guidelines for developing and implementing a sustainable Urban Mobility Plan (SUMP) (2014)
22. Fistola, R., Gallo, M., La Rocca, R.A., Raimondo, M.: Soft mobility in the "oblique city. In town and infrastructure planning for safety and urban quality; Taylor & Francis Group: London, UK, pp. 319–326 (2018). https://doi.org/10.1201/9781351173360-41

23. Holden, E., Gilpin, G., Banister, D.: Sustainable mobility at thirty. Sustainability **11** (2019). https://doi.org/10.3390/su11071965
24. Metropolitan city of Genoa: SUMP (2019)
25. Pirlone, F.: I borghi antichi abbandonati. Patrimonio da riscoprire e mettere in sicurezza. Franco Angeli, Italy (2016)

Correction to: SAR and Multispectral Data Contribution to the Monitoring of Wetland Ecosystems Vulnerable to Climate Change

Marco Dubbini⊙, Michaela De Giglio ⊙, and Chiara Salvatori

Correction to:
Chapter "SAR and Multispectral Data Contribution
to the Monitoring of Wetland Ecosystems Vulnerable
to Climate Change" in: E. Borgogno-Mondino
and P. Zamperlin (Eds.): *Geomatics for Green and Digital*
***Transition*, CCIS 1651,**
https://doi.org/10.1007/978-3-031-17439-1_30

In the originally published chapter "SAR and Multispectral Data Contribution to the Monitoring of Wetland Ecosystems Vulnerable to Climate Change" the first-last name order was erroneously reversed for all authors. This has been corrected.

The updated original version of this chapter can be found at
https://doi.org/10.1007/978-3-031-17439-1_30

Author Index

Printed in the United States
by Baker & Taylor Publisher Services